*'Don Roberto: Commander for the King of Aragon in the Two Sicilies'.
Portrait by James Lavery. Glasgow City Art Gallery*

For RBCG with affection and respect

Acknowledgements

One of the hazards of writing biography lies in the choice of subject in whose company one is destined to spend a great deal of time: whether the task is enjoyable and exciting, or tedious and irritating depends almost wholly on their character and circumstances. Even with those whose lives are already in the public domain accidents can happen: the researcher may come across something in the unpublished sources putting them at odds with the subject, thereby destroying most of the pleasure in the work. I have been most fortunate : the more I enquired into the life and experiences of Robert Cunninghame Graham, the more I liked him.

I am most grateful to Lady Polwarth, Cunninghame Graham's great niece and literary executor for permission to quote from family papers deposited in the National Library of Scotland. Her admiration for him has been life long and she has written her own account of him. I have to thank Mr Colin G. Cunninghame Graham for kindly allowing me to use quotes from his great uncle's letters and other family papers in the Scottish Record Office.

Extracts from reports by George Auldjo Jamieson, Curator Bonis of the Bontine Estate; from the Loch Papers, and from the Gartmore estate papers appear by kind permission of the Keeper of the Records of Scotland. Quotations from the papers of William Morris and John Burns are by permission of the British Library. I am grateful for permission to quote from Foreign and Home Office records in the National Archives at Kew.

In the United States I have to thank the Harry Ransom Humanities Research Center of the University of Texas at Austin for permission to reproduce extracts from the correspondence of Anne Elizabeth Bontine with Edward Garnett and from the letters of Gabrielle Cunninghame Graham to Mary Evans. I was given much help in the time I spent at Dartmouth College, Hanover, New Hampshire and I am grateful for permission to quote from the Herbert Faulkner West collection in the Rauner Special Collections Library at the College. The New York Public Library proved a source of much vital information

Many people shared their knowledge with me in the (far too long) time it took to finish this book. I owe special thanks to Mrs Shirley Toulson, Dr Richard Hitchcock, Tom Bean, Robert Bennett and John and Barbara Parker.

List of Contents

Chapter One	Inheritance	Page 7
Chapter Two	Tutelage	Page 27
Chapter Three	Enterprise	Page 47
Chapter Four	Friendship	Page 67
Chapter Five	Marriage	Page 83
Chapter Six	Laird of Gartmore	Page 111
Chapter Seven	Member of Parliament	Page 133
Chapter Eight	Politician	Page 151
Chapter Nine	Bloody Sunday	Page 171
Chapter Ten	The People's Hero	Page 191
Chapter Eleven	The New Militants	Page 209
Chapter Twelve	Journeys in Spain	Page 229
Chapter Thirteen	Morocco	Page 249
Chapter Fourteen	Literary matters	Page 275
Chapter Fifteen	Return to South America	Page 295
Chapter Sixteen	Nationalism	Page 317

List of Illustrations

Cover	Portrait of Robert Cunninghame Graham in old age By James McBey. National Portrait Gallery, London.
Frontispiece.	'Don Roberto, Commander for the King of Aragon in the Two Sicilies'. By John Lavery. Glasgow City Art Gallery.
Page 21	Inchmahome Priory, Lake of Menteith. Historic Scotland
Page 38	Robert in gaucho dress National Library of Scotland
Page 88	Masham, North Yorkshire Gary Keat
Page 90	Caroline Horsfall as a young girl. University of Michigan Library.
Page 152	Robert Cunninghame Graham, Sketch by George Washington Lambert. National Portrait Gallery, London.
Page 164	Cunninghame Graham in middle age, Sketch by Harry Furniss. National Portrait Gallery, London.
Page 210	Portrait of Gabrielle Cunninghame Graham by Jacomb-Hood. In private ownership
Page 268	Robert Cunninghame Graham in Moroccan dress. National Library of Scotland
Page 278	'The Fencer' by William Rothenstein. Dunedin Art Gallery, New Zealand.
Page 283	Map of Adrar. National Library of Scotland.
Page 290	Gabrielle Cunninghame Graham. University of Michigan Library.
Page 310	Cunninghame Graham and Mrs Elizabeth Dummett. Dartmouth College Library.
Page 334	Graves of Robert and Gabrielle Cunninghame Graham. Inchmahome Priory. Historic Scotland.

Chapter One

Inheritance

His appearance would have made him conspicuous at any time, in any place: to Victorians confined whether in factories or drawing rooms, Robert Bontine Cunninghame Graham represented freedom, adventure, romance. He was tall and strong, with penetrating eyes in a weatherbeaten face, and famously abundant dark brown hair for which, when he was a Member of Parliament the factory girls in his constituency christened him 'the curly headed darling'(1). His bearing matched these striking looks. When the journalist, Frank Harris, first encountered him in 1885, Graham impressed him as much more than a very handsome man: he was picturesque and had an air. 'He might have been the subject of a portrait.. of some Spanish noble who had followed Cortez', Harris wrote. He sensed a certain reserve in Graham, of pride, of conscious intelligence: 'He was someone, as the French say'(2).

The intensity of his physical presence was very attractive to artists. Among those who painted him were William Rothenstein and John Lavery, and there is a bust by Jacob Epstein.(3) Lavery described Graham as a master in the rare art of personality, the quality every portrait painter looked for but all too often failed to find. Lavery chose to translate this forceful presence into paint in the manner of Velasquez. The sitter's pleasure at this sympathetic image of himself inspired him to name the painting,' Don Roberto, Commander for the King of Aragon in the Two Sicilies'.(4) The reference was to the Spanish blood he had inherited on his mother's side which was partly responsible for his decision when little more than a boy to go adventuring in South America. He called himself Roberto in his letters home which were sprinkled with Spanish phrases. Later on it suited him as an epithet because it emphasized that aspect of his career he was resolved to keep before the public to the exclusion of much else. Its echo caught the public's fancy too: as he grew old and famous there were ways in which Don Roberto could be held to resemble Don Quixote. Many who knew him left it at that, even some who were often in his company. Cunninghame Graham's tightly defended personality was complemented by his manner which, though wonderfully polite, discouraged questions. Those who sought to understand him turned to his books and articles which he freely acknowledged to be autobiographical.

As far as these went they were brilliantly evocative of his exploits at different periods; as a traveller in remote and exotic countries; as a lover of horses whose expertise was matched by a scholar's knowledge of their history; as the champion in the 1880s of the unemployed, the first politician to promote Socialist measures in the House of Commons. He was, besides, a staunch friend of Ireland in her struggle for Home Rule. In that context he was a potential danger to the good order of the realm for his speeches moved the crowd, and he was uninhibited about the means to be used to achieve their aim. The power he briefly exercised over workers teeming in the mines, steelworks, and factories along the Clyde seemed to foreshadow the rise of a Scottish Parnell.(5) That was his public image; there were other matters - adventures, enterprises - that he kept to himself. He was, for instance, a seeker after treasure, beyond mountains, on the edge of deserts. In all these accomplishments he was guided by a simple creed: one that apparently gave him the greatest freedom of action; 'the best right a man can have is to be happy after the way that pleases him most'(6) he wrote. If this might seem selfishly indifferent to the claims of family and friends, one can say in his defence that he spent years of his life, ran down his sadly limited resources, and exhausted his nervous energy in the encouragement of others to attempt their own dash for freedom.

One who benefited from Robert Cunninghame Graham's role as an enabler was Joseph Conrad who became a friend. Graham was one of the first people to recognize and promote the Polish writer's early works. Conrad, the novelist, observing Graham, the man of action found much to intrigue him (as did Bernard Shaw who put him into more than one of his plays). Conrad drew on Graham's character and experience for one of the central figures in 'Nostromo', the novel he set in South America. Don Carlos Gould, 'King' of Sulaco, administrator of the silver mine, is a portrait of Graham (as, to a certain extent, Dona Emilia Gould is of Graham's wife). Their correspondence shows that Conrad was privy to one of Graham's greatest anxieties; the debt ridden estate in Scotland he inherited from his father. In 'Nostromo' this dreadful burden is represented by the concession to the São Tomé silver mine which Charles Gould takes on after the death of his father. Because the mine destroyed the elder Gould, Charles accepts it as his fate to restore and work it. 'The mine had been the cause of an absurd moral disaster; its working must be made a serious moral success'(7), Conrad wrote. As with Gould, so with Graham and his moral duty which was inescapably connected to his family inheritance. By the time he and Conrad met in the late 1890s, Graham was involved in a desperate struggle to repair the ruin his forbears had brought about. Conrad, who was one of the few people to know the extent of the disaster Graham had been obliged to face, gave meaning to his friend's conduct in explaining that of Charles Gould. 'Action is consolatory. It is the enemy of thought, and the friend of flattering illusions. Only in control of our own action can we find the sense of mastery over the Fates'.(8) The more one learns of Graham's history, the more perceptive this assessment will appear.

When Robert Bontine Cunninghame Graham was born on 24 May 1852 his future seemed assured. As the eldest grandchild, in the fullness of time he would succeed as tenth laird of Gartmore, an estate on the Lake of Menteith near Stirling in Scotland which had been in his family for more than 300 years. As a boy the prospect was exciting: the moment he saw the place he fell in love with it. Growing up, he could look forward to that happy state when duty coincides with inclination. Later on, when he became a writer, Gartmore was always in his mind's eye, and he delighted in describing it. 'What I have set down I have set down half in idleness, half out of that affection which is common in men and trees for the soil in which they have been for ages rooted',(9) he explained in his first book. Gartmore House, 'a perfect specimen of a Georgian mansion', stood on a hill commanding a view of the Lake of Menteith and of the low, flat, watery expanse known as the Flanders Moss. What cultivable land there was - all hillocks, humps, and rushy parks (fields) was cut off by the encircling hills, the Campsies to the south; to the north the Grampians and the long shoulder of Ben Lomond. Robert came to know the place in all the moods inspired by the changing seasons, and the weather. Sometimes thick white mists rose from the depths of the Flanders Moss giving it a mysterious air, as of a white and steamy sea breaking against the barrier of the two chains of hills. These mists, impalpable and strange, shrouded the district from the world, 'as if they wished to keep it from all prying eyes, safe and inviolate',(10) he wrote. Safest of all - a sanctuary - was Inchmahome, the largest of three islands in the lake, on which there was a ruined Priory. There was a fortress on Inchtalla; Inchuan was an outcrop of rock on which the dogs belonging to the guardians formerly were kennelled. The Augustinian Priory on Inchmahome was founded in the 13th century by Walter Comyn, Earl of Menteith, the most important province in medieval Scotland. By marriage and descent the earldom came into the Graham family and with it a claim to the Scottish throne that could be traced back through the highly complicated Stewart line to King Robert II. In 1651, after Charles I had succeeded to the Crown, he removed the threat to his position allegedly posed by the rival branch by reducing the earl of Menteith to a lesser status. But the claim persisted and would descend to Robert in due course.

Outside the house a fine beech avenue led to three stones where, by tradition, stood the gallows on which, in the mid eighteenth century, the fifth laird of Gartmore, Nicol Graham, hanged the men he caught stealing his sheep and cattle. Of all his ancestors on his father's side Nicol Graham was the one Robert most admired: in following whose example he supposed he would, in due course, take greatest satisfaction. Laird Nicol had secured the estate and its people against disaster at a harsh and dangerous time. Gartmore stood on the line where the Lowlands met the Highlands; upon a frontier - the first of many Robert was to know - dividing settled country from a wilderness. The house was only two miles from the Pass of Aberfoyle where began the rule of the Macgregors, ancient enemies of the Grahams. Twice in Nicol Graham's lifetime; in 1715 and 1745 this wild country had offered a refuge for Jacobites fleeing from the collapse of the Stewart cause. A resolute, shrewd and pragmatic man, Nicol was well placed to observe the effect of these turbulent events upon the local population. He had been 21 in 1715 at the coming of the Old Pretender, and in his prime when Prince Charles Edward landed in the west in 1745. He held himself aloof from both rebellions and condemned their leaders for the extra hardship their cause brought to men and woman already suffering extreme poverty. In 1747, a year after George II's troops had slaughtered many of the Prince's followers on Culloden Moor, he published a devastating indictment of the society which had brought the country to its desperate state.

'An Inquiry into the Causes which facilitate the Rise and progress of Rebellions and Insurrections in the Highlands of Scotland etc.'(11) was written from the standpoint of a lifelong Whig and dedicated to his friend, the recently deceased Prime Minister, Sir Robert Walpole. As a political statement it had great influence upon his descendant, Robert Cunninghame Graham who, when he entered Parliament in 1886 echoed its angry concern on behalf of the common people. In the mid eighteenth century the local economy was based on cattle, a means of exchange it was impossible to secure except by a system Nicol Graham did not hesitate to call blackmail. As he described it, the practice was for Highlanders above the Pass of Aberfoyle to extort money from the Lowland farmers as the price of 'protecting' their sheep and cattle, while by night, driving off these same beasts. He was the first to identify some of the Captains of the so-called Watch, including 'one Robert M'Greiger who assumed the name of Campbell but was commonly called Rob Roy'(12) - a figure immortalized by Sir Walter Scott in the seventh of his Waverley novels published in 1817. That, seventy years after it had been published, the Inquiry fell into the hands of a writer who used it to create a romantic myth about the Jacobites was an irony Robert Cunninghame Graham failed to appreciate. His own considerable body of work about Scotland and its history was distinguished by a lack of nostalgia for what he thought of as a cult which, before the days of Walter Scott, was quite unknown. 'Those who lived near the Highland Line looked upon the inhabitants 'above the Pass' as the early settlers in Vermont and Maine looked on the Indians. There was in neither case any good Highlander or Indian unless he happened to be dead',(13) he wrote in his account of Gartmore and its lairds.

Nicol Graham lived another thirty years after the collapse of the '45 during which time the Highlands were subdued, often bloodily. His firm grasp upon the estate freed his sons to live as they pleased. The eldest, William, died young and without issue, leaving the second son, Robert, who spent fourteen years in Jamaica where he had gone in 1752, aged only 17. He prospered on the island, planting sugar, and became a prominent member of the Assembly. In about 1770 the frail health of his wife obliged him to return to Scotland. At about this time he entered into possession of the estate of Ardoch in Dumbartonshire which a relative settled on him with the understanding that he would take the surname of Bontine. From this time on the eldest son of the laird of Gartmore was known by that name. From the windswept weatherbeaten old house at Ardoch on the north bank of the Clyde, the new Mr Robert Bontine looked out across the river at the great mansion of Finlaystone, directly opposite, where his mother, Nicol Graham's wife, had been born Lady Margaret Cunninghame, a daughter of the 12th earl of Glencairn

Six years later, when Nicol died, he changed his name again, becoming Robert Graham, sixth laird of Gartmore. In 1796, at the death of the childless 15th earl of Glencairn, he inherited Finlaystone when he added the earl's family name to his own. Now he was Robert Cunninghame Graham, first of that name. 'He had reached the summit', his namesake, the modern Robert wrote, 'his estates now stretched from Renfrewshire where Finlaystone was situated across the Clyde to Ardoch, then by way of Gallingad…to Gartmore, and down to Kippen but a few miles from Stirling'(14). The sixth laird also owned land in Lanarkshire, in Old Monkland parish, to the east of Glasgow, and had retained possession of a plantation in Jamaica. Gartmore House bore witness to his increasing prosperity: it was enlarged and the new drawing room embellished with Italian stucco work. Laird Robert also diverted himself writing poems, one of which beginning, 'If doughty deeds my lady please' found its way into anthologies. He engaged in politics, 'the favourite sport of Scottish landed proprietors', continuing the Whig tradition of his father. Elected MP for Stirlingshire in 1795 or 6, he was credited with introducing a Bill of Rights. This sank without trace beyond a rumour that, to some extent, it foreshadowed the great Reform Bill of 1832.

The time in which this Robert lived was peaceful, and he was blessed with good luck in the affairs of the estate. But his success also proceeded from his nature: like his father he was steadfast, capable and judicious. While Nicol had been famously dour, Robert was remembered as an affectionate husband, a warm and hospitable friend. Temperament was to play a disproportionate role in the fate of members of the Cunninghame Graham family, as no one more than the subject of this biography was to find. It was a great misfortune, therefore, that the seventh laird failed to inherit his father's moderation.

In 1925 when Robert Cunninghame Graham published an account of his 18th century forbears, he drew on letters preserved at Gartmore House. Among these were several, dated 1792 and 93, by the sixth laird to the 17 year old heir, William Bontine, at Neuchâtel where he had been sent to learn German. These complained of William's extravagance, idleness and love of show, and expressed anxiety about the fate of Gartmore should he not reform(15). The situation was more precarious than the writer knew; four years later death came to him suddenly at the age of 58. Gartmore, Ardoch, Finlaystone, and all the other lands, passed to William Bontine. He was only 22 at his inheritance (when he assumed the name of Cunninghame Graham); his time as seventh laird of Gartmore was to last for nearly fifty years.

One of the positive results of his expensive taste was the replacement in the early nineteenth century of the grim old corbelled house at Ardoch with a charming version of a plantation bungalow. Pleasing though this was, the cost of building it placed a heavy burden on the estate. As his family grew large - he had nine children by two wives - his debts grew even larger, for he became a gambler and a speculator. These excesses, joined to irascibility, estranged him from some of his family and eventually frightened his creditors into claiming back their money.

By 1833 Laird William had fallen so far in debt he was obliged to place his affairs in the hands of trustees and take refuge from his creditors on the Continent. He settled in Florence where, in 1839, he became involved in the notorious affair known as the Ireland forgeries (after the engraver whose pseudonym it was). At home, at Gartmore, William who was good with his hands, had amused himself with a turning lathe. To pass the time in exile he perfected a machine that copied pictures and engravings. One of his sons by his second wife worked for a bank in Florence, and was introduced to Ireland. The engraver was already involved in plot to exploit the system of letters of credit issued by the London banking firm of Glyn, Halifax and Mills. Travellers who obtained these before leaving home could have them cashed by the firm's agents on the Continent simply by endorsing them. The conspirators in Florence obtained a genuine example whose signature William Cunninghame Graham reproduced by means of his machine: from these copies were made which the Ireland gang planned to present for cash in Belgium and the Rhineland. The scheme, by which they nearly succeeded in defrauding banks of hitherto unimaginable sums of money, was exposed in The Times of 26 May 1840 when William Cunninghame Graham was identified by name(16).

Though it was not suggested that, in copying the letter he was guilty of intent to defraud, he was known in the family ever after as The Swindler. In order to avoid the notoriety the English newspapers fixed upon their name, his eldest son, another Robert Bontine, found it expedient, as well as cheaper to live abroad. During his father's lifetime he spent some years in Frankfurt and at Brussels. In 1845 when the Swindler died this Robert succeeded as eighth laird of Gartmore. His conduct of affairs was to have an important effect upon the subject of this biography for he was Robert Cunninghame Graham's grandfather. A cautious and frugal man, with the help of the family solicitor, Arthur Campbell, he began the difficult task of restoring the fortunes of the estate. His first return to Gartmore House was greeted by the tenants with rejoicing - short lived - for they had to be told he could not afford to stay.(17) The house had to be let for the rent it would bring in while the laird would make his home in England at Leamington Spa. There his wife and daughters could go into society while Mr Cunninghame Graham (as he now was) ,passed his time in hunting. His finances remained precarious; like many Scottish estates Gartmore was already burdened with annuities payable to his female relatives, the many daughters of the seventh laird, while his own family was large; he had three sons and four daughters.

The heir was born in 1825; according to the sequence now established his name was William Bontine. He was not sent to school but, during his family's exile on the Continent, put to a tutor in Market Bosworth, a small town in Leicestershire, the finest hunting county. He was passionately fond of hunting, as of all field sports on which he expended his large reserves of energy. When, in middle age, his doctors persuaded him to write an account of himself as an adolescent he described a nature that was restless, exuberant and self confident, rather like that of the Swindler, his grandfather. According to this narrative(18), at the age of 15 William wanted to be as great a traveller as Columbus, and perhaps the founder of an empire. On reading 'Robinson Crusoe' he said he thought, 'should my Empire prove a failure I might at least make some island somewhere the rival of Juan Fernandez'. His volatility was a worry to his family who coped with it by humouring him. When he was 17 his father wanted him to go to university but William refused. Instead he undertook to spend a year in Weimar learning German. He passed the time there hunting, fishing, and falling in love with Fraulein von Goethe, the great man's pretty granddaughter. He had the entree to the ducal court where, his narrative recalled, he played at Blindman's Buff with the young Tsar of Russia and his bride.(19) But he grew restive and left before the time appointed by his father. Back home in England he joined the Army and, to everyone's relief, found the swashbuckling life of a Cornet of Horse exactly to his taste. In 1845 his regiment, the Scots Greys, was sent to Ireland.

Forty years on, after he had become a Member of Parliament, his son, Robert, would spend six weeks in Pentonville Prison for demonstrating in

Trafalgar Square on behalf of the Irish people's demand for Home Rule. Whereas William Bontine apparently had no qualms about the part he, as an Army officer, was called upon to play in keeping order among the starving tenant farmers. His most vivid memory was of dining, dancing, and - of course - hunting in between periods of duty in places like Galway which struck him as wretched and tumbledown. The country houses where he stayed were islands in a sea of desolation for Connaught in the west where the regiment was stationed first was one of the worst areas of famine that occurred when the potato harvest failed. In 1847 the Scots Greys were transferred to Waterford, and it was there that William met with an injury that was to have very serious consequences for his son, as yet unborn. Outside the barracks he and a fellow officer became involved in an argument with an Irishman passing by. It came to blows, and William was hit on the head with an iron shod stick. 'When my head was washed the Doctor looked very grave and said, 'I am afraid Mr Bontine...the skull is fractured. You may perhaps not feel it now but I am afraid you may feel it afterwards'(20).

Apparently his recovery was complete when, in 1851, he resigned his commission to marry Miss Anne Elizabeth Elphinstone Fleeming. Such was his devotion to the Army that, saying goodbye at the barracks, he nearly cried. 'I had to spend an hour or two with Wright [a family friend] drinking cherry brandy before I could face my intended with sufficient composure not to make her jealous of the dear old regiment'.(21) Looking back in middle age it seemed to him he had been caught up in a process that was not only irreversible but precipitate. 'A winter in the shires, a month in London, three weeks in Canterbury [where the wedding took place] and the fatal knot was tied. We lived fast in those days'(22).

His fiancée's progress towards the wedding was far less smooth. It seemed likely at one time that the engagement would be broken off on the advice of her uncle and guardian, the Hon. Mountstuart Elphinstone. He was doubtful of the 'steadiness'- a favourite word of his - of William Bontine, and he disliked the prospect of an engagement lasting two years which the young man's father, Mr Cunninghame Graham, advocated on the grounds that he could not afford to make a financial settlement any sooner. Mountstuart Elphinstone lectured the bride's mother on the evils of delay when the couple might risk falling out of love. 'Mr Bontine might do many things which would not entitle [his fiancée] to break the engagement yet would entirely alter her feelings towards him'.(23) He put the problem squarely to his niece; 'the question now is are you likely to repent incurring the manifold and obvious risks of so long an engagement, or the pain and sacrifice of breaking it off at the present time?'(24). His forthrightness was a compliment to her good sense; though Anne Elizabeth (as we shall call her) was only 22 he had faith in her judgement, justifiably so. Her very long, sad, and often tragic life was to show <u>her</u> steadiness would never be in doubt.

Uncle and niece were very fond of one another. In so far as she had a home in the years immediately preceding her marriage, it was with him at Hookwood, a house on the Downs near Limpsfield in Surrey to which he had retired in 1847 - according to his biographer (25)- depriving the nation of one of its best loved and wisest counsellors. His great service to his country had taken place in India where he had gone in 1802 at the age of 17 and from which he returned in 1835, the highly respected Governor of Bombay. A supremely capable administrator, who had done much to devise the system whereby the British accomplished the next to impossible feat of governing a sub-continent, he was also a scholar whose retirement was devoted to an eagerly awaited History of India. Yet he was never too immersed in Asian studies not to spare time for his family from which he had been separated for so long. He was as aimiably attentive to the problems they brought him as he had been scrupulous in fulfilling his duties as a proconsul. Though he was unmarried Hookwood was a well conducted household which Anne Elizabeth, known to him as Missy, found to her taste.

She was already distinguished by what her uncle called her 'independent, bachelor like ideas' (26) - a love of reading, and of solitude, a passion for discourse when she could hold her own with Hookwood's eminent visitors. Besides politics, history, music, art, and gardening, the letters she wrote to her 'dearest Uncle Mount' whenever she was away, were full of tart and perceptive gossip which they both enjoyed. These visits were a tedious necessity to Anne Elizabeth who hated being disturbed. However, as a spinster who was not particularly pretty, and certainly not rich; whose father had died ten years before, and whose mother had recently remarried, it was obviously her duty to go a little into society for the sake of her relatives and friends who were anxious to see her 'safely 'married. There was a certain condescension in their attitude to her which she endured in public with good grace while taking their measure in her letters to her uncle.

The world she briefly entered on these occasions might fairly be described as glittering. Her chaperone was not her mother but an elderly cousin of Mountstuart's whose husband's connections at this time were on the point of once more ruling France. In 1817 the not so young and exceedingly prim Scottish demoiselle, Margaret Mercer Elphinstone, captured for a husband - and to everyone's astonishment - held on to - one of the most actively amorous men in Europe, a Frenchman of renown who had come to England after Waterloo. August Joseph Charles de la Billarderie, Comte de Flahaut, aide de camp to Napoleon I, was generally supposed to be Tallyrand's illegitimate son. He was the father, by Hortense de Beauharnais, Queen of Holland, of the Duc de Morny. In 1851 the Duc's half brother, Louis Napoleon Buonaparte, seized power in France by means of a <u>coup d'état</u>, when the Comte de Flahaut was restored to the highest favour. It was at his London house the previous year that Anne Elizabeth stayed for a season as a debutante. In spite of being very grand the Flahauts were kind to her, she told Uncle Mount. But though she was taken to balls she did not capture a single eligible young man. 'Madame de Flahaut has a propensity to sit behind doors which is rather against one's chance of being <u>found out</u> and asked to dance'(27), she explained.

Though the season ended in July Anne Elizabeth could not return to Hookwood until she had paid a visit to her mother, Catalina, who lived with her new husband, Captain James Katon RN at Harbledown near Canterbury. While there was no question of her daughter making her home with them until she married in her turn, relations between the three were easy and affectionate. Mother and daughter kept in touch by letter and much of their correspondence has survived. It is a most important source of what we know of the tragedy that overwhelmed his family when Robert Cunninghame Graham was a boy. Its effect upon him was so extreme that after he grew up he fabricated an alternative version of his boyhood in which his maternal grandmother, Catalina Katon, was the presiding adult. (28). This was a device to obliterate an acutely distressing experience, one that social convention demanded be concealed. The story emerges from the letters between Anne Elizabeth and her mother which may be called the Bontine correspondence since most of them were written after she married Robert's father. It often contradicts the later version.

The point of departure in either case was Catalina's marriage to her first husband, Anne Elizabeth's father. This event had taken place long ago in Spain. Doña Catalina Paulina Alesandro was born in 1800 to a family that had come from Italy in the 16th century to settle at Cadiz. (29) According to her grandson, Robert, this was the place to which Catalina often brought him as a child, which became his second, Spanish home. Yet none of his books or articles give any hint of what the Alesandro house was like beyond the fact that there were fine horses for him to ride. When she was 16 Doña Catalina married a Captain in the Royal Navy whose ship was stationed in the Mediterranean at the time. He was an elder brother of Mountstuart Elphinstone and, like the Cunninghame Graham heir, he bore another name. Captain the Hon. Charles Elphinstone Fleeming was the second son of the 11th Lord Elphinstone whose family seat was at Cumbernauld House east of Glasgow. His choice of the Navy as a career probably owed much to the eminence of his uncle, Admiral Lord Keith, (Madame de Flahaut's father) whose success against the French during the Napoleonic Wars made him a national hero second only to Lord Nelson.

Charles Elphinstone Fleeming was a strikingly handsome, bold, and headstrong man, committed to doing exactly as he pleased. Though he was immensely attractive to women and many of the stories that clung about him concerned young ladies frantic to elope with him, somehow he contrived to remain a bachelor until the age of 42 when he married Doña Catalina who was more than young enough to be his daughter. They had a son and four daughters, the youngest of whom, Anne Elizabeth, was born in 1828. By that time Charles had become an Admiral and was in command on the West Indian station. His last daughter arrived just as his flagship, HMS Barham, came to anchor in the open roadstead of La Guaira, off the coast of Venezuela. Until Anne Elizabeth was three, she and her mother and the other children lived up at the capital, Caracas, while the Admiral patrolled the Caribbean. The Spanish Empire was in the final process of collapse: Admiral Fleeming was present at the siege of Maracaibo, the last place held by Spain in the New World. Afterwards he helped to mediate in the dispute that flared up between the Liberator, Simon Bolivar, and his lieutenant in the war against the Spanish, José Antonio Paez, who was determined to create a Republic of Venezuela independent of Bolivar. Doña Catalina never tired of explaining how much the Venezuelans appreciated the Admiral's diplomacy; hearing these stories as a boy Robert thought they might have asked his grandfather to stay on and govern them; he would have been just as good at it as Paez or Bolivar. The Admiral's personality haunted him: here was a man whose great ability had been recognized; who did much as he pleased in spite of naval discipline; who had been happy in the way that suited him. When he was little his grandfather's portrait hung in his bedroom; painted after his return from South America in 1831 it showed the Admiral dressed in a high necked coat with a black silk stock and curly white hair, as he had looked when, as MP for Stirlingshire, he sat in the Reform Parliament.(30)

Charles Fleeming's last post in the Navy was as Governor of Greenwich Hospital; he died in 1840 when Anne Elizabeth was 12.(31) His widow, Catalina, still comparatively young, was courted by his Flag Lieutenant, Captain Katon. They married in 1849 and settled at Harbledown. It was while she was staying with them the following autumn that Anne Elizabeth was introduced to William Bontine.

Two months later their engagement was announced and skirmishing began between the older members of their respective families over the marriage settlement. Besides his anxiety over the 'steadiness' of William Bontine, Mountstuart Elphinstone was very concerned to protect his niece's position after marriage in the event of her husband's incapacity or death. We do not know how Anne Elizabeth responded to her uncle's doubts about William's character, or what her opinion was regarding the danger of an engagement lasting two years. As things turned out she did not have to make a choice; the problem was suddenly resolved when Mr Cunninghame Graham discovered that funds were available for an immediate settlement after all. The wedding took place in Canterbury on 21 June 1851, and the Bontines left for the Continent that same evening(32).

For the next nine months the newly married pair trundled across Europe in a diligence, accompanied by a maid who, William complained, gave him more trouble than a sergeant of dragoons. They also had a small Skye terrier whose name was Moss; he rode beside the coachman on the box. Whenever they stopped somewhere for a few days Moss kept Anne Elizabeth company as she read and sketched and wrote letters home. She did not care to associate with some of the English who frequented Continental watering places, she told her mother, and the Strix was apt to go off on his own, hunting, fishing, and making a man's party to the nearest gaming tables. It is impossible to say what owl-like qualities earned William this name; apparently his friends and relations rarely called him anything else. One word stands out in the letters that came to Harbledown from France, Germany, Austria, Switzerland, and Italy; that word is kind. 'The Strix is very kind and dear' Anne Elizabeth never tired of repeating. Her emphasis on the kindness of a husband to his wife may have been as much as modesty would allow in referring to her status as a newly married woman, and must have reassured her mother and her uncle. Yet, as the journey progressed, there was rather too much about kindness to the neglect of William's other qualities. He was still a stranger; they had spent only a few weeks together before the marriage.(33)

One thing was clear; his restlessness had not abated. Anne Elizabeth was seven months pregnant before he could be persuaded to turn his face to

England. In April 1852 they arrived in London and moved into a rented house where, little more than a month later, their first son was born. 'The Baby's name is Robert' his mother wrote to Mountstuart Elphinstone, 'which is not only a frightful name in itself but all the abbreviations of it are rather worse. I only dare say this out of the hearing of the family who are all called Robert, nearly'.(34) The baby gave her a good excuse to settle down. Of all the houses belonging to the Cunninghame Graham family only one was available. William's father, the present laird, had first call on Gartmore, and Ardoch had been farmed out since 1845. In October, 1852 the Bontines went north to take possession of Finlaystone, where they were to spend the happiest years of their married life.

There is an affectionate description of Finlaystone in the first book of stories Robert had published. 'An old house in Scotland perched on a rock above the Clyde, and set about with trees...under which John Knox is said to have preached.' Some of the trees were laurels which he remembered, 'as tall as houses'.(35) These appear in the letters his mother wrote to Mountstuart Elphinstone while he was still a baby. In 1852 when she arrived Finlaystone had been neglected for years; behind the laurels the ground floor rooms were damp and dark; the gardens were rank and overgrown, while the gilded Glencairn coronet on the Georgian stables was almost obscured by dirt. 'Open your views and do not spare the laurels' Uncle Mount briskly advised, 'they...block the circulation of air'. After a year of hard work during which they renovated many, but not all, of the rooms, Anne Elizabeth was able to report to him that the house was nearly comfortable 'if it were not for the rats which...dispute possession with us'. Her chief anxiety was the threat of a visit from Madame de Flahaut because of the very sophisticated servants she was sure to bring with her. After that visit was successfully completed she asked Uncle Mount to recommend some books: suddenly she had time for reading. Her second son, Charles Elphinstone Fleeming Bontine, arrived on 1 January 1854.(36)

Robert and Charles were inseparable as children and, it seems, extremely happy. Finlaystone, however shabby, was a splendid place for two little boys. Of course they learned to ride as soon as their legs were long enough to straddle a pony. Their mother, too, was content - outwardly and for the present - clearing and restoring the different areas of garden, one of which was furnished with curious stone vases. She had inherited Admiral Fleeming's passion for botanical research and transferred this enthusiasm to her eldest son. When Robert began his own travels in regions largely unexplored, he was careful to identify the plants and trees, and the uses to which they might be put; these details and the Latin version of their names are in the books he wrote, at the foot of almost every page.

These were not mere lists but part of the structure that sustained his writing. His imagination took its point of departure from a basis of fact, closely observed and thoroughly understood. The process began when he was a child at Finlaystone. He could look down from the rock above the Clyde upon steamers passing between the fairway marks opposite the house. The river, not yet artificially embanked, took a winding course from Glasgow to the Atlantic Ocean. The beach below was scattered with flotsam which it was Robert's habit to examine. The items he turned over in his hands gave him a sense of the world beyond the mountains that closed his view. 'One day upon the sands I found the outside covering of a cocoanut and launched it on the Clyde just opposite to where the roofless house of Ardoch stood, and watched it vanish into nothing, after the fashion of an Irish peasant woman on the quay at Cork watching the vessel take her son away, and just as sure as she of the return'(37).

Indoors he was usually to be found with his nose in an endless variety of books, amassing facts like pebbles on a beach. 'What an immense amount of information his small head has collected'(38) a visitor exclaimed when Robert was only seven. This was Henry Brougham Loch, a cousin of the Elphinstones, a close and dear friend of Anne Elizabeth, as of Robert after he grew up. In 1859 he was 32, two years younger than William Bontine but already the hero of more perilous adventures and bold exploits than anything Robert might read about in books. Henry's remarkable career had begun in 1854 with the outbreak of the Crimean War. He had served before Sevastopol as Adjutant of the famously irregular Skinner's Horse whose mission was to harry the Russians on their flanks. Even so, the stories he told Robert and Charles of these events, while undeniably exciting, could be matched by almost every returning soldier of the expeditionary force. It was what happened next that made Cousin Henry a superlatively romantic figure to the Bontine boys.

In 1857 he had been appointed private secretary to a fellow Scot, the Earl of Elgin and Kincardine, leader of an embassy to the Far East whose object was to open ports to British trade - by force if necessary. He was, therefore, one of the very few people who had been to China. He had been present at the bombardment of Canton and, after its capitulation, come face with its erstwhile master, the enormous, ferocious and spectacularly dirty Commissioner Yeh. He had sailed with the fleet up the Peiho River, through the flat, brown, dusty countryside of Northern China towards the capital, Peking. When at last, by agreeing to negotiate with Elgin, the Chinese called a halt to the British advance at Tientsin, it had been Henry Loch's duty to take down the terms of the Treaty that opened ports to the hated foreigner.

Afterwards the Mission turned its ships towards one of the most fantastic and mysterious countries in the world - Japan, an ancient Empire with a half remembered civilisation which had been closed to foreigners for two hundred years. As recently as 1854 Commander Perry with his black American ships had prized the oyster open. Though Perry had gone no further than Nagasaki Bay the Shogun's government knew it was only a matter of time before other well armed and determined foreigners demanded entry to a country that had no effective means of repelling them. Consequently, when it arrived, Elgin's Mission was most hospitably received and invited to Edo, the administrative capital where negotiations aimed at establishing trade between the two maritime countries proceeded very amicably and with jokes. After the treaty was signed on 26 August 1858, Henry Loch was ordered to take it back to England. Shortly after his return he fell ill and went to Finlaystone to recuperate. There, in the absence of their parents who were at Gartmore with the laird, Robert and Charles 'looked after' him, a task they accomplished, he told their mother, by means of rapt attention to his stories. While what he had to say to them of China was, perforce, selective, his impressions of Japan altogether were benign. As it had appeared to him Japanese society was peaceful, quaint and orderly. This could hardly have been otherwise given the fact that every member of it, from the commissioners in charge of negotiations down to the attendants in the Buddhist temple in which the British lodged while they were in Edo, were under the strictest orders to make themselves agreeable to the Westerners. The Mission was overwhelmed with gifts and taken shopping in the bazaars which, according to Henry's colleague, Laurence Oliphant, were particularly well supplied with toys -'wonderful Jacks in the box, representations of animals, beautifully executed in straw, models of norimons (sedan chairs) and Japanese houses...little porcelain figures whose heads wagged and tongues shot out unexpectedly; tortoises whose heads, legs, and tails were in perpetual motion, ludicrous picture books, grotesque masks and sham headdresses. Enough absurd contrivances ...to create a revolution in the nurseries of England.' (39) It is likely that Henry who was not yet married, brought some of these marvellous toys back for the two little boys at Finlaystone.

The Bontine family was to depend very much on Henry Loch a few years later, at a time of great adversity. But in 1860 he was nearly lost to them. Early in the year he was recalled to China to join the Anglo-French force assembled to punish Peking for its failure to ratify the Treaty of Tientsin. He was captured and thrown into prison where he was tortured and narrowly escaped execution. Graphic accounts of his ordeal filled the London papers, causing Anne Elizabeth much anguish. He was released in October 1860 and repatriated. His letters to Finlaystone during this dangerous excursion contain the earliest surviving indication that all was not well with William Bontine: they refer to a pain the Strix is suffering which is having a bad effect upon his peace of mind.(40)

His temper was, as yet, no more than an inconvenient aspect of William Bontine's character, one that Robert's mother, on the occasions she could not conceal it, loyally excused. At other times the Strix was kind and affectionate towards his family who reciprocated. He was often away from home; hunting and fishing in Ireland, or making journeys on the Continent arranged at short notice with a few male friends. He thought himself lucky that, after 1854, he was once more able to indulge that passion for all things military he had had to put aside in order to be married. The outbreak of the Crimean War brought new measures to strengthen the home defences. As a Major in the Renfrewshire Militia William was liable to be posted anywhere in the United Kingdom threatened with disturbance and was much involved with training younger men. He was also a Deputy Lieutenant of the county and a Justice of the Peace. In 1859, having primed himself with books on political economy recommended by Uncle Mount, he stood for Parliament as a radical but failed to get elected.

These were the usual preoccupations of a country gentleman but the Strix had others that did not commend themselves to his wife. He was much in the company of his younger brother, Bobby (Robert Cunninghame Cunninghame(sic) Graham) and of William Hope, husband of his only sister, Margaret. These two, but Hope especially, were rabid speculators. Hope had served in the Crimean War and for his bravery in the unsuccessful attack upon the fortress known as the Redan, had won the highest honour the nation could bestow. It was only to be expected that Colonel Hope V.C. would exercise a disproportionate influence upon the military minded William Bontine. Mines - of coal or slate, railways, ranches, the reclamation of land from the sea on the very remote and underpopulated island of Majorca, were some of the subjects that occupied their discussions after dinner in the smoking room. 'Pray Heaven these convulsions of nature succeed and you become a millionairess'(41), a friend who overheard them talking, wrote to Anne Elizabeth.

Alarming though they were she had no cause to fear anything might come of these ideas during the lifetime of her husband's father. Mr Cunninghame Graham was securely in control - of the family as of the estate: years of prudent management had done much to restore the equilibrium of both. Even so, in 1861 the eighth laird decided that financial considerations called for Finlaystone to be given up. The loss of the 'owl's nest' was a grievous blow to Robert's parents, more especially to the Strix himself. Among the Bontine letters are several written when he was engaged in the dismal business of clearing up and packing. Some of their furniture was sent to Gartmore but everything else had to be thrown away; old toys, discarded fishing rods, straw hats - the catalogue evoked in him extravagant regret for the happy life so abruptly terminated.(42)

The birth of a third son, Malise, six years after Charles meant there were now five in the Bontine family whose older members had grown accustomed to a spacious existence at Finlaystone. Their home now was another rented house in London, 13 Chesham Place. Meanwhile at Leamington Spa Robert's grandfather, the laird, fell ill and summoned his eldest son to be in constant attendance at his bedside. Robert, aged eight, was sent to school; Hill House at Warwick, not far from Leamington. He took cheerfully to this new regime which held the balance between instruction and exercise. 'I have begun Xenophon and Homer and Horace, and like them pretty well 'he announced in the same breath that he reported an improvement in his efforts at gymnastics. In later years he often referred affectionately to the Headmaster, Dr Bickmore, who gave him an early taste for history and the habit of collecting old and rare books.(43)

The slow but inexorable progress of the laird's illness 'very much bothered' William Bontine. Mr Cunninghame Graham did not die until the winter of 1863 by which time the Strix was afflicted by blinding headaches. Even as he entered into his inheritance as ninth laird of Gartmore, his temper worsened until it became uncontrollable at times. The situation was acutely difficult: the family solicitor struggling to keep the estate on an even keel while his new master ran up debts without informing him. In these circumstances the rent to be brought in by letting Gartmore House was more than ever necessary. Nevertheless Anne Elizabeth and Robert were allowed a brief visit there in April 1864.(44)

According to the evidence available, this was the first opportunity Robert had to acquaint himself with the house and lands to which he was now the next in line. He and his mother travelled overnight by train from London reaching Stirling at 8 a.m. and Gartmore in the afternoon. Thousands of daffodils were out and azaleas coming, Anne Elizabeth told her mother. But the marks of age and neglect were visible in Gartmore House: it was more than thirty years since Robert's family had been able to live there permanently. Either it had been let for short periods to wealthy Glasgow businessmen, or it had stood empty, time past preserved within its doors. 'All through the house the smell of damp, of Kingwood furniture, of roses dried in bowls blended and formed a scent which I shall smell as long as life endures', Robert wrote. The house was sparsely furnished, many of the paintings and much of the fine furniture bought in the prosperous 18th century had gone to auction to pay the debts of the Swindler, Robert's great grandfather. Among the random pieces that remained were curiosities picked up by his bachelor great uncles who had served abroad. Of the books in the 'darkish and dampish' library most had been bought by one of these uncles in India. His imagination was excited by traces of their exotic origin. 'On their yellowing leaves were stains of insects from the East and now and then a grass or flower from Hyderabad or Kolapur, as pencilled notes in the margin said'.(45) There were, too, books on heraldry in which he traced his ancestry back to the Earls of Menteith, and was confronted by the ancient claim to royal descent. This must have excited any boy, let alone one as impressionable as Robert was. But he was also reticent and, as his father's illness ran its dreadful course, would become increasingly reserved. Nothing could have persuaded him to expose himself to ridicule by acknowledging the truth about himself. It was that, from this early age, his attitude to life was governed by noblesse oblige. Instead he disguised his dedication under a cloak of sarcasm and wit. The consequence was that people did not know how to take him: to some he seemed an outright cynic; to others when they were admitted to his confidence, as Conrad was, he seemed a figure from the age of chivalry.(46)

Inchmahome Priory in the Lake of Menteith. Historic Scotland.

Knowing this one can understand the powerful attraction the island of Inchmahome held for him. It was his Avalon, a place where Kings and Queens had congregated; an island abounding in relics of the past which he soon perceived as more virtuous than, and preferable to, the present - an idea that was greatly to influence his adult self. In April, 1363, King David II had married Margaret Drummond in the chapel of the Priory. In 1547 the 4 year old Mary Queen of Scots had been brought to Inchmahome for safety after the battle of Pinkie. There was a bower of box on the island; grown huge with the years it was said to have existed in her time. When, at the Reformation the Priory was dissolved, the Chapter House received the graves of the Earls of Menteith and their Countesses. The island was particularly beautiful in late spring; bluebells were thick upon the grass under the flowering chestnut trees. When Robert first encountered them they had grown stag headed, and he feared that they might fall. He yearned for the time, long past, when ospreys nested in their branches and pine martens hunted along the shore(47).

Robert was out all day riding and fishing while he could, Anne Elizabeth told her mother. 'It seems so sad to let this place now that I have made it comfortable. The house is so clean, airy and nice after 13 Chesham Place'. 'The Strix is in Ireland, I don't exactly know where' she added, 'he left a kind note for me about putting things away' (48). Kind was still the word to which she clung for reassurance, and emphasized when speaking of her husband to her mother and her friends. Over the years it had come to signify all was well with the Bontine family for the Strix, when kind, was also calm and rational. Their son, Robert, came to value kindness more than any other quality, higher even, than love. It was his great misfortune as a child to have to watch kindness give way to suspicion, fear, and anger when the balance of his father's mind was violently disturbed. In the summer of 1864 William's rages became so extreme it was feared he would do himself and others harm so he was put under restraint. The worst aspect of this cruel illness was that, during the attacks he was infuriated by those he loved best. Crueller still, after he recovered he was aware of how badly he had behaved. 'Do not come to see me until I am well' one of his letters urged his wife, 'Do not come'.(49)

During one of his lucid periods William expressed a wish that, should he become wholly incapacitated his brother, Bobby and Colonel Hope should take charge of his affairs. The proposal horrified Anne Elizabeth who did not want her sons to come under the influence of men she regarded as reckless and extravagant. The consequence was that a rift developed between her and the rest of the Cunninghame Graham family. The question of who should control Gartmore and the Bontine boys was left in abeyance at the time because the doctors held out every hope that, after a period of rest and seclusion, the Strix would be completely cured. The family did agree one thing; the following September, when Robert would be 13, he would enter Harrow where he would remain until he was 16. He and Charles (who was also entered for the College), spent Christmas 1864 with their grandmother, Laura Cunninghame Graham at Leamington where they had a tutor, Mr Gulliver, to whom they were attached.(50)

The next three years were miserable and ended in a catastrophe that Robert afterwards chose to forget. When the illness was first recognized, no one, least of all the Strix himself, wanted to accept that his conditions was irreversible. In the spring of 1865, when the doctors pronounced him fit again and the bars were taken off his bedroom windows, he resumed his place as head of the family. As such his word was law. After months of confinement he was impatient to be off so Anne Elizabeth was obliged to prepare for a long sojourn on the Continent. Robert and Charles went with their parents for the first part of the journey during which Anne Elizabeth wrote frequently to her mother, letters that reveal how she and the boys had to take the greatest care not to upset their father whose temper was still extremely volatile. Excitement was forbidden. Towns like Wiesbaden had to be avoided for, though they had the best accommodation, they also offered gaming tables from which the Strix had to be protected at all costs.(51) In late August the boys went home to get ready for school, leaving their parents to press on through Austria and Hungary to Florence where they were to spend the winter.

Robert, who was in the Headmaster, Dr Butler's House, found the first term at Harrow 'dreadfully hard' and got up at 3 a.m. to cram. A contemporary remembered him as quiet, reserved and 'rather exclusive'(52). His best friend was Francis - Frank - Villiers, a cousin of Henry Loch's new wife. His father's only surviving letter dates from this time. The Strix urged his eldest son to take up fencing, the best exercise in the world 'it gives a man confidence'(53). Robert took to it at once and became a lifelong enthusiast. Sadly, William Bontine could not be content with offering advice from a distance; as the autumn progressed he became impatient to see his sons. Arrangements had been made for them to spend Christmas with their maternal grandmother, Doña Catalina. She and her husband, who was now an Admiral, had moved to Ryde on the Isle of Wight. But at the last moment, and in the face of strenuous opposition from their Cunninghame Graham relatives, Robert and Charles were summoned to join their parents. It was a cold and weary journey overland to Italy in winter and their spirits must have sunk when the Bontines greeted them and they realized that William's symptoms had returned. He spent much of his time riding aimlessly about while Anne Elizabeth kept up a loyal pretence that nothing was amiss. William's erratic behaviour often confounded her; for instance she had become involved in rehearsals for a concert to be given by members of the English colony in Florence. Just as she was dressed and ready to set out for the performance 'The Strix forbade it which caused a lot of comment'(54).

Robert and Charles went back to England after Christmas leaving their parents to continue their unhappy sojourn. Robert found the next quarter at Harrow much easier and even began to enjoy himself. 'I like it very much. I was very stupid not to think I would' he wrote, 'the only thing I do not like is that one day the work is easy and short that (sic) a baby could do it and another day it is long and hard'(55); he was touchingly anxious not to be a worry to his parents. In the summer he played cricket for his house while always looking forward to the holidays. Every time he wrote he begged to know if he would be going to Gartmore.

In March 1866 his parents reached Paris on their way home. It was the heyday of the Second Empire and M. de Flahaut was now President of the Legion of Honour and a generous host to his wife's Scottish relatives. 'He gave us the Emperor's box at the theatre', William wrote, 'and a seat at the races in the Bois de Boulogne'. It was the last time poor William would take part in such amusements. In April he and Anne Elizabeth arrived in London where they stayed a month during which doctors were summoned who feigned a pretext to examine him. In June they went home to Scotland. 'I was taken ill at Gartmore in August (1866) 'William wrote years later. Seized by a sudden fit of rage he attacked Anne Elizabeth with a sword(56).

Notes to Chapter One

1. National Library of Scotland: Acc.11335/71, E. Garnett to RBCG ,2 Jan. 1898.
2. Harris, F., 'Contemporary Portraits, Third Series', pub. by the author, New York, 1920. p. 45.
3. For example; John Lavery, Cunninghame Graham on 'Pampa' ; William Rothenstein 'The Fencer'; Jacob Epstein.
4. Lavery, J., 'The Life of a Painter', Cassell, 1940, p.88 et seq.
5. See for example; Airdrie Advertiser, various reports of the crisis in the coal mines 1886, 87.
6. Cunninghame Graham, R.B., 'A Vanished Arcadia: Being some account of the Jesuits in Paraguay, 1607 - 1767' Heinemann, 1901, Preface.
7. Conrad, J., 'Nostromo', Penguin, 1963, p.66.
8. Ibid.
9. Cunninghame Graham, R.B., 'Notes on the District of Menteith for Tourists and Others', Adam & Charles Black, 1895, p.ix.
10. Cunninghame Graham, R.B. Mist in Menteith in 'Rodeo: A collection of the Tales and Sketches of Robert Bontine Cunninghame Graham selected by A.F. Tschiffely', Heinemann, 1936, p.383.
11. Part printed in Cunnninghame Graham, R.B., 'Doughty Deeds: An Account of the Life of Robert Graham of Gartmore, Poet and Politician, 1735 - 1797. Drawn from his Letter Books and Correspondence', Heinemann, 1925.
12. Ibid.
13. Ibid., p. 14. And see Scott, W., 'Rob Roy', 1829 ed. Oxford University Press, p. xxxvii.
14. 'Doughty Deeds' op.cit., p.162.
15. ibid., pp 156 58.
16. For the Ireland affair see Three Banks Review Dec. 1949.
17. Papers deposited by the Rt. Hon. Lady Polwarth in the National Library of Scotland - Acc.11335/1-203, including correspondence between RBCG, his mother, Anne Elizabeth Fleeming/Bontine; his father, William Bontine; his grandmother, Mrs Katon, and others. Acc.11335/52, Anna Cunninghame Graham to RBCG, 1 July 1893.
18. ibid., Acc.11335/7, one of a series of handwritten exercise books by William Bontine; 'Five Years in Ireland'.
19. Ibid. Acc.11335/6, W. Bontine, 'Reminiscences of Germany'.

20. Ibid., Acc.11335/7, 'Five Years in Ireland , Addenda'.
21. Ibid.
22. Ibid., Acc.11335/14.
23. NLS, MS 10288, Mountstuart Elphinstone to Mrs Katon, 15 Oct. 1850.
24. ibid., Mountstuart Elphinstone corr; ME to AE Fleeming, 15 Oct. 1850.
25. Colebrooke, T.E., 'Life of the Hon. Mountstuart Elphinstone', J. Murray, 1884.
26. NLS, MS 10288, ME to Mrs Katon, 31 Oct. 1851.
27. ibid., AEF to ME, 23 July 1850.
28. e.g. Tschiffely, A.F., 'Don Roberto' Heinemann, 1937. (based on conversations with RBCG in 1934 - 36,).
29. NLS, Acc.11335/12, birth certificate, 16 June 1800.
30. Cunninghame Graham, R.B., The Admiral in 'Hope', Duckworth, 1910, p.220 et seq., Lady Dunedin in John O'London's Weekly, 3 Dec. 1937.
31. The Times, 2 Nov. 1840.
32. NLS; MS 10288, ME to AEF 15 Oct. 1850.
33. ibid., Acc.11335/12, AEB to Mrs Katon, various dates 1851/52.
34. ibid, Acc.11335/26, AEB to ME 1 April 1853.
35. Cunninghame Graham, R.B., 'Heather Jock in 'The Ipane', T.Fisher Unwin, 18999, pp. 183-84.
36. NLS; MS 10288, ME to AEB, Oct. 1852; and AEB to ME 4 Dec. 1853.
37. Heather Jock, op. cit.
38. NLS, Acc.11335/31, H. Loch to AEB, 25 Aug. 1859.
39. Oliphant, L., 'Elgin's Mission to China and Japan', Oxford in Asia Historical Reprints, 1970, Vol. II, pp. 217-18.
40. NLS, Acc. 11335/31, Loch to AEB, - June 1860.
41. Ibid., Acc.11335/29, G. Moir to AEB, 12 Feb. 1863.
42. ibid., Acc.11335/8, W.Bontine to AEB, n.d.
43. ibid., Acc11335/19,RBCG to AEB 10 Feb. 1865.
44. ibid., Acc.11335/6, W. Bontine, 'Reminiscences' op.cit.
45. Cunninghame Graham R.B., Miss Christian Jean in 'His People', Duckworth,1906.
46. Davies, K., and L., 'The Collected Letters of Joseph Conrad', Cambridge U.P. 1983, Vol. I, p. 424.
47. 'Doughty Deeds', op.cit.
48. NLS, Acc.11335/12, AEB to Mrs Katon, 14 April 1864.
49. ibid., Acc.11335/8, W. Bontine to AEB, nd.
50. Scottish Record Office; CS 46/143/1868. AEB to Mrs Katon, August 1865.
51. ibid.
52. Cotton Minchin, J.G., 'Old Harrow Days' Methuen, 1898, p. 273.
53. NLS, Acc.11335/8, W. Bontine to RBCG, - 0ct. 1865.
54. ibid., Acc.11335/12, AEB to Mrs Katon, - Feb. 1866.
55. ibid., Acc.11335/19, RBCG to AEB, - Feb. 1866.
56. ibid., Acc.11335/6, W. Bontine,' Reminiscences', op.cit.

Chapter Two

Tutelage

Horrifying though it was, William's attack upon his wife was merciful in one respect: it absolved his family from having to pretend that everything was as it should have been. It is clear from a letter written by his grandmother on receipt of the telegram from Gartmore asking urgently for help, that the fourteen year old Robert had long been aware of the possibility that his father might be violent. 'How sad it must be for the poor dear boys to see their father in that state', Catalina (not a tactful person) wrote to Anne Elizabeth, 'particularly for poor dear Robert who is now old enough to feel it much. He sometimes used to speak to me about his father and ask me if I thought he would be in that state again'. For her part she had long suspected Anne Elizabeth was the victim of ill treatment, but had said nothing. Now - 'something must be done ... for really you cannot go on leading such a miserable life and exposed to so much danger'.(1). Something <u>was</u> done that dismayed the Bontine family and weighed on their conscience for many years. The Strix, whose nature found its solace in the freedom of the open air, and in constant changes of scene, was confined for the rest of his life in a house near Dumfries with a doctor always in attendance - this was his island, his Juan Fernandez, to which rescue never came. To see him imprisoned was pain enough for they were very fond of him, but in the autumn of 1866 they had to face another ordeal. At the age of 38 Anne Elizabeth found herself pregnant with a child conceived the previous July, a few weeks prior to the attack. She survived the birth in February, 1867 but the baby, a girl, was stillborn (2).

Robert, at school, fell ill, failed an exam and was rebuked for bad behaviour. The summer of 1867 was the last at Harrow for both boys; the family could no longer afford the fees. Charles, who had always been destined for the Royal Navy, found a home on board the training ship, HMS Britannia. Robert was enrolled with a tutor, the Revd. Mr Bradly, who lived in Southgate. In later life he never admitted to the months he spent in that unremarkable London suburb, but it was while he was there that he conceived a plan to emigrate to South America as soon as he was able. (3).

The splendidly romantic history of that continent (which he may have studied under Mr Bradly), was to engage him as a scholar and a writer all his life. At 15 he was just of an age to be thrilled by the adventures of the <u>conquistadores</u>; when he grew older he did not fail to address the more controversial issues - the treatment of the Indians for example. As Doña Catalina's grandson he had special interest from the start: the Enterprise of the Indies could be said to have begun when Christopher Columbus set sail from Cadiz, the port where she was born; while the Admiral, his admired grandfather, had been present at the last act, the siege of Maracaibo (4). More recently, in order to report to his ship which was on the Pacific station, one of Henry Loch's brothers, Granville Gower Loch, had crossed the Argentine on horseback.(5). The opening of that country to foreign capital during the last ten years meant that, by the late 1860s many Scots knew of some compatriot who had tried his hand at sheep farming on the <u>pampas,</u> the vast southern plains. However, for the most part these were men of some substance. Robert's use of the verb, to emigrate, suggests that he had succumbed to propaganda, widespread in the newspapers of the time, offering incentives to working men whose labour was being sought to develop land in the republics bordering on the Rio de la Plata. One of the firms prominent in recruiting emigrants at the time, Robinson and Fleming (of which more later), was well known to Robert's uncle, Bobby Cunninghame Graham. (6). It may be that in his penniless condition Robert fixed on the scheme's advantages - a free passage, help with acquiring land on arrival - as a means to escape while neglecting to consider whether the life of a manual labourer would really suit him.

The older members of his family firmly opposed the idea, while his mother was acutely anxious as to what might befall him if he went. Even supposing his refusal to contemplate any other course of action succeeded in bringing her round, he had no hope at all of departing for the New World unless he could secure permission from the authority that, after January 1868, ruled every aspect of his life. An irksome supervision was fixed upon Robert in that year which lasted until long after he succeeded as tenth laird. It was the result of the renewed dispute between his mother and her in laws as to who should take charge of his father's affairs. ('I wish, my dearest, that you had never had anything to do with those horrid [Grahams] for it has been little else than misery to you', Catalina burst out at this point).(7). In December 1867 Robert's uncle Bobby, his grandmother, Laura Cunninghame Graham, his aunts, and Colonel Hope, petitioned the Court of Session to appoint their candidate, a Mr Buchanan, to take charge of William's affairs. Anne Elizabeth rejected him and cross petitioned for one of her own relatives who lived not far from Gartmore. The Court chose neither but appointed a distinguished Edinburgh accountant, George Auldjo Jamieson, as <u>Curator Bonis</u>. (8). However, Robert's mother could at least take comfort from the fact that one of the Trustees of the Bontine estate, also appointed at this time, was her close friend and cousin, Henry Loch. (9). He had reached a plateau in the upward course of his career: in 1867 and for many years to come he was Governor of the Isle of Man.

Jamieson's duty as <u>Curator</u> was to ensure the security and welfare of his ward, William Bontine (he was never known as Cunninghame Graham in spite of having succeeded as ninth laird): to administer his estates against the day when he might hope to be restored to health and competence. The care of William's wife and sons, though obviously important, was secondary. The first task was to rescue Gartmore from the financial chaos to which William's speculative activities had reduced it. Jamieson was required to send reports of progress to the Court of Session: these had to be detailed, even down to the sums of pocket money doled out to the boys. The <u>Curator</u> could not authorize any change of circumstance without special application to the Accountant of the Court, and so its papers, preserved in the Scottish Record Office, are a primary source for what happened to Robert and his family after 1867: as with the Bontine correspondence they often contradict the later, published version.(10).

The strict and formal procedure of the Court had a devastating effect upon the adolescent boy: he could do nothing without Jamieson's knowledge and consent. More particularly when, as heir, he might have been learning the duties of an owner of a large estate, he was excluded from participation in its affairs almost as if he were his father's rival. The inheritance in which he had delighted for so short a time was snatched away by lawyers and accountants: while his father lived - and William was only 42 when the <u>Curator</u> was appointed - Robert must be an exile from beloved Gartmore. At the same time he became the object of nervous attention by the older members of his family who - understandably perhaps - feared he might have inherited something of his father's temperament. At 15 he was perceived to be naturally high spirited, bold, energetic, caustic and funny, but not quite 'steady', indeed at times alarmingly morose. While Charles was happy as a midshipman, and Malise who was seven, remained in his mother's care, no one had any idea of what was to become of Robert except the boy himself. As <u>Curator</u> Jamieson had to weigh what was best for him against what was financially possible. Almost as soon as he took charge he was forced to conclude that the cost of Mr Bradly's fees could no longer be sustained. At Easter 1868 Robert was packed off to Brussels to the care of the Chaplain to the British Embassy, the Revd. Mr Jenkins, who had been highly recommended to his mother. Although money was so tight, in response to Robert's urgent plea the wherewithal was found for extra tuition in fencing, and in Spanish, a language he set himself to learn to prepare for South America. The letters he wrote from Brussels are uncharacteristically brief and uninformative: they mostly complain of the misery of a rough sea crossing - he was always a bad sailor. Since he was obliged to go home for the holidays he became all too well acquainted with the weather in the English Channel. (11).

The expenses he incurred while staying with his mother were paid separately by the <u>Curator</u>. Anne Elizabeth had only £500 a year from the estate for herself and her youngest son. (12). With Malise and Homer, her devoted German maid, she moved to London where she addressed herself to those bachelor like ideas that had endeared her to Uncle Mount, and which did something now to console her in her *de facto* widowhood. In 1860 when her brother John succeeded as the 14th Lord Elphinstone, she had been granted the style of a peer's daughter. Now, as far as she was able within the strict financial limits imposed by the Court of Session, the Hon. Mrs Bontine invited writers and artists to her modest house in Ebury Street, and was seen at concerts and the theatre. She spent her summer holidays with her mother, Catalina, and her stepfather, Admiral James Katon, on the Isle of Wight. In July 1868 the Court approved a payment of £3 for Robert's fare to join his family on the Island.(13). Up to that time his visits there had not been frequent. Catalina's letters to his mother are full of excuses as to why she could not accommodate her grandsons - the Admiral's gout, her own poor health, lack of beds, damp rooms - were some of the circumstances that prevailed against a visit when Robert was a little boy.

The Katons occupied a tall house at Ryde commanding a wide view of naval traffic in and out of Portsmouth dockyard on which the Admiral kept an expert, loving eye. As described by Robert in the sketch, 'A Sailor, Old Style',

James Katon's time in the Navy had begun at the age of 12 or 13 and, until he made landfall on the Isle of Wight some 40 years later, he had always been at sea. His career had been far less flamboyant than that of Robert's grandfather, Charles Fleeming, under whom he had served for years as Flag Officer in HMS Barham. 'Treated as he had been ...to all the rigours of the Admiralty, now freezing off Newfoundland, and again melting off St Helena or Port Royal, lacking advancement always, and seeing others younger than himself put over him by intent or chance, he never grumbled at his luck. In fact I think he thought himself a lucky man always to have been employed and to have been Flag Captain in the Channel for a brief space of time', Robert wrote. In spite of Katon's unassuming manner he held his grandmother's second husband in the greatest affection and respect. 'Of such as he was is the kingdom of the sailor's heaven; that is if single mindedness and kindness, with a high sense of honour and charity which, though it naturally began at home, extended to the limits of the world, entitles a man to a free pass.' (14). The sketch is a tribute to the healing effect of James Katon's strong common sense and kindness upon Robert in the aftermath of the tragedy that had grievously wounded him. Katon, who was merely his stepgrandfather, did better for him than the older members of his own family who sent him off to Brussels by himself, there to recover as best he could.

Admiral Katon had witnessed the tragedy at first hand, for it was he who hurried north to Gartmore in response to the message, 'Come immediately'.(15). Now, two years later, he set himself to distract the Bontine boys in the best way that he knew. As Robert described it the process began with a walk in windy weather on Ryde pier; 'The Admiral was sure to stop and say to some old mariner, 'Nice day for a sail ', and then we trembled in our shoes. Sometimes the owner of the abominable craft in which we passed so many hours limp and green...would answer. 'Lor' Admiral it does blow a leetle fresh for the young gentlemen'. This sometimes was a respite and at others served but as an incentive, and we used to put to sea seated down in a sort of well where we saw nothing but at the same time received plenty of salt water down our backs, shivering miserably. At times one or the other of us steered, jamming the [boat] about across the Solent in the agonies of sea sickness till we relapsed upon the seat inert and miserable'. Still they liked it, Robert remembered, 'and I am certain the Admiral enjoyed it hugely saying it did us twice the good of any medicine'. (16).

By such simple means Katon taught Robert a lesson he took to heart. As he described his Graham relations they were sportsmen who, however dedicated, had no particular profession. Katon was the first person he knew well wholly caught up in a subject that demanded expert knowledge, application, and practical skill: from the exercise of which he had not only earned his living but manifestly derived satisfaction and delight. The sense of fitness of things to their purpose which Katon demonstrated, continued the process begun on the shore at Finlaystone which distinguished Robert as a writer later on. It became a measure of worth for him; one that he applied to people in all walks of life. Those in whom he sensed integrity of the sort he first identified in Katon - gauchos on the pampas; miners in Lanarkshire; metal workers in the Black

Country; certain writers and painters - received his sympathy and, upon occasion, help; while those whom he perceived to be lacking this essential quality - many politicians, almost all businessmen - found themselves the objects of his coruscating wit.

Even so, in spite of this crucial influence, when describing his relationship as a boy with his grandmother, Doña Catalina, Robert never mentioned Katon whose presence in her life did not fit the facts as he chose to represent them later on. But his stepgrandfather was important in another , very particular way. Katon's stories of the old Barham in which he had sailed under Charles Fleeming awoke in Robert an echo of the far distant places and remarkable things both men had seen. - 'the Spanish Main...long raking schooners with tapering masts...barracoons and slaves...the Blue Mountains and Port Royal.. enormous sharks that followed boats...[sailors] with heavy rings beaten out on a marlinspike from a doubloon'.(17). There is more than a trace of self mockery in this but, in 1868 ,these romantic images unsettled Robert; they set him thinking how, in his turn, he must be off and fend for himself rather than relying on the bounty of the Court of Session. The constraints it imposed on him appeared intolerable when he considered how old he was already. Charles Fleeming had gone to sea by the time he was eleven; James Katon not much older; Mounstuart Elphinstone was 17 when he sailed for India. At virtually the same age Robert was trapped at home by the disapproval of his family as to his plan for emigration and the <u>Curator's</u> indecision. He was obliged to sit out 1869 in Brussels where he practised Spanish, and lost himself in whatever books he could obtain on the history, topography, geology, flora and fauna, manners and customs of the various countries of the South American continent. When he rejoined his mother and brothers for the holidays they perceived in him such a vivid representation of what he had read they christened him the Gaucho.

That is how he was referred to in letters between his mother and the first young woman with whom he fell in love. In 1867 or 68 the Countess Harley Teleki came back to England where she had been born, to live with her widowed mother, Lady Langdale. We do not know why she left her husband, Count Alexander Teleki, but the letters suggest that she found life on his vast estates in Poland insupportable. Though she was considerably younger than Anne Elizabeth whom she called Anita, the two quickly became fast friends. The Countess was not so well disposed to Robert who too visibly adored her. 'We cannot agree about the spoony Gaucho', she told Anne Elizabeth, 'He <u>is</u> a gentleman all round, that I grant you, and on that account can I tolerate him. But nevertheless he bores me more unutterably than anybody I have met for a long time. I have no patience with such a maundering donkey'.(18). Robert had to content himself with gazing at her whenever they met. By 1869 he and his family were frequent visitors to Lady Langdale's country house, Eynwood near Hereford where, in his father's boots and a borrowed hat he was able to go hunting. Miladi, as Harley's mother was known to everyone, including Harley, was the only daughter and heir of the Earl of Oxford; as such she was immensely rich and grand - grander, even, than Madame de Flahaut. Miladi was a cross Harley had to bear, even as Anne Elizabeth had to put up with her mother in law, Laura Cunninghame Graham. Both old ladies were noted for their acid tongues and overbearing ways. Harley's letters condoling with Anne Elizabeth on this point also sympathized with Robert's lack of progress in persuading his grandmother and Uncle Bobby to let him go to South America.

Early in 1870 Harley was obliged to accompany her mother on a trip by boat up the Nile. 'How I wish...the party were you and I with two men who would really suit us', she wrote candidly to Anne Elizabeth. It was composed instead of Miladi, two maids, a dragoman, and two young male cousins who bored her almost as much as Robert. Distance softened her attitude to him; from Cairo she sent him an account of how she had climbed a pyramid. In March she wrote from Luxor in answer to a letter from Anne Elizabeth telling her the Grahams had relented. 'I am so glad the Gaucho should (sic) go and see South America... It will keep him out of mischief, ie the neighbourhood of Bobby Graham and Mr Hope for a time. He will see for himself, or if he does not like it, Mr Jamieson's idea of an irregular Indian regiment does not seem a bad one'.(19). When Robert returned from South America Harley now looked forward to seeing him at Eynwood.

As this letter implied, consent had at last been given for Robert, not to emigrate, but to go for a few months only to a ranch some 200 miles up country from Buenos Aires in the province of Entre Ríos. It was run by two Scots, James and Edward Ogilvy who were relatives of another of his mother's friends, Blanche , the Countess of Airlie. The idea of Robert learning the rudiments of cattle ranching in this way seems to have originated with her. On 17 March 1870 the Curator sent a carefully worded application to the Accountant of the Court for special powers to advance a grant not exceeding £300 for Robert's outfit and fare. Jamieson explained that Robert had wanted to go to South America ever since he had been at Southgate. 'Against this inclination Mrs Bontine and the other relatives of the young gentleman exercised every influence they possessed, and whatever the Curator could do, he did, to influence Mr Graham's views towards a course of life less adventurous and more in accordance with his position and prospects. All parties interested in Mr Graham's welfare, entertained the hope that as he became older the predeliction in favour of South America would disappear, but this has not been the case and the desire of the young man to go to Buenos Aires appears as strong now as it did when the idea was originally suggested by him.' The subject had become very anxious and pressing in the last few weeks, Jamieson went on: while Robert had yielded a ready hearing to all those interested in him, he remained determined on his course. He was not sure he would like it when he got there but, 'he cannot settle down until he tries it.'. (20). Reading between the lines, there had obviously been an almighty row before, with the help of the formidable Lady Airlie, Robert got his way. Years later he told his friend and biographer, Aimée Tschiffely, that his mother had surrendered because of her alarm at the fits of depression that, increasingly, took hold of him.

The Accountant's response was less than enthusiastic: if the young man had been going out to settle, and the money required was for a permanent outfit, he probably would not have hesitated to advance it without further ado. But, he feared, a brief sojourn would not result in any lasting benefit. However, 'as the eldest son, of course Mr Robert Graham should be dealt with liberally', he minuted. A canny man, he decided to refer the matter up to the Lord Ordinary himself. (21). His Lordship took the broader view, and was minded to consent, so in April 1870 Robert embarked upon the entrancing preliminaries to any and every expedition; taking lists round London outfitters where they ticked off clothes and equipment - a gun, a saddle, waterproof carriage aprons - the sort of thing they regarded as essential to an active outdoor life south of the Equator. He was observed below stairs at his grandmother's house at Leamington Spa learning how to cook and to bake bread; he was also said to be hemming dusters and, more usefully perhaps, darning stockings. He sailed in the SS Patagonia on 13 May. The crossing took three weeks, during which he celebrated his eighteenth birthday. Not that he cared: he was sick up to the time the ship entered the shallow, muddy inland sea that is the estuary of the Rio de la Plata.

On 8 June they docked at Montevideo in the Republic of Uruguay. 'There is a revolution here,' Robert's first letter on landing artlessly informed his mother, 'and one in Entre Ríos so we are rather uncertain of our movements'. (22). It did not occur to him - then, or later - that he might temper bad news to spare those at home, especially his mother. His letter arrived as she was mourning the death of another dear traveller. After returning down the Nile Lady Langdale had insisted on her daughter accompanying her to Syria though Harley, as she wrote to Anne Elizabeth, only wanted to go home. She was unwell, though she managed to conceal the fact from Miladi until the party arrived in Damascus at the beginning of May. There, as a result of having contracted 'an illness of the country', she died. (23).

In the light of this new disaster it was as well that Anne Elizabeth could not yet know that Robert had arrived at a moment of increased danger in a region that was one of the most disordered and violent in the world. The republics bordering on the Plata, the Argentine Confederation and Uruguay (whose eastern part was known in those days as the Banda Oriental), not only had a well deserved reputation for political turbulence, but more than their fair share of natural catastrophes - storms, floods, drought, pestilence, disease - as well as being subject to attack by hostile Indians. In the first three months of 1870 things had come to such a pitch that the senior British representative in the area, Her Majesty's Consul (soon to be Chargé d'Affaires) at Buenos Aires, H.G. Macdonell, privately urged Whitehall to take immediate steps to halt the flow of immigrants. Macdonell's dispatches argued that, at a time of renewed civil war, and in view of the Argentine government's notorious indifference to the welfare of foreigners, the lives and property of British subjects could not be guaranteed. If they could not buy immunity settlers in the camp (the country at large beyond the few towns) risked forcible conscription into armed bands that preyed on bystanders on behalf of one or another of the factions. Macdonell listed the names of travellers deserving of his protection who had disappeared, and more than one who had been murdered (24).

In London the Commissioners of Emigration needed no further persuasion: they were already looking for excuses to discredit propaganda of the sort Robert had encountered in favour of emigration to the Rio de la Plata. The Colonial Office held the view that British workers belonged in British colonies

- Canada, Australia, New Zealand or, at a pinch, the United States. South America was a waste of effort and resources; the climate was unsuitable and those who did commit themselves would undoubtedly be swamped by the Spanish, Portuguese, and Italians now arriving by the thousands in the Argentine. However since the drive to recruit English, Scots, Welsh, and Irish labourers was well under way, and reasonably successful, a considerable effort would have to be made if would-be emigrants were to be discouraged. And, when rumours of the British government's intention began to circulate in Buenos Aires, the idea found no favour with foreign merchants (a number of whom were Scots) who feared their livelihood would be endangered. Some sort of counter attack was needed. (25). And so Macdonell was told to write a report on the whole condition of the country as it was in 1870 at the precise moment when Robert Cunninghame Graham disembarked at Montevideo. It was published two years later as a Parliamentary Paper; 'Remarks on the River Plate Republics as a Field for British Emigration'. (26). Much of what it had to say was relevant to Robert's adventures in the next 18 months.

The Report began by denouncing the exaggeration and misrepresentation persistently produced in certain newspapers, articles and pamphlets about the Argentine. In accordance with the desire of HM Emigration Commissioners, Macdonell wrote, his observations would be based on the reliable experience of persons long resident in the country. In order of importance its industries were sheep farming, cattle farming, agriculture, mining and commerce. Sheep farming was the most lucrative occupation of British settlers, among whom were many Scots and Irish but this was true only of the province of Buenos Aires where, of late, healthier sheep and better wool had been produced by crossing the native pampa sheep with Leicesters and South Downs. Where this had not been done - Entre Ríos for example - the settlers were having difficulty in surviving.

As to cattle farming, Macdonell was at pains to warn newly arrived immigrants not to attempt it without a thorough apprenticeship. 'The cattle being wild it requires a good horseman and one expert with the lasso, to catch them for the purpose of marking and slaughtering them'. (27). Herds of between 2,000 and 3,000 roamed the plains unattended except for a horseman occasionally riding round to prevent them straying. At night they were brought in and fenced in the neighbourhood of the estancia house. On good land the long horned Spanish cattle would double in weight in 3 1/2 to 4 years. Few survived that long; their meat was extremely tough and there was no point in breeding from them. Not until the 1880s when refrigeration proved successful would new strains be imported to yield beef that was tender and fat. In 1879 and for many years to come the cattle were still machines for the production of leather for which there was a high demand in Europe. From December to May the slaughter houses were constantly employed in the gruesome bloody business of obtaining hides under appalling conditions of dispatching the beasts and disposal of the waste. Much of the meat was salted and dried and sent for consumption by slaves in Cuba and in Puerto Rico. According to Macdonell, in 1869 Buenos Aires province produced 680,000 hides, Entre Ríos 400,000.

Everything about cattle farming appeared simple and primitive, Macdonell remarked, and it had undoubtedly proved most profitable to natives of the Argentine, many of whom had made large fortunes at it. But, he went on, 'strange to say, few if any foreigners have succeeded in the business thought there is no apparent reason why they should have been less successful in cattle than in sheep farming'. (28). Really he was in no doubt as to the reason, at which he had already hinted, and which his Report addressed when it came to discuss the nature of the people of the Argentine. While most English settlers were already experienced in breeding sheep, and needed little, if any, outside help, the peculiar conditions attached to rearing cattle on the vast, unfenced plains, the <u>pampas</u>, made it essential to employ skilled horsemen; these were, necessarily, natives of the camp, of mixed Spanish and Indian blood; the celebrated gauchos. As a race they were notoriously wild; ungovernable, except by one of their own kind, the <u>capataz</u>, the foreman, an heroic figure who, by superior strength, skill, and daring forced them to submit to his orders(29).

Macdonell's purpose being to discourage emigration he was extreme in his denunciation of the people of the Argentine. Those of the town who were mostly of pure descent from the Spanish conquerors were urbane and intelligent, he wrote, 'but as a rule idle, corrupt and very jealous of foreign, especially English, innovation and interference.' As for the inhabitant of the camp, the gaucho, he was illiterate, rude, greedy of money, addicted to gambling, implacable and revengeful, distrusting the foreigner as much as the townsman and more openly displaying his hostility. 'With such it is impossible to hold faith; they are the originators of all the disturbances that afflict the country and at times little better than paid assassins.'. (30).

Very broadly speaking, for most of the 19th century a confused and violent struggle, complicated by blood feuds, had been waged between the Unitarians - supporters of a strong central government at Buenos Aires - and its fierce opponents, the Federalists who favoured a much looser system that worked to their advantage. The Federal leaders were gauchos, <u>caudillos</u> (dictators) whose power in their own territory was absolute. Two of the gaucho leaders, Juan Manuel de Rosas, and Justo José de Urquiza, were exceptional men who forced their own order on the whole country for a time; Rosas ruled as dictator from 1835 to 1852 when he was overthrown by Urquiza. The latter's firm rule promised stability in the Argentine and this brought foreign capital in to the country and encouraged the development of agriculture, especially sheep farming. The significance of the latest revolution in Entre Ríos, news of which excited Robert on his arrival in June, 1870, was that it seemed to herald a collapse into the old anarchic ways. In 1861, when Urquiza had been defeated in battle by a Unitarian leader, he had been allowed to go home to Entre Ríos where, for the next nine years, those who took over from him in Buenos Aires allowed him to govern as he pleased. In April 1870 his flamboyant and despotic ways finally provoked the opposition of another gaucho leader, López Jordán, who had him assassinated. By the time Robert arrived at Montevideo a few weeks later Entre Ríos was in uproar as government forces from Buenos Aires struggled to overcome Jordán's troops.

The southern winter had set in when Robert left Montevideo bound for the Ogilvys' ranch. Though it had long been a place he was eager to see, there is no evidence that he called at Buenos Aires which lay about 150 miles from Montevideo across the estuary on its southern shore. Macdonell's recent dispatches had warned of yellow fever at the capital and it is possible, in order to avoid the sickness, and spare himself the obligatory period in quarantine, Robert continued straight on to the mouth of the River Uruguay. (31). With the other two great rivers of the Plata system, the Paraná and the Paraguay, it was the only means of transport into the tierra adentro, the 'inside country'. Guayleguaychú, the nearest centre of population to the Ogilvys' ranch, lay a night's journey up the Uruguay by stern wheel paddle steamer. Robert stayed on deck to watch its progress and to observe the sleeping passengers; gauchos who lay with their heads pillowed on saddles, their long silver handled knives close to hand. His attentiveness to their appearance and bearing was to be more valuable than, on that first river voyage, he could know. He was arriving in this remote and backward region at a turning point in its history. When, some years later, he came to describe the gauchos' primitive, unusual, brutal and - in his view - entirely comprehensible way of life, it had vanished utterly.

After the broad yellow waters of the estuary the Uruguay was narrow, overarched with trees, the channel frequently interrupted by sandbanks, shoals, and floating debris. 'A thick white mist rose from the stream which shrouded both banks and rose half way up the masts and funnel leaving the tops of trees floating like islands in the air. Upon the highest branches cormorants and vultures sat asleep which at the passing of the boat awoke and screamed'. To Robert the hours of the night passed like days, and very silently, broken only by the pilot's nasal cry as the stream shoaled, or by 'the faint distant neigh of some wild stallion gathering up his mares'. Shortly after daybreak the steamer made fast to a rough plank dock on the Argentine side of the Uruguay. The river marked the frontier with the Banda Oriental - a country also in revolt and even more disturbed than the Argentine - so the first persons Robert saw coming through the mist were a number of sleepy soldiers smoking cigarettes. 'A man dressed in uniform stepped from the pier on to the deck, went down below and in a little while came up again with an air of having done his duty to the State'. The formalities completed, the passengers disembarked, each with a bag or saddle according to his next means of transport. Those with luggage, including Robert, should have been met at the dock by a diligence which was late; drawn by six horses, it arrived in a cloud of dust. They scaled it 'as if it were a fortress' and were jolted to the town. Stuck like a chessboard on a table, on a plain some three miles from the river, with its flat topped white painted houses and streets intersecting one another into squares, Guayleguaychú had an Oriental look. The centre of administration and trade for a large area of Entre Ríos it boasted a church with a dome, a plaza embellished with orange trees, two hotels, several general stores, numerous bars, a police station, a low round building where cock fights were staged, and the house where, more than thirty years before, the Italian guerilla leader, Giuseppe Garibaldi, had briefly been imprisoned and tortured so severely his legs were dislocated . (He had been fighting on the side of insurgent forces in one of the numerous revolts by the province against its centre that raged across the region for so many years). (32).

What struck Robert most about this gaucho town was the preponderance of horses: no one went about on foot, even the one beggar bestrode a miserably thin horse. 'Horses pervaded all the place, in every open space they fed attached to ropes, in all the yards they stood up to the fetlocks in black mud, or in hot dust according to the season of the year, and ate alfalfa... Men dressed in loose black cashmere trousers, with high patent-leather boots, the tops all worked in patterns...their ponchos fluttering in the wind, rode past on silver mounted saddles...Their horses..snorted and passaged at the strange sights of town, tried to whip round and spring across the street like goats if a dog stirred or a door fastened with a bang. Their riders... assumed the far off look of an ineffable content which horsemen, mounted on a horse that does them credit, put on quite naturally in every quarter of the world'.(33). Of the two hotels in Gualeguaychú the one frequented by the young English cattle farmers, the Fonda del Vapor, was where he met the Ogilvys. Their ranch, the Estancia de Santa Anita, lay about 45 miles away across rolling park like country. There were no roads or bridges, only the tracks of bullock carts which converged at fords. 'A man could ride to Corrientes (600 miles) without an obstacle to stop him on the way but flooded rivers if it should choose to rain, or want of water if there was a drought' (34). If, as is likely, the Ogilvy establishment followed the pattern of other <u>estancias</u>, the white painted house stood in a grove of peach trees whose fruit was always hard like turnips), on a rise overlooking a corral made of split wooden rails bound with strips of hide. An <u>ombú</u> tree grew like a giant umbrella beside the well, at a safe distance from the house on which, if bad luck was to be avoided, its shadow must not fall. Also at a certain distance was the <u>palenque</u>, the hitching post, marking the boundary where, by convention, strangers halted until they received an invitation to approach. (35).

Robert spent his time at the ranch reading the books his mother regularly sent him and riding about. His letters home did not mention what, if anything, he learned about the farming practices of James and Edward Ogilvy; sheep and cattle scarcely interested him; he was absorbed in watching the gauchos. In that beautiful but empty and remote countryside their lives were necessarily austere. Horses were a gaucho's chief preoccupation and delight; a good horse enhanced his standing among his fellows, it was an object for barter as well as his only means of transport. The cattle he tended on horseback provided most of his other needs, including food and fuel. Beef was the staple of his diet; there were no vegetables and no fruit beside the unrewarding peach. Corn was not grown so bread, outside the town, was unobtainable, as was dairy produce except on rare occasions. Then the gaucho method as described by Robert, was to tie a bag of milk to the saddle and gallop about until the butter came. (36). Almost everything the gauchos used, or wore, was made from animals they reared or hunted. Their huts were furnished with skins and hides; they used skulls as seats, slept on piles of hides, and cooked and warmed themselves at fires made of grass, bones, and dung. This rigour commended them to Robert who also approved their one extravagance - the silver ornaments they lavished on their horses' accoutrements, and on their weapons they carried with a swagger Robert was quick to adopt as he did their clothes. There is a photograph of him wearing a flat and rakish hat and the chiripá (cloth folded to form baggy trousers), armed with a long knife and a whip; a figure to banish all thought of the outfit he brought with him - waterproof carriage aprons were hardly the thing in Entre Ríos.(37).

Graham in gaucho dress. National Library of Scotland.

Robert's ability to communicate in Spanish with the gauchos; his admiration of their special skills and knowledge; his obvious love of horses, won their tolerance, allowing him an opportunity to approach them given to few outsiders. This privilege was not for the squeamish or fainthearted. The gauchos regarded human life as worth very little: they would knife a man at the slightest provocation and when drunk they were extremely volatile, while their favourite pursuit of ostrich hunting was acutely dangerous. Robert confessed to an agony of fear each time he found himself mounted on a half wild horse, one of a line galloping at a band of ostriches. These were brought down by means of the bolas, three lead balls fastened to strings of twisted hide flung to entangle the bird's elongated legs. Not infrequently what stumbled and fell was the horse when its rider turned a somersault. The trick then was to land on your feet retaining hold of the bridle. To find yourself on the vast empty plain, injured, and abandoned by your mount was, almost inevitably, to perish(38). To know that his survival depended on his horse marked a new stage in Robert's lifelong attachment to the species. Some of the horses he was to own were to be better friends to him than many people. He liked to dwell on the fact that the Argentine mustangs were descendants of the very small number of horses that had been left behind in Buenos Aires in 1537. The year before Pedro de Mendoza had brought out eleven ships with 2000 settlers and many horses and cattle in the hope that the hitherto neglected Plata estuary would prove the starting point for an easy overland route to the vastly rich mines of silver rumoured to lie inland. But the site of Buenos Aires was not well chosen: the Indians were hostile, and there was little food available. After two thirds of the Spaniards had succumbed to famine, disease, or death by violence it was decided to remove to a safer place far into the interior on the River Paraguay. Named in honour of Nuestra Senora de la Asuncion this was to become the first permanent settlement in that part of the continent. In 1537 the move from Buenos Aires was made by river boat; those horses that could not be caught and coaxed on board - perhaps seven mares and two stallions - were left to roam the pampas where, with a favourable climate and abundant grass, they multiplied prodigiously. Their descendants were small in stature, ponies by English standards, but of great strength and stamina, capable of 90 to 100 miles a day over trackless country. (39).

One of Robert's excursions from the estancia was to San José, headquarters of the late governor of Entre Ríos, Don Justo de Urquiza who had liked to be known as Napoleon del Sur. His palace, a crenellated house in the Moorish/Spanish style, stood at the centre of a vast estate overrun by animals that were entirely fearless; deer too lazy to run at the approach of humans; ostriches stalking near the house like fowl; wart hogs tame as ducks, the result of years of abstention from hunting decreed by Urquiza whose quarry was exclusively human. 'Nothing was chased, shot, caught with the bolas, snared or annoyed by order of the General', Robert wrote, 'all the gauchos knew his punishments. The first offence a fine; the next to be staked out between four posts with fresh hide ropes which the hot sun contracted; the third deprived of horses and obliged to march among the infantry (to go on foot was shame and disgrace to a gaucho); the fourth and last, death by the knife, for cartridges were dear and knives and cutting throats a subject for a jest amongst a population to whom the sight of blood was constant from its youth'.(40).

The members of Urquiza's guard struck Robert as wilder, even, than the horses they rode. They were long haired with their naked feet stuffed into boots made from the hind leg of a horse. 'Their toes protruding grasped the stirrup like a vice, and from their heels dangled and jingled huge and rusty spurs which clattered on the ground like fetters when they walked'. The gauchos told Robert they liked Urquiza; he had been their leader and his rule had not been so bloody in comparison with many of the 'liberators' and 'patriots' who abounded in the Argentine. He might have died a natural death had it not been for his son who was arrogant and greedy, and whose offences were used by Urquiza's opponents to stir up animosity against him. 'One López Jordán, a man who had seen service on the frontier drew to himself some followers and went about plundering and killing cattle, waving the national flag and talking loudly of the rights of man'. In April 1870 Urquiza prepared to take the field against him but was murdered by a band of Jordan's followers who came at him in the ballroom of his palace at San José. A few weeks after the event Robert was shown the room by one of the assassins. The walls were panelled in enormous frames of looking glass; the ceiling thickly coated with gold; the chandelier was large enough for a cathedral and the table tops were glass. The drawing room at San José was furnished with statuettes of Napoleon Buonaparte at various stages in his career; he was the inspiration of every general in South America. (41).

After Urquiza's death order collapsed in Entre Ríos. In September 1870 a member of Macdonell's staff reported that the province was in a wretched state of civil war. (42). Rival bands of Jordán's followers and government troops directed from Buenos Aires were roaming about, mostly avoiding one another, but stealing horses and slaughtering cattle. Whoever was unfortunate enough to come in their way was either forced to ride with them, or risked being executed after the manner of the country: that is to say his throat was cut 'just as they cut a sheep's, driving the knife in at the point with the edge outwards, and bending back the head'. While it is not clear if Robert himself was obliged to join one of the factions for a time, there can be no doubt that this demonstration of the arbitrary nature of political power shocked and intimidated him. Fathers and sons and brothers fought on opposite sides; 'the claims of party as a general rule proved stronger than the call of blood', he wrote, 'not infrequently it chanced that friends were called upon to kill each other, and did so...without a qualm of conscience' (43).

These months of fear and neglect transformed life on the great brown plains of Entre Ríos. Herds of tame mares began to run wild while the cattle became fierce as buffaloes; anyone who lost his horse had to make long detours, for to approach them was as dangerous as to come near a tiger or a lion. The sheep were close herded by armed men. Now the deer and ostrich that had been fearless when Robert saw them at San José, ran if they saw a man even a mile away. If forced to ascend a rise he and his companions dismounted and, creeping on all fours, surveyed the country cautiously; having made sure that all was quiet on the plain below they remained as short a time as possible standing against the sky. If, at the crossing of a river, where thick belts of trees obscured the view, two travellers came upon each other face to face, they greeted one another warily and crossed at sufficient distance to escape a sudden shot, then galloped for a mile or so until they could be sure they had not been followed. At the sight of a band of men on the horizon people fled to the woods driving their horses with them, abandoning their houses to the protection of the dogs.(44).

In spite of these hazards, in September 1870, Robert told his mother he was about to depart on an expedition into the Banda Oriental. The letter gave no forwarding address, an omission that provoked her to a rare complaint: she hated not knowing where he was. Six months later he wrote to say his plans had been frustrated by the disturbances which prevailed around him; he had not been able to get about at all. The summer which he had apparently spent at the Ogilvys' ranch, had been exceptionally dry; the only water for many miles had been at the Estancia de Santa Anita. 'It is a very curious sight to watch the wild horses, cattle, and deer come down to drink in thousands' Robert wrote, 'they come down with clouds of dust and a noise like thunder with the galloping on the hard ground, and then they bathe and fling about.'. One evening he caught a fine horse that had been a long time wild. 'I think the best thing I can do now is to come home as I think I see my way to a good thing now', he went on in the letter dated 10 February (1871). 'Ogilvy and another <u>Escoces</u> (Scot) having had all their cattle killed, horses destroyed, & lost everything by the war are going about the country buying hides and wool & making immense profits by it. They have proposed to take me into partnership which might be thought of when I come home and can explain everything properly. At all events say nothing about it now', he warned his mother; she was to ask Jamieson to send him out the money for his passage home.(45) The <u>Curator</u> duly applied to the Accountant for £80, and this was forwarded by banker's draft. Weeks passed and when Robert did not acknowledge it Jamieson made enquiries only to receive the disquieting news that he had not collected it. (46). Time went by and it seemed that he had vanished. His family were desperate to discover what had become of him. Had he been caught up in the revolution? Had he met with an accident? His last letter contained a vivid account of how he had nearly been bucked off a frightened horse in the middle of a ramshackle town far out in the camp. Was he lying injured somewhere unable to communicate? Or, like Countess Teleki, had he succumbed to an illness of the country? The Grahams applied to the British Consulate in Buenos Aires for information. At that very moment as it happened the capital was overwhelmed by an outbreak of yellow fever so virulent Macdonell compared it to the Great Plague of London. (47). Business and trade had come to a standstill while those who could fled into the camp, thus spreading the infection. In June Anne Elizabeth's anxiety turned to despair when a report reached her that Robert was gravely ill, not with the notorious Yellow Jack, a disease of the tropics, but one that was known and feared in Europe - typhus fever.

The Victorians knew typhus to be extremely contagious (it was spread by lice and fleas), and very serious: they had no remedy for it. Recovery depended on the victim's constitution, supported by the most careful nursing. According to that famous compendium, Mrs Beeton's 'Book of Household Management', typhus fever attacked people whose system had been weakened by depression, overwork, and anxiety; those who were badly fed, who suffered loss of harvest, or the hardships of war, or civil strife, or commercial distress were often its chief victims. The symptoms included severe headache, nausea, languor, aching of the limbs and, above all, a very high temperature. In modern times, with modern medicines, the death rate can still be as high as 40%; in an age which knew nothing of antibiotics, the only possible treatment was careful nursing joined to scrupulous cleanliness. 'All noises must be stopped' Mrs Beeton instructed her readers, 'all creases of sheets should be smooothed and the back rubbed with Balsam of Peru or lavender water...Milk must be the chief article of diet... an egg or two may be beaten up in it.. Beef tea, broths, jellies, extract of beef, custards, may be given'. (48).

Nothing of the sort was available to Robert as he lay, consumed with fever, at the Estancia de Santa Anita. His misfortune was the result of act of kindness. He had gone to fetch medicine and bread from Gualeguaychú for the overseer of a neighbouring ranch who had already succumbed to the disease. On his way back he had crossed a river and afterwards watched by the man's bedside without changing his wet clothes. It was the middle of August before James Ogilvy could tell Anne Elizabeth that he was recovering; he had been very seriously ill. 'For two months my brother and I took care of him and as soon as he could bear the journey we got a carriage to convey him to Dr Forbes house in Concepción del Uruguay (further up river from Gualeguaychú) where he is at present. I have advised him to go home as soon as he is strong enough to bear the journey...it would scarcely be prudent for him to knock about the country any more' (50).

The note of optimism previously sounded by Robert as to the Ogilvys' business affairs is missing from this letter, nor did James make any reference to the proposed partnership. Like many of his compatriots he had become wholly disillusioned about conditions in Entre Ríos and his comments exactly confirmed the reports Macdonell was sending to the Foreign Office. (51). 'Revolutions in South American Republics are of too frequent occurrence as my Brother and I have found to our cost, to induce anyone to invest much capital in them, at all events in stock, and I am afraid there is no hope of getting any compensation from the Government...as the Argentine Minister says he will pay no claim for any damage done by the rebels and the same with regard to the National forces unless you have receipts and he also stated that he considered foreigners in some degree as rebels for carrying on business in a province which was in rebellion against the National government.'(52).

This calamity seems to have precipitated the collapse of Edward Ogilvy who started drinking heavily. This, Macdonell noted, was often the case with young men of good family exiled to a wilderness where they became unable to fend for themselves. According to Robert, by October Edward was in a state bordering on Delirium Tremens. 'James and I have been trying to get him out of town (Guayleguaychú) but it is no use' he told his mother. 'I am getting much stronger again' he reassured her, 'but am still a fearfull(sic) object without any hair' - it had fallen out as a result of the very high fever. 'I had a very bad fall the other day from a wild horse' , he went on relentlessly, 'which I foolishly mounted before I was strong enough. The brute fell on top of me and squashed me a good deal.' He told her he was on the point of leaving on a journey of some 300 miles into the interior; to Córdoba where, to celebrate the arrival of a railway line from Buenos Aires, there was a large exhibition. 'Seeing that horses are very scarce there on account of the great quantity of foreigners that are in the city to see the exhibition & the inroads of the Indians who carry off all they can lay hands on, I have therefore bought thirty or forty horses at twenty dollars apiece & hope to sell them there at about eighty or a hundred dollars each. I expect to be away about a month & I will come home as soon as I return'.(53).

The route to Córdoba lay to the west, across the vast and trackless plains, the pampas. It was Robert's first sight of them: they were like nothing he had ever seen; he was to dwell on the memory all his life. 'All grass and sky, and sky and grass, and still more sky and grass...an ocean of tall grass...'. He thought they looked just as they must have looked on the morning of the seventh day when the Creator rested and' looking earthwards saw that it was good'. The ancient Quecha Indians did well to name the plains with the word signifying space, he wrote, 'for all was spacious - earth, sky, the waving continent of grass, the enormous herds of cattle and of horses; the strange effects of light; the fierce and blinding storms and, above all, the feeling in men's minds of freedom, and of being face to face with nature, under those southern skies'. (54).

Córdoba was unlike any place Robert had encountered in South America up to that time; an old city on a high, eastward facing plain with many fine buildings in the Moorish style. Some 400 miles inland from the Rio de la Plata, it was an outpost of Spanish civilisation that had been established from the west. It had been founded in 1573 by colonists who came across the Andes from Peru. The university, one of the oldest in Latin America, dated from 1614; for two hundred years the city and its hinterland were ruled by Jesuits who built a fine church, laid out spacious gardens, and even provided public baths with running water. To ride into this aristocratic, urbane centre after many months of the most primitive existence in the camp and more than a week driving horses on the plain, must have been a remarkable experience by any standards. For Robert especially, to have been confronted by symbols of power exercised by the immediate successors of the conquistadores, whose great adventure had inspired him to come to South America; to find himself, for instance, at the beginning of the road that lead across the Andes to the former Viceroyalty of Peru, must have been a supreme moment. Yet we cannot be certain he ever saw Córdoba for the simple reason that there is no further mention of it in his letters and, more significantly, he did not describe it in his work. One can only speculate about what happened. We know he set out from Guayleguaychú in October 1871; the British Vice Consul, Dr Wells, saw him just before he left. (55). Perhaps, having embarked upon the long and exceedingly arduous journey Robert found his strength was still not up to it and, somewhere along the way, quietly abandoned the whole enterprise. There would be other occasions in his life whose outcome only he would know.

Be that as it may, it is a matter of record that he returned to England early in the New Year; on 12 January his ship docked at Liverpool from where he continued to his mother's house in London. He at once began discussions with his family as to what occupation he might undertake next. The impossibility of finding anything to his taste at home for which he was even remotely qualified made these conversations very anxious. They were also prolonged and inconclusive because his mother and his uncle Bobby lacked authority in the matter. The only effective means of controlling him - giving or withholding money - was not in their hands but rested with his father's guardian, George Auldjo Jamieson. By the end of 1871 Robert had exhausted all his funds; he could not have got to London if Jamieson had not sent £10 to Liverpool for his fare. This payment had to be reported to the Court of Session which also required a detailed account of the extra cost incurred as a result of his attack of typhus fever. By this it appeared that the original advance of £300 had been almost doubled. The doctor's fee alone was £100; 'he went 18 leagues into the country and remained two weeks with Mr Graham' Jamieson explained (56). In spite of this unhappy outcome the Court must have considered the experience sufficiently worthwhile; six months later it approved an urgent plea by

Jamieson for an advance of money to enable Robert to return to South America. This time his destination was the even more remote and exceedingly strange country of Paraguay.

Notes to Chapter Two

1. NLS,Acc.11335/17 Catalina to AEB, 21 Aug. 1866.
2. SRO; CS 96/2407. NLS, Acc. 11335/12, Hay Erskine to his sister; 'Poor dear Missy has got over her confinement well, but the child, a girl, did not survive.' 21 Feb. 1867.
3. SRO; CS 96/2410. Note.
4. Cunninghame Graham, R.B., The Admiral in 'Hope', op.cit
5. Loch, G., 'The Family of Loch', Edinburgh, 1934.
6. NLS Acc.11335/20; RBCG to AEB, 6 Mar. 1873, 'Uncle Bobby's friends'.
7. Ibid.,acc.11335/20, Catalina to AEB, 1 Feb. 1868.
8. SRO; CS 46/143, 12 and 23 Dec. 1867; SRO, GD22/2/83, 'Memorial for George Auldjo Jamieson' , p.3.
9. SRO: Loch papers,GD 268/99, 'Bontine estate'.
10. SRO; CS 96/2407 -2422;CS 46/143, 1868 -1883. GD 22/2/83.
11. NLS Acc.11335/20, RBCG to AEB, various dates, 1868-1869.
12. She had, besides, her marriage settlement over which Mountstuart Elphinstone had taken so much trouble in 1851.
13. SRO; CS 96/2407, 16 July 1868.
14. Cunninghame Graham, R.B., A Sailor, Old Style in 'Hope', op.cit. pp 84 - 102.
15. NLS,Acc.11335/17, Catalina to AEB 21 Aug. 1866.
16. Cunninghame Graham, R.B., A Sailor, Old Style
17. Ibid.
18. NLS, Acc.11335/30; Teleki to AEB, 8 Feb. 1869; 2.Jan. 1870.
19. ibid., the same to the same, 14 Mar. 1870
20. SRO; CS 96/2409; 46/143 ; 17 Mar. 1870.
21. ibid.
22. NLS, Acc.11335/20,; RBCG to AEB 9 June 1870.
23. ibid. Acc.11335/30, Lady Langdale to AEB. From Piraeus, n.d. (June 1870).
24. PRO; FO 6/302, various dates in 1870.
25. ibid.
26. Parliamentary Papers, 1872, 35th vol. LXX, 'Remarks on the River Plate Republics as a Field for British Emigration' by Mr Macdonell, HM Charge d' Affaires at Buenos Ayres.
27. ibid.
28. ibid.
29. See, Cunninghame Graham, R.B., A Vanishing Race, in 'Father Archangel of Scotland', Black, 1896, pp 166- 184.
30. Macdonell, op.cit.
31. PRO, FO 566/197/125-6.

32. Cunninghame Graham R.B, Gualeguaychú in 'His People', Duckworth, 1906, pp 130-148.
33. ibid.
34. ibid.
35. Cunninghame Graham, R.B., La Tapera in 'Progress', Duckworth, 1905, pp 85-94.
36. Cunninghame Graham, R.B Acc.11335/20;RBCG to AEB, - - 1870.
37. NLS,Acc.11335/203, photograph.
38. Cunninghame Graham, R.B., The Bolas in 'The Ipane', T.Fisher Unwin, 1899, pp 84-97.
39. Cunninghame Graham, R.B., The Horses of the Pampas in 'Father Archangel of Scotland' , op.cit.
40. Cunninghame Graham, R.B., San José in 'Progress', op.cit. pp 62-84.
41. ibid.
42. PRO, FO 566/106 15. Sept. 1870.
43. Cunninghame Graham, R.B., A Silhouette in 'Rodeo, op.cit. pp 88-98.
44. ibid.
45. NLS,Acc.11335/34, AEB to Charles Cunninghame Graham, 7 Sept. 1870.
46. SRO; CS 96/2410, Note.
47. PRO; FO 566/107, Mar/April 1871.
48. Beeton, Isabella, 'The Book of Household Management', Ward, Lock & Co.,1888, p. 1577.
49. Tschiffely, op.cit., p. 56.
50. NLS, Acc.11335/29; James Ogilvy to AEB, 20 Aug 1871.
51. PRO; FO 566/40, Sept., Oct., 1871.
52. NLS, Acc.11335/29, J. Ogilvy to AEB, 20 Aug. 1871.
53. ibid.,Acc.11335/20, RBCG to AEB, 10 Oct. 1871.
54. Cunninghame Graham, R.B., La Pampa in 'Rodeo', op.cit., pp 65 - 72.
55. Letter to AEB, quoted verbatim in Tschiffely, op.cit., NB the author has not been able to trace this in PRO.
56. SRO; CS 96/2410 Note.

Chapter Three

Enterprise

Robert's invitation to Paraguay came at the very last moment. In his request for special powers to advance the cost of his outfit and fare, dated 11 July 1872, the <u>Curator</u> asked the Accountant for an immediate decision because the party was to sail very shortly. Jamieson did his best to obtain a favourable reply: the young man would hear of no alternative, he told the Accountant; he was not to go unsupervised but at the behest, and in the company of a connection by marriage, Captain Ross Grove. In support of the application he attached a balance sheet of the income and expenditure of the Bontine estate in the year to September 1871, showing a surplus of £1.l0.1. In his opinion, Jamieson minuted, this favourable result might allow a sum of no more than £150 to be laid out for Paraguay.(1).

Captain Ross Grove was a representative of the London trading firm of Holland, Jacques (his father was its Company Secretary).(2). He was going out to explore the potential for business in Paraguay now that the war between that country and its neighbours united against it - Brazil, the Argentine, and Uruguay - was over. This war which had raged from 1865 to 1870 was as savage and destructive as the worst European war in the whole nineteenth century; it had been a catastrophe for Paraguay; by the time it ended almost the entire male population of fighting age had perished. These facts were known in England since the various engagements between the two sides had been extensively reported in the newspapers and books had been written; the most famous of which was 'Letters from the Battlefields of Paraguay' by the scholar and explorer, Richard Burton. (3). With her voracious appetite for books it is likely that Anne Elizabeth had read it. If it made her anxious as to Robert's safety in a country where two years after the end of the war, conditions were generally described as wretched and miserable, she did not allow it to be known, but confined her expression of regret at this new venture to the fact that it did not seem to her to promise any substantial improvement in his situation. The activities of Holland, Jacques were far too speculative for her liking - much the sort of thing that had led the Strix astray. And the 38 year old Captain Grove who had earned his spurs in the 42nd Foot, the Black Watch, during the Crimean War, was apparently cast in the same mould as her brothers-in-law, Bobby Cunninghame Graham and the - to her - detestable Colonel Hope. Yet it was to her side of the family that he was connected. His wife, Emily, was a granddaughter of Admiral Fleeming's sister, Keith Elphinstone. (4). Keith had married David Erskine whose home was Cardross on the opposite side of the Lake of Menteith to Gartmore. In the mid nineteenth century the Erskines suffered a similar decline in their fortunes as the Cunninghame Grahams. Like Gartmore Cardross had to be let while the owners lived elsewhere.(5). The cousins were close and, when Robert and Charles were small, they were often left in charge of Emily Grove's unmarried sister, Helen Erskine. Perhaps it was

Aunt Helen (who had shares in Holland, Jacques) (6), who found this way for Robert to fulfil his keen desire to return to South America. 'For my part I should have much preferred to see Robert employed in a more civilized part of the World and nearer home', Uncle Bobby Cunninghame Graham told Mr Jamieson.

The Curator's sense of urgency proved unfounded: it was late in the autumn before Robert finally departed for Paraguay. He spent most of the summer at his mother's house in London then, in September, made a dash across the Atlantic to see his brother, Charles, who was stationed at Halifax, Nova Scotia. It was early November before he returned, via New York, where he took passage in the steamer, SS Alps. The voyage is described in one of the first stories he had published. The experience was typical of the misery that afflicted him whenever he put to sea - though not all the ships he sailed in were as dilapidated as the Alps. The weather was rough and he was sick; the only nourishment he could face were cups of arrowroot laced with whisky; the only book he had to read was Spenser's 'Fairie Queene'. The air in his cabin was stifling; 'Lamp smoking, drops of moisture on my pillow, rats running across the floor, a dense steamy feeling which made one sleepy, crumbs of biscuit in the bedclothes, a futile tin basin floating in the cabin, a brandy bottle propped between a Bible and a sponge on the fixed washing stand'. If, in the rare intervals of the storm he ventured on deck, it was to return to his bunk wet through when he fell back into a trance of sleeping, waking, brandy, arrowroot and 'Fairie Queene'. Yet he confessed he liked the voyage; it was an adventure that pleased his restless spirit, and he hoped for a sight of Iceland, a country he longed to visit. As soon as they entered the calmer waters of the Clyde he went up on deck; the landmarks were poignantly familiar though he made no mention in the story of the ship passing Ardoch and Finlaystone. (8).

Instead he wrote that ten days at home in London flew by in a whirl of theatres, dress clothes, good dinners and the unaccustomed feel of comfort. On 29 November 1872 he was back on board the Alps when she left for Montevideo. Her first port of call was Pauillac on the Garonne where she took on Basque emigrants. Robert, whose £31 fare entitled him to a cabin, pitied them for their cramped accommodation - tiers of bunks specially fitted 'after the fashion in which sheep make their railway journeys'. (9). Seasickness kept him in bed for five days while they cleared the Bay of Biscay and headed south for Lisbon. More emigrants boarded there; farmers from the hills of Galicia, part of the mass exodus happening all over Southern Europe. Drawn by tales of wealth to be acquired on the far side of the Atlantic whole villages were on the move, the houses closed and left, as Robert fancied, for wolves to scamper through the deserted streets on winter nights. His easy command of languages made him the only passenger able to communicate with the emigrants so he was obliged to leave his bunk to interpret for them. He found them jammed like sardines on the deck, surrounded by their luggage, some of which struck him as singularly unnecessary. Almost every family was hampered with a great wicker bird cage, 'though they were going to a land of parrots, macaws, toucans, humming birds and flying spots of jewelled rainbow, compared to which the birds of Europe all seemed made of sackcloth or of mackintosh'. (10). One day he had to call more than a hundred of them to answer to their names and give their details to be submitted to the authorities on landing. Just before Christmas he spent all day in the rigging watching for a sight of Rio de Janeiro where the ship touched on 23 December. The temperature on deck was 120 degrees and he feared they would be quarantined when they got to 'Monte'. They were, and he spent the obligatory five days on board the ship in harbour, being unwilling to waste good money on the lazaretto. (11).

Travellers for Paraguay faced another long journey by river steamer nearly one thousand miles into the interior. However, Robert was told to await further instructions before proceeding. He whiled away the time in the manner that came most naturally to him - in riding. He had had a bad accident, he told his mother on 23 January; a horse had lashed out and caught him above the ankle; he had been in bed for a week after fainting from the pain. In March he was in the camp, at San Pedro de Durazno, hoping for a job on a friend's estancia; he had had another fall from a horse; his foot had become entangled in the stirrup and he had been dragged. At last, towards the end of April, he received a list of questions from Holland, Jacques to answer which he would have to go to Paraguay. 'As I am doing nothing here to make money I might as well try what I can do up there', he told Anne Elizabeth. Some of the questions - on the natural products of the country for example - were simple enough, others might prove awkward, and he warned his mother not to talk about them. He was to try to find ut how long the present Government would last, and to assess the social and political standing of certain people. 'Travelling through Paraguay and asking questions will suit me very well. I have asked Mr Jamieson what he thinks, as the prospect of being paid in proportion to my efforts is rather vague.'. But it was better than nothing and he vowed to do his best as he had been idle for so long. In a rare departure from his customary reserve regarding the unenviable situation he was in as a result of his father's illness, he added; 'it must be allowed that until now I have scarcely had any lelgitimate oppening (sic).(12).

This 'oppening' was not as straightforward as Mr Jamieson might have wished. Holland, Jacques were thinking of investing in the yerba trade, a Government monopoly. They had been offered a share in the concession granted to Alcorta & Co., a firm with headquarters in the capital, Asunción, whose head, Don Sinforiano Alcorta ,was related to the then Vice President. Yerba mate, Paraguayan tea was, and is, a popular drink in many parts of South America. In those days the method of producing it was neither complicated nor expensive. Branches of the shrub, ilex paraguayensis which often grew to thirty feet, were put over an open fire. When the leaves were dry they were stripped, coarsely pounded, and rammed into sacks. To make the tea some of the powder was put into a gourd, boiling water poured over it, and the resulting infusion, described as 'pleasantly astringent' sucked through a tube. (13). However, as a consequence of the war, the forests where the plant grew, the yerbales - had been so completely neglected that, according to Richard Burton, the resource that had once provided half the country's exports, was now procured with difficulty, and at a prohibitive price.

As in 1870 the first part of Robert's journey from Montevideo was across the Plata estuary; this time the steamer made a little to the south and entered the mouth of the Paraná, which formed the western boundary of the Argentine province of Entre Ríos, as the Uruguay did the eastern. The Paraná was notorious for the many islands ships had to negotiate, and for the floating rafts of debris that threatened to entangle them. As nothing else could do the length and slowness of the journey up to Corrientes on the border between the Argentine and Paraguay impressed on Robert the extreme remoteness of the place. A little north of Corrientes where the Paraná trended sharply east, the steamer left it to continue by the river Paraguay up to Asunción. The sun was rising as she crossed the border and passed the fort at Curupaity which had offered a famously stubborn defence against the invading forces in the late war. Consequently, Robert's first sight of Paraguayan territory was a ruined town on a bluff above the river with torn and shattered houses, a church with a sagging roof damaged by shells, and a tower that seemed about to topple over, a scene that struck him as stark and miserable. 'We stood upon the deck...as we took our morning mate, all gazing curiously at the ruins of a place that was a household word in South America. As we forged past fighting the current, as near the bank as it was safe to go, for the masts and funnels of several gunboats stuck up like artificial shoals, the commander...took off his cap and stood bareheaded until we had passed the church'. (15). The commander's father had been one of the many casualties suffered by the Allies in the course of the war; he had been killed three years before when Brazilian ironclad ships had forced a passage past the fort at Curupaity. As the journey continued into Paraguay Robert realized why it had taken the combined forces of Brazil, the Argentine and Uruguay so long to overcome the defences; the first obstacle was the fierce current that came with a speed of almost eight knots against them; the second the fact that almost all the way to Asunción the only channel deep enough for ironclads ran on the Paraguayan side under cliffs from which the guns of a well placed battery could sink them.

From Curupaity there were still two hundred miles to go, north to Asunción, a journey that took many days of frustratingly slow progress through the still and silent landscape. Because, in order to control the custom dues, trade had been confined to the capital for many years, there had been no incentive for towns to grow up along the eastern bank of the river, while the western marked the edge of the great wilderness, the Chaco. It was swamp, intersected with lakes and backwaters in which lay alligators, eels, and stinging rays, a prehistoric landscape whose climate Robert found almost unbearably humid; the heavy air was dank with insects against whose stings and bites there was no protection, nothing to do but scratch and curse. There was little enough evidence of civilisation on the Paraguayan side; 'no roads, no paths, no landmarks, but here and there at intervals of many leagues a clearing in the forest where some straggling settlement [existed], more rarely still the walls of a deserted Jesuit mission or church' (16). The interminable voyage, the lifeless country through which they passed, the heat, brought Robert to the verge of melancholy, for him the next worst thing to anger, a threat to his well being his mother feared. In a recent letter she had coupled a warning against drinking spirits with the admonition that he was not to get into 'rages'.(17).

His relief on discerning the red tiled roofs of Asunción may be imagined. When, on disembarking, he was confronted with a tramway running from the docks to a railway station it seemed to him he had arrived in an urban place; one in which there were services and buildings common to the capitals of countries less remote, such as a bank, a post office, and a telegraph station, together with offices of the many Consuls accredited to the Government. Yet he soon perceived that there was something very odd about Asunción. Founded in 1535 it was the oldest city east of the Andes; for many generations the most important, the seat of government of the whole immense region ruled by Spain. Not a few of the houses and public buildings dated from that time, like the Jesuit College where the present government had its offices. But here and there, in the midst of the plain and solid buildings rose a number of conspicuously new ones, flamboyant edifices, like the theatre that would not have been out of place on the Champs Elysées, and a vast unfinished palace whose outer walls ran the length of several streets. However, many of these buildings were mere facades; the theatre had no roof, while the ceremonial balcony of the palace gave on to a grass grown square. Robert had only to look out across the mile wide Bay of Asunción at the thick waving grass and dilapidated palm trees of the Chaco on the far bank of the river to realize that, in this place, civilisation was sporadic. What he had seen on the way up the river; what now confronted him were manifestations of Paraguay's remarkable history. It had followed a different course from that of its neighbours, culminating in the virtual destruction of the state after defeat in war, and with the death of the greater part of its able bodied men. The fort at Curupaity, the Jesuit missions decaying in the forest; the attempt to rebuild Asunción in the likeness of Paris under the Second Empire; these things awoke in Robert a desire to enquire further as to how and why they had come about. In pursuit of this he was to become one of the few people writing in English, with first hand knowledge of Paraguay, who also went to the trouble to acquaint himself with Spanish sources. Using this material he produced two books as well as sketches dealing with different periods in the country's history, including the war, whose devatation struck him so forcibly at his first sight of Paraguay. (18).

The unity imposed by the Spanish conquest on the territory east of the Andes - all of it known as Paraguay - lasted just under one hundred years. In 1620 it was divided into two: Paraguay proper which was ruled from Asunción, and the Rio de la Plata whose capital was Buenos Aires. Spanish officials at both these places remained under the control of the Viceroys of Peru whose judicial authority was exercised from the eccentrically remote and small town of Charcas, high in the mountains, a fortnight's journey to the west of Asunción. In the seventeenth century this enormous distance facilitated the rise to power in both administrative regions of the Society of Jesus. Charged with converting the native Guarani Indians to Christianity the Jesuits evolved a method whose unique combination of paternalism and semi-communism has always fascinated political theorists, as it did Robert Cunninghame Graham when he encountered its physical remains. Upon arriving in Paraguay he was already familiar with the distinctive pattern of the villages - the reducciones - established by the Fathers; he had stumbled across some of the ruins in the course of the long rides he made in the neighbouring province of Entre Ríos during 1871. Each village was constructed as a square. The church and storehouses stood at one end while the dwellings of the Indian inhabitants, side by side under one enormously long roof, formed the other three. The space in the centre was covered by grass close cropped by sheep. As directed by the two priests in charge, the lives of the inhabitants were diligent and devout; every day they went in procession to the fields, singing hymns. The land they tilled was owned in common and its produce went to the support of all. At their most numerous there were thirty of these villages, containing from 80,000 to 100,000 Indians. Though he saw them when they lay in ruins Robert was struck by the air of calm and rest and melancholy that pervaded them, 'as if you had landed (and been left) on Juan Fernandez'.(19). This, however, was an illusion born of the contrast with the ocean of billowing grass he had been riding over. Really the reducciones were exposed to pillage and destruction when the able bodied would be carried off as slaves. Chief among their enemies were the Mamelucos, the piratical inhabitants of São Paolo on the coast of Brazil who regularily harassed the missions closest to them. In 1631, by which time they had destroyed six villages and carried off several thousand Indians, the Jesuit, Father Ruiz de Montoya, took the desperate step of leading those still at risk - some 12,000 people - down the River Paraná to a place beyond the Paulistas' reach. Robert Cunninghame Graham was to be the first writer to make an account of this brave journey accessible to English readers. His history of the Jesuits in Paraguay 'A Vanished Arcadia' would draw on unpublished manuscripts held at the Archive of the Indies, as well as the more familiar Spanish chronicles.(2).

    The missions that received the survivors of the exodus were never entirely secure. Their inhabitants were envied for the prosperity that came to them as the result of combined labour on the remarkably fertile soil, and this envy was intensified by the kind of rumour always current in South America - which excited the conquistadores - rumours of enormous wealth derived from mines. These were supposed to have been discovered by the Jesuits who hid the silver, gold, and copper they produced in the mission villages. But the Society's chief offence was that the Council of the Indies authorized its priests and their charges to carry arms. Necessary though this concession was for self defence, it was strongly resented by the Spanish officials and members of the hierarchy at Asunción. Their distaste for this mark of a state within a state was further stimulated by reports from Europe of the influence the Society was believed to exercise over the government of countries like Spain, France, and Portugal. When, in 1767, Carlos III of Spain , convinced the Jesuits were plotting to overthrow him, issued sealed orders to be opened simultaneously in every Spanish colony, nowhere were these received with greater satisfaction than in Asunción. On 2 April 1767, acting on these orders, the Governor sent troops to turn the Fathers out of the reducciones. No secret treasure was found, and their departure marked the beginning of a long decay, though many Indians clung to the villages and to the way of life they had been taught.(21). A generation later the shock waves of the French Revolution, followed by

Napoleon Buonaparte's dismissal of the Bourbons from the Spanish throne, hastened the process of disintegration which eventually ended in Spain's withdrawal from the continent of South America. Almost all the territories formerly subject to the Viceroys gained freedom as republics but the price they paid was high - generations of bitter civil strife as factions arose and overturned one another. Paraguay was the exception; from the beginning of the nineteenth century, and for more than fifty years, there was no dissension because there was no freedom within her borders.

In 1810 there had been an unsuccessful attempt by one of the factions at Buenos Aires to annex Paraguay. The opposition to it was led by a lawyer of Asunción, José Gaspar Rodriguez Francia who assumed power as dictator. He was an austere man, imbued, it was said, with the ideals of the French Revolution, astute and apparently pragmatic in the grasp he had of commerce, agriculture, and administration. Yet he had an unusual approach to problems. Every ruler of Paraguay was faced with the possibility of conflict with her neighbours because the country blocked their lines of communication. Paradoxically, in the vast and underpopulated continent where there were, as yet, no barriers of any kind, the movement of traffic was limited to those few rivers that were navigable. The western boundary of Paraguay was formed by the river of the same name; navigation on it had to be shared by the Empire of Brazil since it was the only feasible route to her northern province of Mato Grosso. At the same time Paraguay's only route to the Plata estuary and the open sea was down the River Paraná through the Argentine Republic. When the government at Buenos Aires proposed to raise the duty charged on vessels out of Asunción, instead of negotiating, Dr Francia solved the problem by effectively abolishing it. He stopped the traffic, closed his borders and forced the Paraguayan economy into self sufficiency : 'he shut up the country so completely that not a single native could quit it and the few foreigners who succeeded in getting in had marvellous difficulty in getting out again.'(22). Francia allowed only a few trading vessels to come part way up the river, took what he wanted from their cargoes, especially arms and ammunition, paid for it in yerba, and sent them on their way.

Those who objected were made to repent in the cruellest manner. For, while he showed no obvious desire to exploit power on his own behalf - he lived very frugally - he exacted the greatest respect and submission to his person as the living symbol of the Paraguayan nation. Because Asunción was the only town of any size in the whole country the inhabitants had the concept of nationhood constantly before them, and were frequently called upon to demonstrate their allegiance to it. For instance, though they dressed in simple cotton shirts and white trousers the law required every Paraguayan male to wear a tall black shiny hat for the sole purpose of doffing it whenever 'El Supremo's carriage hove in sight along the sandy streets.

After Francia died in 1840 he was succeeded by another lawyer, the 47 year old Carlos Antonio López. For the next twenty years he was confirmed in office each time the nation voted. Reputedly a cousin of Dr Francia, this first López was far more easy going - at least at the beginning of his regime - and left much business to his ministers, many of whom were members of his family. And unlike his predecessor, Carlos Antonio was eager for Paraguay to take her place among the nations of the world. It was to prove very unfortunate that his first requirement for international prestige was a standing army, and naval patrols along the river frontier. Keen to make up for lost time the regime bought ships and <u>matériel</u>, and engaged British engineeers to build arsenals and docks, lay down a railway and keep the engines of the gunboats on the river running. Most unfortunate of all was the fact that Carlos Antonio put his eldest son, the 18 year old Francisco Solano López in command of his large new army. As time went by the existence of this army; the building of forts along the River Paraguay; the squabbling over territory, pointed to the outbreak of a war. When it came in 1865 what made it particularly savage and destructive of the Paraguayan people was the character of their leader, the second López. By then he was the country's President, its third dictator in fifty years, having seized power at his father's death three years before.

Towards the end of his life Robert Cunninghame Graham wrote a book, 'Portrait of a Dictator' accusing López of conduct amounting to genocide. His evidence was based on assertions made to him in Asunción in 1873 by survivors of the war. Some were British; Scots and English marine and railway engineers, doctors, draughtsmen, builders, who had come to Paraguay under contract to the government, and who had been trapped in the country at the outbreak of the war. One was a young apothecary, George Masterman, who had been accused of conspiring against Francisco López, imprisoned and tortured. His book, 'Seven Eventful Years in Paraguay' furnished Robert with many details (25). 'Portrait of a Dictator' followed Masterman in tracing the origin of the war to the period of 18 months the young General had spent in Paris as Minister Plenipotentiary of Paraguay. In 1854 López 'suddenly emerging from the semi-barbarism of a remote and almost unknown republic, was dazzled by the parade and glitter, the false glory and proud memories of wars and warriors he found around him', Masterman wrote, 'and was fired by the ambition of making the brave and devoted people he knew he would one day be called upon to rule, a nation to be feared and courted as the dominant power in South America.' (26). In 1854 Louis Napoleon Buonaparte was at the height of his popularity as Emperor of the French, and the cult of his uncle, the first Napoleon, as soldier, revolutionary hero, and democrat, everywhere prevailed. General Francisco López arrived in Paris at the moment when, as protector of the Holy Places in Jerusalem, Napoleon III had embarked upon a war with Russia in the Crimea, and was proposing to lead the troops against Sevastopol in person. The Parisians who saluted his public appearances were captivated by the beautiful woman at his side; the new Empress, Eugénie de Montijo, whom he had married the previous year. In these circumstances it was hardly surprising that the young López should measure himself for the mantle of the Buonapartes. He followed precedent in this; the cult had always had the greatest appeal for South American leaders. In Mexico, for example, General Santa Ana; nearer home, in Entre Rios, General Urquiza. But General López had one advantage over them, like Napoleon III he acquired a formidable consort. In his case it was the tall and beautiful Irishwoman, Eliza Eloisa Lynch, whom he met in Paris. According to Robert Cunninghame Graham, who met her, her ambition equalled his, while in wit and knowledge of the world she far exceeded López.

Robert's account of her in 'Portrait of a Dictator' did not wholly endorse the sweeping condemnation voiced by the foreign community to him in Asunción after the war. He agreed with Masterman that her role in the unfolding of events after Francisco López took power was crucial , and he portrayed her influence as ultimately disastrous. By flattering the Marshal/President (as López decreed he should be known after the outbreak of the war), by publicly deferring to him, she pushed him to enterprises she must have known were beyond him and ruinous to a small country like Paraguay. But that was a comment on her judgement, not a criticism of her courage or spirit, qualities even her enemies acknowledged and which won Robert's admiration. His interest was engaged by the unusual position she occupied while López ruled in Paraguay, a position which owed nothing to social convention as it was normally defined; which, in fact, ran counter to it. Eliza's story was that she had been unable to obtain a divorce from her husband, a French government official whom she had married in 1850 at the very early age of 15, and so she had resumed her maiden name. As Madame Lynch she had followed her General to South America and born him children on whom he doted. These children, together with her formidable personality, earned her a place at the Marshal/President's side. Of course there was gossip. One may wonder why, once she had arrived in the most remote capital of the New World she did not re-invent her past and claim the automatic respectability conferred by widowhood. The answer may be, either that too many people knew her history or, that she felt sufficiently secure to ignore gossip. In any case there was a difference in attitude between the Paraguayans who, in the time of Francia, had been taught that marriage was an empty ceremony, and the expatriates in Asunción, especially the British, who reflected the strict and formal rules of their own society. That there was an alternative to these rules, a greater freedom, was something Robert welcomed. Probably Eliza Lynch was the first woman he encountered who lived by this alternative: she was certainly not the last. In 'Portrait of a Dictator' he endorsed the allegation that, at the time she met Francisco López, she had been one of the lights of the <u>demi monde</u> whose court was almost as brilliant as the Tuileries, a court where well educated women were to be found, as he described them 'loose in their morals, but refined and quite correct in their behaviour, able to join in intellectual conversation and run a salon'. (27). This world was far more fun than the other, Robert wrote. The passage is revealing as to the kind of manners he valued in women, as is the suggestion that those who sold themselves openly for money were entering into a transaction no different from the one 'society' dignified with the name of marriage.

López' dream of empire inspired a programme of ceremonial building that imitated Haussman's Paris. At his accession Asunción was much the same cluster of single story buildings with red tiled roofs and deep eaves the <u>conquistadores</u> had known three hundred years before. By 1863 work had begun on an immense palace from whose balcony the Marshal/President intended to review his troops together with the people assembled to demonstrate allegiance. Disaster might have been avoided if only his eye had rested there. But, encouraged by Madame Lynch, his ambition prompted him to intervene in international affairs. As leader of such a strategically placed country he decided it fell to him to dictate the balance of power over the region - a delusion that made him an object of ridicule in the Buenos Aires newspapers, but which brought war and devastation to Paraguay. Peace in the area was frequently disturbed as a result of bickering between the republics of Spanish origin, the Argentine and Uruguay, and the Brazilian Empire which had been settled by the Portuguese. Brazil was suspected of a desire to extend her southern frontier to the Plata estuary, a move that naturally found no favour in Buenos Aires. At the same time Uruguay, whose territory stood in the way of such an expansion, was tormented by a running civil war, unrest that gave Brazil a pretext for sending in troops whenever she deemed it expedient.

In October 1864, when Brazilian forces once more crossed the Uruguayan border, López issued a statement about the threat to the equilibrium of the area that was not taken seriously at the time. (28). However, when hostilities broke out in earnest between Brazil and Uruguay, López perceived this statement to have been an ultimatum, giving him grounds for sending troops into the Brazilian province of Mato Grosso and, a little later, into the Argentine at Corrientes. He had not bargained for the result which was that all his neighbours turned on him and formed a Triple Alliance dedicated to the overthrow of his government though they professed no animosity towards the people of Paraguay. An invading force was assembled but was delayed for weeks and months by many difficulties; the unlooked for strength of the Paraguayan defences; the remarkable fighting spirit of López' army; the indecision of the Allied leaders. According to 'Portrait of a Dictator', the grim conditions of disease and hunger; the savage slaughter whenever battle was joined; the destitution suffered by women and children after every able bodied male above the age of 10 was forced into the Paraguayan army, made the war the most terrible and pathetic event the New World had ever known - far worse than the American Civil War for example.(29). By 1867 it was estimated that 80,000 Paraguayans had died from disease alone. Thousands more perished as the Allies, who themselves suffered many casualties, struggled to force a passage to Asunción. Worse was to come.

As the Paraguayan army gave ground before their enemies López exacted retribution from those officers he considered to have failed him: their wives and children were imprisoned, as were the families of deserters who, themselves, were shot. By 1868 when the Allies were drawing near the capital López had turned on members of his own family whom he accused of conspiring to replace him; he had his younger brother put to death, his brother in law also, while his mother and sisters were abused. The alleged plot also served as an excuse to persecute foreigners like Masterman who lived to describe how he was tortured; others merely vanished. When Robert heard the survivors tell their stories he judged that the loss of Asunción which López ordered to be evacuated before the arrival of the Allies, drove him out of his mind. The defeat of the Paraguayan army at the battle of Las Lomas Valentinas on Christmas Day 1868 removed the last obstacle. The Allied troops found Asunción, which had never been fortified, empty, the only movement that of thin, attenuated cats and dogs, 'gone wild like little tigers'. The Paraguayans who had been ordered to abandon the city for the outlying villages told Robert of the utter misery they suffered in camping in torrential rain when hunger and sickness overcame them. Even so, they were not allowed to rest but, as López turned his face to the north, were driven before him like a flock of sheep. As they advanced the villages through which they passed were razed, the surplus animals slaughtered, while the wounded and those who could go no further were dispatched with lances, wielded, more often than not, by soldiers who were only twelve years old. By moving gradually further north, and with the help of supplies arriving down a trail from distant Bolivia, López was able to elude his pursuers. He came to a halt at Cerro Cora, a large natural amphitheatre on the border with Brazil where he and a few followers remained for more than a year. But on 1 April 1870 Brazilian soldiers came upon his camp unexpectedly. They cut López down as he was attempting to escape across a stream. Those who told of his end never failed to describe how Eliza Lynch took handfuls of earth to cover his dead body. (30).

The extent to which the Paraguayans suffered was revealed in a dispatch which reached the Foreign Office in 1867 long before López abandoned Asunción. It was written by the British Secretary of Legation at Buenos Aires - whose name, it is interesting to note, was Gould - in the course of an official visit to Asunción to procure the release or better treatment of British citizens held in Paraguay. Though he was rebuffed Gould was able to give Whitehall the first reliable account of the situation. 'The whole country is ruined, and all but depopulated. Everything is seized for the use of the government. The cattle on most of the estates have entirely disappeared. All the horses, even the mares have been taken away... Many estates have been altogether abandoned... Measles, smallpox and cholera, besides privations of all sorts have reduced the population of this unfortunate country by more than a third.'(31) In 1873 when Robert arrived in Asunción the consequences of the war were still everywhere to be seen. Since it had been unable to meet demands for reparation the country was still occupied. Brazilian gunboats lay at anchor in the port; Brazilian soldiers stood smoking in the shade guarding prisoners cutting grass. There were not many prisoners. Women did everything, Robert noticed; gathered the crops; tended the flocks; shot; fished; hunted. The train that covered the short distance from Asunción to its only destination, Paraguiri, was driven by a man, a Belgian engineer, but it was stoked by two women, naked but for the <u>tupoi</u>, the long loose white cotton shift worn by Paraguayan women. Steadfast and brave they might be but in spite of their efforts they were scarcely holding their own. According to a report in a recent Buenos Aires newspaper, the truth of which Robert was shortly to confirm in person, the rural districts of Paraguay were deserted and going to waste; brushwood and scrub were growing up in place of sugar cane, maize, and mandioca, and the forest was invading the suburbs of Asunción. In the market place women and girls were selling vegetables at famine prices. The houses were ruinous and the streets full of potholes, 'yet many would still die for López'.(32).

To anyone other than a Paraguayan this last assertion seemed hardly believable but it was true; most citizens looked upon Francisco Solano López as a supremely heroic leader fighting to preserve the independence and integrity of their country against the aggression of their neighbours. Convinced that their cause was just they had sacrificed everything in defending it. The extent to which the situation was accepted was underlined in the memoirs of Lieutenant Colonel George Thompson. He was a Scottish engineer contracted to the government of Carlos Antonio López who constructed the forts at Curupaity and Humaita that famously withstood the Allied invasion. On the outbreak of war he accepted a commision in the Paraguayan army and was appointed <u>aide de camp</u> to the Marshal/President. His book, 'The War in Paraguay', published in 1869, gave a lucid account of Paraguayan resistance, including the many battles he observed from close quarters. While in the end he came to regard López as a monster, his memoirs make it clear he did not form this view until 1868,by which time the war was well advanced and Lopez had begun reprisals against those he suspected of conspiring to overthrow him. If, from his privileged position Thompson failed for three years to detect conduct unbecoming in the high command, it was hardly likely the rank and file would either. There was no opposition to the regime; the only newspaper was controlled by López while Madame Lynch was an extremely effective propagandist on his behalf. (33).

The Surgeon General of the Paraguayan army was another Scot, Dr William Stewart who hailed from Galashiels. In peacetime, as personal physician to Madame Lynch and her children ,he had taken precedence over all other foreigners in Asunción. Stewart remained with the army until the battle of Las Lomas Valentinas when he surrendered to the Allies and they agreed to repatriate him. He broke his journey home at Rio de Janeiro where he was granted an audience with the Emperor, Pedro II. Reports of this interview which appeared in the Brazilian papers were the first to reveal how Francisco López had turned his fury on his own people. In 1873 Stewart's name headed the list of people Holland, Jacques had asked Robert to investigate. The Doctor was the go-between with Alcorta & Company in whose concession they were interested. As soon as Robert arrived in Asuncion Stewart asked him out to stay in his large but dilapidated <u>quinta</u> two miles from town. The invitation came as a relief to Robert whose funds were running low. 'Dr Stewart holds a very good general position in Paraguay; he is universally respected both by Paraguayans and by foreigners; he is reported very rich, that is, for Paraguay', he told Holland,Jacques. It had not always been so. Like Ross Grove and William Hope, Stewart had served in the Crimean War. Afterwards he travelled out to Paraguay with a group of Frenchmen and their families whom Carlos Antonio had invited to found a colony. Like so many other enterprises that aimed to make a profit out of importing Europeans to work virgin land, <u>nueva</u> Bordeaux did not flourish, and when it collapsed, Stewart was reputedly left penniless. However, marriage to a Paraguayan lady of Spanish descent brought land in various parts of the country on which, in the usual way, there were rumoured to be mines. In 1872, while he was still in London after the end of the war, he applied to be appointed British Consul in Asunción. The moment was ill chosen; the Foreign Office could not yet bring itself to such an act of reconciliation, and Stewart returned to Paraguay without benefit of office. But he had plenty of other irons in the fire.(34).

Robert found him and his brother, George, very kind and civil. Their hospitality encouraged him to believe his luck had changed at last. 'I think a great deal is to be done here', he wrote happily to his mother in July 1873. Dr Stewart wanted him to go down to Corrientes to fetch up a troop of mules which were much in demand since the loss of nearly all the horses in the war. 'I hope to make some money by the mules... and of course Ross Grove's people will have to pay me pretty well'. His first task for them was to try to get the time limit on the Alcorta concession extended. This called for an almost daily visit to the government offices where he waited on the pleasure of one or another high official; they were always <u>infermo</u>, he complained. 'The soldiers all know Bunnyand Don Roberto. Bunny follows me about and comes when he is called'. Bunny or, in Portuguese (which Robert spoke almost as well as Spanish), O Bonee, was the grey that became a beloved companion, the first horse to inspire the endearment that appears so often in his letters, the highest gaucho term of praise: 'he says his name is <u>pingo</u> and he is the tamest horse in South America.' (35). Robert did not begrudge the time spent hanging about; the terms of the Alcorta concession were, potentially, very favourable. There was to be an exemption from duty for ten years on all imported goods, and for five years on all exports - ie. the <u>yerba</u>. The concessionaires would have the right to exploit all products of the territory in question except minerals. In return they had to undertake to people it with four hundred families of emigrants; 'either European or North American, of known good conduct and lawful calling, each family being composed of five souls.' The clause that Robert had to try to have extended was that which stipulated the agreement should lapse unless thirty five families were introduced in the first year.(36). Since the concession, signed in October 1872, was already nine months old there was no possibility that, if Holland, Jacques took it over, they could recruit and train even a small number of settlers before the year was out. Obviously a decision was urgent but could scarcely be made without a reliable survey of the land in question. There was no one on the spot so, in late July, Robert with Bunny set out from Asuncion on a journey of two hundred miles south and east to the Alto (Upper) Paraná where Alcorta & Co. had been granted some sixty square miles of land formerly belonging to the López family. That he left in a hurry may be supposed from the fact that he forgot to take his rifle.

It was a formidable undertaking for anyone, let alone a 21 year old new to the country and travelling alone. So thick was the canopy of trees in the forest that the track ran for miles almost in the dark. Sometimes it broke into clearings where the settlements had been deserted. 'The fences were all broken, and peccaries had rooted up the crops. The oranges lay rotting under the trees and as you passed along the solitary trail...flocks of green parrots took wing from where they had been feeding in the deserted fields and troops of monkeys howled'. In all that long, mosquito haunted ride he saw few people and fewer animals. Occasionally he came across a family living alone on the edge of a clearing but the only livestock they had about the house were chickens. Very occasionally he encountered an Argentine horseman travelling towards Asunción, or a Brazilian mounted on a mule, but all the country people went on foot. Robert was reminded of the legend that the Marshall/President had met his death at Cerro Cora riding the last native Paraguayan horse. In any case neglect and the climate had conspired to destroy what little grass there was for the remaining few to eat. Tigers (jaguars) lay in wait for them; they had to be protected at night against vampire bats; bathed at sunrise and sunset to keep away the flying, crawling insects, and , somehow, persuaded to avoid snakes and poisonous weeds; 'a man who had a horse became a slave and passed his time caring for him'. (37).

As he walked Bunny cautiously along the deeply rutted tracks Robert passed long processions of women whose low cut sack like garment (the <u>tupoi</u>), and black hair cut squarely across the forehead and hanging down their backs gave them a medieval air. All were barefoot and smoked thick cigars which they kept lighted at the torch their leader carried to scare away the jaguars. On seeing the red haired slender and pale young man, 'sometimes they all saluted, sometimes they only smiled and showed their teeth, and sometimes one would say amid the laughter of all the rest, 'we all want husbands' and added something else in Guarani that made a laugh run rippling down the line'. (38). One is led to suppose that, if any such suggestion were more than a joke, Robert was agreeable. His letters are discreet but it is clear from his written work that, as a youth in South America, his attitude to sex was simple: if it was available he indulged in it; no description by him of his travels is complete without some reference to the 'china' girls who plied this trade. The convention of the time forbade frankness in such matters but a strong sensuality pervades everything he wrote.

Sex was an antidote to loneliness and fear, neither of which was allowed a mention in his letters home. But, years later, when he came to write about this journey to the Alto Paraná, isolation was its theme, and he vividly recalled how oppressive he had found it. 'The snakes, the humming birds, the alligators basking in the creeks, the whir of insects and the metallic croaking of the frogs, the air of being in the grip of all powerful vegetation reduced a man travelling alone through the green solitude to nothingness. One felt as if in that wealth of vegetation and strange birds and beasts, one's horse was the only living thing that was of the same nature as oneself.' (39). The heat pouring down from the sun met the heat rising from the red sandy soil and focussed on his face drying the blood drawn by innumerable flies into hard sticky flakes. Hours of heat brought on intervals of dozing from which he awoke just in time to save his balance, shuddering to think what would happen if he fell and was left miles from any habitation. He comforted himself with the knowledge that Bunny would never abandon him. This interdependence of man and beast became of great significance in his life, bringing consolation in the want of friends and, upon the death of a particularly beloved horse, great anguish. An episode that occurred in the course of this journey left such an imprint on his mind he reproduced it in more than one of his books.

One day he came upon a clearing inhabited by a solitary Paraguayan who welcomed him and put everything he had at his disposal. Unusually he had a horse, a roan that answered Bunny when he neighed. In the evening when Bunny was brought back from his bathe in the river the roan snapped his halter, came galloping to meet him and stood with his nostrils close against the other's nose. Robert's host told him the roan had gone six months without seeing another of his kind, and, somewhat against Robert's better judgement, persuaded him to let them loose together. 'For hours the horses played, leaping about like lambs, galloping to and fro'. At nightfall they were tethered close to one another when they stood with their heads resting on each other's shoulder. Over supper the man told Robert how, in the time of Carlos Antonio López he had been imprisoned in Asunción, in solitary confinement for two years and how, on the day he was released, he went up to the first man he met and embraced him. That was why he was sympathetic to the horse's plight. 'This day has been a fiesta for him, and now let us repeat the rosary and then to bed'. In the morning, as he rode away, Robert was saddened by the shrill high neighing of the roan.(40).

As he approached the Paraná conditions became somewhat pesky, he told his mother. Sleeping out in the continually pouring rain had brought on rheumatism which made getting on and off a horse extremely painful. The stony ground that was in such contrast to the splendid turf of Entre Ríos meant that Bunny had to be shod. The shortage of food was also pesky; he had had nothing to eat for most of the time but oranges and mandioca, a singularly uninteresting diet. If he had not met an Italian who lent him a gun to replace the one he left behind he would have had very little meat. The Italian was very nice, he told Anne Elizabeth; he was 'a sort of gentleman and served in the Crimea'. (41). The Italian appears in his stories as Enrico Clerici, who had followed Garabaldi and who now kept a bar in Itapua, a settlement on the bank above the Paraná. Students of Conrad's work have acclaimed him as the origin of Giorgio Viola. Robert's base was to be an estancia not far from Itapua, belonging to Dr Stewart, called the Potrero San Antonio. From there he sent letters of 'extreme length, dullness and promptitude' to Holland,Jacques via the steamers on the Paraná. The Alcorta concession lay further up the river but it was nearly a month before he could start for it. He had been out of action, the result he told his mother - predictably - of a strain received when riding a wild horse. The enforced rest gave time for letters from home to arrive. As well as news of the death of aunt, these informed him that a Mrs Barclay Allardice was mounting a determined attempt to claim the Earldom of Airth (which involved the Earldom of Menteith). The Curator was deliberating as to whether the Bontine estate could afford to counter claim. Robert's response was practical, if bitter. 'I care very little about the Menteith peerage as long as no one else gets it....As entertainment I would rather have a handful of maize with Bunny out on the plains'. In view of the death of his aunt he apologized for not writing on black edged paper but such things were not obtainable on the Alto Paraná.

Much of his report to Holland, Jacques concerning the Alcorta concession is now too faded to be legible, but enough remains to demonstrate the thoroughness with which he set about the task. The land was situated in the region which had given sanctuary from the Mamelucos to the followers of Father de Montoya. Robert had to decide which of two villages founded by the

Jesuits, Jésus or La Trinidad, could be adapted for use by a colony of settlers. The port for Jésus was larger, and the water deeper, but the road to the village was bad and the houses of sun dried brick were crumbling. La Trinidad had been built on the crest of a hill and struck Robert as particularily eerie. Having fought his way through overgrown fields and pastures he found himself in what had obviously been a place of some importance. He counted three churches, one large, a college, and various administrative buildings. These, and the houses facing on the square, had been constructed of immense blocks of sandstone, evenly dressed, still massive in appearance. When darkness overtook him in La Trinidad he tied Bunny to a tuft of grass and lay down beside him. He could do nothing but watch as moonlight revealed a jaguar that stole out of the church, down the stone steps, across the plaza near him, to vanish in the forest. The next day he set about making contact with the few inhabitants of La Trinidad., Indians living in miserable poverty. His Guarani, though not as good as Dr Stewart's - who spoke it fluently but, to his ear with the accent of Galashiels - nevertheless enabled him to make friends with them. They assured him that the land was very fertile, and had once produced several crops a year of maize, tobacco, indigo, and sugar cane. Robert rode miles in search of yerbales but found none on Alcorta's land. Nor did he succeed in pinning down rumours of copper deposits beside the river which, in spite of the clause reserving minerals to the government, interested Holland, Jacques. 'I made most minute enquires as well as searching myself', he reported, 'but everyone informed me that copper...had never been heard of near La Trinidad although the elder López sent down an exploring party from Asunción'. (43).

    He was back in the capital at the beginning of November but seems to have left it almost immediately on another journey of inspection. Holland, Jacques had not yet come to a decision about the Alcorta concession when, through Dr Stewart, they were offered another tract of land at Chiriguelo in the far north of the country near Cerro Cora where Francisco López met his death. No details have survived of this expedition beyond the fact that ,after he reached Chiriguelo, Robert made a point of continuing to Cerro Cora. It was a long hard ride along a narrow track through a dense forest and he was parched and hungry when he came out into the open. His relief turned to pity when he considered the fate of López. A considerable stream ran across the floor of the vast amphitheatre, an essential feature in deciding the Marshal/President to take refuge there. But Robert could see how, as soon as the Brazilians stumbled upon his presence, Cerro Cora became a trap, 'a natural corral' and the stream the final obstacle that defeated him.(44). As for the land at Chiriguelo, it was a far better proposition to his now experienced eye than the Alcorta concession. 'I am coming home at once on business', he told his mother on 20 December 1873; 'I think I am going to drop in for a pretty good thing... Dr Stewart and I have got [Holland,Jacques] a concession to work yerba from the Paraguayan government. I have just returned from inspecting it rather thin and a good deal bothered with the rhoomatics (sic).' (45). As a mark of the seriousness with which he regarded this new project he asked Anne Elizabeth to get him a writing master for the few months he expected to be home; the first necessity in business was legible handwriting. His was not; his mother frequently reproached him for the 'cuneiform characters' she was called upon to decipher. (This biographer can only say his letters at this period of his life are easy to read compared with those he wrote as he grew older).

When he returned to London Robert found Holland, Jacques well pleased with his efforts on their behalf. However, while he and Ross Grove discussed how much money would be needed to finance the first stage of a colony, the firm remained very cautious about investing in Paraguay.(46). Robert decided to look for support elsewhere and approached the firm of Robinson Fleming - 'Uncle Bobby's friends'. It was a mistake: their connection with Paraguay had recently proved disastrous. In 1872 they had advertised the so-called Lincolnshire Farmers scheme whereby they contracted to deliver two shiploads of farm labourers from that county to Paraguay. The prospectus was no less encouraging than those they had published about the Argentine in the 1860s ,and equally misleading. Among the 900 men, women and children who sailed for Paraguay in October 1872, few hailed from Lincolnshire or had ever seen a farm. Most had been hastily recruited from among the unemployed and destitute on the streets of London. As soon as they arrived in Asunción they were bundled on to the train to Paraguiri from whence they were taken to Itapé where Robinson Fleming's agent was hard put to feed them. Many fell sick and soon, as the official report put it, 'the graves equalled the number of the tents'. The affair became an international scandal when some 200 of the men made their own way across the Paraná into the Argentine where their emaciated condition aroused much adverse comment. Even more shocking to the official mind was the fact that about one hundred of those left behind, men and girls, took refuge in a shed where, huddled together for warmth, the risk of promiscuity was said to be extreme. Eventually they were brought back to Asunción where the Italian Consul gave them food paid for out of his own pocket. The Foreign Office papers recording this sorry affair did not neglect to explore the possibility of blame. But the conclusion was that Robinson Fleming had done nothing illegal and could not be arraigned except at the bar of public opinion. In England the outcry was so great it virtually put an end to all such schemes. (47). As Anne Elizabeth told Robert while he was still in Paraguay, The Times was particularly vociferous. She was inclined to dismiss its warning about unfounded promises, an insalubrious climate, and crops that Europeans would find difficult to work, as propaganda planted on the Editor by rival Emigrant Societies.(48)

Robert seems to have agreed with her; at any rate he persevered in his approach to Robinson Fleming for several months after he returned to London, and with some success. In August 1874, George Stewart, writing from Asunción, noted that the firm had expressed its willingness to enter the yerba mate trade. A new concession would be required: Stewart believed the Paraguayan government might be favourable but warned Robert that he would not proceed until the various parties had come to a firm decision. He was at the end of his patience with his English contacts. 'Having already laid before our friends what we were in a position to recommend as sound investments in Paraguay, and failing to arrive at any practical conclusion, it is, I fear, in consequence of the general distrust in everything concerned with this country, only wasting your time as well as mine, and uselessly troubling other people, to push the matter at present'.(49).

This discouraging letter was not the only reason why Robert did not fulfil his intention of returning to Paraguay. When the <u>Curator</u> was called upon to account to the Court for the £150 advanced in 1872 he wrote; 'Mr Graham...went...but unfortunately not long after his arrival there his health again gave way and this, added to the unsettled state of the country, left him no alternative but to return to England'. Precisely why Robert's health gave cause for concern is not known, but this was a theme that would recur.(50).

Notes to Chapter Three

1. SRO CS 46/143, 11 July 1872; CS 96/2412
2. Burke's 'Landed Gentry' Grove Ross of Invercharron.
3. Tinsley Bros, 1870.
4. Named after her uncle, Admiral Lord Keith.
5. Burke, op.cit., Erskine, formerly of Cardross. And see; Erskine, Mrs Stuart, ed., 'Memoirs of Sir David Erskine of Cardross' , Fisher Unwin, 1926.
6. Flint, J.E., 'Sir George Goldie and the Making of Nigeria', Oxford University Press, 1960, p.26.
7. Quoted in Watts and Davies, op. cit., p. 21.
8. Cunninghame Graham, R.B., SS Atlas in 'The Ipane', op.cit., pp 98 - 120.
9. ibid.
10. ibid.
11. NLS, Acc.11335/20; RBCG to AEB, 26 Dec. 1872.
12. ibid., the same to the same, 23 Jan., 11 Mar., 20 April 1873.
13. Cunninghame Graham, R.B., 'A Vanished Arcadia, Being some Account of the Jesuits in Paraguay 1607 - 1767', Century edition, p 228 n.
14. Burton, op.cit., p. 453.
15. Cunninghame Graham, R.B., 'Portrait of a Dictator Francisco Solano López (Paraguay 1865 - 1870)' Heinemann, 1933, p. 219.
16. Masterman, George, 'Seven Eventful Years in Paraguay', Sampson, Low, Son and Marston, 1869, p.10.
17. NLS,Acc.11335/48 AEB to RBCG, 12 Dec. 1872.
18. Cunninghame Graham, R.B., 'A Vanished Arcadia', op.cit.,; 'Portrait of a Dictator', op.cit.
19. Cunninghame Graham, R.B. and Gabrielle, 'Father Archangel of Scotland and other essays', Black, 1896, p.87.
20. Cunninghame Graham, R.B., 'A Vanished Arcadia', op.cit. pp 78 - 85.
21. ibid, pp 258 - 279.
22. Masterman, op.cit., p. 31.
23. ibid.
24. Cunninghame Graham, R.B., 'Portrait', and see Masterman, op.cit.
25. ibid.

26. ibid, p.24; Cunninghame Graham, R.B., 'Portrait', preface.
27. ibid., p. 100.
28. ibid., p. 128.
29. Masterman, op.cit., p.1.
30. Cunninghame Graham, R.B., 'Portrait', p.245.
31. Quoted in Masterman, op.cit., p. 98.
32. PRO FO 59/35; cutting from Buenos Aires Standard 1 Aug. 1872.
33. Thompson, G., 'The War in Paraguay', Longmans Green, 1869. Note. F.S. López was declared a National Hero <u>sin ejemplar</u> by Decree number 66 of 1 March 1936.
34. Kolinski, C.J., 'Independence or Death; the story of the Paraguayan War,' University of Florida Press, 1905, p. 198.
35. NLS,Acc. 11335/20, RBCG to AEB, 23 July 1873.
36. NLS,Acc.11335/56, Copy Alcorta concession.
37. Cunninghame Graham, R.B., A Meeting in 'Rodeo', op.cit., pp 107 - 110.
38. ibid.
39. ibid.
40. ibid.
41. Cunninghame Graham, R.B., Cruz Alta in 'Thirteen Stories', Heinemann, 1900, p.60.
42. NLS,Acc.11335/20, ; RBCG to AEB, 4 Nov. 1873.
43. ibid.,Acc.11335/56, RBCG to Holland, Jacques, n.d. but Nov. 1873.
44. Cunninghame Graham, R.B., 'Portrait', op.cit., pp 260 -261.
45. NLS,Acc.11335/20, RBCG to AEB, 4 Nov. 1873.
46. ibid.,Acc.11335/56, RBCG to Holland, Jacques, various dates.
47. PRO FO 59/35, Paraguay, 1872 - 74 contains much information on the Lincolnshire Farmers affair.
48. NLS,Acc.11335/48, AEB to RBCG, 24 April 1873.
49. ibid.,Acc.11335/56, G. Stewart to RBCG, 21 Aug. 1874.
50. SRO CS 46/143/10, 10 March 1875.

Chapter Four

Friendship

It was now eight years since William Bontine had been put under restraint, and the prospect of him resuming his place as head of the family seemed remote. Everything possible continued to be done to alleviate the burden of his confinement. Dr Sharpe, with whom he played innumerable games of golf, lived in at Eccles House, Thornhill, where he was the only patient, and there were random visits from other doctors to see that all was in order. Anne Elizabeth made regular journeys north to Dumfries to see her husband. 'Poor Papa was not nearly as well [in mind] as formerly', she wrote, shortly before Robert returned from Paraguay; 'a very sad visit. His health seemed good'. (1). The Strix was only 49; he might be spared for many years and while he lived the Bontine estate must continue in administration. Even though Robert had come of age the previous year the Curator remained in charge of his affairs, paying all the bills. In July 1874 he advanced £15 as Robert's share of a trip to Iceland with his brother. (2). The family had seen little of Charles in the past few years while he served abroad; his amiable presence was always a tonic to them, and he and Robert, 'Lee Cat and Bob Cat', got on as well together now as they did when they were small. The trip would be a welcome interruption to the task of finding Robert something else to do.

Iceland had come to the attention of the English reading public as the result of the interest taken by William Morris in her history as it was written down in the 12th century sagas. Morris had been greatly moved by the courage and endurance in the face of almost impossible odds of the heathen Icelanders as they were depicted in these ancient narratives. His cycle of verse tales, 'The Earthly Paradise' containing passages in the form of sagas, caused a sensation when it began to appear in 1869. (3). Though he was abroad for some of the time Robert kept abreast of the reviews by means of the journals - the Fortnightly and the Saturday Review and the Pall Mall Budget - sent him by his mother. Morris's passionate denunciation of what he called the filth of civilisation (4) whereby the acts of selfish industrialists and greedy tradesmen threatened to destroy everything of beauty and traditional worth, was a revelation to Robert, as it was to many of his contemporaries. The theme was in keeping with his nostalgia for his own ancestral past, which he had experienced at its most intense on the island of Inchmahome. Later it confronted him each time, on returning from some far distant country as yet untouched by industry, his ship traversed the riverside slums of Liverpool or Glasgow. Later still it was to be a crucial element in his support for socialism whose first and only voice he was in Parliament during the turbulent mid-eighties (to the scandal of the Liberals who elected him), when he acknowledged William Morris as the foremost of his mentors.(5).

According to Morris's biographer, the socialist historian, E.P. Thompson, prior to his discovery of the Norse legends, Morris had regarded the human condition with profound pessimism since he believed nothing could halt the rush to self destruction. As a shield against the present which he detested, he had immersed himself in the art of the Middle Ages. Iceland changed all that. What Thompson called the self indulgent melancholy of romanticism in decline was banished when Morris perceived that, before the coming of Christianity at the end of the 10th century, the Norsemen had worshipped courage - courage, 'not in the presence of hope and success', Thompson wrote, 'but in the face of failure and defeat and hostile fate'. (6). The insight into a totally different culture persuaded Morris that his contemporaries might also be capable of resistance to the evils of their own time; that, in the end, they would be moved to violence. Belief in impending revolution now encouraged him to begin a struggle against the two greatest evils; poverty and inequality, a struggle in which, ten years later as a Member of Parliament, Robert Cunnninghame Graham was to join. Of the two future political activists who travelled to Iceland in the early 1870s, Robert was the one who had already suffered tragedy on the scale represented in the sagas. Though he was only 22 - fifteen years younger than Morris - he had already confronted his own hostile fate with courage and, outwardly at least, born it with equanimity. In South America he had watched men endure civil strife, death, and deprivation, as the sagas instructed them to do, bravely and with self restraint.

His visit to Iceland was brief and afterwards he wrote very little about it. One story, Snaekoll's Saga has survived.(7). It describes a triumph of courage and tenacity over adverse conditions of weather and terrain, and - as every saga should - the doom that awaits excessive pride. Iceland's volcanic landscape was very dangerous to travellers; 'a terrible shore indeed' Morris wrote at his first sight of the island from the sea, 'a great mass of dark grey mountains worked into pyramids and shelves, looking as if they had been built and half ruined'.(8). These shelves were the jokulls, the tremendous ice and lava plateaux where no man lived and nothing grew. In Robert's saga the desire to distinguish himself from his fellow men drove Thorgrimur Hjaltalin to attempt the first crossing of the Vatna Jokull. His only companion would be his pony, Snaekoll. In telling the story Robert took care to emphasize the Icelanders' total dependence on their ponies. They were the only means of locomotion; they did all the work from transporting food, and timber for the houses, to carrying a dead man's coffin strapped on their back from his isolated farm to the nearest consecrated ground. As in South America men's lives frequently depended on them. In Robert's view this entitled them to a recognized place in the scheme of things; to consideration at the very least, while he would have given them the kind of trust and affection he had bestowed on Bunny. Thorgrimur Hjaltalin's offence was that he placed an unreasonable demand on his pony, Snaekoll; everyone knew the journey across the Vatna Jokull was impossible. Somewhere in that high and desolate region a hostile fate took its revenge; Thorgrimur Hjaltalin was never seen again but, after what was clearly a terrible ordeal, Snaekoll appeared on the far side of the Vatna Jokull where he lived on for many years. The saga ends with a sudden sensational twist vindicating Snaekoll (the pony is understood to have survived by eating its master), leaving the reader in no doubt of Robert's passionate belief that, just as much as men, animals had rights.

On his return from Iceland Robert went to stay with his mother in London where something like an ultimatum seems to have been issued. 'I have come to the conclusion that I had better go out to Ceylon', he wrote to the Curator on 10 December 1874, 'do you think you could get me money to go out there and also for my expenses during the time in which I shall be obliged to travel about the country before I can find any place to establish myself in?' 'I have heard very good reports of the coffee plantations of Ceylon from many sources', the letter continued, stiffly, as if dictated by another hand, an impression that is reinforced by the postscript, which reads like a capitulation. 'Owing to the very disturbed condition of South America I have been reluctantly compelled to give up all hope of succeeding there'. The best possible decision in the circumstances, Jamieson remarked, on forwarding the letter to the Accountant. If the Court was minded to advance the necessary sum the young man would leave for Ceylon as soon as possible (9). We do not know what these circumstances were, or why they overrode all other considerations. Robert's health had not been good, and it was barely a year after his return from a particularly hard and often lonely undertaking. Had he offended that he must hurried into exile in a part of the world that had not previously attracted his attention? One, moreover, where a horse was no more than useful means of reviewing serried ranks of coffee bushes.

Whatever prompted the proposal it was not carried out. Though he may have set out for Ceylon Robert got no further east than Gibraltar where Charles had now been posted. While they were together there in June 1875 Robert made the acquaintance of another naval lieutenant who was to become one of his greatest friends. At 26 George Morton Mansel was three years older; 'tall, dark and nervous, with round prominent eyes, a sparse moustache, and a skin tanned by the sun to a brick dark red' (10). Irascible and rough tongued, he was also kind, steadfast, and ready for anything. His home was the ancient manor house at Puncknowle in Dorset. His maternal grandfather, the Revd. George Clutterbuck Frome had been Vicar of the equally ancient church that stood hard by the house. George's father, Morton Grove Mansel, had been a soldier but died when George was very young (11). The two young men now set out together from Gibraltar on an expedition down the coast of Africa. Not much is known about it, apparently Robert departed without informing Mr Jamieson, and no letters have survived - if they were sent. The first port of call was Mogador, where Robert had his first encounter with the Moors whose brutal, backward, idiosyncratic, and furiously picturesque state of being at once, and for always, seized hold of his imagination. The Arab way of life, the religion of Islam, was to be of great significance to him. In his forties Morocco became his second home, the setting for what may be called his Greenmantle period when, dressed as an Arab, he enquired into strategically sensitive areas of the country, and did his best to persuade his influential friends to conduct British foreign policy in Morocco's best interest.

After Mogador the ship departed to the south, sailing between the island of Lanzarote and the mainland. This was a lonely shore; for hundreds of miles past Cape Juby and Cape Bogador, down to Rio d'Oro and beyond there were no harbours, and scarcely an inlet where ships might safely anchor, nothing but surf crashing on to unmarked sand. But there were regions inland, as yet unknown to Europeans, that were rumoured to be immensely rich. Though this coast was remote and inhospitable, as we shall see, moves were already under way in England to try to open trade with the interior. (13). This too was something Robert would become involved in during the time he lived in Morocco: he would devote much effort to an attempt to gain a foothold on the coast he saw during this voyage with Mansel. However, in 1875 the only moving object visible from the ship was an occasional Arab mounted on a camel, or a troop of ostriches. They did not encounter people until they had sailed much further south when the true purpose of the voyage was revealed; their ship was a slaver. Whenever the opportunity presented itself the captain kidnapped natives whom he sold to Brazilian traders for transport to their Empire in South America where slavery was legal. They appeared on the ship's manifest as 'rolls of tobacco'.(14). These unfortunate men and women were seized from the towns along the creeks and rivers of Senegal, the Gold Coast, and the Niger delta; wherever the ship anchored in search of goods to barter - taking off palm oil, ivory, gum copal, beeswax, gold dust, and ostrich feathers, in exchange for gin, rum, musical boxes, beads, bells, looking glasses, cheap German clocks, and French indecent prints, these last for the chieftains. Once seen, the unequal and degrading nature of this trade was something Robert never forgot. (15).

Long weeks of desperately hot and humid weather confined to a small coasting vessel must test any relationship. Yet on their return to Gibraltar Robert and George liked one another's company well enough to decide to go into partnership. They talked of ranching. The support of a friend of his own age probably counted for a good deal in the decision Robert made; to defy his family; to abandon Ceylon and go where he really wanted, to the great southern plains of the Argentine. Where Mansel was concerned, Robert's enthusiasm joined to his own taste for adventure prompted him to take the considerable step of resigning from the Navy. His was the greater challenge; like Charles Cunninghame Graham, for most of his life he had been at sea; it left its mark on him even after he became a rancher. Though he rode as well as anyone (bar Robert), and as the saying went, slept in his spurs, it was always obvious that he had been a sailor.

In January 1876 they took passage in RMS Douro from Lisbon where Mansel's naval colleagues gave them a farewell dinner on board HMS Black Prince. Going ashore they passed under the stern of the flagship, 'all the fellows on deck were waving'. The voyage out was propitious; for once the sea was calm, exceptionally so for Robert practised fencing every day, a skill requiring perfect balance. And he pursued his new found interest in the East by means of Edward Fitzgerald's famous translation of the 'Rubaiyat of Omar Khayam'. As the Icelandic sagas did, these 12th century Persian aphorisms warned of the malevolent fate awaiting man; all the more reason, in Omar's view why one should take full advantage while one could of earthly joys like wine and love. As he told his mother in a letter written at sea, Robert derived much consolation from this positive approach to an otherwise hopeless situation. (Mansel, who also read the book pointed out that wine was forbidden by the Koran).(16).

The Douro called at Rio de Janeiro and Montevideo before anchoring off Buenos Aires on 2 February 1876. No land was visible; because the Plata estuary was so shallow ocean going ships could approach no nearer than fifteen miles. All Robert and George could see from the Douro were a number of vessels flying different flags - English, French, American, Genoese - rolling about in the choppy yellow water, a stomach churning sight they had to endure for another week. "Quarantine is the only time in a man's life when he can read Chaucer all through', was Robert's only comment. (17). As soon as they were cleared for landing a whaleboat took them, soaked with spray, towards the city. The land it had been built on was so low a single line of houses with nothing visible behind was all that could be seen from the water. The first proper view of Buenos Aires came when they mounted the dilapidated wooden pier that, Robert fancied, had existed since the time of Pedro de Mendoza. However its days were numbered: a new one was shortly to replace it in order to cope with the greatly increased traffic. In recent years, as the result of the influx of emigrants like the Basques and Galicians Robert had encountered on his previous voyage, the city had begun to expand rapidly. In 1876 it was briefly poised between the ancient and the new.

Most of the houses were as they always had been; low, with flat roofs, and painted white which, as in Gualeyguaychú, gave the town an Oriental air. But here and there a tall new block of apartments built by the French (who were investing heavily) broke the harmonious line, prompting Robert to denounce them as vulgar - the worst term in his book - unsuitable both to the place and the people. The intersecting streets with pavements three feet high, looked more like dry canals than thoroughfares. These flooded when it rained and men with planks appeared who charged for a crossing from one side to the other. The opportunity would not be theirs for much longer: tramways had just been laid down and were still so unexpected that a boy blowing a horn galloped in front of each car. Very shortly, faced with a ride on a horse or a tram, most citizens opted for the latter. However, as of this moment, Robert was glad to see that horses were still indispensable. 'One of the chief sights of the place...was the great square before the Stock Exchange. Hundreds of horses stood about hobbled, all with their reins fastened behind the cantle of the saddle making them arch their necks like rocking horses. They seldom moved as they were so tightly hobbled.'. Anyone who wanted to approach the Exchange - the busiest in South America - had to push and slap his way among the horses. Their appearance aroused Robert's envy and desire. 'Every horse you saw...had a mouth like silk, the kind of mouth a man in Europe dreams of but never sees; and here, even the horses that the poorest rode, all had it, and all bent their necks as if they had been put through all the airs of the best <u>manège</u> in the world'. The owners and riders, businessmen and stockbrokers, were hardly less interesting. As one accustomed to the rigid demands of dress at home Robert was fascinated by the outrageously casual appearance of the male passers by (women, except for the poorest, were seldom seen). All were in black; black suits and soft black felt hats that Robert, already something of a dandy, roundly condemned for making them look like Maltese ship chandlers or touts in the Levant. Nearly everyone wore turned down collars, cut very low upon the neck and kept in place by narrow neckties like a shoe string, and no one carried a stick. Walking sticks were the mark of a greenhorn, Robert decided. This attire was quite as much of a uniform as a high stiff collar and a bowler hat in London. Even the sheep and cattle farmers changed their well cut, well worn tweeds for a black suit and hat and black string tie as soon as they arrived in Buenos Aires from the camp. (18). Robert met them at the place where he and George stayed; Claraz's Hotel at the corner of the Calle de Cangallo near the fashionable shops and the two great plazas. In the whole of his life this eccentric inn was one of the places that gave him the most pleasure.

This was due to the congenial atmosphere rather than the standard of service or accommodation, though the view from his small cell-like room across thirty miles of river to the Republic of Uruguay on the other side could not be equalled. Regulars chose their own rooms; they 'strode into the place with a Basque porter carrying their saddles, took off their pistols, hung them on their beds, and called for a drink...stamping about the brick courtyard in their long riding boots and spurs.'. As all the rooms looked out on to the yard the fashion was to leave the doors open so as to converse while lying on the bed. This ease delighted Robert: in some respects, he thought, the place was like a school with the difference that one was pretty sure to learn something worth knowing. The guests were commercial travellers, mining engineers, and Scots and English cattle farmers from the southern pampas. The commercial travellers were French who deigned to speak no other language but their own. Consquently the farmers 'mostly offshoots of county families' had to make shift in French or Spanish or Italian: in those days of mass emigration from Southern Europe English was hardly spoken. There was nowhere to go at night except the brothels which, Robert did not fail to establish, were numerous, catering for all tastes and pockets. Otherwise guests at Claraz's Hotel stayed in, playing billiards and telling stories while drinking maté, rum punch or a sizzling mixture of white curacao, gum, gin, bitters, and lemon juice. (19).

The proprietor, Georges Claraz, was a tall, black bearded, Swiss whom Robert thought singularly unfitted for such a boisterous profession. Well educated and with a bent for science, over the years he had wandered from Mexico down to Patagonia observing the lie of the land and collecting plants. The impression one gets is of a calm, self contained, rather formidable personality. Whenever his guests became too much for him Claraz retired to his quarters above the archway into the yard where he kept his books and natural history collection. He was engaged upon a comprehensive survey of the natural resources of the province of Buenos Aires, the first volume of which had been published in 1863. (20). From his experience and contacts Claraz could tell Robert and George Mansel all they wanted to know about their next objective, the English colony on the Sauce Grande some 500 miles south of Buenos Aires. Founded in 1868 on potentially fertile land fifty miles from the port of Bahia Blanca, the colony was still struggling because of its proximity to hostile Indian territory. Although the Argentine government had offered generous terms to attract the English, it failed to protect the colony against Indian raids. In 1871 when these had become more than usually frequent and damaging, the colonists asked Claraz to intervene on their behalf in Buenos Aires. His protest was in vain; the British Consul whom he approached did nothing but complain of the Argentine Government's 'wilful neglect' of the settlers. Consequently, when Robert and George arrived in Buenos Aires Claraz was obliged to warn them that the Sauce Grande was still an extremely dangerous place. (21).

That was no longer the case in the region Robert had come to know so well during his previous sojourn in the country. By 1874 peace had broken out in Entre Ríos: the rebel gaucho bands whose depredations he had observed at close quarters, had begun to disintegrate as a result of the slow but effective process of a commercial blockade. When the goods they had been accustomed to requisition - wool, hides, tallow - lost their value because no one would buy them, the rebels were deprived of occupation as well as profit. A tremendous change began to overtake the country: the gaucho way of life was about to disappear. 'The wielder of the long knife and lasso has almost ceased to play a prominent part in the political history of the country and the gaucho of the pampas must needs give way before authority supported by the disciplined soldier and his breech loading rifle' a dispatch from Buenos Aires told the Foreign Office (somewhat portentously) that same year. (22). The Indians took longer to subdue and drastic means were used: the policy adopted by the officer in command, General Julio Roca, was known as 'The Conquest of the Desert'. This campaign had two more years to run when , in March 1876, the two apprentice ranchers arrived on the southern pampas. Although several colonists had left after the worst of the Indian raids, about 50 English remained in the region watered by the Sauce Grande, Sauce Chico and the river Naposta. Their establishments were widely scattered; like those Robert had seen in Entre Ríos they were islands in a sea of grass that flowed around and up to them. But these were distinguished by a deep ditch all round, and some had a small brass cannon with which they signalled to their neighbours whenever a malon (the term for a raid), was in prospect.

These occurred in daylight, never in the dark. 'Once seen never forgotten,' Robert wrote, 'For hours before the Indians actually appeared troops of wild horses and of cattle, herds of deer and bands of ostriches preceded them, fleeing as before a prairie fire. Then in the distance arose a cloud of dust. As it came nearer through it flashed the heads of the lances, twenty feet in length the Indians carried. They usually rode barebacked... yelling and striking their hands upon their mouths. This made their yells sharper and like the howling of a pack of wolves. Around their bodies smeared with ostrich grease they carried three or four pairs of bolas, known to the gauchos as Las Tres Marias. With these...they hardly ever failed to entangle the hind legs of a horse, or to break a Christian's skull.' The Indians always rode in a great semicircle with the chief warriors in the middle. 'They used to pass so rapidly it seemed like a dream. The looker-on who generally sheltered himself in a thicket of tall pampa grass holding his horse whose head was muffled...hardly could believe that in a moment death had passed him by'. The Indians lanced everyone they met, sparing only the girls whom they carried off into the tierra adentro mounted before them on their horses' necks. 'On their retreat from an invasion they drove before them herds of cattle and of horses and left behind a trail of ruin and of blood'.(23).

This peril prompted a spirit of resistance among the settlers whose leaders were two Scots; Hay Edwards and his cousin, John Walker, known as Facón Grande and Facón Chico (facón was the gaucho word for the knife every man carried). Facón Grande affected a sword bayonet stuck through his belt, extending fore and aft, like the lateen sail of a Levantine fishing boat. His long hair, ragged beard, and gaucho costume gave him the look of a desperado, but Robert marked him as a cool headed man who had faith in the country and was determined not to be forced out. John Walker, Facón Chico, he of the smaller knife, was the shorter man, soberly dressed and his manner was almost meek. But show him an Indian and he was a devil. (24). When Robert and George encountered the two Scots the Indians were once more on the warpath. In March Robert wrote to say they had just driven off 100,000 head of cattle and burnt the camp for miles around. Accordingly , he and Mansel - who was very taken with South America - had decided to go in search of new stock to re-supply the settlers by which means they hoped to make some money. Though in this they followed the course adopted by the Ogilvys after the rebel gaucho raids in Entre Ríos, Robert and George found it less rewarding and very arduous. The raids had occurred so widely they had to ride far afield to find more cattle, spending long hours in the saddle, sleeping out at night in the bitter cold of the southern winter and with very little food. After two months they were quite 'knocked up' and with little profit for their pains. (25).

It is not clear whether, during these months, they came across a suitable place to settle. There is no contemporary evidence for the report in Tschiffely's biography that they bought a ranch on the Sauce Chico, on the edge of the Sierra de la Ventana.(26). There was scarcely time for that. By 21 June they had left the area and were no longer even in the Argentine. They had returned to Buenos Aires and crossed the Plata estuary to Montevideo. From there Robert wrote to his mother to say he and Mansel were on their way to Brazil expecting 'to make a good thing'. (27). This new idea had first occurred to them on their way out when the ship called at Rio and they had been impressed by the splendid appearance of the Brazilian cavalry. Horses were at a premium they were told; ones like these cost 80 dollars apiece. Robert already knew the going price for horses in the Banda Oriental was a fraction of that. Why not take horses from the Republic in the south to the Empire in the north? He knew he might acquire them at Durazno where they were cheap. and where he had friends, having been stranded there in 1873 waiting for the summons from Holland, Jacques. Now, three years later, he and Mansel made for the estancia on the river Yi,just outside the town belonging to two Scots, the brothers Witham, whose house Robert had helped to build. After much discussion they and their friends decided the enterprise was feasible notwithstanding the distance on the map from Durazno to Rio de Janeiro was 800 miles.

There was another difficulty; one that, in writing to his mother, Robert bracketed, as if dismissing it. 'If anything comes up and I am wanted home, word must be sent to the English Consul in Rio where I expect to be in about two months (that is to say if the journey is possible by land)'. No one knew if it was possible or not because travellers normally went round by sea. 'Many say it is not possible' he told his mother candidly. (28). There was a special reason why he might be called home. Shortly after his latest departure for South America his uncle, Bobby Cunninghame Graham, had brought an action to have himself replace the <u>Curator Bonis</u>, George Auldjo Jamieson, as administrator of the estate of his brother, William Bontine. As William's heir, Robert was advised to counter claim, Jamieson representing him in his absence. The prospect of being out of touch with his litigious relatives made the long journey into unknown country additionally attractive. (29).

Robert and George were delayed at Durazno by rain and floods. But by the middle of August they had collected a troop of 80 horses, a dozen of which came especially cheap, at three dollars apiece. They were hardly a bargain having been left to roam unattended for too long. They were semi-wild, apt to bolt at the slightest pretext when they caused the rest of the troop to scatter. Rounding them up sometimes took the two partners and the men they hired to accompany them the best part of a day. As a result the journey north was far slower than Robert had anticipated. The first part, towards the frontier, was reasonably well known since mules, which were in demand in Brazil for transport, were regularly driven up from Entre Ríos and Uruguay towards the great fair at Surucaba in the Sertão, the forest region north of São Paolo. (30). But the two partners found the going hard and, at river crossings, dangerous. Often the horses refused to enter the water. 'Then, sending out a yoke of oxen to swim first we pressed on them and made them plunge and kept dead silence, whilst a naked man on the other bank called to them and whistled in a minor key; for horses swimming, so the gauchos say, see nothing and head straight for a voice if it calls soothingly. And whilst they swam men in canoes lay down the stream to stop them drifting, and others swimming by their side, splashed water in their faces if they tried to turn.'. In the middle of the stream a favourite grey mare put up her head and snorted, beat the water with her feet and then sank slowly standing quite upright as she disappeared. After this disaster they approached each crossing with foreboding, especially at the frontier with Brazil. There were guards at the usual place but, in Robert's phrase they, 'being businessmen' crossed in the dark led by a smuggler who took them by devious paths to a ford where they swam, waded, and struggled through the mud. A thick cane brake came next when several of their best horses made off; they had to be abandoned for to pursue them meant losing all the rest.

The river crossing brought them to another world when the difference was in the attitude of the inhabitants to the passer by. Those Brazilians they had already met, who had settled in the Banda Oriental, conformed to the custom of that side of the river; 'that is they practised hospitality after the gaucho fashion, taking no money from the wayfaring man for a piece of beef; they lent a horse...their women showed themselves occasionally; and not being able to hold slaves they were obliged to adopt a different tone to men in general than that they practised in the Empire of Brazil'. In Brazil, in 1876, slavery was legal (hence the traffic from West Africa that Robert and Mansel had so recently encountered); men still carried swords, and women were kept in the strictest seclusion. Travellers fared poorly since it was almost impossible to buy food at the fazenda, (ranch) houses whose great iron studded doors were closed against the world. Those who were allowed to enter scarcely ever got beyond the sparsely furnished guest chamber where, as they ate, they were watched by the owner whose relief at their departure was as obvious as their own. Robert was dismayed by the fazenderos attitude; it was almost as if they were forcing him to beg. He and Mansel decided they should carry their own food for the crossing of the mountains that lay ahead. They bought a horse tame enough to carry packs; had a bullock slaughtered and the meat jerked; made bags out of the hide and filled them with the meat. Soaked in orange juice to make it slightly less tough, this had to suffice until, after burning hot days and freezing nights and ceaseless watch upon the horses, they came out upon a plateau called the Encima de la Sierra. At the far end was a town, Cruz Alta. Here they were obliged to pause; it was a month since they had left Durazno; the horses were thin and, for the time being, they could go no further.

Cruz Alta straggled along three sandy streets which led to a square. At the corner was the store, after the barber and the chemist, the chief meeting place. When Robert called in there half an hour's conversation (in Portuguese) with the owner shattered all their plans. '... to take horses on to Rio was impossible, the country after San (São) Paolo being one dense forest, and even if the horses stood the change of climate the trip would take a year, thus running off with any profit we might expect. Moreover it appeared that mules were in demand throughout Brazil but, horses, till past São Paolo five hundred miles ahead, but little valued and almost as cheap though much inferior in breed to those bred on the plains of Uruguay' The storekeeper told them to lose no time in teaching all their horses to eat salt, for without it they would sicken and die as there was some malign quality in the pasture beyond the mountains that salt alone could cure. 'Naturally, he had the cheapest salt in the whole town.'

After briefly considering - and rejecting - the idea that they should press on come what may, and however long it took, they acknowledged that, for the time being at least, they would have to stay where they were. The horses were driven to an enclosed pasture some distance from the town and the two partners settled down to wait for them to regain condition so they might be sold. Weeks passed while they occupied themselves as best they could -' riding into Cruz Alta now and then and eating cakes at the confectioner's, drinking innumerable glasses of sweet Malaga, laying in stores of cigarettes, frequenting all the dances far and near, joining in cattle markings, races...anything that happened'. They heard how Cruz Alta had declined since the days when 36,000 mules used to be over wintered there and, in spring, moved on to Sucuraba where they were sold to merchants from upper Brazil. But the numbers had halved due in part to continued fighting between the factions in Uruguay, but mostly to the fact that steamboats now carried all kinds of goods, including mules, from the Plata estuary along the coast to São Paolo. Christmas came while they lingered and the troop of horses gradually diminished. Some died of snakebite, some were sold. On Christmas Day they went to Mass in the church on the plaza where every tree had a horse or a mule tied to it.

Shortly afterwards things began to move. On 27 December Robert wrote to Anne Elizabeth to say that the last of the horses had been sold to a local man. He and George were about to strike the back trail with six 'pingoes' and one pack horse, 'cheerful but flat broke. It was exactly four months since he had had anything to read except an old almanack in Portuguese he knew by heart. Cruz Alta was lovely but boring; they had been obliged to endure nine days of prayer and singing to herald Christmas and he found the Brazilian inhabitants almost as disagreeable as the Scotch. In their ragged clothes he and George resembled Robinson Crusoe but the horses on which they were about to depart were in fine fettle. 'I never was so glad to leave a place...' (31). They did not intend to return the way they had come. The plan, which he did not reveal to his mother, was to ride north toward the Argentine province of Corrientes and cross the Paraná at Itapua, the town Robert had last seen in 1873 when reconnoitering the Alcorta concession. This journey was to bring him something of more value than the notional profit from selling horses; it was to provide the groundwork for a history of the Jesuits in Paraguay. The subject had been much in his mind during the past four months. Cruz Alta was on the route taken in the 17th century by the Mameluco bands when they seized Indians from Jesuit villages on the Upper Paraná and took them as slaves to São Paolo.

It was not surprising that, during months of enforced idleness in Cruz Alta, and before, Robert thought of writing. He was already aware that the kind of experience he had had in the past few years in South America was given to very few, and that the remarkable way of life he had observed - in Entre Ríos, for example - was passing. It is likely that Anne Elizabeth encouraged him to begin. The first reference he made to the possibility, which occurred in his August letter from Durazno, reads like a response to such a proposition. 'Decidedly it is reserved for me to be the Bret Harte of the South, but in Spanish or in English ', he asked her. (32). The comparison was apt. Harte had made his reputation as a reporter on the San Francisco Chronicle in the roaring sixties when his account of life in the mining camps, bars, and brothels of the Far West gained a following among readers whose lives never would embrace such picturesque and thrilling roughness and disorder. At the age of 24 Robert was about to begin the long hard struggle to develop a talent he hardly dared hope he possessed, and about which he was modest in the extreme. Even after a measure of success and praise had come to him in his fifties he remained unsure as to how well he wrote, and guarded about his motive in so doing.

The journey from Cruz Alta across the Brazilian province of Rio Grande do Sul towards the river Uruguay was uneventful. 'We camped at lonely ranchos inhabited ... by free negroes or by the side of woods, choosing if possible some little cove in the wood in which we tied the horses, building a fire in the mouth, laid down and slept after concocting a vile beverage bought in Cruz Alta under the name of tea but made, I think, of birch leaves.' Crossing the Uruguay into Corrientes (where Jesuit missions had proliferated), they found it virtually deserted; a wide expanse of tall grass interspersed with islands of trees, with the occasional band of ostriches scudding by. After three days they came to Candelaria, a small town on the east bank of the Paraná which, as Robert discovered when he came to examine the archives held in Spain, was founded on 2 February - Candlemas Day - 1665. It had been the centre of administration for the whole huge area under Jesuit control; the official residence of the Superior who exercised temporal, as well as spiritual authority over 100,000 Indians in the mission villages. In those days La Candelaria stood at the centre of a network of roads wide enough for carts that led in all directions; to Corrientes, to Asuncion, to the Salto Grande on the Upper Paraná. Relays of post horses were stationed along these roads, and fleets of boats and canoes plied the Uruguay and the Paraná with cargoes of <u>yerba</u> and tobacco, hides, timber, cotton and linen cloth - goods manufactured in the villages. All this disappeared after the Jesuits were expelled in 1767. When Robert and George Mansel rode into Candelaria they found it a sleepy gaucho town with empty sandy streets and a horse at every door. Only the fine large church remained in use; the other buildings of the Jesuits lay in ruins. The river Paraná was quiet; a few Indian canoes brought sweet potatoes and fruit to sell, returning home empty or with a tin pail or two, a looking glass; the kind of cheap and simple objects Robert deplored as being specially made in Europe to exploit the needs of frontier people. However, in terms of what they had missed in the past four months the place appeared a metropolis to the two young men. 'In Candelaria...we sat down to a regular meal in a building called 'El Hotel Internacional'; drank wine of a suspicious kind and seemed to have arrived in Paris so great the change to the wild camps beside the forest, or the nights passed in the lonely ranchos of the hilly district of Brazil.'

After two days a ferry took them and their horses across the Paraná, here a mile wide, to Itapua in Paraguay where Robert briefly renewed his acquaintance with Enrico Clerici who still kept a <u>pulperia</u> in the little town. Then he and Mansel set out for Asunción in the direction Robert had followed three years before, across the province of Misiones where there were many villages remaining from the Jesuit period. In the hundred years since the Fathers had been expelled, their good wide road had deteriorated into a narrow sunken path through forest so thick the young men were afraid of getting lost. Nevertheless when rumours came to them of some outlying village where old Jesuit books might have been preserved, Robert was always prepared to deviate in search of them. Though, sadly, they found no books or other documents in these isolated places, they saw that more than a memory remained of the former way of life. The village of Santa Rosa, for example, had a curious wooden church, built by the Fathers, with columns hewn from the trunks of massive trees, and with images of saints made in the 17th century remaining in the choir and nave. Though donkeys played in the grass grown plaza the great bell in the church tower still rang the Angelus. On hearing it the Indians took off their hats and murmured whatever they thought appropriate for an <u>oracion</u>. 'Thus did ceremony always much more important than mere faith, continue', Robert remarked. (33).

When, later, he came to write 'A Vanished Arcadia', contrary to the accepted belief that they had exploited the Indians, it was his contention that the Fathers had done their best to protect their charges from the much worse fate that would have been theirs left to the mercy of the Spanish administration. He was led to this belief partly from what he saw and heard on this journey through the Paraguayan villages in the early months of 1877 when his ability to understand Guarani, joined to his lively interest in the subject gave him the opportunity to asssess evidence beyond the reach of most historians. That the Indians continued to perform the ancient duties even if they did not fully understand them, he took as an indication that they were at peace with this particular memory. The manner in which they responded to his questions was another. 'Not once but many times have aged Indians told me of what their fathers used to say about the Jesuits, and they themselves always spoke of them with respect and kindness'.

A more recent and violent era came to mind in Santa Maria Mayor where their arrival coincided with the annual festival of the Virgin. Some fifty miles from Itapua, it was the largest of the Jesuit villages, at one time housing several thousand Indians. Now less than a hundred lived there and fewer still in the surrounding forest. When they began to arrive for the festival Robert saw that nearly all the males were boys, who had been too young to fight in Francisco López' war and who were outnumbered thirteen to one by the women and the girls who vied for their attention. A few old men came riding in: 'they too had bands of women trotting by their sides, all of them anxious to unsaddle, to take the horses down to bathe, or to perform any small office the men required of them'. They all went into the dark neglected church where an old Indian read prayers from a Book of Hours, pronouncing the Latin as if it had been Guarani, after which they sang 'Las Flores a Maria'. When the service was over and they filed out the only noise was the sound of their naked feet slapping a little on the wooden steps.

The marks of war were also evident when they reached Paraguiri, the terminus of the railway from Asunción. Nearly seven years after the collapse of López, business remained at a standstill in Paraguay, and Robert saw that there were only a few sacks of yerba, and of tobacco to go up to the capital by train. But there were six or eight empty trucks for the people, again mostly women who were going in search of work. On these they swarmed 'seated like flies upon the top and sides, dangling their legs outside like people on a wharf, talking incessantly, all dressed in white and everyone, down to the smallest children, smoking large cigars'. Because only running repairs had been done to the damage caused to the track and bridges during the late war, the journey of under fifty miles took six hours. But that was too fast for Robert and George who did not want their journey to end. Ignoring the train, they continued on horseback, riding slowly even after the churches and unfinished palaces of Asunción appeared on the horizon; a view they found oppressive. 'Not that we minded that our fortunes were not made, but vaguely felt that for the last five months we had lived a time which, in our lives, we should not see again, and fearing, rather than looking forward to all the approaching change'.(35). As usual Robert was reluctant to be parted from the horses, the Bay Overo and the Pateador, that had carried them so far and like Bunny before them, had become old friends, never tied at night for he had come to trust them not to stray.

He was unhappy that the horses had to be left behind in Asunción though he had every intention of sending for them in due course. Following the plan made at Cruz Alta he and George now took passage on a river steamer bound for Buenos Aires where they must have arrived in late March or early

April 1877. If, as Tschiffely has it, they had bought a ranch on the Sauce Chico the previous year it was surely time to be getting back to it. Mansel may have gone, though that is not certain, but Robert can scarcely have ridden hundreds of miles there and back for, by May, he was home in England.

The reason for his return, as Jamieson explained to the Court of Session, was the impossibility of keeping himself informed of the proceedings brought by his Uncle Bobby claiming the office of Curator at law over William Bontine. Robert also claimed it and, after much wrangling a joint minute had been drawn up in his absence. Robert had such difficulty communicating from South America, and deciding whether he should agree to the proposed settlement, Jamieson explained that, in May 1877, he returned to England. The affair had caused Anne Elizabeth much anxiety: she was still strongly opposed to Bobby Cunninghame Graham taking control of her husband's affairs. Agreement proving impossible to reach, Mr Jamieson continued his supervision of the Bontine estate. He did, however, put certain changes forward for the consideration of the Court of Session. Robert was now 25, an age when young men might be expected to settle down - though, he hastened to add ,this was far from certain in his case. 'At least for the present he has resolved to remain here' Jamieson minuted cautiously. 'He has at present no means of livelihood and, instead of paying sums from time to time for his maintenance, the writer is satisfied it would be better for Mr Graham to receive a fixed allowance.' He proposed and the Court agreed, that this should be £250 a year. This was hardly generous even for a young man who for the greater part of the last seven years, had lived at subsistence level. But the principle meant everything to Robert who, for the first time in his life, found himself possessed of the means to follow his own inclination without reference to persons having the authority to stop him. At once he set about making plans for the immediate future. Contrary to Jamieson's assurance to the Court they contained not the least provision for settling down.

Notes to Chapter Four

1. NLS, Acc.11335/34, AEB to Charles C.G.
2. SRO; CS 96/2413, f,36.
3. Morris, W., 'The Earthly Paradise' F.S.Ellis, Vols I &II, 1868; III &1V, 1870.
4. Justice, 16 June 1884, 'How I became a Socialist'.
5. See Below; Chapter 8.
6. Thompson, E.P., 'William Morris: Romantic to Revolutionary', Pantheon Books, 1976, p.182.
7. Cunninghame Graham, R.B., Snaekoll's Saga in 'The Ipane', op.cit., pp 204 - 225.
8. Morris, W., 'Journals', 13 July 1871.
9. SRO, CS 46/143 10 March 1875.
10. Cunninghame Graham, R.B., Anastasio Lucena in 'A Hatchment', Duckworth, 1913, pp 131 - 143.
11. Burke, ed., 'Landed Gentry'; Mansel of Punckknowle

12. Note. Cunninghame Graham was one of the models for Sandy Arbuthnot in John Buchan's 'Greenmantle', See below Chapter 13.
13. For the history of the North West Africa Company see; PRO FO 84/1500, and FO99, Morocco political corr. And see Parsons F.V., 'The North West African Company and the British Government 1875 - 95' in The Historical Journal, 1,2 (1958), pp 136 - 153.
14. Tschiffely, op.cit., p. 98. And see Bensusan, S.L., 'Don Roberto' in Quarterly Review, April, 1938.
15. Cunninghame Graham, R.B., Bristol Fashion in 'The Ipane', op.cit., pp 121 - 142.
16. NLS, Acc.11335/20, RBCG to AEB, 19 Jan. (1876).
17. ibid., 3 Feb. 1876.
18. Cunninghame Graham, R.B., Le Chef in 'His People', op.cit., pp 64 - 95.
19. ibid.
20. Claraz, Georges, 'Ensayos de un concociemento geognostico-fisico de la Provincia de Buenos Aires, 1863; Vol I, La Cordillera.'
21. PRO FO 6/302/ 187, 8 Apr. 1871. And see correspondence between Claraz, Macdonell, and Argentine Government in Parliamentary Papers, 1872, LXX.
22. Parl. Papers, 1876, LXXIII; F. R. St John to Foreign Office.
23. Cunninghame Graham, R.B., 'José Antonio Paez', Heinemann, 1929, p.67.
24. Cunninghame Graham, R.B., Facón Grande in 'Mirages', Heinemann, 1936, pp 169 - 182. And see Graham-Yooll, A., 'The Forgotten Colony', Hutchinson, 1981.
25. 'He spends all day on pingo', NLS, Acc.11335/20, RBCG to AEB, 26 May (1876).
26. Tschiffely, op.cit., pp 104, 128.
27. NLS, Acc.11335/20, RBCG to AEB, 21 June 1876.
28. ibid., 'Colonists letter to his mother', 5 Aug. 1876.
29. SRO, CS 46/143 , 29 June 1877. And see NLS,Acc.11335/50, Admiral Sir .J. Erskine to RBCG 3 May 1877.
30. What follows is taken from Cunninghame Graham, R.B., Cruz Alta in 'Thirteen Stories', Heinemann, 1900, pp 1 - 84.
31. NLS, Acc.11335/20, RBCG to AEB, 27 Dec. 1876.
32. ibid., the same to the same, 5 Aug 1876.
33. Cunninghame Graham, R.B., Feast Day in Santa Maria Mayor in 'Brought Forward', Duckworth,1916, pp 164 - 184.
34. Cunninghame Graham, R.B., 'A Vanished Arcadia', op.cit., p. 211.
35. Cunninghame Graham, R.B., Cruz Alta, op.cit.
36. SRO, CS 46/143, 29 June 1877.

Chapter Five

Marriage

When Robert and George Mansel parted company at the end of their adventures in Brazil and Paraguay, they fully expected to see each other again soon when they would begin another joint enterprise - shipping horses from the River Plate country to the British Isles. Even before the long and anxious deliberations about his father and the Bontine estate were concluded Robert began to explore the possibilities of this new trade. By December 1877 he had identified a demand and, in cheerful anticipation of a speedy return to South America, sent news of his progress to 'Don Jorge'. From his mother's house in Ebury Street he told Mansel he had got an order from a tramway company for 50 horses on approval; several friends wanted ponies, and he was in negotiations with the Turkish Embassy and with the English Army. 'There is an awful scare for horses at present [war with Russia was rumoured to be imminent] and I am in hopes of getting a contract'. He had been to the sales at Worcester Park and judged the horses there far inferior to those they had driven to Cruz Alta. As soon as he could make arrangements about shipping he would send Mansel money to pay for enquiries about prospective purchases. 'However in the meantime mention my ideas to nobody as we might be forestalled...I expect to have everything ready to sail about the 20th January and will send you dajory (French for money) before I sail'. Mansel was to sound a man called Power to see if he might be available for he would be the best person to superintend the horses on the Atlantic voyage . 'Find out how the pateador and the bajo are [the horses they had been obliged to leave behind in Paraguay] and what I owe..for the pateador's keep and what it would cost to send them to Buenos Aires by steam or sailing vessel. I intend to send you dajory to get them both (if they are still alive) ... we shall want two good horses in BA as we shall have to live in some small house in the suburbs. I should like to have the pateador again and you would like the bajo overo'..' Hang on wherever you are for a short time longer' Robert urged his friend ,and draw on me for dajory if you are hard up. Draw through the London and River Plate Bank and remember my name is Bontine'. Hoping to see you soon, he concluded and signed the letter Roberto C. Graham Bontine.(1)

His caution was to no avail; as he had feared his plans were forestalled; not by rivals in Buenos Aires, but by his relatives who contrived to see that he did not leave for South America in January, 1878. Precisely what happened to prevent him is not known, but by the following month he was installed in his mother's house at 32 Ebury Street where he was to be induced to settle down. That this was the intention can be assumed from the Curator's application for two special payments over and above his £250 allowance. One, for £42, was for the entrance fee and first year's subscription to the Devonshire Club; the other £50 to buy a horse and stable it in the vicinity of Ebury Street. These two attributes were crucial to any transformation from wild explorer to young man about town.(2)

According to its rules the Devonshire Club was' a Political Club in strict connection with, and designed to promote, the objects of the Liberal Party'.(3) Its membership was limited to 1,500 among whom sitting MPs were given preference. It was, therefore, the ideal starting point for a young man whose family wanted to see him continue their long tradition of service to the nation in the Whig tradition. Several of Anne Elizabeth's relatives were already members, including the Marquis of Lansdowne whose support for the candidate must have been very influential.. That the young man had not , so far, shown the slightest inclination for such a role, and should he suddenly acquire it, did not possess the financial means to nurse a constituency, let alone fight an election, did not deter his family.

In June he and his mother went their separate ways; Anne Elizabeth to pay her first visit to Dieppe, Robert to join Charles as a guest on board HMS Northumberland at Vigo in Galicia where the Fleet was showing the flag. Vigo- soon to be his place of exile - struck Robert as very little changed since Drake attacked it three hundred years before. Vigo Bay with its long fiord-like inlet, steep hills and pine trees down to the water's edge,was one of the chief points of departure for Spanish emigrants to the River Plate Almost everyone spoke English there. 'After seeing Vigo I begin to understand Pizarro and Cortez better than I did', he told Anne Elizabeth 'America was not conquered or colonized by Andalucians. The Northern Spaniards (from Galicia and the neighbouring province of Estramadura) are not nearly so amusing and he(sic) is much more of a man for a colonist or a solider than the Southerner' . (4) As these comments show he had already begun to contemplate writing about the <u>conquistadores</u>, drawing on what he had seen of their presence in South America. Now he had to enlarge this knowledge by studying the records held in Spain, at the castle of Simancas near Valladolid. From Vigo he made the first of many visits there. Presumably the cost of these journeys was met from his regular allowance for there was no mention of his new occupation in the next report by the <u>Curator</u> to the Court of Session. The only event Jamieson noted was the death on 30 November 1878 of Robert's grandmother, Laura Cunninghame Graham, widow of the eighth laird. In February 1879 Jamieson suggested to the Court that some of the £1500 that had been her jointure should go towards the doubling of Anne Elizabeth's allowance to £1.000 p.a. 'It must be kept in view that Mrs Bontine provides out of her income a house in London in which her sons find a home when they are in London, and the Curator is satisfied that this is an arrangement from which much advantage is derived', he remarked . At the same time he delivered another long cool look at the prospects of the Bontine heir . 'Mr R. C. Graham...has been brought up to no profession and has not succeeded as yet in establishing himself in any independent position, though he has made great exertions to do so...' The Accountant was asked to approve an extra £150 bringing Robert's total annual allowance up to £400.(5)

It was now eleven years since Jamieson had taken control of the Gartmore estate during which time his many reports to the Court show that the welfare of William Bontine's wife and sons greatly exercised him. No doubt he also kept in mind the advice of the Accountant delivered all those years ago - 'as the eldest son of course Mr Robert Graham should be dealt with liberally'. This makes it more extraordinary that his latest report made no mention at all of the dramatic change in Robert's circumstances that had occurred four months previously - his marriage on 24 October 1878. No application was made for funds to support a wife; no extra money was forthcoming. From the information that has survived it looks as though the Curator was not informed about the marriage; certainly the Court was not.

The only contemporary document is the crucial one, the marriage certificate which provides only the bare details required by law. For the rest, years later, the story as he wanted it to be known, was dictated by Robert to his biographers; Herbert Faulkner West whose book 'A Modern Conquistador ',was published in 1932 and Aimée Tschiffely whose 'Don Roberto' appeared in 1937. Tschiffely's account takes as its starting point the visit to Northern Spain in the summer of 1878 and the first attempt at historical research.. 'From Spain', Tschiffely continued, 'Robert once more returned to Paris. ... one day he rode a horse which gave him a certain amount of trouble and when the animal suddenly began to prance about wildly, it nearly knocked over a young lady who happened to be near. Don Roberto immediately dismounted to apologize and being somewhat embarrassed, he inadvertently spoke to her in Spanish. To his surprise and delight she answered in the same language, and then for a while the two chatted and arranged to meet again the next day. As this was a case of love at first sight things happened quickly'.(6)

The only thing we know for sure that happened was their marriage at the Registry Office in the Strand on 24 October. The groom ,who signed himself Roberto Graham Cunningham Bontine (sic), gave his age (correctly) as 26; his condition as bachelor; his rank or profession as gentleman; and his residence at the time as the Devonshire Club, St James's Street. His father's name, rank or profession, which was also required, appeared as William Graham Bontine, Officer in the Army. The bride, who signed herself Gabrielle Marie de La Balmondière, gave her age (incorrectly) as 19 - she was three months short of 21 - and her condition as spinster. She was not required to state her rank or profession. Her residence at the time was Havell's Hotel in the Strand. Her father was described as Francis de La Balmondière (deceased); his rank or profession as Merchant. The marriage, by licence, was conducted by the Registrar, Charles F Dorrell in the presence of two witnesses, Anthony Hart and J.E. Harper, making their one and only appearance in this story.

The procedure by which the licence had been obtained had been laid down in 1836 when the law had been revised to take account of marriage between Dissenters. Three weeks notice had to be given to the Registrar of the district in which one of the parties was living at the time, together with a declaration that he or she had resided there for 15 days immediately prior to the date on the licence; that there was no impediment to the marriage of the persons concerned; and that the necessary consents had been obtained. The notice did not have to be exhibited beforehand and the marriage certificate was available for collection 24 hours later. So, apart from the principals, no one needed to know the marriage had taken place unless one of the parties to the marriage was a minor. In that case a declaration of consent by a parent or guardian was required. As the bride in this case represented herself as being under 21 such a declaration must have been forthcoming . As we now know that Francis de La Balmondière had never existed , the identity of the person who vouched for her is unusually important. His or her name would be a very important guarantee of the credentials of the bride; in this particular and unusual case he or she might provide some clue to the very curious question of why Robert's bride married him under a false identity, which they both maintained in public , thought not in private,for the rest of their lives.

Gabrielle de La Balmondière was not a name to be inscribed on the marriage register and instantly forgotten. To contemporary theatre goers for example, it would evoke an image of romance, calling to mind a demoiselle in one of the wildly popular costume plays set in medieval France that, as they followed one another at the Lyceum in the late 1870s, established Henry Irving as the most successful actor manager of the day. In any circumstances it is a most unusual name. Yet it belonged to an individual well known in London society at the time. It was known to Robert's mother in whose interest those of her descendants acquainted with the story maintained the whole affair was instigated. According to them, by disguising the origins of the bride, she was to be saved the embarrassment of the world knowing Robert had married beneath him. However, from a close reading of the correspondence that has survived it would appear that Anne Elizabeth was the moving spirit in the whole affair helped by that useful person, Captain Ross Grove. Although by then he and his wife, Emily, were living apart he was still a welcome visitor at 32 Ebury Street. His name appears in the letters Anne Elizabeth wrote during Robert's sojourn in Paraguay; he brings her news of Holland Jacques' contacts with her son; he offers to find Robert a job in Russia on his return. Each time Ross Grove's name is mentioned it is coupled with that of another woman - Lina - who appears to be equally in favour with Anne Elizabeth. it is not clear whether Lina had taken Emily's place, or fulfilled some other function in the Grove household such as governess to the couple's two young daughters thus accounting for her constant presence. (7). In these circumstances it is interesting that the only Labalmondière known to London society at the time had a daughter, Lina, born in 1852 and baptized at St Martins in the Fields. Her father was Colonel Douglas Labalmondière, who, in 1878 when it was considered necessary to provide Robert's intended bride with a new identity, was Assistant Commissioner of the Metropolitan Police.

It will probably never be known if it was the Colonel, posing as the bride's guardian and a relation of her father,who provided the necessary form of consent for the marriage of a minor, or, separately testified to her identity, proof of which was required for persons under 23. Nor has the writer traced any connection between Robert Cunninghame Graham and the Assistant Commissioner prior to the marriage. But evidence does exist that some five years later the Grahams and the Labalmondières frequented the Grosvenor Gallery in Bond Street where portraits of Mrs Douglas Labalmondière, her daughter, Margaret, Gabrielle, Robert Cunninghame Graham and Anne

Elizabeth Bontine appeared in successive summer exhibitions, a circumstance that surely must have been avoided if either party was exercised about the past. And as social equals doubtless they met on other occasions, while the only volume of Gabrielle's diary that has survived, suggests that she may have known his daughter. Labalmondière's forbears were French aristocrats who , like the first Robert Cunninghame Graham, in the eighteenth century made fortunes in the Caribbean. Douglas was born in 1815 after his father, Joseph Julian Labalmondière had settled in Bath where, like the non existent Francis, he became a merchant. After Eton and Sandhurst Douglas had a distinguished career in the Army serving part of the time in Ireland. In 1850 he joined the Metropolitan Police and six years later was promoted to Assistant Commissioner. Six months after that he figured in a most intriguing episode which provides the link with Gabrielle. The parish register of St Martin in the Fields records the baptism on 11 August 1851 of a girl named Lina ; the father's name was Douglas Labalmondière, the mother was simply described as Caroline. In 1856 Caroline was nowhere in evidence when the new Assistant Commissioner, now aged 41, married the 20 year old Margaret Paget, daughter of John Moore Paget Esquire of Cranmore Hall, East Cranmore, Somerset. Douglas appeared on the marriage certificate not as a widower, but a bachelor. So was Lina illegitimate? And does this suggest a certain lack of inhibition in his character that eased his conscience when he was called upon to falsify a declaration in support of the Graham marriage? In June 1888 the Grahams were in London. On 21 June Gabrielle noted in her diary , 'Lina came at 10 p.m. Was weak enough to ask her to dine with me and go to the Play.' If this was Lina Labalmondière she would have been 37. Gabrielle who, by then, had been married to Robert for nine years, was 30 (8)

So who was this mysterious girl whom Robert chose above the many who set their caps at him ? 'One of the handsomest boys I ever saw' , was how one of his mother's friends remembered him at about this time. (9) That was not the only reason why young ladies sighed over him; as well as handsome, he was funny, clever and kind; he made no secret of the fact he liked the company of women; he was very well connected and the heir to large estates that for all they knew had already provided him with sufficient income to indulge his taste for high adventure and, they did not doubt - would in due course support the kind of life appropriate to someone in his position.   Gabrielle's true identity remained unknown until the 1980s. Robert told Tschiffely and Herbert Faulkner West that she had been born in Chile of a Spanish mother and a French father. Orphaned at the age of 12 she had come to Paris where an aunt had placed her in a convent. Except for one other detail nothing more was ever said about her origin; that detail was, however, crucial . As Tschiffely put it, she spoke with a slight accent, 'neither French nor Spanish but most attractive and charming as foreign accents can be, especially with ladies'.(10) This performance - for that is what it was - moved W.B. Yeats to call her 'the little bright American', while Friedrich Engels referred to her, in what tone of voice we do not know, as 'La Espagnola'. (11) In fact neither French nor Spanish was her mother tongue; she came from Yorkshire. Her name was Caroline Stansfield Horsfall; she was born on 22 January 1858, the second daughter of Dr Henry

Horsfall of Masham in the North Riding. This was the place her sister Grace made the setting for a novel recounting some of Caroline/ Gabrielle's adventures and called it Beckdale, 'a sleepy hamlet upon the rim of Wensleydale', a cluster of slate roofs in a valley with the spire of a church rising from their midst. The nearest town ,which Grace called Bishopthorpe, was Ripon, ten miles away across the moor.(12)

The town of Masham in North Yorkshire. Gary Keat.

Caroline's father was the doctor here almost from the time he qualified until his death; the kind of place it was, together with the fact that he and his wife, Mary, hardly ever left it even to go so far as Ripon was perceived by Grace, to have been the chief cause of conflict in the family . As parents 'they were ... bound by [Masham's] conventions, its prejudices, its ignorances; their outlook obscured, their judgement impaired, their view as limited as if Beckdale Moor were indeed to be the utmost boundary of their world', she wrote in the first chapter of her novel. In religion they were strictly Evangelical and this, together with the strain of providing for twelve children, (4 boys,8 girls) turned Henry into an anxious father whose response when challenged was unyielding. He was most often challenged by Caroline who was the cleverest in the family, brighter by far than he or her mother, original, tempestuous, hell bent on having her own way. As the eldest daughter living at home Caroline was required to help with the other children. But 'she didn't like children and hated looking after them and had more than once expressed her wish that Herod had been alive when they were born...' Grace wrote. Whenever she could she disappeared into her own room where she flung herself on the bed with a book, 'and presently forgot in the glorious stuff she was reading her own identity as a struggling country doctor's daughter in a miserable little town like Beckdale that confined her like a prison.' (13) Miserable is an exaggeration, prompted by hatred born of despair. In fact Masham was unusually well endowed with books According to the Post Office Directory for 1872, when Caroline was 14, as well as a circulating library , Masham had a Mechanics Institute (with a house for the librarian,) and the Hall Reading Room with over 1600 books . There were three schools; a national school , a grammar school for boys, and in Park Street, where the Horsfalls lived, a school for girls. (14)

Education was essential to the Horsfall girls. Because their parents were unable to support them they knew that, once they reached the age of 17 or 18, they would have to go out into the world and earn a living in the only way open to them - as governesses. But Caroline was determined it would not be her fate; '[she] made it only too apparent she judged it a degradation to be a governess'. By the age of 14 what Grace called 'her rage for study' had put her far in advance of other girls of her age from whom she held herself aloof, living largely in her own imagination. The superb self confidence that marked her every action was not mere egotism or vanity, her sister shrewdly judged; it was born of the consciousness that she was unusually gifted. Her greatest fear, that the circumstances of her birth in Masham would prevent her from fulfilling this potential caused her to adopt the most extreme solution - to cast aside the doctor's daughter for another identity altogether. Besides the usual accomplishments of a young lady - water colour painting, singing, speaking foreign languages - at all of which she excelled, her chief delight was in staging plays in which, inevitably, she took the leading part . Those she wrote herself were full of detail ; she had a passionate love of realism Grace remembered. With striking good looks and a most attractive voice she was already well prepared for the role she was determined must be hers . Yet it seems she reached the age of 16 without her parents realising how much her heart was set upon the stage. When this was made known to them it provoked a crisis of unprecedented proportions. (15)

Caroline could not have delivered a greater blow had she proposed to walk the streets : the theatre was anathema to Evangelicals who equated all its works with vice. Caroline's mother tried to talk her out of her desire but found the task beyond her: in spite of herself she found the intensity of her daughter's feeling very moving. [Caroline] 'refused even to contemplate being a governess' Grace wrote, 'she would be an actress or nothing'. Mary Horsfall had to fall back on the dangers of the stage of which she had no direct knowledge having never been inside a theatre in her life. Yet she knew she had good reason for alarm; she had only to look at Caroline . 'The mother in her was afraid when she saw the surprising vivacity and attractiveness with which the glow of ambition touched her girl, when she considered her slim virginal body not only extraordinarily graceful in its womanly immaturities but strangely provocative' - a description which, in confirming the sensuality revealed in early photographs of Caroline/Gabrielle, is surprisingly frank for the time. As the weeks went by and the crisis was not resolved Caroline's refusal to take any part in household affairs, her sulks, her storms gradually wore her parents down to the point where her father grudgingly agreed to consider her enrolment in a school of acting. This was very reassuring to her mother who had been a teacher 'But [Caroline] would have none of it' Grace wrote, 'The thought of a school was loathsome to her. She conceived a state of bondage; a set of fools imposing rules and trying to teach the unteachable...' (16) Caroline was not prepared to argue any longer. It was December when she made her first attempt at persuasion; the following March she ran away.

According to Grace's narrative, Caroline who was tall for a girl, dressed in some of her brothers' clothes, and having cut off her long hair, she and a boy cousin, who doted on her, set off on foot for Bishopsthorpe/Ripon across the moor. But their absence was discovered; her father chased and caught them before they had gone very far. 'I shall only run away again' Caroline is supposed to have told him whereupon he locked her into the spare room for the many weeks it took for her hair to grow long again. The younger children remembered that time as the most dreadful experience of their childhood; 'Papa always cross, Mama always crying, the door of the spare room always locked with the key on the outside'. Dr Horsfall did not neglect measures to safeguard Caroline's health during this period; she had a constant supply of books and regular periods of exercise supervised by her mother. 'When the children were out in the afternoon it was [Mary's] sad duty to take her daughter for a constitutional about the fields or round and round the old walled garden. ...as they paced the garden walks side by side 'Mrs Horsfall- in the sober dress she had of late affected - might have been a novice mistress, reasoning into quietude and resignation some restless postulant (it is likely this passage marks the nearest Caroline/Gabrielle ever came to convent life)

Caroline Horsfall. University of Michigan Library.

Caroline's imprisonment lasted seven months until her father was persuaded to release her for the sake of her mother whose own health was badly affected by the affair. Caroline was sent to her grandmother at Bishopthorpe/Ripon under whose strict regime it was claimed she began to come to terms with fate. So much progress did she appear to make in the desired direction that her grandmother was even able to persuade her to take a post as governess to some children who,-in the novel- live at the Bishopsthorpe Deanery. This was the opportunity she needed to escape a second time. Unlike far away Beckdale/ Masham, Bishopsthorpe/ Ripon was on the direct London railway line; provided now with money from her earnings as a governess, Caroline took a ticket to Kings Cross where she lost no time in seeking out a famous actor manager (who bears a strong resemblance to the real Henry Irving) in whose company she hoped to be enrolled. Unfortunately for her, when she asked for him at the theatre she was redirected to his home in St John's Wood where his wife saw her waiting in the hall. As was her habit when attractive females approached her husband she took up her post at the keyhole of the room in which the interview took place. In the knowledge that his wife was listening, the great man asked Caroline to come to him at the theatre in three days time when he would be sure to hear her story. But, as Grace told it in the novel, the story had a swift and tragic end. Three days was an eternity to Caroline who had exhausted all her money. Deeply disappointed she left the actor manager's house to wander aimlessly round the streets. Light headed with hunger and cold, confused by the unaccustomed traffic ,she did not see a brewer's dray approaching before it was too late and died under its wheels.(17)

So Caroline was written out of the novel before the appearance of a character representing her future husband. It would be fair to assume that this was deliberate: that the time and place of her meeting with Robert had to remain a secret. It may even be that the whole purpose of her new identity was not so much to conceal who she was or where she came from, but what she had been doing between her second flight from Masham and the marriage at the Registry Office in the Strand.   To speculate along these lines is to assume that what Grace chose to write about her elder sister was essentially true. It is this writer's opinion that it was as accurate as it could be given the fact that it was published in 1919, nearly 40 years after the events it describes which can be dated to 1875. Grace herself was not born until March 1875. She had, however, two sources on which to draw; one the older members of her family; the other Caroline. We have evidence that Robert was fond of Grace and kept in touch with her after Gabrielle died in 1906, and until his own death thirty years later. He may have encouraged her in what she wrote about Caroline; and provided some details .(18)

Grace Horsfall was seventeen years younger than Caroline. According to the Register of Baptisms of St Mary's all the Horsfall children, except the eldest, Mary, who was born before they moved to Masham, and Grace, were baptised by the Vicar . The Register has a note to the effect that Grace was baptized privately and three years later on 3 March 1878 ,received into the church at the same time as her younger brother, Charles Edward , was baptized. Grace married an Irishman, Doctor Stevenson and had one child, Martha, who is the source of most of what is known about Gabrielle's relations with her family apart from Grace's novel (which she wrote under the name George Stevenson). According to notes Martha made in 1986, Grace and Gabrielle met quite often. Their mother, Mary Horsfall, was in the habit of making mysterious trips to York where, it is supposed, she also met Gabrielle. Martha also referred to an incident at Hyères in the South of France when Grace was staying with Gabrielle: something happened that so upset her she left immediately .(19)

Was it the revelation that she was not Caroline/Gabrielle's much younger sister but her illegitimate daughter, conceived on the first occasion Caroline bolted? Was it to conceal the pregnancy that Caroline was locked in the spare room in Park Street for seven months, seen by no one but her father and mother? That long isolation seems too harsh a punishment for the offence of running away even for so wicked a purpose as going on the stage, while the shame her parents were described as feeling was a response out of all proportion . The date of Grace's birth, 6 March 1875; the fact that she was the only Horsfall child to be baptized privately; her reception into the Church , aged three, in 1878, these details could suggest that ,like many other Victorian parents with large families, the Horsfalls passed off a daughter's illegitimate child as their own, in order to avoid a scandal. Caroline's intellect, her originality; her success in everything she attempted, to say nothing of her attractiveness to men, had made her greatly disliked by the ladies of that small community; who 'were as ready to destroy her reputation as domestic hens to set upon and kill a disabled hawk' (20) To see her disgraced in such a manner would have pleased them in no small measure.

Grace chose to dispose of her stage struck heroine through sudden death, a device that relieved her from further explanation. In real life some three years had to elapse between the flight from Masham and the marriage to Robert Cunninghame Graham. We can only speculate as to what happened during that time but it is reasonable to suppose that if Caroline did not find a place in the theatre - or even if she did - as a very attractive, solitary female she suffered a fate Victorians were quick to describe as worse than death . It has been said that the purpose of the masquerade as Gabrielle de la Balmondière was to spare Robert's family , particularly his mother, the pain of knowing he had married out of his social class. Caroline was not the heiress Anne Elizabeth may have hoped her son would marry, but given what we know about her origin there seems no good reason to conceal it unless Robert's mother was the most virulent of snobs. Prostitution on the other hand was of an altogether different degree of undesirability - unmentionable in most circles. If there was any possibility that Caroline had been reduced to such a level a new identity might have been the only way to rehabilitate her .Of this more in due course. To return to Tschiffely's account; he had the newly married pair spend the autumn and winter of 1878/79 at Gartmore; in the spring they decided to try their luck ranching in the United States. Tschiffely made it seem light hearted - two young people undertaking an adventure; Robert's letters suggest it was far from that.

In the first place, as papers held in the Scottish Record Office show, for legal and financial reasons connected with the administration of the Bontine estate, Robert was not allowed to live at Gartmore during his father's lifetime (21). then, in consequence of his marriage to someone his family considered unsuitable he found himself with even less control over his personal affairs than formerly. In particular his freedom of movement was restricted by lack of money. His allowance was now controlled by Robert Wright, a barrister who had long been a close friend and adviser to his mother. Henceforth, if he wanted money he was obliged to let Wright know exactly where he was. In February 1879, for example, he wrote to Anne Elizabeth from the Fonda del Oriente in Spain (the place is not identified in the letter). Gabrielle was very ill; he had the doctor to pay, please could she ask Wright to send dajory? The next letter, in April, was from Bremerhaven in Germany where Robert and Gabrielle were on board the SS Braunschweig, an emigrant ship about to sail for New Orleans. Gabrielle does not figure in the letter which is Robert's farewell to Anne Elizabeth whom he had not seen during the brief visit he made to London after leaving Spain and before he arrived in Germany. He had, however, dined with Mr Wright. (22)

On reaching New Orleans Robert began a series of letters to his mother, the originals of which are preserved in the National Library of Scotland. Gabrielle is nowhere mentioned: all Robert does is done alone. Yet when Tschiffely reproduced extracts from these same letters in his 1937 biography at least one reference to Robert's wife had been written in. The conclusion must be that though more than fifty years had passed since the marriage Robert was still not willing for Tschiffely to reveal the circumstances. 'I arrived yesterday' was how the first letter from New Orleans began. As with so many of the German immigrants who had been their fellow passengers on board the Braunschweig, the city was the last manifestation of sophisticated urban life they would experience before continuing to the place where the new life they were expected to embrace would begin. For Robert and Gabrielle the journey lay across the shallow Gulf of Mexico to Brownsville, a town in the far south west of Texas on the Rio Grande which formed the frontier with Mexico. They had been there almost a week when Robert wrote somewhat shakily to his mother - he had still not recovered from the three day passage in a flat bottomed steamboat - 'I am trying to get a small place for breeding mules', he told her. There was a good wooden house on the land in question with a garden, 'which is a good thing'. This was an allusion to the wife he did not otherwise mention. Brought up among the gardens and orchards of Masham Gabrielle had green fingers; gardening was to become one of her greatest pleasures. (23).

In the circumstances prevailing at the time the breeding of mules was a sensible choice of occupation. Although the railways had already begun their rapid penetration of the South West, transport still depended on four footed animals. Mules were less susceptible to disease than horses and the men who drove them swore they did three times the work on half the food. But this particular venture came to nothing when the Bontines realized what dangers they might run. Brownsville's proximity to the Mexican border put it under constant threat from raids by bandits. Mexico had long been in a state of anarchy: lives and property were everywhere at risk; a stranger in the towns was eyed for his potential worth; no one went unaccompanied into the sparsely populated countryside. So, though Robert and Gabrielle liked what they saw of Matamoros, a town on the Mexican side of the Rio Grande, they decided to move north, further into Texas, taking only one souvenir of Brownsville with them. This was Jack a stray fox terrier that had attached himself to them: he was to become a much loved part of their existence for many years. In the same letter as he asked Mr Wright to forward his allowance, Robert reported their departure from Brownsville. After 190 miles of very sandy going along the almost landlocked Laguna Madre - when Jack's short legs grew tired after fifty leagues he was given a ride on the stage - they arrived in Corpus Christi, the chief town of Nueces County on the bay of the same name. It was a typical mushroom town superimposed on an old Spanish settlement. With its frame houses made in the North, numbered in pieces, railed South, and put together 'like a Chinese puzzle' it looked to Robert very like one of the places Bret Harte was fond of describing. 'I have got a nig servant and have taken a nice little house planted round with tamarisks and oleanders while I am looking for a suitable location [to settle]', he told his mother (24). On 27 June he bought 100 acres of uncleared land on Nueces Bay, four miles north of Corpus; on 5 August he and Gabrielle jointly sold it to an American doctor for $1500, the same price as Robert paid. The excuse was that they had discovered it was not suitable for his purpose; instead of breeding mules this had now become the export of horses to the contacts he had already made at home in England. Corpus was not adapted for shipping horses; the harbour was too shallow to admit anything but small schooners, and all along the coast it was the same. So 'unless shipping horses started on very favourable terms I don't think it would succeed'. (25).

Nothing else turned up. On 3 August he told Anne Elizabeth he was thinking of moving to San Antonio de Bexar some 150 miles to the northwest. '[Corpus Christi] is not very healthy and is rather dangerous to live in. Times are very bad, worse than ever I saw them at the worst in the River Plate. The country is very ugly, all covered with dense low scrub and not such a thing as an open pampa. The people are revolting and mean to a degree. The Mexicans are the only redeeming feature and they are not strictly agreeable as they are chiefly thieves and murderers. The pitiful wooden houses are most repulsive and I long to see one of the white Spanish houses of the River Plate. They say San Antonio is the most endurable place in Texas. I wish I had gone down to Mexico from Brownsville', he wrote in a rare outburst, the measure of his growing discontent with the situation he and his wife were in. 'Words are inadequate for the citizens about here, their meanness, hypocrisy and assassination being beyond all bounds', he continued; 'I don't believe in Italy, in the Middle Ages there was so much assassination as there is in Texas today. Every day there is one or two and such a thing as a fair fight is unknown.' (26). This criticism could have been prompted by his concern for the safety of his wife. Really it was more: the expression of his acute distaste for the culture of violence permeating every aspect of Texan society at the time - it was the heyday of gunfighters like Billy the Kid. At that precise moment Texas was one of the most turbulent places in the while United States; every kind of conflict was resolved by violence.

Besides the people and the landscape the climate did not suit him. 'the heat is simply awful & the hardest to bear I ever experienced. Owing I suppose to the country being so sandy' he told Anne Elizabeth. As soon as he and Gabrielle set out for San Antonio the longstanding drought was broken by heavy rain which turned the sand to mud , heavy going for the horses so that the 150 miles took them seventeen days. His spirits should have revived on arriving there for, by Texan standards, it was an ancient place, Spanish by origin and in appearance; with a high proportion of Hispanics among its population. Yet, if not as dire as Corpus Christi San Antonio also disappointed him. He continued depressed, with a most uncharacteristic tendency to grumble. The reader of these letters is forced to conclude that, left to his own devices Texas was the last place he would have chosen to begin a new life. But his family believed that in such a rapidly expanding place where many foreigners, including English, were in the course of settling, the opportunity existed for him to secure some kind of diplomatic post - as a Vice Consul for example, or a Queen's Messenger, both of which were possibilities being pushed by Mr Wright. Robert was not disposed to take the idea seriously. Of course he was perfectly qualified, he teased, - he could speak French and German (badly) ride, and had no political or religious convictions that could not be promptly altered. His interest lay elsewhere - in the history of the conquistadores which he already had in mind, and he lost no time in exploring the possibility of a journey into Mexico. Very soon after arriving in San Antonio - 'There is complete peace in the Republic...I am confidently assured by the Mexican Consul', he told Anne Elizabeth, a conclusion into which more than a little wishful thinking on his and the Consul's part had entered. Porfirio Diaz who had recently become President, would eventually bring peace, but in 1879 Mexico continued disturbed and very dangerous. Nevertheless Robert and Gabrielle began to look about for a means of going there. He said nothing of his plans in his letters to his mother, and very little about his activities in San Antonio; their place was taken by a stream of chat about the kind of literary and political affairs that interested Anne Elizabeth at home in England, as if to distract her from his more serious affairs. 'Pingo sends his love' was how his letters mostly ended, with never a mention of his wife.(27)

Nor did Gabrielle figure in the report he sent when they were already about a month into their next adventure. From Monterrey, some 200 miles south of the Mexican/US border on 19 January 1881 he told Anne Elizabeth how, for the first time since leaving San Antonio, *he* was in a civilized place. The journey into Mexico had been difficult because winter had set in and the cold was awful, moreover he had had a dispute with the capataz of the wagon train carrying bales of cotton which he had joined in San Antonio. He had been obliged to wait a week for another southbound convoy. After being delayed a further fortnight at the frontier he had been allowed to ride with the Mexican commander going to pay the troops stationed in Monterrey. Mexico was living up to his expectations; the trail so far across a spur of the Rocky Mountains was spectacular, while the towns were far more Spanish in character than those he had seen on the River Plate.

Again there was not the slightest mention of his companion in this letter. However the original bears a note he added years later ; 'with Gabrielle and 'Jack', and, as was his custom, signed it with his brand. (28). Gabrielle left her own account of this same journey in an article, 'The Waggon Train'. Although it was not published until two years after her death, it was obviously in her mind to write it at the time. Gabrielle was further advanced than Robert in her desire to become a writer, with greater confidence in her ability, and much less inhibited in acknowledging her ambition. Her description of the two month long journey from Texas to Mexico City relied for its effect on observation of people and places along the way. Countless films romanticizing the Wild West have made such accounts almost too familiar nowadays. But it made an impression on contemporary readers, the more so since its author claimed no special dispensation from the hardships of the journey as a woman. Probably it was one of Gabrielle's first attempts at writing. What cannot be denied is the special sense of pleasure it conveys. With the freedom to ride for miles over open, unfenced country came another. Liberated by the fact of travelling in the wild from the need to pretend she was someone other than she was, the masquerade was abandoned for a time and, as we shall see, Gabrielle gave way to Caroline.

'The waggon trains which go from San Antonio de Bexar (Texas) to the interior of Mexico present to the European or the Yankee from the Northern States a sight sufficiently curious', Gabrielle began. 'The waggons are large and solidly built, with ponderous wheels, and covered with tilts of white canvas to protect the merchandise from the weather. They are capable of carrying an enormous burden, and may be considered the ships of the Mexican deserts, as they are in fact. Each waggon is drawn by a team of from ten to twenty mules, harnessed in two rows of four abreast, with a couple of wheelers, one of which is ridden by the driver, whose traps and necessities for the journey dangle over the wheels or from the back. These consist of cooking utensils, ropes for mending broken harness, and spare boots with bright red or yellow tops; whilst his rifle is carefully slung in front, near at hand, ready for immediate use'. The style which does not vary struck Robert later as almost childish, though he was forced to admit its truthfulness. After nearly one thousand miles with the waggon train they arrived at the railhead in the Valley of Mexico thoroughly tired out. 'As we take our tickets at the station for Mexico [City] we are pleased to have arrived at our destination without the [waggon] train having been robbed en route - an occurrence always likely to happen in Mexico. Mexico [City] strikes us as being a large, handsome, somewhat French looking town and when we find ourselves in a comfortable French hotel, luxuriously supping on cotelettes a la milanaise and a bottle of burgundy we are thoroughly able to appreciate the comforts of civilisation', Gabrielle concluded.

Later on when Robert began to use his knowledge of exotic places as the background to his literary work, though it was among the most remarkable, Mexico City hardly figured. Instead he chose to portray it as conquistadores like Bernal Diaz de Castillo had seen it three hundred and fifty years before, using Diaz' words rather than his own. However, interrupting his account of Cortez' temporary retreat from the city in 1520 when one of the Spaniards,

Pedro de Alvaredo, escaped the Aztecs by using his lance to leap across a canal, is a brief glimpse of the two modern travellers. 'The first thing I saw in Mexico on my way to the post office after a journey of two months from Texas, having left my wife tired out and seated on the kerbstone holding my rifle and my horse, was a plate let into the wall with the inscription 'here was Alvaredo's leap'. (29). This was the kind of thing they had come so far to see. Robert's aim in visiting sites on the high plain bordered by the Sierra Nevada and the Sierra de Guadarrama which forms the Valley of Mexico where the events of the Conquest occurred, as well as the principal libraries in the capital, was to enlarge upon the knowledge he had already gained from the Spanish archives at Simancas 18 months before. The reason Tschiffely's 'Don Roberto' mentions nothing of this most important aspect of their sojourn may be explained by the fact that duties connected with his inheritance shortly overtook Robert, delaying his debut as a writer for many years. And when, at last, he was free to fulfill his ambition, what he wrote about Mexico was not the most successful of his work. In the absence of information volunteered by his subject Tschiffely fell back upon suggesting that, while they stayed in Mexico, Robert and Gabrielle turned their respective abilities to earning money; he by giving fencing lessons, she by teaching French, painting, and the guitar. It seems unlikely they would have bothered so long as credit was available. From the Curator's regular report for 1880 we know that Robert was still in receipt of his not insubstantial allowance of £400 a year, and that Jamieson knew by then he was in Mexico. But the Court of Session remained in ignorance (as Jamieson probably also did) that the heir to the Bontine estate was now married.(30)

One further glimpse of Mexico City, as it was at the moment of their leaving, appears at the beginning of Robert's story, 'A Hegira', published twenty years later, in 1900. In this he expressed his fury at the manner in which the Indians were being treated by the Hispanics and Americans. 'The giant cypresses, tall even in the time of Montezuma, the castle of Chalpultepec upon its rock (an island in the plain of Mexico), the panorama of the great city backed by the mountain range; the two volcanoes, Popocatepetl and Ixtaccihuatl, and the lakes; the tigers in their cages did not interest me so much as a small courtyard in which, ironed and guarded, a band of Indians of the Apache tribe were kept confined. Six warriors, a woman and a boy, captured close to Chihuahua, and sent to Mexico, the Lord knows why; for generally an Apache captured was shot at once, following the frontier rule which, without difference of race was held on both sides of the Rio Grande, that a good Indian must needs be dead'. The piece must rank with the most powerful polemic in the English language against the cruelty practised one upon another by members of the human race. The Indians in question were Mescalero Apaches from the country astride the Rio Grande much reduced by hunger and harsh treatment; 'naked except for a breech clout, their eyes apparently opaque and looking at you without sight but seeing everything, and their demeanour less reassuring than that of tigers in the cage hard by'. Fully aware of how dangerous they were, Robert approached them as he would tigers - or any other animal - that is to say with respect. 'I asked the nearest if he was a Mescalero and received the answer 'Mescalero-hay' and for a moment a gleam shone through their eyes, but vanished instantly as when the light dies out of the wire in an electric lamp'. Their case seemed hopeless; in fetters, closely guarded, confined in a fortress at the summit of an isolated rock, even if they succeeded in escaping they were six or seven hundred miles from their own country to the north.

Yet they did escape, having murdered two of their guards, and fled along the route parallel to the one Robert and Gabrielle had to follow on their own journey back to Texas. In 'A Hegira' Robert contrasts their progress with that of himself and Gabrielle; they are constantly in the background, their unseen presence a cause for alarm. 'In my mind's eye I saw the Mescaleros trotting like wolves all through the night along the base [of the Sierra Madre}, sleeping by day in holes, killing a sheep or goat when chance occurred, and following one another silent and stoical in their tramp towards the north'.(31)

This, while he and Gabrielle, having joined a mule train, rode north along the normal route via San Juan del Rio, San Luis Potosi, La Pareda, Matehuela and Saltillo. 'Day followed day as in a ship at sea; the wagons rolling on across the plains and I jogging on my horse, half sleeping in the sun, or stretched at night, half dozing on a tilt, almost lost count of time.' Part of the way lay through a wild and stony desert where everything was covered with the whitish dust of alkali. They saw the domes of San Luis Potosi long before they reached it and found it full of fine buildings, churches, and palaces from the time when its mines of silver had made it wealthy, set among gardens, groves of pepper trees and palms, and flowering shrubs. It was a city of enormous distances, Robert wrote in 'A Hegira'; 'of gurgling water led in stucco channels by the side of every street, of long expanses of adobe walls, of immense plazas, of churches and of bells, of countless convents; hedged in by mountains to the west, mouth of the 'tierra caliente' to the east, and to the north the stopping place for the long trains of wagons carrying cotton from the States'. But they soon tired of its squares, its long dark streets, its crowds of people, and left before daylight for the north. It was then that, crossing a sandy track, the <u>capataz</u> saw the tracks of the Mescaleros. When they stopped for the siesta they met a band of Mexicans who announced the death of one of them. They had found him sitting on a stone too tired to move and shot him, after which they hanged him by his heels from a tree. When Gabrielle and Robert came up with the body they found it covered with bullet wounds. 'Half starved he looked and so reduced that from the bullet holes but little blood had run; his feet were bloody and his face hanging an inch or two above the ground, distorted; flies buzzed about him and in the sky a faint black line on the horizon showed that the vultures had already scented food'. After Saltillo came Monterrey, Juarez, and Las Navas, from where the mountains that marked the beginning of the Apache country were visible. The surviving Mescaleros had been seen passing Las Navas; two men and a woman carrying in her arms a little dog. 'I knew that in the mountains the three Indians were safe.. and I wished them luck after their hegira, planning with such courage, carried out so well' It was not to be. The next day they met a Texan who told them he had surprised the Indians the day before and, even though he could never bear to kill a squaw, 'though I've often seen it done', shot all three. He would have shot the dog which flew at him but refrained at the request of the Indian woman who was his concubine (whom he said he would have married if she had not been a Catholic) The Bontines found the bedraggled dog guarding the Indians' grave and tried to get it to follow them. In vain. (32)

It was May before Robert and Gabrielle arrived back in San Antonio, their journey having taken fifty days. What happened next is hard to explain. The couple separated; Gabrielle remaining in Texas while Robert took ship for the Argentine, apparently in response to an invitation from George Mansel to join him in a new attempt at ranching. He and Robert had been in touch the previous autumn while the Bontines were pursuing their somewhat aimless existence in San Antonio. Mansel wrote from Entre Ríos where he was helping to run a ranch not far from Gualeyguechú. George condoled with Robert for having fallen among Texans. His own news was grim: there had been no rain since March and he had lost 50 out of 400 head of cattle in consequence. His contract would be up in August 1880 and he would not go in for another; 'it is too great a gêne being boxed up with a low class Scotchman', he told Robert. By the time he wrote again in December his thoughts about his future had advanced. 'What do you think of renting an *estancia* of two leagues with all the stock on it at a fixed rent and a capital between us of about £1,000?' he asked Robert. 'We are a little hitched at present in the negociations for want of funds but I think we shall be able to see our way through it on the make or break principle'. The letter goes on to discuss the pros and cons of a Queen's Messengership. Such jobs had once been a pretty soft option but, Mansel warned Robert, as the Foreign Office had recently cut the salary and reduced the numbers they had the remaining Messengers 'pretty constantly on the trot'.(33)

The 'we' in the letter probably were Mansel's real or prospective partners whom he did not name; but Robert seems to have read it, rightly or wrongly, as an invitation to himself to join in. It is likely that he did not receive it before he and Gabrielle left San Antonio on their way to Mexico, but found it waiting for him on his return. The moment may have been decisive. He had found it hard to endure Texas before the Mexican journey; now, faced with the need to remain in a place he disliked in order to earn some kind of living, he may have seized upon Mansel's letter as a means of escape. In August when he wrote his first letter since arriving to his wife, he had acquired a troop of horses, identified a suitable property, and ridden the hundred miles to Buenos Aires where he had sampled all the entertainments the city had to offer. Every line of the letter testifies to a revival in his spirits on returning to the place he preferred above all others - 'country for country the River Plate is the best of all of them'. But this time things were different; it remained for him to persuade his wife to join him.

Wholly unlike their later correspondence the letter was formal in its approach, stilted even, suggesting that Robert was unsure of the response. 'My dear Caroline', it began 'I have long promised to write to you but have been so much occupied I have never done so yet'. 'This is a charming part of the country', he went on, coaxingly, 'splendid open plains for miles; all over long Pampa grass and absolutely covered with horses and cattle; in the distance there are a range of low hills, a very nice little river... goes right past the house and falls into the Paraná about three miles below the house where there is a shipping place for Buenos Ayres which is about 100 miles off. The house is built round a patio in the old Spanish style and the courtyard is planted with orange and lemon trees'. The ranch was stocked with a large number of cattle and he had already had time to collect some 40 head of tame horses.

'Buenos Ayres is rather dull now', Robert continued, 'the Opera troupe has left and there is only the French company at the Alcajar and a rather dreary Spanish one at the Colon. I wonder how you can still stay among those odious Yankees in Texas when down here is so much nicer and we might have such horse and ostrich hunts and also deer hunts together. If you can come just drop me a line to say by what steamer you are coming and I will meet you at the Hotel de Provence, Calle Cangalo, with a tropilla of horses and we will gallop out'. The letter was signed 'Roberto el gaucho', with a postscript, '...bring Jack with you'.(34)

The proposal obviously did not suit Caroline for Robert was back in San Antonio before the end of the month. We do not know how she received him, or even if she stayed to greet him before leaving for New Orleans where she spent the next eight months. The reason for her departure remains unknown but it would have been quite in keeping with the character of Caroline, as described in 'Benjy' if, faced with a situation not to her liking, she bolted leaving her husband to his own devices. 'I am very ill' he told his mother in a letter written shortly after his return to San Antonio; confined to bed with inflammation of the kidneys, he was unable to sit up. Like so many other misadventures that afflicted him in the course of his travels abroad, he explained it as the result of a fall from a horse. Sick and alone in San Antonio, he was also in debt and very bothered by it. 'About the bills 'he wrote to Anne Elizabeth at the end of September, 'I cannot hear of you paying either of them', and - in a very rare allusion to his married state - 'you have already payed far too much for *us*'. He had only just recovered when a further blow fell. In October his mother wrote to tell him how desperately ill his maternal grandmother, Catalina Katon, was; a few days later she had to tell him she was dead. 'This is a sad letter for you to read. You have the comfort of remembering her great love for you and *of knowing she died in ignorance of anything that might have grieved her in yr lot*'.(35) His lot was to have been sent into exile in order to conceal the circumstances of his marriage.

Also in October Robert told Mr Wright there was no chance of a Consulship for him and, 'I am afraid the Messengership is more than doubtful.' (36). He was getting reconciled to Texas; Mexico was a much nicer country but he hated being cooped up in towns as one had to be for safety's sake when living there. Probably it was during this period that he made the acquaintance of Colonel Bill Cody - Buffalo Bill - whose Wild West show was playing in San Antonio at the very beginning of its long career. He also seems to have spent some time roaming across Texas and neighbouring states tracing the passage of Hernando de Soto, the conquistador whom he followed possibly even into Arkansas,with a view to the book he was eventually to write (37). Tschiffely and others have it that in the autumn of 1880 he went into partnership with a Mexican Greek with whom he bought a ranch some distance from San Antonio which was plundered by Indians and all its cattle driven off. There hardly was time for this, nor is there any mention of it in his letters home. These refer to Mr Wright's continued efforts to find him a Consulship. 'A paid one is impossible' he told his mother in the New Year, the only prospect was of a lesser post, unpaid. He was thinking of a trip to Cuba to escape the malaria prevalent in San Antonio from which he was now suffering. On 22 January he told Mr Wright he had abandoned any idea of going to Havana because of the expense. Texas was in the grip of awful cold and snow. (38)

At this point his mother appears to have realized how desperate Robert had become. She lost no time in sending his brother to his rescue; 'paid Mr Charles Cunninghame Graham's expenses of going to America and back, 23 February to 27 April, looking after Mr Bontine; £174' the Curator's accounts noted.(39). As a result of seeing Robert, Charles and Anne Elizabeth came to the conclusion that he and Gabrielle (whom Charles seems to have visited in New Orleans) must leave the United States. They were not to return to England but go as quickly as possible to Vigo, a decision Robert accepted with relief. In a postscript to a letter by Charles from San Antonio he wrote, 'How jolly it will be in Spain, not in the least resembling Texas'. (40) The two left America in May to be met by Anne Elizabeth at Dieppe. Although he had been away for more than two years Robert was not encouraged to see the other members of his family, or his friends; after a brief stay in Dieppe he and Gabrielle went on to their next place of exile. Their failure to appear in London caused considerable comment. For instance Malise told his mother that Blanche Fane, an old and close friend of hers, had asked him to go and see her. 'I went today. I said no more than necessary about the Bob subject and that only in answer to her questions wh. I rather snubbed. She asked why you were at Dieppe; I told her Homer (AE's maid) was not quite well and that the house was not quite ready. I said also in answer to her question that you had not heard any additional details about Bob' (41)

There were two reasons why Robert's immediate family were reluctant to have him exposed to the curious. One was his poor state of health. According to the Curator who had him examined by a doctor shortly after his return from the United States he would have to live quietly for some time. The other was the continuing problem posed by Gabrielle. What little evidence remains suggests that both these reasons were taken into account by Anne Elizabeth in proposing that the couple should live in Spain, and that the two were related. Robert had not embarked on the Texan venture of his own free will; the death of his much loved grandmother; his failure to obtain the diplomatic post urged upon him by his family; lack of success in any direction, and a series of debilitating illnesses contributed to his growing unhappiness. But the most important factor in the failure of his health and spirits probably was the fear he might be permanently separated from his wife. Everything Robert was to write, whether thinly disguised as fiction, or in the form of letters to Gabrielle proclaims her as, henceforth, the most important person in his life.

He never concealed the fact that, the histories excepted, all his work was autobiographical. Though he did not begin to write until he was in his forties, thereafter he produced a series of dazzlingly effective sketches based on the people and places he had known. The people were shrewdly observed; their lives - in South America, in Spain, in Morocco provided the inspiration for his narrative. Nearly all his subjects were men; women hardly figured. A couple of eccentric aunts, an affectionate reference to George Mansel's mother (42) this - with one exception - was all he attempted; those he knew best - his mother, Catalina - have no presence in his work. Their exclusion underlines the importance of the exception, the woman who occupies the centre of the stage in more than one sketch whom he describes with sympathy and admiration, and no wonder, for she - the intelligent, kindhearted, reasonably well educated, brave, and independent -minded cocotte - is a portrait of his wife.

Such candour may seem remarkable, shocking even, especially for the times. But truth telling was an essential part of Robert's character and would become the hall mark of his behaviour as a Member of Parliament. The reason for the revelation concerning Gabrielle was twofold; generally to express his detestation of marriage as an institution by representing the so-called 'fallen' women as normal human beings; specifically, to rebuke those who had presumed to confer a bogus respectability on the person he had chosen for his wife. So they would be in no doubt as to his intention he had recourse to the convention of the roman á clef. Those who knew Gabrielle would have had no hesitation in identifying her with the English woman faisant la cocotte in New Orleans who appears in the sketch 'A Hundred in the Shade'.(43) The woman, who does not use her real name, is tall, like Gabrielle; she is good at conversation; she has taste; she likes furniture and collects china; she plays the piano, not very well but has a good voice; she speaks French, German, Spanish, and Italian. A significant clue lies in the list of her books - Dante's 'Vita Nova'; the 'Heptameron' -these are the same Grace Stevenson described in 'Benjy'. 'Manon Lescaut' which is also on her shelves is the story of a young man and a girl who elope to Louisiana, while the volume of poetry is by Adah Isaacs Menken who, like Gabrielle was an actress, a poet, and a fine horsewoman. Robert makes her a Catholic - 'not that she cared too much for her religion, but as she said, the Mass with all there is about it, lights, incense, and the tradition of antiquity, appealed to her on the aesthetic side.' Gabrielle's Catholicism was very much as here described; she came to it via the High Anglicanism she and her brother, William Horsfall, adopted in Masham in defiance of their father's Evangelical fervour. (44)

'Yes, well, yes, I got to love her, and to look forward to our long talks on books and china, pictures and the like,' was how the man in 'A Hundred in the Shade' described his relationship with the Englishwoman in New Orleans. As a description of how the marriage of Robert and Gabrielle developed this also rings true: his letters speak of the pleasure he took in conversations with her; of how much quicker she was in appreciating art and literature than he was. Elise, the cocotte in two earlier sketches, 'Un Monsieur' and 'Un Autre Monsieur' (45) is not so closely identified, possibly because they appeared while Anne Elizabeth was still alive, whereas 'A Hundred in the Shade' was not published until immediately after her death. But she possesses two of Gabrielle's distinctive characteristics: the habit of haunting museums to teach herself about painting, and her love of clothes. 'I was a mannequin in a great

Paris shop', Elise is made to say, 'I am,you see, both tall and elegant...I was born with...an innate sense of elegance in dress.' Whether Gabrielle herself worked as a mannequin during the years between her flight from Masham and her marriage, one cannot say. But someone taught Robert to write convincingly about the subtleties of dress - the absolute necessity of good stays for example (46) - a skill he could hardly have acquired from his fencing partners at Angelo's, or playing bridge at the Devonshire. Gabrielle's letters to him are full of the problems posed by being well turned out in an age when every gentlewoman had her clothes made; her elegance was not acquired cheaply; the amount she spent became a by word in the Cunninghame Graham family.

Lack of money had always been Robert's chief worry; all his adult life had been spent in a conscientious attempt to relieve the Bontine estate from the necessity of supporting him. Later on it was his great misfortune that, of all the lairds of Gartmore, some spendthrift, some penny pinching, he was the one with the greatest detestation of falling into debt, and the one who inherited the greatest burden of it. While they were growing up his brother, Charles, had been the one to receive the occasional word of reproof for extravagance from the <u>Curator</u>; Robert (so far as we know), never. (47) The only time he exceeded his allowance was in 1873 when the expenses of his typhus fever at Gualeyguachú had to be paid. Now, on his return from Texas, Jamieson was obliged to make an application to the Court of Session for special powers to borrow a sum not exceeding £2,000 to pay off the debts incurred in the United States. And, since his present allowance of £400 a year when burdened with the interest of that debt, would be quite insufficient for his maintenance in a position suitable to the heir of the Ardoch and Gartmore estates, Jamieson asked for an additional £100 to bring it up to £500 a year. It must be noted that, in making this application, Jamieson made no reference to Gabrielle. That was left to the Accountant who, in agreeing the increase, made a passing reference to the fact that Mr Bontine was now married. But, canny as ever, he referred the request for the £2,000 loan to the Court to decide on the grounds that Robert might die before the ward, his father, and there was no way of insuring against this. (48).

£2,000 was five times Robert's annual allowance; no wonder he was in despair. It is hard to imagine how it was incurred; one suggestion lays the blame on Gabrielle and her alleged taste for extravagant living. But, however free with money they may have been in San Antonio and Mexico City, they would have been hard put to spend the whole amount. The explanation must lie with some kind of business transaction that went wrong - a partnership with the mysterious Mexican-Greek; an investment that lost its value; a venture by Gabrielle who, as we shall see, was a born entrepreneur. Whatever the explanation the outcome was favourable. 'Mr Jamieson wrote this morning to say the Court had increased my allowance to £500 a year and were going to pay the debt too', Robert told his mother on 30 July (49) By that time he and Gabrielle (with Jack) had moved in to the Quinta de la Grana where they were to spend two of the happiest years of their lives. Visitors from England whose own drawing rooms, in the fashion of the time, were heavily carpeted, smothered in curtains, beaded and befringed, found the former granary alarmingly bare. But it was warm and sunny, lying as it did along the side of hill overlooking the bay of Vigo and the islands. Most of their time was spent on the terrace where Gabrielle arranged olive jars planted with flowers. For several weeks after they moved in she was very unwell with fever, ague, and a bad cough - symptoms that were to return many times in the years to come, as did opthalmia. Following the meeting in Dieppe relations with Anne Elizabeth seem to have improved - temporarily at least. 'Gabrielle sends her best love', was how this letter ended.

In those days and for many years to come Spain was untouched by the modern world, unvisited, unknown. 'We find the natural manners and customs unchanged since the Middle Ages, virtually unaltered to what they were when the Moors and the Spaniards lived side by side together in the heart of the Peninsula' (50) The quotation is from a lecture on Spain given by Gabrielle at Newcastle on Tyne in 1890. She began with a description of Vigo, its landlocked bay, its serried ranks of houses clinging to a steep rocky cliff; the kind of thing, she told her audience, most of them would only have encountered previously as scenery for plays put on by Irving at the Lyceum Theatre. On the top of the cliff was the plaza surrounded by old granite palaces, the town houses of the local gentry. Badly paved and narrow streets led to the Alameda, the public garden looking down upon the bay, an inland lake shut in by mountains, studded with the white sails of fishing boats coming in from the open sea. 'It is hot, the atmosphere balsamic with the scent of pine woods, and the fresh salt smell of the sea'. As to the Spanish character, Gabrielle took issue with Richard Ford, author of the famous, 'A Handbook to Spain' for exaggeration to the point of making it seem grotesque. 'I for my part see more to respect, to love, to admire, in the proud, self respecting dignity, the simple sober habits, the native good manners and kindness which are the characteristics of all classes of the nation'(51) Sobriety, as in the case of Robert's own countrymen, sometimes left an unfortunate impression on strangers. Of all the inhabitants of the Peninsula the Galicians were renowned for a sobriety so extreme it might be described as dourness - Galicia the Grahams often said was another Scotland. They were to have a constant reminder of this regional characteristic in the woman who came to keep house for them at about this time. Peregrina Collazo's local knowledge - she was a native of Vigo - made life much easier and cheaper for them and because of her presence at the Casa de la Grana they were the more quickly accepted by the townspeople. Peregrina became particularly attached to Gabrielle but the relationship between mistress and maid was not an easy one. Peregrina was much given to very trying fits of sulking, while her refusal to carry out orders which she did not like frequently caused Gabrielle to threaten to dismiss her. (52)

But life on the whole was very pleasant and far from lonely. One of the first visitors at the Casa de la Grana was Malise, now a student of theology at Oriel College, Oxford. He was spending the long vacation travelling round Spain and arrived at Vigo thoroughly exhausted after long hard days in a diligence infested with fleas. Beyond a short description of the house and its incomparable view, the letter he wrote to Anne Elizabeth from Vigo was uninformative;' Bob seems very well so does Gabrielle' was all he had to say this time upon the 'subject'. (53) The next letter she received was from Robert who told her George Mansel had been to see them on his way home to Dorset from the Argentine. He had asked them to visit him and his mother at Puncknowle which they would do in October, after a week in London and some time with the aunts at Leamington Spa. From this it seems young Mrs Bontine was to be introduced to the family gradually. Their long absence from home was obviously causing gossip, as Robert reminded his mother. 'I think more suspicion will be evoked by us living so far away as Vigo', he told her, 'Mansel seemed to think it very odd but he was very pet [Grahamspeak for nice] on the whole. He came and camped here for a day'.(54)

Robert was to look back on the visit to the Manor House at Puncknowle as the happiest occasion in his life. So far as anyone can tell this was the point - to put it very simply - at which he and Gabrielle fell properly in love; their letters, once constrained, as in the manner of his to her from the Argentine, afterwards became full of warmth and affection. There is one crucial piece of information indicating that this visit to Puncknowle was of the greatest importance in the marriage: it is Robert's pet name for his wife, and the one Gabrielle asked her closest friends to use - this was 'Chid', short for Chideock, a village on the side of a steep hill, west of Puncknowle, near the sea. Whatever happened there was always to be remembered. More than twenty years later, at the end of her life the woman who had been born Caroline Stansfield Horsfall, signed her will 'Gabrielle Chideock Cunninghame Graham' (55)

Another long remembered visit was to Wales in the spring of 1882. While staying at Chapel Arthog they fell in with a painter, Bernard Evans and his wife, Mary. Evans' landscapes were regularly hung at the Royal Academy' Summer Exhibition and at the Grosvenor Gallery in Bond Street so his offer of tuition delighted Gabrielle who was trying to improve her style. She and Mary Evans wrote frequently to one another for many years. Their letters reveal that, by the summer of 1882 the Bontines' exile was nearly over. They were free to visit London where they rented a flat in the Vauxhall Bridge Road. Possibly it was the Evans who introduced their new friends to the Grosvenor Gallery which now rapidly became a favourite place of resort for both of them, but more particularly Gabrielle who could indulge her passion for pictures and artists to her heart's content. It had been founded in 1877 by a Scots baronet, Sir Coutts Lindsay, who transformed a warehouse into a series of well lit rooms finished in gilt and crimson that housed a Summer and a Winter Exhibition. Lindsay, who was himself a painter, wanted to enable his fellow artists to exhibit their work unencumbered by the strict and stuffy rules imposed by the Royal Academy. Among those who came over to him were Alma Tadema, G.F. Watts, Albert Hunt (father of the more famous Violet), Millais, Edward Burne Jones, and Walter Crane. The leading light, however, was the irascible, volatile, witty and sarcastic James McNeil Whistler whose eccentricities kept the habitués of the Grosvenor, among them Oscar Wilde, Bernard Shaw, and Walter Crane in a state of pleasurable commotion. The easy going atmosphere at the Grosvenor owed much to the exuberant personality of its manager, Charles Hallé, and also to the fact that there was a restaurant beneath the Picture Gallery where ladies might lunch unchaperoned. The Grosvenor was noted for the number of woman artists whose works were entered in the Summer Exhibition; if Gabrielle had ambitions in that direction so far as is known she did not achieve them. However, like the Labalmondière ladies and her mother in law she was successful in another respect: the 1880s saw the zenith of the aesthetic movement when to have one's portrait painted and exhibited at the 'greenery, yallery Grosvenor Gallery'(as 'Patience' had it) was to be in the height of fashion. Where Robert was concerned, the Grosvenor was his introduction to the world of contemporary art among whose practitioners he was to make lifelong friends. Not a painter himself, nevertheless a highly developed sense of form, colour, and movement enlivened all his written work, while the facility he possessed, of putting an artist's vision into words would frequently be employed on behalf of friends like John Lavery, William Rothenstein, and the young Australian, Mortimer Menpes , who as one of Whistler's young disciples was the means whereby Robert came to be on friendly terms with the most celebrated painter of his day.

In September 1882 the young Bontines went to Scotland where Robert saw his father. Now aged 57 William Bontine was not in good health. The whole of the visit was spent at Lochend, a house belonging to Robert's Erskine cousins, on the shore of Lake Menteith, opposite Gartmore. It was presided over by Cousin John - Admiral Sir John Erskine, whose mother, Keith Elphinstone, was Uncle Mount's youngest sister. While there Gabrielle painted a picture of the gate of the Priory on the island of Inchmahome (a short boat ride from Lochend),had it framed and presented it to Cousin John. The Admiral was touched; he became one of Gabrielle's staunchest admirers in the family and wrote her chatty letters signed 'Yours affectionately'.(57)

As letters to her show Gabrielle inspired affection in all sorts of people. Among her correspondents were the Mother Superior of a London convent to whom she sent presents of flowers and game; a botanist with whom she discussed specimens from the Flanders Moss at Gartmore; a mining engineer in Spain who wrote her clumsily flirtatious letters; and members of the English colony at Oporto whom she and Robert got to know in the course of several visits there while they were living at Vigo. (58). The British Consul at Oporto was the celebrated Oswald Crawfurd, by origin a Scot, an old friend of Robert's parents. His first wife, Margaret - Meta - was Richard Ford's daughter. She and Gabrielle became fast friends; both were keen gardeners and exchanged plants; both collected porcelain. Then in his mid fifties, Crawfurd had been Consul at Oporto since 1867 during while time he had become a successful writer, turning out novels, essays, and poetry as well as several well regarded books about Portugal, while contributing to The Times. Like Bernard Evans who helped Gabrielle with her painting, Oswald Crawfurd encouraged her belief that she had the talent to become a writer.(59)

Meanwhile Robert had begun a fierce battle to take control of his father's affairs, including the management of the Ardoch and Gartmore estates on the grounds that the costs incurred by Jamieson, as <u>Curator</u> were excessive. Should he be successful he and Gabrielle intended to return to live at Gartmore House. His family were very much opposed : they foresaw a descent into financial instability should Jamieson be dismissed. Consequently, in March 1883,

Anne Elizabeth Bontine, her brother in law, Robert Cunninghame Cunninghame Graham (Uncle Bobby) and Robert Wright asked Jamieson to take Counsel's opinion on the matter. This effectively disposed of it. For, though Counsel agreed Robert had the right to become Tutor at Law to William Bontine in which capacity he would control the whole estate, he would not be able to charge for his services; he could not pay himself his existing allowance of £500 a year; he would not be able to live rent free at Gartmore House which, for the benefit of the estate, must continue to be let to Sir Gerald Fitzgerald for £750 a year.(60) The rebuff seems to have strained relations between Robert and his mother whose attitude towards Gabrielle continued very cool. This in contrast to the welcome Anne Elizabeth gave the girl Charles had just married. 'Too heavenly pet and talks incessantly and is always kind and sweet to me' was the verdict on Barbara Bagot. Anne Elizabeth was not told when, in the summer of 1883, Robert and Gabrielle left Spain for a rented house, Milland Farm, near Liphook in Hampshire. While they were there news came of the death of William Bontine on 6 September at Eccles House near Dumfries where he had been closely confined for the last 16 years.

Notes to Chapter Five

1. National Library of Scotland; Acc. 11335/77; RBCG to Mansel, 29.12.1877
2. Scottish Record Office; CS 96 2418, 1 Feb. 1878
3. Rules of the Devonshire Club
4. NLS,Acc.11335/20; RBCG to AEB, 29 July 1878
5. SRO,CS46/143, 24 Feb. 1879. Note. After Charles inherited a substantial sum of money he no longer received an allowance from the Court of Session.
6. West, H.F., 'A Modern Conquistador: Robert Bontine Cunninghame Graham: His Life and Works', Cranley and Day, 1932. Tschiffely, A.F., 'Don Roberto', Heinemann, 1937,
7. NLS, Acc. 11335/48, AEB to RBCG, - Feb. 1873, 24 Apr 1873.
8. The author is very grateful to Christine M. Thomas of the Archives Branch of the Metropolitan Police for information about Colonel D.P. Labalmondière and his daughter, Lina. And see NLS, Acc. 11335/ 135 (Gabrielle's diary for 1888) So far as the 'de' is concerned, it probably was added for ease of pronunciation.
9. Collier, E.F., ed., 'A Victorian Diarist' (Lady Monkswell), John Murray, 1944, p. 146.
10. Tschiffely, op.cit., p. 138.
11. Wade, A., ed., 'The Letters of W.B. Yeats', Hart Davis, 1954, pp 6364. Bottigelli, E., ed., 'Friedrich Engels, Paul and Laura Lafargue; Correspondance', Editions sociales, 1956-59, Vol III, p. 179.
12. Stevenson, George, 'Benjy', John Lane/The Bodley Head, 1919. Note. A short essay 'The Soul and the Sunbeam' stands before the second part of 'Benjy'. This was written by Gabrielle Cunninghame Graham in 1888; copies of it are among RBCG's papers with a note to the effect that he thought it one of the best things she ever did.
13. ibid.
14. Kelly, E.R., 'Post Office Directory of North and East Ridings 1872'.
15. Stevenson, op.cit., pp 105-6.

16. ibid., pp 108-9.
17. ibid., p. 150.
18. Dr Richard Hitchcock of Exeter University has several books in his possession by Robert Cunninghame Graham which establish the connection. For instance, a copy of 'José Antonio Paez', Heinemann, 1929, is inscribed 'To Grace from RB Cunninghame Graham'. 'Redeemed and other sketches', Heinemann, 1927, has 'Grace from RB Cunninghame Graham. With best love, Oct 24/1927'. And 'Cartagena and the banks of the Sinu', Heinemann, 1922, has 'Grace H. Stevenson from RB Cunninghame Graham'. I am most grateful to Dr Hitchcock for this information.
19. Horsfall Family Papers, Martha Stevenson's notes.
20. Stevenson, op.cit. p. 84.
21. SRO, GD 22/2/83 'A Memorial for G.A. Jamieson'. Tschiffely, op.cit., p. 139.
22. NLS, Acc. 11335/23, RBCG to AEB, - Feb. 1879.
23. ibid., - Apr. 1879.
24. ibid.
25. ibid., RBCG to AEB 3 Aug. 1879. Note; Tschiffely omits any reference to the trade being in horses.
26. NLS, Acc. 11335/23, RBCG to AEB, 3 Aug. 1879.
27. ibid., RBCG t AEB, 27 Aug. 1879; 21 Oct. 1879, 1 Nov. 1879.
28. ibid., RBCG to AEB, 19 Jan. 1880.
29. Cunninghame Graham, Gabrielle, The Waggon Train in 'The Christ of Toro', Eveleigh Nash, 1908. Cunninghame Graham, R.B., 'Bernal Diaz del Castillo: Being some Account of Him, Taken from His True History of the Conquest of New Spain' Nash, 1915, p. 128.
30. SRO, CS 46/143, 8 Mar. 1880.
31. Cunninghame Graham, R.B., A Hegira in 'Thirteen Stories', Heinemann, 1900, 110 - 132.
32. ibid.
33. NLS, Acc. 11335/77, Mansel to RBCG, 13 Oct.1879, 10 Dec. 1879.
34. NLS, Acc. 11335/136, RBCG to Caroline; date not easily legible; 2 or 20 Aug. 1880 (2 Aug. makes more sense in the context).
35. NLS, Acc. 11335/23, AEB to RBCG, 12 Oct. 1880, 14 Oct. 1880.
36. ibid., RBCG to Wright, 21 Oct. 1880, To AEB 3 Aug. 1889, 29 Sept. 1880
37. Cunninghame Graham, R.B., 'Hernando de Soto: Together with an Account of one of his Captains, Gonçalo Silvestre', Heinemann, 1903.
38. NLS,Acc. 11335/23, RBCG to Wright, 12 Jan. 1881.
39. SRO, CS 46/143, 8 July 1881; CS 96/2420, f. 36, 18 June 1881.
40. NLS, Acc. 11335/23, Charles C.G. to Admiral Katon, 13 Apr. 1881 (postscript by RBCG).
41. ibid., Acc. 11335/38, Malise to AEB, 30 Apr. 1881.
42. Cunninghame Graham, R.B., A Hatchment in 'Hope' (Elizabeth Mansel). Cunninghame Graham, R.B., Aunt Eleanor in 'Charity' op.cit., 12-24. His Aunt Alexia appears in A Moral Victory in 'Rodeo', op.cit., 367 - 374.

43. Cunninghame Graham, R.B., A Hundred in the Shade in 'Redeemed' Heinemann, 1927. Note. This sketch was first published in the Saturday Review of 5 May 1925. His mother , Anne Elizabeth Bontine, had died two months previously.
44. e.g., Stevenson, op.cit., pp 201 - 205.
45. Cunninghame Graham, R.B., Un Monsieur in 'Hope', 163-174. Un Autre Monsieur in 'Charity', 163-176.
46. ibid.
47. NLS, Acc. 11335/34, Jamieson to AEB, 15 July 1870.
48. SRO, CS 46/143, 8 July 1881.
49. NLS, Acc. 11335/20, RBCG to AEB, 30 July 1881
50. Cunninghame Graham, Gabrielle, 'Spain A Lecture Delivered by Mrs Cunninghame Graham in the Tyneside Theatre, March 9 1890'.
51. ibid.
52. e.g. NLS, Acc. 11335/55, Gab to RBCG, 7 May 1889.
53. ibid., Acc. 11335/38, Malise to AEB, 7 Sept. 1881.
54. ibid., Acc.11335/20, RBCG to AEB, 6 Oct. [1881]
55. SRO, SC/36/5 ff 280-281. 22 Jan. 1906.
56. The Harry Ransom Humanities Research Center, University of Texas at Austin. MS Graham RBC, Misc., Gabriela Cunninghame Graham to Mrs Bernard Evans.For the Grosvenor Gallery see, Newall, C., 'The Grosvenor Gallery Exhibitions' Cambridge UP, 1995. the portrait of Miss Margaret Labalmondière was no 291 in the 1884 exhibition; of Mrs Douglas Labalmondière, no 193 in 1885 exhibition. And see Jacomb-Hood, G., 'With Brush and Pencil', J. Murray, 1925, p. 73.
57. NLS, Acc. 11335/20, RBCG to AEB, 7 Sept. 1881; ibid., Acc. 11335/141, 14 Oct. 1882.
58. ibid., Acc. 11335/141, 1,8. 14, 23.
59. ibid., 18 (part letter, n.d.)
60. SRO, GD 22/2/83, 'Memorial for G.A. Jamieson'.

Chapter Six

Laird of Gartmore

'Perhaps you will have seen the announcement in the papers of the death of my husband's poor father', Gabrielle wrote to Mary Evans on 12 September on paper thickly edged with black. 'He died without pain on the 6th and was buried yesterday in the family burial ground at Gartmore.' This was a green enclosure surrounded by a stone wall at some distance from the house overlooking the Lake of Menteith; it contained the graves of some of William's predecessors. 'We have succeeded to an estate of £10,000 a year', Gabrielle continued, 'but so great are the embarrassments connected with it that we are at this moment poorer and more hard up for money than when we left Milland Farm to come to Scotland'. This was no more than the truth but to draw attention to such matters was a striking departure from good form. And she persisted in this candid vein: 'I am going to...Milland Farm tomorrow as the expense of stopping about in houses is enormous and.. I wish to help my husband as much as possible. Of course he will have to be continually in Edinburgh wrangling with the lawyers'. (1).

In fact there was no wrangling in the next few weeks, rather an effort by those concerned to do the best they could in a difficult situation. 'I was sorry to hear young Bontine is likely to be so badly off', one of the trustees wrote to Henry Loch who was an executor. (2). A glance at the balance sheet drawn up by the <u>Curator</u> revealed the extent of the problem. 'Assets, £14,720.14s.10d; Liabilities, £94,050.8s.3d Included in the latter were loans and charges outstanding from the time of Robert's grandfather, the eighth laird. In addition to his debts money had to be found to meet his instruction that each of his four daughters(Robert's aunts) who remained unmarried at his death should receive £200 a year from the estate. By 1883, of the sisters, Mary was dead and Margaret had a husband, albeit William Hope who was deep in debt on his own account. Anne and Charlotte were maiden ladies of more than a certain age who had come to rely on their annuities. Then there was Robert's mother for whom substantial provision was made in William Bontine's will. Anne Elizabeth was to have £1200 a year; £1,000 for mourning garments, and plate and linen for her new establishment as a widow (a provision that Mounstuart Elphinstone had caused to be written into her marriage contract). Charles and Malise were each to receive £10,000. (3).

Faced with demands he could not hope to meet, Robert turned to Henry Loch. 'My father's affairs are quite dreadfully involved', he complained. What was he to do, for instance, about the promissory notes amounting to £1500 given by William Bontine to the doctor who looked after him at Eccles House? 'I must tell you that Dr Sharpe and his wife have behaved in the most kind and even affectionate manner to my father, and they are people of strict honesty'. Robert knew the notes were not binding in a legal sense, 'or perhaps even in a moral sense', but he was anxious to do the right thing. He also consulted Cousin Henry about the £5,000 worth of fees owing to the <u>Curator</u> and to Arthur Campbell, the family solicitor. Campbell who had helped his grandfather repair the damage done by the excesses of the Swindler, had been obliged to look on as William Bontine squandered hard won resources at the behest of his brother-in-law, William Hope - 'the VCs' unhelpful behaviour figures largely in the correspondence with Henry Loch. Robert was touched when Loch turned over to him the dressing case he had been left in William Bontine's will. It was one of the few things he remembered seeing his father use: he promised to find Henry something from Gartmore to replace it. (4).

The house was occupied by tenants so, for the time being, Robert had to content himself with a view of it across the lake from Lochend where he spent October. It was not a happy time: riding about in the autumn cold gave him a chill which developed into bronchitis; unusually for him he took to his bed from where he wrote to his 'chère petite femme'. He was up to his eyes in business he told her, and very worried about money: it cost six shillings a day to hire a pony, to buy one would be cheaper. He also feared he would have to find a new factor to manage the estate: the present one would be sure to want an increase in pay which he could not afford. (5). Burdensome though these were, these concerns were simple compared to the task of reconciling Gabrielle to the life he as laird, she as mistress, of Gartmore would soon be called upon to lead. He was already aware that she was not looking forward to it; he feared that under pressure she would bolt (as she had from Masham); his letters from Lochend were careful to offer support and a means of escape. When Gabrielle complained of an icy reception by Anne Elizabeth in London he replied in terms that left no doubt as to whose side he was on. 'As regards...my mother, <u>do not bother yourself and I wonder you called at all</u>. Both you and I are greatly liked here and as we shall, I suppose, spend our life between here and Spain, <u>it is all we want</u>'. He urged her to take great care of herself (could she have been pregnant?); she should go back to Milland Farm where it was warmer than in London, sit by the fire, read and draw until he could join her and they would go to Spain. The letter was signed, 'ton petit mari qui t'aime'. It did not suffice; Gabrielle continued disturbed to the point where she seems to have suggested some kind of financial venture whose recklessness alarmed him. 'Do try and look matters in the face, <u>all</u> our future depends on the next six months as, if we play the fool now, not even the sale of Ardoch will clear us'. (6).

His tetchiness is explained by the fact that he had just received a letter from the <u>Curator</u> whose contents were a shock to him. He had enquired when they might take possession of Gartmore; the response was not encouraging. Jamieson warned him that he must not count on having more than £800 a year; even this was by no means guaranteed for it depended on the rents, a part of which was already earmarked for the repayment of loans and for annuities: 'a fluctuation of revenue by no means extravagant would leave you with no income'. Jamieson remarked. 'In these circumstances in reply to your enquiry I must set clearly before you my opinion that it is not practically possible for you to reside with comfort at Gartmore with the income now at your disposal. I do not say it is absolutely impossible, for nothing of the kind can be said to be so if one resolves to endure the discomfort inseparable from the attempt - but knowing you as I think I do I am satisfied your life at Gartmore under such circumstances would become intolerable and the attempt so made would probably engender a permanent distaste for your life there which you ought not to run the risk of creating'. In the event the Curator's advice, based on a shrewd assessment of the young man's temperament, proved exactly right. 'I do not think, therefore,' Jamieson continued in this letter,' that there can be the least doubt that you ought to contemplate the sale of Ardoch as soon as a favourable opportunity occurs'.(7). With the sale in prospect Jamieson thought Robert might safely move in to Gartmore House and even incur a little debt because, as the market was at the time, he expected the price to rise. The Dumbartonshire estate was entailed so there would be some delay while the legal position was unravelled. This allowed Robert and Gabrielle to escape to Spain for the coming winter.

They spent several weeks travelling about before settling in at Vigo. At the Casa de la Grana Robert found letters from Lindsay, Jamieson and Haldane containing even more sober news. The agricultural depression which had made its appearance following the disastrously wet year of 1879 was tightening its grip on Scotland as well as England. And a flood of cheap imports was driving down the price of home grown products; rents could only follow. Thus, in a letter dated 20 February 1884, forwarding a draft on Coutts Bank for £200m Jamieson warned Robert that one of the farmers on the Gartmore estate had recently gone bankrupt. At Martinmas, when the farm was re-let they would have to accept a lower rent. When did Robert think he would be coming home? The answer was in April, after a visit to Paris. Three weeks later they were 'stopping' with the Speirs (more cousins) at Laurel Hill in Stirling, and getting ready to move in to Gartmore House.

'I am busier than I ever was in my life before, seeing servants and buying stores,' Gabrielle told Mary Evans on 15 May. Engaging servants was a task that always provoked a crisis, 'the maid agony' was how Gabrielle described it. More than once she took on servants only to dismiss them a day or two later when they failed to please. This was a hazard faced by every employer but Gabrielle seems to have been unusually bad at judging character. As far as the maids themselves were concerned, besides an always demanding, occasionally tempestuous, mistress, they had to cope with her deputy, a housekeeper who was vigilant, dour, and a foreigner to boot. Though she spoke only Spanish Peregrina Collazo was brought from Vigo to supervise the Scottish household. Its full complement of servants was a cook; two maids to wait at table, and three laundrymaids who, as well as doing the washing and ironing, cleaned the house between them. Keys were held by Gabrielle to the Bread Room, the Paraffin Room, the Dairy Room, the Meat Safe, and the Potato Room. Peregrina, who acted as her personal maid, kept her company in Robert's absence. (9). He was out all day riding round the farms, saluted by everyone he met - as 'Laird' by his tenants (Gabrielle was 'Leddy'), as 'Gartmore' by his neighbours. As he rode he saw how badly off some of the people were, and how unpromising the assets. The high lands on the estate were clay; stiff and poor, fit for grazing and little else. Lower down the soil was better and, with effort, would yield a decent crop of potatoes. But these fetched so little at the time it was scarcely worth growing them in quantity. The farmers also grew 'neps', turnips, on which to feed the cattle and some corn. They were crying out for expensive improvements; better drainage, lime, more fencing, new steadings, repairs to dairies, piggeries, barns, and - sometimes last of all - to houses. Nor did the laird's responsibility end there: one of Robert's first acts after he inherited was to sign a deed for a new school with a house and garden at Kippen in the south of his domain. Under Scots law all heritors had a duty to provide a school within the parish; if they failed the presbytery could report them to the Commissioners of Supply who had powers of compulsion.

Among the other villages and small settlements on the estate were Balfron, high and remote on a plateau below the Campsies; Buchlyvie, the nearest railway station to Gartmore House, and Port of Menteith where you took the boat over to the island of Inchmahome. Next to the jetty at the Port was an hotel and hard by, right on the shore of the lake, the Graham mausoleum. Stonebuilt, its elegance was almost frivolous - if such a word may be used of such a place - beside the gaunt new church whose congregation had celebrated its completion five years previously. In Gartmore village itself, at the top of its steep main street, were two churches whose congregations were often at each other's throats. As Robert understood their attitude, one thing only united them - disapproval of the laird. This fancy was to grow on him and, over the years, their concerted influence became a burden. (11). But in 1884 he approached his tenants as individuals whose particular existence and behaviour he observed with a sympathetic, if ironic, eye. The farmers he encountered when riding about the Gartmore estate seemed to him to have acquired a distinctive character as a result of the kind of life they were called upon to lead. The most striking example was the man who farmed a few acres in the depths of the Flanders Moss. At his first approach Robert was appalled at the signs of poverty and disorder; evidence that conditions in the Moss were as hard and extreme as in any mountain glen. It seemed a mark of desperation that anyone should try to cultivate the place at all; 'scattered drainpipes lying in the fields looked like relics of a battlefield of agriculture in which the forces of the modern world had been defeated in the contest with the moss'. In place of fences there were piles of brushwood fastened with rusty wire to crooked posts, with cast off ploughs and carts standing in the gaps as gates. A scanty crop of oats grew, like rice, in standing water, while a few turnips and potatoes, black with disease, shared a row with weeds. The place was as primitive as a Highland steading and, though he was not a Celt by origin, it seemed to Robert the farmer had assumed the appearance and some of the characteristics of the Highlander. 'Tall and shock headed and freckled on the red patches of skin which a rough crop of beard and whiskers left exposed, his eyes looked out upon the world as if he had a sort of second sight begot of whisky and of loneliness'. (12).

In complete contrast was the tenant of the farm above Balfron with whom, over the years, Robert formed what he called a bickering friendship. The point always at issue between them was whether the farmer could stand to continue as things were; poor seasons, bad markets, sheep with foot rot or with fluke, potatoes so diseased the smell in the fields was tangible. Though it lay so high all his attempts at drainage were in vain: the land stayed wet, wet as Loch Lomond, he lamented. These manifold complaints had a single object - a reduction in the rent. When Robert refused, but offered to take the farm back next Martinmas, the answer was always No, for this was a man who recognized a bargain. He was a careful tenant; 'an air of neatness without homeliness pervaded everything. Carts with their shafts upright stood under sheds and on a rope stretched from the stable to the byre hung braxy (diseased) sheep, their bodies black and shrunken, their skins new flayed and pink, fluttering about like kites'. (13). His grey stone house had a blue slate roof and was squarely planted down upon the road, details that tell us it was new. Our eyes have become so accustomed to this kind of house it seems to complement the Scottish landscape but in Robert's time it was just beginning to replace the old thatched cottages with their whitewashed walls. He hated all such houses; to him they seemed not homes but mere corrals, one sign among many of creeping industrialization.

A passion for saving money led this particular farmer to walk whereever he went. In a place where everyone of any consequence went on horseback, walking was euphemistically known as travelling. In those days of economic hardship the Gartmore estate (a long day's walk from Glasgow) was visited by many 'travellers' whose history Robert made a point of getting from them. His knowledge of tramps, pedlars, and other 'going aboot' persons stood him in good stead when he came to write regularly for the literary journals. If no plot came to him he could always make do with a description of the man they called Heather Jock or - one who claimed his own ancestry - the Beggar Earl. William Brodie, bred a weaver at the Bridge of Weir, when he was thrown out of work first turned pedlar, then became a wandering singer and buffoon which calling was announced by the curious headdress that he wore; 'like an Inca of Peru stuck all about with pheasants' and peacocks' feathers, bits of looking glass adorned with heather and fastened underneath his jaws with a black ribbon... in his hand a rude Caduceus made of a hazel stick and in the centre a flat tin heart set round with jingling bells and terminating in a tuft of ling.' Thus attired, for the rest of his life Heather Jock travelled about singing Annie Laurie - the only song he knew - at races, meetings, fairs, trysts; in country houses and at farms. According to Robert, everywhere he went he was most welcome. (14).

The Beggar Earl lived in the time of Nicol Graham and was briefly well known in Edinburgh where, as a youth, he studied medicine. In 1744 he appeared at an election of a Scottish peer (to sit, according to the Act of Union as one of 16 representative Scottish peers in the House of Lords). He told the assembly he was the rightful Earl of Menteith and claimed the right to vote. 'From that time till his death he never dropped his claim attending all elections of a Scottish peer until he got weary of the game.' And then he took to wandering about his earldom; 'a little man, a little clean man, that went round about through the country... a man asking charity. He went into farmhouses and asked for victuals, what they would give him, and into gentlemen's houses'. He carried papers with him that, however destitute, he would never sell. Robert was certain that these told of the Beggar Earl's ancestors (who were also his) 'mail clad knights who fought at Flodden, counselled kings with the half

Highland cunning of their race, and generally opposed the Southrons who, impotent to conquer us in war, yet have filched from us most of our national character by the soft arts of peace.' The Earl was remembered most of all for his death in the snow on a high tract of moorland overlooking Loch Lomond. He was found with his back against a stone wall, his beloved parchments in his hand; his old white pony shivering by his side.(15)

His descendant, on his own return to the District of Menteith, received a welcome that seemed to augur far more favourably. On 22 August 1884 a meeting took place in Gartmore village schoolroom, the report of which filled eight columns in the <u>Stirling Advertiser</u>. (16). The occasion was a dinner to welcome the new young laird to whom the paper (whose Editor, W.B. Cook was a guest) referred as Mr Graham Bontine. 'There was a general desire in the district to give him a public welcome and the arrangements for a dinner were entrusted to a committee. It went into the matter with the greatest heartiness and energy'. On the wall behind the Chairman's table were displayed the arms of the Grahams neatly worked in holly leaves with the family motto' For Right and Reason', while at the other end of the room were the Glencairn arms. 'The table decorations were highly elegant and the entire appearance of the room was superior to anything previously seen in Gartmore. Before the proceedings commenced Mrs Graham Bontine paid a visit to the schoolroom to witness the preparations for the banquet and it may safely be said that scarcely any villager failed to take a peep of the room in its festive character, so strong was the interest excited by the auspicious event'.

At 2 p.m. some seventy tenants, feuars(17) and their guests sat down to a banquet purveyed 'under considerable difficulty but to general satisfaction' by the landlord of the Black Bull Inn. The dinner eaten and cleared away the proposing of toasts began. Responses were made by representatives of every interest present with one exception. Apart from the laird himself no members of his family were there. His brothers, Charles and Malise, his uncle Bobby, his cousin, Admiral Erskine, sent their apologies which, when they were read out, effectively absolved those present from dwelling on the misfortunes of the recent past. The speakers chose instead to look much further into history for ways to encourage their guest of honour. One after another they recalled the years of security and prosperity in the late 18th century under Robert Cunninghame Graham, first of that name. Praise of the sixth laird was a measure of the hope and expectation they laid on Robert, the tenth. More especially, since they knew he proposed to make his home at Gartmore, they looked to him to represent them in the wider world, a role filled by the first Robert as MP for Stirlingshire. Their anticipation was confirmed by the presence at the top table of three local MPs, two Liberals and a Conservative. (18).

That members of the opposing parties consented to sit down together at that particular time must be a matter for congratulation and a tribute to the good sense of the company assembled, the Chairman remarked. He was William McOnie, Lord Provost of Glasgow, whose invitation to preside stemmed from the fact that he was the second Lord Provost in forty years to have been born and bred in Gartmore; who left the village at an early age and found a fortune in Glasgow. (19). For those who stayed at home Glasgow rather than Edinburgh, was the nearest point of contact with urban life; the centre to which they turned for essentials only a city could supply; whose turbulent affairs reported in their newspapers provided welcome relief from agricultural preoccupations. Robert held it in affection as the place of arrival home in Scotland and when Gartmore palled (as it would) of temporary escape from his troublesome responsibilities. His family's connection with its ancient University had been crowned by the election in 1785 of the first Robert Cunninghame Graham as Lord Rector (succeeding Edmund Burke). His Whiggish cast of mind was commemorated by the Gartmore Gold Medal awarded annually for the best essay on 'Political Liberty'.(20). In August 1884 that particular subject was much in people's minds. Earlier in the year a Bill to extend the franchise had been introduced by the Liberal Government under Gladstone. The Conservatives used their majority in the House of Lords to block it, provoking a serious constitutional crisis. The country at large was restive and bad tempered; it was sixteen years since the last Reform Act and a head of pressure had built up for wider change. Frustration turned to bitter resentment against the peers; as the summer progressed marches and rallies promoted the call for abolition of the unelected Second Chamber. The longer the crisis remained unresolved the more explosive it became, prompting the Chairman of the Gartmore dinner to warn the speakers not to mention politics.

While giving every appearance of obeying this order, Sir Donald Currie speaking for the MPs present, blandly subverted it. He made no reference to the House of Lords but spoke vaguely and with enthusiasm of the people's will for reform. At the end of a skilful speech, to loud acclaim, he reminded his audience that the foundation of social order depended on this will; on, in the words of the motto displayed behind Robert's head, the people's right and reason. This social order , he contrived to infer, was secure as long as the Liberal Party was in power. It had been in power in Scotland for more than fifty years; since the passing of the first Reform Act in 1832, and it had been confirmed most recently at the general election of 1880 when, out of the 60 Scottish seats, the Conservatives had won only seven: enough Gladstone cheerily remarked to fill a first class railway carriage, but no more. As a prospective Liberal candidate Robert was fortunate in securing Currie's interest. One of the leading shipowners in the country, having built up the Castle Line trading to South Africa, he had privileged access to the Prime Minister since Gladstone enjoyed cruising on his yachts. Currie who was born in Greenock and began his shipping business there was an archetypal Scottish Liberal MP. The great majority of them were businessmen, entrepreneurs, propelled to fortune by the explosive growth of industry that had reached its peak towards the end of the 1870s. Not the least of Robert's attractions to the Party managers was that his election would break this mould, would help to form a bridge over the wide gulf that existed between members of the Scottish aristocracy whom the Act of Union had seduced with English money and English ways, and the common people whose expectations had been transformed in the last fifty years.

On 6 September, two weeks after the Gartmore dinner, the most intimidating of the nationwide franchise demonstrations took place in Glasgow. More than 200,000 working men, bearing symbols of their trades, marched in procession to Glasgow Green where they heard their leaders denounce the Lords' resistance to the Bill. We do not know if Robert was present though it is likely that he was; such an occasion would hardly be missed by a 'prentice politician' which is how he had taken to describing himself. If it was the first time he had seen the vast open space filled with orderly and slow moving crowds, it would not be the last for the Green was often to provide him with a platform of his own. Now in September 1884 the mass demonstration in Glasgow heartened those who, like him, believed it was high time for the people to be given a greater measure of responsibility . The message was well understood at Westminster where a special autumn session of Parliament was convened to give effect to a compromise reached after much manoevring behind the scenes. Gladstone, the Prime Minister, and the Marquis of Salisbury, Leader of the Opposition, agreed that the reintroduction of the franchise Bill to the Commons would be matched by an Act for the redistribution of seats - a point scored by Lord Salisbury for, at subsequent elections this arrangement would favour the Conservatives. Though much was heard of the slogan 'Mend them or end them' the House of Lords was left alone. The legislation which came into effect at the beginning of 1885 gave the vote to another two million adult males effectively doubling the electorate. Groups of workers - miners, cotton spinners, railwaymen, agricultural labourers and, in Scotland, crofters, became entitled to vote for the first time. The number of Scottish seats was raised from 60 to 72; seven of these were in Glasgow. Efficient organisation by the Liberal Party's agent in the West of Scotland, W.P. Adam - a cousin and close friend of Anne Elizabeth Bontine - meant that the Liberal Party would have a large advantage there in the next election. By the summer of 1885 everyone knew it would not be long delayed. News of Gordon's death at Khartoum the previous February had begun the rapid disintegration of Gladstone's second administration. On 9 June the Government lost a vote on the beer duty when 39 members of Parnell's Irish party voted with the Tories and some seventy radicals abstained. Gladstone was replaced by Salisbury (to Queen Victoria's undisguised relief) and a general election called for November.

Robert Bontine Cunninghame Graham (as he had now decided to be known), was adopted as the Liberal candidate for the Camlachie division of Glasgow, a safe enough seat it might be thought since the city had returned only one Conservative to Parliament in the last 52 years. It lay at the heart of Glasgow's East end - the Camlachie Burn ran through the Green, but the pleasant rural location these names suggest was a cruel deception. The burn had long been imprisoned in a tunnel which wound its invisible way through a dark and dirty muddle of smoking chimneys and dilapidated buildings. Camlachie's inhabitants were principally engaged in spinning cotton and making clay pipes. Since the dwellings lay next to the factories there was no escape at night from the noise and smell of overcrowded streets. Many of the people thus confined had begun life in the open air as crofters, farmers, agricultural labourers who had been forced to the city when the land could no longer support their growing families; most retained links with their place of origin. Some were still crofters who chose to submit to factory discipline for part of the year in order to scrape enough together to see them through at home. All had a vivid sense of the hardship those left behind on the land had to endure. In 1885 while reform of the system of land tenure had long been of close concern to the inhabitants of Camlachie, recent events had made it a major preoccupation in Scotland generally, to the extent that it was to be a crucial issue in the forthcoming general election.

Three years previously widespread protest by local inhabitants of the island of Skye against the eviction of crofters by certain landlords had provoked riots and arrests. The disturbances, so serious they became known as the Crofters' War, forced the Government to take action. In 1883 a Commission under Francis, Lord Napier and Ettrick, a former Governor of Madras, was appointed to enquire into the whole state of crofting in the Highlands and Islands. (21). In the course of the next 18 months the Commissioners travelled the length and breadth of the region taking detailed evidence from landowners and their agents, factors, gamekeepers, storekeepers and fishermen as well as crofters. Their report which ran to over 3,000 pages shocked the nation by revealing that under the established system crofters were little more than serfs; they could not vote; they had no security of tenure; no written leases, not even the protection of custom long upheld; their landlords did as they pleased while complaining of their tenants' inertia; of how they ignored schemes devised at great expense to help them.

The evidence which was reported daily in the newspapers as it was given aroused great public indignation because it showed to what a state of despair the people of the Highlands and Islands had been reduced by hunger, cold, and disease. The underlying cause was overpopulation of unproductive land, but blame was perceived to lie with greedy landlords who cleared the people from their estates in order to replace them with sheep, or to forest the land for deer. Insult was added to injury when most of the landowners called before the Commission were seen to be outsiders; wealthy Lowlanders or Englishmen absent for most of the time. Though the Cunninghame Graham lands lay below the Highland line there were special reasons why Robert followed the debate with the closest interest. His deepest sympathy was engaged; in their struggle with hostile elements the crofters resembled other isolated people he had reason to admire - the gauchos of the pampa, the Icelanders. As they described it to the Commission their commitment to their austere way of life seemed to him, as to many of his countrymen, in whom the sense of place was strong, both natural and admirable. In Scotland the idea that men and women whose families had for centuries held to one place, should command special consideration from the owners of that place, was of ancient origin, springing from the interdependence of a chieftain and his clansmen. In 1884 there was widespread agreement - though also loud dissent - with the proposition that the current relationship of crofters with their landlords ought to be of mutual advantage - the one should not exploit the other. But a more particular reason for Robert's interest was the fact that one of the chief dissenters from this proposition which he so eagerly supported was none other than the Curator of the Gartmore estate, George Auldjo Jamieson. Called before the Commission in October 1883 Jamieson put the view - deeply resented by the crofters - that the land belonged to those who came by it through inheritance or purchase, and that they could do as they pleased with it.(22)

Jamieson regarded himself as an expert in the subject having presented a pamphlet on its historical, economic, and legal aspects to the Royal Society. His findings were based on experience he had gained as <u>Curator</u> of a Highland estate near Dingwall over which he had presided since 1867 (23). Under pressure from Commissioners he admitted he had ordered the eviction of many families during those years for the purpose of amalgamating crofts in order to command a higher rent. Though he argued (as he did in the case of Gartmore) that he had done nothing without the approval of the Accountant of the Court of Session, he did not deny that the people involved had suffered hardship. 'The idea that the predecessors of the present crofters have any real right in the soil is contradicted by all the evidence of history' he declared. It was put to him by Charles Fraser-Mackintosh MP, one of the members of the Commission, that the interest of the State required crofters to remain in their homes, not to emigrate since the nation depended on them to swell the ranks of the Army in time of war. If the crofters presently had no rights in their land should not the State step in to protect them? 'Certainly not', Jamieson replied, 'I can see no such duty devolving on the State'. The very idea made his hackles rise; it seemed to him to lead inescapably to a system of direct communism - shocking thought; 'you have no halting place', he warned. In his view the only wise policy was to cooperate with the law of economics which, requiring profit, dictated that the land must be worked to its fullest potential, whatever that might be. (24).

Jamieson's belief that the supremacy of landlords should continue not unnaturally disposed his ward to take the contrary view. From this moment on Robert cleaved to the principle of cooperation which many crofters already saw as the best way forward. One of their leaders, John Murdoch, whose eloquence joined to common sense captivated Robert when first they met, told the Napier Commission that, while apathy was a major problem, the overbearing attitude of landowners was far worse. No expenditure of mere money could compensate for the cramping effect of being kept in leading strings; 'The first thing the crofters want is the revival of the spirit of the people, the second the calling forth of their intelligence, common sense and enterprise, the third definite legislative protection from interference'. (25). For Robert Cunninghame Graham these words defined the right approach to solving problems; the one he would adopt as soon as he found himself in Parliament. They also made such an impression on members of the Napier Commission, especially the Chairman, that the principle they represented was enshrined in the Report published in September 1884. Describing those crofters who had appeared before them as men of intelligence, high moral standing, and industrious habits such as no country could afford to lose through emigration, the Commissioners proposed a system whereby the crofting townships were to be recognized as distinct communities, having protected powers to negotiate change of use of land with the owners, as well as other rights to be exercised collectively. Uproar and outrage greeted this suggestion which, to people like Jamieson, smacked of nothing less than communism, and it was not implemented. But the idea of self help, of collective action thus aired aroused an instant response in some quarters; it was a point on which, apprentice politician though he was, Robert Cunninghame Graham could speak with real authority. He had seen vestiges of a similar - though more benevolent - kind of tutelage to that imposed on the crofters, in the Jesuit missions of Paraguay. Though he recognized that the <u>reducciones</u> had preserved the Indians from a much worse fate at the hands of the Spanish, he was also prepared to say that the price had been loss of independence, freedom curtailed, and a smothering sense of apathy.

Immediately to the west of Camlachie, his prospective constituency, was Glasgow, Blackfriars, whose Liberal candidate at the forthcoming election was as anxious to see the most far reaching proposals of the Napier Report implemented as Robert was himself. This was Lord Edmond Fitzmaurice whose distinguished careeer as Under Secretary of State for Foreign Affairs had been cut short by Gladstone's resignation. Lord Edmond's mother was Madame de Flahaut so it was as his cousin as well as a political ally that the candidate for Camlachie occupied a seat on the platform at his meetings. Lord Edmond was famously radical in his attitude towards reform: he wanted the machinery of government brought closer to the people. His support for the crofters in their struggle against the landlords was given piquancy by the fact that his elder brother (probably the most exalted of Robert's many cousins) was the Marquis of Landsdowne who possessed one of the largest estates in Ireland. Besides a Conservative, Lord Edmond was opposed by one of the five candidates sponsored by the Crofters' Party; the first 'common peoples' political organisation truly independent of both leading parties to emerge for many years. As the election campaign got under way Robert regularly attended its meetings.

The Crofters' Party had its beginning at a meeting held in Glasgow Town Hall at Easter 1881 by the Irish National Land League which was addressed by the Irish Parliamentary Party leader, Charles Stuart Parnell. Among those who heard him denounce landlordism in Ireland were members of various Highland societies. Parnell's cold contempt for all things English awoke a response in them; they decided to band together in defence of the crofters even then under threat of eviction in Skye. The most active of these groups were the Scottish Land Restoration League and the Highland Land League, they and others joined together as the Federation of Celtic Societies. Their leaders for the most part were professional men; lawyers, doctors, civil servants. James Shaw Maxwell was a Glasgow barrister who earned the gratitude of the Skye crofters by defending their interests in 1882. Gavin Clark was a doctor with a special interest in the land question, who had been a member of the First International; Charles Fraser-Mackintosh, who served as a member of the Napier Commission, was Liberal MP for Inverness Burghs; Angus Sutherland, founder of the Scottish Land Restoration League was a schoolmaster. (26). John Murdoch was a retired Customs and Excise Officer. In 1873 he had begun to publish the <u>Highlander</u>, a newspaper which sought to convert its readers to the Editor's passionate belief in Scotland's separate identity as a nation. To that end it devoted much space to Celtic literature, language, and history, deriving its air of authority from Murdoch's unrivalled knowledge of the region - he was brought up on Islay. Following the outbreak of the so-called

Crofters' War Murdoch was the prime mover in the decision to send delegates round the worst affected crofting counties in advance of the Napier Commission to urge the people to join together to present their case. And he was one of the first Scots activists to look to events in Ireland as showing the way forward for the cause of his own country. He was acquainted with Parnell, having accompanied him to the United States in 1881, a fact that, on the outbreak of the Crofters' War, prompted the landowners to accuse him of involvement in the Fenian conspiracy to overthrow British rule in Ireland. (27).

Towards the end of the 1870s, following Parnell's accession to the leadership of the Irish Parliamentary Party, bitter unrest over the arbitrary treatment of the Irish peasants by their English landlords escalated into a widespread land war. By 1880 this was such a threat to order that the newly elected Liberal government was obliged, greatly against its inclination, to introduce severely repressive measures. At the same time it was hoped that a Land Act granting fixity of tenure, free sale by a tenant of his interest in the land, and fair rents would mitigate the effect, and finally resolve the problem, of coercion. But as a measure of State intervention in a private contract the Act was bitterly criticized. It was keenly examined in Scotland where thousands of Irish had settled after the famine years of the 1840s and drawn by the industrial boom. Some Scots denounced the Act as a dangerous incitement of tenants on their side of the water - the Duke of Argyll resigned from the Cabinet for this reason. Others welcomed it precisely because it offered the hope of a solution to the crofting problem. For example, in an emotional speech before the Napier Commission, Professor John Stuart Blackie, a much loved figure widely known for his nationalist sympathies, hailed it as an act of justice and generosity and called for it to be extended to the Highlands and Islands.(28).

The subject came to dominate discussion at the meetings held in Glasgow during the 1885 general election campaign. Well aware of the value of publicity in recruiting supporters to their cause the Crofters' Party leaders chose speakers of note likely to attract large audiences in the run up to the polls. Among them were Michael Davitt, founder of the Irish National Land League who, unlike Parnell, believed in the wholesale nationalisation of land, and an American of similar persuasion who was even more famous; Henry George, mention of whose book, 'Progress and Poverty', arguing for a single tax on land, was on everyone's lips at the time. (29). As a member of the landowning class wholeheartedly in favour of the crofters' cause - a bird of rare plumage - Robert Cunninghame Graham received a special welcome at these meetings. Background joined to experience gave him the advantage of a foot in both camps. His family was related to the man responsible for the most disastrous 'improvement' of the century. As land agent to the Duke of Sutherland James Loch (cousin Henry's father), had obliged some 15,000 people to leave their glens for new settlements by the sea where their lives were supposed to become more productive through fishing and gathering kelp. These were the notorious Sutherland clearances which, in his evidence to the Napier Commission, John Murdoch quoted as the most telling illustration of the misuse of capital (30). However, while Robert's descent was privileged, his practical experience lay with who most certainly were not. He had first hand knowledge of the fate that awaited many Highlanders when the land could no longer support them: he had been an emigrant; had sailed in the overcrowded ships; had made shift to survive in a wilderness. He had fought alongside Scots against the Indians on the Sauce Grande; herded cattle with them in Entre Ríos and shared their homesickness. The programme he submitted to the electors of Camlachie reflected these concerns. He called for reform of the land laws; the abolition of primogeniture and entail; the repeal of the Game Laws; the right of free access to mountain areas in Scotland and, above all, a Bill on the lines of the Irish Land Act of 1881 to redress the particular grievances of the crofters. (31).

Most of the industrial towns in the West of Scotland had Highland Clubs or Leagues by means of which the exiles kept in touch with one another and raised money to help the less fortunate among them. In August 1885 one of these clubs in the town of Coatbridge, centre of the newly created constituency of North West Lanarkshire, invited Robert Cunninghame Graham to speak to them. Of all the extraordinary places he encountered in the course of his life Coatbridge, a mere eight miles east of Glasgow, was the most remarkable and sinister, so fearful that even those who reaped spectacular rewards from exploiting its natural resources described it as the worst place out of Hell. It was Scotland's Birmingham; the locomotive of the industrial boom. When Robert came to know the town its pre-eminence was on the wane; the coal was nearly worked out, the iron ore depleted, but the fouling of the place by smoke and slag and slurry was increasing year by year. It was a by-product of the vast industrial complex that, after 1830, grew up on a narrow strip of land beside the Monkland Canal, two miles from the ancient burgh of Airdrie. There some 4,000 acres had been found to contain the celebrated blackband ironstone - iron nodules in a bed of coal - which produced vast profits for those who won the race to work it. By the end of the 1870s when the peak of production was reached, as well as mines the area contained 41 blast furnaces, 8 malleable iron works, 113 puddling furnaces, 19 steel rolling mills, and an indeterminate number of brick works. These were only yards from the rows of workers' houses, shops, and - wherever the ironmasters' diktat did not run - public houses. There was no peace in Coatbridge six days out of seven. 'There was a continual noise from the mass of heavy machinery; this and the pounding of steam hammers seemed to make... the very ground vibrate under one's feet'. Much of this ground was covered by huge mounds of spoil still hot beneath its crust which gave off a sulphurous vapour. At night the sky was red with furnaces flaring like volcanoes. Railways belonging to different companies criss- crossed the town; they were built on high embankments cutting streets off from one another; the high banks shut the houses in adding to the oppressive atmosphere in which some 25,000 people were obliged to conduct their whole existence. (32).

In the time of their greatest prosperity, towards the end of the 18th century, the Cunninghame Grahams had a connection with this place: they owned the estate of Lochwood which lay north of the Monkland Canal.(33). The unexpected death of the sixth laird forced its sale to a Lanarkshire farmer, Alexander Baird. This piece of family history might have been supposed to offer Robert an easy introduction to his speech. He did not mention it. His audience was composed almost entirely of working men conscious of their new responsibility as voters: while he did not deny his privileged origin he sought to win them over by focussing on the years - he was vague as to how many - he had spent in the democratic atmosphere of various South American republics where, he insisted, he had abandoned every pretension of the class into which he had been born. Thoughtfully attired in well cut tweeds and soft hat, his appearance strengthened this impression; he was the very model of an English farmer newly arrived in Buenos Aires from the camp, and it was as the 'ranchman' that the local paper often wrote of him. (34). His demeanour was equally informal; his earnestness was tempered with a stream of jokes. Though he said he came before them as a novice in the art of politics, he was unusually well informed about its history, especially in Scotland, and eager to impart it which he did with an absence of condescending that endeared him to those present. In those days the Liberal Party embraced a wide spectrum of opinion from what was not quite yet called the right to the equally uncategorized left. So, though he was the official Liberal candidate for Camlachie, Robert was free to advocate measures the Crofters' party favoured. When he finished presenting his programme of land reform he was startled by the warmth of his reception. The outcome of this venture was an invitation from the Liberal Association of Coatbridge to stand as candidate for North West Lanarkshire. The Camlachie Liberals seem to have raised no objection, and the Crofters' Party leaders were delighted at the change (which they may have instigated).(35). By putting Robert up in North West Lanarkshire the contest between him and the Conservative promised to focus attention on their cause. He and his new opponent, John Baird of Knoydart, were almost equally matched - in age, in education, in occupation - while holding dramatically different views on the crucial question of the ownership of land. If Robert was already a hero in the eyes of his supporters, the other had recently shown himself a villain on the same account.

John Baird was the same age as Robert Cunninghame Graham and had been at Harrow at the same time. He was a member of the family that had created the wealth of Coatbridge. His grandfather, Alexander Baird of Lochwood, began life as a farmer but also carried coal to Glasgow by the Monkland Canal. In the first years of the nineteenth century, which saw the long minority of William Cunninghame Graham, seventh laird of Gartmore, the coalmasters realized what huge profits would result from further exploitation of the blackband ironstone. In 1828 Alexander Baird and three of his seven sons built the first furnace to employ the hot blast process newly invented by their friend, J. B. Neilson. In the next few years, as the seventh laird of Gartmore languished on exile on the Continent, the firm, now William Baird & Co., built 15 blast furnaces in quick succession near to the Canal. At the same time, in order to ensure a constant supply of raw material, the Baird brothers bought up all the land they could lay hands on in the parishes of Old and New Monkland. Over the next four decades this land, between Airdrie and Coatbridge, was crammed with the cumbersome machinery needed to produce a marvellous diversity of objects serving new uses. Among them were brass fittings for the gas industry; tubes for the water industry; cast iron pipes; spades and shovels for navvies building railways; coils; springs for the mattresses now replacing feather beds.

The wealth created was tremendous; the Bairds disposed of their substantial share of it in two directions.

The provision of amenities for their employees - libraries, baths, temperance halls, churches of every denomination - was not a purely philanthropic gesture, (though as Conservatives in the image of Sir Robert Peel they were genuinely concerned to help those less fortunate than themselves). It was also a means to control the swarming population of Coatbridge which fell into three ill assorted groups. Until the beginning of the nineteenth century the miners, who originated in the area, had suffered unbelievably harsh conditions. Now they were fiercely protective of their interests and inclined to hold themselves apart. They had little to do, for example, with the Scots from other parts of the country who chose factory routine as a lesser evil than subsistence agriculture. This second group's sober way of life, its Presbyterian religion, put it at odds with the third, the Irish, many of whom had been brought over as strikebreakers whenever the ironmasters' interests clashed with that of their workers. By the time Robert knew it, Coatbridge contained the highest proportion in Great Britain of Irish, Catholic and Protestant, to the rest of its population. The naturally uninhibited behaviour of the many young single men among them was a source of much annoyance to the good Scots burghers; one Chief Magistrate condemned the whole of them as 'most vicious, turbulent, and disaffected' (36).

No doubt the Bairds derived much satisfaction from the substantial buildings they erected in Coatbridge (the houses were not built to last; as the mineral reserves were exhausted in one place they, like the works, were relocated). But they sought their pleasure elsewhere. In the ten years from 1853, in a triumphant return to the land in one generation, Alexander Baird of Lochwood's sons between them spent, at current prices, £1 million on Scottish estates. James, the second son, paid £90,000 for a vast domain on the spectacularly beautiful and remote peninsula of Knoydart opposite the island of Skye. In due course this passed to his nephew, John, who had been brought up as befitted a member of the landed gentry. In 1883 young Mr Baird of Knoydart figured as a witness before the Napier Commission. Sharply questioned as to his behaviour, he did not trouble to conceal his irritation. He could not let farms at reasonable rents to local people; he did not want Southerners, so the farms on Knoydart were left empty. He would not allow the people to re-inhabit crofts that had fallen out of use because 'their presence would be an injury to the land'. He had nothing good to say of - or to - the crofters. He was very much annoyed, for instance, when they refused to fish as he instructed them to do. 'I called the heads of the families together one day and rather abused them', he declared. (37). His obduracy caused a sensation at the time so, two years later, when he put up for North West Lanarkshire, the Crofters' Party leaders scented blood. When they also considered that he belonged to the Conservative Party that bore the stigma of responsibility for the Act of Union, the odds against him beating their man seemed formidable.

Meanwhile Robert's popularity surged. His meetings were crowded; latecomers had to wait outside the halls where he spoke, among them many women eager to catch a glimpse of the 'curly headed darling'.(38). His handsome appearance and his jokes were not the only things to titillate the crowd;

some of his ideas were sensational. While the call in his manifesto for free education and religious equality(including the disestablishment of the Church of Scotland), was shared by other radicals, his demand that class monopoly be extinguished touched upon territory that was only just beginning to be mapped. (39). Nevertheless the means of achieving such a transformation lay to hand, he told his audiences, in the implementation of reforms already mooted to deal with the crofting problem. At their fullest extent such reforms could sweep away the feudal system in Britain which, in his opinion, was the source of many evils. Free trade in agricultural products was a success (though not to him as a landowner) why not extend it to agricultural holdings? Why stop at abolishing primogeniture and entail? Why not introduce a cheap method of conveyancing so that anyone who wanted could buy and sell land? Why not let municipal corporations buy up land cheaply in city centres and elect local people to new boards with power to sell such land to anyone who wanted it? Some of Robert's phrases came straight from the Napier Report; others - greedy capitalists, downtrodden wage slaves - were terms of the class war. The ready manner in which they came to him was partly the result of reading the London journals; Justice published since January 1884 by the Social Democratic Federation; The Commonweal begun a year later by one of Robert's heroes, William Morris.

This language caused the Liberal establishment of Coatbridge to wonder what kind of cuckoo they had invited into their nest. The extent of their doubt was revealed for everyone to see - and to read in the Airdrie Advertiser afterwards - on 17 September when Robert made an appearance at the Theatre Royal, Coatbridge when he was introduced by Andrew Stewart, Chairman of his sponsors, the local Liberal Association. As Managing Director and part owner of the huge Clyde Iron Tube Works Stewart was an ironmaster on a par with the Bairds whose company, he left his audience in no doubt, he much preferred. He had been abroad when the Association adopted Mr Cunninghame Graham as their candidate, he said, or he would have advised his members 'to delay a little, to consider further'. Nevertheless it was his duty as a Liberal voter to go with the majority and so he would. But he must remind those present that John Baird, the Conservative candidate, came from a family whose intelligence and ability had created Coatbridge; they should not forget how much the town owed them. This calculated snub set a match to Robert's temper so when he came to speak he threw caution aside and mounted a slashing attack upon the capitalist system - of which Stewart was an archetypal member - for delivering prosperity to the few at the expense of the many. He did not hesitate to lay the blame on individuals; the Duke of Hamilton for taking a 'monstrous' income out of the Lanarkshire mines to be spent 'God knows how' while 30,000 men (some of whom were present) toiled underground for a bare subsistence. He compared the £1,000 a day delivered to the Duke of Westminster in London ground rents with the pittance earned by the match workers of the East End (whose plight would not reach the newspapers for another three years). 'What I should like to see,' he said, 'is that capital should be made to disgorge some of the wealth it has made out of the working classes'. The change would be brought about by 'that dangerous and socialistic measure' free education. It was the key to his policy; the enabling system from which all else would follow, and he set it before his audience with a directness that was new. Free education would mean self sacrifice, he told them, education must be paid for by the State, not by the Church, or churches. 'We are the State and it is the State's duty - that is to say our duty - to see that none of its citizens grow up ignorant'. It was to education they all must look to refine the people; shorten the hours of labour; join them all in the demand for proper dwelling houses and, finally, open their eyes to the fact that their strength must lie in co-operation. (40).

He was careful to insist that measures condemned by politicians (one of whom was Charles Bradlaugh) as imported into England by foreign socialists fleeing persecution on the Continent were, in fact, indigenous and of long standing. The payment of MPs for example which together with the provision of election expenses on the rates, he deemed essential if the people were ever to be properly represented in Parliament. A method of payment had existed in the reign of Henry III, he told his audience, and had prevailed until the advent of the Glorious - so-called - Revolution when it was abolished. At the same time William of Orange and his 'needy, greedy Dutch adventurers' completed the plundering of the land begun under the incompetent Stuarts (there spoke the claimant to the Earldom of Menteith). In a hall where the 'classes' as represented by the platform party, faced the 'masses' in the shape of hundreds of ,by now elated ,working men waving their hats and handkerchiefs, talk of revolution past was sufficiently disturbing. But the climax of their excitement came when Robert turned to foreign affairs. In the light of the catastrophe at Khartoum the subject was one on which no Liberal cared to dwell while John Baird was naturally making much of the different manner in which a Conservative government would have acted. So far as Robert was concerned, his inability to support his party's record overseas had already caused disquiet: it was interpreted - rightly - that he was anti-war. This exposed him to the charge that he would not fight to defend his country or the Empire. Well aware that such an accusation could destroy his chances of election he moved to deny it with sincerity and passion. When he advocated non-intervention in foreign affairs, he said, it was not in a spirit of indifference to the Empire on which every true Briton looked with pride - 'there does not live a man so dead to self respect and love of country'. What he deprecated was the promotion of useless wars to push class or political interests. Should war ever be necessary - 'which God forbid it ever should 'to maintain commerce, to uphold the Empire, or 'in the interests of the great mass of the people' of course he would play his part. This statement of a belief formed by the brutal sights he had seen in South America, especially in ravaged Paraguay, was greeted by loud and prolonged cheering from a large part of the audience which was beside itself with approval, excitement, affection, and relief. His sincerity had brought them to such a pitch of enthusiasm that they were - for the moment - his to command.

This euphoria was not general: when it fell to a member of the committee to move a vote of confidence in the candidate yet another note of warning was sounded from the platform. Not everyone found it possible to agree with Mr Graham, the speaker opined; he was a very advanced radical indeed.

However in Coatbridge they had sensibly resolved to make the best of things: 'by voting for Mr Baird of Knoydart we do what we can to saddle ourselves with Lord Salisbury and Lord Randolph Churchill. By voting for Mr Graham we do what we can to bring in a good sound Liberal government under Mr Gladstone'. And so the vote was put;' the audience rose en masse 'the Airdrie Advertiser wrote, 'an innumerable number of hands being held out, and a deafening round of applause being given for Mr Graham'. (41).

John Baird's meetings were sedate by comparison but they too were well attended. Though at the time he appeared before the Napier Commission he had insisted that Knoydart was his home in order to establish the fact that he was no absentee landlord, he was also, as the Airdrie Advertiser put it 'well entrenched' in Lanarkshire. Brought up at Lochwood House his face was familiar to almost everyone in the neighbourhood of Coatbridge. As an Elder of the Church of Scotland he was a hero in the eyes of those who were passionately opposed to its disestablishment, which Robert supported, albeit without enthusiasm. As a member of Airdrie School Board John Baird's activities were regularly reported in the local paper; Robert on the other hand had never held public office. Above all Baird had the advantage with regard to the most urgent and vexatious issue of the campaign. Both candidates declared themselves in favour of the greatest measure of self government for Ireland that wisdom could devise but, at a time of persistent rumour concerning an alliance between Parnell and Salisbury aimed at resolving the problem of coercion, Baird was far more likely to appeal to Irish voters. Robert was sympathetic to their plight while remaining cautiously detached. He pointed out that, because reforms and conciliatory gestures towards the Irish were always so long delayed they appeared to have been extorted by the threat of force . He called for the Irish to be treated as the British would wish to be treated - 'as men and citizens not as children', to which end the 'exasperating and puerile' Viceregal system at Dublin Castle should be abolished, and the Irish given full power to manage their own affairs. In spite of these sensible remarks he was continually heckled on this issue; he had to confess he was not in favour of full independence for the Irish since he felt it would mean the collapse of the Union and of the Empire. He was not a supporter of Parnell. He did not want the return of Grattan's Parliament. He was bitterly reproached for appearing on the same platform with Lord Edmond Fitzmaurice whose call for the reform of parliamentary procedure was resented by the Irish as an attempt to curb Parnell. (42). Robert's excuse: that he was merely supporting a relative failed to redeem him in the eyes of the Irish in Coatbridge. Then, on 21 November, came the blow he recognized as fatal to his chances of election. Parnell issued an order to his newly enfranchised rank and file in Britain that, in seats where a Conservative was opposed by a Liberal or a radical, they were to cast their votes in favour of the former since the Conservative Party now offered the best hope of progress towards a united Ireland. This ukase was unexpected and, in some quarters, unwelcome. In particular John Ferguson, Secretary of the Glasgow Branch of the Irish National League, a tough and independent minded Ulster Protestant, refused to endorse it, continuing to advise his members to vote for Cunninghame Graham in North West Lanarkshire. (43).

In the last weeks of the campaign Robert had the support of two dashing figures; Lieutenant Charles Cunninghame Graham RN was constantly at his side as was Gabrielle. Her elegance of dress - perceived as quintessentially foreign - her prettily accented English, intrigued and pleased the crowd, while her rapt attention to Robert's speeches prompted them to give her much of the credit for his determined support of votes for women. But the person who would have thrown herself with the greatest fervour into the campaign, whose Liberal credentials were impeccable, was absent. Anne Elizabeth Bontine remained in London nursing her youngest son who had been ailing since the beginning of the year. In September she had accompanied him to Switzerland in the hope that the mountain air would restore his damaged lungs. Malise' life had been quite different from that of his much older, more robust brothers. While between adventures Bob and Charlie flashed like birds of paradise in and out of their mother's house in London, Malise had spent his school holidays at home. The Bontine correspondence shows how close he and his mother were, sharing a love of the theatre and a passion for music. Growing up in the years of his father's illness and incarceration he was Anne Elizabeth's dear companion in the long drawn out and brave attempt to make the best of things. His life, like hers, was circumscribed by lack of money. After Winchester he went up to Oriel College, Oxford in 1879 to study theology with the intention of taking Holy Orders. His allowance of £300 had to be found at the same time as the Gartmore estate was called upon to repay the £2000 of Robert's debts in America, when rents were falling. When Malise came down he had nothing to live on. The Curator who had hoped the Church would immediately enfold him, was, with difficulty persuaded to advance £100. In 1884 Malise was rescued from this uncomfortable position by the offer of a curacy at St John's Winchester where he quickly made himself well liked.

Shortly afterwards his health started to give way. By the autumn of 1885, after his return from Switzerland, Anne Elizabeth had to tell his brothers that the disease could not be checked. In the North West Lanarkshire campaign Robert's last appearance was at Swinton on 24 November when his Chairman read out a speech his maternal grandfather, Admiral Fleeming, had made in 1832, 'in order to prove that Mr Cunninghame Graham comes of a thoroughly Liberal family'. (45). When the meeting was over Robert and Gabrielle left Scotland.. Polling in the general election took place over a period of days and the results were announced whenever they were known. By the time North West Lanarkshire voted on 4 December a pronounced swing towards the Liberals was evident. Not so in Coatbridge and its neighbourhood. When the votes were counted John Baird proved to have reaped the benefit of the Irish vote. He was the winner with 4545, a majority of 1103 over Robert Cunninghame Graham who was not present to concede victory. He and Gabrielle were with his mother in London where, aged only 25, Malise had died the week before.

Notes to Chapter Six

1. Harry Ransom Humanities Center, the University of Texas at Austin (hereinafter Austin). G.C. (Gabrielle) Graham Bontine to Mrs (Mary) Evans. 12 Sept. 1883.
2. SRO: GD 268/99/41. C.W. Fitzwilliam to Henry Loch, 16 Nov. 1883.
3. SRO; GD 22/1/260, 9 April 1884.
4. SRO; GD 268/99/13, RBCG to Loch, 26 Sept. 1883.
5. NLS, Acc.11335/136, RBCG to Gab., 26 Sept 1883, 1 Oct. 1883.
6. ibid., same to the same,13 Oct. 1883 (his italics).
7. SRO; GD 22/2/99, Jamieson to RBCG., 8 Oct. 1883.
8. NLS; Acc. 11335/185, Lindsay, Jamieson & Haldane to RBCG., 1 Feb. 1884, 10 Apr. 1884.
9. Austin: Gab. to Mrs Evans, 11 Feb. 1884, 15 May 1884, And see SRO, GD 22/2/98.
10. NLS. Acc.11335/185, Lindsay, Jamieson & Haldane, various dates.
11. See, for instance, Cunninghame Graham, R.B., Salvagia in 'The Ipane', op.cit., pp 189-203.
12. Cunninghame Graham, R.B., Pollybaglan in 'Progress', Duckworth, 1905, pp 251 - 259.
13. Cunninghame Graham, R.B., A Traveller in 'Progress', op.cit., pp 260 - 268.
14. Cunninghame Graham, R.B., Heather Jock in 'The Ipane', op.cit., pp 174-187.
15. Cunninghame Graham, R.B., The Beggar Earl in 'A Hatchment' op.cit., pp 183 - 194.
16. <u>Stirling Advertiser</u>, 30 Aug. 1884.
17. Note. Under 16th century Scots law, in return for an annual payment called a feu, to a superior - the laird of Gartmore in this case - feuars held their farms in perpetuity and with the right of sale.
18. They were Donald Currie, Joseph Bolton, and Archibald Orr Ewing. For Currie see below. Bolton was Liberal MP for Stirlingshire 1880 - 1892. A merchant in the East India trade he was President of Glasgow Chamber of Commerce. Sir Archibald Orr Ewing was Conservative MP for Dunbartonshire, 1868 - 1892.
19. McOnie was born at Gartmore in 1813, the son of a butcher to the trade who bought cattle from drovers passing nearby. After the family moved to Glasgow he set up an engineering works making machinery for the sugar trade. He was knighted in 1888.
20. Cunninghame Graham, R.B., 'Doughty Deeds', op.cit., p 129.
21. Parliamentary Papers, 1884. 'Report by the Commissioners of Inquiry into the Condition of the Crofters and Cottars in the Highlands and Islands of Scotland Volume XXXII to Vol. XXXVI'. (Napier Report).
22. ibid., Vol XXXVI, p. 3209.
23. The estate belonged to Mackenzie of Kilcoy.
24. Napier Report; Vol. XXXVI, pp. 3209, 3214.
25. ibid., Vol. XXXII, p. 3093.
26. Crowley, D.W., 'The Crofters' Party 1885 - 1892' in Scottish Historical Review, Vol. 35, pp.110 - 126.
27. Napier Report, Vol. XXXII, p. 3093.
28. ibid.
29. Crowley, op.cit.
30. Napier Report, Vol XXXII p 3215, Murdoch on Sutherland clearances

31. NLS, Acc.11335/203, poster, 'The Liberal Candidate for North West Lanarkshire'.
32. Drummond P., and Smith, J., 'Coatbridge: Three Centuries of Change', Monklands Library Services Department, 1983.
33. Cunninghame Graham, R.B., 'Doughty Deeds', op.cit., p. 162.
34. <u>Airdrie Advertiser</u> and <u>Linlithgow Standard</u>.
35. ibid., 15 Aug. 1885.
36. Drummond and Smith, op.cit.
37. Napier Report. Vol. XXXIII, p.505.
38. NLS, Acc.11335/71, E.Garnett to RBCG., 2 Jan. 1898.
39. NLS, Acc.11335/203,, poster, op.cit.,
40. <u>Airdrie Advertiser</u>, 12. Sept. 1885.
41. ibid., 17 Oct. 1885.
42. ibid., 23 Oct 1885.
43. Crowley, op.cit.,
44. SRO; CS 46/143/7, 1884.
45. <u>Airdrie Advertiser</u>, 28 Nov. 1885.

Chapter Seven

Member of Parliament

'My dear Mrs Evans', Gabrielle wrote on 13 December, 'the illness and death of my brother-in-law, and the ill success of my husband's Election have put all thought of writing to you out of my head. I was in London at the time of my brother-in-law's death and it quite upset me, and Mr Graham was in dreadful grief. Then immediately after came the defeat, which too has been somewhat of a blow - at all events a great disappointment'. Robert's distress was intensified by the sight of Anne Elizabeth mourning someone very dear to her for the second time in two years. On the other hand his disappointment at not being elected to Parliament was tempered by messages of continuing support. Deputations from various clubs and societies in the constituency waited upon him at Gartmore where they presented him with tokens of their esteem - an umbrella for himself, a purse for Gabrielle. These had to be placed in the balance against unfavourable comment in some newspapers castigating him for losing one of the safest seats in the country by his reckless proposals and extreme language. It was exactly the sort of thing a novice in politics ought to have avoided. It occurred in January, a month of darkness, loneliness and gloom for Gabrielle had bolted. 'Scotland does not seem to suit me very well in the winter', she told Mary Evans. Her plan was to go with a friend to Cannes and on into Italy. 'Mr Graham will stay at Gartmore. I don't like leaving him but he will stay and like a limpet will not be moved'.(1)

So, in the unmercifully short dark days of January 1886 only the laird was in residence at Gartmore. After breakfast when, finally, it was light, with Jack the fox terrier at his heels Robert rode out around the farms. Or if, remarkably, the cloud had lifted he and Pampa took the back road to the snow covered hills and Loch Katrine. The horse was already as much of a beloved companion to him as Bunny had been in Paraguay. Pampa was a young, black Argentine mustang that, according to the story Robert told, he had encountered with a shock of recognition pulling a tram in Glasgow. (2). From this unbecoming servitude he had liberated Pampa on the spot. As he related it their encounter had the same element of surprise leading to good fortune as his version of the first time his grandfather, Admiral Fleeming, saw Doña Catalina, his future wife; and his own near accident in Paris with Gabrielle - <u>equus ex machina</u> as it were. The other member of the Gartmore family in those days was Talla, the Iceland pony Gabrielle rode.

In the evenings after supper Robert retired to the book room whose fusty atmosphere bore witness to the years when no one had entered it. There he was confronted by the pile of papers Lindsay, Jamieson and Haldane had considerately withheld during the election campaign. They made anxious reading. Although there was money in hand from selling feus, Jamieson warned him he had overspent his income for the year to September 1885 by £1161.3.4, to which must be added £620.0.0, the cost of the campaign. The weather had been bad; the Gartmore farmers had lost numbers of sheep from standing on wet ground; consequently some were asking for a reduction in their rent; several were badly in arrears. The death of Malise was a severe financial blow; his trustees required £10,000 to settle his estate, money which would have to be raised by an additional mortgage secured on Gartmore. At the same time cash had to be found for the half yearly payments of the annuities due to Anne Elizabeth and her two sisters-in-law. The situation remained as it had been at the time he inherited; the only way to solve the problem was by the sale of Ardoch. But that, Robert told Jamieson on 1 February, was not worth pursuing for the moment since the economic situation generally was so dire.(3). In Scotland the raging boom in shipbuilding had collapsed; in 1885 35% less tonnage was constructed on the Clyde than in the previous year. Iron production was also sharply down; thousands were out of work in Glasgow and, in Lanarkshire, miners' wages had been reduced for lack of demand for coal. The slump was also affecting England.

A week later on 8 February Robert's London club, the Devonshire, was one of several attacked by an angry crowd of working men. Its windows were broken and, for several minutes, stones lying ready to mend the roadway were turned into missiles that rattled and bounced into the library and smoking room before the men moved on to Piccadilly where they broke into some shops. We do not know if Robert was in London at the time but his mother was; she and Homer, her maid, were alone in the house in Chester Square on the far side of Hyde Park - barely a mile away. As the newspapers reported it the event was not only the worst disturbance in the capital for many years, but it had sinister implications for the future. For the first time mass unemployment - the word itself was only just coming into use - was associated in the public mind with looting and the destruction of property. For several days at the darkest period of the year London was in the grip of panic; 'the all pervading black fog heightened the feeling of unease which culminated in a rumour that 50,000 men were marching from Deptford and Greenwich towards the West End wrecking and looting as they went', the Annual Register reported. (4).

The event lead to a hardening in the authorities' attitude towards the task of keeping public order that was to bear heavily on those concerned to preserve the right of free speech which they feared was under threat as never before. As a leading protagonist in this contest Robert Cunninghame Graham was soon to pay dearly for his opposition to the new measures of control. The four leaders of the 8 February riot - Henry Hyndman, Henry Champion, John Burns, and John Williams - were to become his friends and colleagues in the struggle; one, John Burns, was to share a prison sentence with him. In April 1886 these four stood trial at the Old Bailey charged with seditious intention in calling the meeting that got so seriously out of control. The jury heard evidence of a clash between two factions holding meetings at the same time in Trafalgar Square in the presence of a crowd of more than 15,000 onlookers. The first was called by the Fair Traders - a group of seamen, dockers, and men from other waterside industries badly affected by the loss of work in the West India docks as the result of foreign competition. Their speakers called for a Minister for Commerce, a measure of protection for English made goods, outdoor relief for agricultural workers, for whose plight they expressed much sympathy, and public works to provide employment. From their platform on the other side of the Square Hyndman, Champion and other Social Democratic Federation members castigated the Fair Traders for interfering in the real job of overthrowing capitalism and - not without reason - accused them of taking Tory money for the purpose.(5). In particular Burns, a powerful and emotional speaker, worked himself up to the point of declaring that to hang landlords and others who exploited workers was a waste of good rope. Scuffles broke out and the Fair Traders' platform was overturned. Hyndman called for the meeting to continue in the larger open space of Hyde Park and Burns, who was carrying a red flag, set off down Pall Mall to St James's followed by an excited crowd. As they passed the Tory stronghold of the Carlton Club they were jeered by 'gentlemen' standing in the windows; behaviour it is hard to believe was copied by the famously radical members of the Devonshire which, even so, was one of the next targets after the Carlton Club of the by now infuriated marchers.(6).

When order was restored over £7,000 worth of damage was found to have been done. Shops in the vicinity of Piccadilly and Oxford Street rushed to install steel shutters, and banks reduced the amount of cash they kept in hand. The police were severely criticized; the attack on the clubs had only been possible because they were elsewhere - defending the Mall when their orders had been to block off Pall Mall. Superintendent Walker, the man in charge, was ridiculed. His method on the day, as always, had been to mingle with the crowd in plain clothes. So successfully had he mingled that he could not be found to give orders when they were needed, and he had had his own pocket picked.(7). The new Liberal Government hastily retired the 69 year old Walker and named a former soldier to the post of Metropolitan Police Commissioner. Sir Charles Warren's appointment was a signal of the Government's intention to deal firmly with the situation on the streets. His stiff necked personality was to have a disproportionate effect upon subsequent events including those in which Robert Cunninghame Graham played a major part. Hyndman was cock a hoop at the violent outcome of the 8 February demonstration; to him it represented progress in the right direction. 'Once the idea is planted in the minds of working men that nothing can put them right except an entire revolution of the existing order of society, they will not be easy to stop before they have made a clean sweep of the classes who have fattened so long on the plunder of the people', he told Joseph Burgess, a sympathetic journalist (later Editor of the Workman's Times)(8). Printed in the Pall Mall Gazette, these remarks provoked further apprehension with the result that many of its readers looked forwards to the trial of Hyndman and his three colleagues as the occasion when they would, deservedly, suffer the full penalty of the law. At the same time the serious nature of the charge gave pause to fellow activists and those like Robert, not yet engaged ,but in growing sympathy with the new movement.

The four accused came from very different backgrounds. Hyndman was regarded by a devoted handful of his followers as a sort of god, according to Bernard Shaw. '..he was a leading figure in any assembly and took that view of himself with perfect self confidence. Altogether an assuming man quite naturally and unconsciously', Shaw wrote, adding that Hyndman could talk about anything with a fluency that left William Morris - though obviously not himself - nowhere. (9). Shaw, who enjoyed paradoxes, fixed Hyndman' image for posterity as managing director of a private company whose object, nevertheless, was to ensure that sooner rather than later the English working man would rise in bloody revolution. As a rich man advocating the downfall of the system that created wealth, his own included, Hyndman was not at all unusual. In those early days there were very few working men in the Social Democratic Federation. Of the four accused as a result of the events of 8 February only Jack Williams had emerged from the workhouse where he had been brought up without education or a skill. John Burns (who after 8 February became famous as 'the man with the red flag'),was a foreman engineer who had spent 1879 to 1881 in Africa working for Sir George Goldie's Niger Company; Henry Champion was the son of a Major General in the Indian Army. It was dislike of what was perceived as Hyndman's overbearing attitude, not his belief, that, in 1884 caused Morris, Eleanor Marx, Ernest Belfort Bax and other members of the SDF to secede and form the Socialist League.

Arrogance was a charge also laid against Henry Champion with whom Robert was to work in close association in the years to come. The two had much in common - background, education, even temperament. (11). Both Champion's parents descended from the Highland family of Urquhart that, like the Grahams and Elphinstones had a tradition of service overseas, and produced a number of scholarly eccentrics ,the latest of whom, David Urquhart, had died in 1877. As an enthusiast in the field of politics Champion was an Urquhart through and through. So far as school was concerned he derived even less benefit from his time at Marlborough than Robert had at Harrow. His decision to enlist in the unfashionable Royal Artillery was unwelcome to his family as Robert's dash to South America had been to his mother and the Curator. Champion was 18 when his regiment was sent to India Upon the outbreak of the Second Afghan War in 1879, it was ordered up to Quetta in Baluchistan where there was little fighting but a great deal of outdoor sport. Champion stayed there until, in 1881 a severe attack of typhoid fever caused him to be invalided home. A visit to the East End of London in the company of a friend where he was confronted by scenes of poverty, sickness and overcrowding he had not dreamt existed ,shocked and overwhelmed him. Shortly afterwards he accompanied the friend on a visit to the United States where he was introduced to Henry George and became for ever afterwards a fervent advocate of the nationalization of land. Circumstantial evidence suggests this friend was another famous Scots eccentric, Thomas Davidson, who roamed the world setting up branches of his Fellowship of the New Life wherever he encountered persons desirous of changing society for the better. Davidson had made his home in America but was in England in 1881, the year Henry Champion became Secretary of the English branch of the Fellowship.(12). Its members were considering founding an ideal colony in some remote part of the world - South America was an option. When the late Dr Henry Pelling was engaged in research for his 'Origins of the Labour Party' Champion's widow told him that, among her husband's papers were letters from Robert Cunninghame Graham. These, alas, have disappeared but they may have contained advice for

Champion as to which part of South America might suit New Life colonists. (13). The idea came to nothing and, as is well known, the Fellowship split: the more hard headed of the members departing to form the Fabian Society.

Champion was not among them, In 1882, his convalescence at an end, he resumed his Army duties at Portsmouth. As Adjutant his afternoons were free so the 22 year old sat down to what he afterwards regarded as his real education. The books he read were all of a kind: Adam Smith, Ricardo, Karl Marx (<u>Das Kapital</u> in French translation); Mill. 'Gradually, step by step I was driven to Socialism and also to conclude that I must leave the Army', he explained, years later. In 1882 England was at war in Egypt and Champion's military training prevailed over his instinct as an Urquhart - 'it isnt quite the thing to throw up one's commission just at the moment when one is ordered to the front'. So he waited, expecting to sail for Egypt at any moment. On 17 September he opened the newspaper to read of a tremendous victory by the English at the battle of Tel el Kebir. That same day he handed in his resignation; that same night he was 'preaching Socialism' on Clerkenwell Green.(14). From then on he was one of the most effective propagandists of the new belief, becoming, albeit for a brief period, Secretary of the SDF. Unlike Robert Cunninghame Graham whose lack of money was to be a serious handicap to his political career, Champion disposed of funds which he put at the disposal of his colleagues - the expenses of John Burns' unsuccessful attempt to become MP for Battersea in 1885 were paid by Champion ,for example. At first his money came from his family: it was they who, in 1884, provided the wherewithal for <u>Justice</u> to be printed. Later on he had recourse to wealthy manufacturers and other interested persons whose desire to keep their contributions secret caused Champion's motives to be questioned and his activities regarded with considerable suspicion, even by his own colleagues. (15).

According to Joseph Burgess the Government regarded the disturbances of 8 February as a wonderful opportunity to circumscribe the activities of the SDF. (16). That hope was frustrated by the legal process. When Hyndman, Champion, Burns, and Williams came up at the Old Bailey in April, the presiding Judge, Mr Justice Cave, put a different perspective on the situation. Seditious intention with which they were charged was a crime against society nearly allied to treason, and it frequently led to treason, he told the jury. But, he warned them, the public had great latitude given them for voicing criticism; 'an intention to show that Her Majesty has been mislead or mistaken in her measures, or to point out errors or defects in the government, or to point out matters that have been productive of hate or ill will between Her Majesty's subjects is NOT a seditious intention'. Cave directed them to take a broad, or even generous view of the case; they were not to attach too much importance to isolated phrases - here he expressed his belief that John Burns' strong language arose from sincere distress at the condition of the unemployed. (17). This robust affirmation of the essentially law abiding nature of the English, joined to the fact that , according to Shaw, the foreman of the jury was a Christian Socialist, 'in whose hands the rest were like sheep', won the accused an acquittal. (18). As a direct consequence of the riot efforts were made to alleviate distress among the unemployed and an appeal for funds to help their dependants by the Lord Mayor of London received a large response. Then, at that very moment, public interest in a problem destined to grow worse was blown away by a tremendous new idea.

Gladstone's decision to introduce measures aimed at granting Home Rule for Ireland which leaked to the press towards the end of 1885 shocked members of the Liberal Party to say nothing of the country at large. When, after long and agonizing debate in a nervous House of Commons the Bill was defeated at its second reading on 8 June 1886 the Prime Minister's response was to ask the Queen for a dissolution. She demurred on the grounds that his current administration had lasted less than six months but Gladstone insisted feeling that honour demanded nothing less. (19) Consequently a a second general election in less than a year was called for July. When Robert Cunninghame Graham once more offered himself for election in North West Lanarkshire it was under the label, not simply of the Liberal Party,but as a Ministerialist, signifying his support for Gladstone's version of Home Rule. (The many members of the Liberal Party ,including Cabinet Ministers like Joseph Chamberlain and the Marquis of Hartington who bitterly opposed Home Rule added Unionist to their names; they and their Conservative allies were often referred to as the Unionist Party.) The nub of the Irish policy favoured by Ministerialists was the demand for a separate assembly in Ireland to control internal affairs, including the police, customs, and education; defence and foreign policy being reserved to Westminster. This measure was described by Robert Cunninghame Graham as a simple act of justice for Ireland; one, moreover, that ought to be extended to Scotland and Wales. The issue that caused many Liberals, including Chamberlain, to withdraw their support from Gladstone - whether the Irish would continue to sit at Westminster and vote on purely English matters - apparently did not worry him. To those who denounced Gladstone's conversion to Home Rule as the act of a dotard whose intellect was waning (Gladstone was 75), in a speech at Coatbridge Robert declared the Prime Minister had more sanity in his little finger than was in the united brains of the whole Tory party. (20). This was much more the kind of language the local Liberal Association yearned to hear from him; that, given his family connection, they thought they had a right to expect. In 1878 it had been Robert's relative, W.P. Adam, who together with the wildly popular Earl of Rosebery, had persuaded Gladstone to stand for a Scottish seat - Midlothian, a constituency at the centre of Edinburgh where, in the campaign of 1880, the Grand Old Man had achieved his greatest popular success. Though Adam was dead by the time Robert put up for Parliament the connection reassured those who might otherwise have taken fright at the accusation that he was a 'mongrel' politician who did not scruple to take ideas from sources that were, to say the least, unorthodox.(21).

July was the month of the most important Orange demonstrations in Coatbridge so when Robert arrived to begin his campaign he found the Irish section of the population already in a state of high excitement. The town was given up to bands like the Sunnyside Blues marching to fife and drum in honour of King Billy. The police were out in force but sometimes failed to prevent a confrontation between Protestant and Catholic when heads as well as drums were broken. Robert's contribution was to say what had hitherto been carefully left unsaid. At a meeting in a playground (the school itself having proved too small for the number that arrived to hear him), he warned his audience they had no choice but to vote for him: the alternative was too awful. Either Gladstone would be returned and introduce Home Rule, or he would lose and there would be another 20 years of coercion under Lord Salisbury. If the latter he asked them to consider what might happen as the people's will grew stronger - it was his firm belief that it would. If the Scots, for example, had to put up with half the annoyances presently visited upon the Irish in the name of government 'blood would flow from John o' Groats to the Solway'. This violent turn of phrase provoked an immediate condemnation from his opponent, the sitting MP, John Baird of Knoydart. 'The Scots are a law abiding people' Baird declared- a thought most definitely fathered by the wish. (22). In the light of Gladstone's concession to the Irish, whoever fell to govern Scotland would confront a potentially dangerous situation beside which the recent Skye riots would pale into insignificance. If, for example, a Scottish Parnell were to arise and unite grievances regarding land tenure with a general demand for greater political independence, the Scots' famous predeliction for respectability and the constraint it had hitherto imposed upon the politically minded in the community, might be sorely tested. Well aware of this the more cautious of the Scottish Liberal party members and two of its leading papers, the Scotsman and the Glasgow Herald ,now abandoned Gladstone and cleaved to the Union as the best hope of avoiding disaster. As a result of all this ,in certain constituencies there were now three candidates ;Liberal Unionist versus Ministerialist, as well as Conservative.

That was not the case in North West Lanarkshire where the contest was a repetition of the straight fight of the previous election. Polling took place over more than two weeks in the country at large and North West Lanarkshire was one of the last places to vote. For several days beforehand it was rumoured that Gladstone had suffered a rebuff though on what scale was not clear to those who had to rely on newspapers for the result. The Prime Minister was better informed;' the defeat is a smash' he wrote on 8 July, the eve of the poll in Robert's constituency. (23). That same evening the Ministerialist candidate was rapturously received when he spoke for the last time. According to the Airdrie Advertiser he shared the platform with his wife and 'several Reverends' - a useful collection of Nonconformist Ministers there to affirm their support for Home Rule. They were less enthusiastic about the candidate's performance in their own particular interest. Robert ducked issues connected with the Presbyterian religion whose effect upon the Scottish character he privately deplored. Cornered as he sometimes was after he became a MP he went to great lengths to conceal his dislike of the mean and narrow way of life John Knox had fixed upon the nation. But after he had left the House of Commons, 'going to Church with us replaces charity', he complained, 'a man may cheat and drink, be cruel to animals, avaricious, anything you please, so that he goes to church he still remains a Christian and enters Heaven by his faith alone'. (24). Catholicism, on the other hand, drew kind words from him. His long experience of countries of Hispanic origin had accustomed him to its form and practice; it had been the mainstay of not a few of his friends; it was his wife's chosen faith; the time in which it had been Scotland's was to him the most distinguished in her history.;

Friday, 9 July was full of noise and movement in Coatbridge. Bands played as voters were transported to their local school where the polling booths had been set up. All kinds of conveyance were pressed into use; according to the <u>Airdrie Advertiser</u> the 'masses' were crammed onto lorries which had rows of seats installed for the occasion, while the 'classes' proceeded by carriage, trap, or gig. Each proclaimed its allegiance with flags and bunting; red for Home Rule; red, white, and blue for the Tories and the Union ; each had a tail of small boys prancing and shouting in its wake. Large hoardings on every street urged a vote for Baird, or for Cunninghame Graham. Towards lunchtime Robert and Gabrielle drove to the polls in an open carriage and were loudly cheered. As soon as they were decently out of the way John Baird and his wife appeared to a no less warm reception. The polls closed at 8 p.m. and by ten the result was posted in the window of Mr Pettigrew, Stationer, in the main street of Coatbridge. Alphabetically it read, Baird 3698, Graham, 4033 (25).

The news of Graham's narrow victory was the signal for groups of his and Baird's supporters to go on the rampage in the town, their behaviour anxiously monitored by the large force of police and military the Sheriff, in consultation with the Chief Constable, had drafted in to Coatbridge. In the last two weeks appalling sectarian riots had broken out in Belfast - it was now a city virtually out of control. The Scots were acutely aware that, in a town like Coatbridge, rivalry between political groups could quickly become a confrontation between Nationalists and Orangemen. In fact, though the situation was extremely tense for the next two hours, by midnight the crowds had dispersed without serious incident. Robert Cunninghame Graham was not in evidence, having chosen to sit out the count at the George Hotel in Glasgow where his supporters went to congratulate him in the morning. He awoke to find himself out of step again: more than one third of the 72 seats in Scotland had seceded to the Liberal Unionists while he had held on for Gladstone, though with a majority of only 334. In striking such a blow it must have seemed to him he had secured his own position. It was barely three years since he had been a wanderer, an exile as so many Scots were doomed to be.

Now, aged 34, newly in possession of his ancestral estates, favourably regarded by his neighbours, saluted by a large section of the 'masses' warmly responding to a power of communication that had come upon him unawares, he found himself the official Liberal MP for one of the most important seats in the industrial heart of Scotland His victory put him on course for advancement in public life in which he hoped to play a larger part than most members of the class into which he had been born. Their anglophile way of life isolated most of them from their native country; as a result they were not altogether popular with the rest of its inhabitants. Robert Cunninghame Graham seemed different: on becoming laird of Gartmore he had declared his intention of living permanently in Scotland; his commitment to Scottish affairs was already on record in the wholehearted support he had offered to the crofters' movement. He had won his seat in Parliament at a time when the system of governing Scotland had recently been modernized . As soon as the Liberal Government took office in 1881 the Earl of Rosebery (whose radical sentiments had earned him the title of 'the people's peer 'from his fellow Scots)(26), brought pressure on Gladstone to replace the Lord Advocate's regime whereby, he complained, the Scots were governed by lawyers who never left Edinburgh, with a separate department under a Minister with a seat in Cabinet. This initiative coincided with and greatly encouraged , renewed public interest in Scottish nationalism. The outcome disappointed everyone. By 1886 a Scottish Department had been created but its chief was subordinate to the Home Secretary of the day. Nevertheless for a new and energetic Scottish MP, such as Robert hoped to be, the scope for action concerning the affairs of his native land was wider than it had been since the Act of Union.

Seasoned politicians at Westminster viewed the result of the most recent election with foreboding. No party had an overall majority in the new House of Commons; those in favour of Home rule numbered only 191, while on that issue the 78 newly elected Liberal Unionists could be expected to join their opposition to that of the Conservatives who, with 316 seats were the largest single party. Parnell commanded roughly 85 Irish MPs, as before. On 20 July Gladstone resigned the Premiership and was replaced by the Marquis of Salisbury. The change of government meant that Parliament had to be recalled. In the absence of the still stubbornly mourning Queen, it was appointed to be opened by Commission on 6 August when most MPs had usually quit London for the country and its pursuits. Though the Gartmore estate derived much needed income from renting out the shooting rights, the laird himself no longer killed birds or animals for pleasure, having had enough of hunting to survive in South America.(27). The first summer of Robert's existence as a MP was filled, not by shooting parties but by picnics, highly political events at which his suitability as their representative came under further scrutiny by his constituents. The picnic at Gartmore House in the last week of July held for the Band of Hope - an organisation dedicated to instilling an aversion for alcohol in the very young - was just such a demanding occasion. It marked a further stage in Robert's losing battle to remain detached from the temperance movement. With the largest branch in the world of the Good Templars (whose origin was American while the Band was home grown), at Airdrie, and another almost as large at Coatbridge it was a force he must at least placate if he was to be at all effective. He had been open with its adherents during the campaign; he had willingly agreed that drink was a chief cause of poverty; he had thrown away the publicans' vote by supporting measures to control the sale of alcohol, while holding to the position that he was not himself a total abstainer - a statement that must have raised an eyebrow or two among the friends of his youth in South America.

Capitulation followed hard upon the election. The newspaper reported that Mr Cunninghame Graham had taken the occasion of a picnic to announce his decision to forswear drink entirely. (28). The news was bound to gratify his friend and colleague, Gavin Clark who, beside his duties as a crofters' MP, was Editor of the Good Templars magazine. It did not please his wife so well. 'I am a teetotaller in theory but not in practice' ,she confessed to Mary Evans, 'but my husband goes in for it root and branch'. Although she had not been well, she told her friend, she was determined to do her duty at the picnic as Honorary President of the Band of Hope. (29). The day was long remembered by the inhabitants of Gartmore village. The morning saw a procession of charabancs bring over a hundred children up the steep hill to the house where they were to receive prizes for regular attendance throughout the winter at meetings where the evils of drink were vividly brought home to them. The older boys got money, the young ones of both sexes, pencils, pen holders, workbaskets, pocket handkerchiefs. The best liked prize, according to the <u>Airdrie Advertiser,</u> was a cabinet portrait in a plush frame of Gabrielle which was given to the older girls. "The main attraction for the little ones was Mr Graham who gave each and all of them a ride round the park on Mrs Graham's beautiful pony'. This was Talla who, Robert declared in his speech after tea, deserved to be made a member of the Band of Hope. Tea was strawberries and cream and many kinds of cake served on long tables set up outside the gaunt old house with its spectacular view across the Flanders Moss to Stirling Castle floating in the distance. Afterwards they sang hymns and gave three cheers for Mr and Mrs Graham. (30).

There is no record of Robert attending Parliament on or after 6 August so we do not know if he took the oath or, like Charles Bradlaugh, chose to affirm instead. (31). The only trace of him during the brief summer session is that in September he was paired in support of the Bill Parnell vainly tried to bring in to relieve distress among the Irish rural poor. (32). The Bill's rejection paved the way for direct action by Parnell's supporters in Ireland which had dire consequences for the peace of the Union; consequences that, eventually, landed Robert himself in prison. Meanwhile there was more than enough for him to do in Scotland. The Lanarkshire miners were seething with rage at the reduction in their wages of 6d a day due to the low demand for coal. Throughout August and September meetings at Motherwell, Hamilton, Coatbridge and other towns near Glasgow called for the 6d to be restored. These were addressed by Donald Crawford and Stephen Mason, Members for North East and Mid Lanark respectively ,who were sometimes joined on the platform by Charles Bradlaugh vigorously campaigning against the illegal use of truck by Lanarkshire coalmasters. On 25 September wages, hours and truck figured largely on the agenda of the Scottish Miners' Federation conference at which the two Lanark MPs put in an appearance. The chair on that occasion was taken by James Keir Hardie, a 30 year old former miner, now correspondent for a local newspaper. During all this time the new MP for North West Lanarkshire was nowhere to be seen.   Then on 2 October the <u>Airdrie Advertiser</u> announced that Mrs Cunninghame Graham was so seriously ill the doctor had ordered her to Spain (33). By accompanying her Robert was prevented from getting to grips with the manifold problems of his constituents until the month was past.

It was a bad beginning that prompted rumour and undermined his supporters' confidence in him. What could be wrong with his 'wee Spanish wife'? Gabrielle's health was also the subject of much discussion among members of the Graham family, more especially his aunts and great aunts. Her cough alarmed them and its cause - chain smoking - came near to shocking them. But, as they remarked among themselves, she was a foreigner so allowances must be made. So, from Leamington Spa on the couple's first return to Scotland, the Misses Cunninghame Graham wrote kind letters to Robert's wife, ending with greetings in French in which they were fluent, having shared their brother's exile forty years before. But their patience was not infinite and, after a while, they began to sound a little peevish. When one of their number fell too much under the influence of her maid, they summoned Robert to take charge of her affairs. He was to come to Leamington and bring his wife. 'Gabrielle is quite capable to keep her own, and that she must do, seeing after matters and being mistress'.(34). Perhaps it was this kind of pressure, joined to the continuing coolness of Anne Elizabeth that caused Gabrielle once more to bolt. The weeks in Spain did not resolve the problem; on her return Gabrielle told Mrs Evans her doctor said she had been very ill and was even yet not fully recovered. But she would fight resolutely against going abroad again. While in Glasgow to see the doctor she and Robert had gone to a meeting addressed by the Marquis of Aberdeen. 'He spoke fairly well but had no great gift of oratory or conviction...one would say he is a kind little man full of good impulses and with average ability but certainly not one to set any part of the world on fire.' This attempt to cut a Liberal grandee down to size, one who had just won golden opinions during a brief period as Lord Lieutenant in Dublin, reflected Gabrielle's mood of irritation born of apprehension. She feared - rightly as things turned out - that politics and politicians were about to come between her and her husband. (35)

When Parliament reassembled after Christmas, Robert took his seat, not as a faithful Gladstonian, but on the cross benches where his neighbours on one side were five members of the Crofters' Party, on the other the Irish. According to his own account of how he came there - straying about the House of Commons like a new boy at school, he chanced to sit down and was briskly warned off because that seat was Parnell's. Typically, he refused to move whereupon Parnell politely waived his claim. 'This laid the first stone of a desultory friendship,' Robert wrote, 'which lasted until Parnell's death. Occasionally we dined together, not talking very much as we had nothing much in common except a love of horses. (Parnell prided himself on his equestrian skill but Robert maintained he was incapable of getting his stirrup leathers even). In the course of his remarkably eventful life Robert was often asked which of the public figures he had known was the most striking. The answer was, invariably, Parnell who 'stood out as the Old Man of Hoy stands out against the sea'. Watching him in the Commons Robert decided that Parnell's greatest service to the Irish Parliamentary Party lay in the cold contempt he showed for all things English; the way in which his speeches ridiculed the Anglo-Saxon Members. 'Thus did the Chief make it impossible for British [Cabinet] Ministers to take up the Poor Patrick attitude which , in the past, had always been a trump' (36).

Ridicule was one of Robert's weapons; he once memorably described the view from the Commons gallery of the bald heads of Members as that of a nest of ostrich eggs (37). The contempt in which he came to hold his fellow MPs after a short acquaintance was hotter and fiercer than Parnell's. It was demonstrated for the first time when he rose in support of an amendment to the Queen's Speech. The Speech was little more than a catalogue of the problems facing Lord Salisbury's administration. The most urgent was Ireland, newly in a state of uproar as a result of the Plan of Campaign introduced by Parnell's followers (but without his blessing) the previous November in a renewed attempt to help the rural poor whose state continued desperate. The brainchild of Michael Davitt this urged tenants to make their own assessment of what level of rent might be fair and, if the landlord rejected it, to pay the money to a committee that would hold it on their behalf. The Queen's Speech now condemned the Plan as an incitement to tenants to conspire against fulfilling their legal obligations. To combat the violence which was its product stronger measures of coercion would be brought in. In other parts of the United Kingdom the depression in agriculture and industry was hardly less serious than in Ireland but the Speech barely glanced at it. (38). On 1 February Robert was called in support of an Opposition amendment to the effect that '... the want of employment and general distress prevalent among the working classes in England and Ireland deserve the immediate attention of this House'. He began lightly: a debate on the Queen's Speech formed the best occasion for a new Member to lose his political virginity - but quickly turned a blast of withering contempt upon all sections of Society in the course of which he contrived to imply that members of the Royal Family were nothing more than parasites. On glancing over the Speech he said he had been struck with the government's evident desire to do nothing at all. 'Not one word was said...about lightening the taxation under which Her Majesty's lieges presently suffer; not one word to make that taxation more bearable; not one word to bridge over the awful chasm existing between the poor and the rich; not one word of kindly sympathy for those suffering from the present commercial and agricultural depression - nothing but platitudes; nothing but views of society through a little bit of pink glass'. This was a society divided against itself, he charged them, in which one man worked and another enjoyed the fruit; in which capital and luxury made Heaven for 30.000 and Hell for 30 million; whose crowning achievement was London - 'this dreary waste of mud and stucco with its misery, its want and degradation; its prostitution and its glaring social ineqalities'. (39)

    This savage denunciation was delivered with what the Parliamentary sketch writer of Vanity Fair described as an air of chastened melancholy which produced a very different response. 'House kept in continuous uproar formore than half an hour', this reporter (not one to waste words)) noted; 'fogeys and fossils eye him askance and whisper that he ought to be 'put down'; but lovers of originality ...hail him with satisfaction'. (40). Politically the speech was a landmark; a demand for social justice presented to the House of Commons by a member whose allegiance was demonstrably to neither of the two main parties but who spoke with formidable self assurance. Henry Champion thought so much of it that, years later, in the course of describing how he had been a leader of the Socialist movement in the 1880s, he claimed to have written it for Cunninghame Graham to deliver. (41). But those who had followed Robert's progress as a candidate in two general elections recognized it as the natural outcome of what had gone before. It was warmly received in North West

Lanarkshire. 'A wonderful speech,' the <u>Airdrie Advertiser</u> called it; of striking originality and irresistible humour. 'Mr Cunninghame Graham blazes forth, a star of the first magnitude, his quick wittedness and shrewd pungent satire have long been familiar to his constituents, most of whom will doubtless be proud of the fact that their member has now lost his political virginity'. But the manner in which he chose to do so left the paper in some doubt as to whether the Hon. gentleman would ever get any further than the back benches. (42).

If Robert's maiden speech did not endear him to the Liberal Party whips, what happened next was guaranteed to compound his offence. As soon as news reached Westminster that, on 3 February, starving miners had looted shops in Blantyre and the following day in Coatbridge, Robert made an overnight dash for his constituency. His appearance there was viewed as nothing but a nuisance by the Sheriff and as an affront by the coal and ironmasters. Admittedly the situation was dangerous. Since June 1886 when 6d had been cut from the miners' wages without reducing the price of coal, months of argument, the withholding of labour, and demonstrations had failed to solve the problem. By Christmas many pits in Blantyre, Hamilton, Coatbridge and Airdrie were idle, the miners and their wives and children destitute and starving at a moment when the weather was more ferociously cold and stormy than for many years. In spite of their obvious despair the looting of food shops took the authorities by surprise. It was not until evening that reinforcements arrived by special train enabling the miners' rows to be patrolled by mounted police with drawn swords who, under cover of darkness entered houses to arrest suspects in their beds, and remove the bags of flour and lumps of cheese and bacon stowed beneath them. The next day large and sullen groups of miners roamed the streets of Coatbridge and formed a cordon through which the prisoners from Blantyre had to pass to reach the railway station en route to Glasgow. So menacing were these groups that a detachment of Royal Scots drafted in to Coatbridge was issued with 20 rounds of ammunition each while the telegraph office was ordered to remain open all night in case more troops needed to be summoned. (43)

A close watch was kept on the midnight meetings that now took place in Academy Park, Airdrie when some 12,000 miners were addressed by their leaders. Robert Cunninghame Graham's appearance at the later of these meetings and at a huge demonstration on Glasgow Green the Saturday following the food riots marked his progress past the point of no return, as he recognized. 'When I took my ticket at Euston and came here', he told an assembly of his Liberal supporters a few days later, 'I knew I was leaving behind me every chance of rising in political life. What had I, a landlord, to gain by championing the working class? I had everything to lose.' But, he told them, he found the miners in a worse position than he could have believed. 'Would you have me say to these poor starving fellows that I could do nothing for them?' And so he did what he thought best in the course of which he brought down upon his head bitter recriminations. (44).

As far as is known Saturday, 13 February was his first appearance as a speaker in Glasgow's only public forum, though 'roaring on the Green' as he put it, was to become a regular habit in the next few years. He stood accountable for advice that many condemned as rash, and dangerously subversive. 'Having gone so far, having passed through so much misery, if you feel you can you should go on to the bitter end', he told the miners; 'if not you should give in quickly to avoid further suffering.' They had as much right to band together to keep wages up as the masters had to band together to keep them down. This declaration caused the 'classes' to accuse him of making the miners' position worse; there was a real danger that the ironmasters, faced with an increase in the price of their raw material would cut the rate of smelting so that the cause would collapse under tons of unsold coal. Yet his rhetoric was accompanied by some practical suggestions. He proposed a conference to be attended by delegates from every mining district that would draft legislation putting an end to mineral royalties - 'a shameful tax upon communities'. He thought the miners ought to agree a sliding scale of wages with the employers - 5s a day was his figure - more if the miners wanted it; '5s is hardly gorgeous for men toiling eight hours a day in the bowels of the earth'. This speech, widely reported in the press, was condemned, particularly in the industrial Midlands, whose masters jibbed at his frequent reference to rights. Worse was to come. (45).

Four days after the rally on Glasgow Green (which was organised by the local branch of the Socialist League), Robert attended a meeting at Bellshill of the Lanarkshire Miners Association. The principal speaker was its secretary, William Small, who, as miners' agent in Blantyre had witnessed the worst effects of the long drawn out dispute, the riots, and the arrests that followed. His language was bitter. He exhorted the miners' delegates to adopt the same method of self help and direct action as the Irish were currently using under the Plan of Campaign. Instead of watching their families starve the miners should go in a body to the magistrates and ask to be fed. If help was refused they should occupy the prisons and workhouses. Then in a very short time the coalmasters would go down on their knees and ask the miners, For God's sake, return to work. Small assured his audience that 'dynamite was abroad 'the Airdrie Advertiser reported, and 'before many days Scottish miners would raise such a revolution as was never seen in Scotland'. If the old laws were honoured, Small added, the masters would already be in prison as thieves; 'what they needed was Home Rule for Scotland, the sooner they had it the better for all concerned'.(46)

Small went on to announce that arrangements had been made for Michael Davitt to address a series of meetings in Lanarkshire. This was bound to be unwelcome news at Westminster where the Government was still grappling with serious disturbances in Ireland arising from the operation of the Plan of Campaign. Even without Small's (probably fictitious) dynamite, the equation of Davitt and Coatbridge was worrying. During the 1870s suspicion fell upon the Irish population of the town as giving aid and comfort to members of the Fenian conspiracy. In 1870 Davitt had been sentenced to 15 years in prison for taking part in that conspiracy to overthrow British rule in Ireland , of which he served seven in Dartmoor before being released on ticket of leave. As a result of his recent appearances at Crofters Party election meetings his influence was no longer confined to the Irish community in the West of Scotland but was increasingly acknowledged by all those who supported the Highlanders in the fight against their landlords. It was Davitt's passionate belief that if working people would only make common cause they would soon alter the system of government. (47). As if the promise of his imminent arrival was not enough, Small also announced that , the following week, miners would parade in Airdrie, Coatbridge, Hamilton and other towns in Lanarkshire, carrying picks. The dramatic nature of his remarks obscured the fact that, at this same meeting, Robert Cunninghame Graham urged the delegates to negotiate; in spite of his conciliatory remarks he, too, was accused of 'preaching dynamite'. Undeterred , he proceeded to make a round of pits in the neighbourhood when he made his first descent underground. His guide on this occasion was James Keir Hardie. As the dispute dragged on they were much in each other's company. They were together, for instance, at the meeting of the Scottish Miners' Federation in Glasgow on Monday, 21 February, when delegates discussed calling a stoppage lasting three weeks over the whole of Scotland whose object would be to compel the Government to establish a council for miners' wages.(48)

As they soon discovered, the plain truth was they did not have the means to compel any such concession. The best they could do was to recommend the miners return to work on the understanding that the masters would agree to a conference to fix a scale for wages. Graham, who urged them not to compromise their interest by any show of force, or lawlessness of any kind, supported this. The motion to resume work was proposed by William Small. In view of the inequality of the struggle of starvation against plenty, going back would be on the masters' terms, he said. They would go back as an organized body and recruit reinforcements to the union in order , if necessary, to resume the struggle at an early date. His motion denounced the iniquitous system that condemned the miners to a life of privation while the idle classes lived in comfort. By it the miners pledged themselves to educate their members and agitate until the system was removed. This motion, supported by John Bruce Glasier of the Glasgow branch of the Socialist League (motto; educate, agitate, organise) who was present, was passed unanimously. (49).

When the meeting was over Robert went back to London having promised he would champion the miners' cause in the House of Commons. 'He assured them that he had learned much from his interviews with the Lanarkshire men', the <u>Airdrie Advertiser</u> reported; 'and that the result of these would help him much in consideration of political subjects'.(50), These words were well chosen, as his conduct throughout the crisis had been well judged. It won him the respect of men who, because of their life underground had been regarded until quite recently as outside the law, and who still lived very much to themselves. Robert was accepted by them as, previously, he had been accepted by another isolated, idiosyncratic group - the gauchos of the Argentine (51). As far as the Lanarkshire miners were concerned this was due to the nature of his approach to them, described by a young socialist admirer as 'openness of mind, breadth of view, sanity, and discipline' (52). Robert kept his promise to do his best for the miners though the cost in fortune, health, and the happiness of himself and Gabrielle was greater than he could have imagined at the time.

Notes to Chapter Seven

1. Austin: Gab. to M. Evans; 13 Dec. 1885.
2. SRO; GD 22/IV/36, Notes by Sir Angus Cunninghame Graham.
3. NLS;7282/20, 21 Dec. 1885 and 2 Feb. 1886; SRO; GD 22/77/260
4. 'Annual Register', 1886.
5. Burgess, J., 'John Burns: The Rise and Progress of a Rt. Honourable', The Reformers Bookstall, Glasgow, 1911. Note. For evidence that the Fair Traders were financed by the Conservatives, see below, Chapter Nine, p.182.
6. ibid., pp 45,56.
7. Critchley, T.A., 'The Conquest of Violence', Constable, 1970, p.74.
8. Burgess, op.cit., p. 68.
9. Shaw, Bernard, 'Pen Portraits and Reviews', Constable, 1949, p.133.
10. Bax, E.Belfort, 'Reminiscences and Reflexions', Allen & Unwin, 1918, p.280.
11. The best account of Champion is in Pelling, H.; 'Henry Champion, Pioneer of the Labour Party', Cambridge Journal VI, 1953.
12. Douglas, George, 'The House with Green Shutters', The World's Classics, 1938,
13. Champion's reminiscences in the Trident, Melbourne, 1908.
14. ibid.
15. Pelling, H., 'Origins of the Labour Party 1880 - 1900' Macmillan, 1954, pp, 34,35.
16. Cambridge Journal, VI, 1953.
17. Cunningham, Glen, R., 'Reports of cases in Criminal Law, XVI, 1886 - 1890', Horace Cox, 1890.
18. Laurence, Dan H., ed. 'Bernard Shaw Collected Letters 1874-1897', Max Reinhardt, 1965, p. 122.
19. See, for example, Jenkins, R., 'Gladstone',Macmillan,1995, p 556.
20. Airdrie Advertiser, 19 June 1886.
21. ibid., 26 June 1886.
22. ibid.
23. Quoted in Jenkins, R., op.cit., p. 558.
24. Cunninghame Graham, R.B., Salvagia in 'The Ipane', op.cit., pp 188-203.
25. Airdrie Advertiser, 9 July 1886.
26. Rhodes James, R., 'A Biography of Archibald Primrose, 5th Earl of Rosebery', Weidenfeld and Nicolson, 1963, p. 91.
27. Bensusan, S.L., 'Don Roberto', in Quarterly Review, April 1938.
28. Airdrie Advertiser, - Aug. 1886.
29. Austin, Gab. to Mrs Evans, - July 1886.
30. Airdrie Advertiser, - Aug. 1886
31. Note By allowing MPs to affirm Mr Speaker Peel put an end to 6 years of agonized debate during which Bradlaugh had been repeatedly excluded from the House though consistently re-elected as MP for Northampton.
32. Hansard 3rd Series Vol. CCCX , 10.
33. Airdrie Advertiser, 2 Oct. 1886.
34. NLS, Acc.11335/52, Charlotte Cunninghame Graham to RBCG, — 1886.

35. Austin; Gab. to M. Evans, 2 Dec. 1886.
36. Cunninghame Graham, R.B., 'A Memory of Parnell in 'Thirty Tales and Sketches', op.cit., pp 186 - 196.
37. Tschiffely, op.cit., p. 207.
38. Hansard, 3rd Series, CCCX, 3 - 6.
39. ibid., 441 - 445.
40. <u>Vanity Fair</u>, 5 Feb. 1887.
41. the <u>Trident</u>, 1908.
42. <u>Airdrie Advertiser</u>, 5 Feb. 1887.
43. ibid., 12 and 19 Feb. 1887.
44. ibid., 26 Feb. 1887.
45. ibid., 19 Feb. 1887.
46. ibid.
47. Moody,T.W., 'Michael Davitt and the British Labour Movement', Royal Historical Society, 5th Series, 3, 1953.
48. <u>Airdrie Advertiser</u>, 26 Feb 1887.
49. ibid.
50. ibid.
51. See for example, Campbell, A.B., 'The Lanarkshire Miners A Social History of their Trades Unions 1775 - 1874', J. Donald, 1979, intro.
52. Finger, C., 'Seven Horizons', Doubleday Doran, 1930, p. 181.

Chapter Eight

Politician

'Tinkering can do little good. The system must be changed. Still I propose to venture', (1), Robert noted in the margin of one of the Parliamentary blue books that landed on his desk. His purpose was to to bring about a greater measure of social justice, not only for the miners, but in the country at large, acting alone if necessary. He was already privately contemptuous of the Liberal Party; he felt it had lost its way (after he was no longer a MP he described his erstwhile colleagues as 'an amorphous crowd of Nonconformists, Temperance Reformers, deceased Wife's Sister's Monomaniacs and Single Taxers - the dried fruit of outworn politics stranded like jellyfish on a beach') (2). He paid little attention to the Whips and was seldom in the smoking room. His potential allies lay beyond the pale of Westminster, and before the crisis had occurred in Lanarkshire he was in touch with the most influential of them. 'The day Parliament met', William Morris noted in his diary, 'a young and new MP, Cunninghame Graham by name, called on me to pump me on the subject of socialism. We had an agreeable talk'. (3). Much was to flow from this encounter with the man whose interpretation of the Icelandic sagas had provided Robert with a philosophy - of failure dignified by courage, and hardship born with equanimity - that had consoled him at a particularly difficult period of his life.

Morris was then at mid point in his self imposed task of proclaiming the social revolution: an epic undertaking requiring a prodigal expenditure of time, energy, and, not least, money. As the Norsemen had he foresaw a violent end to the world as it was known. Constantly, by lecturing and writing, he drew attention to the particular threat posed by the increasing demands of commerce to man' s fragile relationship with the world around him. Unless equilibrium was restored by men producing what they needed - and no more - the balance of nature would be irrevocably destroyed. One sentence said it all. Under capitalism, Morris lamented the country was 'in part a cinder heap, in part a game reserve when it ought to be a fair green garden.' (4). This was a view to which Robert Cunninghame Graham already subscribed; now he felt he was in a position to do something positive about it. Catching the Speaker's eye on 17 February he condemned the proposal to build a railway from Windermere to Ambleside in the Lake District in terms that echoed those of Morris in the latest <u>Commonweal</u>. Don't destroy one of the country's most beautiful areas for the sake of a railway no one wants, he pleaded; buy the land instead and preserve it for the nation. His effort failed, albeit narrowly, the enabling Bill received a second reading by only 12 votes (5).

Morris had not expected any other outcome. To him Parliament was an institution designed to prevent things being done: a place where cowardice, irresolution, chicanery, and downright lies were constantly in action. 'Parliament exists for the definite purpose of continuing the present evil state of things', he told his friend, Fred Pickles.(6). His temper was not improved by having to decipher letters originating from the House of Commons, a place he warned his followers to avoid. 'I have just had a letter from the MP again', he grumbled to his daughter on 19 February (at the height of the Lanarkshire miners' crisis). 'It is headed, 'private' and 'most confidential' but...it is so badly written that it takes three strong men to read it'. (7). And four weeks later, writing to John Bruce Glasier, Morris remarked, 'Cunninghame Graham is a very queer creature and I can't easily make him out: he seems ambitious and has some decent information.' But, he added, 'I am almost afraid that a man who writes such preposterous illegible scrawl as he does must have a screw loose in him'.(8).

Morris and Glasier were arranging a series of lectures to be given by Morris in Scotland which, so far, had proved a promising field for socialist views. Invited to take the chair at the lecture arranged for Glasgow on 3 April, Robert wavered; though flattered he feared the sensation his appearance would create in North West Lanarkshire; partly because his involvement with socialism was rapidly becoming a controversial issue there; mostly because 3 April was a Sunday. After due consideration he refused the invitation, only to change his mind and turn up after all. The meeting at the Waterloo Rooms in Glasgow attracted about 1,000 people who paid to hear Morris lecture on 'A True or False Society'. Afterwards the Commonweal hailed it as an unique occasion. 'For the first time in the history of Scotland a Scottish MP took part in a political meeting held on a Sunday, and for the first time in the history of Britain, a British MP presided at a Socialist meeting.' (9).

Sketch of Graham by George Washington Lambert. National Portrait Gallery, London.

Morris saluted Robert's courage in publicly flouting the rigours of the Scottish Sabbath. And the latter's performance in the chair on this occasion also won him marks for ease of manner, knowledge, and, as always, wit. Henceforth he was in high demand as chairman at the political gatherings he now began regularly to attend; a man, according to Joseph Burgess, more unlike the typical representative of Labour, it would not be possible to imagine. 'One of the handsomest men of his generation, he might have stepped right out of a canvas by Velasquez', Burgess wrote. 'He was a tall, lithe young man, browned by exposure on the grassy plains of Mexico where he had spent some years ranching, and generally dressed in a suit of brown Melton cloth. His clothes were fashionably cut; he stood erect on somewhat long feet, and he had a habit, as he spoke, of running his aristocratic hands through a thick crop of upstanding dark hair. His face was long and thin, the length accentuated by the high narrow forehead and the pointed brown beard, and he had intuitive eyes which burned and glowed with animation.' (10). The first time the 18 year old Charles Finger, a member of the SDF rank and file, saw Cunninghame Graham was in April 1887 at a meeting to protest against the verdict in the trial of the so-called Chicago Seven. In the course of a demonstration in that city calling for the introduction of the 8 hour working day, a bomb had exploded, killing seven policemen. Though they had not planted it, seven known anarchists were arrested, tried, and sentenced to death. Cunninghame Graham joined William Morris, Annie Besant, the Christian Socialist, Stuart Headlam; the Russian anarchist, Prince Kropotkin, and other leaders of the SDF and the Socialist League in asking the US Supreme Court to grant a reprieve. When he spoke he called attention to the threat to free speech in the Chicago verdict: if guilt by association were ever the rule in England no political activist would be safe from prosecution. And he argued passionately in favour of the eight hour day as the only means of giving back working men sufficient time and energy to educate themselves - as they must if they were ever to govern themselves. The young Charles Finger was thrilled by his performance; many years later Robert's air of vigorous good health and his courteous manner were still fresh in his memory. What impressed him most was his utter sincerity which he compared to that of his other hero, William Morris. (11). The two were well matched. Both were splendidly gifted, sensitive, and compassionate men, but volatile; provoked to short lived fury by foolishness, ignorance and apathy on the part of their fellow human beings. Both were dauntless and strongminded - chivalrous was the word that came most often to the minds of their admirers. Finger thought of Cunninghame Graham accoutred as for battle; 'brandishing a shining sword'; while in describing William Morris Edward Burne Jones put into words a painted image from his medieval landscapes; to him Morris was' a rock of defence to his friends, and a castle on top of that, and a banner on top of that'. (12). As we have already seen, those who observed Robert from a more distant perspective questioned the seriousness of his motives, suspicious of dilletantism. They were confounded when, over the next few months, no one protested more strongly against the repressive measures employed by politicians lost for any constructive solution to sporadic political unrest and continuing widespread economic misery.

Charles Finger, who was active from the beginning of the conflict in 1885, left a perceptive account of how tempers deteriorated. In the beginning, 'the question of unemployment loomed large and...we gloried in every new shut down and lock out and strike. In me and others likeminded were blissful yearnings for the grand smash up. So we rounded up unemployed men, not questioning them very narrowly as to their economic condition and paraded them in a straggly way through the streets carrying banners. The police occasionally contributed a surly 'mustn't stand here'. Sometimes they trod on the heels of those who were defiantly slow to move on. That led to small violence of a mild and Pickwickian kind, to thrustings and elbowings and pushing and threatening and now and then to an arrest'. According to Finger, in the early days the crowd treated the moving on tactics almost as a game. ..' peripatetic orators ...made speeches and framed resolutions to be put to the vote while on the move in front of the police. A meeting might begin near the National Gallery and finish on the corner of Northumberland Avenue'. Then, in September 1885 a moment came when the police cracked down harder than before. This occurred in Dod Street, in Limehouse, one of the principal outdoor meeting places of the SDF. Finger said tempers were under control until someone knocked a policeman's hat off when violence set in for, 'to deprive an Englishman of his head covering is to strike at the root of human endurance . I saw a mighty swaying, a falling of banners, heard the clash of broken glass, yelling, and screaming. The crowd opened up and the police marched off with prisoners. The others ran off, fearful of being identified.' (13). Eight men came up at Thames Magistrates Court where the justice presiding, Mr Saunders, was notoriously fierce. He sentenced one man to two months in prison with hard labour; others were fined 40s or a month's detention. Thus a precedent was created to be followed by other magistrates. The hardship inflicted on wives and children was so great that socialists and radicals were moved jointly to form a Vigilance Association with delegates from the SDF, the Socialist League, Bradlaugh's National Secular Society, the Irish National League and several of the many working men's clubs in the East End. Annie Besant, Vice President of the National Secular Society, one of the most famous speakers of the day, played a leading role. Whenever men were brought up before the magistrates she alerted members to provide bail at short notice. Otherwise those who could not afford it - it was often as much as £50 - went to jail pending the next hearing, leaving their wives and children destitute.

Robert Cunninghame Graham's recruitment to their ranks provided the activists with an alternative means of fighting back - the Parliamentary question. In 1887, with the approach of summer, the situation in the East End deteriorated; socialists who had held meetings without incident during the cold weather now encountered local inhabitants bent on repossessing their own streets. As the Home Secretary later told the House of Commons, the locals objected to their politics, disliked their presence and were unmoved by their eloquence. Matters came to a head in Sancroft Street in Kennington on Sunday, 1 May. The SDF were in the middle of a meeting when a crowd estimated at more than 2,000 was seen to be advancing. The police ordered the SDF to disperse; when they stood their ground the police chased everyone away, and made several arrests. On 3 May Cunninghame Graham asked the Home Secretary 'if the police have special powers to break up Socialist meetings, or if they act in their own authority in so doing?' The reply was a categorical denial; 'the police have received no special instructions of any kind'.(14) In the course of the next week both sides swore to occupy Sancroft Street the following Sunday when the SDF forecast a battle and promised to provide its members with boxes of cartridges. Came the day and the Socialists found themselves face to face with what all parties agreed was a gang of roughs advancing under the banner of 'The Lambeth Anti Socialist Primrose Society'. (15) The police, this time present in strength, ordered the SDF to call off the meeting; its leaders refused, whereupon Sancroft Street was cleared. This order purporting to ban the SDF meeting in advance, and before any violence had occurred, gave rise to widespread misgiving. Many people who were far from sympathetic to the agitators, nevertheless condemned the ban as unlawful; regarding it as a misuse of police authority. Their apprehension prompted a full scale Commons debate on public meetings in the metropolis which took place on 12 May. (16).

This debate and Robert Cunninghame Graham's contribution to it has to be read against the background of events in Ireland where the disturbances consequent upon the implementation of the Plan of Campaign had forced the Conservative government to sanction draconian measures of repression. The necessity for the Bill now before Parliament, was a cause of bitter regret to many Conservatives and it was the object of a fierce attack by members of the Liberal Party. Gladstone called it 'narrow, dark, destructive, retrogressive'. (17). The divided state of society prevailing at the time was addressed by Edward Pickersgill, MP for Bethnal Green South West, when he told the House on 12 May; 'the conduct of the police in itself is serious enough; but it does not stand alone. There are upon many sides indications of an attempt on the part of the privileged classes to put the people down. There is... a spirit of coercion in the air which finds its chief embodiment in a Bill upon which much of our time in this session has been expended, and which also takes on many other forms. We see it in the Boycotting and intimidation which is practised by the Primrose Party, and one cannot travel...in a carriage on a suburban railway without hearing expressions in the same spirit in the terms in which readers of the Globe and the St James Gazette refer to their fellow citizens, terms which I do not hesitate to characterize as inhuman and most unwise'.(18). If this was a timely warning to MPs that the situation must not be allowed to deteriorate further, Cunninghame Graham, who followed Pickersgill, sounded an alarm. His speech was bitterly sarcastic and contemptuous of ministers sitting opposite, and it was delivered in a passion that left the House gasping. He began by stating his belief that Socialist gatherings had been dispersed because those attending them were poor, because their doctrines were not popular and no one cared to stand up and incur the odium of speaking for them. 'England is a free country - thanks to Heaven. It is a free country for a man to starve in - that is a boon you can never take away from him - but it appears in the future it is not going to be a free country to hold public meetings in. What with the closure in the House of Commons, coercion in Ireland, and the suppression of meetings in London we are getting to an almost Russian pitch of freedom. And Sir, should we succeed in arriving at the priceless boon of that freedom we cannot wonder if the people at last shake themselves clear of their apathy and take the matter a little into their own hands. I do not suggest the people of England are ripe for revolution yet; they will be soon enough, especially in the face of the Bills which are now presented to the House, but I ....can see no just motive whatever that - because a man's doctrine or political faith differs in some measure from that held by the rest of the community, free speech which has always been considered the birthright of the Englishman should be denied to him'. He did not criticize the police; they were obliged to do the dirty work of breaking up meetings, work that was repugnant to them. 'Now I think that every Member of this House knows Buffalo Bill - Colonel Cody [whose Wild West show was playing to huge crowds in London at the time] I would suggest very respectfully ...that a select deputation of the Unionist Party should wait upon Colonel Cody to ask for the loan of a few thoroughbred Unionist Indians to coerce the people of London'.(19)

This last suggestion seemed to have no other purpose than to remind the House that here was a man who had ridden with Buffalo Bill Cody, herded cattle on the Texas ranges, and was acquainted with real, not stage, Indians. That it would incur the charge of playing to the gallery - 'making a figure 'was how the <u>Airdrie Advertiser</u> more politely put it - seems not to have occurred to Robert who had not yet grasped the effect his colourful personality and forceful language had upon his audiences. This flaw in his armour was seized on by his enemies who were increasingly concerned to destroy his credibility with the 'masses'. His rare self confidence was portrayed as evidence of an inflated ego, and his justifiable indignation at the parlous state of things, as evidence of the manic disposition he was accused of having inherited from his father.

The Home Secretary ,who spoke directly after him, left the House in no doubt of his distaste for Graham's intemperate language. Henry Matthews rejected any suggestion that he was biased against Socialists or that special instructions had been given to the police. The position as to public order remained as it always had been; the First Commissioner of Police was solely responsible for whatever measures needed to be taken. (20). This confirmation of Sir Charles Warren's powers came a few weeks before London was due to play host to the thousands who flocked to celebrate Queen Victoria's Golden Jubilee. When it occurred in June Warren was perceived to have taken such a grip upon the capital whose streets were lined with thousands of police and special constables, he was compared to the greatest autocrat of all, the Tsar of Russia. Similar - unflattering - comparisons dogged the government during the passage through Parliament of the Irish Crimes Bill. When the Liberals of Coatbridge held a meeting to oppose the Bill at which Robert Cunninghame Graham introduced the principal speaker, (John O'Connor, MP for Tipperary). he was received with huge applause. Far down the list , seconding the vote of thanks, appeared the name of James Keir Hardie, agent for the Ayrshire miners (21). By this time Graham and Hardie had become virtually inseparable in so far as their political activity was concerned. As Bruce Glasier put it, for the next few years 'they went about in harness'. Their alliance was one of the more hopeful developments in an otherwise unpromising situation for miners in the West of Scotland.

The prolonged strike culminating in the Blantyre food riots had produced no lasting improvement in their state. The cut in their pay was restored but only for a few months. By June 1887, with the demand for coal at Glasgow at its lowest for six years ,the coalmasters again docked 6d a day from their wages. In the circumstances of continuing industrial depression the only hope of better conditions lay in the Coal Mines Regulation Bill which began its progress through Parliament in the spring. It had over 50 clauses aimed at revising the rules governing such matters as the provision of lamps, the placing of shafts, the availability of plans showing the changing position of the coal face, the appointment of inspectors, and the need for these men to be truly independent. Because the Bill was a measure introduced by the Liberal opposition with the support of the Irish MPs it was for the Home Secretary to say whether the Government would accept or reject each clause. A yawning gulf was demonstrated to exist at the committee stage between, on the one hand, the Lib Lab MPs - Thomas Burt, William Abraham (called Mabon), Henry Broadhurst and Charles Fenwick - speaking on behalf of the English and Welsh miners - trades union men jealous of their ability to look after their own interests; on the other the Scots; Donald Crawford, Robert Cunninghame Graham and Stephen Mason, MPs for, respectively, North East, North West and Mid Lanark where the miners were still a long way from effective organisation. There, as a sympathetic Irish MP put it, the mines were large concerns, their owners strangers to compassion; 'they make the hardest possible terms with their employés'.(22) Some of the conditions were manifestly unjust, for example the convention whereby they had to supply 22 1/2 cwt to the ton, not 20. Robert Cunninghame Graham asked Matthews whether the new Bill would put an end to this practice which deprived the men of the full reward for their labour. The reply was that such a practice, if it was imposed on the workforce, was already prohibited under existing law. If, on the other hand, miners entered <u>voluntarily</u> into such an arrangement, there was nothing Parliament could do about it.(23)

How willing were these so-called volunteers; what choice did the miners have? This was the kind of awkward question the MP for North West Lanarkshire never shrank from addressing for fear of causing offence. The Commons were discussing the Scots miners' demand that two inspectors be chosen from among their number to examine safety measures in each mine. In drawing attention to the fact that they specially insisted that these inspectors must not be employed in the mine they were to examine, Robert Cunninghame Graham underlined a fact that had been conveniently ignored. His purpose was not to insinuate that the mine owners might be guilty of intimidation, he said, but human nature being what it was he had to warn the House to take the Scots miners' recommendation very seriously. It was not safe to let men review measures in the mine where they worked because 'there are those who have been accustomed all their lives to treat their managers and owners as a sort of superior being and they cannot bring themselves to act contrary to their wishes even when they know justice and right are on their side'. At this very moment the need for more stringent safety measures was tragically demonstrated when on 27 May a huge explosion at Udston colliery, a few miles from Coatbridge, caused the deaths of 74 miners. As the Airdrie Advertiser put it, the explosion (due to fire damp) 'made' 27 widows and 80 orphans (24). An unspecified number of pit ponies also died in this explosion, adding weight to Robert's plea for their better treatment to be written in to the Bill. They were at risk not only from explosions and roof falls, but from overwork and lack of water - in the course of time many had died from thirst. He detested the need for animals to work underground. If he could he would have brought them up out of the dark as he had rescued Pampa from the shafts of the Glasgow tram.

This strong impulse towards freedom lay at the heart of his involvement with the eight hour working day, the cause that preoccupied him above all others in these parliamentary years. To set a limit to the hours men were obliged to work to earn a reasonable wage was to liberate them; to give them a precious commodity - time - to secure the quality of life as all men had a right to know it. He was at one with William Morris when he declared 'I do not want art for a few, any more than education for a few, or freedom for a few' (25). The eight hours movement was slowly gaining ground in Scotland. The first time in his life Keir Hardie went to London was to lobby for this cause. He and his colleagues from the Scottish Miners' Federation received a warm welcome at the Commons from Cunninghame Graham and the two other Lanarkshire MPs. But they were an embarrassment to the Lib Labs - Burt, Mabon, Broadhurst and Fenwick - who did not want a clause stipulating an eight hour day included in the Bill but did not want to say so. Their prevarication during the first stage of the discussion caused the clause to fail. When a second opportunity arose later in the summer Henry Broadhurst, MP for West Nottingham, Chairman of the TUC, told the House he would not vote for the reintroduction of the clause. He was in favour of an eight hour day when it could be obtained by agreement with the employer. 'But the question is whether the State is to be called on to do for the miners what they are perfectly able to do for themselves. If we ask the State to regulate the hours of labour for adults, we shall afterwards have to ask for State interference in the matter of wages, and then we may have to ask the State to intervene to settle how wages are to be expended. To support this proposal would be to condemn the whole system of trades unionism which is one of the great triumphs won by labour in this country'. (26).

State intervention was anathema to Liberals and Broadhurst was paraded at elections at the very model of a Liberal working man. Bradlaugh, a giant by comparison, was beholden to no party but he, too, savaged the proposals in a speech that betrayed the full measure of his dislike of the socialists who supported it whom he described as 'those who encourage men to rely on Parliament to do for them what they ought to do for themselves' (27). Robert Cunninghame Graham was moved to fury by these speeches; his protective instinct was aroused; he never forgave Henry Broadhurst for, in his opinion, abdicating his responsibility as a union leader. So, when he rose he vehemently denied the suggestion that many Scots were not in favour of State interference with hours of labour in mines. They had no time to organize themselves as it was said they should; 'are our men to be pushed, day by day to starvation while this organisation is growing up? ... You talk of freedom and say we are not to interfere with adult labour, but how otherwise are we to interfere between the rich and poor man? Your freedom of contract is all on one side...If all the miners had the same mental power as the Member for Northampton (Bradlaugh, that epitome of a self educated man), I should be the last to ask for State interference but these men stand in a vastly different position and I say that it is not in their interest alone but in that of employers that the eight hour system should become law'. The proposal was a moderate one and would be carried sooner or later, he warned the House. 'I can tell [the Home Secretary] they look forward to the time when the Government will take over the mines and machinery and work them for the benefit of the people and not for the selfish ends of a few capitalists'. Laughter and cheers greeted this peroration; in all probability the first time nationalization of the coal mining industry was taken seriously by anyone in the House of Commons. (28).

The amendment in favour of the eight hour day was lost by 171 votes to 81, a disappointing result to those who had supported it, but far from the humiliation Robert's enemies represented it to be. During the Bill's progress he made altogether 19 interventions on behalf of better conditions for the miners which his colleagues on the Opposition benches treated with respect. But his efforts were singled out for ridicule by a London daily paper whose Parliamentary sketch for 17 August was headed 'Mr Cunninghame Graham's eccentricities" Its reproduction, three days later, in the <u>Airdrie Advertiser</u> damaged his standing in the constituency : it made him out to be ignorant as well as awkward; a hobbledehoy whose influence in Parliament counted for very little. The paper described him as making frantic efforts to figure in the discussion of the Bill, to which end he rushed wildly about the lobby, 'always bareheaded, at a pace seldom seen in Parliamentary circles' and, when in the Chamber bobbed anxiously up and down in a vain attempt to speak. Eventually the Chairman of Committees, (who was presiding at this stage) accused him of having no idea of the correct procedure, and asked him to sit down. After that rare rebuke, the paper said, 'the MP for North West Lanarkshire vanished like a bubble that is blown upon'. (29).

Embarrassment was not the cause of this sudden exit; Robert had other urgent things to do. He had become closely involved in an attempt to save the life of a young Jewish man condemned to hang for a most brutal murder. The execution was fixed for Monday, 22 August; by the time the sketch appeared four days at most were left in which to obtain a reprieve. Graham's rapid progress through the lobby, his impatient efforts to catch the Speaker's eye; his obvious agitation were dictated by the horror of a situation that threatened to overwhelm all those caught up in it. The condemned man was a 22 year old Pole, Israel Lipski, who had arrived in the East End of London from Warsaw two years previously, one of thousands of Jews fleeing persecution on the Continent. On 28 June he had been discovered unconscious under the bed of Miriam Angel, also from Warsaw, a married woman who was judged to have died from suffocation as a result of having had nitric acid poured down her throat. A postmortem examination produced evidence, albeit inconclusive, that she had been raped. Lipski, who occupied a room in the same lodging house in

Whitechapel as Mrs Angel and her husband, had also swallowed nitric acid, though not a fatal dose. Those who came to see why Mrs Angel had not appeared at her usual time (her husband having gone out early) were obliged to force the door of the room which appeared to have been locked from the inside. At the trial which took place on 29 and 30 July before Mr Justice Fitzjames Stephen, the prosecution alleged that Lipski's motive had been robbery and/or a sudden impulse of lust produced by the sight of Mrs Angel lying on her bed by means of a small window on the stairs leading to his room. Lipski who pleaded not guilty claimed that the murder had been committed by men known to him whom he named. Having killed Mrs Angel, he said, they attacked him and fled, leaving him to be discovered at the scene.

Lipski was found guilty on 30 July and sentenced to hang two weeks later. The verdict was greeted by an outburst of fury and revulsion prompted by the unprecedented revelation in the Pall Mall Gazette that, no sooner had he doffed the black cap, than the judge began to doubt whether Lipski was the murderer. 'I have never known a worse or more curious case', Mr Justice Fitzjames Stephen wrote to his wife during the days he was obliged to remain in London pending the Home Secretary's response to requests for a reprieve. These were orchestrated by W.T. Stead, the Pall Mall's Editor. He and his supporters were much encouraged when Robert Cunninghame Graham published his belief that Lipski was innocent. On Saturday, 13 August he put down a question to the Home Secretary drawing attention to the doubt attributed to Fitzjames Stephen which had appeared in the Pall Mall Gazette of the previous day. This put extra pressure on Matthews who was also under attack by Lipski's solicitor who did not accept the verdict. That afternoon Robert was one of a number of MPs who met Mattthews and his Permanent Secretary, Godfrey Lushington, when the Home Secretary assured those present 'he would keep his mind open to the last moment and would not allow the law to take its course if he saw the slightest grounds for altering his decision'.

Unease about the irreversible nature of the sentence was widespread. Lipski impressed all who met him as a particularly upright and straightforward young man whose assertion of innocence had the ring of truth about it. The manner in which the case had been conducted also aroused considerable misgiving. To go into detail here would be to confuse the reader who is referred to the brilliantly argued account of the trial and its effect upon public opinion in 'The Trials of Israel Lipski' by Martin Friedland. (30). A third cause of anxiety; one to which Robert Cunninghame Graham drew particular attention when pleading for a reprieve, was the fact that Lipski and many of the witnesses barely understood English. Their evidence at the trial was given in a mixture of Yiddish and Polish and all transactions had to be translated. Although Mr Justice Stephen angrily rejected the Pall Mall's report that he had doubts about the case, the Saturday before the Monday when Lipski was due to be hanged, he sent a long telegram to the Home Secretary suggesting a week's respite. To his wife he wrote;...' have decided to return to town tomorrow, after thinking over and over Lipski's case. I decided at last ..to telegraph to Matthews to respite the man for a week; to satisfy the public and avoid the appearance of haste. I do not doubt the man's guilt' '(31).

Robert Cunninghame Graham lost no time in making use of the extra seven days. In circulating a petition to MPs he did not ask for a full pardon but for the sentence to be commuted to one of life imprisonment on the grounds that the prosecution had failed to prove beyond reasonable doubt that Lipski was the murderer. The response encouraged him. 'With barely two hundred MPs in town I have been able in two days to get a petition signed by 78 Members representing all shades of political opinion', he told the Jewish World.(32). By Friday evening, when it was given to Matthews, 110 MPs had signed, including Charles Parnell. However not one of the seven recently elected Jewish MPs put his name to it. Graham kept up the pressure in the Commons by asking Matthews that same evening if the respite would be extended. Matthews answered No. Graham then asked if, in view of the petition by MPs he would reconsider that decision? Matthews again answered No. 'I must formally protest against interference with the normal course of the administration of justice by questions in the House' he said. (33). This appeal for protection was supported by loud cheers, a hint Graham chose to ignore. The next day, Saturday (the House was sitting due to pressure of business), he presented a second petition he had organized in Whitechapel and surrounding districts with 2,000 signatures; 'praying for a further respite for the condemned man, Lipski'. Matthews was not in the Chamber but the Leader of the House, W.H. Smith, rose to protest against what he called further harassment of the Home Secretary who, he said, was 'acting on a deep sense of his own responsibility.' Courtney, Chairman of Committees then expressed surprise at Graham's bringing the petition to the Commons when it was addressed to a particular Minister. At that the Speaker intervened: if what Courtney said was true the petition was altogether irregular and no notice could be taken of it. Robert apologized; 'May I enquire what course I have to adopt?' Courtney's response was to remove the petition from the table and hand it back to him. Unabashed he hurried off to Hatfield House to argue the case with the Prime Minister (34). but Salisbury who had no desire to become embroiled in a crisis that had escalated to the point where it threatened the reputation of his Home Secretary, refused to see him. (35).

The danger to Matthews lay in the possibility that if he allowed the execution to proceed, some new fact might afterwards emerge casting further doubt on the justice of the sentence, or even, proving Lipski's innocence. Professor Friedland emphasizes how little was known of the persons concerned. 'What is patent to everybody is that the case is now involved in too much uncertainty to make the execution of the prisoner at all safe', the Daily Telegraph wrote. The Methodist Times considered it morally impossible to hang him, while the Jewish press, without exception called for a reprieve. There was a risk that, as the time for Lipski to be hanged approached, tension would erupt in demonstrations. The trial had renewed public disquiet at the appalling conditions under which East Enders were obliged to live. The exceptionally harsh winter of 1886/87 had come at the end of a three year period that one economist has described as probably the worse continuous sequence of unemployment before the First World War. (36). The fact that those born there had now to compete for jobs with a rapidly increasing number of Jewish refugees aroused fears - openly expressed in the Pall Mall Gazette - that the incomers might encounter the kind of systematic persecution they had already suffered in Russia and in Poland.

On Sunday, 21 August Matthews and Fitzjames Stephen were together all day at the Home Office struggling to decide whether Lipski should hang the next morning, or his sentence be commuted to penal servitude for life. At 5 p.m. their predicament was sensationally resolved with the arrival of a confession signed by Lipski. We do not know how Robert took the news. Shock mingled with disgust at the procedure which must now follow, probably struck him even before pity for the condemned man. He was familiar with death inflicted as revenge or retribution: he had seen men shot in South America. But compared with the gruesome ritual of 'the law taking its course' which now began in Newgate Prison, culminating in the execution at 8 a.m. on Monday, 22 August, their end was enviably swift. An Editorial in the Commonweal over the names of William Morris and Ernest Belfort Bax probably expressed his thoughts. 'There is nothing to be surprised at in Lipski's confession. Indeed it is just what was to be expected; those who have never believed in his guilt have no need to do so now, the evidence is entirely against such a hypothesis; but that under the circumstances the world should be given to understand that he has confessed and 'admitted the justice of his sentence', was absolutely essential to the stability of the government, of the system of capital punishment, and to the credit of our judicial machinery generally.' (37). It is likely that Robert's belief in Lipski's innocence was based on personal knowledge - his status as a MP securing him access to the prisoner. Professor Friedland did not have that advantage but, from an exhaustive study of the papers, he noted glaring discrepancies between the evidence heard in court and Lipski's confession. These led him to suppose that it was a deliberate act of suicide to avoid life imprisonment which the 22 year old had said he would rather die than endure. (38).

The Home Secretary received much praise for his conduct of a most difficult affair. As his chief tormentor in the House of Commons the MP for North West Lanarkshire was sharply criticized: Fitzjames Stephen called him 'a parliamentary black guard'. The questions he put to Matthews were denounced as more than any Minister should be called upon to bear in the discharge of his duty. Consequently, for the next 80 years, until capital punishment was abolished in 1965, it was a parliamentary rule that no questions be asked about the prerogative of mercy while the Home Secretary was deciding whether a reprieve should, or should not, be granted.

While all this was going on the Irish Crimes Bill had been passed into law. Almost at once the Irish Secretary, Arthur Balfour, was obliged to make use of it to keep order in the face of widespread disturbances provoked by the withholding of rent under the Plan of Campaign. Certain offences, including boycotting, intimidation, and resistance to eviction ,were made subject to courts of summary jurisdiction, while Lords Lieutenant acquired the power to proclaim the Act in force in their separate areas. Within those areas certain associations might be proscribed as dangerous when their members became liable to prosecution. According to a report by Sir Charles Warren (of which more later) (39), the passing of the Crimes Act provoked a particularily hostile response in

London. The truce that had briefly obtained during the Queen's Jubilee, gave way to further tense encounters on the streets when the police were abused for acting as instruments of a government allegedly bent on repression. Parnell did his best to warn his followers on both sides of the water that to challenge the provisions of the new Act was to risk disaster. Robert Cunninghame Graham was among those who heard him deliver such a warning at a dinner in his honour at the National Liberal Club (40). Like the others present he was dismayed at the 'Chief's' appearance. White and shivering, Parnell was already in the grip of the illness that, a few weeks later, forced him to lie up in a place unknown even to his closest allies, an abdication that lasted until the beginning of 1888. In any case he would have been hard put to restrain his by now infuriated countrymen. One of the first actions Balfour took was to ban the Irish National League. On August a huge protest was arranged at the Rotunda, Dublin's principal meeting place, to be addressed by Michael Davitt, John Dillon, and William O'Brien, leading spirits of the Plan of Campaign. Robert Cunninghame Graham was one of several Scottish MPs who crossed the water to lend their support. Though he was invited to speak he did not do so. Years later he told Wilfrid Scawen Blunt why he failed to grasp the opportunity - a gift to a rising politician with nationalist aspirations. 'We [Gabrielle was with him] were so disgusted with that awful deputation (that we joined in Dublin) their vulgarity, their want of tact, their commonness, that I said I had a cold and would not speak (we did not know you ,ie Blunt, were to speak) and after driving once round Dublin...came straight home and were sick crossing...' (41). This may have been the true explanation; on the other hand it may have been that upon arrival Robert found himself on the point of collapse and unable to face the proceedings: it was less than a week since Lipski had been hanged. He may have been persuaded to leave by Gabrielle. Once round the city and back to the boat sounds as if she decided to resolve the situation in the way she often did, and bolted, taking Robert with her.

A week later he was back at Westminster where the Coal Mines Regulation Bill had returned to the Commons from the Upper House minus several of the clauses for which he had campaigned. In particular their Lordships had removed provision for improving safety, including inspections to be made by independent inspectors, a change the Government was content to leave unchallenged. Robert Cunninghame Graham's objection was savage. The Lords, not being elected, should not dare to dictate to the Commons, he told MPs assembled for the last sitting of the session on 16 September. Mr Speaker Peel ruled the word 'dictate' unconstitutional: he ordered Graham to withdraw it and apologize. Graham said his conscience would not allow him to do either. The Speaker therefore ordered his suspension for the remainder of the session, a penalty that lacked its customary force because as soon as the debate ended Parliament was to be prorogued. (42). This time comment, which raged for a day or two, was far more favourable to the new Member. By suspending him for a matter of minutes only the Speaker was considered to have brought the rules into some ridicule. A plea of conscience was taken very seriously by the House. While Graham's inexperience had tried their patience during the session no one doubted his sincerity. And the point he raised about the

Lords was of continuing concern: the monumental row over their opposition to the most recent extension of the franchise was still fresh in people's minds. As the first Scottish MP to be named by the Speaker (in contrast to the Irish who made a habit of it) Robert found himself once more the object of attention from the parliamentary sketch writers. 'Mr Cunninghame Graham is one of the best known of the young Scottish Members', the <u>Scottish Leader</u> wrote. 'He has made a peculiar position for himself in the House. He has absolutely nothing of the professional politician about him but he can bring members from the lobbies when he rises to speak and he can keep them there. He is generally entertaining, he is sometimes trenchant, and he is always racy. Many critics set him down as an eccentric, and so he is if originality and even fancifulness can be so represented. It is however more accurate to describe Mr Cunninghame Graham as unconventional; certainly if he is eccentric as the Tory critics insist, his eccentricity is of a very practical kind as can be testified by political organisers in Scotland...and by the miners whom he has served with a degree of assiduity and usefulness not exceeded by more direct representatives of the working men'. Mr Graham's mannerisms were pronounced, the <u>Leader</u> admitted; foreign to the orthodox and ponderous parliamentary style so much affected on the Tory benches, but if these were notable they were not offensive by reason of affectation; 'for of that vice the Honorable gentleman is perfectly innocent'. 'Nature fashioned Mr Cunninghame Graham to be a brooder on the principles of government, a fitter out of new constitutions', the <u>Edinburgh Dispatch</u> declared. All praised his good manners demonstrated by the graceful way in which he gave way to other speakers, the mark of 'an old world courtliness worthy of Black Rod'. (43.)

The recess, which was to last for three months, came as a badly needed respite after a most exhausting session when, in order to complete its business, the House regularly sat until well past midnight, sometimes not rising until 5 a.m. For Robert personally it had been the most testing introduction a newcomer could possibly have undergone. Even so the programme he now set himself meant that he could not retreat to Gartmore for more than a few days at a time. He planned to use the ensuing weeks to establish himself as an independent voice on behalf of working men in Scotland. His activities since he had arrived at Westminster had made many of them well disposed to listen to him. They knew they needed help: the recession showed no sign of easing and they were still at odds with their employers over wages and conditions. So, for Robert, October was a furiously busy month of meetings as, often accompa-

Sketch of Graham by Harry Furniss. National Portrait Gallery, London.

164

nied by James Keir Hardie, he went about the mining districts delivering one particular message. This was that Parliament was dominated by men antagonistic to the working class; while that state of affairs prevailed legislation beneficial to themselves and other groups - the crofters for example - would never be enacted. They must realize that it was in their best interest to seek out and elect representatives from among their own number. Sometimes lapsing into broad Scots (in which he was at ease and fluent) to drive the point home, he told them 'Corbies dinna pike oot ither corbies een'. By the end of the month his popularity had again begun to soar. Crowds turned up at his meetings almost as if another election campaign were under way. The number of his engagements often caused him to be late of an evening when his audience whiled away the time they had to wait admiring Gabrielle who came early to the platform.(44).

The heightened atmosphere was partly due to recent events in Ireland. On 9 September William O'Brien, MP. ,Editor of United Ireland, had come up before the magistrates at Mitchelstown in Co. Tipperary charged under the new Crimes Act with making inflammatory speeches. An angry crowd that had gathered to protest against the proceedings was fired on by the police; three men were killed and others wounded. The incident caused a huge outcry; 'Remember Mitchelstown' became an all purpose slogan for opposition to the policy of coercion. O'Brien who was known to be suffering from TB, was imprisoned at Cork but, after the Lord Mayor of that city made it clear he would mount a daily protest, was removed to Tullamore Jail which the authorities hoped would prove more secure. On 12 October the Coatbridge Junior Liberals held a meeting to add their voice to the general condemnation of Mitchelstown . Robert ,who arrived accompanied by a brass band, was greeted by shouts of 'here comes the gallant Graham'. He delivered a rousing speech in the course of which he allowed himself to appear far more favourable to nationalism than on any previous occasion. Ireland blocked the way to all reform in Scotland, he said; Ireland would not let them deal with the land question; Ireland would not let them frame an eight hours bill; Ireland would not let them address the drink question. The Irish parliamentary party had embarked on its blocking action because its members knew that if attention was diverted from Ireland's just claims those claims would be shelved. He believed Irish and Scots interests were identical and the way to advance them was through Home Rule. Some people thought Scotland was contented and the Scots only wished to make money, he told the Junior Liberals, but the crofters, the miners, the ironworkers, the factory workers, and the men who looked to a solution of the drink question all had problems to be solved and these would be solved far quicker by the Scots themselves than at Westminster. 'Although they did not suffer such wrongs as they did in Ireland still these were sufficient reasons for the cry of Home Rule and a Scottish Parliament'. Whereas during the election campaign he had refused to be drawn on the question of whether Irish MPs should continue to sit at Westminster after they had a parliament in Dublin, now he was in favour of what amounted to regional assemblies for all four parts of the realm - 'the sooner they take the management of English affairs out of Westminster and place it at York or elsewhere, the better'. (44)

From Coatbridge he moved on to Broxbourne where the shale miners had been locked out after 18 weeks of a wage dispute. Before Parliament rose he had tabled a question on their behalf protesting at the use of evictions as a means whereby the employers hoped to force them to capitulate. Now, six weeks later, they were faced with strike breaking by men imported from elsewhere - 'blacknebs' was the local word. Robert told them their only hope of challenging the employers was to overcome their natural tendency to hold themselves apart from other groups and join the growing movement towards a union. He was able to assure them this would be to their advantage, he said, because he had just spent several days at the annual conference of miners' delegates from England, Wales, and Scotland which took place at Edinburgh. In the course of the proceedings the Scots' delegates had won a vote for the first time; a development that the <u>Pall Mall Gazette</u> regarded as highly significant. The miners' organisation consisted of two factions, the newspaper told its readers; one around Thomas Burt and Charles Fenwick, and including most of the officials of the English miners' organisation. This was the party in power but it was seriously threatened by a rising band, mainly of Scots. The chiefs of this new party were James Keir Hardie, James Chisholm Robertson, and William Small. 'They are strongly tinctured with Socialism and utterly opposed to the policy of the Lib Lab MPs who objected to Parliament being asked to pass an eight hours Bill.' On the last day of the conference Small proposed such a bill be introduced and pressed forward. This was opposed by Burt and Fenwick but carried by 213,000 to 160,000 votes. 'This is the first victory of the new section and it is regarded as most important' the <u>Pall Mall Gazette</u> remarked. 'It is said to be not unlikely that a Scottish Labour Party will be formed before long and that Mr R.B. Cunninghame Graham will be their leader. The Hon. gentleman is gaining enormous popularity with the Scottish workers, and especially the miners.' (45). He was certainly trying hard: some thought too hard. If he went on at the rate of ten speeches a week he would be talked out by the time he got back to Coatbridge, the <u>Airdrie Advertiser</u> commented. In fact a period of silence was approaching; one that would be forced upon him.

At the end of the second week in November he was obliged to cancel engagements in the North in order to join his Socialist friends and allies at a most important meeting at the Home Office. While he had been preoccupied in Scotland during the recess Trafalgar Square had been taken over by a large and determined army of the unemployed who made it their base for daily meetings. They were addressed by Robert's colleagues in the Vigilance Association - William Morris, Annie Besant, Bernard Shaw and others - on the need for self help, and the means of finding work. After the speeches were over they went off to lobby influential people like the magistrates at Bow Street, or the Lord Mayor ('that infernal scoundrel' was how one of their leaders described him), or simply to show themselves as a group in the City or the West End. At first they marched in hundreds through the streets and back to the Square, later more than a thousand took part on each occasion. Towards the end of October, as tempers worsened, the Metropolitan Police Commissioner urged the time had come to call a halt and clear the Square. Warren was particularly anxious to prevent the demonstration planned to coincide with the largest procession of the year - the Lord Mayor's Show on 9 November. He wanted to avoid a repetition of the near disaster of the previous year when the SDF had organized a contingent of unemployed to bring up the rear of the Show, always a magnificent display of gilded carriages, top hats, tricornes - the usual appurtenances of wealth and municipal glory. On that occasion, when these gave way to flat caps and shabby bowlers (no one would have dreamed of going bareheaded) the crowd waiting in Trafalgar Square was moved to such indignation at the contrast scuffles broke out. A serious riot was only avoided by Warren giving orders for the police to clear the Square, which they did with the help of a posse of Horse Guards summoned in haste from Whitehall.

He proposed to take even fewer chances this time. On Monday, 7 November, without prior consultation with the Home Office, he issued a proclamation whereby no person, unless officially part of the Lord Mayor's procession, would be allowed to deliver a speech, or carry a banner in any of the streets through which the Show must pass, including Trafalgar Square. This ukase caused a sensation because it seemed to confirm the charges of dictatorship by the police the activists had already made against Warren. The sharpest reaction came from the delegates to a new umbrella organisation, the Metropolitan Radical Federation, whose members were virtually the same as those belonging to the Vigilance Association. The MRF's immediate purpose was to hold a demonstration in Trafalgar Square on Sunday, 13 November to protest against the treatment in Tullamore Jail of William O' Brien MP. As soon as Warren's proclamation appeared on placards in the London streets, the MRF demanded an assurance from the Home Secretary that their demonstration would be allowed to go ahead. A meeting was arranged for Friday, 11 November. But, when the delegates, including Annie Besant, Edward Aveling, Eleanor Marx, and Robert Cunninghame Graham , arrived at the Home Office in Whitehall, they were told Matthews would not see them. As a Member of Parliament Graham insisted he be admitted to the presence and so he was, but unaccompanied. The encounter cannot have been pleasant for either man: it was only a few weeks since they had been leading protagonists in the case of Israel Lipski; subsequently they had come to verbal blows about the miners, now here they were confronting one another in what promised to be a most tremendous row involving a point of national pride - freedom of speech and unimpeded access to the most important open space in the capital - that lay within a few hundred yards of the Houses of Parliament.

When the tête á tête was over the MRF delegates were given to understand the outcome was consent for their arrangements for Sunday's meeting in the Square. Robert Cunninghame Graham certainly believed that Matthews now welcomed the occasion as an opportunity to test the legality of such meetings via the courts. (46). He issued a statement to the press saying that he intended to be in Trafalgar Square on Sunday 13 November when he would speak on purpose to challenge Warren's right to proscribe the demonstration on the day of the Lord Mayor's Show. This was reported in Saturday's <u>Airdrie Advertiser</u>, but with a rider to the sensational effect that 'the authorities will prevent the meeting by a strong force of police and military'.(47) Matthews, it seemed, had also spoken to the press . At the eleventh hour he had once more changed his mind, apparently without imparting that information to the MRF, or to Cunninghame Graham. By that the scene was set for the confrontation which afterwards caused the events of 13 November 1887 always to be known as Bloody Sunday.

Notes to Chapter Eight

1. Herbert Faulkner West Papers;Rauner Special Collections Library, Dartmouth College, Hanover, New Hampshire; Series I, 'Board of Trade Report on the Nailmakers of S. Staffs. and E. Worcs.', RBCG holograph note in margin.
2. Cunninghame Graham, R.B., A Memory of Parnell in 'Rodeo', op. cit.
3. BL Add. 45335, Morris Diary, 7 Feb. 1887.
4. Quoted in Lindsay, J., 'William Morris', Constable, 1975, p. 258.
5. Hansard, 3rd Series, Vol. Col. 1744.
6. Lindsay, op.cit., p. 358; Pickles was a founder member of the Bradford branch of the Socialist League.
7. Kelvin, J., ed., 'Collected Letters of William Morris', Princeton, 1987; Morris to Jenny, 19 Feb. 1887.
8. Morris, May, 'William Morris', II, p.210
9. The Commonweal, 9 Apr. 1887.
10. Burgess, op.cit., p. 137.
11. Finger, op.cit., p. 181.
12. Quoted in Lindsay, op.cit., p. 238.
13. Finger, op.cit., p. 156.
14 Hansard, 3rd Series, CCCXIV, Col. 693.
15. ibid., Col 1746.
16. ibid.
17 Airdrie Advertiser, 11 June 1887.
18. Hansard, 3rd Series, CCCXIV, Col. 1746.
19. ibid., Col. 1756. This passage refers to the time limit on debates introduced to counter delaying tactics used by the Irish Parliamentary party.
20. Hansard, 3rd Series, CCCXIV, Col. 1758.
21. Airdrie Advertiser, 30 April 1887.
22. Glasier, J. Bruce, 'J. Keir Hardie A Memorial', ILP 1919, p. 20.
23. Hansard, 3rd Series, CCCXVI, Col. 1786.
24. ibid., CCCXIX Cols 512, 592.
25. Airdrie Advertiser, 4 June 1887.
26. Morris, W., 'The Lesser Arts, Lecture, 1877.
27. Hansard, 3rd Series, CCCXIX, col. 909.
28. ibid. Col. 912.
29. ibid., Col. 907.30. Airdrie Advertiser, 20Aug. 1887.
30. Friedland, M., 'The Trials of Israel Lipski', Macmillan, 1984.
31. Friedland, op.cit., p. 134.

32. ibid. p 161.
33. Hansard, CCCXIX, cols. 253,364.
34. ibid. col. 1255
35. Friedland, op.cit., p. 175.
36. Rostow, W.W., 'British Economy of the 19th Century', Clarendon Press, 1948, p.16.
37. The <u>Commonweal</u>, 24 Aug. 1887.
38. Friedland, op.cit., p 170ff.
39. PRO HO 144/294/A47976
40. <u>Airdrie Advertiser</u> - July 1887
41. W. Sussex Record Office; Blunt papers, RBCG to Blunt, 22 Sept 1912.
42. <u>Airdrie Advertiser</u>, 17 Sept. 1887.
43. ibid.
44. ibid., 15 Oct. 1887
45. ibid.

46. ibid. 3 March 1888. Statement by Harry Smith, parliamentary candidate for Falkirk Burghs.
47. <u>Airdrie Advertiser</u>, 12 Nov. 1887.

Chapter Nine

Bloody Sunday

Up to 13 November Cunninghame Graham's political career might be described as distinguished more by dash than calculation; however justified his actions they had been taken heedless of the cost to his reputation. This time he paused, conscious that to take part in an advance upon Trafalgar Square in defiance of a ban by the authorities was a very serious undertaking. On entering Parliament he had taken an oath of loyalty to the Crown; now he was to ignore an order by one of Her Majesties' Ministers, one reported to involve the illegal use of force; a development he, like other delegates of the Metropolitan Radical Federation deplored but was powerless to prevent. Yet it was widely known that he had telegraphed to James Timms, the Federation's Secretary, asking to speak on 13 November; his credibility depended on him turning up.(1) He took comfort from the thought that his situation, though more exposed, was not in essence different from that of other MPs; all of whom the MRF had invited to attend Sunday's demonstration. Looking back on these events Robert said he had been convinced that Matthews' decision to countermand the arrangements approved on 11 November would so anger Liberal MPs as to cause them to call out their constituents to occupy the Square on Sunday. That they were in a mood to take such drastic action he believed from what he had heard and read during the recess of their attitude towards the rapidly worsening Irish situation. It had seemed to him that the Liberal leaders were preparing to confront the Government over its policy of coercion. 'Members of my party, men whom I respected and believed to be in earnest', he said, 'had spoken of what they would do to help the Irish.'(2) In particular, when Gladstone told the National Liberal Federation at Nottingham on 17 October 1887, that coercion would not be confined to Ireland but applied in England if the English remained supine, Robert took this both as a warning and a call to action. He was taken aback when he discovered he was the only MP who intended to be present. Though he gave the benefit of the doubt to two colleagues, Walter McClaren and Charles Conybeare (3) who said they would have attended if they had not been unavoidably engaged elsewhere, he dismissed the rest as 'mere politicians crawling to Downing Street'. He might have entertained even more doubts as to the wisdom of his own involvement had he not been so completely occupied in Scotland during the recess that he was out of touch with colleagues and events elsewhere. Those who had been following the crisis since the summer could have told him how dangerous it promised to become. As it happened he plunged straight in just as it came to a head with Warren's order to prohibit access to Trafalgar Square on the day of the Lord Mayor's Show. When Matthews reneged on the arrangements with the MRF a confrontation was unavoidable.

    Home Office papers made available in 1987 (4) show there was a very serious difference of opinion between, on the one hand, Matthews and his

Permanent Under Secretary, Godfrey Lushington, who were very uneasy at even a temporary ban on access to Trafalgar Square, and the Metropolitan Police Commissioner whose first concern was the maintenance of order. As the autumn advanced this had become increasingly difficult. The Square was regularly in chaos as a result of the daily meetings of the unemployed; ordinary people were prevented from going about their business; access to Charing Cross station and the Underground was impeded; ladies had to refrain from shopping from fear of being jostled. By the third week in October Warren had become very impatient with what he regarded as Matthews' fatal propensity to vacillate. When another large demonstration of the unemployed was called for Sunday, 23 October, Warren demanded it be stopped. He told the Home Secretary he had received a memorial from householders and firms in and about Trafalgar Square praying for an end to its occupation by turbulent and noisy people. 'It is not that I apprehend an organized movement from the Socialists themselves or any other organized body', Warren wrote on 22 October, 'but it is from the roughs and criminals who always attach themselves to large processions...that I anticipate serious damage to property. During the past ten days it is only by the most strenuous effort that we have prevented shops being looted and the language used by speakers at the various meetings has been more frank and open in recommending the poorer classes to help themselves to the wealth of the affluent than in former years'.(5)

This time Matthews' response was unequivocal. 'Sir Charles Warren should not attempt to prevent any orderly body of persons from meeting or making speeches on 23 October'. (6) Nothing untoward did occur at that demonstration but Warren obviously decided it was time to take matters entirely into his own hands; hence the ban on the day of the Lord Mayor's Show. For some time past he had been trying to assemble evidence to suggest that the regular demonstrations in the Square were part of a conspiracy against the Government. Police shorthand writers were stationed incognito at the daily meetings to record anything remotely provocative in the speakers' language. One who swam into the net when Chairman for the Day was a prominent member of the Socialist League, James Allman (others who performed this office were William Morris and Henry Hyndman). Arrested on suspicion of seditious language on 4 November he was hurried off to Holloway Prison only to be rescued by Annie Besant who produced a solicitor just in time to have the charge dismissed for lack of evidence. In an attempt to avert further incidents of this kind, the Law Officers advised Home Office officials that the instructions they had previously given Warren had not sufficiently stressed the need for substantial evidence, 'which must come from independent persons' before any public meeting could be dispersed on grounds of illegality.(7) It was at this moment of high seriousness that Gladstone intervened. As well as recording what speakers said in Trafalgar Square the police had been going about taking the names of bystanders, a much disliked measure. To general laughter and acclaim Gladstone now suggested that, if asked, people should confess to being called Walker after the Superintendent of that name. This was suspiciously like a joke, something that Matthews could have done without and must have felt was unfair given his efforts to curb Warren. But these took place behind the scenes; all the public could see was Warren apparently assuming the mantle of a dictator. 'Police law in England' was the Commonweal's response, 'the Government are undoubtedly introducing Continental ideas as regards the supremacy of the police'.(8)

In truth, though Cunninghame Graham, for one, had condemned Warren's tactics in keeping order during the Jubilee as achieving a positively Russian level of autocracy, many Londoners were grateful to the Commissioner for exercising such close supervision. (9) And, in the months that followed, a large section of the population looked to him to protect them during the increasingly well organized demonstrations of the unemployed in Trafalgar Square. The problem was, among a crowd of uniformly poverty stricken men, how to distinguish between those intent on exercising what they believed to be their right of protest in a public place from the criminal element that, in those days of severe unrest in Ireland, might well have included not only thieves but terrorists carrying bombs. It was not surprising that these incomers to the Square aroused suspicion for they were as strange to its inhabitants as if they had come from a foreign country. Although in 1883 the famous 'Bitter Cry of Outcast London' had brought the appalling conditions in which people east of Aldgate were obliged to live to the attention of their more fortunate neighbours, few of these had yet ventured past the frontier of the City. (10) While activists like Annie Besant, Stuart Headlam, Bernard Shaw, Henry Champion and Cunninghame Graham himself already knew their way about the teeming streets, it would be some years yet before every self respecting charitable and religious organisation had its own 'mission' to the people of the East End.

The Press, more especially the Pall Mall Gazette, also raised an outcry over the fact that Warren was a soldier by profession who, if left unchecked by politicians, would soon have London groaning under martial law. In fact several other senior police officers including his immediate predecessor, Sir Edmund Henderson K.C.B., and Henderson's Assistant, Douglas Labalmondière, had also been Army men. In Warren's case, however, the apprehension was well founded for he was determined to the point of obstinacy to do what he conceived was his duty whether or not it accorded with the views of his superiors. This unswerving approach to his responsibilities sprang partly from habits acquired during long service in remote parts of the Empire, but also from the keen religious and moral sense instilled in him by his upbringing in the Cathedral Close at Bangor where his great uncle was Bishop and his grandfather the Dean. That he was an exceedingly devout Anglican goes far to explain the unusual vehemence of his language in his official reports. As the Chartists had discovered forty years before, a most effective way of gaining public sympathy was to have those concerned parade to church on Sundays. So, on 23 October the unemployed marched to Westminster Abbey from Trafalgar Square. Some failed to doff their caps on entering the building, others talked and smoked during the service. 'These people are the veriest scum of the population', Warren fulminated; their behaviour threatened a reign of terror in the London streets, he told the Home Secretary. 'I am keeping the peace at the present time by escorting these roughs on all occasions with a large number of men amounting to about 2,000 who are either taken from their beats...or from night duty. This has now been going on for 18 days and it is quite impossible that it can continue much longer without the men being quite worn out and so harassed that there will be danger of them losing their tempers.'(11)

Warren was not accustomed to interference by civil servants. Until 1887 whatever action he had chosen to pursue in the course of his military career had always proved the right one. Twenty years before, as a young Lieutenant in the Royal Engineers, he led an expedition to the Holy Land where he faced down stiff opposition from the Turkish authorities in order to explore and map unknown territory for his sponsors, the Palestine Exploration Fund. In 1882 it fell to him to search for Professor Edward Palmer who disappeared in the Sinai Peninsula while on a secret mission to discover how far the local Arabs would support the British in their attempt to suppress Colonel Arabi's revolt in Egypt. He was rewarded with a knighthood, not so much for finding the bodies of Palmer and his companions, as for his initiative in bringing to justice the Bedouin who robbed and killed them. In 1884 he offered to lead an expedition to rescue General Gordon (a fellow Royal Engineer) from Khartoum. The Liberal Government having had the same idea, Lord Wolseley got the job but Warren was sent to deal with another dangerous situation in South Africa. Boers known as filibusters had begun to seize land across the Vaal River where they set up two independent republics; Stellaland, a small area in the neighbourhood of Vryburg, and Goschen which covered most of what was better known as Bechuanaland. Warren's orders were to eject the Boers, pacify the region where settlers of English origin were on the point of war with the intruders, reinstate the Africans in their farms, and hold the country until its future might be determined. As Special Commissioner he controlled civil and military forces; the police and the Army were his to command. His success was dazzling. In four months he sailed to South Africa with an expeditionary force; recruited volunteers; moved 5,000 men 570 miles by rail and marched them a further 350 through waterless country; dug wells, installed telegraph lines; persuaded President Kruger to recall the filibusters from Goschen; cleared Stellaland without a fight, and began arrangements for a Bechuanaland Protectorate. Though his methods were criticized as unnecessarily harsh in the Legislative Assembly at the Cape by no less a person than Cecil Rhodes, Warren had the backing of the British Secretary for War, Hugh Childers. In 1886, when Childers briefly became Home Secretary, he chose Warren to take over the Metropolitan Police from Henderson whose head was forfeit as the result of Superintendent Walker's incompetence.(12) But the fall of the Liberal Government swept Childers out of office when Lord Salisbury's choice of Home Secretary fell on Henry Matthews. The fact that Matthews was a Roman Catholic (the first to sit in Cabinet) was only one of the many points of friction between him and that latter day Ironside, Sir Charles Warren. According to Matthews' Private Secretary, Evelyn Ruggles-Brise, 'Warren was the finest man we had in Whitehall but probably the worst appointment because he <u>must</u> be independent and the Commissioner of Police is held in very tight bonds by the Home Office. Matthews was an exceedingly capable lawyer but quite incapable of dealing with men: he was a regular Gallio in his attitude to Warren's complaints.'(13)

By the morning of 13 November most of those intending to be present at the demonstration knew the police would try to stop them gaining access to Trafalgar Square and that the encounter could result in numbers getting arrested. But in the light of two pieces of recent information personal considerations had all but ceased to matter. The first came from Tullamore Jail where William O'Brien's condition had grown so much worse he had been removed to the prison infirmary. As he was known to be suffering from tuberculosis this gave extra point to the resolution protesting at his treatment which was to be proposed as soon as the demonstrators were assembled in the Square. The second was a devastating blow; news from America that the long campaign to save the Chicago Seven had failed; the executions had been carried out on Friday. Saturday's newspapers in London were full of descriptions of the last moments of the men on the gallows; details that, even after a hundred years, are sickening to read. Consequently the mood of those gathered for the march to Trafalgar Square on the following day could not have been bleaker. Each of the component parts of the MRF (the Irish National League, the Socialist League, the Social Democratic Federation, the National Secular Society and various working men's clubs) had its own point of assembly in the East End to which they repaired in the morning with bands and banners. They intended to approach Trafalgar Square at the same time but from different directions. However Warren was ready with the plan he had wanted to implement two weeks previously. As he had already explained to Matthews this was 'to break up all processions proceeding to Trafalgar Square when they have arrived within a radius of about a mile, as was done on 9 November [1886]'(14)

His second line of defence was to station men shoulder to shoulder all around the Square leaving the central area clear. As now it was below the level of the surrounding streets, cut off from them by a stone parapet broken in places by steps. As now a street divided the sunken area from the steps of the National Gallery. The Square was one of the very few open spaces in the capital suitable for those large gatherings by which the process of democracy was normally fulfilled. Speakers standing between the lions on the plinth of Nelson's Column were easily visible to the crowd below, while by lifting their eyes they could see down Whitehall to the Houses of Parliament - too short a distance for their rulers' comfort.(15) This time Warren intended to disperse the crowd before its ardour could be reinforced by speeches. It was a strategy that made heavy demands on the limited number of police available, a fact the Home Office acknowledged by appealing to forces elsewhere in the country to send constables to London for the occasion. This idea, which flew in the face of the principle that every locality raised and controlled its own force, commended itself to hardly anyone but the embattled Warren. Leeds, Liverpool, and Birmingham refused point blank. Manchester Watch Committee asked to be excused on the grounds that Hyndman was due to speak in Stevenson Square that day and every man they had would be needed there. That left one alternative; one the Prime Minister particularly disliked but was persuaded to approve - the use of soldiers. A contingent of Life Guards and another of Horse

Guards was ordered to hold itself in reserve and out of sight of the crowds of spectators who, by early Sunday afternoon had taken up positions in the windows and even on the roofs of the hotels and banks and other businesses that, in those days, made Trafalgar Square a busy commercial centre. Most of them got there either by Underground or on the buses that continued to come and go along the southern edge of the Square throughout the afternoon.

Among these spectators were Gabrielle Cunninghame Graham and Sir Edward Reed, Liberal MP for Cardiff . She watched from the Metropole Hotel; he from Morley's. Both were to give evidence of what they saw done to Robert Cunninghame Graham after he reached the Square. Up to that point his movements are not easy to reconstruct; he was vague about timing, probably deliberately. We know that, following his discussion with the Home Secretary he went down to Stoke on Trent to fulfil a prior engagement to speak at a miners' meeting. Telegrams sent to him there warned him of Matthews' change of mind, and of the fact that arms might be carried by some going to Sunday's demonstration. Apparently he did not come back up to London until Sunday morning; he did not appear at Clerkenwell Green where William Morris and Annie Besant addressed a group of marchers. The aim of this group, once they reached the Square, was to take up a prominent position on the steps of St Martins in the Fields where Graham was to have joined them. Sir Charles Warren decreed otherwise. Those marchers who started from Deptford, Fulham and Bermondsey had to cross the river; they were met and scattered on Westminster Bridge. North of the Thames the Clerkenwell Green contingent advanced without hindrance until it reached Seven Dials where several streets converge at the top of Shaftesbury Avenue. Police issuing from those streets fell on the marchers, truncheons flailing. 'The women were much in the way', Shaw told Morris (who had not accompanied the march from Clerkenwell). 'The police charged us the moment they saw Mrs Taylor. But you should have seen that high hearted host run. Running hardly expresses our collective action. We <u>skedaddled</u> and never drew rein until we were safe on Hampstead Heath or thereabouts'.(16)

A few bold and determined individuals from this group then made their own way into the Square. Annie Besant was one. Her object was to get arrested 'to obtain the decision of the High Court of Justice and, if necessary, the High Court of Appeal on the interference of the Commissioner of the Police with any user of the Square', she explained later.(17) She went up to the cordon of police guarding the central area round Nelson's Column. 'I pressed quietly against their line (Annie had been thoroughly well brought up), and was seized by five of them whereupon I said I was one of the speakers and would submit to arrest.' In fact she had already been recognized. Forewarned as to her unlimited capacity for making trouble, and in the knowledge that Bradlaugh would deal with any legal matter arising from her being taken into custody, an inspector hastily gave orders that she be left strictly unmolested. This encounter took place in the street in front of the National Gallery, north of the defended area. Cunninghame Graham, whose intention was the same as Annie's, made his attempt in the south. He too was instantly recognized but he met with an altogether different response.

Having left Gabrielle in the safety of the Metropole Hotel, he had made his way to Charing Cross Underground Station where he met John Burns. At his trial he insisted the encounter was by chance - conspiracy was a very serious offence - but John Burgess maintained the two had planned to meet.(18) Several independent witnesses corroborated the official report of what happened next. For instance, Charles Finger said that about four o'clock he saw Graham arm in arm with Burns in front of some 150 men at the south east corner of the Square. Hatless, his dark brown (Finger said red) hair was easy to spot among a sea of caps. Just as they reached the pavement on the Trafalgar Square side Burns, who was a big and sturdy man, let go Graham's arm and, getting behind him, pushed him forward onto the line of police. At the same time Graham was heard to shout something which the prosecution at his trial insisted was 'now for the Square'. (19) What followed was graphically described by Sir Edward Reed in a letter that appeared in The Times on Monday morning to be copied by dozens of other papers, including the Airdrie Advertiser. Having watched from an upstairs window Reed could say the conduct of the police was very good, admirable even, 'but I must say Mr Graham was treated with much needless violence and brutality'. Reed made no complaint of the actual arrest, though he could not see the necessity of striking him across the head in the process, 'but what I do complain of is, after his arrest was complete one policeman after another , two certainly but I think no more, stepped up from behind and struck him on the head with a violence and brutality shocking to behold. Even after this and when some 5 or 6 policemen were dragging him on to the Square, another from behind seized him most needlessly by the hair (the abundance of which perhaps tempted him) and dragged his head back and in that manner he was forced forward many yards'.(20)

Faint from the large wound on the back of his head Robert was kept a prisoner in the central area of the Square during the next phase. In his official report Warren maintained that it was his arrest and that of Burns about 4.15 p.m. that determined him to bring in the soldiers. Up to that point Warren himself had cut a very conspicuous figure in the thick of things; mounted on a splendid horse he had ridden to and fro, followed by his own mounted escort. Among John Burns' papers in the British Library is an account by an anonymous man of the advent of the troops. He had been on the steps of Morley's Hotel intending to see the 'fun', and as a farmer's son said he had been upset by the sight of men with sticks tormenting the police horses. He got on a bus and went backward and forward to Piccadily twice until the third time it was stopped by the struggle surrounding Graham and Burns. 'You and Cunninghame Graham were in the front', he told Burns, 'Just one pace onward, hardly without stirring foot the first cordon of police [guarding the central area] was broken through, the second was broken through. The police in front and behind had scattered through the crowd and were using their truncheons. I saw you and Graham... his head was bleeding fearfully. The Horse Guards walked up just then, the officer gave a command. The mounted soldiers began to walk at a much quicker pace. All around, from every part of the Square the booing and screaming was fearful. Again at the very same spot he gave another command and they began to trot. The screams and the shrieks I heard in my ears for many months. Again at the same spot he gave another command. It was a wild cavalry charge around the Square. The panic-stricken people tried to get away but loud above the clattering of the horses' hooves and the rattling of their accoutrements were the frightened mad screams of the poor people. The Square was now cleared indeed and I got down from the bus and with a heavy heart hurried away as quickly as I could for home.'(21) Though a magistrate was standing by ready to read the Riot Act it was not needed: the demonstrators were in full retreat. Altogether 300 people were arrested; 73 were treated in Charing Cross Hospital for injuries received; 50 in Westminster Hospital, including 3 policemen; 30 in St Thomas'. It might have been far worse as William Morris pointed out; if the demonstrators had succeeded in getting past the police cordon into the centre of the Square there might have been a massacre to rival Peterloo, 'for they were in a pinfold at the mercy of police and soldiers'.(22)

Robert Cunninghame Graham and John Burns were taken off to Bow Street where they were locked together in a small narrow cell whose stone floor was covered in straw; the only way for light and air to enter was by means of a square in the door which was covered by a shutter for the greater part of the time. These details are from a letter by Robert's mother writing at the first opportunity to Barbara, his sister in law who, like the rest of the family, was anxiously waiting for news. Anne Elizabeth Bontine had gone to Bow Street first thing on Monday morning escorted by her nephew, Adrian Hope, and had been allowed to see the prisoners. 'Robert's head is bandaged, the wound is on top of his head', she told Barbara, 'he is in tremendous spirits making even the police inspector laugh. I felt it no laughing matter'. (23) It was a brave attempt to reassure the younger woman. Anne Elizabeth's laconic account concealed shock and great foreboding. Her happiness had been destroyed by a blow to her husband's head. Now the Strix's son was bruised and bloody from a similar brutal attack - what dreadful consequences might there be this time? In court she found Robert's aunt, Margaret Hope, who was there with her husband the VC, whom Anne Elizabeth had not seen for 25 years ,'and should not care if I never saw him again'.(24) Gabrielle was also present having made her own way to Bow Street. In a furious letter to _The Times_ she described what she had seen from the Metropole Hotel. A perfectly orderly and well behaved crowd would have held a perfectly orderly and constitutional meeting but for the 'imperial and autocratic warrant of the Home Secretary and Sir Charles Warren'. Her husband had merely tried to vindicate the right of free expression of opinion but he had been brutally beaten about the head. Wounded and bruised all over he had been kept like a common thief all night at Bow Street. An added insult was that, though his case had been scheduled to come on at 10.30 a.m she and his other relatives and friends had been obliged to listen to a succession of broken heads, drunken women, etc. until 2 in the afternoon. 'Now Sir', she addressed the Editor of _The Times_' How is it that he, a Scottish MP, was not accompanied by metropolitan MPs, by those Liberal MPs who, holding the same views, talk loudly when they can do it with safety but the moment it is to be put to its logical conclusion, they vanish. My husband acted nobly and bravely. The first steps to the fearful coercion and tyranny which has embittered Ireland for so long have now been taken in London. The people are to be coerced. Their rights of open air demonstration; their expression of indignation at a man dying of consumption in an Irish jail is to be suppressed by the Riot Act and charges by cavalry and mounted police. The Government has gone too far now', Gabrielle concluded, 'and I am sure my husband will have the sympathy of all brave Scotchmen who hate injustice and coercion'.(25)

About forty of those arrested were charged at Bow Street that Monday morning; some were sentenced on the spot; hard labour for one, two or three months was usual; six months if found in possession of a weapon; one man got five years penal servitude for wounding a policeman. When Burns and Graham finally came up, in the afternoon, both cases were adjourned to 22 November. In response to an urgent message from Robert, R.B. Haldane, then a rising young barrister left a consultation at his chambers in Lincoln's Inn to stand bail. Among others who rushed to Bow Street were William Morris, Walter Crane, and Oscar Wilde. The long wait had taken its toll of both prisoners. 'Poor Robert looked so worn and ill in the Court but so handsome notwithstanding his bandage' , Anne Elizabeth told Barbara. 'One of his eyes is shut up. Gabrielle who I really was sorry for was in one of her best moods. I asked her to come back to lunch with me but she was too busy, she said.' As soon as he was free Robert went to see a doctor about his head wound. From his surgery he issued a statement to the press insisting that he had not been part of the socialists' demonstrations; he had not even known they intended to march; his presence had been solely to affirm the right of free speech in Trafalgar Square, and to support the MRF resolution on behalf of William O'Brien. Although he had been roughly treated by the police he felt no animus towards them, merely pity for the dreadful job they had to do. With regard to Gladstone (who had called on every citizen to preserve the peace) he felt the Liberal leader had been ill advised not to make more of the crisis. For himself he would vindicate his action in the House of Commons. Afterwards, with Gabrielle and his mother he repaired to the Metropole Hotel in Trafalgar Square where, besieged by well wishers, they stayed until 22 November. As the Airdrie Advertiser told its readers under the headline 'Increased notoriety of Mr Cunninghame Graham', he was about the best talked of man in London; his past career and personal abilities and peculiarities much canvassed. 'I heard this Tuesday morning the veracious statement that he had spent years on the plains with Buffalo Bill and that he had at length struck a gold mine and become a millionaire' the Advertiser's London correspondent wrote. 'If any enterprising publisher would bring out his portrait and a page or two of his adventures he would get a large street sale'. But, the newspaper went on, its readers would be shocked to hear that, in spite of sufficient bail and an undertaking not to take part in any public demonstrations their MP was under constant surveillance at the Metropole Hotel, a detective in plain clothes being stationed in the hall, another at the entrance - a piece of impertinence in the Advertiser's view.(26)

The Pall Mall Gazette's headline over 8 1/2 pages of reports was, 'At the point of a bayonet'. Its Editor, W.T. Stead, described the action of the police, backed by the Horse and Life Guards as nothing less than a coup d'état; when the country realized what had been done in its name to innocent people the

Government would fall. On the other hand The Times which had been running daily accounts for the last few weeks under the headline 'The Police and the Mob' now congratulated Warren on a remarkable success. No meeting had been held in the Square; no procession had got near it; the Riot Act had not been read; no one had been killed. This was small comfort for the man responsible to Parliament for the alleged brutality of the police including one incident above all others; the one that caused the greatest sensation - the attack from behind upon a Member of Parliament already under restraint by five policemen. That was the Home Secretary's responsibility and the Department's papers show that he began to address it as soon as he saw Monday's newspapers. He had been reading the Pall Mall Gazette and Sir Edward Reed's letter in The Times Matthews told Lushington, his Permanent Under Secretary, which led him to conclude that Warren ought to publish a report on the proceedings at once in order to show what, if any, misconduct there had been by the police; he should pay special attention to any incident showing premeditated violence or illegal or mischievous purpose by the participants. If there had been any alleged excesses by the police the report should either excuse them or condemn them. If Sir Edward's report, that Cunninghame Graham was struck from behind by two policemen was true, these men should be punished. 'A dangerous feeling may grow up against the police if the public gets to believe that they are allowed to indulge in brutalities unchecked', Matthews told Lushington...' I should much like to get a verdict of a jury on the side of the authorities' he went on. 'Any case of an aggrieved kind, if we can only be supplied with proof of it should be sent for trial at the earliest opportunity. Throughout all these meetings [he meant those that had taken place daily in the Square for the past six weeks] I have not had brought before me a report of a single case of the kind one would wish to try. It will not do to rest on decisions of Police Magistrates'.(27)

Such a case it now transpired was that of John Burns and Robert Cunninghame Graham but time was needed to prepare it. So, when they came up at Bow Street on 22 November they were told to return a week later. Robert's response to this unexpected reprieve was to make a dash for home. Alerted by telegram that he would be arriving in Glasgow on Wednesday evening, his supporters prepared a hero's welcome. Preceded by a brass band members of the branch of the Irish National League whose President he was, marched in procession to Central Station already crowded with well wishers awaiting the arrival of the London train. When the Grahams appeared; 'the Hon. gentleman looked pale and weakly and on removing his hat in acknowledgement of the loud cheers that greeted him, it was noticed that his head was still covered by a dark silk bandage.' the Airdrie Advertiser told its readers. Robert and Gabrielle were greeted by the Secretary of the Irish National League, John Ferguson and his wife. After a small girl had presented a bouquet all four got into a carriage drawn by two greys and set off behind the band. Upon emerging into Hope Street a crowd estimated at 8,000 people brought the carriage to a standstill while men climbed up to shake Robert by the hand. By the light of street lamps cheers were given for Graham, Gladstone, Parnell and John Dillon, followed by groans for Salisbury, Matthews and Warren. When the carriage reached the HQ of the League Robert was urged to say a few words. Though, as he told them, he was still weak from the attentions of the London police, he managed more than a few. Given the circumstances it was not surprising he struck a slightly frantic note. He said he had been beaten and thrown like a dog at the foot of the lions in Trafalgar Square because he had dared speak for the public against the tyranny of landlords and capitalists. Coercion was coming to England and the people would have to band together to protect their rights. A Government that tried to interfere with the liberties of the people could not in the end succeed; and here Robert reminded his audience that the events of what had quickly come to be called Bloody Sunday had taken place less than 300 yards from where Charles Stuart had lost his head. In modern times, he said, a man opened a coal mine and made the people his slaves. Would it be bad if they banded together and hanged him? Nervous laughter seemed the best response to this, after which, to everyone's relief, his voice gave out.(28).

Next day he and Gabrielle received a smaller but, by most accounts, equally enthusiastic welcome at Balfron station when they were met by over 70 tenants and feuars who escorted them up to the door of Gartmore House. Not everyone was gratified by their return. A letter appeared in the local press claiming that the people at Balfron had been obliged to turn out for fear of the laird's displeasure; that while he lost no opportunity to advise others how they should manage their estates the Gartmore lands were sorely in need of improvement; and that in the matter of hiring and firing servants he had shown himself hasty and unsympathetic. The writer left no doubt in his readers' minds that the laird of Gartmore was hard pressed for money. Had he not driven home on this occasion in 'a machine not much better than a wheelbarrow, the only one of which he is possessed and drawn by a mongrel of some indeterminate breed?'(29) This diatribe drew a response from one of the Gartmore tenants who denounced its author as a man well known to harbour a grievance against the Graham family. (30) Nevertheless it was not the last time such things would be aired.

Robert was back in London for 30 November when he and Burns came up on remand. His defence was conducted by Herbert Asquith, a young barrister whose struggle to become established at the bar had been greatly assisted by his recent election to Parliament as Liberal MP for East Fife, in which capacity he was becoming a formidable critic of the Government's Irish policy. Asquith aimed to show that his client had been exercising a legitimate right of public assembly in Trafalgar Square. Burns defended himself, as he had when he was one of the four accused of causing the famous riot of 8 February 1886 which cast its long shadow over this latest incident. The prosecution was in the hands of Harry Poland, Treasury Counsel, whose pursuit of criminals, while unrelenting, was generally agreed to be conspicuously fair. On this occasion, though Poland pressed the principal witness for the defence, Sir Edward Reed, very hard, he failed to shake his account of the brutality visited by the police on Graham which was to be an important mitigating factor. And when it came to his cross examination of another defence witness, Charles Bradlaugh, he suffered a spectacular reverse. Bradlaugh testified to the frequent meetings he had held in Trafalgar Square that, owing to careful organisation and close control, had never led to violence. In order to refute him Poland raised the meeting of 8 February 1886 which had undeniably ended in violence. Bradlaugh, who had not been involved, seized the opportunity to make a sensational accusation: that the Fair Traders had been paid by the Tory Party to discredit the SDF. Poland was taken aback; 'Speak of what you know', he ordered. 'I do', said Bradlaugh, 'I saw the cheque'. At that , according to the court reporter, 'the prosecution was abruptly terminated'. But in the end the prosecution won the day. Burns and Graham were sent for trial on three counts; of riot; of unlawful assembly; of assaulting the police in the execution of their duty. The last charge rested on the evidence of two constables who had formed part of the cordon round the central area of the Square. They insisted Graham had punched them in the face, having been pushed in their way by Burns.(31) The penalty for riot and for assaulting the police was normally two years in prison with hard labour.

It was a frightening prospect that no one underestimated. 'An English prison is torture, and is meant to be so', William Morris warned Georgiana Burne Jones à propos of the trial.(32) It was scheduled for the New Year, condemning Robert and Gabrielle to a tense and nervous Christmas which they spent at Gartmore. Although he had not yet recovered from his injuries Robert made several forays into the outside world to speak at political gatherings where the ordeal he was to undergo earned him much sympathy. Gabrielle, who stayed at home, spent most of the brief daylight out of doors, walking, riding, planting apple and pear trees to form an orchard and planning the more formal garden she hoped to establish - rabbits and roe deer permitting - at the corner of the house outside the book room. Deep snow and ice followed by high winds and heavy rain hampered these activities, often driving her indoors where as was her habit she fell to berating the maids; this time one in particular, Jeannie, whose box upon inspection was found to contain items she had pilfered. These details are from Gabrielle's diary for 1888 (the only volume to survive). (33) As well as noting her daily activities it gives a running account of the state of her physical and mental health (revealed as extremely volatile), as well as her often difficult relations with her husband's family. Although she used a Spanish phrase or two - to protect her meaning from prying eyes - English is the language of the diary with nothing to suggest it came less than naturally to her. An interval of spring like weather marked the end of this peaceful interlude. London was very cold and foggy when they arrived on Friday 13 January. Two days later Gabrielle's health had deteriorated, as had her spirits. 'Very unwell all day. Lying about in a dressing gown. Sent for Theodore W (her doctor) in the afternoon. Said I had pleurisy. Fearful day. Black E. wind. London is fearful in winter'. Nevertheless she was up early on Monday to be at the Old Bailey by 10.30 a.m. when her husband's trial began. Other interested parties were assembled - 'Had lunch with my dreadful M in L'. That relations between Anne Elizabeth and Gabrielle were more difficult than usual seems to be confirmed by the fact that on the following day, Tuesday, Anne Elizabeth sat with Charles and Barbara Cunninghame Graham in one part of the court while in quite another a determinedly cheerful Gabrielle received the homage of friends and well wishers.(34)

The seriousness of the occasion was not in doubt. The Attorney General appeared for the Crown. Asquith again represented Graham, and Burns conducted his own defence, albeit with advice from a friendly barrister. According to his diary, he was not at all well on the day he spoke, 'but in spite of a headache stuck to my cross examination of Warren and other witnesses', a process that took all day. (35) The headache did not prevent him scoring many points against Warren to the undisguised pleasure of many of those in court. According to the <u>Airdrie Advertiser</u> Warren, who had been assured and even aggressive when questioned by Asquith, grew 'decidedly snappish' when pressed by Burns to give precise details of the 'roughs' and to describe the various acts of looting in Trafalgar Square, both of which he had cited as grounds for banning meetings there. When Burns finished 'Sir Charles descended flushed and annoyed from the box'.(36) When Robert's turn came his composure gained the approval of a reporter from the new radical newspaper, the <u>Star</u>. 'He coolly took off his hat, laid down his stick, pulled off his overcoat, struck his fingers through his hair and settled down to have a calm survey of the historic court room. Graham is a striking figure as he stands in the dock with his fine breezy head of hair undivided by a parting - in the artistic disorder of which his opponents would see a touch of revolutionary unkemptness - and his moustachios to match. He is over middle height and although not strongly built is decidedly wiry. His features are clear cut - his nose sharp and his eyes keen.'(37)

On his behalf Asquith argued that his purpose on the day had been to attend a lawful meeting in a public place that had long been recognized as such. And that what he had shouted was not' Now for the Square' as a leader encouraging his followers (to whom the indictment referred to as evil disposed persons whose names were unknown) but a polite announcement viz;- 'I have come to attend a meeting in the Square'. This was undeniably far fetched and the Court was not convinced. The judge, Mr Justice Charles, then proceeded to instruct the jury on the nature of the separate charges of riot and unlawful assembly. A riot was a disturbance of the peace by at least three persons who, with the intent to help one another against any person who opposed them in the execution of some enterprise or other, actually executed that enterprise in a violent and turbulent manner to the alarm of the people. An unlawful assembly (an ancient and rarely used term) was an assembly of persons with the intent of carrying out any purpose, lawful or unlawful, in such a manner as to give firm and courageous persons in the neighbourhood, ground to apprehend a breach of the peace in consequence of it. Charles told the jury they had to decide whether the defendants simply went quietly to the Square to ask leave to hold a meeting, intending to come away again, or if they went there deliberately to assert their alleged, or real, rights; it mattered not which, by forcible means dangerous to the peace. If the second the jury had to consider if they had sufficiently executed their purpose to constitute them rioters. If they did not think so they could find them participators in an unlawful assembly. This was a signal to the jury to be merciful which they heeded. They found Graham and Burns guilty of unlawful assembly; not guilty of riot or of assaulting the police. Anne Elizabeth was convinced that this more lenient verdict was due to an effort behind the scenes of her old friend, Robert Wright who, since 1883 had occupied the very influential position of junior Counsel to the Treasury.(38)

All the same Sir Charles Warren was entirely vindicated. It was held that the Metropolitan Police Commissioner was a magistrate, mainly responsible for the preservation of peace and order in London. According to the law, if he stupidly or negligently failed to take the necessary precautions to keep the peace he could be proceeded against in a criminal court. He was, therefore, fully justified in forbidding a meeting in a public place if he had reasonable grounds for believing it would disturb the peace. It was further held that, though Trafalgar Square was a public place vested in the Crown, where public meetings had been held in the past, the law recognized no right of holding meetings for the purpose of discussing any question, social, political, or religious.

The sentence followed hard upon the verdict - six weeks in prison though mercifully without hard labour. That Burns who for the first two days of the trial had worn a frock coat like everyone else, on the third appeared in a blue serge jacket, was taken as meaning the accused had expected something of the sort: 'he is a careful man', the Airdrie Advertiser explained.(39) Both of them, but more particularily Robert had had a narrow escape. If, as a Member of Parliament he had been convicted of either of the other two charges - riot and assaulting the police - his career at Westminster would have come to an abrupt end. Unlawful assembly was such an arcane offence some of the sting was drawn from the conviction. Even so he found himself the object of severe criticism by those who felt strongly that one who assisted in making the laws should not assist in breaking them. 'Graham must expect for some time to come to be a pariah among MPs' William Morris commented in the Commonweal. 'To do him justice he is not likely to care much about that'.(40)

Taken down from the dock Burns and Graham were conducted through a series of underground passages connecting the Old Bailey with Newgate Prison. In response to a plea by Asquith to Mr Justice Charles, Pattie Burns and Gabrielle were allowed to say goodbye to their husbands. They were shocked to find them already behind bars, each with a warder at his elbow. Robert gave Gabrielle a letter for the Pall Mall Gazette. After thanks for its efforts to defend free speech, it registered his defiance of the verdict and the sentence. 'When daffodils begin to peer it is a nuisance for a politician to have to live retired for six weeks', he began; however, to an ex-ranchman neither prison food nor clothes would be a punishment. More seriously it castigated the Government for its folly in turning what might have been an insignificant civil broil into a full blown catastrophe by which it precipitated 'by a good ten years the close grips that must finish the struggle, I hope a constitutional one, between the rich and poor.' (41) Until transport arrived to take them the short distance to Pentonville where they were to serve their time, they were held in a room across the corridor from the condemned cell whose last occupant had been Israel Lipski. At Pentonville where they arrived late in the evening they were stripped, searched, weighed ,bathed, and given a set of old but clean underclothes and a new jacket and trousers marked with the broad arrow. Thus attired they were conducted each to his own cell where, the door locked upon them, they were left to cope as best they could with the harsh reality of solitary confinement.

Finished in 1843 Pentonville was a model prison. That is to say it had been specially designed to put into effect the theory - widely held - that the quickest way to make a criminal see the error of his ways was to shut him up alone for most, and sometimes all, of his time. Those in charge of him were to use what little contact they had with him in exhortation, while he was always to keep silent. Thus isolated and humiliated his thoughts would naturally turn to repentance. One new member of the criminal class thought otherwise. 'How crass it is to shut men up in vast hotels(Pentonville had 520 cells) withdrawing them from any possible influence which might ever change their lives, Robert wrote, 'and to confine them in a white washed cell with windows of Dutch glass, gas, and a Bible, table, chair, little square salt box, wooden spoon, tin pan, schedule of rules, hell in their hearts, a pound of oakum in their hands, condemned to silence and to count the days, pricking them off under the ventilator with a bent nail or pin'.(42) The food they received was part of the punishment. Upon arrival he and Burns were put on Number 2 diet, designed for men without hard labour, women, and boys under 16. It consisted of a daily ration of 5 ounces of bread and a pint of gruel. On Sundays and Wednesdays this was supplemented by suet pudding; on Mondays and Fridays by potatoes and on Tuesdays, Thursdays and Saturdays by soup. When Robert complained of hunger he was transferred to Number 3 which allowed cooked beef without bone on Mondays and Fridays. When he complained of cold he was given an extra blanket and as a concession, a mattress.(43) This was a luxury most prisoners received only after months of good behaviour. John Burns fared rather better in the beginning. No sooner had they entered Pentonville than he was found to be suffering from jaundice which caused his removal to the prison infirmary. Though Robert had a bladder infection he was judged fit enough to undergo the full rigour of his sentence. To be shut up in such a place was a severe ordeal. 'Day follows day with 'skilly', exercise, with chapel, with dreary dullness, and with counting hours', he wrote. 'Night follows night, and when the light goes out the tramping up and down the cells begins, the rappings, and the mysterious code by which prisoners communicate sound through the building like an imprisoned woodpecker tapping to be free; tremendous nights of eight and forty hours, a twisting, turning, rising oft, and lying down to rise again, of watching, counting up to a million, walking about and touching every single article; of thinking upon every base action of one's life, of breaking out a-cursing like a drab; then falling to a fitful, unrefreshing sleep which seems to last but a minute and then the morning bell'. (44) But however isolated he thought himself the world outside was far from forgetting him. Tributes and testimonials to him and Burns for their defence of free speech appeared on every side. At the same time much was made in the newspapers of past incidents in Robert's life; the time in Entre Ríos for example when he fell ill of typhus as a result of having swum a river to bring help to a sick neighbour, quoted to show his latest exploit in Trafalgar Square was entirely in character. However, while keen to let its readers know how their MP was faring in Pentonville, the <u>Airdrie Advertiser</u> continued somewhat tongue in cheek about him. His solicitor had been to see him and given the paper an account of his appearance. 'his beautiful auburn moustaches have not been touched, nor has the prison barber laid violent scissors on his attractive beard and flowing locks', it reported. According to the solicitor Robert told him life in prison was 'very jolly'.(45)

It was hardly that for Gabrielle who now found herself called upon to play a new supporting role; that of almost as much of a martyr to the cause as Robert himself. Every good socialist and radical wanted to do their bit to help her. Thus Annie Besant told William Stead she had called on Mrs Graham; 'she was so glad to see me poor little thing'.(46) It was unfortunate for Gabrielle that she was suddenly in demand when she had not fully recovered from the pleurisy diagnosed before the trial. According to her diary, as soon as she had said goodbye to Robert she retired to bed for three days getting up only on her birthday, 22 January. Dutifully thereafter she went out and about; to a political meeting in Camberwell; to spend the day with the fashionably radical Duke and Duchess of St Albans; to call on Mary Costelloe - 'Disliked her exceedingly' - the diary noted - and, suitably chaperoned, to call on Stead at the offices of the Pall Mall Gazette.(47) In the aftermath of Bloody Sunday he was beside himself with excitement not so much at the way things had gone - too many of the marchers had failed to confront the police for that - but at the way he thought the situation might now develop. Like Robert Cunninghame Graham Stead believed the existing order of society must be replaced, by violence if necessary, and that the effect of Bloody Sunday would be to advance this upheaval by a significant number of years. He made no secret of the fact that he felt called upon to lead the people towards this goal, and that in the PMG he possessed the means. A newspaper, he wrote in 1886, was more powerful than the other estates of the realm. 'An editor is the uncrowned king of an educated democracy, his paper the great court in which all grievances are heard and all abuses brought to the light of open criticism'.(48)

There was truth in this much to some people's dismay. As the New York Sun remarked some time after these events, Londoners did not like being told that between 1884 and 1888 Stead came nearer to governing Great Britain than any other individual. The trouble was that Stead's personality was such an unbridled mixture of bizarre emotions it made them nervous. Kind and generous, compassionate towards those labouring under the evils of an unjust society, he was also turbulent, brash, hyperactive, and given to melancholia. Married to a devoted wife who gave him six children he indulged in exaggerated guilt each of the many times he fell for another woman. According to Shaw 'he was a puritan who brooded so intensely on sex his brain had gone maggoty; sex and sin being in his view synonymous.'(49) Among men his conversation was notoriously Rabelaisian (as was Robert's). (50) Stead's greatest moment of notoriety of which he was exceedingly proud, had come in 1885 following a series of articles in the PMG with the title 'The Maiden Tribute of Modern Babylon', exposing the scandal of juvenile prostitution. Stead had paid £3 for a little girl ostensibly for sex, taken her to a brothel where she was examined, certified to be a virgin and put to bed. Stead returned a little later with a Salvation Army woman officer to whose care he entrusted her. The enormous outcry this escapade aroused resulted in the hasty passing of the Criminal Law Amendment Act which raised the age of consent from 13 to 16. Because on abducting the child Stead had ignored what laws existed, he was sentenced to three months in Holloway Jail which he served in a mood of exaltation. It was a matter of public knowledge that each year on the anniversary he recalled the thrill of sacrifice by wearing prison clothes. When Burns and Graham were sent to Pentonville Stead was able to relive his own experience of incarceration under the guise of enlisting suppport for them. As the wife of a political prisoner Gabrielle was naturally the object of much sympathetic interest. As soon as Stead discovered she was also young and pretty he directed the full force of his unlikely charm upon her.

This certainly did not lie in his physical appearance. At the age of 36 Stead was a tall, thin, unkempt figure, shambling along in an unbearably loud suit and a shabby sealskin hat. His voice proclaimed his Northern origin and his manners were peculiarly his own - when moved he burst into tears no matter where, or with whom he was. But he was a genius in detecting what it was that people valued about themselves; in drawing them out and in showing them appreciation. A number of highly intelligent women became attached to him in this way. Among them were Madame Olga Novikoff, an unofficial ambassadress for Tsarist Russia; a masterful woman she had great influence over Stead. Annie Besant was another used to having her own way but not where Stead was concerned. At this particular moment she was in hot pursuit having conceived a violent passion for him. (51) Though he replied patiently and sympathetically to a spate of letters, hers was a feeling he did not share. Gabrielle's appearance when this awkward situation was at its height must have been a welcome distraction, providing Stead with a legitimate opportunity to help and advise a most attractive woman, bereft for the time being of her husband. The newcomer, moreover, was quite as intelligent as Annie Besant, just as attractive, and eleven years younger. The language of his letters to Gabrielle reveals how much Stead was enjoying the situation. 'I often think of you, my dear widowed heroine,' he wrote on one occasion, 'and hope that the good God is helping you to bear the proud but weighty burden for His sake'. 'I telegraphed you today in the vain hope that I might see you, for I am in rather low spirits and felt as if it would have been inspiring to see your face and tell you the latest news from Pentonville', he wrote on another. So far as Gabrielle was concerned their relationship offered something she wanted very much and had long been trying to achieve - recognition as a writer; the opportunity to see her work in print. Fully aware of this Stead proposed she should write an article for the third number of <u>The Link</u>, the journal of the Law and Liberty League.(52)

When it was set on foot immediately after Bloody Sunday this organisation, masterminded by Stead, attracted interest from most radical and socialist groups, including the Socialist League, the SDF and the Fabian Society. The <u>Link</u> was to be the means whereby the League would establish units of control in every parliamentary constituency whose aim would be to work towards an entirely new moral order to replace the existing Government. Members would begin by monitoring the behaviour of the police, Poor Law guardians, landlords - any citizen in a position of influence - in order to report and condemn via the Link behaviour that did not meet their strict requirements. Stead, whose dearest wish was to become the founder of a new Church, and who was a fanatical admirer of Oliver Cromwell, named these units Ironside Circles. This was enough to persuade the leaders of the SDF that the whole idea was profoundly antidemocratic; on 14 January Justice warned its readers that the proposed Centres and Circles were essentially secret societies with which they should not get involved.(53)

Acknowledging Gabrielle's MS on 14 February Stead described it - with less than his usual enthusiasm - as 'very nice and bright'. It had been posted from Gartmore whither Gabrielle had gone on 30 January, much to the relief of her mother-in-law, the last person to see any advantage at all in a connection between Robert's wife and the notorious Editor of the PMG. 'Mrs Graham went to Scotland on Monday night' , Anne Elizabeth told Pattie Burns, 'she is far from well and the doctor thought she would be better out of London. She will find plenty to do in Scotland and that is the best thing to make the time pass quickly. A fortnight is gone today'. (54) Gabrielle arrived at Gartmore to find the weather had turned cold again. On 1 February she wrote, 'Went a little into the garden. Lovely day, snow on the hills, bright and clear. Campbell burning leaves. Nothing out but some hellebores and aconites. Saw Grant (the factor) about business in the afternoon. Wrote to Jamieson for money. Wrote letters and did accounts.' The diary shows that Gabrielle much preferred action out of doors to business inside. 'Arranged papers and arranged papers' she wrote wearily one day.(55) It was embarrassing to have to apply to the Curator for cash which was not always readily available. On this occasion, as on others, Jamieson sent a cheque, not to Gabrielle, but to Grant who was required to enter the amount in the books before signing the money over to his mistress.(56) The Gartmore estate was still heavily encumbered with debt, hence Jamieson's continuing grip on the Graham finances. However there was one direction in which Gabrielle was beginning to make progress on her own account. On 7 February she was received with acclaim when she deputized for Robert at a meeting in Coatbridge of the local Liberal Association which was attended by an unusually large number of working men. A report of her speech appeared in the PMG; this time Stead's congratulations were sincere. (57)

8 February was the second anniversary of the riot of 1886, the occasion when John Burns had become famous as the man with the red flag. His diary recorded the solitary manner in which he celebrated the occasion (he had been returned to his cell by then, having recovered from jaundice). After singing the Marseillaise and the Carmagnole, he inscribed 'Long Live Socialism" 'Ca ira, and 'John Burns' on the wall, then, 'Released from prison' he wrote on Saturday, 18 February. 'Took out messages although watched when changing my clothes. Received by William Morris, Annie Besant, and Michael Davitt'. (58) Wise in the ways of prison authorities they and a few others had been outside the gates of Pentonville since 6 a.m. When Burns and Graham appeared an hour later their first and only thought was food. Adjourning to the nearest coffee shop on the Caledonian Road they fell upon meat pies and bread and butter which was all that was available until bacon and eggs arrived. Some time

later Charles and Barbara Cunninghame Graham drove up in a cab, followed shortly after by Anne Elizabeth. On seeing her Robert struggled up out of the narrow pew. 'The lady fell on his heart without a word', the Standard told its readers; 'All right, mother' was the ex-prisoner's response. Arriving last Gabrielle was observed to deliver kisses all round.(59).

Notes to Chapter Nine

1. Airdrie Advertiser 12 Nov. 1887
2. The Commonweal 10 Nov. 1888.
3. Walter McClaren was Liberal MP for Crewe. John Bright was his grandfather. Charles Conybeare, a barrister, almost as much of a hothead as RBCG, was Liberal MP for Camborne.
4. PRO,HO; 144/204/A47976
5. Critchley, TA., 'The Conquest of Violence', Constable, 1970, p.154
6. PRO,HO;144/204/A47976/8
7. ibid., A47976/8
8. The Commonweal, 22 Oct. 1887.
9. Hansard, CCCXIV col. 1758.
10. Mearns A., (pseudonym of William Preston) 'The Bitter Cry of Outcast London', London, 1883.
11. PRO,HO; 144/204/A47976/42e
12. Williams, W.W., 'The Life of Sir Charles Warren', Blackwell, 1941
13. ibid., p.220
14. PRO,HO;144/204/A47976/43e
15. Note. For instance, on 2 August 1880 when Bradlaugh asked a crowd of 15,000 in the Square for a vote in favour of his being allowed to take the Parliamentary oath and so his seat, several thousand of his audience interpreted this as an invitation to escort him to the Commons there and then. They surged out of the Square, down Whitehall to Palace Yard where police had to struggle to keep them out.
16. Laurence, Dan H., ed 'Bernard Shaw. Collected Letters 1874 - 1897', p. 177. Shaw to Morris, 22 Nov. 1887.
17. PRO,HO;144/204/A47976/53
18. Glen, R.C., ed., Reports of Cases in Criminal Law 1886 - 1890. Vol XVI, H. Cox, 1890. Regina v. Graham and Burns, Jan. 16,17, 18, 1888.
19. Finger, op.cit., p. 188.
20. The Times, 14 Nov. 1887.
21. BL, Add. 46288, ff 53-58.
22. The Commonweal, 19 Nov. 1887
23. NLS Acc 11335 /34, AEB to Barbara CG, 14 Nov. 1887.
24. ibid.
25. Airdrie Advertiser, 21 Jan. 1888.
26. Ibid.
27. Pall Mall Gazette, 14 Nov. 1887.

28. <u>Airdrie Advertiser</u>, 26 Nov. 1887
29. ibid.
30. ibid.
31. Ibid., 3 Dec. 1887
32. Kelvin, J., ed., 'Collected Letters of William Morris', Princeton U. Press, 1987 Vol II, Morris to G. Burne Jones, 14 Jan. 1888.
33. NLS Acc 11335/135 Diary for 1888.
34. ibid., 16 Jan. 1888, and see <u>Airdrie Advertiser</u>, 21 Jan. 1888.
35. BL, Add. 463101, 16 Jan. 1888.
36. <u>Airdrie Advertiser</u>, 21 Jan. 1888
37. The <u>Star</u>, 16 Jan. 1888..
38. Glen, op.cit., pp 420-435. NLS,Acc.11335/34; AEB to Barbara CG, 14 Nov. 1887.
39. <u>Airdrie Advertiser</u>, 21 Jan. 1888.
40. The <u>Commonweal</u>, 26 Nov. 1887
41. <u>Airdrie Advertiser</u>, 21 Jan. 1888.
42. Cunninghame Graham, R.B., Sursum Corda in 'Success', Duckworth 1902
43. PRO,HO;144/294/A47976/19
44. Cunninghame Graham, 'Success' op.cit.
45. <u>Airdrie Advertiser</u>, 28 Jan. 1888.
46. Stead Papers, Churchill College, Cambridge, Besant to Stead, 22 Jan.1888.
47. NLS Acc 11335,/135, Diary 23 Jan. 1888.
48. Stead,W.T., 'Government by Journalism', in <u>Pall Mall Gazette</u>,—1886
49. Pearson, H., 'Bernard Shaw His Life and Personality', Reprint Society,1948, p. 108.
50. Holroyd, M., 'Augustus John A Biography' Penguin, 1976, p.171. 'Graham delivering a string of improper stories all decently clothed in his impenetrable Scottish dialect'.
51. Stead papers, Churchill College, Besant/ Stead Correspondence.
52. NSL Acc 11335/141, Stead to Gab.C.G. 11 Feb. 1888.
53. The <u>Commonweal</u>, 26 Nov. 1887.
54. BL Add. 46288,f 88; AEB to Mrs Burns, 1 Feb.1888
55. NLS Acc 11335 /135, Gab diary 31 Jan. 1888, 2 Feb. 1888
56. ibid.,Acc.11335/141
57 BL Add 46310.
58. The <u>Standard</u>, 20 Feb 1888

Chapter Ten

The People's Hero

A few hours only after his release Robert and Gabrielle visited the offices of the PMG. 'Mr Graham says that since his incarceration he has increased in weight but no one would say so to look at him', the paper reported. 'He looks somewhat worn and wan. He is only 35 but his hair has greyed... His voice also sounds somewhat hollow and hoarse due partly to disuse and partly to a cold. The usual exuberance of high spirits which distinguishes the young laird of Gartmore was subdued into a quiet cheerfulness'. (1). Visibly exhausted and, in reality, downcast, Robert was obliged to preserve an air of cheerfulness throughout the celebrations organised to mark his and Burns' release. These were mandatory; the opportunity to register continuing defiance of the government. At 6 p.m on Saturday there was a tea party; 'a confused affair' , according to William Morris, 'and no wonder as the place was crammed but as a meeting was as enthusiastic as possible, in fact the audience cheered the prisoners so much they could hardly speak' (2). When they did the faintness of their voices betrayed their debilitated state. Two days later they were guests of honour at the meeting called by the Law and Liberty League at Allen's Riding School on the Edgware Road, an important occasion, Morris noted; the presence of William O'Brien emphasizing the closeness of the Irish to radicals and socialists: 'it brings London coercion in line with Irish'. Morris, who arrived ten minutes before the meeting was due to begin, was dismayed to find the place so full he could not get in; 'however I thought I must try; so I left the others and dived among the crowd, who were very civil though like packed herrings in a barrel and they handed me along so that at last I got through' (3). On the platform he found Michael Davitt and Robert Cunninghame Graham; Burns and O'Brien coming later; 'everybody was in a huge state of excitement, and cheered everybody they recognized. I did not have to speak after all as Davitt (who was Chairman) put on various MPs who were not down on the programme to speak and some of them were very long winded. There was a bit of a row at the end.'. The row was caused by Hyndman who attacked Liberal Members of Parliament for not being present and, subsequently, those Liberal MPs who were present for their craven lack of support on 13 November. Morris thought this injudicious of him: having been asked to come, they had; 'and we were therefore prepared to accept their repentance, I suppose. Mrs Besant spoke very well, so did Graham, Burns was successful in holding the audience though he was too long, he was very well received'.(4). Burns, whose robust and vivid language was no small part of his growing reputation as a political leader was very much on form, developing the theme that had preoccupied him in his prison cell. The French chose the Bastille in which some of their fellow creatures were suffering for daring to oppose the Executive Government as a symbol to crystallize and galvanize their aspirations, Burns told his audience. They whom he now addressed could make Trafalgar Square their revolutionary square and let their Bastille be Pentonville prison. And when they had captured Trafalgar Square - and he intended to be one of those to do it - let the celebration of their capture of their open air town hall - their Trafalgar Square revolution - be the demolition of their Bastille - that cursed prison at Pentonville...' the embodiment of all that is bad in the worst possible forms of government and the system of society'(5). At some stage in these turbulent proceedings Robert left for the Commons in order to put a question to the Home Secretary as to whether Warren's ukase forbidding meetings in Trafalgar Square was still in force. Matthews replied it had not been revoked. Robert then asked whether Her Majesty's government had any reasonable ground of apprehension in prohibiting the meeting on 13 November. Matthews did not reply and, although Hansard indicated an attempt by Robert to press this crucial point he obviously did not succeed. (6). He was not up to a fight at that particular moment. He was suffering from inflammation of the bladder which prevented him from sleeping; the reason why, he thought, he was so hoarse. On 24 February Gabrielle warned Burns; 'he must not speak; his voice sounds weak and hollow. I am anxious about him and rely on you to prevent it'.(7)

    He had to save his strength for the next ordeal. On 1 March the Commons were to begin a two day debate on 'Public Meetings in the Metropolis' the second in under a year. A rumour to the effect that Graham's tailor had made a replica of his Pentonville suit for him to wear to the House <u>a la</u> Stead caused much foreboding among MPs. The potential ghastliness of such an appearance had already been revealed by a cartoon in <u>St Stephen's Review</u>, 'The Convict', showing a belligerent looking Graham, arms akimbo, stiffly encased in a suit of broad arrows. (8). And when he and the Prime Minister encountered one another; 'Are you thinking where to put the guillotine', Salisbury demanded. 'In Trafalgar Square of course' was the prompt response. (9). Very much beyond a joke was the article hot from the press in February's <u>Contemporary Review</u> called - with a certain lack of tact - 'Has the Liberal Party a future?' As far as is known, though Robert's efforts to become a writer began as early as his sojourn in the Argentine, this was the first time his name appeared in print. It was a promise of things to come that would make him far more famous than his exploits in the House, while the content of the article foretold a change in the landscape of politics that he did much himself to bring about. If the Liberal Party's purpose was to redress social inequities, pass good laws, remove the stigma of poverty, stand between the poor and the police, the employed and the employer, tenant and landlord, may it live 1,000 years. If not let it go. <u>Laissez faire</u> was pretty device in a book but a poor thing in practice; '<u>Laissez faire</u> the Factory Acts and <u>laissez faire</u> the Irish and the Highland landlords, <u>laissez faire</u> the chaos of London nogovernment and you will in a short time have to face a civil war or revolution', Robert warned the Party. Of late the Liberals had concerned themselves too little with the condition of the people question. 'I doubt all optimistic views. I believe that never before in England have relations between the State and the people been so intimate and strained. I doubt whether the Spirit of Hate and Fear animating the one and the Spirit of Menace and Discontent the other have ever encountered each other before with such virulent pressure as at this moment' The people disliked and distrusted politicians, Liberal as well as Tory and there was now a debate among intelligent workmen throughout the nation on such subjects as the nationalization of capital and land, State regulation of hours and wages. The miners were foremost in adopting the new direction. They were not idiots. They understood Marx when he wrote that there would be enough for all were it more evenly distributed. 'The new democracy seems not to reverence Liberalism as we once knew it', Robert noted, but Gladstone. It is the name, the personality of the man that holds the voters.' His very shortcomings were condoned while his colleagues were Tories at heart posing as Liberal leaders. The poor were bludgeoned in London, the crofters driven to desperation and they did and said nothing. If the Party was to have a future it must get rid of these nobodies and show it had no fear of modern thought. It must pledge itself to an eight hours Bill, institute municipal government for London, nationalize the land and begin public works for the unemployed. Then, with good luck it might regain the confidence of the people; 'That is to say if some other party has not been beforehand in the field'. (10).

Such openly expressed contempt for those to whom, as an official Liberal, he had owed allegiance, was unforgivable. Ranks were closed against him on that account rather than the simple fact that he had found himself in prison. The first confrontation after the article appeared was on 1 March when the House began to debate the events of Bloody Sunday. An Opposition motion in the name of the former Attorney General, Sir Charles Russell, called for a Select Committee to examine the whole question of public meetings in London and especially the limits of the Executive's right to interfere with them. Bradlaugh added an amendment calling for an enquiry into police conduct on 13 November. In rejecting the demand on behalf of the Government, the Home Secretary, Henry Matthews, insisted that the measures used had been justified by the extent of the threat to public order on the day. After describing the mounting unrest in and around the Square ,especially the scenes of disorder at Westminster Abbey on Sunday, 23 October, he told the House that James Timms, Secretary of the MRF had had 60,000 to 70,000 men ready to come in 60 or 70 organized processions to bear down on Trafalgar Square at the same hour on 13 November, 'and the defendants [Burns and Graham] who were convicted were manifestly waiting for those processions and have since boasted in letters and speeches that 'if our man had come to the scratch we should have carried the Square like a dose of salts.' Police considerations determined the Government's actions on 13 November Matthews insisted. He and his colleagues had done what was necessary to prevent a repetition of scenes that happened two years previously, on 8 February 1886, 'which certainly were a disgrace to the Metropolis.' Referring to the series of demonstrations by the unemployed in Trafalgar Square he said it was unsafe to allow persons to go on being massed day by day in the very centre of accumulated wealth, in the midst of the most crowded thoroughfares, in a place where preservation of order amongst thousands of persons was a task of the greatest difficulty, and where only a sheet of plate glass stood between the depredators and goods of the greatest value.'(11)

'Stayed at the H of C until midnight', Gabrielle noted in her diary for 1 March (12). The following day's proceedings were opened by the Attorney General, Sir Richard Webster, who like Matthews, insisted on the absolute necessity of meeting force with force on 13 November. As evidence of the desperate threat to public order he quoted John Burns' call to his followers to make Trafalgar Square their revolutionary Square and Pentonville Prison their Bastille. What would the House think of the Government if, confronted by a man capable of such language, and supposed to be a leader of thousands, it at once withdrew the order forbidding meetings in the Square? Put like that the Government's case looked formidable and Sir Charles Russell was quick to reassure Liberal voters by emphasizing that the Opposition had no quarrel with the verdict in the Burns and Graham trial. In that he was supported by most of the Liberal newspapers, while even Anne Elizabeth was forced to admit to Barbara that Robert had brought his troubles on himself though, she hastened to add, that did not excuse brutality by the police.

2 March was another long day for Gabrielle in the Ladies' Gallery. The Speaker contrived not to let his eye fall on her husband until very near the end of the whole debate by which time he was exhausted. 'I was ill but managed to get it all out' he told Burns who, somewhat surprisingly, was not present to support his fellow convict (13). On getting to his feet Robert tried to strike a note of moderation. He wished to free those involved from the aspersions cast on them of being revolutionary. He would not attack the police or government only the social system which had forced the best of its young men into the police and the best of its young women on to the streets. In spite of his resolve this was controversial enough, even more so was his accusation that the police had been kept without food on 13 November to create hatred between them and the demonstrators. Free speech was essential in a place as crowded as London, he went on ,more sensibly, a safety valve without which secret societies would grow up as in Russia. Turning to the evidence of riotous intention presented by the Government, he asked what sort of riot could it have been when 60,000 men were to have assembled and all the properties which the Hon. and Learned Attorney could produce in court (at his trial) were two pokers, a piece of iron, and a piece of wood with nails in it? There had indeed been an illegal assembly, he went on, warmer now, an assembly of 4,000 police and soldiers in the middle of the metropolis for no adequate reason and in time of high peace. He would admit it was bad taste for the unemployed to parade their insolent starvation in the face of the rich and trading portions of the town. They should have starved in their garrets as he had no doubt many members of Her Majesty's Government and most of the upper classes would have wished them to do. [cries of Order, Order and Divide]. If to be a revolutionary was to wish to ameliorate the condition of the poor of London, to wish for a more democratic form of government, to wish that MPs should be paid for their services, ...then he was a revolutionary. But it was a calumny that he had urged men to break the law. With his customary courtesy he thanked the House for listening to a man struggling with weakness, trying to place before them what he considered a most serious Constitutional question. He ended by warning them the time would come when he would hold a meeting of as many men as Trafalgar

Square would hold; when the Government, Whig or Tory - so greatly would public opinion have changed by then - would be only too glad to assist him in preserving law and order on that occasion. (14). When he sat down; 'you never heard such a noise, even at the roughest meeting', he told Burns. (15)

It was an audacious performance and, for the time being, if not the pariah foretold by Morris, he became persona non grata among influential people - members of Brooks's Club, for example. 'Thanks for your kind letter' he wrote to R.B. Haldane a day after the debate. 'I do not care in the least about being blackballed but I am much obliged to you for your advice. Please take my name off the candidates' list. What I like about Brooks's is the old look of the place and the Chippendale furniture, but then, if I remember right you cannot give a stranger a cup of cold water for Jesus' sake and my only use for a club is to take a [?] friend in to dine'. (16). Haldane also fell a victim to the unpopularity currently afflicting clever young men - as well as standing bail for Robert he had given evidence in his favour at the trial. The 32 year old Haldane had hoped to celebrate the New Year by becoming a QC. He was sorry the Lord Chancellor had not complied with the application, Lord McNaughton, a Lord of Appeal, told him; he did not know on what grounds - 'youth or Cunninghame Graham, or both combined'. (17)

The debate ended in defeat for the Opposition. The motion for a Select Committee was lost by 316 votes to 224, and Bradlaugh's call for an enquiry into the conduct of the police by 322 to 207. (18). The result was another blow to the activists: public support was felt to be ebbing away. Stead told Gabrielle there were difficulties about finding a hall for the meeting to welcome Robert and John Burns on their release from prison. More than one establishment had refused, including Exeter Hall. (19) 'Some sort of meeting is to be held' William Morris wrote, 'but one must not forget that there are very few people indeed who care for the subject at all.'(20). In the event Allen's Riding School was crowded but Morris continued depressed. 'I am not in a good temper with myself' he told Georgiana Burne Jones a fortnight after the Commons debate, 'I can't shake off the feeling that I might have done much more in these recent matters than I have...I feel beaten and humbled'. (21) But there were some who felt there was still all to play for, though tactics might have to be changed. One was Robert Cunninghame Graham. 'Now to business', he told John Burns on 12 March. 'My idea is to force the Government to pass a Coercion Act for London. It is plain there is no active resistance in the people but that does not preclude passive resistance. Meetings should be held if possible day after day in Clerkenwell Square and other places of that sort. As soon as they get large the Government will stop them' (22). Should the Government oblige the hoped for response was a coming together of groups of people similarily oppressed - the Irish and English working class whose common interest Michael Davitt had been strenuously promoting. Robert Cunninghame Graham's contribution would be to galvanize the Scots, especially the miners, though, for the time being, he was too ill to take an active part. After the Commons debate he had been obliged to cancel all his engagements. 'The kicking I received on 13 November has brought on a very painful affliction of the bladder and I must be quiet or it will last all my life', he told Coatbridge Liberal Association who had been expecting him to address them. (23). Here, perhaps, he stretched a point. The kicking may have aggravated a long standing problem, rather than causing it. His prison record shows he was provided with a catheter to deal with what was described as 'an old stricture'.(24) 'Don't you envy me a month's rest from the National Gas Works at Westminster?' he asked Haldane. (25) On 5 March he and Gabrielle made the long train journey, third class, from Euston to Glasgow. In spite of the late hour of their arrival many supporters were at the station to meet them, including, according to Gabrielle's diary, 'That wretch, Mcghee' - Richard Mcghee, a close friend and correspondent of Michael Davitt and John Ferguson.(26) His presence signalled that, although the constituency Liberal Party would see nothing of their MP during his enforced rest, his more recent political colleagues were to have ready access to him. The arrival home was another triumphal occasion; crowds escorted the carriage from Balfron station up to Gartmore House where the horses were taken out of the traces so that forty stout men might drag it down the drive to the front door. 'Donny Grant [the factor's son] fell under the carriage wheels', Gabrielle's diary noted. After an address of welcome there was dancing on the lawn in front of the house and refreshments were served to all comers. As soon as it was dark bonfires flared on the neighbouring hills. (27)

The first three days after their return home are blank in Gabrielle's diary; it resumed on 10 March; 'I gave Margaret notice. Crocuses out and blue anenomes in my little garden'. For the next few days a bitter North East wind brought snow, keeping her indoors where Robert was feverishly writing letters. (28). His purpose was to revive interest in the strategy he had been outlining to the Scottish workers when Bloody Sunday so rudely intervened. Now four months later he and his colleagues were impatient to put it to the test via the ballot box. Since, in normal circumstances, a general election was still a long time away, the only hope they had was of a by election. Almost before Robert had fully recovered his strength a search was begun for a likely opportunity - they already had a candidate. On 14 March, a day of bitter cold and snow and a high tempestuous wind, 'R in Glasgow about Keir Hardie's election' Gabrielle recorded. Also present at this meeting were the two Ulstermen, John Ferguson and Richard McGhee and two of the Scots miners' leaders; James Chisholm Robertson, Secretary of the Stirlingshire miners, himself a parliamentary candidate for that county; Catholic, self educated, fiery, Chisholm Robertson was a force to be reckoned with among the miners; and Robert Smillie of Larkhill colliery in Lanarkshire, a lifelong trade unionist, a future President of the Scottish Miners' Federation. (29) Their discussion resulted in a manifesto signed by Robert Cunninghame Graham MP published in the Airdrie Advertiser of 17 March, St Patrick's Day - a date of some importance to a significant number of those to whom it was addressed. Under the heading 'To the voters of Mid Lanark' it began,' Owing to the unfortunate retirement of your esteemed Member, Mr Stephen Mason, a safe Liberal seat is vacant.'. Mid Lanark was particularly a democratic seat, Cunninghame Graham declared; particularly fitted to be represented by a man of the people. 'In no constituency in Scotland have the 'classes' less power'. The Liberal Party was the instrument by which the people had obtained the franchise, something the Party had always maintained must be used and not allowed to rust away...Miners in 1885 and 1886 had sacrificed causes close to their hearts (the 8 hour working day for example) in order to return the Liberal Party to power. Now was the time for Liberal Associations in Mid Lanark to show their gratitude by helping the party of labour return the first working man's representative in Scotland.

Two days later Robert was one of the speakers at a St Patrick's Day rally on Glasgow Green presided over by John Ferguson. As this was the first occasion Keir Hardie appeared in public as a candidate for Mid Lanark, Robert took the opportunity to commend him as an honest man; one who, knowing the vicissitudes of labour, could best represent working men in Parliament. On such a day the chief purpose of the rally was to proclaim Home Rule for Ireland, and this was done to great acclaim by Michael Davitt. (30). The celebrations over, Davitt applied himself to the more immediate business of Mid Lanark. Returning to London he sought Parnell's support for Hardie. The 'Chief' equivocated, caught between, on the one hand, a desire not to offend the Scots miners and other workers (as his ukase to vote Conservative had done in 1885), on the other the necessity of refraining from any action likely to upset Gladstone's more nervous followers on whom must depend the current hope of progress towards Home Rule. Davitt also approached Francis Schnadhorst, chief organiser of the National Liberal Federation and received an altogether unenthusiastic response, Schnadhorst being already convinced that for the National Liberal Party to support Hardie would allow the Conservatives to win the seat.(31). In Glasgow John Ferguson was coming to the same conclusion. A strong minded individual with a high regard for his own ability, he was accustomed to making decisions that went unopposed. However, in 1885 his public defiance of Parnell's ukase had got him into trouble with branches of the Irish National League other than the one in Glasgow he controlled; they were particularly affronted by his insistence on support for the official Liberal candidate in North West Lanarkshire. Since then, Cunninghame Graham's metamorphosis into a socialist and, more recently, his conduct over Bloody Sunday, seems to have altered Ferguson's opinion to the point where he decided prudence must prevail over loyalty to a colleague, even one who had shown himself as brave as Graham had. It has to be remembered that the driving force behind all Ferguson's manoeuvres was the fact that he was the secret representative in Scotland of the Council of the Irish Republican Brotherhood whose supreme objective was to bring about Home Rule for Ireland. (32). In spite of their public pronouncements in its favour Ferguson had now become persuaded that Graham and Hardie would do the cause more harm than good. So, while paying lip service to the similarity between labour and liberal ideas and aims, Ferguson took steps behind the scenes to ensure Hardie would not become the official Liberal party candidate at Mid Lanark. According to Robert Smillie it was Ferguson, 'an adroit wire puller' who got into communication with a young Liberal, J.W. Philips, then on his honeymoon, but known to be in search of a seat in Parliament, and invited him to come immediately to the constituency. (33)

Ferguson's very private thoughts coincided with the deliberations - also intended to be private- of the Mid Lanark Liberal Association but which were reported in the <u>Airdrie Advertiser</u>. The paper made it clear that members had taken umbrage against the Cunninghame Graham manifesto which they saw as an attempt by an outsider to tell them what to do; one moreover who had not only declared himself a socialist but was the author of the savage denunciation of their leaders in the recent <u>Contemporary Review</u>. To make matters worse, by issuing the manifesto in mid March Graham and his colleagues had jumped the gun, making it appear they were pushing the sitting member out before he had come to a final decision.. Although he had only represented Mid Lanark since the 1885 election, Stephen Mason was popular in the constituency, not least among the miners whose cause he had championed in the Commons and at the pithead. 'Would it not be better to have made certain the Hon. Member is to retire before the electors of Mid Lanark are thrown into all the excitement of a contested election and one that appears likely to be waged with very considerable keenness if not considerable bitterness?' the <u>Advertiser</u> asked on 7 April, three weeks after the manifesto's first appearance.(34) At that particular moment something like a Liberal primary was under way as no less than four aspiring politicians ; John Sinclair, Stewart Macliver, John Wynford Philips and James Keir Hardie were at large in the constituency. On 9 April when the Council of the local Liberal Association met, Philips was chosen as their candidate by 70 votes to 0 but with 22 abstentions. After this the Chairman called on all members by closing ranks behind him to defeat the tactics of those who sought to interfere from outside the constituency. 'The Liberal Association of Mid Lanark have split the difference between Captain Sinclair (who had received much support from the <u>North British Daily Mail</u>) and Keir Hardie by selecting a complete outsider' the <u>Pall Mall Gazette</u> remarked. 'Mr Philips is a young gentleman comparatively fresh from Oxford who stood for East Wiltshire at the last election and who has just been censured by that constituency for throwing them over in favour of Lanark. He is possessed of considerable assurance and ability, has an excellent presence, is the heir to a baronetcy and married to a rich, clever and charming wife. He will no doubt make a good fight of it but we doubt if the selection of an untried candidate is likely to lessen Mr Keir Hardie's resolution to split the party'.(35) In spite of his failure to be endorsed by the local Liberals Hardie's persistence in continuing the fight at Mid Lanark as an independent candidate was due above all to his own determination; he thought by splitting the vote he would force the Liberals to come to terms with him and his somewhat motley band of supporters. But it was also a decision pressed upon him by his close associate of the past few years, Robert Cunninghame Graham.(34)

When Parnell shortly told the Irish National League to vote for Philips, Robert must have recognized there was about to be a repition of the 1885 disaster at Coatbridge. Yet he took no steps to deal with it. As the Mid Lanark by election got properly under way there was something in his behaviour that gave his friends and colleagues private cause for alarm. His temper was more than usually volatile, his tone frenetic; his response to hecklers unpredictable and all too often intemperate. Those who knew him well were naturally inclined to explain this behaviour as the result of the severe blow to the head on Bloody Sunday, an effect that could have serious consequences for his entire future. A glimpse of how things were in the middle of the campaign betraying Robert's disturbed state of mind, was captured by the Airdrie Advertiser in its report of a meeting on 24 April. Headed 'Scene with Mr Cunninghame Graham at Shotts' (a conglomeration of villages cheek by jowl with ironworks and quarries), the paper described how Hardie and Graham arrived at a very crowded meeting when the latter called for a Chairman to be appointed. No one could be got to take the chair so Graham said he would do it himself. He had done it often in the diggings in America and thousands of times in Scotland and in England (laughter and cheers greeted this blatant untruth). From the chair Graham called for more working class men in Parliament. Questions were invited but none put. Hardie then addressed the meeting and was well received. Graham then called for a vote as between the official Liberal (Philips) and a miner (Hardie). 'There was a majority for those voting for the miner but many did not vote' the Advertiser ominously reported. As they were about to disperse one, Peter Forrest, challenged Robert from the floor, objecting to a statement he was alleged to have made saying miners were paid no more than 12s a week. He knew Graham was a little light in the head, Forrest declared; no doubt that was the reason he had made such a misleading statement. He, Forrest, would give £1 for every miner who took home only 12s. Mr Graham in an excited manner said he had been insulted' the reporter noted, whereupon he lauched into a furious diatribe. 'He might be light in the head but he was heavy at heart when he saw the condition of the working class, when he knew the large towns were thronged with prostitutes. Thousands were tramping the London streets with only bare stones to lay their head on and the wind to fill their stomachs. If a man was to be termed light in the head for feeling for the miseries of his fellow countrymen, then he thanked God for it'. Embarrassment was the general reaction among the crowd to the fervent manner in which he spoke. As for the subject that had figured so prominently in his recent speeches; to mention prostitutes at all was to break a powerful taboo.(36)

    The outburst at Shotts further damaged the chances of the independent labour candidate. Probably it was the reason why Henry Champion warned Hardie to stay away from Cunninghame Graham for the remainder of the campaign. National officers of the Liberal Party now rushed to Glasgow to attempt to persuade Hardie to avoid every political tactictian's nightmare - splitting the vote. But neither their arguments, nor the secret offer of a safe seat at the next election with a salary of £300 a year persuaded Hardie to withdraw. (37) His campaign struggled on with the help of speakers like Tom Mann of the SDF and John Lincoln Mahon of the Socialist League. Charles Conybeare, the ultra radical MP for Camborne who - for whatever reason - had not joined the Trafalgar Square demonstration, did appear at Mid Lanark in the early stages . But he was already very uneasy about the means of funding Hardie's campaign. 'Where do they get the money from? We have a clear right to know' he insisted to Cunninghame Graham.(38) His misgivings were shared by others due to the appearance at Mid Lanark of the mysterious Maltman Barry, Champion's alter ego. They feared it foretold a repetition of the notorious Tory Gold disaster that engulfed the SDF in 1885. As Secretary at the time Champion provided Hyndman with £400 to pay the expenses of three SDF candidates at the general election in November. As always Champion did not feel it necessary to say where the money came from. Early in December the Pall Mall Gazette revealed it came from Maltman Barry, a paid agent of the Tory party whose aim, freely confessed ,was to split the Liberal vote in favour of the Tories. Although rank and file members of the SDF ,the Fabian Society, and the Socialist League were deeply dismayed by the public furore which followed, Champion continued his close association with a man whom they regarded as unscrupulous and, very likely, a rogue. Irish by origin, a journalist by profession Barry was a political operator whose presence spelled trouble. While making himself useful to Tory grandees he professed Marxist ideas (like Gavin Clark he had attended the First International where both of them had been particularily interested in the land question); his dearest wish, however, was for Irish Home Rule. All of which explains why he was well known to , though not well regarded by, those of Hardie's present supporters, including Robert Cunninghame Graham, who had come together at the formation of the Crofters' Party.(38)

Hyndman credited Barry with complete control over Champion and great influence in the case of Keir Hardie, John Burns, 'and even Graham'. But in his memoirs he absolved Robert from the charge of short cut intrigue which he laid on all other politicians who came too close to Maltman Barry. (39) Perhaps he never knew that in 1888 Robert was caught out in a financial transaction that bore the hallmark of the Irishman. This concerned the anonymous donation to Hardie's expenses at Mid Lanark that so worried Charles Conybeare. After the by election and following pressure by the North British Daily Mail, Robert was obliged to confess he had laundered £300 given him by Champion through his private bank account. 'Having been returned as a Liberal I personally would take no money' he told the Mail 'but then I am not a working man and have means to express my opinions. I do not know where Mr Champion got the £300 nor do I care a single farthing.' Nor did he ever care; he was to resort to the same device to protect the anonymity of donors for the rest of his political career. (40) After the damage had been done it emerged that the £300 had come, not from Maltman Barry, but from Margaret Harkness, a convert to socialism which doctrine she regarded with the same ardour she bestowed on Champion's person at the time. A cousin of the numerous Potter sisters Maggie Harkness had the edge on even Beatrice (the future Mrs Sidney Webb) in practical experience of the poor. Under the pseudonym, John Law ,by 1888 she had several closely observed and able novels to her credit set against the background of appalling conditions in the East End. According to John Burns writing a few months after the Mid Lanark by election' the lady is very energetic for the poor; her sympathies outrun her discretion' he noted, tactful even to his diary.(41) Gabrielle was less tolerant. 'The Harkness' as she always called her seemed to her a driven woman whose demands upon her husband in the name of politics she resented. (42) As for the by election, the time it required, Robert's frequent absences put Gabrielle into a very bad temper. Mal Naza....Mid Lanark she grumbled to the diary on 6 April. The weather at Gartmore was splendid and she was happily sowing seeds and moving plants in the garden when Robert decreed they must return to London to drum up support for Hardie. 'Most sorry to leave' Gabrielle wrote, 'the place is beautiful, and for what - bustle, noise and worry'.(43) Back in London by 9 April 'bothering about Mid Lanark' took Robert away from her most days. That he was conscious of her loneliness appears from the fact that he invited her to accompany him on several occasions when he received visitors at the House of Commons in an attempt to enlist them to go to Scotland to speak for Hardie. Gabrielle's diary testifies to his lack of success. On 20 April (when the election was only a week away) she noted 'A fine day but rather fresh. Walked down (to the Commons) by St James's Park to see Conybeare. Saw him and learned that none of them would go to Mid Lanark.' Two days later, with only a maid for company she went - or perhaps was sent by a husband whose patience was exhausted - to Paris.(44)

The poll that took place on 27 April has become a landmark in that it was the first time the future leader of the Labour Party offered himself as a candidate for Parliament. As has almost been forgotten the election was a victory for the young man, J.W. Phillips ,who got 3847 votes to the Conservative's 2917. Hardie came a miserable third with 617, a result good Liberals hailed as nothing short of a deliverance. Yet, according to an analysis by Dr J.G. Kellas, Hardie took 20% of the native Liberal vote, representing a majority of the non-Irish electors. (45) Hardie refused to be downcast; he toured the constituency telling the 617 that, in days to come the great Liberal victory at Mid Lanark would be remembered only for the stand they made. Looking far into the future was a habit of his for which he became famous, and it was as something of a prophet and seer that, after his death at the early age of 59, Robert Cunninghame Graham always remembered him. Yet Hardie's faith in the gift of second sight was something Robert privately deplored: he felt it had an adverse effect upon the former's popularity. 'A belief in the supernatural ...is to be avoided by the judicious' he advised another young rising politician, John Burns. (46) However, in the dismal aftermath of the Mid Lanark by election he was as upbeat about the future as the defeated candidate himself. His demeanour at the meeting held the day after the result was announced stayed in Robert Smillie's mind for years afterwards. Smillie and his colleagues were understandably downcast; not so Graham. 'He thought we should go on to finance a new and independent party'.(47) In fact Robert was euphoric at the prospect of cutting loose from the Liberals and going on alone to form the long awaited Scottish Labour Party whose advent he had already publicized in an interview with a reporter from the Glasgow Evening News. The reporter was impressed. Mr Cunninghame Graham sprang into notoriety because ofr his eccentricities, he told his readers, but these appeared to him mere effervescence. The Scottish Labour Party's programme might contain controversial elements but Mr Graham himself struck him as a man of affairs who knew what he was about.(48)

The next step was a meeting on 19 May attended by representatives of interested parties - crofters, miners, land reformers, members of Ferguson's Home Government branch in Glasgow of the Irish National League; they were empowered to elect officers. These were presented to the public at a meeting in

Glasgow on 25 August when the Scottish Parliamentary Labour Party (its full title) was officially inaugurated. Robert's leading role was recognized by the office of President. Dr Gavin Clark and John Ferguson were Vice Presidents; James Shaw Maxwell, Chairman, and James Keir Hardie, Secretary. (49). Afterwards it was said - unkindly - that the officers forbore to be seen together in public in case they were taken for a full dress rally of the party. According to the <u>Commonweal</u> the rank and file - such as they were - were made up of 'land reformers, Social Democrats, miners' agents, and advanced Radicals'. Of the latter by far the most advanced was the President himself. Cunninghame Graham had tried to include the nationalization of the means of production and the nationalization of the land in the new party's platform but the other members had declared him out of order. As it stood the party's programme was a mixture of State socialism and ordinary radical reform, the <u>Commonweal</u> reported.(50) This was something Robert accepted, albeit without enthusiasm, in the hope that opinion among the members would eventually shift in his direction. That thought also occurred to Henry Hyndman, the SDF leader, who hailed the advent of the Scottish Labour Party as a definite step forward for socialism, due in no small part to Cunninghame Graham's integrity of purpose. 'At the beginning and throughout [Graham] was dead against any compromise with the Liberals', Hyndman remarked, 'and though his friendship with Maltman Barry and Champion and one or two other short cut intriguers placed him more than once in a very awkward position, he always remained personally quite straight and vigorous in his opposition alike to Liberal humbug and Tory reaction'. It seemed probably to Hyndman that 'regardless of abuse by Radicals and sneers about Tory gold, Scotland, by far the best educated portion of the United Kingdom would...take the lead in the political arena on behalf of the disinherited class'. (51) In fact by the summer of 1888 much had already been done on behalf of a certain section of that class and much more was to follow as the impulse towards self help among groups of workers so far excluded from the existing trades union movement gathered pace.

That summer Cunninghame Graham and Keir Hardie regularily turned up at an early stage of any protest only to find Henry Champion already to the fore. In the years since he had left the Army Champion had made it part of his self imposed mission to travel the country gathering information on conditions in factories and workshops (as with regard to foreign affairs his relative, David Urquhart did). Before the partnership of Sydney and Beatrice Webb Champion was probably the best and most widely informed of any private citizen in this field. In June 1888 he launched a monthly magazine, the <u>Labour Elector</u>, whose aim was to bring the harsh and unfair practices of employers against their workforce to public attention. Among the industries critically examined by Champion as Editor in the first few copies were nail and chain making in the Black Country, the production of chemicals at Brunner Mond's huge works at Northwich in Cheshire, and, most famously, the match factory owned by Bryant and May at Bow in the East End of London. The miserable conditions their employees were obliged to endure had long been known to Champion and his colleagues. (52) Open opposition came in July when Bryant and May's largely female workforce suddenly went on strike. A series of rallies and marches from Bow to the West End, vigorously promoted by Annie Besant in the Link, and publicized in the Elector, awoke public sympathy; among those who spoke for the match girls on platforms and at street corners was Robert Cunninghame Graham. The help he was now giving Champion behind the scenes with his new journal was his first taste of regular campaigning journalism; the first success Bryant and May's speedy capitulation in the face of public indignation which shamed them into raising the match girls' wages. In the course of the next few months he adopted one cause as peculiarly his own - that of the nail and chain makers at Cradley Heath in the Black Country. They tried to mount a strike for higher wages in July but had insufficient resources to sustain it.

For at least as long as the last fifty years the vile conditions in which the people of Cradley Heath had lived and worked had been obvious to anyone who cared to look in their direction. Many had. 'Disraeli called it Hell Hole', Robert wrote, Royal Commissions not a few have reported on it. Radicals have questioned about it. Philanthropists have sighed and passed on. Clergymen of various denominations have passed lives of modest usefulness endeavouring to divert the minds of the people from the ills they endure in this world to the prospective happiness they may enjoy in the next. But nothing has, so far as I am aware, ever been attempted in a practical way to improve their condition'. Then, as a result of the attempted strike, an official enquiry by the Labour Correspondent of the Board of Trade once more drew attention to the very urgent need for reform. It was in the margin of his copy that Robert scribbled the words already quoted as applying to a wider context; 'Tinkering can do little good. The system must be changed. Still I propose to venture'. The opportunity soon arose. The report, entitled 'The condition of Nail Makers and small Chain makers in South Staffordshire and East Worcestshire' was presented to the Commons on 9 November and ordered to be printed as a Parliamentary Paper when Members might debate it. It was damming. Having considered that 'for at least the last 150 years the conditions of the nailors has been wretched in the extreme...except the abatement of the truck system and the excessive employment of children, all the evils then complained of...exist today, intensified to some extent by increased population and the pressure of outside competition.' The domestic workshop system which still prevailed in the making of nails and small chains was the root of all evil the Board of Trade's Correspondent reported: he called for a Royal Commission of Enquiry to be appointed and for the House of Lords Committee into Sweating - sitting at the time - to add the subject to its already long agenda.(53)

In a pamphlet published shortly after the Board of Trade report appeared Robert Cunninghame Graham gave a devastating glimpse of what its Correspondent meant by evil. Cradley Heath, when he visited it, struck him as infinitely worse than anything he had encountered at Coatbridge. 'Let me try to place it before you', he wrote, 'A long straggling poverty stricken red brick Worcestshire village. Houses all aslant with the subsidences of the coal workings underneath. Houses, yes, houses because people live in them. But such dens. Ill ventilated, squalid, insanitary, crowded; an air of listlessness hanging on everything. Not a pig, not a chicken, not a dog to be seen...Something picturesque withal about these wretched houses, something old world about the shops where the people slave. Something of pre-machinery days in the deliberate tenacity with which the chains are made. The crowded little workshop, with its four or five 'hearths', its bellows, its anvils, its trough of black water, its miserable baby cradled in a starch box. The pile of chains in the corner, the fire of small coals, the thin, sweating girl, or boy, or old man. The roof without ceiling, the smell of bad drainage, the fumes of reeking human beings pent in a close space - such is a Cradley Heath workshop. Mud , dirt, desolation, unpaved streets, filthy courts, narrow reeking alleys, thin, unkempt women, listless men with open shirts showing their hairy chests. Mud, dirt, dirt and more mud...Work, work, always; ever increasing, badly paid, from early dawn till after dark; from childhood to old age, and this is the chain they forge. Stunted forms, flattened figures, sallow complexion, twisted legs from working the treadle hammer... are the outward and visible signs of which the chain and nail makers' dull, dogged, despairing resignation, born of apathy and hunger is the inward and spiritual grace.' This sublime patience had but one reward, Robert wrote- neglect. If there had been park railings to pull down or landlords to boycott, their grievances would long since have been addressed. As it was, while everyone agreed that the small domestic workshops in the Black Country were grotesquely out of date, one could not simply impose a factory system on the industry; that would not deal with the middlemen, the foggers, who took such a large share of the profits. 'To introduce the factory system without legislation would do more harm than good. The factory system under some benevolent, go-as-you-please, supply and demand, church and chapel going capitalist would indeed be handing over the poor people to be more sweated than ever... for without doubt there is still marrow in their bones for the clever man of business to extract if he had the chance. The factory system I look for is one under the direct control of a local authority created by the Government and elected by the nail and chain makers themselves.'

This was the sort of scheme put forward in a later section of the pamphlet by John Lincoln Mahon, a young engineer of Irish origin, with a taste for political theory. Described by E.P. Thompson as a 'floating agitator', Mahon had become involved with the crofters' struggle in 1883 and was a member of the Scottish Land and Labour League. In London he attended the Hammersmith branch of the Socialist League and was for a short while its Secretary. He resigned in 1885 when he took up a job in a gun factory in Bradford. At first his attitude to Parliament reflected that of William Morris - he saw no usefulness or good in it. However, after 1886 he was often in the company of Robert Cunninghame Graham when his attitude began to alter. In 1887 he published a programme for the prospective Labour party which had the benefit of a typically sparkling Graham introduction; now, in 1888 he added his name to the Cradley Heath pamphlet with detailed proposals for the reform of the system.(54)

In mid November the affairs of the nail and chain makers were temporarily eclipsed by the first anniversary of Bloody Sunday. This same day also saw the resignation of Sir Charles Warren. The reason for his departure was the continuing antipathy between him and Henry Matthews: the Government was forced to admit that his reluctance to take direction from the Home Secretary was hampering the efficient performance of its duties by the Metropolitan Police. So far as the general public was concerned, by and large it had supported Warren's measures the previous year. Now, suddenly, it turned against him as a result of the failure by the police to catch Jack the Ripper, the individual supposedly responsible for the series of horrific murders that occurred in Whitechapel during September and October 1888. That Warren's departure was imminent was fairly widely known. That his downfall came exactly a year after his great triumph in Trafalgar Square was a cause of huge rejoicing to the radicals and socialists who had not ceased to inveigh against him and who on 13 November gathered on Clerkenwell Green to commemorate the events of Bloody Sunday. On moving off some of the crowd were involved in a fracas outside the nearby police station. The following evening Robert Cunninghame Graham rose in the House of Commons to protest against alleged police brutality in dealing with the assembly at Clerkenwell. He quoted a newspaper report of between 15,000 and 16,000 people who, at the end of the proceedings, had been scattered, and some of them beaten by mounted police. Though present at the rally he did not himself witness that particular incident. However, these reports of it seem to have reawakened disturbing memories of his own part in the previous year's riots, and upset him to the point where he lost all sense of proportion. In a performance that caused many of those who heard him to doubt the balance of his mind, he warned MPs that the people would turn in the end, and that they would have some frightful event like that which led to the execution of the Chicago Seven to debate. And then he said 'For the past year I have pleaded at many private meetings with men of the more violent section of advance in this country on behalf of the Rt Hon. Gentleman, the Home Secretary, and do not hesitate to say before God and this House I have stood between death and the Rt. Hon. Gent. the Home Secretary, many times'. This hint of assassination, in the context of his speech, was dangerously close to a threat. On rising Matthews chose to ignore it. No one had been hurt at Clerkenwell and no complaints had been made; the incident in question had been caused by a few police horses becoming restive.(55)

Robert's next appearance in the Commons was on 29 November when he gave notice of moving the adjournment in order that the Board of Trade report on Cradley Heath might be debated. At this Brooke Robinson, Tory member for Dudley ,which included Cradley Heath, put down a notice of motion the effect of which was to prevent the adjournment being moved. On 1 December Robert asked the First Lord of the Treasury, W.H. Smith, if he would give time for Robinson's motion to be discussed. When Smith refused on the grounds that the Government was already dealing with the matter by referring it to the Lords' Committee on Sweating, a furiously angry Cunninghame Graham described the whole affair as a 'dishonourable trick'. 'The Hon. Member is conducting himself in a most unusual and unparliamentary manner in making use of language of that kind', the Speaker warned; 'I must request him to withdraw the expression'. 'I never withdraw 'Graham replied, 'I simply said what I mean' . The Speaker twice more asked him to withdraw .' I refuse, Sir, to withdraw it' 'Then I must ask the Hon Member to withdraw from the

House'. 'Certainly Sir I will go to Cradley Heath' was Graham's parting shot which drew a 'bravo' from Charles Conybeare (who had also been to Cradley Heath in defiance of the convention that Members did not trespass on one another's territory).(56)

Conybeare had to continue the story of what happened next in the second part of the Cradley Heath pamphlet. Brooke Robinson did eventually bring on his motion but at the impossible hour of 2 a.m. on 8 December when he castigated Robert for not being present. An indignant Conybeare rose to tell the House that Graham had been called urgently to Scotland where his wife was desperately ill, something Robinson should have known since it had been widely reported in the press. This news had caused the Graham's friends to make enquiries. The only surviving letter of thanks for their concern shows Robert in the grip of high anxiety. On 14 December he wrote to thank a Mr Smith for his kindness. 'Mrs Graham is, I grieve to say, so seriously ill that I start tomorrow for Spain. I fear there is little chance of her ultimate recovery. What I regret is that our sudden departure will prevent me from raising the case of the Cradley Heath people on the Appropriations Bill. With much sorrow that the reports are too true.'(57)

Here is a puzzle. We now know that diabetes ran in the Horsfall family; Grace Stevenson suffered from it; the youngest daughter, Dorothy, died from it aged only 18. Gabrielle herself was destined to succumb to it but not for another twenty years during which time she led a remarkably active life. The letter she wrote to Mary Evans from Gartmore on Christmas Eve 1888 was not that of a sick woman nor was there any sense of urgency in her reference to their plans for spending the Parliamentary recess in either Italy or Spain.(58) With hindsight one may suppose that this time it was Robert who bolted, using the sudden illness of his wife as an excuse for escaping a situation that had become intolerable to him, and which, given the highly nervous state he was so obviously in ,posed a threat to his reputation. It was not the first time he had dropped out of sight to avoid disaster. Of course the blame was laid upon the injury he had received in Trafalgar Square. There might have been another explanation. The infection of the bladder might not yet have cleared, in which case he might still have been subject to the intermittent high fever that affected its victim's judgement. With regard to Gabrielle, to look back at her diary for 1888 is to perceive that, while she did not conduct herself like a woman who had just been told she was suffering from a very serious disease she was very far from all right.

Notes to Chapter Ten

1. Pall Mall Gazette, 18 Feb.1888. Reproduced in the Airdrie Advertiser, 25 Feb. 1888.
2. Kelvin, J., ed., op.cit.,Vol.II, p.746.
3. ibid., Morris to Jenny, 23 Feb. 1888.
4. ibid.
5. BL Add. 46310, (Burns' diary), 18 Feb. 1888
6. Hansard, 3rd series, CCCXXII Col 879.

7. BL Add 46284, Gab. CG to Burns, 29 Feb. 1888.
8. <u>St Stephen's Review</u> , 28 Jan. 1888. (reproduced in Watts & Davies, op.cit., p. 74).
9. Tschiffely, op.cit., p.233.
10. <u>Contemporary Review</u>, February 1888.
11. Hansard, 3rd series, CCCXXII, 1 March 1888, Cols 1879 - 1899.
12. NLS, Acc. 11335/135, Gab diary, 1 March 1888.
13. BL Add. 46284, RBCG to Burns, 12 March 1888.
14. Hansard, 3rd series, CCCXXIII, Col. 127.
15. BL Add. 46284, RBCG to Burns, 12 March 1888.
16. NLS, Acc.5903, RBCG to Haldane, 4 March 1888.
17. Sommer, D., 'Haldane of Cloan. His Life and Times 1856-1928'.
18. Hansard, 3rd series, CCCXXIII.
19. NLS Acc. 11335/141, Stead to Gabrielle.
20. Kelvin, J., ed., op.cit., Vol II, Morris to Jenny, 10 Feb. 1888.
21. ibid., II, p.755, Morris to G. Burne Jones, 17 March 1888.
22. BL. Add.46284, RBCG to Burns, 12 March 1888.
23. <u>Airdrie Advertiser</u>, 3 March 1888.
24. PRO. HO, 144/A47976/19.
25. NLS , Acc. 5903, RBCG to Haldane, 12 March 1888.
26. NLS, Acc. 11335/135,Gab. Diary, 5 March 1888. Note. Richard McGhee was an Ulster Protestant with advanced views on social questions. See, Moody,T.W., 'Michael Davitt and the British Labour Movement 1882 - 1906' in Transactions of the Royal Historical Society. 5th series, 3, 1953.
27. NLS, Acc 11335/135, Gab. Diary, 6 March 1888.
28. ibid., 19 March 1888.
29. ibid., 14 March 1888
30. <u>Airdrie Advertiser</u>, 17 March 1888.
31. Kellas, J.G., 'The Mid Lanark by election and the Scottish Labour Party' in Parliamentary Affairs, 18, 1964/65, pp. 318 -329.
32. Moody, T.W., 'Davitt and Irish Revolution 1846 -1882', Clarendon Press, 1981, p. 88.
33. Smillie, R., 'My Life for Labour'; Mills and Boon, 1924, pp 290,291.
34. <u>Airdrie Advertiser</u>, 7 and 14 April 1888.
35. <u>Pall Mall Gazette</u> 28 April 1888.
36. <u>Airdrie Advertiser</u> 28 April 1888.
37. Pelling,H., 'Henry Champion' in Cambridge Journal, VI, 1953.
38. London School of Economics, Francis Johnson Corr., Conybeare to RBCG, 20 April 1888.
39. Hyndman, H., 'Further Reminiscences', Macmillan, 1912, p.242.
40. <u>Airdrie Advertiser</u>, 23 June 1888. And see, BL Add 46288, RBCG to Burns 10 Feb 1891 (sending a cheque for £10 passed through his bank 'so the donor can remain anonymous').
41. BL, Add.46310 Burns diary .
42. NLS Acc 11335/55, Gab. to RBCG 'Has the Harkness committed her last atrocity on you?' 25 Feb. 1891.

43. NLS Acc. 11335/135, Gab. Diary, 22 April 22 May.
44. ibid
45. Kellas, op.cit..
46. Cunninghame Graham, R.B., 'With the North East Wind' (on Hardie's funeral) in Brought Forward, Duckworth, 1916, pp 51-59.
47. Smillie, op.cit., p 293.
48. Glasgow Evening News, reproduced in Airdrie Advertiser, 21 April 1888.
49. Kellas, op. cit.
50. The Commonweal
51. Hyndman, op.cit., p. 242.
52. Justice
53. Parliamentary Papers. (Board of Trade Report)
54. Cunninghame Graham, R.B. MP. 'The Nail and Chainmakers A Plea by RB Cunninghame Graham MP. A Protest by C.A.V. Conybeare, A Proposal by J.L. Mahon' The Labour Platform Series Number 2 (1888)
55. Hansard
56. ibid.
57. Austin; RBC G to Smith, 14 December 1888
58. Austin; Gab. CG to Mary Evans, 24 December 1888.

Chapter Eleven

The New Militants

It was Robert's great misfortune that two of the people he loved best were destroyed by illness. His father's incapacity formed the dark background to his youth, while one of the diseases his contemporaries most feared overtook his wife. Diabetes ran in the Horsfall family; towards the end of her life Gabrielle was condemned to knowing she could not recover and died at the early age of 48 (1). But in 1888 when Robert's anxiety caused him to abandon his parliamentary duties in such haste, diabetes had almost certainly not been diagnosed. The symptoms were there: frequent chest infections when pneumonia threatened; diarrohea that left her dangerously weak; for some considerable time these were treated as first causes which might, in themselves, prove fatal. There were other signs of her condition, less serious, none the less damaging in the effect they had upon Gabrielle's relations with those around her. She grew increasingly irritable; trivialities put her out of temper. 'Had a row with Peregrina and beat her' the diary recorded, and, 'Was very cross with poor Robert over some indigestible rhubarb tart I eat (sic). She began to resent the claims Parliament made upon her husband; of necessity she was often left alone and, though she made gallant attempts to occupy her time - window shopping down Regent Street, long bus rides to inspect churches in the remoter parts of London; whole days spent in the British Museum, or the National Gallery - 'my loneliness does oppress me', she told her diary (2). Yet there were many occasions connected with his political interests she could share ; she appeared on the platform at his meetings, or spoke as a committed socialist in her own right when he took the chair. She was seen with Robert at marches and rallies in the East End - the meeting at Bow in support of the match girls , for example - she wrote letters to the newspapers; she was one of the speakers on Saturday evenings at Kelmscott House in Hammersmith in the uncomfortable and gloomy lecture room Morris had made out of his long narrow coach house, and she wrote pamphlets whose tone was a touch schoolmarmish and whose theme - after Morris - was the utter iniquity of capitalism and modern commerce. (3). Add to this the attention she received in the aftermath of Bloody Sunday as the gallant wife of the principal hero and she seemed poised to become, at least, an understudy to socialism's leading lady, Annie Besant. But she lacked Annie's fire, endurance, and consistency; the disease from which she suffered saw to that. The changes in her mood were even reflected in her appearance. The sketch that accompanied her furious letter to <u>The Times</u> in defence of Robert over Bloody Sunday was of an alert, vigorous, and capable young woman, curiously modern in appearance due to her cropped hair, whom one could easily imagine cycling in pursuit of Bernard Shaw (4). By contrast her portrait by George Jacomb-Hood conveys introspection and, even, religiosity. The eye is carried to a crucifix behind the dark head of a peaky Spanish looking woman who barely supports the painter's gaze.

Portrait of Gabrielle by George Jacomb-Hood. In private hands.

Whatever the nature of this particular attack Gabrielle had recovered by the end of December. Nothing untoward occurred during the Christmas recess which the Grahams spent in Spain. In Madrid Robert visited the Chamber of Deputies and made contact with Spanish socialists and anarchists with whom he kept in touch after returning home. Now that the Labour Elector appeared weekly instead of monthly he was commissioned to keep a watching brief on Continental politics. Almost every week he had to report the arrest, imprisonment, in some cases torture of French, Italian, and Spanish activists whose respective governments saw them as a threat to the established order. On too many occasions anarchists' meetings had ended in violence and death. The most notorious and recent involving bombs was the one for which the seven Chicago anarchists had been tried. Following the execution of three of them in November 1887, and for a long time to come, anarchism stood no chance of a fair hearing. It was against this background of terrorism abroad and severe disaffection among the Irish at home that his contemporaries had to assess Robert's casual references to his own connection with what he called 'men of violence'. Like much else in the remarkable adventure that had so far been his life the truth of this could not positively be established: there might be an element of fantasy in these claims, yet it might all be true. What could be said for sure was that disturbed state he was seen to be in during the Mid Lanark by election was again apparent in some of the interjections he made in the House of Commons in November. Nor did it escape the notice of a new and very shrewd acquaintance he made while in London 'seeing about Cradley Heath'. (5)

'Cunninghame Graham was here last Sunday week', Friedrich Engels wrote to Karl Marx' daughter, Laura Lafargue, on 2 January 1889; 'a nice fellow but always in want of a manager, otherwise brave to foolhardiness, altogether much of an English Blanquist' (6) From this one may conclude Engels had not missed the hint of violence that marked Robert after Bloody Sunday. Louis Auguste Blanqui, who died in 1881, had spent half his life in prison and been twice condemned to death for his attempts to overthrow successive French governments in order to replace them with a communist republic of the most extreme kind. In 1870 the Communards elected Blanqui to the insurgent government of Paris, a position he was unable to assume being still in prison for mounting a demonstration against Napoleon III Blanqui's flair for political journalism had been the means of recruiting followers; this was a skill that, when Engels met him, Robert was fast acquiring. In 1889 it won him the entrée to 100 Regent's Park Road where Engels held court among the followers of his friend the late Karl Marx. 'Engels has been resident in England for nearly 50 years', Hyndman wrote, 'and since the foundation of the 'International' in 1864 his personal influence has been more baneful than his literary work has been useful to the Socialist movement. He has been head of the Marxist clique - far more Marxist than Marx himself - which has never ceased to intrigue and vilify any Social-Democrat organisation not under its direct control'. Among the members of what he called this mutual admiration society Hyndman counted Engels himself, Henry Champion, Maltman Barry, Marx' youngest daughter, Eleanor, her lover, Edward Aveling, Keir Hardie, Margaret Harkness, and John Burns. Closely associated with them' though happily he is opposed to their methods in some particulars [is] Cunninghame Graham' (7) So, while Graham here stood accused of consorting with (so far as Hyndman was concerned) the enemy, the SDF leader once more excused him from the full rigour of his disapproval. Hyndman's forbearance was the more surprising since Robert was not only on the opposite side from him in the furious row that occupied socialists prior to the 100th anniversary of the French Revolution but secured a much more important role than Hyndman in the celebrations.

Only one idea commended itself - the coming together in Paris of workers on 14 July 1889, one hundred years to the day after the fall of the Bastille. It proving impossible to agree which group should have the honour of making the arrangements, two separate congresses, meeting separately, were the result. One to which trades unionists from many different countries, but not France, were summoned called itself the International Workers' Congress; it was supported by Hyndman's SDF and the Fabian Society. The other, composed of French trades unionists and the French Workers' Party called itself the International Socialist Labour Congress and was supported by followers of Karl Marx. From it sprang the Second International. Robert Cunninghame Graham was given the signal honour of presiding at the latter on the last day, 20 July. Among the other 19 delegates from Britain was Keir Hardie for the Ayrshire Miners (it was the first time he had been abroad). The most important act for the Marxist Congress was to call for the 8 hour day to be made universal and that May 1 each year should be the day on which workers would demonstrate in its favour. In his report to the <u>Labour Elector</u> Robert gave a vivid description of the deliberations. The 400 or so delegates met in a large music hall, the Fantaisies Parisiennes near the Gard du Nord. A high platform at one end ; on each side a row of boxes, when it was filled with people it seemed to him to reproduce exactly the National Assembly of 1789. From his seat as President he strained to see the delegates through a cloud of tobacco smoke which he likened to cannon smoke over a battlefield. The speeches pleased him for their total lack of similarity to those he was obliged to endure in the House of Commons. Those in Paris he described as fierce, logical, commonplace, sturdy and workmanlike; scorning rhetoric they addressed practicalities like hours of work, wages, sanitary and safety measures, and were received with frantic and prolonged applause. The chief benefit of the congress, he told the readers of the Elector lay in the fact that men who had read of each other, men like Bebel and Liebknecht from Germany, Lavroff from Russia, Guesde from France, Cipriani from Italy and William Morris from England met, talked, and smoked together.

This was Robert at his most informed and sympathetic; the pity was that those who read him would be confined to the very small number of English working men who subscribed to the Labour Elector, a situation Engels deplored. 'Apart from the Star (the new radical paper edited by T.P. O'Connor), we have only the Labour Elector, a very obscure and very shady paper run on money from unavowed sources and therefore very suspect',(9) he told Paul Lafargue when assessing the Marxist' advantage in the run up to the Paris congress. In a move to counter this kind of attitude, in an editorial on 6 July Henry Champion announced a change in the paper's ownership; the Elector was so successful in reaching members of the working class its power was too great to be vested in the hands of one man , by which he meant himself.. Henceforth it would be run by a committee; he would be Editor; Tom Mann of the Amalgamated Society of Engineers, Secretary; John Burns , Treasurer with George Bateman of the Compositors, William Parnell of the Cabinetmakers, and Robert Cunninghame Graham, M.P The paper's finest hour followed hard upon this move when members of the new management committee found themselves caught up in the sudden and extraordinary surge of feeling that brought thousands out on to the streets of the East End of London in repeated demonstrations of support for what has ever since been known as the Great Dock Strike.

The Elector of Saturday 3 August carried an announcement to the effect that the following day Robert Cunninghame Graham MP and John Burns would address the first of a series of meetings in Canning Town of regular hands employed at the London and St Katherine Docks and the East and West India Dock Company. 'These men are anxious to combine and…are sorely in need of a trade union' , the paper reported, giving details of the hours worked and wages paid to stevedores, tugboatmen, lightermen and guards. The hours were long - more than 12 a day and the pay low: after hearing what Graham and Burns had to say the men voted overwhelmingly to proceed to form a union. However bad their conditions were at least they knew they would have something to take home at the end of the day. The casual labourers did not; their only hope was to wait at the dock gates until a ganger came to them when he wanted men; 'the struggling and fighting of the wretched competitors for work was the saddest sight I ever saw' Joseph Burgess wrote. (10)

The wage for casual labour was fivepence an hour and a man might be turned off with one hour's work after standing at the gate for a day in order to get a turn at all. So far the plight of men like these had not attracted attention even from so well informed an observer as Henry Champion. Suddenly they could endure no longer. On 13 August a dispute about the rate for a certain cargo at the West India Docks aroused such anger among the casual labourers they went in a body to the only man they thought might help them. This was Ben Tillett who, two years previously had formed a small society for teawarehousemen.. The 'casuals' urged Tillett to do what he could for them. On their behalf he put a demand to the employers for an increase to 6d an hour and a minimum period of employment of four hours. As the men continued very angry they attracted growing support from the regular dock employees, now well on the way to uniting among themselves. Tillett appealed for help to other union organisers; among those who responded was Tom Mann who joined the group of dockers' leaders that made its headquarters at The Wade's Arms in Poplar. Mann's colleagues on the <u>Elector</u> naturally joined him. Years later Mann recalled how incongruous Cunninghame Graham 'a West End dude' appeared among the working men in the snug behind the bar (10) In an attempt to win public support they had recourse to the tactics used by the unemployed in Trafalgar Square two years previously; each day a procession of strikers and their supporters marched five abreast to a public place like Tower Hill to hear speeches. The weather was hot and soon thousands turned out to demonstrate their sympathy. Now, as before, the most effective speaker was John Burns, the red flag that was his emblem in 1886 having given way to an equally conspicuous straw hat. As much as he was able given the demands of his parliamentary duties Robert was present at these meetings, and he and Gabrielle made a point of turning up at the dock gates in the early mornings to encourage the thin ranks of pickets in their attempt to hold the line against the large force of blackleg labour drafted in to keep the ships moving. 'Revolution was not made with rosewater' Tom Mann remembered Graham shouting hoarsely; 'I call upon you to paralyse all industry in every trade in the metropolis'. Later in the month when a Joint Committee of employers met the dockers' representatives to discuss their demands it fell to Graham to keep the anxious crowd outside in check. That meant standing on a wagon to see and be seen, telling stories, telling jokes until, after six long, hot and exhausting hours that particular meeting broke up without agreement. (11)

In between he and Keir Hardie made one of a series of visits to Newcastle where, with the help of Joseph Cowen Editor of the <u>Newcastle Chronicle,</u> they were hoping to contrive the dismissal at the general election of the city's MPs Thomas Burt and Charles Fenwick for their refusal to endorse the 8 hour day. On 3 September the focus shifted to Dundee where members of the Trades Union Congress were assembling for their annual gathering. Henry Broadhurst, Secretary of the Parliamentary Committee was their chief antagonist and, for the third year running, Hardie signalled his intention of moving a vote of censure against him. In his memoirs Broadhurst described these attacks as extremely bitter and unfair. Hardie and his socialist colleagues including Champion, Burns, Mann and Cunninghame Graham were out to discredit him, he complained; their one aim was to prove he had been a traitor to the cause. 'A newspaper called the Labour Elector was especially conspicuous for its undisguised and venomous attacks. Paragraphs criticising my action appeared in nearly every column and the homes of trade- union officials and other workmen...were flooded with this journal'. (12) At Dundee the mood was acrimonious even before the proceedings began. Hardie and Cunnninghame Graham had few friends among the delegates, who for the most part were members of craft unions, long established in their working practices and ill disposed to change. Many were contemptuous of the attempt to bring unskilled workers under the TUC umbrella. As an observer Miss Beatrice Potter placed herself most definitely in the Broadhurst camp. The new militants were trying to overthrow the craft union leaders and commit the unions to independent political action, she wrote, making no attempt to conceal her disapproval. She objected to the 'filthy personalities, envy and malice of the socialist speakers...; a crew of wretches, beardless enthusiasts and dreamers of all ages.' Cunninghame Graham whom she saw at breakfast poring over proofs of the Labour Elector, she roundly denounced as 'a cross between an aristocrat and a barber's block... a poseur but also an enthusiast, above all an unmitigated fool'. (13) She shortly had the pleasure of seeing Graham's protege, Keir Hardie, soundly beaten in his latest attempt to unseat Broadhurst. Even so his speech was respectfully received and rumour had it that, had Burns and Mann been present to support him, he might have come very much closer to success.

While Congress was still in session news came of the unexpected death of J.F. B Frith, Liberal MP for Dundee. At once the cry was heard that John Burns, leader of the striking London dockers, hero of the hour, must succeed him. It was another turning point in his career: his part in the event of Bloody Sunday had been the means of his election to represent Battersea on the London County Council, Parliament,no less, now beckoned. Among his supporters in Dundee for the Congress, beside Hardie and Robert and Gabrielle Cunninghame Graham, were Eleanor Marx and Edward Aveling. These five now threw themselves into an attempt to persuade the Dundee factory workers that Burns must be their Parliamentary representative. On 5 September a meeting was held in the Tally Street Hall for the purpose of nominating Burns as candidate for Dundee in the by- election. According to David Lowe, a journalist colleague of Keir Hardie, a lifelong socialist, the proceedings were very lively. His description throws a great deal of light on Robert's mood at this time. 'The chair was occupied by Graham but only for a few minutes, because ere the business was scarcely under way he got into hot water. One of the audience enquired whether Burns was to be run as a Liberal and the question not being answered to the satisfaction of certain parties, the meeting got slightly out of hand.

'Graham lost his temper and in a towering rage told the faithful that they were only fit to be represented by capitalists, and thereupon he bounced out of the hall. Hardie whispered to a young man [John Carnegie] to follow him, then quietly took the chair. The meeting was soon brought round... and we were willing (without qualification) to take a hand in the contest. Meanwhile Graham went striding on like a man possessed out past the Nine Wells with

John Carnegie at his heels. At last he cooled down and deigned to offer John a few epigrams on the stupidity of the working class. The return journey was more leisurely and when they reached the foot of Tally Street Graham stopped... and looked up at the hall. John said nothing and Graham walked away again. This little comedy occurred several times until [Carnegie] proposed they should go and see how the meeting was getting on, and they entered the hall to find the meeting unanimous for Burns'.

'A telegram was dispatched that same night asking Burns to contest the constituency and a reply was received next morning acceding to the request', Lowe continued, 'Public feeling was aroused and a mass meeting of Socialists, Labourists, and sympathisers was held ...at which a resolution was carried unanimously endorsing the candidature of John Burns. The speakers were [Robert Cunninghame] Graham and Hardie.' That evening another meeting was held at which 250 names were handed in to form an election committee. However immediately afterwards a letter was received from Burns which shocked the new Committee. 'He began to water his assent and stipulated that the approval of all the Trades Unions and Labour bodies should be guaranteed before he entered upon the contest' [an impossible condition] 'Meanwhile the Liberals had been interviewing some of their prominent men who, without exception, refused to stand against Burns' According to Lowe it was at this interesting moment that Edward Marjoribanks, the Liberal whip [and Robert's pet hate when they were both at Harrow] arrived in Dundee, stayed some hours during which he knocked a few Liberal heads together and departed, all in one day. 'It was supposed he returned to London where he made an offer of the Battersea seat at the first election to Burns, on condition that he withdrew from Dundee. At any rate a letter [from Burns] was received the following day withdrawing his name and giving as his reason that he was to contest Battersea of which he had a preference. Our men at once requisitioned Tom Mann to stand [at Dundee] but he declined and eventually our committee and enthusiasm collapsed like a cask without a hoop'(14).

And so in such a haphazard manner was a repetition of the Mid Lanark affair avoided. Burns' prevarication must have been a shock: to Robert especially. In the two years since they had been in Pentonville together he had regarded the younger man as his political protégé; he had had him down to the Commons, chaired his meetings; got him engagements to lecture - at Kelmscott House for example; and most recently, as we have seen, shared a platform with him in the Labour Elector's campaign to persuade unskilled workmen to form unions. On this occasion Burns showed himself the more practical of the two; Dundee would have been a disaster. If he had agreed to stand he would have stirred up all the bitterness Hardie did at Mid Lanark and more beside. Burns was a Londoner, born in Battersea; after Bloody Sunday he resigned from the SDF and founded the Battersea Labour League which paid the expenses for his election to the London County Council in 1888. Apart from the fact he was keen to represent Battersea, he would have been out of place in a Scottish constituency and, without financial support, hard put to sustain the demands of one so remote from Westminster as Dundee. Nevertheless, in spite of these legitimate objections his closest colleagues, Robert most of all, had to admit that the episode was disquieting in so far as it revealed a new and unfamiliar aspect of Burns' character. It seemed he was calculating, ruthless even, and more obstinate than they had imagined possible; they were surprised at the force of his political ambition, in the pursuit of which, to their dawning dismay, a rather too lively self interest had begun to appear.

He who suffered most from the Dundee affair was Robert Cunninghame Graham against whom the Liberal Party at large now began a savage campaign of denigration. While Burns' candidature at Dundee was still in play some local members of that party went so far as offering to support him on the understanding that Cunninghame Graham and Hardie would be asked to absent themselves from the constituency. On 12 September a leader in the Glasgow Daily Mail revived the accusation made against Hardie at Mid Lanark, this time directing it at Graham to the effect that he was using Tory gold to scupper Liberal chances at by elections. [The fact that Maltman Barry was now a sub editor on the Labour Elector lent a certain credence to this accusation]. The Mail called on the Liberals of North West Lanarkshire to turn their MP out. (15). His commitment to that constituency was already the subject of debate among those loyal to him. Earlier in the year a rumour had gone the rounds of Coatbridge that he would not offer himself as their representative at the next election [which must be held by 1892 at the latest], now his supporters called on him to reassure them that he had no intention of deserting North West Lanarkshire.(16)

Their unease was justified; things were going badly wrong with their MP. Robert's chief problem was an acute shortage of money. By 1889 his general financial situation was so bad he was hard put to justify the expense of continuing in an occupation that was less attractive to him than before. 'I am sometimes disgusted with the whole job, the jealousies and petty spite', he told John Burns, however he felt obliged to soldier on for the moment, believing he had duty to hold the line until working men were elected to the House of Commons in sufficient numbers to make their voice heard. Their failure to respond to his prompting often infuriated him; 'I fear the English working classes are born slaves' (17) he told Burns. To make sacrifices on behalf of men who would not help themselves was hard. Moreover Robert, who had always keenly felt the injustice of having to bear the burden of debt incurred by his predecessors as lairds of Gartmore, now found himself charged with the cost of extra parliamentary activities on behalf of the public at large. He made no secret of the fact that Asquith's fee for defending him at the Old Bailey after Bloody Sunday was nearly £2,000, a sum he had to find at a time when the agricultural depression showed no sign of ending. 'Sir, my thanks for your kind letter and offer of help', he wrote to Sir Charles Dilke on 29 April 1889, 'There are very few people who even ask to help one. I have also to thank you for the delicate way in which you offer to help me. However I think...that if my constituents..will not pay my expenses I cannot go on with Parliament. I shall not like to accept so great a favour from any man' (18). Dilke's motive in making such an offer probably stemmed partly from a disinclination to see a useful man wasted for lack of something he disposed of in abundance – Dilke was a wealthy man. He was also, though a Liberal who had held high office, out of politics altogether for the moment; unlikely therefore to be troubled by Robert's skirmishes with the Party grandees. In 1885 Dilke, who had been Under Secretary for Foreign Affairs in Gladstone's second government, suffered instant public disgrace as the result of being named as co-respondent in the divorce of Donald Crawford, Member for North East Lanarkshire. Crawford's wife, Virginia, was named as Dilke's mistress.

Financial troubles were enough to explain the state of high irritability Robert was in; there were, however, other causes. One was physical: he was exhausted from the constant travelling up and down the country , endlessly repeating the call for an 8 hour working day. However much he believed in it he had been at it so long his patience was sorely tested. Correspondence was a penance; 'writing for hours to newspapers and labour candidates', he grumbled to Burns; he must have help and someone other than himself must act as spokesman for 'the advanced party' (19). Now, too, he began to suffer severe attacks of rheumatism, the result his doctor told him, of all those arduous journeys in South America. The other cause of his uncertain temper was foreboding as to the state of his marriage. As usual that autumn in the brief intervals he had from political engagements Robert made for Gartmore. Gabrielle was not there, unaccompanied except by Peregrina, she had gone to Spain. 'I am pleased to hear you contemplate publishing a novel', Keir Hardie had told her the previous year, and went on to offer some cloudy thoughts on inner consciousness and the hidden springs of life. The project would develop into a life of St Teresa of Avila which occupied Gabrielle for the next five years during which she and Robert were frequently apart. (20)

His own inclination was increasingly for change, for escape not only from his parliamentary and political duties but from his responsibilities as laird of Gartmore. A rumour he was pleased to encourage had it he would return to ranching in America. When this reached the <u>Airdrie Advertiser</u> his long suffering supporters in Coatbridge had to deny it as best they could: in spite of their requests for information he would not give them any hint of his plans for the next election. He seldom appeared in the constituency, leaving Keir Hardie to represent him. Yet when he did attend a gathering of supporters of the Scottish Labour Party in October he was still able to rouse the audience to such a pitch of enthusiasm they hailed him as their own Parnell (21). Signals like this were taken sufficiently seriously by the Liberal Party tacticians for Edward Marjoribanks to offer by-election deals to the SLP over several marginal seats [at Partick in February 1890 for example] the object being, as always, to avoid splitting the vote and letting the Tories in.

These negotiations together with the progress of his 8 hour bill through the Commons, and his normal constituency duties, amounted to a crowded schedule. Yet by mid-November weeks before Parliament went into recess, Robert had departed to join Gabrielle at Valencia in the hope that warmer weather would ease his stiffness. From Spain they went to Lisbon where he interviewed Portuguese socialists for the <u>Labour Elector</u> and in the same article reflected on the foolishness of the Brazilians turning out a perfectly good Emperor. Dom Pedro whom Robert had last seen riding about his Imperial capital of Rio de Janeiro, was now back home in exile - 'a good European turned out and a lot of greedy rogues put in'. In spite of these forthright remarks the article lacked its customary verve as if its author was hard put to summon up an interest in Lisbon's political affairs. 'I could write plenty more', he remarked somewhat defensively, 'if I was not right over a stable in which two mules are fighting and if I had not, for want of blotting paper, to get up at the end of each sheet and take a little sand out of the wall with a knife to dry what I have written'. (22) Here, suddenly, after years of arid polemic, was a brief glimpse of a new kind of writing that was beginning to come more often and more easily to him: to say what he saw; to describe what he, and not others, did, he discovered was intensely satisfying.

The sight of Dom Pedro provoked an attack of acute nostalgia for the old free way of life in South America. However, at that very moment, just as it seemed youth and excitement lay behind him, he and Gabrielle made the acquaintance of a country that disposed of vast spaces, largely unexplored, but which lay open to a seasoned horseman. That country was Morocco. 'I have seen what England was like in the Middle Ages', Robert told readers of the Elector after spending Christmas 1889 in Tangier. Twelve miles across the Straits from Gibraltar and he had entered a time warp where the mistakes of modern life had yet to be committed. Not that everything was satisfactory, he hastened to assure his readers. Public affairs were mismanaged and there was great injustice. A large proportion of the scum of Europe was gathered in Tangier. There were no roads, no railways and little education. But there was, besides, no great push for advancement, no great hurry; no one felt obliged to conform - one Moor was very unlike another - something that made for happiness he felt. 'Is not a country where each man cultivates his own little plot, sits in his own little shop, works at his own loom, wields his own hammer at his own forge nearer to Socialism than England?' he demanded, describing a situation William Morris must have approved. (23). He laid plans to explore further as soon as he was able.

On their return the Grahams found all London in a state of uproar. On 24 December a petition for divorce from his wife, Kitty, had been filed by Captain William O'Shea MP naming Charles Stuart Parnell as co-respondent. Such news must always have caused a sensation but it was the greater for its timing - the very moment Parnell stood higher in the esteem of friend and enemy alike than at any previous moment in his career. Although in December 1889 the Commission appointed by the Government to enquire into his conduct of Irish affairs had not yet published its report, Parnell had already been triumphantly vindicated in the matter of the letter printed in The Times over his signature purporting to approve the murders in Phoenix Park in 1882 of Lord Frederick Cavendish and his companion.(24) In February 1889 this had been shown to be a forgery. Ten months later Parnell paid his first visit to Hawarden where on 18 and 19 December he and its master, as Leader of the Opposition, held discussions about Home Rule for Ireland, now to be introduced as soon as the Liberal Party returned to Government. 'Nothing could be more satisfactory than [Parnell's] conversation', Gladstone purred, 'full as I thought of great sense from beginning to end'. (25). Five days later he had to eat these words: there was nothing sensible about Parnell's new predicament.

Nevertheless the Irish leader preserved his customary aloof and contemptuous stance in public as though nothing of consequence had occurred. Privately he assured Gladstone and colleagues like Michael Davitt, that O'Shea's accusations had no substance. So long as the facts were not established there was little anyone could, or would, say on his behalf.

Society did not tolerate open discussion about divorce. In these circumstances the article signed Robert Cunninghame Graham MP which appeared in the Labour Elector of 25 January 1890, caused another sensation. Its savage contempt for those who presumed to condemn the Irish leader recalled Charles Bradlaugh in his heyday as Iconoclast. 'Yes I know Thou shalt not commit Adultery', it began' That is to say Thou shalt not be found out'. He had no opinion on the case, Robert remarked; it could not matter to him, or to Home Rule for Ireland, yet he heard an attempt was to be made to destroy the policy by casting aspersions on Mr Parnell's character. 'Is this as it should be? Perhaps Mr Stead will say yes. Perhaps the great Nonconformist Party will say yes . I say No.' Parnell's only offence was to have been found out. 'If he has been found out...Look round the House of Commons, Look at the well fed, idle, rich men in it and then ask me to believe they are all earnest practisers of social purity'. Had Parnell been an obscure member of the Irish Party, 'some McHafferty or O'Rafferty or some member for Ballyshaughsguttery, is one to suppose anyone would have cared a farthing? It is because on the Liberal posterior the imprint of Parnell's boot is to be traced...that this freezing tone has come over so many of his quondam allies, assuming for the sake of argument the O'Shea thesis'. Comparing the present attitude towards Parnell with similar treatment of Charles Dilke, Robert went on: 'What! Hunt an adulterer from public life and take a sweater to your chaste arms? The thing is ridiculous in a state of society where marriage itself is too often a clerical absolved prostitution - in a society where we see a Prince marry his daughter to a boon companion ...and no one raise a word of disgust or contempt'. The reference was to the recent wedding of Princess Louise, aged 22, eldest child of the Prince and Princess of Wales, to the 40 year old Earl of Fife when the bride was seen to be in tears throughout the ceremony. (26).

Such sentiments were to be expected from a young man who had gone to prison for his part in Bloody Sunday; a 'sort of wild creature who has been making himself most offensive in the House, more Irish than the Irish themselves'. Thus Lady Monkswell in her diary, whose husband was a close friend of Anne Elizabeth Bontine. Nothing would convince her Parnell was innocent either of political crimes or of seducing another man's wife. Lady Monkswell regarded him with horror - that animal' , she called him, and when Lord Monkswell's duty obliged him to attend a lunch for Gladstone at which the Irish leader was present 'Bob actually...shook hands with a man upon whose head rests at least a hundred murders'. (27) Many others shared her view. The fraught atmosphere was not conducive to serious political discussion and so progress towards an Irish solution came to an abrupt halt pending the divorce hearing. That was not until November 1890 when the verdict brought the precarious edifice Ireland's future was supposed to inhabit crashing down, and with it the modest outbuilding Robert Cunninghame Graham and his Scottish Labour Party colleagues had been busily constructing.

In the months that intervened between his defence of Parnell in the Labour Elector and the case, Robert had much to do in his capacity as a Scottish Labour Party leader. In March he threw himself into helping the Liverpool dockers force the shipowners to improve wages. In spite of valiant efforts by himself and the Ulsterman, McHugh, they were unable to rouse the public to the same pitch of enthusiasm that had helped to secure victory in London. The Times laid the same charge upon Graham as, by publishing the Piggot forgeries, it had on Parnell - of advocating the use of violence by others to achieve his own ends. (28). He was unrepentant. 'Things are bad here' he told John Burns from Liverpool on 20 March,' There is no food, no money. The blackguard newspapers boycott and the blasted public sympathy is a quality not to be found'. (29) Two days later he wrote 'All goes badly. Public sympathy be dammed. Davitt comes this afternoon'. Davitt's arrival in Liverpool was the signal for both sides to open serious negotiations. Though Robert's letters to Burns written during the strike demonstrate his strong desire to see the hero of the London dockers' battle give a repeat performance in Liverpool, Burns stayed away, pleading illness. Burns was becoming increasingly his own man. To Robert's often expressed annoyance he failed to answer letters; he did not write letters when asked to do so; he would not turn up at meetings. By the summer of 1890 there were rumours he was going to 'do a Bradlaugh' and turn a Liberal Party man. 'Haldane, smart fellow, is saying it', Robert warned him; it was damaging because it made it appear Burns was nothing without the Liberals. 'Send a denial at once to the Glasgow Herald that you are a follower of the Grand Old Man', Burns was instructed (30). Came the autumn and Robert's thoughts turned towards the next general election. 'I write with a special object', he told Burns in September 1890, 'You will find yourself very lonely and also much hampered in the next Parliament all alone. I shall not be in it as I have no money for another election. Now the ablest man beside yourself in the whole Labour Movement is Keir Hardie. Do help him in West Ham both for your own sake in Parliament and his. I of course should have liked to see him represent miners but that is impossible for the Scottish miners have no money to run him. Therefore it is good policy to get him in anywhere. I should have liked to have been there too (though I hate the place), as I have fought and beaten them for a hearing this year as he will have to do. However I cannot manage it.' (31)

In fact he could- and did - but by the time the election was held circumstances had changed and he stood, intending to be beaten. What happened first was that on 18 November 1890 Captain O'Shea was granted a decree nisi whereupon all those who had hounded Parnell from the moment O'Shea was known to be suing for divorce, considered themselves entirely vindicated. Parnell did not instruct counsel or attend the hearing. O'Shea's evidence which contained some misleading statements was heard without cross examination. As soon as the verdict was known politicians had to decide how to deal with a situation in which the leader of the Irish Parliamentary Party now stood revealed not only as the guilty party in a divorce, but as one who had betrayed his closest colleagues by pretending ignorance of O'Shea's charges. Robert Cunninghame Graham's correspondence with John Burns contains several references to Parnell in the months before the hearing which show that he was one of the privileged few to whom the Irish leader personally declared his innocence (32) Yet he seems to have taken the court's verdict to the contrary as a matter of course: if it did not surprise him it did not shock him either. According to more than one of his biographers that was also Gladstone's private reaction. But he was the principal public figure called upon to give expression to the prevailing sense of outrage that greeted the decree. Many factions, of which the most prominent was the so-called Nonconformist Party - as Robert had foretold it would be - were clamouring for Parnell's head. The Irish leadership election was due on 25 November. On 24 November Gladstone wrote a private letter to John Morley but which was intended to be shown to Parnell before the election, with the calculated result that he would immediately fall on his sword. It contained a carefully constructed phrase to the effect that if Parnell remained leader of the Irish Party Gladstone would find it impossible to continue as leader of the Liberal Party. The plan misfired: Parnell did not see the letter until after he had been re-elected leader by the Irish MPs. The letter was given to the press when the crucial phrase caused a major political sensation. The following day Robert saw the Irish leader enter the chamber of the House of Commons. 'I walked forward and shook hands with Parnell before the whole House. Not a man of them all would speak to him', Robert told Gabrielle (33) Disaster greeted these events. The Irish party split; Parnell became Gladstone's bitter enemy; those who had been closely engaged in discussions about Ireland's future began to suspect that Home Rule must now be postponed for a considerable length of time [though they could not have imagined for exactly how long]. Robert Cunninghame Graham saw at once what a blow had been dealt to his own party's plans. 'The Parnell split has, I fear, killed the Labour Party in Scotland', he told Burns on 15 December (34). That was in strict confidence; for the sake of the SLP they had to carry on but, for Robert, the task now became increasingly difficult. On 30 December Burns was told he would not be able to attend the opening of Parliament because he was crippled with rheumatism. He had been able to get to only one of the recent meetings in Glasgow and only because two men had carried him to the platform. 'The Doctor is afraid I will not get right'. In February 1891, in the course of advising Burns they must be ready to help Edward Aveling if he decided to contest Northampton at the general election, he confessed he had been ill again: he was thinking of taking a run abroad. No need to balance the relative claims of Italy or Spain; this time there was only one possible destination - Tangier from where he wrote to Burns on 24 March. He was alone Gabrielle having gone to spend Holy Week in Seville. His leg was bad but he felt a trip into the interior on horseback would do him good. 'France and England and Spain are struggling for the supremacy of this country - the pre-eminence of either would be a curse' (35)

His health was much improved by this brief sojourn in the clear air and the rolling empty spaces of the Mahgreb, and also by the prospect that there might be money to be made there. This had to be done somehow and soon if

Gartmore was to be saved from ruin. It was a task that would need all the strength he had, and if he were to succeed he must break out of the constraint of the last six years. To disengage himself from the responsibilities he had acquired would not be easy. As time went on the answer appeared to reside in the forthcoming general election.

In the meantime he continued his activities in support of the socialist movement. On 1 May he made a quick dash to Paris to join a march to the Chamber of Deputies. On 3 May he was back in London as one of the speakers at a rally in Hyde Park in support of the 8 hour working day where he shared Platform number 6 with Edward Aveling. Afterwards he was invited back to 100 Regents Park Road where he joined the household in a <u>Maibowl.</u> ' We put in four bottles Mosell, 2 of Claret and champagne. Late in the evening Cunninghame Graham actually had 2 or 3 glasses of it - he seems to have left his teetotalism at Tangiers' Engels told Laura Lafargue. (36) On 9 May Robert crossed over to Calais to join the protest in commemoration of the previous year's incident when the Army, attempting to disperse a group of miners on strike in the industrial town of Fourmies shot and killed ten people, including women and children. However, as soon as the procession got under way he was arrested amid scenes of great excitement and escorted to the ferry by a troop of chasseurs. ' My dearest Chid', he wrote to Gabrielle, as soon as he got home, ' I was expelled from France yesterday. The bother of it is I cannot now pass through France without being arrested as long as Castres is Minister'.(37)

At some time in the summer of 1891 an offer by a friend to pay his expenses determined Robert to accept an invitation from the Liberals of Camlachie, to be their candidate at the general election , at which a feeling of relief could be detected in North West Lanarkshire; ' Neither fish, flesh, nor good red herring, being sometimes Conservative, sometimes Liberal and sometimes a nobody' was the response of one constituent who dismissed him as a faddist.(38) Then, on 6 October news came that Parnell had died, less than a year after O'Shea had obtained his divorce. The immediate cause was inflammation of the lungs but Robert chose to blame the leader of the Liberal Party 'that hypocrite' for his action in throwing Parnell to the Nonconformist wolves. In an appreciation of Parnell Robert predicted - accurately as things have turned out - that in so doing Gladstone shut off Home Rule for a hundred years. 'Not that I think that Gladstone did not believe in Ireland's wrongs', he explained, 'but that he did not wish to see an Irish parliament led by a man far stronger than himself.' (39). Privately he told John Burns he wished Gladstone had died instead of Parnell. The Liberal leader's second capital offence in his eyes occurred in June 1892, in the run up to the general election, when he refused to receive a delegation from the London Trades Council who wanted to discuss the 8 hours working day. Gladstone regarded such issues as merely another manifestation of what he called 'that leaning towards socialism of both parties which I radically disapprove' (40) On hearing the outcome a furious Cunninghame Graham demanded an audience and persuaded Gladstone to see the men after all. It may be that this was the occasion of which Robert often spoke with pride when he succeeded in staring down the GOM (41). Be that as it may, when they came into the presence, the Trades Council delegates failed to live up to the occasion. 'They got absolutely nothing from him' the <u>Glasgow Evening News</u> reported; 'he asked them more questions than they asked him and succeeded in rendering the 8 hours and its advocates ridiculous in the eyes of the country'. (42)

There were many such diverting moments during the campaign which got under way in June. In Camlachie the contest deteriorated into farce with the Liberal Party taking every fall. Afterwards no one was in any doubt as to who deserved the blame - 'that scarecrow, Cunninghame Graham'. (43) Yet things had begun so well. So far as anyone knew Camlachie was a safe Liberal seat. In 1885 when Robert deserted it for North West Lanarkshire, it had been won by a businessman, Hugh Watt. However safe a figure he may have seemed at the time, subsequently he embarked on a series of risky enterprises, the details of which he kept to himself. By 1892 enough had emerged to ensure that, although Watt was eager to retain the seat, the Liberal Association decided to draft in Cunninghame Graham to replace him. Watt thereupon announced he would stand as an Independent Democrat. No doubt the Liberals of Camlachie believed that, with a MP of six years standing they were well out in front of other parties. They soon discovered how wrong they were: their horse did not fall at the first hurdle, he crashed straight through it and had to be disqualified. As soon as the campaign began Robert abandoned all pretence of support for the leaders of the party that had given him his nomination. He denounced them for shameless platering, for shuffling, for, in particular, juggling Ireland in their own selfish interests. At Gladstone he levelled insults that, in the opinion of the <u>Glasgow Observer</u> [the Liberal Catholic paper], 'would have come badly from a Salisbury Tory'. (44). His own description of himself was as the Liberal, Labour, and Trades Council candidate for the Camlachie division of Glasgow. The local politicians jibbed at that; in a very short time John McCulloch became the Gladstonian candidate for the same constituency, and Graham popped up with a new label - that of the Independent Labour Party. (45)

The appearance of five other candidates in the same interest [Henry Champion in Aberdeen; R. Brodie for the College division of Glasgow; Chisholm Robertson in Stirlingshire; Bennet Burleigh in Tradeston, and John Wilson in Central Edinburgh] moved Gladstone to accuse them of a desire to punish the Liberal party for concentrating on Ireland to the alleged neglect of the working man. 'The Irish question *is* a labour question', he insisted, 'for the Irishmen are ...a nation of labourers and this is the most urgent part of the Irish question'. The Irish were the most needy; they were oppressed by unequal laws, insulted by open breaches of privilege; deprived of institutions of local government. 'Let it then be understood', Gladstone thundered, 'that any Liberal voter who cooperates in bringing about the return of a Tory candidate votes against the Irish nation, and especially against the Irish labourer'. (46) With five candidates in Camlachie - Labour, Gladstonian Liberal, Independent Democrat and Liberal Unionist - it was beginning to look as if a split vote would let the Tories in. As in the case of Mid-Lanark and Dundee Edward Majoribanks was hastily sent north to see if he could retrieve the situation, not only in Camlachie but in the four other seats where an ILP candidate was standing.

His efforts in Camlachie were unavailing for which the Glasgow Observer awarded him a large share of the blame. Mr Marjoribanks treated Cunninghame Graham with misplaced tenderness, it complained; 'the local [Liberal] leaders acted with promptitude and energy but the party wirepullers displayed towards their deserter a deference...that was both undeserved on his part and mischievous in its public effect'. Graham richly deserved cashiering at the hands of the local Liberals. 'He fostered treason to Liberalism wherever he found opportunity and then cried out like an injured innocent when the Liberals ..turned on him and rent him....refusing all approach to amicable arrangement his party.[the ILP]..broke up a meeting Mr Marjoribanks held to bring about Liberal unity. And even then insulted, flouted, baffled, Mr M had no word for Mr G other than a platonic regret that he could hardly regard him in the next House as a Liberal member. Admirable Christianity but bad political warfare'. the paper concluded. (47) The Glasgow Evening News published a profile of the maverick. Robert Gallingad Bontine Cunninghame Graham 'began to struggle against the adverse fate which imposed such a lengthy and high sounding collection of names in 1852, it remarked, and went on to explain that he married a Spanish lady 'a helpmeet as volatile as himself'. In Parliament Graham appeared a strange mixture of English pluck, Scottish determination, and Spanish temper. In appearance every inch the aristocrat he declared himself a friend of the people. There were some on the side of Gladstone who would gladly buy him over but he would not name his price. (48). Those of its readers who heard Robert, but more especially Gabrielle, in full rant on the hustings would have had no doubt what the author of the profile meant by 'volatile'. Both denounced the Liberal Party and its leaders with a degree of savage contempt that left their audiences gasping. One speech in particular, by Gabrielle, to the Glasgow branch of the Irish National League seemed calculated to cause the maximum ill feeling. She began by contrasting labour supporters - men of far reaching aspirations - with their Liberal opponents whom she described as 'miserable piddling party hacks, dull heavy beery brained dullards who would sell their souls if they had any'. Addressing men whose allegiance was to Michael Davitt she eulogized the dead Parnell]whose denial of his role in the O'Shea divorce had destroyed Davitt's trust in him]. Gladstone had murdered Parnell, Gabrielle insisted, 'he waited until Parnell was at bay' when he saw how the Nonconformist vote was going he turned to stab a wounded desperate man.' (49) Her impassioned effort was to no avail; according to the Glasgow Observer the Irish voted as one man for Cross, the Liberal Unionist.(50)

The Cunninghame Grahams were nowhere in evidence during the last week of the campaign, alone of all the candidates Robert did not put in an appearance. The result was a disaster for the Gladstonians as well as the ILP. Cross gained the seat. Robert who polled 906 votes out of a total of 7624, told his supporters he was glad to have split the vote; the ILP intended to go on doing so. The Liberal defeat at Camlachie would go far to destroy the existence in Scotland of the Gladstonian myth , he declared. (51) Camlachie was sold by traitors, the <u>Glasgow Observer</u> remarked; Graham knew all along he had no chance of winning. Why stand? Was it revenge for some slight by Liberal leaders? Or was he acting in concert with the Tory? (52). As for North West Lanarkshire where Robert had given his blessing to his successor, the new official Liberal candidate well in advance of the election, it fell to the Tory, Graeme Whitelaw by the narrow margin of 90 votes. This caused the <u>Airdrie Advertiser</u> to write its former MP off as a deserter.

Yet while reproaches were heaped upon him for his failure to live up to expectations in Scotland, he could claim a large part of the credit for a successful campaign in a London constituency whereby the future leader of the Labour Party entered Parliament for the first time. His defiance of the police on Bloody Sunday and, more recently, his efforts on behalf of the dockers during the great strike of the previous summer had made the name of Cunninghame Graham one to conjure with in the East End. Consequently, when the official Liberal candidate for West Ham, Hume Webster, committed suicide early in 1890 following the collapse of a business venture, Robert's immediate attempt to have Keir Hardie drafted in his place gained momentum from the start. Though the situation briefly resembled that of Mid Lanark, Hardie's most recent biographer, the late Caroline Benn, wrote, 'National Liberal bosses such as Schnadhorst knew that Hardie would not withdraw, and that forcing their own candidate into the field would mean the Tory retained the seat. Reluctantly, at the last minute, they left the field to Hardie'. (53)

Part of the reason for Robert's poor result at Camlachie was probably due to the fact that he spent a good deal of time speaking for Hardie in West Ham, a place that appalled him nearly as much as Coatbridge and Cradley Heath. 'Street upon street of half crooked brick abominations falsely called houses, here and there a little 'Bethel' chapel...row upon row of stalls at night when the stale vegetables are sold...on one side lines of endless docks, and on the other, lines of endless misery', he remarked.(54)

Polling took place in West Ham on 4 July when Hardie won by 5,268 to the Tory's 4,036, causing Friedrich Engels to declare; 'the spell which the great Liberal Party cast over the English workers for almost forty years is broken'. (55). Robert had to wait another week to hear his own fate at Camlachie. Another spell was broken there, which had kept him tied for six years to a place he had always regarded with ambivalence. In the circumstances prevailing at the time - his low state of health, his urgent need for money, the damaged prospects of the Scottish Labour Party - his first reaction to his dismissal probably was relief; now he had time to rest, to reflect; time to decide whether he was pleased or sorry.

Notes to Chapter Eleven

1. Horsfall Family Papers; in private hands. RBCG to Miss Mary Horsfall, 11 Sept. 1906, 'Your sister was ill for long of diabetes'. Grace Stevenson had the disease and the youngest Horsfall daughter, Dorothy, died of it in 1896 at the age of 18.
2. NLS, Acc.11335/135, GCG Diary; various dates e.g. 22 April, 14 June, 25 June 1888.

3. e.g. Cunninghame Graham, G.C., 'Readjustments', 'Art and Socialism'.
4. As an illustration to a reprint of a letter to The Times, in the Pall Mall Budget, 17 Nov.1887
5. NLS, Acc.22335/135, GCG Diary, 21 and 23 Dec. 1888.
6. Bottigelli, E. ed., 'Friedrich Engels, Paul and Laura Lafargue: Correspondance' Laurence and Wishart, 3 Vols., 9159 -1963, Engels to Laura, 2 Jan. 1889.II, p. 183
7. Kapp, Y., 'Eleanor Marx' Vol II pp 456-57.
8. Labour Elector, 27 July 1889
9. ibid.
10. Bottigelli, op.cit.,Engels to Paul Lafargue, 11 May 1889, II, p 241.
11. ibid., II, p 303.
12. Torr, D., 'Tom Mann and his times', Laurence &Wishart, 1956, p. 290.
13. Tsuzuki, C., 'Tom Mann', Clarendon Press, 1991, p 63
14. Broadhurst, H., 'From a Stonemason's bench to a Cabinet bench', Hutchinson, 1901, p. 219.
15. Mackenzie, N., and J., eds., 'The Diary of Beatrice Webb', I, 1873 - 1892', Virago, p. 69.
16. Labour Elector, 14 Sept. 1889; Burgess, op.cit., pp 116-18.
17. Glasgow Daily Mail quoted in Labour Elector, 12 Sept. 1889.
18. Airdrie Advertiser, 23 Feb. 1889, 16 March 1889.
19. Burns Papers; BL Add.46284, RBCG to Burns, 17 Aug. 1891.
20. NLS, Acc.11335/141, Hardie to GCG, - May 1888.
21 Airdrie Advertiser, 26 Oct. 1889.
22. Labour Elector, 21 Dec. 1889.
23. ibid., 11 Jan. 1890.
24. The Times, 18 April 1887.
25 Matthew, H.C.G., 'Gladstone 12875 - 1898 'Clarendon Press, 1994, p. 312.
26. Labour Elector, 25 Jan. 1890.
27. Collier, E.F.C., ed., 'A Victorian Diarist (Lady Monkswell), 1873-1895' J. Murray , 1944, p. 152.
28. quoted in Labour Elector, 22 June 1889.
29. Burns Papers, BL, Add. 46284, RBCG to Burns, 20 March 1890.
30. ibid., 30 Sept. 1890.
31. ibid., 18 Aug. 1890.
32. NLS, Acc.11225/136, RBCG to GCG, various, undated, but 1890.
33. Matthew, op.cit., pp314-15. NLS, Acc.11335/136, RBCG to GCG, n.d. but 26 Nov. 1890.
34. Burns Papers, BL. Add.46284, 15 Dec. 1890.
35. ibid.,the same to the same, 30 Dec. 1890.
36, Bottigelli, op.cit., Engels to Laura Lafargue, 3 May 1891, III, p 56.
37. NLS, Acc.1335/136, RBCG to GCG, 11 May 1891.
38. Airdrie Advertiser, 17 Feb. 1892.

39. Cunninghame Graham R.B., A Memory of Parnell, in 'Rodeo', Heinemann, 1936, pp 413-430.
40. quoted in Matthews, op.cit., p. 257
41. Burns papers, BL. Add. 46824, 8 Oct. 1891.
42. Glasgow Evening News, 17 June 1892. And see, Shannon R., 'Gladstone Heroic Minister 1865 - 1898' Allen Lane/ Penguin, 1998, p 513.
43. Glasgow Observer, 9 July 1892,
44. ibid.
45. Glasgow Evening News, 8 June 1892. Note. Although the ILP was not formally constituted until the following year the name was already in use.
46. Glasgow Observer, 23 July 1892
47. ibid., 9 July 1892.
48. Glasgow Evening News, 2 and 6 July 1892.
49. Glasgow Observer, 9 July 1892. Note. Davitt was convinced the key to Home Rule for Ireland was to continue to support the Gladstone Liberals.
50. Glasgow Evening News, 8 July 1892.
51. Glasgow Observer, 9 July 1892.
52. Benn, Caroline, 'Keir Hardie', Hutchinson, 1992, pp 85-6.
53. ibid., p 86.
54. Marx and Engels, 'Selected Works', Vol III, p. 452

Chapter Twelve

Journeys in Spain

When in 1892 the electors of Camlachie relieved Robert of his parliamentary duties, he had been laird of Gartmore for nearly nine years. Though at the time he inherited he was apprehensive about the future of the estate, he was mercifully unaware of how bad things would become by the end of the 1880s, a decade which saw the intensification of the agricultural depression, the worst of the century. Landowners and their tenants had to contend with a succession of cold, grey summers and harsh winters at a time when fresh meat and other produce from the far corners of the world had begun to invade their markets. Low prices meant pressure for rents to be reduced: their fall was steep and sustained, leading to a sharp decline in the value of land. Gartmore did not escape its share of these misfortunes. At the same time special circumstances made the task of keeping the estate afloat virtually impossible. The first charge on the income from rents was Anne Elizabeth Bontine's jointure of £1200 a year together with the £200 each due to Charlotte and Anne Cunninghame Graham, the unmarried daughters of the eighth laird. Then came over £1.000 p.a. worth of interest on loans, leaving Robert with under £2,000 for every other eventuality. This was sharply reduced by the cost of fighting three parliamentary elections which he put at roughly £1,000 a time, and the fee for his defence by Herbert Asquith at the Old Bailey in 1888 - nearly £2,000. As Lindsay, Jamieson and Haldane did not fail to warn him, by 1889 Robert was getting into debt on his own account. At the same time the mortgages secured on Gartmore, Gallingad and Ardoch that had sustained the lifestyle of his predecessors remained outstanding. Salvation, it was thought, lay in the sale of Ardoch, the estate opposite Finlaystone on the banks of the Clyde. In 1885 a detailed valuation of the houses, farms and other assets, including a tile factory and a quarry was drawn up and the estate advertised for sale as a whole at £100,000. There were no offers, even when, two years later, the price was reduced to £85,000 Eventually smaller lots were sold, the colonial Georgian Ardoch Cottage going to a private individual. (1).

Robert's resolve to extricate himself from this appalling situation was consistently supported by Gabrielle ; while their approach was pragmatic the means they applied were sometimes unusual. The immediate task was sufficiently straightforward. They had to increase income while reducing expenditure on behalf of the estate and personally. On their own behalf they looked to make money wherever they could. One of their more successful enterprises was trading in rare objects from countries seldom visited by their contemporaries but to which their special interests took them. Gabrielle had a good eye for furniture, carpets and objets d' art which she picked up cheaply while researching her biography of Santa Teresa in the remoter parts of Estramadura and Castille. Similarly Robert acquired rugs and leather goods in the souks of Tangier and Fez, and tapestries in Seville, some of which were auctioned at

Christies (2). Gabrielle bought a microscope and embarked on an erudite correspondence with a Glasgow doctor, an expert in bryology, who proposed to put her in touch with someone who might consider exploiting the Flanders Moss for commercial purposes (3). Robert pressed his Uncle Bobby for information about the Majorca Land Scheme in which William Bontine had sunk £5,000 at the behest of his brother in law, William Hope. Even some of what had disappeared would be a godsend in his present circumstances. Letters between them in April 1893 reveal that it was hardly fair to accuse William Bontine of throwing money away on this particular occasion. The scheme was directed by John La Trobe Bateman, the distinguished civil engineer who, in 1856, had begun work on bringing water to Glasgow from Loch Katrine, just five miles from Gartmore, probably the occasion when William Bontine first encountered him. Towards the end of his career Bateman turned his attention to developing land in Spain and Majorca. Some 5,000 acres of the Albufera were to be reclaimed from the sea in Majorca and brought under cultivation. According to Uncle Bobby some £300,000 was spent. 'You can take it there was no flaw in the engineering works' he remarked, when explaining that, so far as he knew, it had been a disastrous failure 'I always thought the people concerned did not understand Spain or cosas d'Hispania (sic)'. That was his last word on the subject his beleaguered nephew was forced to abandon as leading nowhere.(4)

So far as the estate was concerned, shortly after he became laird Robert introduced a fundamental change in the way the land was managed. Whenever he could, instead of letting farms to tenants, he sold feus. The procedure was practised only in Scotland under a very complicated feudal law. Whereas in England a lease had finite term, a feu, once granted by the landowner, was almost always in perpetuity. The feuar, having made a downpayment on entering the land had to pay the landowner a small sum each year at Whitsuntide and Martinmas. Under this system the landowner was relieved from much of the expense involved in renting land and in those specially difficult times, of the necessity of taking back farms whose tenants went bankrupt - as not a few of the Gartmore farmers did during the 80s and 90s. At the same time the owner had to reconcile himself to a significant loss of control over part of his estate that, more often than not, had kept its integrity for generations. Moreover, once the land was feued, all possibility of a greater return , if and when times improved, vanished. Money received in down payments on feued land went to reduce the general level of debt Robert had inherited while the twice yearly payments due in perpetuity - £40 here, £20 there - provided a welcome, if small, addition to his income. Even so his finances remained very precarious.

The ultimate solution was for him to divest himself of all his encumbrances - to sell Gartmore as well as Ardoch. The first time he seems to have touched upon the subject was in 1891. The fact that there was no male heir to Gartmore may have influenced him. He and Gabrielle were childless after 13 years of marriage while Charles and Barbara had a daughter, Olave, born in 1883. The precarious state of Robert's health, physical as well as mental, following upon his prison term, as well as that of Gabrielle, probably also made him inclined to free himself of the irksome responsibilities of laird. Nevertheless it would be an act of violence, cutting him off from what had been the central purpose of his life. The prospect caused consternation among his relatives. Anne Elizabeth did as she usually did in times of crisis - sent for Mr Wright, now a judge in Leeds. Even Charles was moved to remonstrate in a letter that reveals his good nature and his abiding affection for his elder brother. 'Kit [Anne Elizabeth] has just shown me your letter about las cosas de Gartmore', he wrote in December 1891... He had not referred to Robert's plight before due to embarrassment that he could not help him financially as that would not be fair to Barbara and Uff [Olave}. Everything to do with Gartmore was absolutely Robert's; 'your life is quite as good as mine and in my opinion better'. However before he took such a step as to sell, Charles urged Robert to go to Leeds to see Wright whose advice , he thought, was good. Charles suggested Robert should try one of the schemes Wright proposed. Even if he did sell Gartmore the surplus after paying off the debts would be nothing, and Robert would be without a house. 'Kit has been dreadfully worried and will, I know, do all in her power, but after such a miserable life as she has had I cannot think she is in any way called upon to take any step which would cripple herself'. (5)

Anne Elizabeth feared for her jointure, as her two sisters in law did for their annuities, were the Gartmore rents to be substantially reduced or cease. As Charles pointed out, with mortgages to be paid off from the proceeds of a sale there would not be enough surplus capital to provide Robert with a reasonable income, let alone themselves. Their dependent state, a serious impediment to any decisive action, had been imposed upon Robert by his predecessors. While over the years since he inherited he had become more or less resigned to the twice yearly drain on his scanty income, the unfairness of it angered Gabrielle. 'I suppose it was never intended that Mr Graham was to maintain these ladies on any income but that of Gartmore. The moment there is no surplus income their jointure must be affected', she noted grimly in the Gartmore letter book. (6)

In the spring of 1893, deaf to pleas that he should consult Mr Wright, Robert dismissed Messrs Lindsay, Jamieson and Haldane from the management of the estate saying he could no longer afford their fees. It was with 'a sort of hereditary pleasure' that he told George Campbell WS he would like him to undertake the task(7). Campbell's grandfather had been legal adviser to the eighth laird, and his father had acted in the same capacity for William Bontine. The fact that George Campbell asked for exactly the same fee as Jamieson's firm had charged - £100- suggests there was another reason for dispensing with the services of the man who, as Curator Bonis had supervised the affairs of the Bontine estate for 25 years. During that time Jamieson had become a legendary figure among Edinburgh accountants, hugely successful in everything he touched. He had spent years supervising the administration of estates whose owners, like William Bontine, were incapable of doing it themselves, he had, in consequence, great influence among the Scottish gentry. As a Director of the Royal Bank of Scotland he had even greater influence over the disposal of capital: after 1878 large amounts of Scottish money began to flow into ranching in Texas and mining in Arizona, something for which Jamieson was personally responsible. In these circumstances the fact that he apparently had nothing to do with Robert's Texan venture seems to this writer to indicate that he was not told about it until long after it began. Jamieson, who was a devout Episcopalian, dour, and agonisingly earnest, was notorious for his lack of tact in dealing with his clients. At the same time Robert's long years of exile from Gartmore had made him more than usually touchy on the subject; it was not surprising, therefore, that by 1893 he wanted nothing more than to see the back of Jamieson. Notwithstanding the letter he wrote dated 25 February 1893 was scrupulously polite. 'For some time as you know my affairs have been steadily growing worse, this, of course, is neither your fault nor mine; it is incumbent on me if I wish to preserve the place (wh. is my ambition) to exercise the very strictest economy in <u>everything</u> and in pursuance I have gradually reduced my expenses both personal and with reference to the estate...having now dismissed every superfluous servant and having made myself..master of all the details (which are simple enough of management) I have come to the conclusion that, as I am quite without employment, I had better, in order further to economize, take the management of my own affairs entirely into my own hands. Naturally after the 5 and 20 years you have been connected with this property, it is with great reluctance that I see myself compelled to take this step but the circumstances are desperate. I wish you most clearly to understand that I in no way complain either of your management or charges but that in my position I am totally unable to pay any fees for management at all' The letter ended with the request for the return of all papers, documents, rent ledgers and cash books. (8)

As soon as they reached Gartmore the documents were redirected to George Campbell because, although Robert let Jamieson believe he would be his own manager, Campbell was asked to act in that capacity. He was to collect rents, make payments such as taxes, insurance and mortgage interest, interview tenants and advise on legal matters. In March, as a matter of urgency, he was asked to arrange an overdraft of £2,000 to meet the running expenses of the estate. Payment was due in May; rents did not come in until June. Campbell was uneasy about replacing Jamieson and unhappy with the fee: £100 was scarcely enough for all that work. The response from Gartmore was imperious. Campbell was not to tell the tenants Jamieson had gone; the fee was quite sufficient given the fact the laird would direct him in the smallest detail. 'What I ask you to do for me is in reality not a very troublesome matter'. This kind of tone hardly made for an auspicious beginning; worse was to come. At the beginning of April when Campbell warned Robert that the selling of feus had reached a point where the bondholders felt their interest might be prejudiced, he provoked a furious outburst. Robert accused him of an attempt to grab the management of the estate for himself by threatening to call in the mortgages, a move that , as laird, would ruin him. But, 'I wish you to understand distinctly that I am not a man to be influenced by threats', Campbell was told. At the same time as he dismissed Campbell and ordered him to send back all the papers, Robert let it be known that he had taken the fatal decision - Gartmore was to be sold. (9)

A letter from Gabrielle to Anne Elizabeth written two days later reveals the fraught state both Grahams were in. It was an invitation to Robert's mother to come and see the place before they went; 'for go we must. We cannot even get an advance to tide us over from Whitsuntide to the end of June'. All Robert had told her about their difficulties was moderately stated; 'I am sure that you never can have had the least idea of them. There are two alternatives before us; either to hang on in a most miserable way for at the most, the <u>very</u> most, four or five years and then be sold up and have to go to starvation or beggary, or sell now when, although the agricultural depression is bad, there is still a chance of our selling and having something to live on'. Having begun in this forthright manner Gabrielle went on to speak her mind on the most delicate of subjects - the burden of responsibility that bore so heavily on her husband. 'Gartmore, perhaps because of the struggle I have had here and the poverty we have fought against, has become endeared to me', she told her mother in law,' but ruin in the near future if we go on striving is inevitable. I do not think that any two people would have, or could have, struggled for so long and after all we too must be considered and not become a holocaust to hereditary prejudices'. (10)

In fact there was no sale in 1893; the Grahams stayed on for another seven years. It is not clear what saved them from the ruin they insisted was staring them in the face. Perhaps the bondholders were reassured as to their security. Perhaps the calling in of the mortgages really was merely a device to halt or slow the sale of feus. However, on the evidence of the correspondence in the Gartmore Letter Book, another possibility suggests itself - that the crisis was largely imaginary, a product of the overwrought state of mind afflicting one or another of the pair. Many pages have been torn out of the Book; of those copies that remain all are in Gabrielle's hand while the signature is Robert's. The conclusion must be that both subscribed to what was written. From this it appears that in 1893 and afterwards the business of the estate was conducted in such a manner as to suggest the laird and his wife were suspicious of all comers. Their approach reveals that the chief casualty of the battle to survive was their sense of proportion; they hectored tenants and bullied tradespeople in a desperate attempt to keep Gartmore and themselves afloat. 'Mr Graham and I have learned in the severest school, that of poverty, to be economical', Gabrielle wrote in 1895. 'We live here in a way that you would scarcely believe and as no two people in our position would live. We have two women servants, no horses, no carriages, no shootings, no society. Everything is regulated by the strictest economy. We do the whole business of the estate ourselves as we cannot afford even to keep a clerk. My life is spent in an office. Mercifully I am a good accountant and can keep the books and do all the office work. My husband and I never leave home together; it is years since we have done so. When one is away the other remains to attend to the business. We are simply factors for the Bondholders and Annuitants.' Gabrielle made a point of being present when the feuars came, twice a year, to Gartmore House where they handed over the money due. Since this was not something other lairds' wives took upon themselves it was greatly talked about in the neighbourhood ,and it provoked much adverse criticism among members of Robert's family. (11)

He hardly cared; he and Gabrielle, together with <u>la familia</u> - Pampa, Talla and Jack - were sufficient unto themselves at Gartmore and, however difficult the circumstances in these years, testing his patience to the limit, it was at that particular moment that he embarked upon the second career that was to bring him lasting fame. Writing was an obvious means of making extra money, as well as convenient for people living in the country with, as Robert told Jamieson, not much else to do. But writing is an act of will, requiring three main qualities; Robert possessed energy and patience but was deficient in the third, self confidence which he never quite achieved even in the days when he was compared to Guy de Maupassant. Yet he was always conscious that he had it in him to be a writer, knowledge that in itself was a burden, for persons thus endowed suffer guilt if they do not at least attempt to fulfil their potential. 'I have tried two or three times to make a magazine article of the Mexican journey, but find I have no talent whatever in that line...I think I have no literary ability whatever', he told his mother gloomily in 1880. (12) Sixteen years later the Mexican journey was the basis for one of his earliest sketches Un Pelado, which was also one of the finest. Would-be writers are often urged to begin by describing what they know; advice that Robert followed in his first book published in 1895. 'Notes upon the District of Menteith for Tourists and Others' was the archetypal slim volume whose aim was to describe the geography, history, flora and fauna of that part of the world Robert knew and loved best.(13) In the process of performing this deceptively simple task he provided an impression of Scotland and the Scots so totally unlike any other productions with the same theme that he surprised and delighted his readers - especially if they were English. 'The wittiest little book to come out for a long time' the Saturday Review enthused. There were few things more depressing to those wise Scots who had followed the time honoured habit of deserting their native land than a visit to it; the reviewer opined; 'the gloomy climate and the gloomy religion may nurture sturdy values but they rob the face and character of amiable qualities'. Graham had exposed the Scottish character and its history with an ingenious reference to grave yards. 'Some like your quiet corner under a yew tree close to some Norman church in England' Robert wrote, and described a place where the Vicar's pony grazed, where grass grew long and lush in summer and swifts wheeled overhead'. What is it that makes a Scots churchyard so different', he demanded, 'It may be the knowledge that the sleepers' souls are all in torment - for none could possibly escape the penalties so liberally dispensed to them in life in church'. 'Mr Graham has found his vocation', the Saturday announced; 'we hope he will cease to 'fash' himself with politics and give us many another book, small or great, but like this discursive, poetical, full of ingenuous reflection and pleasant distortion of history'. (14)

Shortly after this the Saturday Review was bought by Frank Harris, one of the greatest editors of the day, not a man to hide his light under a bushel. His memoirs list the new writers he engaged; 'What a crew of talent to get together on one paper before they were at all appreciated elsewhere' he congratulated himself, '[HG] Wells and [Bernard] Shaw, Chalmers Mitchell, D.S. McColl and Cunninghame Graham, I think the best staff ever seen on any weekly paper in the world'. (15). Harris who kept a string of horses for his own use in London first encountered Graham riding Pampa in Hyde Park during the 1880s when his literary talent was untried. But one had only to read his political articles and Commons speeches to recognize the promise that was there. This was put to the test on 12 September 1896 when Harris published the first of many pieces signed by Robert Cunninghame Graham in the Saturday Review. The sketch, Salvagia continued the theme begun in 'Notes upon the District of Menteith'; that Scotland had never recovered from the terrible damage done to its national character by the religious reforms of John Knox which removed all warmth and pleasure from its way of life. Robert had little good to say of modern Scotland or the Scots whose meanness and narrow mindedness he described with the same withering contempt hitherto reserved for capitalists, sweaters, businessmen and some politicians. This disaffection with his native land probably had its origin in the manifold problems he was then enduring just as his bitter complaints about the dismal weather reflected the sequence of cold winters and wet summers prevailing at the time. His portrait of Gart-na-cloich, the village in Salvagia was scathing, despite the fact that, since the article appeared over his signature, most of his readers would have no difficulty in recognising the settlement at the gates of Gartmore House. 'A straggling street looking upon a moor, bordered by slated living boxes...Two churches and two public houses, and a feud between the congregations of each church as bitter as that between the clients of the rival inns...No trees, no flowers, no industry... Much faith and little charity, the tongue of every man wagging against his neighbour like a bell-buoy on a shoal. At the street corner groups of men stand spitting.' (16)

Robert's notoriety as the hero/villain of Bloody Sunday ensured that 'Notes upon the District of Menteith' was widely reviewed in the newspapers as well as the weeklies with encouraging results. 'So far as I am able to decipher your cryptogram I am very glad you are in good spirits and making writing pay', Uncle Bobby wrote in December 1895.(17) Robert's sudden appearance in the role of author was bound to surprise many of his friends and acquaintances. While his political articles already had much of the force and style of his later work, very few of his contemporaries, and fewer still of what have to be termed his social equals, took the Labour Elector, Justice or The People's Press. The Saturday Review was a different matter: discussed in the London clubs and, if not always read, at least laid out on the table in the library of every country house in Britain. In the next few years after his first appearance with Salvagia, the Saturday published some of his finest sketches, including Un Pelado, Heather Jock, and Snaekoll's Saga. These put him on the way slowly to becoming a writer of repute.(18)

In 1896 Adam and Charles Black published the first collection of Cunninghame Graham sketches. 'Father Archangel of Scotland' was a joint effort by Robert and Gabrielle. In De Heretico Comburendo, a description of the Colleges at Valladolid where young men from Scotland and England went to be prepared for the priesthood, Robert returned to the theme addressed by the 'Notes'. He described the Rector of the Scottish College as a Scot of Scots, 'with the geniality that Presbyterianism seems to have crushed out of the modern Scotsman'. He looked back with nostalgia to the older Scotland that was poor and furnished soldiers and adventurers to the rest of Europe. The Scotland which vanished after Culloden and was replaced by factories and mines, progress and money, and an air of commonplace, exceeding all the world. 'No one in his wildest fits of patriotism ever talked of Merrie Scotland. Did Knox kill merriment even as Macbeth did murder sleep?' he wondered. Now, too, he began to draw on his adventures in South America. <u>A Vanishing Race</u> was a rather too ambitious picture of the gauchos and their way of life. <u>The Horses of the Pampas</u> was more successful; he wrote as someone who knew these horses; who had ridden them; who had followed their particular and unusual history in the region, who loved and admired them. '[The pampas horse] is part of me, I live on him and with him; he forms my chiefest subject of conversation, he is my best friend, more constant far than man, and far exceeding woman'. <u>In The Tarumensian Woods</u> was a portrait of the Jesuit missions in Paraguay. Reviewing their history Robert rejected the view of the eighteenth century writers, Bonpland and Azara, that the communistic rule imposed by the Jesuits had made the Indians idle and thriftless; on the contrary he believed they had done much good, endured many perils, and were the only people whose mere presence did not bring death amongst the Indians. 'I hope to try to prove [this] at some length in the proper time and place', he promised. These and other sketches in 'Father Archangel of Scotland' take the side of indigenous people against exploitation. This was a cause Robert had already vehemently endorsed in public.(19) In a letter to the <u>Daily Graphic</u>, headed 'Ghosts Dancing', Robert referred to the news that the Sioux were gathering in Dakota to defence their tribal lands from further encroachments by the white man. 'Better that they should come and smoke and dance, dance for ten days without food or water, better that they should die fighting than by disease or whisky', he wrote furiously. 'Outrages they will commit, of that there is a certainty, but all they do can scarce atone for all that they and theirs have suffered. Tricked by all, outwitted, plundered by the Christian speculator, better that they should die fighting and join the Ghosts who went before them.' (20).

Three of the sketches in 'Father Archangel' were by Gabrielle, drawing on her travels in Spain during the previous six years. <u>Yuste</u> was a description of the remote monastery where the Emperor, Charles V of Spain had spent his last few months. <u>The Batuecas</u> described an even more remote place; a ruined convent founded by Santa Teresa. <u>La Vera de Plasencia</u> was set in one of the few towns in Estramadura, country through which Gabrielle had ridden on a donkey in the course of her research. Adam and Charles Black of Soho Square were her publishers before they were Robert's; in 1891 they had agreed to her proposal of a biography of Santa Teresa of Avila and had stuck firmly to their decision in spite of the many difficulties that occurred in the course of its preparation. On the face of it a biography of a Carmelite nun, subject to visions, who called herself Teresa de Jesus because she believed she was the bride of Christ, and set down these visions in explicit language, might hardly be said to fit comfortably into their list, the greater part of which consisted of explorers' tales, books of geography, and maps. Nor could it be said they stood to profit by taking on an author who was not only completely unknown, but Catholic as well as female. These aspects do not appear to have deterred them - rather the contrary. 'We understand that your proposed work is not orthodox and have no objection to it on that account', one of their first letters told Gabrielle cheerfully (21). As all publishers must, they knew the current state of the market . In 1891 and for some years previously unorthodoxy was all the rage. Alternative religion, Eastern ideas and beliefs, the doctrines of Hermes Trismegistus, Philo, and Origen, for example were the objects of serious study while table rapping, seances, the calling up of beings from the other side with the help of mediums was a very popular way for fashionable people to amuse themselves. Gabrielle was a member of the Sesame Club for ladies which met in the Marchioness of Ripon's drawing room to hear lectures on religious and philosophical subjects. Among the men who came as guests were Bernard Shaw, Thomas Huxley and W.B. Yeats. In 1888 Madame Blavatsky published 'The Secret Doctrine', which, in weaving together religion, superstition and magic with the greatest panache, caught the mood of the moment and won followers for her Theosophical Society. Gabrielle possessed books on Theosopy and, years after her death, was claimed to have been a member of the Society. There is no evidence that she was; Catholicism remained her chosen faith. Furthermore though, as we shall see, she drew many parallels between her life and that of Teresa of Avila, as far as anyone can tell she did not subscribe to the Theosophical belief in reincarnation. The poetry she began to write during the 1880s was gently melancholic about life in general, expressing vague regret for what might have been, for those who had been dear to her and were no more. Robert who was immensely proud of her abilities in that - and every other - direction, published a book of her poems very soon after her death and distributed it among their friends It is as 'Chilean Poetess' that his wife is most often described in the books of reference that notice him.

We do not know when Gabrielle dropped the idea of writing the novel she had mentioned to Keir Hardie but her diary shows that she started work on the biography in the summer of 1888.(22) On 15 July she notes that she had been in the Reading Room of the British Museum where she saw the facsimile it possesses of Teresa's life in manuscript which Philip II of Spain had caused to be placed in a special casket in the Escorial the key of which he always carried with him. Books were to be a particular difficulty, the British Museum collection was strictly limited; Gabrielle would have to buy most of those she needed. This meant haunting the shops in the Charing Cross Road, most of whose stock she dismissed as rubbish, and making frequent sorties to the Euston Road where she knew an old bookman who could occasionally get her what she wanted. The task before her was immense: her subject was a leading figure in the Spanish Counter Reformation, caught up in the tumult that accompanied the Inquisition. There were two points of reference for English readers to whom Spain and Spanish history were unfamiliar. Teresa's life which began in 1515 ,spanned most of the reign of Henry VIII and continued into that of Edward VI, Mary ,and Elizabeth. Mary's husband, Philip II of Spain, was king in his own country for much of that time, outliving Teresa who died in 1582. And there were 40 Carmelite friaries in England at the Dissolution of the Monasteries. For the rest Gabrielle would have to describe a country unvisited, a people unknown to most of the rest of Europe, and events determined by religious beliefs that the English, and more particularly the Scots, had violently rejected.

Though a great part of Teresa's existence was spent behind the walls of a Carmelite convent, under obedience to the superiors of her order, she became an active participant in the events that were convulsing the Church in Spain in the mid 16th century. The reason why her life was controversial, and exciting, lay in her dual nature. At the same time as she experienced spiritual insight to a degree granted to very few, and was capable of conveying her vision in language that touched the hearts of many, she was a woman of strong practical ability, shrewd, and resolute in everything she chose to do; otherwise she would never have succeeded in reforming the Carmelite Order and founding a series of nunneries in which her reforms were faithfully observed. A flair for business, a liking for affairs, was something Gabrielle whose own inclination lay in that direction, could well understand: she devoted a large part of her research to this side of Teresa's character. The unorthodox aspect of her book, which so much commended itself to the brothers Black, lay in her approach to Teresa's account of her mystical experiences. Gabrielle was quick to remark those passages in which Teresa referred to her visions as the effect of ill health; passages previously glossed over. 'We have endeavoured to show the various and contradictory impulses and emotions of a strong and vigorous intellect and character which was led away but never wholly vanquished by the tremors of mysticism' Gabrielle wrote; '[Teresa's] judgement prevented her from becoming the victim of delusion, never sure herself of the reality or origin of her visions she never ascribed to them any other than a very minor importance' (23) This was an approach her husband wholeheartedly approved; those lives of Teresa written from a purely religious or sentimental standpoint seemed to him to diminish her. 'It may be that whilst dwelling on the virtues of the woman, the merits of the saint may appear more clearly', Robert wrote in his Introduction to Gabrielle's book. (24)

There was another, striking, similarity between biographer and subject. Teresa's father, a member of an old Castilian family, many of whose young men went to the Indies as <u>conquistadores</u>, doted on his imaginative and headstrong daughter. In 1523, when Teresa was eight she ran away accompanied by her brother, was brought home by her father and kept under close surveillance. At the age of eighteen she ran away again to the Convent of the Encarnacion in Avila, brought home once more she told her father she wanted to be a nun. Parental opposition, reinforced by a further period of confinement, failed to change her mind and she was finally allowed to have her way. Reading this one wonders if the tale of Caroline Horsfall's flight from Masham is altogether contemporary with the 19th century, or if it owes anything to the history of the 16th century nun who, as she came to know her better, became a heroine to Gabrielle?

'Santa Teresa' was conceived on a large scale. As well as attempting to explain the psychological basis for a world famous religious experience and the historical background to the events of the Saint's life, it was intended to provide an account of the major figures involved with her. Nor would it neglect the physical aspect of the country which seemed to Gabrielle always to have had a crucial influence on the character and behaviour of the Spanish people - little altered in the three hundred years since the period in question. Consequently, one of the first tasks she set herself was to become closely acquainted with all the places connected with Teresa. Beginning in May 1889 she made two, sometimes three visits a year to Spain, staying in fondas, often in very poor and remote parts of the country. Her only companion on most of these journeys was Peregrina; beside his parliamentary duties, the agreement that one of them should always be on hand to deal with affairs at Gartmore, meant that Robert could not go with her. The separation was painful to both of them. 'My dearest Chid, your little face looked so sad over the ship's side', Robert wrote on seeing her off at Glasgow on one occasion. 'When will you be back?' was a frequently recurring question, 'Jack and Tal and Pampa send their love'. For her part Gabrielle sent letters often written in pencil in the train; 'It is awfully dreary travelling alone'. Always eager for news from home she constantly sent Robert instructions as to her next address - 'Write as legibly as you can and write at once...I wish I was home and selling the feus'. Her letters reveal how taxing these journeys were, even in the beginning when she was in relatively good health and anxious to begin research. The first time she went to Spain her chief concern was whether as a young (and very attractive) woman travelling without a male companion she risked attracting attention from other men, something Mrs Cunninghame Graham of Gartmore must not tolerate. Anything remotely improper would diminish her standing in the eyes of those around her and reflect badly on the man whose well known name she bore. Her relief on completing the voyage from Glasgow to Pauillac in May 1889 without incident was evident in the letter she sent off upon arrival at La Coruña. Everyone on board had been extremely courteous. 'Everyone wanted to do everything for me...A Major Martin Sharpe Hume (who says he knows you) looked after me and was very kind'. (25). Aged 43 Hume's fluent Spanish had been acquired in the course of many visits to his mother's family, long settled in Madrid. A keen volunteer officer, it was as Major Sharpe that he fought with the Turkish contingent in Bulgaria during the Russo-Turkish War and explored the coast of West Africa. Subsequently he travelled extensively in Central and South America. In 1876 the last of the Spanish Humes left him a considerable sum of money on condition he assumed her surname. His new financial independence enabled him to embark upon a second career as a writer of histories based upon material in the Spanish archives. When he met Gabrielle his first book 'A Chronicle of King Henry VIII of England', had just been published. He and her husband, with whom he already had so much in common, were shortly to become close friends for Hume, who had retained an interest in business acquired as a young man, was to help Robert try to persuade the Government in Madrid to grant a concession for trade with Spanish Morocco.

On her arrival in Spain on 6 May Gabrielle hastened to report things were just as easy as they had been on the boat. 'Everybody is absolutely respectful and kind and I have had no difficulty. It is just as easy as travelling in France. Everyone takes me for a Spaniard or a Francesita. Peregrina eats well and drinks more wine that is good for her. I let her do as she likes; it is only for a time and so much of my comfort depends on her'. That letter was written in La Coruña which she found less attractive than Vigo but the people charming;

in particular the women who were far gentler [Peregrina, one remembers, was a native of Vigo]. She intended to send W.T Stead some account of her wanderings; Robert was to make sure he published it.(26) Ponies were the only means of transport to some of the places she needed to see; high in the mountains to which one penetrated by following dried up watercourses, there being no paths, were the remains of some of the 16 convents and 14 monasteries founded by Teresa. Those bridle paths that did exist such as the one from Plasencia to Batuecas, a two days ride, led through cistus, heather, lavender and other fragrant shrubs. At Batuecas she sat talking all night over a log fire in the convent kitchen, the goatherds recounting their narrow escapes from wolves and wild boars. As she rode so her love for Spain increased. 'I don't know how I shall bear it to come back to the chilly fog and respectability and hateful desesperacion which I always feel in London', she told Robert. She hoped he was all right and his 8 hours Bill progressing - 'but this is worth any quantity of 8 hour Bills'. Three weeks later things were not going so well. 'I have lost my voice entirely and my chest rattles fearfully'. Peregrina was in sulks. 'Still I bear it and I shall make use of her as she makes use of me'. She had not recovered by the time she visited Avila where Teresa died on 29 September 1582. The Mother Prioress of the convent showed her the cell, humble, whitewashed, but scattered with tissues of gold and silver and lit by jewelled lamps. Gabrielle was deeply moved; afterwards she told Robert, 'I really do believe Saint Teresa has made me better. As I knelt before her shrine I half doubted I should be able to get back to England alive' (27)

La Coruña was the birthplace and summer home of the leading - indeed the only - Spanish woman writer of the time. Emilia Pardo Bazán's essays and short stories embraced a wide range of subjects - philosophy, chemistry, politics, the condition of women in Spain - while her novels gave her an international reputation. During the 1880s, and taking as her models the French writers Zola, the Goncourt Brothers and Balzac, she wrote books based on careful observation of the real world. La Tribuna, published in 1882 portrays the cigarette factory at La Coruña for example. Gabrielle, who was a member of the Council of the Women's League in England, was commissioned to offer Pardo Bazán honorary membership. At this first encounter she may also have suggested the article 'Women in Spain' which appeared in the Fortnightly Review the following year. Having met her Gabrielle told Robert she felt she had made a friend. So it proved. Aged 37, nearly the same age as Gabrielle, Emilia had agreed to her husband's desire for a separation three years before; he objected to the notoriety he felt she had courted by writing in the way she did. She now lived in Madrid for half the time where she edited a monthly review Nuevo teatro critico. She was able to give Gabrielle much practical help in connection with her book about Santa Teresa - an introduction to the scholar, Sanchez Miguel, who would provide a bibliography; directions as to where to buy the books he recommended most cheaply; advice about how to go about gaining access to the archives at Simancas. In the following years she did much more for her 'little bird' as she called Gabrielle. A woman of great energy she was involved in many aspects of literary and theatrical life in Madrid; time consuming though these were, she submitted to her house being used by Gabrielle as a repository for the antiques - furniture, pictures, carpets - which she picked up cheaply in far flung parts of Spain with the intention of selling them at a profit when she got them back to England. Emilia became her associate for a time; interviewing dealers, arranging transport, collecting money and - a most vexatious business - sending funds to Gabrielle, a procedure that, in the absence of banks in the parts of Spain she frequented, was often very complicated. (28)

The correspondence, unfortunately, is one sided; only Emilia's letters to Gabrielle appear to have survived. Nevertheless it is possible to conclude from these that Gabrielle sometimes pressed her friend too hard, never more so than in her urgent desire to appear upon the stage. The reference has no date which is a pity since it appears to be the only piece of direct evidence linking Gabrielle and Caroline Horsfall in so far as their passion for acting was concerned [their mutual interest in the writing and production of plays can be more readily established]. Emilia had a friend called Mario, the director of a repertory company in Madrid; he was to put on a new play in which a part might be offered to Gabrielle if she suited it. She was obviously beside herself with excitement at the prospect. Emilia had to call for patience; it was not so easy to arrange with the speed she desired. Mario's company would not be playing in Madrid but in the provinces where the first place they would visit would be La Coruña, a town she presumed Gabrielle would not want to appear in. Emilia intended to post her 'Romeo and Juliet' in Spanish, Mario wanted her to learn one of the roles so she could go through it with him; his was the only company in which there was a vacancy for an actress. Apparently nothing came of this.

It is evident from the letters that Emilia discussed her work with Gabrielle and even sent her proofs for translation into English. By the end of the 1880s she had begun to explore a new form of novel, based on the interior life of its characters, their psychological reactions one to another, rather than on a given situation relying for its effect upon a naturalistic background. In 1889 when she met Gabrielle she was well into 'Una cristiana - La puebra', a novel whose heroine sacrifices the possibility of happiness outside marriage in order to uphold her Catholic faith. At the same time she was writing 'La Piedra Angular', (and complaining to Gabrielle how much effort it was costing her). Set in Marineda [La Coruña] it concerns the murder of a man by his wife and lover. One of its themes is the interrelation of the physical and psychological worlds; the central character, Don Pelayo Moragas, the doctor who sets out to save the two murderers from execution by trying to explain their motive, sees human beings as a harmonic whole and believes many physical conditions have a psychological cause, and vice versa. This was the explanation favoured by Gabrielle of Teresa of Avila's visions; in her biography she describes them with respect but leaves no doubt as to her opinion that their origin is sexual.(30) Her publishers were moved to warn her to be guarded in the expression of views like these; 'there is no doubt that a work of this character will be subjected to a most searching and severe criticism' they wrote in October 1893 when the book was nearly ready for the press. While her editor, Dr Black, had no desire to interfere in any way with her individual opinion as Author, he was anxious to secure for it all respect and attention, considering it an important work. 'This being our firm belief we beg you to reconsider carefully any point which Dr Black strongly advocates' But Gabrielle stood firm: what she had written was her honest opinion, the Truth as she saw it; 'as such it must stand'(31)

'Santa Teresa' ran to 800 pages in two volumes. The speed at which it was written recalled the young Caroline Horsfall and her 'rage for study'. Gabrielle had completed fourteen chapters by March 1892, prompting the Blacks to suggest some of the digression about minor characters might be relegated to a footnote, or, even, cut. They also suggested words like 'tetrical, comulgate, and quickfall', the result of translation from the Spanish, should be changed into a common English form. "Santa Teresa' went to press in October 1893 with a view to publication the following March. The Blacks sent Gabrielle a copy of 'The Life and Letters of Madame de Krudener' which they had recently published 'for a lady' to serve as a sample. One question to be settled was how the author wanted her name to appear. While Gabrielle favoured the formal, Mrs Cunninghame Graham, the Blacks wanted her to use her Christian name. Eventually she agreed to the form, Gabriela, which was how Emilia had addressed her on the occasions she did not call her Chid. The decision marked a change in the way she was perceived in public. Hitherto the emphasis had been on the French side of the [fictitious] family to which she claimed to belong, now those who made her acquaintance from this time on knew her as Gabriela. However, to Robert's mother and the rest of his family she remained Gabrielle.

As with Robert's first book reviews of 'Santa Teresa' appeared in several newspapers and journals but Gabrielle's reception was far less favourable than his. It was her bad luck that Frank Harris had not yet bought the <u>Saturday Review</u> . When it came to her book it was still in the habit of chastising authors for letting their pitiful productions see the light of day - the attitude that, according to Harris earned it the name of the <u>Saturday Reviler</u> (32) Nor did gallantry lead the anonymous reviewer to spare female writers; they were fair game for every kind of prejudice with regard to style and content. Mysticism was somewhat foreign to the English temperament, the <u>Saturday</u> reviewer began; he could only think of George Fox, Wycliffe, and Edward Irving. But the English had always been interested observers of Buddhism, Confucianism, and other notable eastern religions. Lately, however, many people had begun to dabble in the somewhat amateur mysticism of Swedenborg 'and other quacks'. There had been previous attempts at writing St Teresa's life in which turgid sentences succeeded sentimental rhapsody, the reviewer remarked. Mrs Cunninghame Graham's style was not free from turgid sentences while her powers of description often ran riot. A large dictionary was necessary to understand her book nor were her words always to be found in one; 'she has a peculiar system of mixing her past and present tense'.

Buried most unfairly in the middle of the piece was the grudging admission that Teresa's adventures made an exciting romance - 'the biography is very readable'. And it was valuable for its account of the peripheral characters - the Duke and Duchess of Alba, the Princess of Eboli, St John of the Cross, Philip II. The surroundings were well described. But in her interpretation of the saint's motive Mrs Cunninghame Graham would have been wiser to stick to the cautious approach others had taken - that Teresa represented the common sense of devotion. 'In her epilogue Mrs Cunninghame Graham makes the dogmatic assertion that there will be no more saints. We suppose she is in possession of some private information on the subject' was the reviewer's parting shot. (33) Gabrielle was deeply upset. By demolishing her style the review contrived to suggest her intention was foolish and her judgement flawed. Suspicion as to who might have written it fell on Oswald Crawfurd as having the necessary knowledge of Spanish history as well as literary pretensions - yet it hardly fits with the encouragement he gave her when she and Robert visited him at Oporto.

Of those who came to her defence the most vehement was Robert's mother. Anne Elizabeth was caustic in her denunciation of the review in the Saturday and another of the same type in the Athenaeum, the work, she thought, of a petty clique. She cross examined her friends and acquaintants in an effort to discover the guilty parties but was not successful. Do not be upset, she told Gabrielle; 'Every book worth anything has been severely reviewed. Gibbon was fallen foul of by the critics of the day. I think of Keats, now acknowledged the greatest of our later poets. Wordsworth treated as though he wrote from an idiot asylum and now with a following nearly as large (though certainly undeserved) as Shelley...Do not mind but sit tight and stick to your guns'. (34) Gabrielle should not have been surprised: family honour came first with her and this was a moment to defend it. Later on, however, she was in the habit of referring to 'Santa Teresa' as 'that weary book'. Mysticism did not appeal to a person of her robust and rational temperament: she thought it complete delusion as a guide to conduct; 'It seems to me only another word for egotism; it is the foundation of sham art and bad literature'. (35)

The book was not well received in Spain; the Church frowned upon it and nothing came of the plan that Emilia should translate it into Spanish. Gabrielle even seems to have suspected her of being involved in a plot by Spanish writers to have the book put on the Index; her letters to Robert in the summer of 1894 warned him to stay away from her. There was another reason for that beside doubts about Emilia's conduct over the book. The Grahams had now become absorbed in a new project they were anxious to keep to themselves; neither Emilia nor any of their other acquaintances in Spain must get wind of it until they were successful. Since they were not nothing more was heard of it until, nine years later, Robert let fall a brief reference in the Saturday Review to a search for a mine in a remote part of Northern Spain in the hope of finding gold left over from the time the Romans worked it. He had found the description in a Spanish version of Pliny the Elder's Historia Naturalis. 'The position was fairly and clearly set down, the very place names scarcely altered, for to that valley no Arabs ever entered as their horses seldom took them far from the flat plains', he explained in the course of reviewing a book about an archaeological expedition. (36)

The experience was obviously one of the most memorable in his life probably because it involved some of the things he liked best - old and rare books, Roman history, an expedition on horseback to a wild and beautiful part of Spain; the always dramatic search for gold that, on this occasion was known to have existed at a particular place. But the very detailed and leisurely piece he wrote long afterwards suggests his pleasure was not confined to the Spanish part of the expedition but began as soon as he took down the book with its description of the mine. A Page of Pliny is notable for its evocation of the Graham's life at Gartmore once business was finished for the day, and for a rare glimpse of Gabrielle as she was in her late thirties. The fact that both of them were caught up in the excitement sitting over the fire in the book room making plans, would have remained in Robert's mind because, in the years that followed, such evenings ceased to happen to the great regret of both of them. (37)

The first paragraph sets the scene, leaving no doubt as to who the characters are. 'My friend, McFarlane lived in a curious old house, far from the world. When you had driven up the long, neglected avenues, you felt that you could pass your life there happily, just as some kind of sailors must have felt when they had been marooned upon a lonely island lost in the South Seas. He and his wife, a studious woman, yet with an adventurous strain, lived quietly as was befitting to their narrow circumstances, due to a fall in agricultural values, which in those days had just begun.' There follows a description of the book room at Gartmore - the long low pillared room with four pillars, double fireplaces, five great windows looking out over steep terraces and rushy parks towards the billowing, brown, Flanders Moss. The long spells of rain that visited that part of the world meant that the damp exuded from the walls, the furniture bloomed, and the grates turned reddish brown with rust. Although Gartmore had long been sold when he wrote A Page of Pliny, Robert could still name the books and the order in which they stood; the Pliny in two folio volumes occupied a lower shelf between Sir Walter Raleigh's 'History of the World', and Gerarde's 'Herbal'. Further on was Sir James Hope's' Scottish Fencing Master, The Parfait Mareschal', a tall Montaigne, bought in Paris from a lead box on one of the quays; Andrade's 'Arte da Cavalheiria', and Garcilasso de la Vega's 'History of Peru' - books proclaiming Robert's special interests; many of them books he had collected; all of them well read except, as he admitted, the Bible in folio which seldom left the shelf.

He gave Gabrielle the credit for the discovery that led to the adventure. Having started reading the 'Historia Naturalis,' but tiring of it, he made it over to her. 'She read and annotated after her custom and in a day or two asked me if I remembered hearing of a Roman gold mine in Galicia upon a journey we had made' He had forgotten so she read him out a passage in which Pliny talked of a gold mine in Lusitania which, in his day, comprised Galicia. 'Then I remembered how the country people used to go down to the sands upon the River Sil and wash for gold, and an infinity of stories we had heard near Carraceido, a little village by a lake, not very far from Villa Franca in the Vierzo, a most neglected part of Spain.' Robert describes how Gabrielle, in half a moment, jumped to the conclusion that the mine described by Pliny and the tales the Spanish peasants told them were of the same place. 'Proud of his clever wife' the narrator allows himself to be convinced. 'Nothing would content [her] but that I should go at once and find the gold mine which she was certain, by the system she had of mental triangulation would be there, waiting for me undisturbed'. Gabrielle argued that no one in Spain had ever taken any notice of Pliny except as 'a troublesome historian about whom boys were bothered when at school' and that, though traditions lingered in the Val de Orras, as she believed the region to be called, no one had thought of making a survey. 'There is something in the confidence of one you live with that, if it does not at once impel belief, still keeps your mind upon the stretch' was how Robert described the manner in which Gabrielle brought him round - doubtless on other occasions as well as this. The upshot was that they agreed Robert should go out to Spain to the place that Pliny indicated and do a survey. He preserved a vivid memory of the time and place of his commitment - an evening, sitting in the semi darkness of the long room, beside a spluttering fire of half green logs, their dogs about them.

So far as the mine itself was concerned the only thing the Grahams lacked was technical expertise. In <u>A Page of Pliny</u> this is supplied by a mining engineer, whom Robert calls Don Tomas Garnard. Described as an acquaintance of the narrator's wife he has spent years prospecting in South America, and often thinks of himself as still in Peru. In real life the mining engineer signed his letters T.J. Barnard; the two that survive are from the summer of 1894, addressed to Gabrielle when both of them, but not Robert, were in Madrid. Gabrielle had in her possession a sample of earth from the mine [how she came by it is not known]. On the strength of a promising assay she invited Barnard to discuss a joint expedition to the Val de Orras. He responded with enthusiasm. The tone of his letters was, in places, alarmingly flirtatious; the idea that he and the very attractive Mrs Cunninghame Graham, accompanied only by her maid, might set out together into one of the wildest parts of Spain had obviously gone to his head, though he never lost sight of the potential profit to be made. 'I tell you candidly', he wrote, 'for anyone else but you I would not now leave Madrid for the journey contemplated, professionally inspect and report on any mining property under a fee of <u>100 guineas paid in advance</u>. In fact just at present I would not do it for money at all. We are now not perfect strangers and you know I would not insult you, your Husband or my dear Wife, by even so much as thinking you could accompany me alone. Your maid, Annie, must go with us. If we break our necks or someone else breaks our heads, Annie must take pot luck with us. .How to get there I must leave to you. But as a Gentleman, a man, I will do my best to protect you and make the journey as agreeable as possible.' Should the journey turn out to be fruitless Barnard promised not to grumble. 'I shall expect from you no more than your graceful Castilian English shrug of the shoulders as tho' you had staked £5 or £15 at roulette <u>pour passer le temps</u> and lost'. Gabrielle's response was to discover a sudden illness prevented her from seeing Barnard or having anything further to do with him. She departed back to Gartmore and Robert took over as leader of the expedition. (38)

Freed from distraction of a female kind the two men got on well together. In <u>A Page of Pliny</u> Robert described how they left Orense in a diligence on one of the hottest days of the year and bumped slowly towards the remote and tiny village of Carraceido in the Val de Orras. 'The Roman mine was a tradition of the place, well known to everyone and in the River Sil, after a flood, people occasionally washed out a pan or two and got a little gold'. Barnard who, like every miner was endowed with optimism that increased with age, decided that Pliny's story must be true. And so it proved. A guide led them to a green glade that ended abruptly in a precipice 'sheer down it went and seemed unfathomable. It looked as if a monstrous bowl had been dug out of the red earth about a quarter of a mile across. A chestnut wood, dark and mysterious in the moonlight covered the bottom of the bowl. Here and there in patches you could see the ground and from the patches towered great pinnacles of dark red earth three or four hundred feet high'. It was a placer working in which the cuttings, waterways, and the remains of sluices constructed by the Romans could still be seen. Further off were ancient dams by which the streams had been harnessed to wash down the hillside nearly two thousand years before. The standing columns were inexplicable but Barnard decided that some earth must be left in them containing gold and quartered the place like a spaniel, looking for the most likely site to dig They spent three days washing pans of earth to get sufficient samples for a scientific assay. Stooping over a stream was bad for Robert's rheumatism and he quickly got bored';' it seemed that in all my life I had done nothing but wash out mud in a tin pan and begin again'. Nevertheless he admitted to a mixture of hope and fear as they watched the samples being fired in a crucible. Sadly, two sacks of earth from the Carraceido mine were reduced to no more than a handful of red dust. (39).

Gabrielle was the more disappointed of the two. 'My dearest Lob, How is that your first letter was so cockahoop and your second so descorazonado [disheartened],?' she wrote, having had 'a sorry downcome' at the news. Still if the mine was no good common sense dictated they should leave it alone. She would return frequently to Spain in the next few years but not to that place and never with her husband. The collapse of their hopes for the Pliny mine was not such a blow to Robert since it left him free to turn his attention to a country he first visited in 1889 whose attraction was, for him, far stronger than that of Spain. Every year until 1906, and at intervals thereafter, he was to spend weeks and sometimes months together in Morocco, a witness at close quarters of the prolonged death agonies of the country's independent government; one of the best informed spectators as the European powers circled for the kill.

Notes to Chapter Twelve

1. SRO, GD 22/2/98, 22/2/106, 22/3/507
2. ibid., GD22/2/98, Gartmore letter book. GCG to Messrs. Lawrie, 4 and 18 July 1892. And see Christie's sale catalogue, 22 March 1899 when Flemish tapestries belonging to RBCG were sold. The author is grateful to Christie's archivist for this information.
3. NLS, Acc. 11335/140; Stirton to GCG., Jan-Feb 1896
4. ibid., Acc.11335/50, RCCG [Uncle Bobby] to RBCG. 10 May 1893.
5. ibid, Acc.11335/53, Charles CG to RBCG, 7 Dec. 1891.
6. SRO, GC22/2/98, GCG note in Letter Book, 30 Sept.1892
7. ibid., - March 1893
8. ibid., RBCG to Lindsay, Jamieson and Haldane, 25 Feb 1893.

9. ibid., RBCG to Campbell, 12 March 1893.
10. NLS Acc. 11335/23, GCG to AEB, 6 Apr. 1893.
11. ibid., Acc 11335/185-201
12. ibid., Acc. 11335/23, RBCG to AEB, 3 July 1880
13. 'Cunninghame Graham, R.B., 'Notes upon the District of Menteith for Tourists and Others', Adam and Charles Black, 1895.
14. The Saturday Review of Politics, Literature, Science and Art, 21 Sept. 1895.
15. Harris, F., 'Contemporary Portraits Third Series, Published by the Author, New York, 1920, pp 47, 54. Harris, F., 'My Life and Loves' , W.H. Allen, 1964, p.704.
16. Salvagia in 'The Ipane', op.cit., pp 188-203.
17. NLS, Acc.11335/50, RCCG [Uncle Bobby] to RBCG, 5 Dec. 1895.
18. Un Pelado in 'The Ipane', op.cit., pp 37-51; Heather Jock in 'The Ipane'op.cit., pp 174 187; Snaekoll's Saga, in 'The Ipane', pp 204-225.
19, Cunninghame Graham, R.B. and G., 'Father Archangel of Scotland', A&C Black, 1896.
20. Daily Graphic, - Dec. 1890. Note. For an account of the Ghost Dance religion see, Brown, Dee, 'Bury My Heart at Wounded Knee', Vintage, 1991, pp 431-438.
21. NLS, Acc. 11335/139, A&C Black to GCG, 4 Jan. 1891.
22. ibid, Acc. 11335/135 (diary), 5 June, 14 and 18 July 1888.
23. Cunninghame Graham, G., 'Santa Teresa', Black, 1894
24. ibid., RBCG Introduction.
25. NLS, Acc 11335/55, GCG to RBCG 6 May 1889, 12 Apr. 1890; n.d. 1897. Acc.11335/136, RBCG to GCG, 7 Apr. 1890.
26. ibid., Acc. 11335/55, GCG to RBCG, 6 May 1889,28 May 1890.
27. ibid., the same to the same, 17 May 1889.
28. ibid., Acc.11335/138, E Pardo Bazán to GCG [in Spanish], various dates.
29. Hemingway, M., 'Emilia Pardo Bazán, the Making of a Novelist' Cambridge University Press, 1983, p. 90.
30. Cunninghame Graham, G., 'Santa Teresa', op.cit. II, p 325.
31. NLS, Acc.11335/139, GCG to A&C Black, 18 Oct. n.y. (1893)
32. Harris, F., 'My Life and Loves', op.cit., p 704. 'The Saturday Review was the most poisonous critic of all lost and new causes'.
33. Saturday Review, 28 July 1894.
34. NLS, Acc. 11335/137, AEB to GCG, 19 Aug. [1894]
35. ibid., Acc. 11335/23, AEB to RBCG, 23 Feb. 1905, à propos Oscar Wilde's book written in prison 'looking for the mystical, in art, in life'.
36. Saturday Review, 7 Feb, 1903
37. Cunninghame Graham, RBCG, A Page of Pliny in 'A Hatchment', Duckworth, 1913, pp 144-182.
38. NLS Acc.11335/140, Barnard to GCG, 5 June 1894 [both letters]
39. A Page of Pliny, op.cit.
40. NLS, Acc.11335/ 55 GCG to RBCG (the mine)

Chapter Thirteen

Morocco

The P & O boat took five days from London to Gibraltar. Depending on the weather in the Bay of Biscay, during that time Robert would either be prostrate in his bunk or clinging apprehensively to the rail. Life returned each time he reached the Rock: the passage from there to Tangier was a few miles across the Straits; every detail of the Spanish and Moroccan coasts sharply outlined in the clear air. Though after 1891 he was to spend weeks and sometimes months each year either in Tangier or travelling in remote areas, Morocco was not the release for which he had yearned whenever his parliamentary duties joined to his family responsibilities came near choking him. His heart was still in South America - 'country for country the River Plate is the best of all of them' (1) Nor was he drawn to it by ties of blood and family as he was to Spain whose language and literature were a part of him in a way that Arabic never could be. Yet his close acquaintance with Tangier's remarkable society over the years gave him much pleasure and many friends. Further afield he became caught up in a bold and romantic venture to exploit the riches people supposed Morocco to possess.

Everyone who went to Tangier struggled to express how strange it was -' thirteen miles from Europe as the gull flies, millions of miles away in feeling and in life' was how Robert put it; and again, 'but thirteen miles from Europe and yet less spoiled with European ways that is Crim-Tartary' (2). Though he was not a painter he had a painter's eye that, from the years of frequenting the Grosvenor and being much with some of the leading artists of the day, was highly developed. He could, moreover, put this painterly aspect into words. 'Tangier la Blanca, Tangier the white. Whitewash and blinding sunlight on the walls; upon the beach, white sand; the people dressed in robes of dusky white, a shroud of white enfolds, a mist as of an older world hangs over it, coming between our mental vision and the due comprehension of the secret of the place.'(3) The New York Hotel where he stayed in the early years and which he described as 'a hostelry that, with the discomforts of a Spanish _fonda_ of those times, still lacked the saving grace of picturesqueness.' was on the beach a little way from town. The distance was desirable: Tangier was spectacularly dirty; its streets slippery with the intestines of sheep and fowl, rotten eggs, dead cats and orange peel. Whenever it rained, which it did often and in torrents, the streets were inches deep in mud. Not that many Europeans walked; in a country where the wheel was unknown and there were no roads, 'whoever could afford five and twenty dollars for a horse equipped himself with boots and spurs and rode about splashing the dirty water of the streets on the foot passengers with as much disregard of consequences as John the Baptist when he performed mass baptism in the Jordan' (4) Every kind of sport associated with Robert's favourite animal could be had in Tangier. The New York Hotel where he stabled his own horse, was the headquarters of the Tangier Hounds, established shortly before his arrival by two unlikely partners who became his lifelong friends. Bernardino de Velasco, Duque de Frias, was Master, and as his First Whip, nominated the painter, Joseph Crawhall; in Robert's expert opinion, both were perfect horsemen. The pack hardly matched their standard. Three couple of mangy looking foxhounds from Gibraltar, several mongrels always referred to as 'the bastards' and three or four half bred fox terriers were the usual complement.

Frias- Dino to his friends- was one of those individuals who bring disaster to their loved ones. In a manner reminiscent of some of Robert's own forbears, he dissipated an inheritance through extravagance leaving his wife to cope with the consequences. What differed was the scale: as well as Duke of Frias, Dino was Hereditary Grand Constable of Castile, Count of Haro and of Oropesa, a Grandee of Spain. His estates, which stretched half over Spain included a palace in Madrid, a villa in Biarritz, and crumbling old houses in several towns. 'What he fancied he would have, no matter at what cost' Robert wrote in a candid account of how he came to shipwreck, which leaves no doubt as to the Duque's charm. After leaving Eton - his mother was English - Dino drifted to Tangier where he became unpaid secretary to the Spanish Minister but spent most of his time with the English colony. Those were carefree days 'for he was at the age when one has bought the world on credit and not received the bill'. He was universally liked in Tangier and according to Robert, everyone who had a horse turned out to follow his mongrel pack of hounds.(5)

As for the First Whip of the Tangier Hunt the sketch Robert published of him was equally frank. A horsy looking man in a faded red hunting coat, his face as weather beaten as his stained dogskin gloves, his air 'of a stud groom in a moderately good place'belied the fact that here was a great artist, a man of genius. One of the finest painters of animals and birds of the late 19th and early 20th century, acknowledged as their master by members of the Glasgow School, in those days Joseph Crawhall was unknown to the general public. Robert described his work as in the line of descent from the great draughtsmen of the caves of Altamira, as well as having some affinity to the art of Japan - a comparison he was qualified to make, having recently been introduced to it by his friend and fellow habitué of the Grosvenor Gallery, Mortimer Menpes. In the 1890s Japanese painters had not yet adopted European rules of perspective that took away much of their claim to originality . The sketch, which was not published until long after Crawhall's death in 1913, contains a perceptive account of the way he went about producing a picture, from the first observation of his subject to the final version. But it also made much of the fact that Crawhall, known as Creeps to all and sundry, found more to answer to his needs in Tangier than a diversity of exotic subjects under an African light.

Crawhall's time in Morocco was the era when Bohemianism captured the public's imagination. The Yellow Book, the 'greenery yallery' Grosvenor Gallery focussed attention on artists' lives. It became fashionable to look upon the greatly talented as set apart from the rest of society - as objects, therefore, worthy of a certain pity - always a suspect emotion. The argument was that the effort to propitiate the force within them drove some artists to sustain themselves by unorthodox means, whose consequence almost always was anti-social behaviour. Crawhall's failing was his shyness, a reserve so extreme John

Lavery named him the Great Silence. His solace was in bouts of drinking whisky. The sketch is brought to its climax with his disappearance for several days when his friends, including Robert, search Tangier in vain for him. Eventually he is found in a brothel described by the author with careful attention to detail (6). One might have supposed that Robert's by now longstanding involvement with the world of art, would have allowed him to dispense with this aspect. To identify the subject by his real name in a sketch that had a wide circulation among people who knew his family would have been an offence against good taste in normal circumstances. Robert had a habit of writing RIP on the letters from friends he preserved, a form of salute to those he had held in affection and respect. Three of those he met in Morocco - Frias, Crawhall, and one other to whom we shall come - were the subjects of a longer appreciation That Robert dared to include material more conventional obituaries would certainly have left out - references to drinking and gambling, for example, seem to this writer to have proceeded from his desire to commemorate a friend whose failings were a part of him, and also from his obsession with the whole picture. To draw attention to the unvarnished truth had been one of the strengths of Cunninghame Graham, the politician; to give the impression of reality was to be even more significant in forming Cunninghame Graham, the writer.

A smarter event even , than the Tangier Hunt was pigsticking which figures in many of the memoirs of the time. The credit for devising it went to Sir John Drummond Hay, British Minister in Tangier for 26 years until his retirement in 1886 when he continued to spend the winters there. Everyone who could sit a horse repaired for five or six days to a camp among cork and olive trees on a hill above a lagoon near the village of Howara; tents and food were supplied by Anselmo of the Hotel Continental. Wild pigs were put up by Arab beaters who drove them towards horsemen armed with spears (7). Those taking part were the leading members of Tangier society and their visitors of every nationality. By profession they were diplomats for as Robert explained, Tangier had more Ministers, Secretaries of Legation, Consuls, Consuls-General and Vice Consuls in proportion to its population than anywhere else in the world. 'Flags of the various nations fluttered from half a hundred houses in the town. Adventurers who styled themselves presidents of Patagonia, kings of Auracania, and other hypothetic states hoisted the flags of their fantastic countries and, whilst their money lasted, if they were presentable, spoke 'diplomatic French', were not seen drunk in public, or committed any flagrant misdemeanour, were received as cordially in the tolerant society of the place, as if they had been representatives of real countries to be found upon the map. The Moors looked on them all with awe mingled with amusement, and regarded them as amiable madmen who, for some purpose of his own ... Allah had endowed with the command of fleets and armies, and with mighty engines of destruction so that it behoved the faithful to walk warily in their dealings with them.' (8).

The mighty engines of destruction were the reason why so many countries felt obliged to keep a presence in Morocco. As the race for naval supremacy gathered pace, Morocco's position at the gateway to the Mediterranean and with a long Atlantic coastline guaranteed that whatever befell the Sultan's government - already perceived to be dangerously unstable and corrupt - would be of crucial importance to the European situation. The Powers feared a collapse leaving a vacuum to be filled by one or another of them, a process that, before it was completed would almost certainly precipitate a war. This was the Moroccan Question so-called - quite as much a threat to peace in Europe as a similar situation in Turkey had been a generation before. France, England and Spain each had a different approach to the problem depending on their history. From 1860 to 1886 England's official attitude had been determined by her forceful and independent minded Minister, Drummond Hay. He was steadfast in his belief that the independence of the Sultan's government must be safeguarded. During that time, with the Royal Navy firmly established at Gibraltar, England was able to preserve a state of benevolent detachment. As for France and Spain, while they were able to tolerate England's hold upon the Rock, they would have been unalterably opposed to any extension of her presence to the west. As it was, their diplomats were in an almost permanent state of uproar during those years over the appearance on her deserted Atlantic coast , of English and Scots traders, harbingers of some undisclosed British purpose, as swallows are of summer.

As a direct descendant of the Prophet Mohammed, His Shereefian Majesty, the Sultan of Morocco, claimed the allegiance of all Muslims who mentioned him in their prayers: a greater number, it was said, than paid the same tribute to the Caliph at Istanbul. This dismissive approach to international boundaries worried the French for, in their advance into Africa, they had already gained Algeria, immediately to the east, and Senegal, far to the south across the Sahara Desert. The threat posed by what was labelled PanIslamism was to become something of an obsession at the Quai d' Orsay. What he saw of it in Morocco also greatly interested Robert Cunninghame Graham; to what effect during the First World War will appear (9). Strategic considerations also bothered Spain but, at the beginning of the 1890s, emotion played the larger part, as it had done for years. 'Morocco must some day belong to Spain', the Spanish Foreign Minister had declared in 1869; 'as long as it cannot belong to Spain it is necessary it should belong to no other nation'.(10) Nothing had changed in the intervening years. When Robert arrived in Tangier, the Spanish Legation's long term objective, far fetched though it seemed for a country not yet recovered from the collapse that followed the loss of her American colonies, was to fix Spanish rule upon as much of Moorish territory that could be wrested from their rivals. The destiny of the two countries, once so close, was held to demand nothing less.

Whichever nation gained an even temporary advantage largely depended on what kind of terms their man on the spot might succeed in establishing with the Sultan and his Viziers. Having become accustomed to a privileged relationship during Hay's long tenure, after he retired the FO officials found themselves obliged to deal with less experienced men on whose discretion they were not altogether sure they should rely. More than one of Hay's successors betrayed a tendency to what, when he was Foreign Secretary, Lord Salisbury identified as <u>ferocitas consularis</u>(11.) One might say in their defence, however, that at a time of rapidly increasing tension and doubt as to the future, it was only common sense to try to get ahead as far as possible. The ultimate solution to the Moroccan Question was perceived to be a Protectorate by one of the Powers when the standing of its representatives would be enhanced by comparison with all the rest. This would have been enough to make Tangier a hotbed of rumour, gossip, and intrigue even without the special efforts of the Makhzen, the Moroccan government, whose principal object was to keep all foreign diplomats shut up in Tangier until it suited them to grant an audience to one Minister at a time. He who was chosen was forced to make a long and arduous journey under armed escort to one of the four seats of government - Rabat, Meknes, Fez or Morocco City [Marrakesh], or even to catch up with the Sultan who might be camped anywhere in the interior watching his army trying to administer discipline to one of the many recalcitrant tribes.

In these circumstances the fundamental task of assessing the present state of the country in order to foretell its future was complicated by the near impossibility of knowing what was going on, private people moving about were sure of a warm welcome from their respective Legations on their return to Tangier. In 1891 Robert Cunninghame Graham began a series of journeys in the company of friends like the painters, William Rothenstein and John Lavery. As someone who could be relied on to keep his eyes open, he was a valuable recruit to the ranks of those on whom the British Legation drew for information. Moreover the guide who accompanied him on several of these occasions was a key figure in Morocco; a most important go-between in the relationship between Christians and Moors, besides acting as official interpreter to the British Minister. It was through Edward 'Bibi' Carleton that Robert's name became known to a number of Moors who wanted to escape from the close grip the Makhzen had fixed upon them in order to do a little business on their own.

There was no jetty at Tangier; like Buenos Ayres in 1871 passengers had to transfer into a smaller boat in order to be rowed ashore. The young man who urged his horse into the shallows to assist the Arab boatmen on the first occasion Robert landed from Gibraltar was to become one of his closest friends. Bibi Carleton, christened Edward Pio by his staunchly Catholic English family, was one of the few 'Roumis' in Morocco to be regarded by the Moors as - almost - one of them. His Arabic was perfect; his English was not; it came less readily to him than did the Spanish he acquired in the Franciscan school. His university was the streets of Tangier 'a divinely beautiful, immoral little place, a miniature Constantinople' Robert remarked when commemorating Bibi. He was at pains to insist that the Carletons were a 'good English family living in reduced circumstances in Tangier' - he wanted to refute some of the epithets Bibi's exploits earned for him - 'Levantine Englishman' was one of the least pejorative.

A favourite of all sections of society Bibi was particularly in demand when riding through the Mellah, the Jewish quarter' of almost any Moorish town when, as Robert put it, a stout black eyed daughter of Israel would hold up for him to see the latest addition to what became widely known as 'the tribe of the Beni Bibi'. With an old mother and sisters to support as well he was obliged to make money. His principal means of doing that in the early years was by acting as a guide to Europeans wishing to explore the interior of Morocco. There were not many - the influx of winter visitors to Tangier was just beginning. Those who took part needed to be fit enough to sit a horse for hours at a time and undaunted by the necessity of swimming it across the frequently recurring fords - Morocco had no roads and hardly any bridges. Robert's expertise with horses, his long experience living rough in South America made him an ideal candidate for Bibi's expeditions. Even more important, and most welcome to the Moors was the courtesy he showed to everyone which they perceived came naturally to him. In Morocco, as he explained to his readers, all men were equal under Allah and his Vicegerent on earth, the Caliph of the hour. It was an attitude he shared with Bibi whom the Moors loved for that reason. 'Bandying jokes with boatmen on the beach, or serving as interpreter before the Sultan, he was equally at home, not in the least abashed by the formalities of the Moorish court, or holding himself superior to the boatmen, except in so far as his personal strength, his quick wits and better education gave him the superiority' (12)

No journey in Morocco was without its perils though these were mostly in the minds of the people living along the way. The Sultan, who owned everything, held them responsible for anything untoward that befell his property. If foreigners who were not supposed to leave Tangier without permission from the Mahkzen suffered loss or damage in the course of moving about, the local inhabitants were forced to compensate them. The consequence was that, if possible, the locals would prevent foreigners from entering their territory or if not, keep a close watch upon them until they left. Robert's first venture beyond Tangier was down the coast to the ancient Portuguese fortified town of Larache, and inland via Arzila to Alcazar el Kebir. Bibi drew up the itinerary, submitted it to the authorities for approval, assembled stores, hired servants, horses and mules and put himself at the head of the line of march. Robert thought him well suited to the occupation of guide. 'Ceaseless good humour, indifference to heat or cold, and the capacity to reduce to order a refractory mule or an insolent camp follower he possessed to a supreme degree'. His own more volatile temper made him less accommodating to the conditions that, often for the sake of prestige - their own and that of their companions - they were obliged to endure. 'On the whole I have enjoyed myself 'he told Gabrielle at the end of one journey, 'but I shall not bother to come again as it is quite different from [South] America. Here one can never get away from people'(13). To sleep without shelter, for example, was quite exceptional for an Arab; even the wandering ones carried tents with them. Thus confined Robert found himself regretting the freedom and solitude he had experienced on the plains of the Argentine; 'one never sleeps so soundly as on a fine night beside a fire, one's head upon a saddle 'he wrote sadly (14).

The necessity of observing such conditions made travelling in Morocco very expensive. The scale on which provision was made can be judged from the memoirs of William Rothenstein. Invited to accompany Robert on a second trip to Alcazar in 1894 the 22 year old artist - 'a nice little fellow, he wants to paint me on Pampa'(17)- was thrilled by the prospect of adventure. 'We were supposed to take guards with us but Graham would not'. However, Robert had a large revolver and Rothenstein a shotgun as well as a small revolver. 'I fancied myself riding with a gun slung over my shoulder and when I discovered that my pony was so trained that I might safely shoot from the saddle, I felt like a Byronic corsair'. William had never ridden before and modestly admitted to being nothing of a rider (a view in which Robert wholeheartedly concurred). They had a cook, three other servants, four mules, and two donkeys to carry their baggage. On the first night at a place called Sidi bu Merelsch a party of villagers arrived and built a great fire close to their tents where they watched all night, 'there were marauders about... and they were afraid for our horses'. Rothenstein had been hoping to paint landscapes but was disappointed when they reached Alcazar el Kebir. From a distance it had looked promising; dazzling white houses surrounded a mosque whose green tiled tower shone like a lizard's back in the sun. At close quarters it proved an unsuitable place for an easel: the narrow streets were shut in by matting hung from roof to roof while the inhabitants took particular pride in a mound of manure 60 feet high; 'quite the filthiest place I have ever been in'.(16)

On their return to Tangier Robert wrote to Gabrielle; 'This journey has done me great good for I am much more cheerful and in better spirits and feel as if all the world was not bounded by Gartmore...' adding, however, 'This I think is my last journey here. Spain is better though the pones [horses] are a great attraction.'(17). Yet he did go back, the following year and many times thereafter, penetrating into the most remote and strangest parts of that strange country where he became acquainted with many of the leading personages. That he was not only willing but able to meet the expense of such journeys at the precise moment Gartmore was teetering on the edge of financial ruin is evidence that their purpose was not for the sake of his health or merely for pleasure. It was not in him to be able to indulge himself while Gabrielle was struggling to help him make ends meet. The conclusion must be that he went to fulfil some kind of task, or tasks , others had proposed

'Travelling for information'was the usefully ambiguous phrase written beside the names of certain visitors to Morocco at this time, not only by officials in Whitehall but in many a Chancellery in Europe (18). Missionaries, doctors, prison visitors, animal welfare activists, naval officers on leave and above all, journalists were approached. 'I want you particularly to find out and let me know the following things....; It would be interesting , as you are in that part of the country, if you would go a little farther and visit...; Please give the Sultan clearly to understand that we will not....' - this was the kind of thing Walter Harris recalled diplomats having said to him in the course of more than thirty years as correspondent of <u>The Times</u> in Morocco. For all that, and much more, he said he had only ever had one payment; £50 from the secret service fund in recognition of these efforts on behalf of his country(19). Certainly there is no trace of any payment to Robert Cunninghame Graham. Yet it is more than likely that several contacts he made involving long journeys away from Tangier were undertaken at the request of persons connected to the Foreign Office in London.

His status as a recent Member of Parliament, well known for his strong anti-imperialist views; the articles he published in widely read and influential English journals continuing the Drummond Hay line as to the absolute necessity for independence for Morocco, must have disposed the Makhzen to look favourably on his presence in the country. At the same time, probably less well known but even more significant were his personal connections with those in daily contact with the makers of British foreign policy. For example, among those to whom he had instant access, by-passing the 'official channels'was his greatest friend at Harrow, Francis Villiers, for some years during the 90s Private Secretary to the Earl of Rosebery, the Foreign Secretary, afterwards Prime Minister. All things considered there could hardly have been anyone whose combination of social standing, knowledge of the country, and taste for adventure made him more suitable to the business of quietly furthering British interests in those parts of Morocco where it seemed France or Spain might get the upper hand, or those so far removed from habitation they had yet to see more than an occasional Arab on a camel passing by.

One of the principal ways in which the rival European Powers measured their progress in the race to dominate the country was in the number of so-called protégés they succeeded in attracting. These were subjects of the Sultan who claimed the protection of a particular foreign flag when they would be exempt from Moroccan law, military service, and taxes. The system had begun as a convenience for native employees of foreign legations and trading firms. However, as the Sultan's government declined further into rapacity and corruption the value of protection soared. Soon it was for sale by every country with a foothold in Tangier while the Powers were forced to bid against each other to secure the country's leading men. France carried off most of the prizes, including the greatest of all - the Grand Shereef of Wazzan, Hadj Abd es-Salem. A direct descendant of the Prophet, in 1884 he accepted a pension from the Quai d'Orsay. Shortly afterwards the French backed a rebellion in his part of Morocco that came very near to deposing the Sultan, Moulay Hassan. In 1892 Robert Cunninghame Graham, accompanied by Bibi Carleton turned up in Wazzan,one of the holiest places in the country, his presence almost certainly in response to an approach by the Foreign Office now anxious to retrieve a situation that was becoming dangerous. Abd es-Salem had just died. His widow, the Shereefa, who was English, (20)had asked Britain to protect his sons, a move that would alter the balance of power in a highly sensitive area of the country. Wazzan was a place of pilgrimage and of sanctuary. When, in 1884, the reigning Grand Shereef, Abd es- Salem became a French protégé much was made in Paris of the number of faithful who paid allegiance to him - far more it was said, than to the Sultan, Moulay Hassan. The <u>coup</u> meant a strong French presence in a city only 60 miles north west of Fez, the political and intellectual heart of Morocco.

Towards the end of 1892 Robert Cunninghame Graham and Bibi Carleton reached Wazzan after a long hard ride in atrocious weather. The only shelter they had there was a small open summer house with a green tiled floor, put at their disposal by the authorities. Its Moorish arch looked on to a garden where the horses and mules stood eating corn. 'Ceaseless rain made the palm trees droop and look unreal.'(21). No details of the meeting with the Shereefa have survived - whether deliberately or not. However their acquaintance must have prospered since he contributed the preface to her memoirs in 1911. His mission on the other hand appears to have had a negative result: the Foreign

Office took no step towards protecting her, while the new Grand Shereef (Abd es-Salem's son by a Moorish wife) became a French protégé. (22)

One day while they were still ensconced in the summer house at Wazzan Robert and Bibi were told a young man was asked for them. Aged about 22, dressed in Moorish clothes, his head was shaven except for a lock 12 inches long dangling from the centre of his crown. He was followed by two greyhounds their feet dyed bright yellow. He and Bibi already knew one another and when he introduced himself as Walter Harris Robert immediately recognized the name. They sat and smoked and drank tea flavoured with mint in the summer house - 'it was the beginning of a 40 year friendship'. Although he had only been in the country since 1887 Harris was already famous throughout Morocco (23). This was partly due to the uncanny ability he possessed of putting on the personality of an Arab - he spoke several dialects like a native - when he proceeded to acquire a closer knowledge of Moroccan history, geography and politics than anyone else alive - partly because he was by nature one of those happy souls whose company is always in demand. Harris was genial, funny, and as Times correspondent, very well informed in all the subjects the Consuls and Vice Consuls were paid to investigate; he was, therefore, one of their first points of reference - occasions when he absorbed whatever they had of use to him. Privately, his graceful manners joined to his charm made him a favourite with the royal families of Greece, Germany, and England, his summer leave from Morocco was often spent among Kings, Queens, and Princes at Bad Homburg. The genuine liking the boy Sultan, Abdul Aziz, who succeeded in 1894, formed for him was to play a role in events that were to come.

Harris' family were Quakers, his father a partner in a London shipping firm. While he was still at Harrow he paid several visits to Morocco during the holidays, it captivated him to the extent that, after a voyage to Japan, he spent most of the rest of his life there. Passionately fond of art and architecture, the pride of his life was the house in Moorish style he began to build shortly after Robert met him. Tilers brought at vast expense from Fez installed patterns copied from the finest palaces in that city. The house stood isolated on the shore to the east of Tangier and one reached it by splashing through the shallow waters of the estuary ,then traversing the forest that, in the course of 30 years grew up around it. Plants and animals also delighted Walter. His many courtyards were green with shrubs and trees in which guinea fowl, peacocks, and the odd cockatoo found shade. Water snakes swam in huge tanks and deer grazed inside the walls of the domain which often gave shelter to wandering tribesmen and their families.(24)

Together the three, now fast friends, went on to Fez which they reached in December 1892. It was already well known to Harris whose dispatches to The Times depended for their authority on frequent contacts with members of the Sultan's entourage who were more often in Fez than any of the other three principal cities. Bibi Carleton had been there earlier in the year as official interpreter to the new British Minister, Sir Charles Euan-Smith, who had been on what he was pleased to call his 'Special Mission' to the Sultan. Sir Charles exaggerated: the occasion was routine, the customary, if sometimes long delayed reception by the Sultan of a newly accredited diplomat but the use of the term special, added to the fact that Euan-Smith had come from Zanzibar where he had presided over the setting up of the British Protectorate, convinced the French and other Powers tht his presence signalled a renewed attempt by the British to produce a similar outcome in Morocco. The international furore this caused took some time to subside. Fez - 'great, noisy, dusty Fez' - was Robert's least favourite Moorish city; its situation in a deep ravine, the dark and tortuous alleyways often running with water that were its only thoroughfares oppressed him; he found it difficult to get on terms with its inhabitants - absorbed in their own affairs the Fezzis made no secret of their dislike of 'Roumis'. The best part of Fez, to him, was as they left it when its dazzlingly white and crenellated walls flanked by towers on which storks stood asleep on one leg appeared silent and ghostly in the early morning air. (25).

After twenty long days ride they reached the southern capital of the country. His first sight of Morocco City on its high plateau, shut in by the great wall of the snow capped Atlas mountains astonished Robert; it was so like Mexico City in situation and in the exhilaration of its atmosphere. One of the few Europeans to penetrate so far, once inside the walls he found it different from anywhere he had previously been. Though it was a space as large as Paris, except for the sublime Kutubieh there was virtually no architecture. 'Sand, sand and more sand in almost every street, in the vast open spaces, in the long winding narrow lanes outside the walls, up to the city gates; sand in your hair, your clothes, the coats of animals. Streets, streets and still more streets of houses in decay... No noise, the footfalls of the mules and camels falling into the sand as rain falls into the sea, with a soft swishing sound...' It was, he found, a city of vast distances, wearisome perspectives, great desolate squares, of gardens miles in length, a place in which one wanted a mule to ride about, for to attempt to labour through the sand on foot would have been a purgatory. Yet it grew on him 'the sound of water ever in your ears, the narrow streets arched over with grape vines, mouth of the Sahara, city of Yusuf ibn Tachfin, town circled with mountains, plain girt, sun beaten, wind swept, ruinous, wearisome, mournful, in the sad sunlight which enshrouds its mouldering walls.' He was to come back to Morocco City again and again to transact whatever business - his own and others - brought him to the country so often. It was the great meeting place to which men from across the High Atlas came and he came to have a great affection for it which he celebrated in a kind of poem. 'Fez and Rabat, Safrou, Salee, and Mogador with Tetuan, Larache, Dar-el-Baida and the rest may have more trade, more art, more beauty, population, importance, industry, rank, faith, architecture or what you will, but none of them enter into your soul as does this heap of ruins, this sandheap, desert town, metropolis of the fantastic world which stretches from its walls across the mountains through the oases of the Sahara '(26). To that add the Atlantic coast with its line of breakers crashing endlessly on to the deserted shore and there was a region largely unknown and even less regarded except by a few enthusiasts whose fantasies concerned its strategic and commercial value. Robert Cunninghame Graham was one of those who saw what might be made of it and, more importantly, what benefit might accrue to its people, mostly wandering tribesmen, nominally subjects of the Sultan of Morocco but who paid no attention to any authority but their own local sheikhs. This territory, its people and affairs were to bring a new dimension to his life during the next ten years and contribute to the creation of something like a legend in his name.

After 1892 and following his release from the House of Commons he was beholden to no one, free to come and go as he pleased. He became a well known figure in Morocco, his presence noted everywhere he went; an adventurer with connections in high places; a Scot among Muslims whose object was to unite them in trade and in politics as they were already united in a common faith. His efforts caught the eye at home of John Buchan who drew partly on him for his most famous character. Sandy Arbuthnot, the wandering Scot in 'Greenmantle', the first of Buchan's modern knights errant, has Robert's striking physical appearance and powerful sexual attraction. Both were tallish with lean, highboned faces, hair like a fox's pelt and brown eyes. Both were highly strung, sensitive, proud and volatile. 'Sandy... would take more than mortal risks and you couldn't scare him by any ordinary terror. But let his old conscience get cross eyed, let him find himself in some situation which in his eyes involved his honour, and he might go stark crazy' Both were fine horsemen who passed easily for Turks or Arabs when suitably disguised. The greatest difference between Robert's career and 'Greenmantle' is that the action in the novel takes place in the Balkans, Turkey and other parts of the Near East while Graham's sphere was Mogreb el Acksa, the far West. And the time is twenty years later, at the onset of the First World War. But the atmosphere is similar: both periods were haunted by the fear of aggression on the part of one European nation; aggression that Islam could do much to resist if the faithful would unite. In both cases there was a vivid sense that war was inevitable. 'A jehad is preparing' is how 'Greenmantle' put it, when the enemy was German. In Graham's earlier time, in Morocco, France was the nation whose territorial ambition was most likely to precipitate disaster.(27).

One of his functions throughout this period was to receive and pass on information about the movements of the French in Morocco and across the border in Algeria. Not much of the correspondence has survived, but the letters that have were written by all sorts of people, Moroccan as well as European - merchants, itinerant traders, desert Arabs, even Vice-Consuls - acting in a strictly unofficial capacity. One of the best informed by virtue of his job as an official interpreter was Bibi Carleton whose letters to Robert were written in two languages; Spanish for business including intelligence reports, English for news of friends and family. The surveillance was by no means all on one side. For instance, 'while at Tangier and when you left for the interior the French sent spies after you 'one letter from a newspaper editor told him (29). Robert's dislike of France began in his childhood when his mother and grandmother told him stories of the atrocities visited upon the Spanish by Napoleon's army of occupation which invaded the Peninsula when Doña Catalina was a girl and whose behaviour was still a vivid memory when Anne Elizabeth was born(30). Consequently a role in thwarting French territorial ambition which by 1892 had become a threat to British interests in other parts of Africa besides Morocco had much appeal for him. As he saw it, part of his function was to let people at home in England know there was an alternative to Britain's official policy which sometimes seemed to be confined to letting France have her way in order to avoid a confrontation. There is a paragraph in the book he wrote in 1898 giving a startlingly frank account of his activities in the past four years which puts this alternative very clearly. 'Into the ethics of the European occupation of Morocco I do not propose to go, but if at any time that occupation should occur, as it is certain that Europe would not see us [Britain] in Tangier, and as the French have thoroughly secured the north, and as the Germans will no doubt bid for some towns upon the coast, it might perhaps be still advisable to seize the south and so control the Sus, secure Morocco City, and thus keep a way open for the Saharan trade... and opening Agadir or some point on the Wad Nun, check French advance' (31)

Lying between the High and Anti Atlas mountains the valley of the River Sus was a lure to enterprising foreigners. One of the most fertile and promising areas of the whole country, a highway for caravans trading to and from the Sahara, it was seldom visited by outsiders. It could be reached without too much hardship via passes across the mountains from the north, or by sea to the port of Agadir near to which the Sus flowed into the Atlantic Ocean. The reasons for its isolation were political and military; the best way in the Makhzen's view to control a region so remote. There were only eight harbours in Morocco that foreign ships were allowed to visit; all were in the north. (32). Agadir near the mouth of the River Sus was closed and had been neglected for many years as had the few other landing places on that coast. But any plan to seize Morocco City would have to envisage bringing men and supplies from some harbour on the Atlantic north across the Atlas mountains. The most likely route went from near Taroudant, the principal inland town of the Sus; a spectacularly steep and high track, it came out on to the plateau less than forty miles from Morocco City. Travelling along this route one had to pass through a village called Tamasluought. In 1893 Robert and Walter Harris rode out from Morocco City to spend a night with Mulai el Hadj, the Sheikh of Tamasluought. This appears to have been the occasion on which the Sheikh was granted British protection. The importance of this new if exceedingly small extension to the Empire could hardly be exaggerated. The Sheikh was a descendant of the Prophet, 'a semi-sacred character, a sort of cross between the Pope and a feudal baron... occupying in the south the position held in the north by the Shereefs of Wazzan', Robert wrote.

The other very important personage he met on this visit had nothing at all to do with holiness. Sidi Bu Bekhr, who had been British consular agent in Morocco City for the last 30 years, was of the world, worldly. Whenever news reached Westminster of his extra curricular activities certain MPs were moved to question whether he was a suitable representative. Robert dismissed them as 'Nonconformist conscience bearers' - the sort of men he held in contempt for hounding Dilke from office and Parnell to his grave. Nevertheless they wanted to know why England continued to be represented by a slave dealer, a brothel keeper, a murderer and - the crime Robert accused them of detesting more than any other since their way of life barred them from joining in - an adulterer. In his opinion Bu Bekr was a true friend of England, a clever scheming politician who knew the right way to play upon successive British

Ministers; he was feared and disliked everywhere north of the Atlas, but also respected because of his success 'for the Moor above all things respects success'. (33)

South of the mountains what might be called these most favoured nation terms did not exist. Instead for some considerable time a number of fiercely independent sheikhs had signified their desire to offer trading concessions in their part of the country to foreign entrepreneurs with or without the backing of their respective governments in return for what was not yet termed venture capital. 'The desert chief is here ...It is not impossible I may be able to get a concession from him and in that case I am certain I could peddle it well in London. But I shall have to go to Las Palmas and on in a fishing boat to Cape Juby. I shall be awfully sick but it will be an interesting trip'.(34). This chief to whom Robert referred in this letter to his mother from Morocco City was Bashir el Bairuk with whom he was to be in contact for a number of years before they eventually signed an agreement. One of the most important sheiks in the south Bairuk's home was Goulimine, a town of more than two thousand people in the Wad Nun, about a hundred miles south of Agadir, but his writ ran over a much larger area; along the Wad Draa, out to the coast by Ifni and down beyond Cape Juby to Cape Bojador. Immediately to the south the low lying land in Tiris and the upland region called Adrar were ruled by Bairuk's father in law, Wold Aidah. South of Adrar on the coast lay French Senegal and further inland the Niger country which had recently come within the British sphere of influence.

Bairuk's father, the late Sheik Mohammed el Bairuk, was known in London where the Foreign Office cursed him as a nuisance. His offence, which had occurred in 1879 was to have granted a strip of land 8 miles long and 2 wide on the shore at Cape Juby to a Scot, Donald Mackenzie, who was possessed of a remarkable idea. By excavating a channel through a barrier of sand running almost immediately behind the Atlantic short the huge shallow depression known as El Juf in the country of Tiris might be flooded so that ships, having taken goods on board in England, could off load them at Timbuctoo on the northernmost bend of the Niger River. Mackenzie's prospectus published in 1875 had two aims. The first was 'to regenerate the dark children of Ham from ignorance and superstition'; the second to discover the Eldorado long rumoured to exist somewhere beyond the Sahara. The first brought him Quaker backing for a series of expeditions he conducted in 1876 and 1878 into the country inland from Cape Juby. Had anything come of this it would have been one of the scientific wonders of the age. Not surprisingly nothing did. Undaunted Mackenzie proceeded to the second object. Two brothers joined him as business partners. Henry Lee was a Director of Manchester Chamber of Commerce,and MP for Southampton. Joseph Lee was knighted for his efforts at international gatherings on behalf of British trade. Together Mackenzie and the Lees founded the North West Africa Company and began operations at the place ceded to Mackenzie by Mohammed el Bairuk. They called it Port Victoria, the Moors, Tarfaya, the various highly placed officials who were constantly having to write minutes about it - the British Foreign Secretary, his permanent officials, the Lords of the Admiralty - Cape Juby. The only independent harbour for hundreds of miles along the Atlantic coast, its presence was a threat - real and imaginary - to many different interests. Spain feared for her rich fishing grounds between Juby and the Canary Islands. The French were convinced it was the first step in a British occupation of the region, including the Sus valley, whose ultimate purpose was a Protectorate over the whole country, and that its more immediate aim was to thwart their plans for a Trans Saharan railway from Algeria to the Atlantic Ocean. The Sultan, Moulay Hassan, was outraged by Bairuk's flouting of the allegiance he, as one of the faithful owed him while his Viziers objected to the British presence as possibly interfering with the trade in slaves from the Sudan.

As soon as the factory was established at Tarfaya it attracted Arabs who arrived, fully armed asking for goods on credit. When the Scots traders refused scuffles broke out; on one of these occasions ,in 1888, a manager was killed. The Company's response was to claim government protection which more than once resulted in a visit to Tarfaya by the nearest Royal Navy warship. This in spite of grave misgivings on the part of Foreign Office and Admiralty officials about the dangers inherent in a show of power in that particular part of Africa.(35). By 1892 the Lee brothers had decided that the North West Africa Company could only continue if granted a Charter on the lines of the one recently conferred on the Royal Niger Company. Otherwise they suggested they might take serious notice of various proposals by other interests; one of these being a partnership with Spain to develop the whole area from Cape Juby down to the Rio de Oro, a Spanish colony.(39) The Foreign Secretary, Lord Salisbury, found himself in a dilemma; to grant a Royal Charter was tantamount to declaring sovereignty over the area in question. Yet its owners, as British citizens, had an absolute right to protection when going about their business peacefully. ' No one has a right to object to recognition of the Company's private property in a tract of land which the Sultan might see fit to make' His Lordship remarked, ' But a recognition of HMs sovereignty over such a tract is a very different matter. It might bring down the Empire of Morocco with a crash'.(36). Part of the trouble was, of course, that Bairuk, not the Sultan had made the grant. 'Nothing displeases me as much [as Tarfaya] Moulay Hassan was reported to have said, ' because the Christians, (May God destroy and ruin them) have governed the whole world... and only remains but this country and they are working to take it whether by money if it suits them, or by conquest'. In 1892 Salisbury's reaction was to prohibit any visits by Foreign Office officials to Tarfaya and at the same time to order that a watch be kept on Spanish movements in the area. One of the people involved in this was Bibi Carleton whose contact was the Captain of HMS Goshawk, on patrol between the Canaries and the African coast. It is more than likely another was Robert Cunninghame Graham.(37)

No one knew more than these two about the venture at Tarfaya. One of Euan-Smith's objectives on his 'special' mission to Fez in the summer of 1892 had been to come to an agreement as to whether the Moroccan government would buy the North West Africa Company out. The only other person beside the Sultan, Moulay Hassan, at these discussions was Carleton in his capacity as official interpreter. (38) As for Graham, he had a number of opportunities to acquaint himself with the course of events at Cape Juby. He was one of the very few of his countrymen to speak Spanish with the result that he gained an immediate insight into perhaps the most significant aspect of the whole affair. His sojourn at Vigo in the early 1880s when the factory at Tarfaya was probably doing better than at any other time, would have shown him the situation from Spain's point of view, Vigo being the point of departure for ships for the Canaries; much of its business was concerned with the Islands. Furthermore, when relations began to deteriorate with the Islanders and the coastal Arabs, the Company's representations were dealt with at Permanent Under Secretary level. In the 80s, as the crisis developed, these were Charles Dilke, a friend, and Lord Edmond Fitzmaurice, a relation. Though both had left office before Robert became most closely involved with Cape Juby, their background knowledge would have been of value should he have been disposed to ask for it.

A creaking old schooner, the Sahara, which had begun life many years before as a Portsmouth patrol boat, made a monthly run from Lanzarote with supplies for Tarfaya/Juby. Passengers were rare but one at least one occasion before the North West Africa Company severed its connection, Cunninghame Graham sailed with her, when his worst fears appear to have been realized. 'Never again by sea beyond Vigo' he told Gabrielle.(38) Yet it was the most discreet way of arriving at Tarfaya, the alternative being a highly conspicuous and expensive expedition overland via the Sus and the Wad Draa. His gloom vanished on stepping ashore: the place was so absurd it delighted him. No trade was being done by order of the Lees who hoped by this means to force the British government to give them their Charter. Arabs who had endured a three week journey by camel across the desert had to bury the wool they had brought to barter for Manchester cotton goods in the sand at a distance from the factory which they were forbidden to approach. The general appearance of the place reminded Robert all too much of Texas;' in front the desert, flat, sandy and grown over with 'sudra' bushes as the prairie was grown over with mesquite...Behind the sea, shipless and desolate, breaking upon the coast in long lines of surf, thundering and roaring ceaselessly. On the horizon a faint blue cloud just indicated the whereabouts of Lanzarote' he wrote (39).

The distaste he felt for the current scramble by businessmen to get their hands on a part of the new continent now emerged. Though the buildings had been in existence for more than ten years, so few people ever reached this lonely shore his was the first description of the place. The ugly square built factory struck him as a piece of Manchester in Africa; 'only redeemed from stark vulgarity by the cannon on the roof'. Three hundred yards to seaward on a sand bank was the fort. Built to defend Tarfaya from attack by Arabs its guns pointed towards the shore. Otherwise the atmosphere was wholly familiar. He found Tarfaya 'a portion of Scotland reft from the mother country in the same way that bits of Cromarty are found scattered about the map' The place was as Scotch as Peebles, Lesmahagow or the Cowcaddens. 'Decent and orderly the Scottish clerks, the tall red bearded manager, Scotch the pioneer known to the Arabs down into the Sahara as 'M'Kenzie'... Order and due precision of accounts, great ledgers, beer upon taps, whiskey served out 'medicinally', prayers upon Sunday, no trifling with Arab women ever allowed, a moral tone, a strict attention to commercial principles, and yet no trade'.(40)

Tarfaya is the background to three of Robert's Moroccan sketches. There were some 26 of these published week by week in London journals like Justice and the Saturday Review. After he became famous they were collected in book form. What might be called the quirkiness of the country has great appeal; the landscapes provide compelling images; the manners of the people are observed with his customary blend of irony and compassion. Yet that sudden flash of insight into character and motive that caused him to be mentioned in the same breath as Balzac and Guy de Maupassant is hardly attempted here, for a particular reason. The Arabs were a race of gentlemen but impenetrable, he wrote - a description that might well be applied to him - 'a frank exterior serves as a watertight bulkhead between them and the world.' He was inhibited in his approach to writing about the Moors because he felt their Muslim faith conferred a unity and status upon them from which he was excluded. He was not a religious man; so far he had found nothing in any denomination to compel his allegiance and much to deplore in the effect some had upon their followers - Nonconformism for example. But upon arrival in Morocco he was intrigued and more than a little beguiled by what he called the stately folly of the whole way of life -' the call to prayers, the half-contemplative, half militant existence led by Mohammedans, the immense simplicity of their hegemony; the idea of a not impossible one God, beyond men's ken, looking down frostily through the stars upon the plains.'(41)

Most successful are the glimpses of Moroccans at a given moment; set pieces in which the young Sultan, Abdul Aziz reviews his troops in splendour in Morocco City; the same monarch seen after his forced abdication in the tawdry surroundings of the Villa Florida at Tangier, or the Shereef of Tamasluought deep in conversation about the meaning of life with his friend, the British Consul. The most interesting because they were connected with his private activities in the country, are those that depict two employees of the North West Africa Company at Tarfaya the place where Robert first encountered them. Spiridon Ayoub and Najim Kisbany were Syrians, Arab by race, Christian by religion. Both were educated at the American College in Beirout whose secular approach produced competent young men much in demand in a variety of professional jobs, and who moved readily from country to country. Spiridon Ayoub worked on a newspaper in Cairo, then moved to London where he taught Arabic. Here he fell in with Donald Mackenzie at the beginning of his Sahara venture. 'Mr Spiridon' as Mackenzie called him, accepted an invitation to go out to Cape Juby as official interpreter. Whether at that time - 1877 or 78 - he was already married to a sister of Sheikh Bashir el Bairuk is not known but the fact that the chief of the region was his brother in law subsequently caused his actions to be closely followed by the Foreign Office. As a consequence of his marriage he converted to Islam and took the name Mohammed el Sabbah. He was Mackenzie's contact with the Bairuk family and it was he who, in 1878, accompanied the Scot on several trips into the unexplored country behind Tarfaya. The most significant of these was along the coast to the Rio de Oro where Spiridon's knowledge of their language facilitated discussions with the Spanish authorities there.

He seems to have been distrusted by practically everyone who did business with him. Though Robert's sketch Sidi bu Zibbala in which he appears as Marion Mohanna, was not published until some years after their brief association, he had not a good word to say for him. His chief offence in everyone's eyes was to have abandoned his Christian faith to become a Muslim - an act whose obvious lack of conviction aroused Robert's distaste, and the Bairuk family's suspicion. (42) Eventually he departed Tarfaya for the Canary Islands. Some years later a second Syrian was employed as interpreter at the factory whom Robert came to know well and described in At Torfaieh. Najim Kisbany was an altogether different character but he, too, was transformed by contact with what went on outside the factory gate. 'The wild old life, the camels, the lean and worthless looking but untiring desert horses, the blue clad, long haired Arabs, with their close bargaining for trifles, and boundless generosity in larger things, the low horizon and pure language spoken by the people...took so firm a grip of him that all his sympathies were outside the fort [at Cape Juby] and his desire was to be like the natives in thought and dress.' Najim, who rose to be manager at Cape Juby, spent all his time off duty with the desert Arabs. But when they asked him why, unlike Spiridon Ayoub, he did not join Islam, his answer earned their respect. His people had been Christians for a thousand years and, though he did not believe it, he would die one, he told them. This steadfastness probably was one of the reasons why Robert chose Najim as his principal assistant in developing the concession Sheik Bashir el Bairuk offered him (43)

The time he spent kicking his heels in Asunción when hoping to obtain the right to work Paraguayan yerba was as nothing compared to the manoevres that went on about trade in Sheik Bairuk's territory. These occupied the best part of three years during which time Robert told his mother 'If I refuse he will take it to someone else'(44) There had been a change of circumstances in Morocco since his first visit to Cape Juby which contributed to an increase in tension between the Powers with the result that the Atlantic coast south of the Atlas began to attract more attention. In 1894 the Sultan, Moulay Hassan, died suddenly; his successor, Abdul Aziz, a boy of about 14, fell completely under the control of the Chamberlain, Bou Hamed, a cruel and rapacious man whose government was regarded by the outside world as leading inevitably to disaster. In 1895 the factory at Cape Juby was bought by the Moroccan government but the partial resumption of trade under the new owners did not end constant speculation as to which nation would be the next to take it over.

London was the most likely place in which to raise capital for such a venture and in spite of the poor success of the North West Africa Company the region's potential was recognized there. However, Sheik el Bashir el Bairuk had already made two visits without result. Then, in 1896, a new and bizarre figure appeared whom Robert had previously encountered a long way from either London or Morocco. This was an Austrian who, when posing as a Turk, which he did from time to time, called himself Abdul Kerim Bey. It was the name he used in 1895 when he set himself up in the Moroccan port of Mogador as

Consul for Patagonia, a region the locals thought was administered by Chile or the Argentine. Robert, who went to considerable trouble in the book he published about Morocco in 1898 to shed light on Kerim Bey's activities, traced their acquaintance back twenty years to when he and George Mansel were hoping to start ranching near Bahia Blanca and the same individual occupied the post of Consul for the fictitious country of Araucania in that city (45) The Austrian's career began in the late 1879s; he first appeared as secretary to a Frenchman with a criminal record who posed as a claimant to the Sultan's throne; afterwards he moved to London and tried to buy arms. By then British Intelligence had discovered his real name was Captain Geyling, and the fact that he was a doctor. He was kept under surveillance with the result that, in 1896, the Foreign Office knew that, for the two years before he moved up to Mogador, he had been living in Goulimine, the Bairuk stronghold in the Wad Nun.

The story of how Kerim Bey went to London with a treaty from the chiefs of Sus to engage in trade with that province can be found in two places; the book, 'Mogreb el Acksa' by Cunninghame Graham, and the Foreign Office file marked Globe Venture Syndicate. According to the first, Kerim Bey's objectives included opening a harbour to which the caravans that had always come from the Sudan and even farther to Mogador, would be diverted to the Sus; supplying its inhabitants with rifles, Bibles, and Manchester goods and working the mines that had long been rumoured to exist there. Among the names supposed to be taking an interest in the Globe Venture Syndicate were Daniel Sassoon and Cecil Rhodes. (46) Kerim Bey's next move was to recruit an assistant to return with him to Morocco where they hoped to get the Sultan's approval before going to the Sus to arrange matters with the local chiefs. According to 'Mogreb el Acksa' a brave man was needed to cope with the difficulties that must arise. Such a one was found; Major Albert Gybbon Spilsbury of the Royal Engineers. As one famous for deploring imperial adventures Robert was uncharacteristically warm in his assessment of Spilsbury. 'Quiet and courteous, a linguist and brave to rashness, he was the very antithesis of Abdul [Kerim Bey] but they started out together on their quest.' Early in 1897 their appearance in Tangier bearing a prospectus for developing the Sus aroused the hackles of the British Minister, Arthur Nicolson. From the moment he met them he was aware that the unpublicized intention of the Globe Venture Syndicate was to supply the Bairuk family and their friends with arms, something neither he nor the Foreign Office had the means of preventing. When Spilsbury and Kerim Bey/Geyling finally caught up with the Sultan at Morocco City in the summer they were refused his approval. Nevertheless they proceeded to Mogador where they had such a quarrel Kerim Bey severed his connection with the syndicate and left the country (47)

Thus abandoned Spilsbury might have been forgiven for returning to London. Instead he went ahead with next stage of the plan and called a meeting of the Sus chieftains at Assaka, a long neglected harbour north of Cape Juby, in order to ratify the draft treaty Geyling had brought to London. He could not have done this without the help of the Globe Venture Syndicate's agent at Mogador, Pepe Ratto. As the proprietor of the International Palm Tree

Sanatorium, the town's leading hotel, he was already well known to Robert who described him as a man of many talents, a south Moroccan version of Bibi Carleton. (48). When Spilsbury arrived in Assaka in September 1897 he found a large number of Sus tribesmen waiting for the commodity they most desired and which , apparently, they knew he would have on board the schooner that brought him from the Canaries - rifles. All was going well, Robert wrote, until an inferior chief rode up at the head of fifty horsemen declaring he would permit no Christian to trade in the land. 'Shots were exchanged and Spilsbury...had to escape on board his schooner and for the present leave the enterprise'. The Sultan's extreme displeasure at this incident was communicated to the British government which, as a result, urged its nationals to keep away from the region south of the Atlas altogether. (49).

By the time it did so Robert was well on his way there. Plans for him to go to Cape Juby via the Sus valley had been made in July. A letter from Walter Harris tells him there should be no difficulty along this route; another from Gabrielle regrets Bibi Carleton cannot go with him as planned (50). As interpreter he had with him instead Hassan Suleiman Lutaif, a Syrian who like Kisbany and Spiridon Ayoub was a Christian; and a Moor from the Rif, Haj Mohammed es Swami who had accompanied him in the past and, it should be noted, spoke Spanish. 'Mogreb el Acksa' is the story of their adventures in October 1897. It turned out to be one of the liveliest and most enjoyable of his books but also the most curious for there was much to be read between the lines by those who knew of his clandestine activities in Morocco. These are partly confirmed by his private papers and by a few passing references in reports by diplomats in Tangier. On the simplest level it was a book of travel of the kind his contemporaries most enjoyed; that is it portrayed an intrepid Englishman [or Scot] outwitting the fanaticism of the inhabitants of a distant and preferably romantic country. Except - and this was typical of Robert - 'Mogreb el Acksa' celebrated not the usual success in this direction but a spectacular failure. Success, as we know from his admiration for the Icelandic sagas was not important; what counted was the manner in which an individual coped with failure. This particular failure was much admired by the English reading public; 'I put it next to Doughty's as a true portrait of Arab ways and far before anything that Burton did', Wilfrid Scawen Blunt remarked. For Joseph Conrad, who praised its skill, pathos, humour, wit, and indignation, it was 'the book of travel of the century'(50)

Sir Richard Burton's most famous exploit was to enter Mecca in 1853 disguised as a Muslim when, had he been revealed as an infidel his life would have been forfeit. Presented with an account of how Robert Cunninghame Graham assumed the personality of a Turkish doctor on leaving Mogador for the Sus, the public at home in England naturally assumed the disguise was to protect him from a similar fate. The old hands in Tangier found this intensely irritating; several went to some trouble in their own books to explain that for a European in Morocco to adopt native dress was a matter of convenience, and that nothing sinister occurred should the wearer be found out. Budgett Meakin, Editor of <u>The Times of Morocco</u> was one.' Clad as a native a European acquainted with the people and their language may travel freely ..through all the open parts of the country without attracting attention, yet without concealing either his nationality or his creed from those with whom he converses. The difference this change of habits and costume makes in one's relations with the natives is enormous, a wide and all but impassable gulf disappears'. And Meakin also remarked; 'It is of the utmost importance that the traveller should have some ostensible object before him, and some 'visible means of subsistence' wherewith to disarm suspicion and appease the curious. For this purpose medicine or trade is best'.(51)

Graham in Moroccan dress. National Library of Scotland.

Robert's declared intention was to visit Taroudant which 'Mogreb el Acksa' persists in describing as a forbidden city. In so far as the whole of Morocco south of the Atlas mountains was closed to foreigners by order of the Makhzen it was indeed forbidden. But it was not unknown to Europeans; for instance Allan Maclean, Consul in Casablanca, had been there with the Sultan's army in 1883; his brother, Kaid Maclean, the Sultan's Army commander, more recently. And unlike Wazzan or Tamasluought it was not particularily significant in religious or political terms. But as an 'ostensible object' it could hardly have been bettered, lying as it did on the road to Goulimine and roughly half way to Cape Juby. That it was nothing more than an excuse was abundantly clear before the party set out. 'Hardly well landed in the town [Mogador] than a report was spread that we were agents of the British government or advance couriers in the interest of the [Globe Venture] syndicate' was how Robert began his tale(52). In so far as he was, indeed, a British agent, the report was true and he took obvious pleasure in not denying it. Whether he was carrying messages on behalf of the Globe Venture Syndicate as well is not known, but he was expecting Major Spilsbury to make another attempt at landing on the coast at any moment the implications of which would be serious. 'The Moors all know when once a European gets a footing in their land, even though that should be brought about by filibustering syndicates financed by London capitalists, that the nation to whom the filibusters belong steps in to guard its subjects and having once stepped in, remains for ever...Therefore their irritation about the Sus was most intense, and the jealousy of foreign travellers never keener'(53) That being so, one may ask why did he choose that particular moment to set out? And why did Arthur Nicolson, whom he visited in Tangier before leaving, not prevent him? And had he wanted to keep his plans to himself he would not have stayed at the International Palm Tree Sanatorium while making his final preparations. Everyone in Mogador knew Pepe Ratto was agent for the Globe Venture Syndicate. His activities on its behalf were monitored at the Foreign Office on the basis of information from the British Legation in Tangier, some of which was supplied by Robert - he and Nicolson were cousins.(54)

There were further explanations regarding the choice of route. Robert had to find an excuse for taking the longest and most difficult in order to obtain the information he wanted. From Mogador one could take the coast road south some sixty miles to the port of Agadir from where it was an easy thirty miles up the Sus Valley to Taroudant. The second, the Bibuwan Pass which was by far the shortest, started from Iminantout some 60 miles inland from Mogador. While they still at the International Palm Tree Sanatorium news came that the tribe that occupied the country beyond Agadir had rebelled and the road beyond was closed. Consequently they made for Iminantout from where it was an easy two days across the mountains to Taroudant. The journey which began on 12 October, was agreeable; the weather was fine, the landscape varied, the people they met harvesting along the way and in the small towns, friendly. But Robert's greatest pleasure was in the company of those who rode with him. Lutaif was an Arab scholar; Mohammed es Swani an old friend who had twice made the pilgrimage to Mecca; there was a great deal to discuss and ample time to do it. It is clear from the letters they wrote him long afterwards that they liked him, as he did them. (55)

When they got to Iminantout they found the local tribes also in revolt so the Bibuwan Pass was closed. Nothing daunted - encouraged one may guess - Robert said he had no choice but to go on to the third and most difficult. They followed the foothills of the Atlas to where Amsmiz, opposite and in sight of Morocco City, marked the beginning of the pass named for the mountain, Tizi n' Test over whose huge shoulder they would have to climb. At Amsmiz, having been content to be recognized as a Christian wearing Moorish clothes thus far along the way, from then on Robert would play the Turkish doctor for all he was worth. This was because their route passed Talaat n' Jacoub the summer palace of the governor of the province, the Caid of Kintafi, into whose hands, his readers were led to believe, he did not wish to fall.

But those with access to his private papers and a decent map of the area might have concluded - as this writer does - that his object was, first, to reconnoitre the Morocco City end of the Tizi n'Test; second, to obtain an audience with the Caid of Kintafi The arrest of himself and his companions when they had already passed beyond the kasbah; their detention in the courtyard for several days before being summoned to see their captor, could have been to divert suspicion, not so much from Robert but from the Caid whose relations with the Makhzen were more than usually difficult at the time. He was responsible for the peace and security of the region in the Sultan's name; east towards the Algerian border as well as south towards the Sus and the Wad Draa. In the last few weeks he had been called upon to demonstrate his loyalty by suppressing the revolt which had flared after Spilsbury's abortive landing at Assaka. Anyone wishing to assess the possibility of establishing a sphere of British influence from Morocco City to the Atlantic coast and taking in the Saharan oases, needed to know precisely where Kintafi stood. If the recent activity of the Globe Venture Syndicate was a harbinger of such a policy, as Robert hinted it might be, their observers would put a high value on obtaining the Caid's reaction to another landing. Robert, who described himself in 'Mogreb el Acksa' as 'the observed of all observers', went so far as to suggest that the people at Talaat n' Jacoub were convinced this was the reason for his appearance there. (56)

There were good reasons why the British might believe the Caid was ripe for turning. He was not an Arab but a Berber; one of their greatest chieftains. He lived in a remote and well defended area among people whose loyalty was to him (so long as he could pay them) not to the Sultan against whom he harboured a grievance. Some years before his death in 1894 Moulay Hassan had invaded his territory and destroyed most of the Berber villages but had not been able to reduced the Caid's own fortress. Instead he was supposed to have won him over by offering him either his sister or his daughter. 'The Caid rendered [the Sultan] henceforth a limited obedience responding to his overlord's demands for taxes and for assistance in the field...but taking care not to rebuild his villages, so that the aforesaid overlord might find a desert through which to pass if the fit took him to again commence hostilities' (57)

Letters smuggled out of Talaat n' Jacoub made sure Robert's captivity was widely known at home.(58) Arthur Nicolson's response to the one he received giving news of his cousin's second term of imprisonment was to assure Lord Salisbury - who cannot have forgotten the first - 'Doubtless the Caid has arrested them on suspicion Mr Cunninghame Graham is connected in some manner with the commercial enterprise in the Sus'. Johnstone, Consul at Mogador had warned Robert of the risks he ran, Nicolson remarked 'but [Graham] is an adventurous traveller and difficult to dissuade from making journeys which he thinks would be interesting.' (59) Behind the blandness lay acute concern at a situation which was rapidly deteriorating. On 9 October, a fortnight before Robert and his companions were released, Nicolson warned Whitehall in a cypher telegram that the Sus tribes were ready to rise if provided with arms. Major Spilsbury was rumored to be collecting such a cargo for a ship he had chartered in Belgium. The Moorish government, which had many spies, must be aware of what was about to happen, Nicolson suggested (60). Lord Salisbury was furious; he told the directors of the Globe Venture Syndicate (whose Chairman, very embarrassingly was a former Ambassador, Sir Edward Thornton) they must not expect HMG to protect them from the consequences of any action taken against the wishes of the Moorish government and in defiance of warnings by the FO. (61)

Robert left Talaat n' Jacoub on 30 October; giving the readers of 'Mogreb el Acksa' to understand that he had no choice but to go back to Morocco City, if not exactly with his tail between his legs, at least in some disorder. But the names of the Moors he made a point of visiting on the way would have told anyone with more than a passing interest in Moroccan politics that his most recent adventure had not caused him to abandon his principal object - 'travelling for information'. He, Lutaif, and es Swani spent their first night of freedom with Mulai el Haj, the Shereef of Tamasluought who, in the four years since Robert and Walter Harris had stayed with him, had become a bitter opponent of Bou Hamed, the country's de facto ruler. Now, the Sheik told them, men south of the Atlas and from the Saharan oases were looking to him for advice and leadership. After leaving Tamasluought and on entering Morocco City the first person on whom Robert called was Sidi bu Bekr, the British agent, whom he found no better disposed to Bou Hamed and his government. Somewhere along the way from Morocco City to the coast he came up with Mulai Othmar, a Sheik from the Sahara, a descendant of the Prophet, whose independent spirit excited his admiration more than that of any other Moor., 'no friend of French or English intervention, the Shereef Mulai Othmar, but a believer in the regeneration of the Moors, by a new intermixture of the desert blood which in times past has often been the salvation of the Arab race' he wrote. Though he could not know it then, during the First World War he would be involved with moves to help men of the same blood free the Middle East from the Turkish yoke. (62)

At Mogador which they reached on 7 November Robert again put up at the International Palm Tree Sanatorium. That enabled him to give Arthur Nicolson on whom he called in Tangier before taking ship for England, news of Pepe Ratto's doings which the Minister sent on to London where an increasingly anxious eye was being kept on the Globe Venture Syndicate. At Casablanca there were rumours that a ship belonging to the Syndicate would land there about 16 November 'Mr Cunninghame Graham brought me a similar report from Mogador' Nicolson telegraphed in cypher, 'but I imagine the reports emanate from the same source which is Mr Ratto, the Agent of Major Spilsbury. I have still doubts whether ...the Company would be able to establish stable and permanent commercial relations with the tribes of the Sus'.(63). Mindful that the second anniversary of the Jameson Raid was due in six weeks time official Whitehall shrank from the suggestion that anything like the coup that had failed so disastrously in South Africa might be repeated in the North.(64). A grip had to be taken on persons like Major Spilsbury whom Robert described as a filibuster [meaning a pirate rather than an unstoppable orator] before he went too far. The moment would be crucial but very tricky; the government could not lightly interfere; nor was the Globe Venture's Chairman, Sir Edward Thornton, disposed to assist his former colleagues. at the FO. He issued a series of statements, each more forthright than the last, regarding the right of the Syndicate to trade in whatever part of the world it chose.(65). As one who had recent and first hand information as to the likely course of events in that part of Morocco, Robert was much in demand on his return to London where he lost no time in asking Spilsbury to come and see him at the Devonshire Club. According to his account of their meeting in 'Mogreb el Acksa' he tried to dissuade Spilsbury from going ahead with his plan to arm the Sus sheikhs. Curiously enough his lack of success did not alter his admiration for the man (66)

On 15 December the steam yacht Tourmaline, registered in the Major's name was ready to sail from Antwerp for India via the Canaries, ostensibly so its owner could avoid the English winter. In fact its cargo was 500 cases of Mauser rifles bought in Holland, 500 cases of cartridges from Austria, and 30 bales of surgical bandages (67). On 28 December Arthur Nicolson was told the Tourmaline was about to land somewhere in Southern Morocco. He sent a private warning to Bou Hamed that arms from Belgium were about to reach the Sus with the request that if any British subject were apprehended, he be handed over to the nearest British consulate (68). What happened in the first week of January 1898 when the Tourmaline began landing its cargo at Akssis, another little used harbour about 20 miles north of the previous landing place, was related by Robert Cunninghame Graham in the Saturday Review (69). The exercise was interrupted from two directions; mounted troops rode up on land and the Moorish gunboat, El Hassani, appeared at sea. Spilsbury escaped in the Tourmaline which was captured later and detained at Gibraltar. Five of his co-conspirators, including a member of the Bairuk family, were taken prisoner on shore and removed to one of the Sultan's dungeons at Fez. The French, the Spanish, and the Germans chose to regard the venture as having the tacit approval of the British Legation in Tangier. The Kaiser expressed his opinion that it seemed to be a repetition of the Jameson Raid. 'His Majesty...made a sarcastic remark about a trade which supplied the Sous (sic) tribes with rifles and ammunition' the British Ambassador in Berlin reported to Lord Salisbury. According to Harold Nicolson the incident left his father who had done so much behind the scenes to try to prevent it, angered and distressed. (70)

It did nothing to deter Robert from continuing his own contacts with the Sus tribes or from pursuing his acquaintance with the Major. Nor was he at all abashed by his apparent humiliation at the hands of the Caid of Kintafi. In the months that followed he would press ahead quietly with his plans for developing Southern Morocco; among those people who figure in the correspondence are Spiridon Ayoub, Najim Kisbany, and Albert Gybbon Spilsbury. At the same time he related their history and adventures in articles for the Saturday Review and in his book, 'Mogreb el Acksa' There were to be other books and many more articles. Now was the time that, with the advice of Edward Garnett, arguably the most perceptive publisher's reader of the day, he discovered how to turn the events of his remarkable life into a form of literature that gave the public much pleasure. As the nineteenth century came to its end Robert Cunninghame Graham, landowner, politician, traveller, secret agent? - a man of many disguises, according to the Saturday Review - was poised to become a literary celebrity.

Notes to Chapter Thirteen

1. NLS, Acc,11335/136 RBCG to GCG, 2 or 20 Aug. 1880.
2. RBCG, Tangier la Blanca in 'The Ipane', op.cit., 143-154.
3. Ibid.,
4. RBCG, Fin de Race, in 'Writ in Sand' 115-152, Heinemann, 1932.
5. ibid.,
6. RBCG Creeps in 'Writ in Sand', op.cit.
7. Meakin, Budgett,' The Land of the Moors', Swan Sonnenschein, 1901.
8. Fin de Race in 'Writ in Sand'.
9. See below, Chapter
10. Parsons, F.W., 'The Origins of the Morocco Question 1880 - 1900' Duckworth, 1976, p.633.
11. ibid.
12. RBCG, Bibi in 'Mirages', Heinemann, 1936.
13. NLS, Acc.11335/136, RBCG to GCG, 4 Jan. 1895.
14. RBCG, 'Mogreb el Acksa', The Century Travellers, 1988 (Heinemann 1898).
15. NLS, Acc. 11335/136, RBCG to GCG, 9 Jan. 1894.
16. Rothenstein, W., 'Men and Memories Recollections of William Rothenstein 1872 - 1900', Faber and Faber, 1931, Vol 1, pp 215-224.
17. NLS, Acc. 11335/136, RBCG to GCG, 4 Jan. 1895.
18. PRO/FO99/ 297
19. Harris, W.B., 'Morocco That Was', Blackwood, 1921, p.28.
20. Aged 30 Miss Emily Keene met Abd es-Salem when she was governess in the Tangier household of Ion Perdicaris. They were married in 1877 and had two sons.
21. Tate Gallery, Lavery Papers, 7245.333, 'W. Harris' By RBCG.
22. Emily, Shereefa of Wazzan, 'My Life Story, 1911.
23. Tate Gallery, 7245.333, 'W. Harris'. Tangier Gazette 13 April 1933 (Harris obit).
24. RBCG, Dar el Jinoun in' Redeemed and Other Sketches', Heinemann, 1928.
25. RBCG Bu Gidri in 'Faith', Duckworth, 1909, 66-80.
26. RBCG, 'Mogreb el Acksa', pp 280,285.
27. Buchan, John, 'Greenmantle' Hodder& Stoughton, 1939, p. 12 et seq., (first published 1916).
28. NLS Acc,11335/65, Abrinez to RBCG, 14 Mar. 1899.
29. See, for example, RBCG War to the Knife in 'Rodeo', Heinemann, 1936 213-218.
30. RBCG, 'Mogreb'.
31. They were Tangier, Tetuan, Casablanca, Larache, Salle, Rabat, Mazagan, Mogador.
32. RBCG El Masgad in 'Brought Forward', 146-163. Mogreb p. 269.
33. NLS, Acc. 11335/21, RBCG to AEB, 15 June 1899.
34. Mackenzie, Donald, 'The Khalifate of the West', Simpkin Marshall,1911 pp 163 et seq. Parsons, F.W., 'The North West Africa Company' in Historical Journal, 1,2, 1958; 'Mogreb' pp 157-59.
35. PRO, FO 99/298 25 Sept 1891
36. Parsons, 'The North West Africa Company.'

37. Parsons, 'Origins' p 439
38. PRO, FO 99/298, Juby Diary 2 June 1891.
39. NLS Acc 11335/136, RBCG to GCG, 4 Jan. 1894.
40. RBCG At Torfaieh in 'The Ipane' 257-273.
41. RBCG, Bu Gidri in 'Faith', op.cit. Sidi bu Ziballah in 'Thirteen Stories' 133-147, Heinemann, 1900.
42. ibid.
43. ibid. PRO,FO 99/357, Nicolson to Salisbury 5 Aug. 1898. ibid., 99/298, N.W. Africa Co. to Currie, 2 Sept 1892.
44. NLS, Acc 11335/21 R to AEB, 15 June 1899
45. RBCG,' Mogreb' p 37 et seq
46. PRO, FO 99/375 Vol 1, 1896 - Feb 1898.
47. 'Mogreb' p. 40
48. PRO, FO 99/375 Spilsbury to Kaid Maclean 11 July 1897
49. 'Mogreb' p 308
50. NLS Acc, 11335/60, Harris to RBCG, 28 July7 1897; Acc. 11335/55 Gab to RBCG 8 Oct 1897
51. 'Mogreb' Introduction
52. Meakin, B., op.cit., p 424
53. 'Mogreb', p 43
54. PRO FO 99/375 Nicolson to FO, 19 Jan 1897
55. NLS Acc 11335/63, Lutaif and es Swani to RBCG, various dates - 1898, 1900, 1922.
56. 'Mogreb' p 53
57. ibid., pp 130-31
58. ibid. p 310
59. PRO FO 99/347, Nicolson to FO 22 Oct 1897
60. ibid, 99/375, Nicolson to FO 9 Oct 1897
61. ibid, Salisbury to Globe Venture Syndicate 10 Oct 1897
62. 'Mogreb' p 300
63. PRO FO 99/374 Nicolson to FO 15 Nov 1897
64. The raid began on 29 December 1895.
65. PRO FO 99/375,2 Sept 1897
66. 'Mogreb' p 321
67. PRO FO 99/375, Plunkett (in Brussels) 15 Dec 1897
68. ibid. Nicolson to Grand Vizier 19 Dec 1897
69. Saturday Review 4 June 1898; 18 June 1898, 11 Feb 1899 in notice of 'Mogreb el Acksa' - The Art of Adventure
70. Nicolson, Harold, op.cit. p 125.

Chapter Fourteen

Literary Matters

By the time Robert took to writing as a regular occupation an earthquake had transformed the English literary landscape. On 27 June 1894 Mudie's, the most influential of the circulating libraries, whose subscribers had underpinned the market for over 40 years dictating which authors should be published, which not, announced a drastic change in policy. 'The Three volume novel does not suit us at any price so well as the One vol and upon the old terms it is no longer possible'(1). This sudden, shocking disappearance left long established publishing houses in disarray; their place to be quickly filled by new firms. Duckworth, Methuen, Heinemann, Hutchinson, T. Fisher Unwin now became household names. Their success depended to a large extent upon the ability of their readers to recognize what it was the public wanted - even before it knew itself - and to take firm hold of those writers who could supply it. Beginners had previously found it very hard to persuade publishers to take a risk on anything that did not promise a large popular success. Now in Edward Garnett, T Fisher Unwin possessed a reader whose unshakeable faith in his own judgement and the ability to detect among piles of MSS the rare one with promise gave him an influence over literary matters quite out of proportion to his age - he was only thirty in 1898. Originality was the criterion he applied when assessing talent while anything that might conceivably appeal to the general public was pronounced beyond the pale.

In May 1898 he approached Robert with the offer that would make his name. T. Fisher Unwin was contemplating a new series to be called The Overseas Library; it would contain sketches and tales about colonial life and English and colonial settlers, emigrants and travellers the world over. Garnett proposed the first volume should consist of pieces by Robert that had already appeared in the Saturday Review. 'The note of the series would be not imperialism' Garnett (who had socialist sympathies) wrote, 'but the inclusion of any work sufficiently artistic to give local life, atmosphere and point of view of the new countries. Such a series would be experimental and probably its volumes would be rather suggestive than finished artistic work'. With this idea in mind he had gone over Robert's sketches and found that some of them were 'absolutely the thing'. 'If I could only find other men doing work in the spirit of 'Un Pelado' [the account of the preparations for the hanging of the Mexican, Jose Maria Mendiola] the idea of the Overseas Library would need explanation to nobody, not even to the British Public'.(2) 'The Ipané' by Robert Cunninghame Graham was published the following year. The title was derived from the sketch placed first, which described life in Paraguay after the defeat of López; its chaotic state symbolized by the Ipané, the ramshackle cargo boat plying between Asunción and Corumba. As well as 'Un Pelado' the collection included 'Tangier la Blanca', 'Heather Jock', 'Snaekoll's Saga', 'At Torfaieh' and 'Niggers' (which first appeared as 'Bloody Niggers'). There too, was the account of William Morris' funeral which had occurred two years previously. 'With the North West Wind' did not remotely qualify for inclusion in such a volume, being an evocation of the English countryside as Morris had perceived and celebrated it, but so moving, so finely written by Robert who had loved him, Garnett could not bring himself to leave it out. 'I have just been reading with delight 'The Ipané' as it came to me in proof' he wrote to Robert in January 1899, 'and again came to me the keen sensation of delight which rushed across me when I first struck across the 'North West Wind' in the <u>Saturday</u>. Then I tore it out of the paper and carried it in my pocket book for months - I was so fond of it and so jealous, as a half formed artist is, saying to myself - this man, this man can <u>write</u>'(3)

  The correspondence between editor and author - who quickly became friends - continued for nearly forty years. Many of the letters from Garnett to his 'dear amigo' contain praise for Robert's work that seems rather extravagant in one whose authority was derived from his gift for constructive but penetrating criticism. For instance 'I admire, I admire fully and deeply' he wrote on reading 'Cruz Alta' the story of the failed attempt by Robert and George Mansel to drive horses north through Uruguay to Brazil; 'it is right, it is inevitable; you will remain alone'. As for 'Aurora la Cujini', Robert's description of a gypsy woman dancing the flamenco in Seville which had a hard time finding a publisher due to the explicit - and stunning - description of the way the men and women watching were sexually aroused, Garnett's excitement was unbridled. (4) 'You infect us with the snaky poison of that woman [Aurora], he wrote, 'the delicious madness. Admirably seen, admirably felt, admirably described, amigo, for the strong emotion works in us too'.(5) Robert's response to this effusion was characteristically modest. It was an impression, nothing more 'that is all I can do'. Aurora was published eventually but at the author's expense and by Leonard Smithers whose reputation was for taking risks.

  The writer Garnett most admired was Turgenev, master of the short story. If Cunninghame Graham would only develop characterisation and plot to add to his existing skills of clarity and close observation he might have some chance of approaching the Russian's level, an exciting possibility. But, in order to do so he would have to conquer the instinct not to express his deepest feelings. 'I want you to think over what there is in yourself and life which you have shrunk from writing', Garnett coaxed, then - '<u>Write</u> it, my dear Amigo, in a journal as though you were communing with yourself, just as Turgenev wrote his 'Sportsmen's Sketches'; Cast it in that loose and fluid form'. (6) If only Robert would apply the kind of insight and feeling expressed in his letters to his literary work Garnett forecast a significant increase in his standing as a writer. Robert would have none of it. 'Now you must understand that I am a man of action and have passed most of my life out of doors', he wrote, 'I am really, <u>pas de blague</u>, extremely diffident of all I write. I never put pen to paper until I was 37'. There was the rub. To make the most of his or her talent a writer needs self assurance above all else, a firm belief in the merit of the work, a quality often mistaken for arrogance by those less gifted, many of whom choose to be affronted by what seems to them presumption.

Garnett's own writing was self conscious and undisciplined. Carried away, he did not consider the effect of phrases like 'snaky poison' and 'delicious madness' which should have made him wince. That he was unhappy at his lack of success in writing plays and novels appears in a letter to his father, Richard Garnett, Keeper of Printed Books at the British Museum. 'I am a discontented flower who would be the earth, and so am fit for nothing.. But I have had an idea in the back of my brain...that it is not impossible to put criticism into living form, rather that it is one's duty to try to do so'.(7) This he did and with conspicuous success. Among the writers he found and promoted were Joseph Conrad, John Galsworthy, W.H. Hudson, and D.H. Lawrence. Yet where Robert was concerned it was not until after his death that Garnett set down the reasons why his work had appealed to him with a degree of candour that is absent from his letters. Some of those he wrote in the course of their long acquaintance give the impression that he was afraid of speaking too frankly for fear of giving offence to someone whose reaction, by virtue of their very different backgrounds, he feared he was not in a position to anticipate. Garnett found it difficult to separate the man from the writer, both of whom he envied. 'Absolutely independent of public opinion and class ties Graham was in the delightful position of social observer without any fish to fry but with means and leisure to speak his mind freely. The charm of his manner, his fine breeding, his gleaming wit, his savoir faire, his Spanish courtesy combined with his Scotch blood to make his personality unique'.(8)

The letters between the two gave Garnett an unrivalled insight into the difficulties over the Gartmore estate Robert was facing at that particular time - the last years of the century. But he was not wholly admitted into the latter's confidence; certain areas of his life remained closed, more especially the tragic events concerning his father, William Bontine. There is no evidence that Garnett knew what had occurred; probably he did not for, after Anne Elizabeth's death he suggested that Robert might write an account of his family with special reference to her and to her mother, Doña Catalina - he knew nothing of either, he complained.(9) Yet while Robert did produce gently ironic portraits of some of his relatives - his grandfather, Admiral Fleeming; his Aunt Alexia; his Uncle Tom; his stepgrandfather, Admiral Katon, nothing was ever forthcoming about the two women nearest to the tragedy and who had the greatest influence on his early life. Nor was he anything but vague about the time he spent in South America beyond giving the impression that it had lasted without a break for a period of years - thirteen was the number Garnett quoted in telling others, and in so doing lent the story his authority as one known to be a friend.

Even if it had not lasted quite that length of time Robert's experience of the region had been prolonged. And in the late 1890s circumstances took him frequently to Spain. Both were places relatively little known in England at the time but whose history was romantic and exciting. Now here was a new writer who, with his command of Spanish and his aptitude for narrative history was equipped to deal with sources so far unknown to the reading public. His longstanding desire to describe what he had seen when he stumbled over the remains of the Jesuit settlements in Paraguay was fulfilled in 1901. 'A Vanished Arcadia: Being some Account of the Jesuits in Paraguay 1607 -1767'(10) which came out in that year, made a strong impression. Painstaking research into hitherto obscure historical events was enlivened by the Graham flair for describing a landscape and its people; the whole coloured by his sympathy as a socialist with a process he judged had preserved the Guarani people from a far worse fate. Many of the sketches he wrote in these years had Spain or Spanish history as their subject; more particularly the effect upon the mother country after 1898 of the disastrous defeat she suffered in the war with the United States over Cuba which occurred in that year. While most English commentators took Washington's side, Robert Cunninghame Graham roundly denounced the Americans for acting like neo-colonialist ruffians.(11)

Impressionism was the fashion as the century drew to a close; among writers as well as artists and, as we have seen, Robert was content to call himself an impressionist in literary matters. Whether or not he would have used the word to describe the guise in which he now began to appear before the public, this, too, was an impression. These were the years in which his beliefs, his work, his appearance created the legend of Don Roberto, the quixotic Spanish adventurer, the dashing <u>hidalgo</u>; an image which fixed itself on people's minds to the point where, as he grew old, it became a caricature. That this melodramatic, Hispanic aspect emerged in his middle years, and not before, was something those who had known him during his time in the House of Commons placed on record. There were various reasons why, with his encouragement, the image rapidly took on a life of its own.(12) In a situation where much interest was aroused by his ancient name, his Scottish estates, details which threatened

'The Fencer', William Rothenstein, Dunedin Art Gallery, New Zealand.

to betray his family tragedy, his quarter Spanish ancestry provided a diversion of which he made increasing use as he became well known.

The artists who painted him at this time almost invariably did so in the trappings of an earlier age. Will Rothenstein chose to represent him as The Fencer. He stands upright, alert to the thrust of his opponent. Many of his contemporaries frequented Angelo's famous establishment in the Strand but few conveyed so perfectly the air of one born to wear a sword. That Robert's personality as well as his appearance gave the impression of belonging to the period of the conquistadores, rather than his own, was underlined when William Strang, one of the leading painter etchers of the day chose him as the model for a series of 30 etchings illustrating Cervantes' 'Don Quixote'. There he sits upon his charger, every inch the wandering knight from the jut of his beard to the hand poised nonchalantly on his hip; ready to confront all comers.(13)

There was something of this attitude in Bernard Shaw's sketch of him as Sergius in 'Arms and the Man' when he borrowed the phrase Robert tossed at the Speaker on departing the House at his command. 'I never withdraw' was an echo of the explanation Edward Garnett received from Robert with regard to a fundamental aspect of his character; 'To a nature like mine capitulation is the one hard thing to bear and I never march out without the honours of war'. To Ford Madox Ford Robert was Don Collar in his novel 'The English Girl'; a man torn between the idea of social reform and a love of picturesque feudalism. (14) And it was as a figure from the age of chivalry that his friend, W.H. Hudson, thought of him. 'You are rather like an Arthurian knight abroad in the great forest of the world', he told Robert, 'in quest of adventures and ready at a moments (sic) notice to lower your lance and joust at any evil minded person that may turn up'. (15) This was to take a broad view, based on the image presented to the world. It was left for Joseph Conrad to provide the most penetrating analysis of the forces that drove the real person. Conrad was in a position to do this because he became a close friend in 1897 - precisely the same time as Garnett. He and Robert corresponded; over 80 of Conrad's letters have been published; Robert's to him have not survived. The result of these exchanges [as has already been pointed out] was the portrait of Charles Gould in 'Nostromo'. Scholars have long debated the sources Conrad used to write his South American masterpiece; his own experience of the continent being limited to a few days ashore from a ship on which he served. Cunninghame Graham was an obvious candidate and the impression is confirmed by the man himself. 'Conrad tells me he has used a story I told him in 'Nostromo', he told Edward Garnett. 'Nostromo' is a dammed bad name,' he grumbled; 'it ought to have been called Costaguana'. In spite of which he praised the book wholeheartedly.(16)

Its setting, a republic in political turmoil, must owe something to Robert's reminiscences of his time in the Argentine in the Seventies while some of Conrad's characters bear a resemblance to people we know Robert knew. Thus it has often been suggested that Giorgio Viola, the Garibaldian hotel keeper, friend of the capataz, Nostromo, is more than probably based on Enrico Clerici, whose pulperia on the river Paraná Robert frequented during his time in Paraguay. And Perez Triana, son of a former Colombian President who, in spite of his position as Ambassador to London, was always badgering Robert for introductions, has long been identified as the model for Costaguana's elder statesman, Don José Avellanos. But those who are acquainted with the unpublished Cunninghame Graham papers will recognize that there is a much closer connection. Like Garnett Conrad was privy to the events that governed Robert's life in the late 1890s. As novelist he took the central issue - the bitter legacy of debt left by the ninth laird, William Bontine, and transformed it into the story of the São Tomé silver mine. Gould's father leaves the concession to work the mine to his son, Charles, whose life becomes wholly subject to it as Robert's life nearly was to Gartmore. Conrad, who had no patience with Robert's optimism makes 'Nostromo' end in tragedy. (17) The Goulds' marriage, ideally happy at the beginning of the novel is irrevocably damaged by Charles' long absences on the business of the mine; his determination to use whatever means there are to make it a success. In the end Emilia, his wife, a much admired figure in Costaguana society, has to acknowledge she faces a life alone in which the qualities that made her respected are certain to be wasted; the marriage will never be repaired; she will never have a child.(18) It is an echo of the fate Conrad foresaw overtaking Gabrielle.

Many of the details Conrad used in his portrait of Emilia Gould appear in the story Robert told the world about his own wife. The first encounter, for example, is very similar. Robert's version was set in Paris, an aunt was involved and a convent. Charles Gould meets Emilia in Italy where she is staying with an aunt whose appearance, in black robes and a white headband, is nun like. The background of both girls is vague; Emilia is an orphan; all we are told is that she was brought up, as Caroline/Gabrielle was, in an atmosphere of intellectual interests, and both are gifted water colour painters. Like Gabrielle Emilia is eager for an unusual life, for adventure, for remote places and great distances. After the Goulds return to Costaguana Emilia accompanies Charles in his search for labour for the mine. 'In her travel-worn riding habit, her face powdered white like a plaster cast, with a further protection of a small silk mask during the heat of the day, she rode on a well-shaped light-footed pony in the centre of a little cavalcade'. No doubt Gabrielle looked much the same on the journey from Texas down into Mexico she and Robert made shortly after their marriage. As the novel progresses Emilia becomes increasingly independent of her husband; from necessity since he is invariably absent at the mine. She has to represent him at the capital, Sulaco where, Conrad explains, the mantle of his family's hereditary position has descended on her. Similarly Gabrielle stood in for Robert in his long absences from Gartmore, a task his family thought she made too much of, and resented. Emilia performs the duty well; she has the fastidious soul of an experienced woman; she is highly gifted in the art of human intercourse just as Gabrielle once was. There is one difference; although Conrad indicates Emilia's promise will be wasted and her fate will be a sad one he leaves the details to the reader's imagination. With Gabrielle the outcome is the same - her energy, her resourcefulness, her efforts on Robert's behalf all go to waste through illness, but her long decline is painfully and precisely recorded in her letters.(19)

The correspondence with Conrad and Garnett show the Grahams continuing the practice whereby one of them was always in residence at Gartmore, leaving the other free for a time to pursue his or her particular interest, a separation neither of them welcomed. But, while Robert's letters show he usually enjoyed his absences from Scotland and was miserable alone at home, Gabrielle was increasingly unhappy wherever she might be. 'My dearest old Lob' she wrote to him in Morocco on one occasion, 'do take care and come back safely, and in future we will go about together as I have felt lately in Spain how lonely one is without the other'. And, when it was her turn to be away; 'I hope you are not very dull at Gartmore; it is a dull place to be left alone in.' (20) After she turned forty in 1898 her visits abroad - mostly to Spain but also France, Switzerland and Italy - became a series of aimless wanderings to places that, at her first encounter, interested, even excited her - only to provoke acute distaste the following day. Her restlessness was a symptom of the disease now gaining on her. As a solitary traveller (Peregrina no longer always accompanied her) her predicament was often frightening. She would fall ill in some remote and miserable <u>fonda</u> from where Robert would receive desperate notes in pencil. 'My dearest Lob, I have had an awful time. From seven at night the day before yesterday to three yesterday, I thought I was going to die. It [pneumonia] came at once...I suffered so much I thought of shooting myself.' At moments like these, Gartmore, however dull, seemed a haven to which she longed to return.(21)

Robert seldom gave a thought to Scotland during his frequent absences when he was kept continually on the go seeing to business of one kind or another. His long drawn out attempt to obtain a concession to develop an area south of the Atlas Mountains from Sheik Bashir el Bairuk was crowned with success when the two of them met in Morocco City in August 1899 to sign the formal agreement. It gave Robert, as the principal party, leave to develop a large area of land lying inland from Cape Juby and extending a long way south, even to the Rio de Oro. Part was the low lying region known as Tiris containing the depression of El Juf that Donald Mackenzie had briefly considered flooding, part was the fertile upland of Adrar whose nomadic population acknowledged Wold Aidyah, Bairuk's father in law as their chief. (22) Both areas were wild and remote but by this time few European Chancelleries were without a map of their most prominent features and their boundaries. Lying to the north of French Senegal and north west of the vast territory that recently come under the control of the Royal Niger Company, they had become of increased interest to the Powers after 1885 when Spain had declared a Protectorate over the best harbour on that part of the coast, the 25 mile long inlet known as the Rio de Oro. One of Robert's first approaches, therefore, was to Joseph Chamberlain with whom he had been on friendly terms during his time in Parliament. 'It is important...to secure this territory before the French step in', he urged.(23) The Royal Niger Company's success in West Africa offered a precedent as to British government support. Chamberlain was a shareholder, and a list of directors is among the Graham papers dealing with Tiris and Adrar. Its Chairman, Sir George Goldie, was yet another Graham family connection via Captain Ross Grove; he of Holland Jacques [on whose behalf

Robert had negotiated the concession to work yerbales in Paraguay in 1874] Holland Jacques also traded to West Africa in those years but got into difficulties and nearly collapsed. George Goldie's first experience of Africa was when he went out to take control of Holland Jacques which he subsequently transformed into the mighty Royal Niger Company. In spite of these advantages Chamberlain approached the issue gingerly, as one still smarting from the aftermath of the Jameson Raid. 'I take a great interest in all that bears on the development of Africa, but there is no doubt whatever that this particular question is a matter entirely for the Foreign Office' he told his former Liberal Party colleague cautiously.(24)

Foreign Office dignitaries were not keen either. Their reluctance to become involved created something of a political vacuum along the length of Morocco's Atlantic coast. Nevertheless there was no shortage of private individuals eager to turn a profit; their eyes were fixed on the valley of the River Sus whose Sheikhs were more than ever eager to see it developed. In May 1899, following his acquittal by a Gibraltar court for his part in the Tourmaline affair, Gybbon Spilsbury approached Robert Cunninghame Graham with a new proposal. The gallant Major intended to press ahead with the Sus concession acquired via Abdul Kerim Bey/ Geyling. Spilsbury sent Robert a plan that, if put even partially into effect, would have seriously destabilized the region. If the British government would not grant him permission to proceed and, at the same time guarantee his safety as a citizen going about his legitimate business, he intended to apply to Spain. He was confident she would supply troops to protect and assist the members of a new syndicate whose object would be to develop every aspect - strategic, commercial, and political - of that huge and exceedingly sensitive territory.(25)

The genuine alarm this created did not subside until Najim Kisbany, keeping watch for Robert in Tangier, assured him Spilsbury's plan had no firm foundation. Shortly after this the Major transferred his attention to the Portuguese territory of Mozambique, a place sufficiently remote to escape the kind of notice his filibustering expeditions usually attracted. In effect, after 1899 he vanished, and with him into the darkest part of Africa, he took one of Robert's closest friends, Dino de Frias. For him the good years had long been over; the bills were rolling in. His gambling debts had all but swallowed up the vast estates in Spain, Most of the time he and his English duchess inhabited a couple of rooms in the New York Hotel, on the beach outside Tangier. Dino spent the next ten years in Mozambique while Maya de Frias and their daughter, Laura, survived as best they might alone, either in a small house in England or among the faded splendours of the family's last remaining Spanish castle, at Oropesa in Castile.(26)

As soon as the agreement with Bashir el Bairouk was signed in Morocco Robert and Kisbany began to discuss the preparations necessary to bring the concession into being. It was no fly by night affair; it would depend on the provision of accurate information - about terrain, climate, population and resources, joined to a credible forecast of what it was hoped to achieve in the way of development. Expeditions would have to be mounted to discover whether there was water enough for profitably large herds of grazing cattle, for example, but above all to prospect for the minerals that had long been rumoured to exist in fabulous quantities. The project, with its maps and plans and detailed reports calls to mind Charles Gould's Costaguana enterprise; it is on the same large scale. As the chief concessionaire Robert would have presided over a territory of similar vastness; in that remote and underpopulated area his responsibilities, like Gould's, would have included matters governments more usually decide; just as Conrad made Gould 'king' of Sulaco, had the Adrar concession come into being so Robert Cunninghame Graham could have found the destiny reserved for him by his ancestry fulfilled in a totally unexpected but curiously suitable manner.

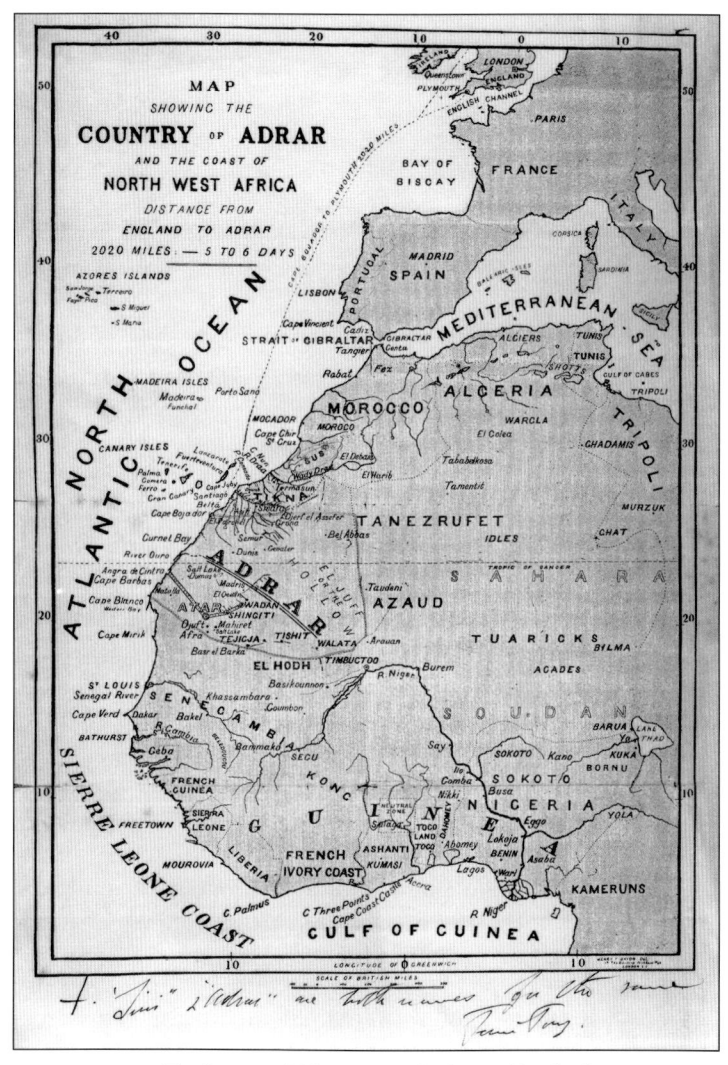

The Country of Adrar. National Library of Scotland.

While Robert kept Conrad and Garnett informed of the latest developments in Southern Morocco, his chief adviser as to how to proceed was Martin Hume. In the years since he had encountered Gabrielle on her first unaccompanied voyage to Spain, Hume had prospered as a writer and a businessman, holding firmly to the belief that if anything was worth the trouble of writing down it deserved a respectable financial return. By 1898 he was established as the leading authority in England on Spanish history and politics and had succeeded Pascal de Gayangos at the Public Record Office as Editor of the Spanish State Papers, one of the most important collections in the national archive. Meanwhile, his vividly written histories of Sir Walter Raleigh and Philip II of Spain, published two years earlier were bringing him a handsome sum. He saw no reason why Cunninghame Graham should not achieve the same level of return. However, as it fell to Hume to review much of Robert's work in these years he grew privately impatient with what he considered major flaws of style. His letters are always forthright and sometimes highly critical; there is nothing of the slightly fawning note one may detect in both Conrad and Garnett: Hume is on terms of social equality as a friend; as a writer he predominates. On receiving 'A Vanished Arcadia' for example, 'All the critics say practically the same' An excellent and entertaining book marred by irritating digressions etc. I suppose you will see my review in the Chronicle. There I, of course, speak much of its excellence and of the author's abounding wit; whilst holding my peace about the digressions (whatever I may think about them)...Seriously between you and me ...the book is far better than I should have thought possible. But O how I panted for a blue pencil, or power to black out passages like a Russian censor. Why Why Why the devil will you handicap yourself so. There ought to be a fortune in your writing and I want to see you get the fortune'.(27)

That there was an even larger fortune to be made in Southern Morocco Hume was in no doubt. He became a partner in the Adrar concession, as did Walter Harris and Bibi Carleton. ' Believe me', Hume wrote, ' there will be no difficulty in disposing of the concession on favourable terms as soon as you can show; 1. That you have the native concession (which you already have). 2. That you have Lord Salisbury's assurance that he regards the territory as Spanish... and 3 That you have at least the beneplacito of the Spanish government. So far as 2 was concerned, a letter from the Foreign Office on behalf of Lord Salisbury among the Graham papers disclaims all interest by the British government in the area in question.(28) Thus was Spain encouraged in the belief that one of the most serious obstacles to the fulfilment of her destiny in Morocco had been removed. As to the beneplacito of her government, that also seemed to come within reach when, in August 1899, the Spanish Minister in Tangier, Emilio de Ojeda. agreed to receive Najim Kisbany on behalf of the concessionaires. He told Kisbany he was willing to put proposals to his government in Madrid provided the Globe Venture Syndicate was not involved. He emphasized the importance of sound financial backing for the enterprise and recommended Spanish or French capital be brought in. He insisted the territory in question must always be considered purely Spanish, be governed by Spanish officials according to Spanish laws , and supervised by Spanish, or, possibly, Rif soldiers. In return Spain would probably grant the exclusive right of trading, of tilling the ground, and of mining. What excited Kisbany more than anything was Ojeda's hint that when , as she shortly hoped to do, Spain moved to repossess and reopen the fishing port of Santa Cruz de Mar Pequeña, she might also hand it to the company to develop. The problem was that, since it had been abandoned many years before, the precise location of Santa Cruz had been forgotten: all anyone knew was that it had been on the Atlantic coast somewhere near Cape Juby. Kisbany emerged with the impression that Ojeda regarded cooperation with a financially strong and independent syndicate as the best protection for a government as weak as Spain against filibusters of whatever nationality. (29)

While all this was going on great changes were about to take place in Scotland. George Mansel was one of the first to hear the news. On 7 September 1900 Robert told him Gartmore had been sold for £126,000 to Sir Charles Cayzer, head of the Clan Shipping line, ' It has been a great wrench but it was sad to see everything in ruins and [have] nothing to repair it with. When I took the old chap over the place yesterday step by step I was appalled at the decay'(30) Signs of this were everywhere; fences were unmended; slagging wires had been dragged by cattle into the middle of the fields, gates were off their hinges and weeds covered up the gravel in the drive. The grass was thick with nettles, the paint of the garden seats blistered by sun and rain; the formal terraces had reverted to grass; roughly mown they had been honeycombed by rabbits. These details are from ' A Braw Day' the sketch not published until 1912 which, in the significance of the occasion and the private misery it describes, may be considered Robert's answer to Garnett's plea that he should set down what touched him most. ' Never before in the long years that he had passed in the old place, had it appeared so much a part of his whole being; as on the day on which he signed the deed of sale. '(31) was how it began. 'Still he felt like a murderer, as judges well may feel when they pronounce death sentences. Perhaps they feel it more than the prisoner, for things we do through fate, and by virtue of the circumstances that hedge our lives about with chains, often affect us more than the actions we perform impelled by no one but ourselves'. As this passage implies, the acute distress caused by the need to take such a decision was made worse by guilt, for by this action Robert prevented his brother and heir, Charles Cunninghame Graham, and Charles' son, Angus, from succeeding in their turn. Charles' reaction was predictably unselfish: he was glad a decision had been taken at last for he knew how it had worried Robert. Selling would have been of little avail if he and Gabrielle had not paid off the debt; he hoped that after sixteen years of struggling, they would now be comfortably off.. Anne Elizabeth Bontine also rallied round though it is clear she felt the loss acutely. on her son's behalf. ' I cannot tell you how much I admire your determination and pluck in sitting down to finish the Jesuits [ie ' A Vanished Arcadia] in the midst of so much mental worry ' she wrote ' I often think that the spirit of some ancestor of the Raleigh period or perhaps a Spaniard who volunteered to go with Columbus or was a friend of Cervantes must have entered into your body for you are so unlike a 19th or 20 century man'. (32) Gabrielle received a somewhat brisker letter. Anne Elizabeth praised her for doing her duty, and more than her duty; she hoped Gabrielle's health would not suffer from what she still had to go through ; then -' You must try to cheer up. I am quite sure you are very sad but it really for the best now the plunge has been taken.' Kind words but afterwards Gabrielle got the blame for having been the moving spirit behind the decision to relinquish something infinitely precious that had been in the Cunninghame Graham family for more than three hundred years.. Her zeal in selling feus was the principal means whereby the debt Robert inherited was paid off, leaving most of the money Sir Charles handed over at his sole disposal. (33)

Gabrielle was sad at leaving the garden, the animals and the birds. Pampa was to be brought down to London where Robert continued to ride him. He was the only survivor from the early years. Jack, the dog that had adopted them in Texas, had long since died, and they had been obliged to have Talla put down in 1898. Robert's distress at the loss of this dearest of animals was acute; the affection in which he held the Iceland pony revealed by Gabrielle's response to his letter describing the last painful moments before it was shot. 'Poor dear little Tal. I shall be the next of the familia, I think'. (34) Altogether it was a dark and miserable time. Their last day in the house was 4 December when she wrote to Robert's mother; 'My dear Mrs Bontine, ...I still live in a dream it is all so rapid... We leave tomorrow. Who would ever imagine that we should be sorry and distressed to leave the sour, dour faces of these people. It is because they are familiar and one had got accustomed to their strange ways. Even their rudeness had ceased to grate on one. I had begun to think they did not mean it and take it as the fashion of the country.' This relenting attitude towards their neighbours did not last; her antagonism soon returned. 'That hated and hateful village,' as she called the settlement at their gates, was a bad influence over everything and everyone at Gartmore; 'I fear Sir Cayser (sic) will not escape from it'.(35)

With their move to a London flat in Margaret Street, near Oxford Circus, a period began in which circumstances came between Robert and Gabrielle. So far as one can tell from reading the papers that have survived, their affection for each other was as strong as ever. Yet it is clear that they began to lead increasingly separate lives. There is no sense of a shared domestic existence in Margaret Street where, between frequent journey s abroad, Gabrielle seems to have lived alone except for the company of the housekeeper, Miss Ward, who became a close friend. From time to time she had visits from a woman whose Christian name only is known but which suggests she was that most intriguing member of the Horsfall family, Caroline/Gabrielle's younger sister, Grace Stevenson. Whenever he was in London, life for Robert took place further west, across Hyde Park, in Chester Square. There, Anne Elizabeth, now 75, and growing more formidable with every year, directed the affairs of her immediate family, their Scottish and Spanish connections, and her many friends. She made no secret of her delight at having her eldest son virtually restored to her; soon her became her dearest companion in all her pursuits, almost as Malise had been. These involved visits to galleries, to concerts, and above all, to the theatre. She had a friend who was a playwright - an increasingly successful one to whose first nights she made a point of going. Robert had known him years before in another context. Now he found himself the playwright's model for a character who so pleased its author he used him in more than one production. Nor was it merely certain traits he reproduced but incidents from Robert's life and maybe even a particular situation that he would have much preferred to remain private. To protest would have been to no avail. 'I am an artist' Bernard Shaw told Mrs Patrick Campbell, 'and as such utterly unscrupulous where I find my model'.(36)

Like Ford Madox Ford Shaw was fascinated by the conflict between idealism and realism demonstrated by Robert's past history. Sergius in 'Arms and the Man', and Hector Hushabye in 'Heartbreak House' are a reflection of this one facet of his nature. Hector, who was given to wearing Arab robes instead of evening dress and makes fencing passes with a sword stick on the slightest provocation, also has Robert's , by now notorious, attractiveness to women. Shaw was determined his audience should recognize the joke. 'I want you on the first night to make up like Cunninghame Graham' he told the actor playing Hector on one occasion; 'he will be in the front row'. (37) Tricks like these were unkind for they suggested he was more extraordinary than was the case; people jumped to conclusions as to why the real person might look and behave as Shaw's character did. 'Graham's head is going wrong' (38) Bruce Glasier put it bluntly. The result of these attentions was a widening gulf between the playwright and his model; Shaw continuing to express admiration for the hero of Bloody Sunday; Robert treating him with growing reserve. Apart from anything else their approach to social questions had diverged. Shaw was all for doing things deliberately; for directing how they should be managed; Robert for leaving them to happen. Shaw took to bycycling on roads; Robert went on giving the horse its head in open country.

One other play must be considered in any discussion of the Shaw/Graham relationship - Pygmalion. A situation in which a young woman from a different class and background whose speech and accent have to be artificially adjusted before the mutual attraction between her and the principal character can be considered desirable, comes very close to the strange history of Robert Cunninghame Graham and Caroline Horsfall. We do not know if Shaw guessed the secret - it seems unlikely he would have been told. And there are other candidates for the role of Eliza - Janey Morris, for example, or Lizzie Siddal, both of whom were coached in the sort of behaviour to which their husbands, William Morris and Dante Gabriel Rossetti were accustomed.(39) Nevertheless, the timing fits, though Pygmalion did not appear until 1912 there are indications Shaw was already thinking about it in 1897. Besides, there is another possible connection with the Grahams. The Professor's mother, a woman of strong common sense, acerbic, authoritative, well read and knowledgeable about the arts, bears a striking resemblance to Anne Elizabeth Bontine. Such a mother set a standard against which it was difficult for younger women to compete - in the Professor's case Mrs Higgins made it possible for him to separate his idealism and sense of beauty from his sexual impulses; he could afford to ignore the necessity of marriage. If Robert thought that Shaw borrowed this situation from observing Anne Elizabeth's ascendancy in Chester Square, he would have been bound to resent it.

Though his mother was intellectually as sharp as ever she was aware of failing powers. 'I do so hate to be old' she told Shaw. One result was that since she was no longer capable of disguising her anxiety Robert's exposure to danger caused her, she became somewhat querulous though to no avail. In 1902 he vanished, much as he had in Entre Ríos all those years ago. In Fez a horse had fallen and crushed his foot so badly he was laid up for more than two months in the greatest discomfort for the weather was hotter than he had ever known - that, at any rate, was what he told her, an old and familiar story, and perhaps even true.(40) It may also have been cover for whatever he was doing in connection with the Adrar concession which, in 1902, was nearer to becoming a going concern than before or after. An agreement between the Spanish and French governments to divide their spheres of influence which would have given Spain the area in question seemed to signal real progress at last. But to the great disappointment of the concessionaires, the Madrid government fell before the necessary documents were signed. Their hopes fluctuated for another two years but were dashed for ever in 1904

By that time Robert's attention had been distracted, his existence blighted in the knowledge that Gabrielle was dying. The doctors seem to have told her what to expect in the early summer of 1903. Robert was in Scotland, staying at the Lake of Menteith Hotel while visiting his former tenants and neighbours. Up to the time this worst of news reached him his letters to Gabrielle had been cheerful; surprised by the warmth of his reception he took comfort for the still enduring pain of losing Gartmore from their vociferous disapproval of Sir Charles Cayzer's doings - a 'beastly' motor boat on the lake, a motor car up in June, electric light, trees felled, eventually an entire reconstruction of the house. Then came the blow for which he had no words ; 'Oh Chid' was all he could say.(41) Yet it cannot have been wholly unexpected. Although she had continued very active since the sale of Gartmore, her judgement was flawed and her ability to concentrate declining. This was especially noticeable in her written work. In 1899 the Yellow Book paid her the compliment of publishing a story with a Spanish background The plot is commonplace, the language wooden. In 1900 she undertook the translation of a well known Spanish play. 'Don Juan Tenorio' became her version of Don Juan. No less a person than the actor manager, Martin Harvey, undertook to bring it to the London stage and lavished very complicated stage effects and scenery on it. The first night was a disaster when the machinery ground to a halt; actors and audience were plunged into silence and darkness, a fiasco for which Gabrielle got a share of the blame.

In 1902 advance notices were published of a new novel by Mrs Cunninghame Graham which Anne Elizabeth, for one, greeted with serious misgivings. 'I rather tremble at the thought of a study of madness' she told Edward Garnett a propos of 'Genera'., Gabrielle's last work.(42) This writer has not succeeded in tracing the MS, However it would appear that it was seen by Dr Cedric Watts, the editor of Conrad's letters to Robert Cunninghame Graham. He describes it as Gabrielle's autobiography, 'breathlessly romanticized'. Genera is a Spanish servant girl who falls in love with Euan, an aristocrat, 1/4 Spanish, 3/4 Scots, as he does with her. When Euan's mother and her friends trick them into separating, Euan goes mad. The action moves between Spain and Scotland when Vigo and Gartmore are instantly recognizable.(43)

One of the worst aspects of the fate that had overtaken Gabrielle was that while it was inevitable, it approached so slowly. A period of waiting had to be endured; it may have been one reason why, in 1903, they began negotiations, conducted as always by Gabrielle, to reacquire Ardoch, the charming white plantation house built by the seventh laird on the shore of the Clyde opposite Finlaystone. The other was plain homesickness; 'I want the North <u>now</u>' Robert complained not long after the move to London. In July 1904 they returned to the place Robert had loved so well when he was a child. Much of the furniture was brought from the stone mausoleum at the Lake of Menteith where it had been stored since the sale of Gartmore. Gabrielle immediately started planning; 'there is another idea which occurs to me re Ardoch, have the whole building on the ground floor raised a few inches from the ground bungalow fashion' she told Robert. 'If I build at Ardoch you are better away. You know how excitable discussion makes me'.(44) Her strength came and went. 'I met Gabrielle at the Whistler exhibition' Anne Elizabeth told Robert in February 1905. 'I thought her looking very ill and she was coughing a good deal. I think she ought to go abroad at once...she would like Taormina'.(45) Three months later, in a letter condoling with Edward Garnett on his father's death Robert wrote' I am under a shadow too. My wife is very very ill and the doctors are not sanguine. Do not write to Margaret Street in case she opens the letter by accident. It is not a quick disease.' (46) Yet she rallied and at the end of June had recovered sufficiently to set out for Avila accompanied by Peregrina. There are no details of what happened to prolong the visit beyond the three weeks originally intended but towards the end of August they started to make their way slowly home. Hendaye on the French side of the border was a place Gabrielle was always pleased to reach when travelling south. Once the train crossed the bridge over the river Bidassoa she knew she was back in Spain. This time she was going north but at Hendaye she was obliged to leave the train and seek refuge in a hotel. Robert was summoned in haste. On 1 September he wrote to Edward Garnett from the Grand Hotel de France et Angleterre.' Querido Amigo, I have little or no hope. You know what these days are. Will you write to my mother for me for I cannot? ' On 9 September he wrote again. 'Mi querido amigo, My poor wife died yesterday. It was a long agony but I am glad to say not with much pain. RIP.' (47) From the Hotel Bellevue on Lake Maggiore where she was staying, Anne Elizabeth was instantly in touch with Garnett; in spite of her offering to go at once to Hendaye, she had been persuaded to remain in Italy. 'Poor poor soul. I truly grieve for her'.(48)

As death is a time for truth the news also went from Hendaye to Gabrielle's own family. On 11 September Robert wrote an apologetic letter to an address in Glasgow. 'Dear Miss Horsfall, I am so sorry. I would have written but on the day of her death I asked your brother Willie [William Horsfall, Vicar of Colgate in Surrey who was also in Hendaye] to do so. Your sister was ill for long of diabetes and suffered much. She was in Spain with old Peregrina, her attached maid, and in France. There she caught dysentery and wired for me to come to Hendaye. I was there for nine days but there was no hope from the first. She died brave, resigned, and peaceful and conscious to within an hour of the end. It has been a dreadful blow to me after 25 years of married life and affection. She is to be buried next Wednesday in the chancel of the ruined priory of Inchmahome on the island in the Lake of Menteith. Many of my people lie there. With kind regards and in great grief'.(49) This, the only letter establishing a direct link between Robert and members of his wife's family, was not taken particularily kindly by Mary Horsfall to whom it was addressed. Apparently William had not seen his sister before she died. 'Poor Carrie' Mary told another member of her family' I am sure from what he [William] says she would have liked to have seen him..' Mary hoped to obtain a picture of her sister's grave 'Of course her burial is very different from anyone else's. I shall watch the [news]papers for I am certain in spite of all the story will come out but we need not mind him [Robert] what I want to find out is what name he has registered her death in for then if other than Papa's or Mama's he can be charged with perjury.' (50) The name on the death certificate was Gabrielle Marie Cunninghame Graham; that she was born Caroline Horsfall would not be made public for another 80 years. If, as Mary Horsfall's remark in this letter suggests, she and Robert had not been legally married, because one or other had a husband or wife living in 1878, it has never been revealed.

Gabrielle Cunninghame Graham of Gartmore. University of Michigan Library.

Robert wrote to Edward Garnett on 25 September, 'No, the funeral was not the worst. Now is the worst. I ordered her coffin alone. I saw to all details in Hendaye and in London and with the old Highland grave digger rolled off the stone over the grave [on Inchmahome] it weighed 800 pounds and helped him at the grave. He rowed the coffin over just as if he had been rowing out fishing, now talking of the crops? now drawing his hand over his eyes and saying she was a bonnie leddie. It is good for a man to do and see all these things but it is not good for him to sit as I am sitting alone tonight. Yes, the people were very fond of us both. Thanks for what you say'.(51) According to the Stirling Sentinel, before the boat set out there had been a service in the Graham mausoleum at the Port of Menteith conducted by a clergyman described without comment or explanation as the Revd William Horsfall from London The incumbent of the local parish church , the Rev Mr M' Lean had to wait to do his part until the coffin was in place within the chancel of the Priory of Inchmahome beside the graves of Walter Comyn, the 12th century Earl of Menteith and his Countess, when he led the prayers Later a plaque was set in the wall above which read '. Los muertos abren los ochos de los vivos'(52)

    Contrary to what Mary Horsfall had expected - and, perhaps, desired - the death and burial of Gabrielle did not provoke any direct challenge to Robert to explain the circumstances of their marriage. Nevertheless there obviously was speculation which surfaced in the form of leading questions ; certain people hinted they could say more if they chose. One was the correspondent of the Stirling Advertiser who in praising Gabrielle's conduct as mistress of Gartmore, referred to his presence at the first homecoming of the young laird and his wife in 1884. Though at the time her native language and descent was believed to be French, this man chose to ignore that aspect and to describe her Spanish self- a disguise she did not assume until well into her biography of Santa Teresa. 'A woman possessing the highest accomplishments and a keen and penetrating intellect which overcame every difficulty that a language foreign to her could present.. her knowledge of the history of 'sunny Spain' was supplemented by an acquaintance with our own country, its manners and customs which few even of our best-educated Scotsmen possess' And he went on 'I am told by a gentleman well qualified to judge...that Mrs Cunninghame Graham, acting in her husband's interest succeeded in mastering the extremely complicated Scottish system of conveyancing [ie feus] which, in the case of anyone without a legal training, is truly marvellous'. According to this report the mourners were surprised Gabrielle was not laid permanently to rest with other members of the Graham family in the mausoleum but taken to Inchmahome Priory. The explanation he gave for this signal honour was that she had a deep affection for the ruins and had been instrumental in having them restored . 'As a relic of her own faith Inchmahome Priory was also dear to Mrs Cunninghame Graham and in his appropriate and touching prayer at her graveside the Rev Mr M'Lean alluded to the fact that she often resorted thither to pray'.(52)

    As correspondent of a local newspaper with many Graham friends and neighbours among its readers this individual could hardly say more. But whoever composed Gabrielle's obituary in The Queen, a journal which had followed her career in socialism and as a supporter of votes for women, was less inhibited. The long pretence would be plain to all who cared to read between these lines which are another echo of Shaw's 'Pygmalion'. 'That Mrs Cunninghame Graham was a Spaniard is notable. English, or any foreign language, except perhaps Italian, presents great difficulties to Spaniards. Few succeed in pronouncing our numerous consonants clearly but Mrs Cunninghame Graham achieved success also as an English writer.' Spanish women were seldom well informed and hardly ever intellectual this writer continued; according to northern ideas their education was severely limited , in which case Gabrielle's superiority in this respect was doubly remarkable.(53)

Anne Elizabeth was another whose mind dwelt on the fact of impersonation. Her well being had been the cause, and she herself the principal in contriving the metamorphosis of Caroline Horsfall. Now , to her evident surprise, the death of the stranger who had become her daughter in law, had brought about another. That much is plain from her letter to Edward Garnett nearly a month after the funeral. 'Robert thinks of poor Gabrielle all the time as she appears to his imagination not as she really was. It is infinitely touching and I am so glad that he pours it all out to me. I understand and it reminds me of when he was a little boy.' Gone for the time being was the dashing figure whose amatory pursuits had been the talk of the London clubs and whose conquests caused Gabrielle once bitterly to end a letter, 'After all the others'. In November Anne Elizabeth wrote again to Garnett; 'I seem to see the real Robert emerging from his temporary eclipse. Though I do not think I ought to say this for the tender loyal nature shown in his deep grief for poor, *unsatisfactory* Gabrielle is the real Robert too.'(54)

Notes to Chapter Fourteen

1. Jefferson, G., 'Edward Garnett. A Life in Literature', Cape,1982, p 39.
2. Acc. 11335/71, Garnett to RBCG, - May 1898.
3. ibid., the same to the same, 20 April 1899.
4. ibid.
5. ibid.
6. ibid., same to the same, 28 Dec 1905
7. Jefferson, op.cit., p 38
8. Austin, microfilm, Garnett, rough notes on RBCG's style
9. NLS, Acc.11335/71, Garnett to RBCG, after AEB's death in 1925
10. Cunninghame Graham, R.B. 'A Vanished Arcadia. Being some account of the Jesuits in Paraguay 1607 - 1767', Heinemann, 1901. On the Cuban War see, Austin, microfilm, RBCG to Garnett, 1 Feb 1899, 2 May 1898.
11. Cunninghame Graham, Gabrielle, 'Spain,'
12. e.g. David Lowe in Glasgow Evening Times, n.d. [cutting]
13. See Strang, W., 'Etchings', George Newnes, 1907, plate 30.
14. Austin, microfilm, RBCG to Garnett, 28 Jan.1899, Ford Madox Ford, 'The English Girl,' Methuen, 1907. p 106.
15. Watts, C.T., ed., 'Joseph Conrad's letters to R.B. Cunninghame Graham'; Cambridge, 1969, p.191.

16. Austin, microfilm, RBCG to EG, 3 and 15 Oct. 1904. For the physical likeness between RBCG and Charles Gould see, Conrad, J., 'Nostromo', Penguin Modern Classics, 1963, pp 52, 53. (First published 1904).
17. ibid., pp 60,61
18. ibid., p. 428
19. ibid., pp 61, 62
20. NLS, Acc. 11335/55, GCG to RBCG n.d.
21. ibid.
22. NLS, Acc. 11225/64, Copy of Treaty with Bashir el Bairouk, 10 Aug. 1899.
23. PRO, FO, 99/391
24. ibid., Chamberlain to RBCG, 10 Mar. 1899.
25. NLS, Acc.11335/64, Spilsbury to RBCG, - Oct. 1899.
26. ibid., Acc. 11335/70, Frias corr. eg 11 and 31 July, 15 Aug. and 21 Aug. 1899.
27. ibid., Acc. 11335/74, Hume to RBCG, 23 Aug. n.y. but 1899.
28. ibid., the same to the same, August 1899.
29. ibid., Acc. 11335/63, Kisbany to RBCG - Aug. 1899.
30. ibid., Acc. 11335/77, RBCG to Mansel - Dec. 1900.
31. Cunninghame Graham, R.B., A Braw Day in 'Charity, op.cit., pp 133-145.
32. NLS, Acc. 11335/48, AEB to RBCG
33. ibid., Acc. 11335/53, Charles CG to RBCG, 22 Aug. 1900.
34. ibid. Acc. 11335/137, GCG to AEB, 4 Dec. 1900.
35. ibid
36. Quoted in Holroyd, M.., 'Bernard Shaw The Lure of Fantasy', III, Chatto & Windus, 1991 p. 153.
37. ibid., p. 23.
38. Glasier, J.B., Diary, 17 Jan. 1897.
39. e.g. McCarthy, Fiona, 'William Morris A Life for Our Times', Faber, 1994, p. 137.
40. NLS, Acc.11335/21, RBCG to AEB, 6 Aug. 1902.
41. ibid., Acc. 11335/136, RBCG to GCG, various dates, Sept. 1903.
42. Austin, AEB to GCG, 6 Apr. 1903.
43. Watts, op.cit., p 145, n. 21.
44. Austin, RBCG to EG, 13 Nov. 1903. NLS, Acc.11335/55, GCG to RBCG,
45. ibid, Acc 11335/48, AEB to RBCG, 28 Feb. 1905
46. Austin, RBCG to EG, 5 June 1906
47. ibid. AEB to EG. 6 Sept. 1906. Note. This date because an alleged mistranslation of a telegram from Spanish into Italian caused AEB to conclude that Gabrielle died three days before she did.
48. Horsfall Family Papers. RBCG to Miss [Mary] Horsfall, 11 Sept. 1906/
49. ibid., M. Horsfall to 'My dear Poppet , 21 Sept. 1906.
50. Austin, RCCG to EG, - Sept. 1906.
51. <u>Stirling Advertiser</u> Funeral report, - Sept.1906
52. The <u>Queen</u>, September 1906.
53. Austin, AEB to EG, 22 Oct. 1906. Taylor italics.

Chapter Fifteen

Return to South America

Robert was 54 when Gabrielle died: in that chilling phrase applied by – mostly- well meaning people to the recently bereaved; his life would never be the same again. Among the letters of condolence was one from Will Rothenstein in which, after expressing his shock he wrote, 'I shall always think of her as I saw her the first time, in a white monk's habit and her black hair over her shoulders and that fire burning deep in her eyes that seems to us so fitting in those who have Spanish blood'. (1) As others do he sought to console himself in the preservation of her memory. In the first weeks following the disaster at Hendaye, he shut himself up at Ardoch to pore over her papers, driven - comforted perhaps - by the thought of publishing the work she left behind. A volume of her poems was shortly printed for circulation to her friends, a new edition of Santa Teresa, with a preface by him, and a Spanish translation took longer to appear. 'Genera' never did; to Anne Elizabeth's profound relief Edward Garnett vetoed it. It was hardly a large enough body of work to preserve the name of Mrs Cunninghame Graham as a writer. As a person 'poor, unsatisfactory Gabrielle' was quickly forgotten in the Graham family circle. The flat in Margaret Street, 'that dreary place of sad memories' was given up for a place in Basil Street nearer to the house Anne Elizabeth ruled in Chester Square. Blamed for the loss of Gartmore, Robert's late wife was hardly ever mentioned there.

If he referred to her in public it was always as 'my wife' never 'Gabrielle'. But in private, away from his mother, his love and grief were bestowed on the woman who had called herself 'Chid', whose letters he spent much time at Ardoch in re-reading. It was the name by which her close friends - Maya de Frias - for example, spoke of her with the deepness sadness and regret.(2) Much was said of her by the people who had known her as mistress of Gartmore, evidence that she stood far higher in their esteem than she had allowed herself to believe. Robert, too, was the object of their sympathy - as he had always been; though that had been obscured from him by the defences of his beleaguered personality. For instance; 'I often think of poor Mr Graham, he is left so lonely and he is so kind' Jemima McLean, one of the Gartmore tenants wrote to Miss Ward in 1911. ' He is so lonely and his hair has gone quite white 'was the kind of thing they all said about him, observing him on his frequent visits when he sat and smoked a cigarette beside the grave on Inchmahome. These were interludes: he remained active in politics, foreign affairs and literature; his views continuing to receive a degree of notice in the press often denied to persons of greater importance but whose powers of expression were inferior to his. Provided his own emotions were aroused , his ability to stir audiences had not abandoned him even though it was fourteen years since he had been in Parliament.

During that time progress had been made towards an objective he had made peculiarly his own, emphasized in his speeches as the only means of achieving social justice - that working men must represent themselves in Parliament. The most spectacular advance towards this goal had occurred at the general election of January 1906 when a Liberal landslide dismissed the Tories after eleven years in office. At the same time no less than 53 members were elected on a class basis. Twenty nine of these had stood under the auspices of the Labour Representation Committee, now they were to sit as an independent party led by Robert's erstwhile protégé, James Keir Hardie. Most of the other 24 were officials of the miners' unions. In the next four years the Liberal Government under Campbell Bannerman enacted legislation that is often characterized as laying the foundation of the welfare state. Among the Bills put forward was an old age pension for every worker; school meals; and, 16 years after Robert had made the cause his own, an eight hour day for miners. Yet, from the beginning and as one of those best qualified to judge - the first MP to advance socialist ideas in Parliament - Graham refused to be impressed. He remained contemptuous of the Liberal Party and its members, his views expressed in terms even more savage than those he had used against Gladstone at Camlachie in 1892. In 1907, for example, 'I entirely disagree with you as to the wave of materialism having receded', he told E.D. Morel, who wanted his support in denouncing the atrocities committed by the Belgians in the Congo;' I have never seen it higher, one of the proofs being that the party which contains all the great Liberal sweaters is now in power. They have always sold everyone who has put their trust in them and will sell you if they get the chance'.(3)

His scepticism saved him from the disillusionment that afflicted other Labour leaders like Hardie and John Bruce Glasier when the new Bills were published. As the late Caroline Benn described them in her biography of Hardie, the measures were pitifully inadequate. ...'The heart of each reform had often disappeared. Provision of school meals was not made compulsory, merely an option for local authorities. A universal old age pension introduced in 1908 after much delay, did not start at sixty but at seventy and was by no means universal or even adequate. Most particularly maintenance for the workless was entirely inadequate and highly selective. In Hardie's view the relief he had pressed for merely 'mocked' the poor. ...Even the eight-hour day legislation...was diluted with endless concessions to employers'(4)

As well as denouncing his former colleagues in the Liberal Party Robert attacked the trades unionists and the Lib Lab MPs for their pusillanimous behaviour towards those in power. 'They are a hopeless lot', he told Wilfrid Scawen Blunt, 'When they get into Parliament they are at once bitten with the absurd idea they are no longer to be working men, but statesmen and try to behave as such. I tell them they would do more good if they came to the House in a body, drunk and tumbling about on the floor'. (5) This outburst derived in part from the defection - as Robert saw it - of one of his close associates of the 1880s. John Burns, hero of Bloody Sunday and the Great Dock Strike, Robert's fellow convict in Pentonville Gaol, was now a Cabinet Minister. His tendency to stray from the path of true socialism which had begun to worry

Hardie and Graham at the time of the Mid Lanark by election, once he entered Parliament in 1892, carried him into the arms of the Liberal Party. His reward came in 1906 when Campbell Bannerman appointed him President of the Board of Trade. 'Poor Burns' Robert remarked; 'so good a fellow and led astray by good natured vanity'. His impatience extended to Keir Hardie with whom he was no longer on good terms. Though he acknowledged Hardie's fine qualities as a man, as a politician Robert felt he should have been firmer in his opposition to the government. (6) It was a situation destined to get worse Barely a year after he became leader, ill health obliged Hardie to hand over to Ramsay Macdonald. The latter's freedom of action was almost immediately curtailed by the fear of a new general election when the advantage won in 1906 might suddenly vanish. The Liberal government had to be supported at all costs.. This awkward situation was the result of the furious opposition mounted in the Lords to the government's programme of reform, culminating in their refusal to pass the so-called Red Flag budget of 1909. As a result the country was in a state of turmoil superficially resembling that of 1884 at the time of the uproar over franchise reform when Robert made his entry into politics. In fact it was a far worse conflict, darker, more bitter, extending to hundreds of thousands of workers across the English Channel as well as at home.

In these circumstances, because the customary means of defending their rights and privileges struck many trades union members as less than adequate a new doctrine began to take hold. Syndicalism had its origin in France where its central idea owed much to anarchism. Direct action was to be the order of the day; strike after strike would undermine parliamentary institutions until a general strike would usher in the ultimate workers' democracy. Parallel with this was the rise in the United States of the International Workers of the World whose immediate aim was to create one enormous union embracing workers everywhere. Syndicalism's chief advocates in Britain were two of the heroes of the Great Dock Strike of 1889 - Tom Mann and Ben Tillett. Cunninghame Graham who had spent hours in their company in the small back room of Wades Arms in Poplar at the time, backed their call to action. He was no stranger to the new ideas; as well as years spent corresponding with anarchists on the Continent he was one of the principal contacts in Britain of members of the IWW. In 1910 Mann and Tillett set themselves to unite the disparate elements of the transport industry into one proactive body. Mann started with the seamen (who were notoriously badly treated), Tillett, Secretary of the Dockers' Union, with the wharfingers, lightermen, stevedores and other waterside occupations. Soon the agitation spread to the railways and the mines.

By the summer of 1911 centres of industry like Manchester, Liverpool, Sheffield, Nottingham and London were in a dangerously volatile state. The weather then turned hotter than it had been for many years. By August the temperature in the narrow streets, ill ventilated factories and back to back houses regularly rose into the nineties causing one observer to doubt the sanity of people trapped in such a way. Yet it was in these extreme circumstances that Mann, Tillett and their colleagues took action, a development that gave Robert Cunninghame Graham cause to hope the working class was at last beginning to see it must stand and fight. A confrontation loomed. The employers were in no mood to give in - strikes were countered by lockouts. Liverpool, where the Shipping Federation was determined not to give way, was badly affected; movement in and around parts of the city like Scotland Road, was brought to a standstill by crowds attending impromptu meetings. Among those who sought to rouse them was Cunninghame Graham no doubt mindful of the occasion in 1889 when he had done the same in virtually the same place. He was fresh from three immense meetings in Glasgow where he found the exhibition of solidarity a great feature of the strike. ' It gave me hope for the future', he told Edward Garnett, 'there has been nothing like it since the Commune of 1870'.(7) There were other, more sinister, similarities with the Paris of those days; riots broke out on 15 August and raged for days; vans taking men arrested for obstruction were besieged on their way to Walton Gaol; troops brought in to clear their passage shot and killed two men. Though in 1889 John Burns had refused Robert's urgent request to come to Liverpool, this time he did and by his presence and patient negotiation calmed the strikers to a point where a settlement was agreed when Robert and other agitators were obliged to withdraw.

Another fundamental change in the political landscape in the last twenty years was that socialism as a belief, and syndicalism even more, demanded perfect allegiance to the exclusion of other doctrines. It was no longer possible for Robert in his speeches to follow a call for socialist measures in government with another for that government to be Scottish or Irish. Notwithstanding the socialism he had embraced in the 80s, as preached by members of the SDF and SL on street corners, in Trafalgar Square; at the gatherings he attended in Regents Park Road, was cosmopolitan, international he had tried to promote a version peculiar to himself, whose details he left a little vague, but with the suggestion that it was somehow home grown. Few among his audiences in the West of Scotland, the Black Country, or London's East End knew enough of socialism at the time to accuse him of inconsistency for speaking of it in the same context as nationalism. But in 1913 he was confronted by the need to choose between these two pillars of his political belief.

Since 1908 two very dissimilar men had been engaged in forming an Irish Transport Workers' Union on syndicalist lines. 'A small silent remorseless desperado, compact of courage and scheming' was R.K. Ensor's estimate of James Connolly and of his colleague, James Larkin,' a voluble, large limbed Irishman who like fighting for its own sake without deeply studying what it was about'.(8) Voluble was an understatement; Larkin's language was that of a prophet seeking to arouse a religious fervour in his audiences; 'half genius, half lunatic' he claimed to have a divine mission to make men and women so discontented with their lot they would go to any lengths to alter it, including violence. The Citizens' Army Larkin and Connolly founded in 1913 as part of their mission , played a major role three years later in the Easter Rising (after which Connolly was executed by the British). In the autumn of 1913 'Larkinism' which relied heavily on sympathy strikes plunged Dublin into chaos Larkin was arrested for sedition and sentenced to seven months in prison at which the transport strike collapsed. But the public would not have him there; their indignation at the sentence caused his release within a fortnight. At once he came to England to campaign for support. He was met by Robert Cunninghame Graham who thought him 'a splendid fellow', appearing beside him on platforms up and down the country; at the Royal Albert Hall; in Edinburgh (where he dodged a Fabian Society meeting in order to do so) and on Glasgow Green. They were often greeted by a storm of boos and, sometimes, missiles. In Ireland ' Larkinism' had been opposed by leaders of the Home Rule movement (causing his followers to look to the nascent Sinn Fein movement). In language as extreme as Larkin's Robert denounced the nationalists whose cause, in the days when he was MP for North West Lanarkshire, he had promoted; with whose leaders, Parnell and Davitt, and afterwards John Redmond, he had been on friendly terms.

The very men who were oppressing the women and children of Dublin were mainly Nationalists, the Glasgow Herald reported him as saying at the City Hall on 10 December 1913. Man did not live by bread alone... and the legitimate desire for nationhood had to be considered. But, he went on, man must have a little bread as well as sunbursts and green flags and Brian Boru and the Celtic movements.... Before Jim Larkin came as saviour among these people they might have waited long enough before Home Rule would do anything for them. This new enthusiasm did not go down well among old fashioned socialists - no point in going to the Fabian Society meeting, he told Edward Garnett; ' they would not have allowed me to speak'.(9)

There were certain beliefs with which Robert as politician and writer had come to be associated in the public mind. When in 1914 changing circumstances caused him to renege on the most significant of these - opposition to a war with Germany, he was savagely attacked, not least by former colleagues. His experience as a young man in Entre Ríos and Paraguay had given him a horror of war as an instrument of realpolitik. In 1885 he told the electors of North West Lanarkshire he could only bring himself to fight for his country if it, or the Empire, was in danger. In 1914 that kind of anti-militarism was shared by many socialists and trades unionists. That such a war involved an alliance between England and France against Germany was an extra source of misgiving. 'I cannot like the French' he told Edmund Gosse as late as 1918, 'I admire them but have no sympathy for them. I think is their excessive egotism and disagreeable manners'. (10) The dislike instilled in him by his grandmother, Catalina, had been confirmed by what he had seen of the French drive for power in Morocco. In 1906 he had come to close quarters with her diplomats when he had attended the conference at Algeciras where they obtained many advantages over other foreign powers with designs on Morocco. And he was in that country in 1911 when, on pretext of suppressing a revolt against the Sultan French troops marched into Fez, the last act before the Mahkzen was replaced by a French Protectorate. That he was well disposed towards Germany became a matter of record when, January 1906 he was a signatory to a letter in The Times calling for understanding between the two powers. It was in response to one by German intellectuals, including several professors deploring statements in the English press that, in the aftermath of the Boer War attributed sinister designs by Germany on England. As well as Cunninghame Graham the English signatories included Thomas Hardy, John Lavery, Jane

Morris, William Rossetti, William Rothenstein, William Strang, Walter Crane, Edward Elgar and Georgina Burne-Jones.(11)

Many of those opposed to war simply refused to believe it could happen so long as international socialism opposed it. If by some chance it did break out workers in every country would combine to bring it swiftly to an end. Keir Hardie was one who thought like this. In the years before 1914 he maintained the working class was strong enough to impose peace merely by threatening social disorder. He and others were overtaken by the rapid escalation of the crisis in the summer of 1914. Not until 2 August when the British Fleet had been brought to a war footing and the Channel closed to German ships, was a mass rally called in protest. Starting from East India Docks, Kentish Town and Westminster groups of trades unionists marched on Trafalgar Square where they were addressed by Henry Hyndman, Ben Tillett and Robert Cunninghame Graham. All three urged their audience to pass a resolution calling on workers everywhere to use their industrial and political strength to ensure war was not declared. Meanwhile a separate crowd had assembled at Admiralty Arch where, according to <u>The Times</u> 'Speeches of Patriotism' were made, 'Rule Britannia' sung and the anti-war protesters nearby not so much routed as constructively ignored. (12) Barely three months later Lieutenant-Colonel R.B. Cunninghame Graham sailed from Liverpool bound for Uruguay as head of a small party charged with buying horses for the British Expeditionary Force in France.

Although motorized transport was already recognized as vital to a successful outcome of the war, there was alarmingly little of it at this stage. Horses were still essential to the three separate arms of combat. They carried the cavalry into battle, hauled the guns and ammunition for the artillery, as well as field ambulances and food wagons, and provided the principal means of moving about for all but the unfortunate infantry. October which saw the Battle of the Marne, had taken a heavy toll of horses - though hardly noticed when set beside the loss of men. Once landed in France a horse's life was inevitably short; often they lasted barely three weeks and died in harness beside the road. The need to find more was pressing, South America the only place where they could be got in large numbers. Besides its leader who refused to be addressed as Colonel and did not wear uniform there were eight members of the Uruguay Remount Commission that reached Montevideo on 12 December. Second in command was the Senior Veterinary Officer who, in spite of his expertise, was ordered to remain there to help with the flood of letters that soon began to come in from horse owners, dealers and contractors in the camp. This office work was made more onerous because most of the letters were in Spanish but, as the official report pointed out 'Mr Graham is perfect in Spanish'. It was one of the reasons why he had been chosen, another was his knowledge of the country and its people, though the most important was his expertise with horses. He lost no time in establishing his headquarters at Fray Bentos on the River Uruguay where the Liebig factory had a landing place with sufficiently deep water and a launch he could borrow.(13) In high spirits at being back he wrote to his brother, Charles; 'thirty five years seem to have vanished as, after a long day on pone, I sit in the deserted plaza and watch a swarm of locusts and some yellow dogs and two negro children. Everything is as I left it except there are more houses and a few motors Pone stands nodding in the sun ..and the great yellow river with the countless islands flows past the high bluff and Gualeyguachú is only two hours away on the other side'.(14) Several weeks now had to be spent contacting owners and arranging for their horses to be brought in for inspection. Though their general health was found to be good few were of sufficient height and weight to pull the guns and ammunition wagons.

It was hardly a combative role yet it was essential to the prosecution of the war and some of his colleagues - John Bruce Glasier was one - sneered at him for betraying a principle he had publicly espoused. (15) His reason was that, given the gruesome fate that awaited the horses he must do his best to see the conditions under which they were transported were the most humane. And like others who had opposed the war, once it had been declared he felt he had to do all he could to see it brought to an end as speedily as possible. Beyond that he had to confess he was enjoying himself. He was delighted to be back among the people who had meant so much to him forty five years before. He was exhilarated to discover that, at the age of 63 he was equal to the considerable physical effort involved (not for him the office work in Montevideo). 'I am nearly always on horseback' he told Will Rothenstein,' from daylight to dusk and nearly always wet through .. This alternates with days in the train, in motors, in diligences and steamboats. Sometimes I sleep in native huts and again in the Plaza Hotel in Buenos Aires (a kind of Ritz). As it has been the wettest season on record - we are nearly always caked in mud, as the corrals we work are sometimes knee deep in mud'.(16) To Anne Elizabeth (now aged 90) he wrote in terms that must have conjured up the boy of 19. 'Today a man was missing and I had to lazo all day, hence my writing is worse than ever, for my hands are very much cut and 'burned' for want of practice. Quite by accident I got on a buck jumper but sat him alright'. (17) In Bopicua, one of the sketches in 'Brought Forward' he described the process of assembling horses in a huge corral where, after a veterinary inspection, they were either given the British government brand or returned to their owners as unfit. In its outward aspect it might have been a long remembered scene from 45 years before - animals graze peacefully in lush pasture; smoke rises from camp fires round which gauchos are seated on buffalo skulls; the river gleams in the distance. Later the horses are rounded up at the very beginning of their long journey. Possibly because the war was still far from over when the sketch was published in 1916 Robert refrains from spelling out what suffering awaits them; the mood is elegaic, not savage as given his love of animals it might well have been. 'The horses smelt the water at the bottom of the hill and the whole five hundred broke into a gallop, manes flying, tails raised high and we, feeling somehow the gallop was the last, raced madly by their side until a hundred yards or so of the great lake. They rushed into the water and all drank greedily, the setting sun falling on their many coloured backs and giving the whole herd the look of a vast tulip field'. (18) 'It was a wonderful sight', he wrote privately to Anne Elizabeth, 'but sad to think it was their last happy day on earth. The Kaiser has much to answer for'.(19)

Not only was the gallop the last those horses were to enjoy, so was the opportunity to drink their fill. The report of the Uruguay Remount Commission makes no secret of the fact that once they had been loaded on to trains for the 20 hours journey to Montevideo water was severely limited. Six cargo ships were chartered there to take 2,232 horses to Europe. Most were carried on the upper decks but some unfortunates had to be consigned to the lower. That part of the Report makes bleak reading. 'No exercise was possible nor could the horses' feet be reached; and it only with much difficulty and the carpenter's assistance that animals could be removed from their stalls in case of need. The watering arrangements were considered to be inadequate. .. The watering of twenty or twenty five horses by one man from a small bucket along very narrow and crowded gangways is apt to result in the animals going short...'(20)

'I am still out here after 7 months', Robert told Wilfrid Blunt on 16 May 1915; 'Always on horseback. Always wet and muddy and tired and overworked. But well and happy, My last ship goes off next week and I then come home. I am bringing a little horse, not because of any special merit, but because most of my work has been done on him and we have both been often very tired together'. After thanking Blunt for his kind words about his latest book, the story of the conquistador, Bernal Diaz, Robert continued; 'If all goes right I hope to take my little horse out of a box at Southampton one day this summer and canter through the woods to see you' [Blunt's house Newbuildings Place was in the New Forest].(21) This little horse probably was El Charja which took the place left by Pampa whose death occurred in 1911 at the age of 31. Both were mustangs, the half wild horse of the South American plains. After Gartmore was sold in 1900 Pampa was moved to stables near London. Dearest of all the animals who shared Robert's life he inspired the dedication to his history, 'The Horses of the Conquest'.

To Pampa
My black Argentine - whom I rode for twenty years without a fall
May the earth lie on him as lightly as he once trod upon its face
Vale...or until so long'.(22)

It was to Blunt that Robert confided his distress at losing Pampa, trusting to the older man's understanding. Blunt's love of horses equalled his; his professional involvement was greater. He and his wife, Lady Anne (Byron's granddaughter) were importers and breeders of Arab horses; over the years they created one of the finest studs in the world. But the two had more in common. They were political allies, sharing a disaffected view regarding the most difficult problems of the day - Ireland and the Near and Middle East. With regard to the first; in the troubled 1880s both had gone to prison for overstepping the bounds of opposition. Blunt's account of his sojourn in Kilmainham Gaol in Dublin was remarkably similar to Robert's description of his tribulations in Pentonville after Bloody Sunday.(23) Though they were mere acquaintances at the time Blunt sent his condolences to his fellow convict and instructed Lady Anne to enquire kindly after Gabrielle. With regard to the second; both believed it essential for the people of the collapsing Ottoman Empire to be brought to self government as speedily as possible as the only way to ensure stability in a region of crucial importance to Britain, extending from India in the East, taking in Palestine, Syria, Turkey, and Egypt to Algeria and Morocco in the West. Blunt's claim to speak with authority owing to many years spent in close touch with Pan-Islamic and Nationalist movements in Egypt and Turkey, was equally true of Cunninghame Graham with regard to the countries of the Mahgreb.

Both had learned at first hand to respect the beliefs and practices of Islam which they held should be given a principal role in any newly established nation. They were critical of Sir Edward Grey, the British Foreign Secretary for paying less attention to this crucial aspect than they thought it deserved, thereby damaging Britain's standing among Muslims. This failure of imagination on the part of Grey was in contrast to an inspired move by the German Kaiser. In 1914 Wilhelm sought to draw Turkey into his embrace by talk of a new world order that Germany would create with the help of Pan-Islamic forces. Here was the theme from Greenmantle' - still in Buchan's head though within two years of publication - whose importance the German Emperor in one of his more exalted moments had seized upon. The propaganda value of such a declaration was immense and the Allies would be hard put to counter it. Even so one member of the British Cabinet knew precisely what should be done. Lord Kitchener, Secretary of State for War, who had just retired from three years as British Agent and Consul General in Egypt to which office he had succeeded after seven years as Commander in Chief in India, told his colleagues the Kaiser's instinct in the matter of Islam would bring far greater rewards than Grey's relatively cool approach. On 14 November 1914 the Sultan, speaking as Caliph, the acknowledged head of Islam on earth, declared a jihad against Germany's enemies, a gesture that was not lost on Kitchener. When, shortly after, the Cabinet discussed the long term future of the Near and Middle East, he urged steps be taken to create a wholly new Caliphate based, not at Istanbul, but at Mecca to which holy city Sherif Hussein, its religious and temporal ruler, had recently returned after years in prison by order of the Sultan who feared the power he possessed over the Arabs of the Hejaz.(24)

Hussein and his sons, the Emirs Ali, Abdullah, Faisal and Zeid , leaders of the Arab revolt against the Turks, are the principal characters - bar one - in T.E. Lawrence's 'Seven Pillars of Wisdom'. While giving the impression of a clear, straightforward narrative Lawrence contrives to leave the time scale of his own involvement extremely vague. In fact he came late to the affair. Early in 1915, a mere Lieutenant, he was posted to the Intelligence Department in Cairo where he was desk bound , working on maps and other military sources of information about Turkish dispositions. He is not likely to have known the full extent of the British effort, already under way, to persuade Hussein to rebel against the Turks who, for their part were expecting the Sherif of Mecca to support the jihad. In the same month it was declared - November 1914 - Kitchener sent a dramatic message to Hussein; 'it may be that an Arab of the true race will assume the Caliphate at Mecca or Medina, and so good will come by the help of God out of all the evil which is now occurring'. Though the public came to regard Lawrence as the prime begetter of the Arab revolt he did not make contact with Hussein or his sons until October 1916 when his Army masters sent him to the Hejaz to encourage Ali, Abdullah and Faisal in their separate commands against the Turks with orders to report back to Cairo.(25)

Long before that, in a letter written from Fray Bentos, Uruguay, and published in the <u>Daily News</u> of 1 March 1915 Robert Cunninghame Graham made a remarkable intervention in the affairs of Arabs half a world away. After explaining what power the religious head of the Muslim faith possessed over the inhabitants of many different countries the letter urged England to take advantage of the unusual opportunity now within her grasp. 'Either proclaim the Grand Sherif of Mecca [Hussein] Caliph which perhaps would be the best of all for he would have no temporal power, or else allow the mantle of Mohammed to fall upon the Sultan we have ourselves proclaimed' - i.e. the Khedive of Egypt.' In either case' the letter went on, 'we should be free for ever from the Turks and their attempts to stir up strife in India upon religious grounds.' And in an appropriately high flown manner the letter ended; 'Therefore, O unknown Editor, for writing from this lost little port upon Uruguay I cannot tell into whose hands this lucubration may be wafted, consult, I pray with the Ulema, Muftis and others learned in the law, on this my poor idea, that I hope yet may fructify if it be Allah's will'. So far as Kitchener was concerned this was timely publicity from a far flung source. The letter would carry weight if only because Graham was well known to readers of the <u>Daily News</u> as an expert on the Arab way of life, and more particularly the paper's special correspondent at the Algeciras conference about Morocco in 1906. (26). That it earned him friendship in what were to be the highest places after the war may be seen in the remnants of a correspondence whose letters came to him in Scotland from 'The Palace, Baghdad' whose signature was, simply,.' Faisal 'It also provided the spur to friendship with the man who laid claim to be the only begetter of the events that placed Faisal on his throne. 'Your letter to the <u>Daily News</u> came to me in Egypt in 1915,' T.E. Lawrence told Graham in 1920. 'I fancy most of it has come off since though the best Khalifates seem to me to be grown not made and so we [he meant himself] have left Hussein of Mecca (Faisal's father) to get his if his wardenship of the Holy Cities is efficient... The Arabs pray for him now in Syria and N. Arabia'. The letter ends with a request for a meeting as Lawrence has a great deal to ask Graham.(27). The latter's reply is among the Graham papers assembled by his first biographer, Herbert Faulkner West at Dartmouth College in New Hampshire. On 7 June 1920, after asking Lawrence to drop the Mr in addressing him, Robert agreed; 'Yes Caliphates grow and are not made. I wrote my letter from Fray Bentos late at night and after a heavy day on horseback and many hours decoding more or less idiotic instructions from the War Office and had no time to revise it. It appeared to me then that it was important to bring the Arabs [into the war]. I did not know then that Allah (for I believe it was he) had you in his eye as a Mahdi'.(28)

Robert returned to England from Uruguay in May 1915 to find the country in a very different frame of mind than when he had left. The war was going badly. The German Army was well established across Northern France and in Belgium, with good lines of supply by rail. It was to remain immovable for the next three years in the face of successive assaults by the British and

French whose cost in killed and wounded was horrendous. Now began the agony of War Office telegrams to relatives and the shock of stumbling across a familiar name in the endless columns printed in the newspapers. In <u>Brought Forward</u>, the leading sketch in the volume of the same name published in 1916 Robert ventured to address this situation. One of the very few attempts by him to convey the authentic voice of working men, in its uneasy representation of their speech it draws attention to the gulf that existed between Graham the aristocrat and the men to whom he had pledged himself to deliver social justice. That his efforts had met with scant encouragement, let alone gratitude while inertia ruled was one of the major disappointments of his life, on a par with the loss of Gartmore. But whereas he could excuse himself from that on the grounds that the actions of people he had never known - his forbears - had made the sale of the estate however long delayed, virtually inevitable, the failure of his personal appeal to working men on which his whole political life had centred was a devastating blow to his self esteem. His mood was evident in the piece he wrote three months after his return from South America. <u>With the North East Wind</u> describing Keir Hardie's funeral in August 1915 has the same form as the lament for William Morris, a device that serves to underline the different degree of respect in which Graham held each man.(29) Everything in <u>With the North West Wind</u> goes to enhance the stature of Morris the piece is a celebration of a marvellous human being. <u>With the North East Wind</u>, on the other hand, though it accords Hardie even higher status; that of prophet and seer, it dismisses him as ineffectual ; someone whose efforts fell far short of what was required. Graham also evokes the colleagues he and Hardie shared in the days when they went about the West of Scotland mining villages together. John Ferguson, the Ulsterman, who defied Parnell's ukase to give him support in his first attempt at North West Lanarkshire; William Small, the miners' agent, whose speeches were as inflammatory as his own; John Burns, Tom Mann, Henry Champion with whom he fought many a battle on the London streets; the reader is reminded all are dead, or superseded; all have gone down into the oblivion that awaits those that live before their time. The author of the sketch does not include himself among them; he is not ready to embrace oblivion; it is evident from the events of the next few years that he was very anxious to continue to play some kind of public role. (30)

  The opportunity came in January 1917. The war was still going badly for the Allies; their troops were in stalemate against the Germans on the Western Front, while civilians at home were going short of food because German submarines had sunk so much merchant shipping. Once more the special qualifications that had taken Robert to Uruguay now earned him a commission from the Board of Trade. He was to go out to Colombia to explore the possibility of buying cattle in large numbers for export as meat to the United Kingdom. Much had to be done: the cattle located and inspected; a suitable port found; perhaps even built; where they would be slaughtered and packing stations erected there on the lines of Messrs Liebig's establishment at Fray Bentos. Arriving at Cartagena in early February he began work at once. Most of the cattle were raised in the Department of Bolivar, in flat country on the banks of the River Sinú. There virgin forest had been cleared and artificial grasses planted for feed. The district was remote and sparsely populated; there were no roads; one either had to ride miles each day along meandering bridle paths, or sit patiently and uncomfortably in a slow moving boat on the river where the temperature in the shade averaged 85 degrees. The conditions were very similar, certainly not less arduous than those he had encountered in Paraguay more than forty years before. His report to the Board of Trade concerning the cattle was as carefully prepared and full of closely observed detail as the one he sent to Holland Jacques on the availability of yerba.(31) There was, however, a new and awkward problem. Virtually all the capital in the country was in the hands of American businessmen who charged prohibitive rates for loans; consequently most transactions with the cattle owners were done in kind, thus making progress in developing the industry very slow. Robert's official position brought him many requests from the people he met for the British government to set up a bank to advance capital against the security of land and stock (32)

In April he left the plains and travelled up into the High Andes, to the capital, Bogotá, a place he seems to have disliked almost more than Texas by reason of its disagreeable climate, excessively high altitude, and melancholy disposition of the inhabitants. His longstanding friendship with the Colombian Ambassador to London, Perez Triana, was most useful in making connections but the people he met in this way struck him as altogether far too subservient to the clerical authorities. At Bogotá he turned his attention to the unpublicised aspect of his mission; to assess the degree of support among its most prominent citizens for Britain and the United States whose support for the Allies was shortly to bring it into the war. A letter written to him twelve months before contained the germ of his present undertaking. He and the British Foreign Secretary, Sir Edward Grey, who were old school friends, often corresponded. In February 1916 Grey told Robert he would like a quiet confidential talk about relations between the South American Republics and their mighty neighbour to the North. Were they justified in regarding Washington as the centre of a spider's web that might, in time, draw them in? Grey foresaw certain advantages if that happened; closer relations with the US might help to counter German ambition.. 'South America is nearer Europe not only in race, religion, language, manners, aspirations and ideals than it is to New York but it is nearer geographically', Grey wrote. In 1905 Americans had not understood why Britain had raised such violent objections to Germany sending a gunboat to Agadir, the port on the Moroccan coast not far from Cape Juby. Yet this move, which provoked a full blown international crisis narrowly avoiding war, posed a real threat to the Monroe Doctrine; ..' the sea distance between Cape Bathurst [on the west coast of Africa] and Pernambuco [on the east coast of South America] is unfortunately small...when a railway is constructed through Morocco German troops could be in Brazil long before those of the US' Grey remarked. (33)

The answer to Grey's query, Robert found was that a great and jealous hatred existed among the population of Colombia for the United States because of her annexation of the Panama Canal Zone in 1903, and the behaviour of some of her citizens towards them since. Consequently, though not ill disposed to the Allied cause a very influential minority, though not exactly pro-German, was unwilling to favour anything identified with America or Americans. In spite of this not very sanguine report, in mid May he was ordered to proceed with choosing a locality for a port to ship cattle and meat products to the UK, and to negotiate concessions for that trade. But the British Minister at Bogotá was careful to warn him to preserve secrecy pending the decision of the Board of Trade Nothing came of his efforts in the end; the enterprise was called off, partly because of the lack of cargo ships [the greater part of Colombia's shipping was German owned] (34)

At Cartagena on 9 June, on the first stage of his journey home, a telegram caught up with him bringing news he half expected and had long feared: his brother, Charles had died the day before. 'It seems impossible to be alone in the world without Charles'he wrote to Anne Elizabeth the same day, '...he was indeed my Pylades. So different to me and much better, yet we understood each other so well. I have no one to speak to but a Spanish bullfighter, perfectly ignorant and yet so kind. I opened the telegram before him and he said '<u>Le accompagno en su dolor</u>' and offered to go out and take a walk with me on the walls; it was at night and the heat great. I went and walked on the walls and thought of all our life from Dr Bickmore's [Headmaster of the school at Leamington Spa] and before and Mr Gulliver [their tutor] and all kind of things. Poor dear Lee Cat, to think of his lying dead in Warwick Square and me so far off. This morning all the company of bullfighters met me in the street and took their hats off and 'accompanied me in my grief'(35). Charles' career which had begun so much more auspiciously than Robert's foundered as a result of his marriage to Barbara Bagot in 1882. Not long after her family began to agitate for him to leave the Navy. Though it was a sacrifice equal to his father, William Bontine's in abandoning the Army to marry Anne Elizabeth, Charles acquiesced, becoming instead an Inspector of Lifeboats. His devotion to the welfare of the men who risked their lives in that service was such that he rose to become Deputy Inspector General. At the same time the years he had spent while in the Navy on the Royal Yacht brought him to the attention of Edward VII who summoned him to court as an extra equerry. Moving in royal circles exposed him to much teasing by his mother and elder brother who liked to make a point of seeing nothing to commend in Queen Victoria or any of her offspring.

The Cunninghame Graham correspondence bears witness to the great affection in which they all held Charles, the most amiable, easy going, and well disposed among them. So it was not the least of the series of misfortunes the family had to bear that he developed heart disease at a relatively early age. His wife, Barbara; his two children, Angus and Olave, his mother, Anne Elizabeth, had to endure the sight of Charles growing weaker and more weary by the month. Robert who was away in Uruguay at this time was spared that aspect only to be confronted on his return by the full measure of how his brother had deteriorated in his absence. When 'Brought Forward' was published a few months later the dedication was to Charles who wrote to say how greatly he was moved. All their lives they had kept in touch; first one, then the other sending letters from distant places. Charles' last one, dated 9 February 1917 reached

Robert at Jamaica on his way to Cartagena, a journey so long and far he went in the knowledge they might never meet again.

His first care on returning home in the summer of 1917 was for his mother whose third great loss by death this was: the Strix in 1884 after 20 years of involuntary widowhood; Malise in 1886 ravaged by TB, now Charles whose cheerful presence had consoled her as old age began to gain on her. She had no idea of giving in. Aged 92 at his death the steadfastness that had marked her as a girl remained, as did her keen perception of what was going on around her. Age and adversity had tried her patience and shortened her temper; she was quick to chide and remonstrate but remained a stranger to self pity. During the war, though her house in Chester Square was subject to raids by German aircraft she stayed put. In September 1917 two houses nearby were hit; 'the servants behaved very well and stayed in the kitchen and were not hysterical' she told Robert. What annoyed her more than anything were her daughter-in-law's efforts to look after her. On one occasion when Barbara came to stay; 'I feel as if I had no volition of my own...as if my life as I used to lead it is at an end. Barbara says she promised you faithfully *to take care of me*...of course it is all kindly meant'. Over the years Barbara had acquired a reputation among her in-laws, Robert included, as one who overindulged in fuss. Yet at her marriage to Charles 35 years previously Anne Elizabeth had greeted her with relief, in the first instance because she was so very different from Gabrielle then still an outcast from her husband's family. Subsequently, after she passed the age of 75 at the turn of the century, she became the object of a considered attempt at kindness from Gabrielle who, as the result of successful speculation on the stock exchange - something Robert left strictly to her, and which was , equally strictly - only temporary - found herself with money at her disposal. She did her best to spend some of it on her mother-in-law, proposing to buy her books and, even, a coupé, a small carriage in which Anne Elizabeth and her lifelong friend, Blanche Fane, could indulge in what they called 'dowagering'.(37)

As has already been said Gabrielle's penchant for financial affairs was not appreciated by her husband's family. But in one respect the Cunninghame Grahams had reason to be grateful to her for it was she who brought to a successful conclusion long drawn out negotiations that restored to them one of their ancestral homes. While the family held on to the land and various appurtenances of the Ardoch estate - farms, mills, quarries - all through the various crises until the death of the ninth laird, William Bontine, the house itself had been sold in the mid nineteenth century. After the move to London in 1900 Robert was deeply homesick. He and Gabrielle cast about for some means of re-establishing a foothold in Scotland. Finlaystone was not an option - far too grand, long gone to other owners. But Ardoch Cottage, the charming plantation style house on the opposite side of the Clyde, built by the first Robert Cunninghame Graham, beckoned. It only remained to persuade its present owner to relinquish it. A series of letters from Gabrielle to Robert kept him abreast of her increasing bids which were finally successful. With them in 1904 when they moved in they brought furniture and paintings from Gartmore that, to make way for the Cayzers, had been stored in the mausoleum at Port of Menteith. Gabrielle's ideas for making Ardoch over (there was an alarming proposal to raise the level of the floor) came to nothing as diabetes tightened its grip on her. (38). Instead it was Anne Elizabeth whom Robert invited to spend time with him there, especially after the death of Charles.

Here, directly opposite the place he had known as a small boy, he was to make his principal home for the years that remained to him. Ardoch suited him; not large, not grand, it was unusual and attractive, with an 18th century air about its well proportioned rooms that were filled with mementoes of his family's long history as well as objects from his own adventure, and - while he was its master - those that Gabrielle had acquired in the course of hers. The oval drawing room looked out on the garden she replanted at their first return. Though apparently secluded at the end of a long drive lined with trees, in fact the house was a short distance from Cardross to the west and Dumbarton to the east. Villas approached from each direction but not too near since they were the result of feuing land belonging to the estate. In 1885 when Jamieson, the Curator, advised Robert to sell this part of his inheritance in order to preserve Gartmore, no buyer was found for the whole. (39). Lots were sold off but at the time the house was bought back a significant of land in farms remained with the result that, in spite of his urge to wander which continued into old age, Robert had the cares of a landowner to call him back to Scotland at frequent intervals. His mother delighted in the house that had been roofless in the days when she had been chatelaine of Finlaystone. 'How very, very pet [Grahamspeak for nice, agreeable] Ardoch was and how more than pet was Khat [Robert]. He spoils me', she wrote on her return to London on one occasion. On another, after seven weeks looking across the Clyde to the house where she had spent her early married life; 'I used to think often …how strange it was that at the very end of my life I should have such happy days and all owing to you', she told Robert. 'So many of the places were associated in my memory with sad things, some of which I thought I had forgotten Now I shall remember them as connected with you'. She was to enjoy Robert's devoted attention for eight more years after Charles died; she survived until 1925 when she died in her sleep aged nearly 97. (40)

Long before that all those who knew him, including his mother, came to accept there was a special friendship between him and a widow of French origin, Mrs Elizabeth 'Toppy' Dummett. They behaved strictly according to the rules, Mrs Dummett being chaperoned at appropriate moments by her unmarried sister, Louisa Miéville. Mrs Dummett was an accomplished horsewoman; some photographs exist of her mounted, in bowler and riding habit. Not graceful - her shoulders are too square for that - the phrase that springs to mind is 'a safe pair of hands'.(41)

On the face of it Robert had survived the war in better condition than many of his contemporaries. Charles had died, it is true, but of natural causes; he had not had to endure the bitterness of mourning a son or other close relative killed in action. His circumstances seemed propitious and likely to remain so. He now disposed of an ancestral house in Scotland free from the burden of debt that had tormented him as a young man. He had a flat in London, in Basil Street, not far from Mrs Dummett who was to be his dear friend, companion and hostess until he died. He had sufficient money to indulge his propensity for giving it away. He possessed a vast and varied array of friends and acquaintances among whom his literary reputation stood high. The only cause for regret, it appeared, were the recurring attacks of rheumatism and neuritis, the result of all those nights spent sleeping on cold and damp ground. And, in so far as these were the occasion for frequent winter visits to warm climates - Ceylon , the Canaries, Venezuela [where he stayed with members of the Vestey family] - even they brought pleasure. In 1918, at the age of 66, having had as 'good' a war as any man of his age dared expect, he was poised to resume his former preoccupation with politics and literature.

Graham with Mrs Elizabeth Dummett in Rotten Row. Dartmouth College Library.

With regard to the first, three days after the Armistice was signed Lloyd George called a general election at which Robert was one of three candidates for Stirling West. This constituency was home; Gartmore stood at the heart of it; in no other could he have been so well known and, most conveniently, it was only an hour or so by chauffeur driven car from Ardoch. To find himself campaigning in these well loved surroundings was something he cannot have anticipated. The end of the war had come sooner than anyone had dared hope. In June 1917 when Robert returned from Colombia U boats were still a menace to shipping - the ship on which he sailed was torpedoed but so close to shore the captain had been able to beach it without loss of life. While the United States had declared war on Germany three months before, it remained for her troops to be transported to the Western Front where the long stalemate between the opposing sides persisted. Though in the course of 1917 the Royal Navy regained control of the Atlantic, Allied planners continued to look to the spring of 1919 as the earliest time when sufficient forces could be assembled to mount an offensive strong enough to break the German Army. However, in the summer of 1918 separate attacks by the British and French on German forward positions round Amiens and Chateau-Thierry proved remarkably successful. When, in September, the newly arrived Americans drove the Germans out of a third salient at St Mihiel both sides recognized the importance of the breakthrough. Nor was it lost on the forces fighting on the Eastern Front where, a few days later, the Bulgarian Army laid down its arms. This was the signal for the Kaiser's representatives to begin negotiations for a general armistice.

If the general election campaign of 1918 is compared to the three previous ones Robert fought it will be seen to resemble most closely the last - at Camlachie in 1892 when, judging by his eccentric behaviour the strength of his commitment to another term in Parliament was, to say the least, questionable. His conduct in 1918 seems to have been equally injudicious, his language similarly intemperate about his opponents, among whom he again numbered Gladstone, the object of his furious disapproval in 1892 but who had now been dead for twenty years. The terms on which he stood in Stirling West created as much bad feeling as they had in Camlachie in 1892. The coalition government that called the election had no desire to be replaced. Its supporters, whether Liberal or Tory, were the beneficiaries of a pact not to oppose each other and were given 'coupons' to distinguish them from other MPs who might favour a return to the two party system. As soon as the election was called the local Liberal Association in Stirling West nominated Cunninghame Graham as the official coalition candidate, a move that so annoyed older members of the party, ever mindful of his cavalier treatment of his predecessors, they refused to share a platform with him. The reproaches they addressed to their officials for acting too precipitately in their choice called to mind the rebuke administered by the Chairman of the Airdrie Liberal Association to his committee in 1885 for having adopted young Mr Graham in his absence. Conservative Central Office was not pleased either, having believed the choice of official coalition candidate had fallen to their man, Sir Harry Hope. For a brief moment it looked as though Cunninghame Graham would resolve the situation by himself; he resigned in protest at the attitude of his Liberal critics; a few days later he returned, invigorated, to the fight under the guise of a non-coalition Liberal. (42)

As, in the aftermath of the war almost every candidate of every persuasion did, he called for retribution. 'Hang the Kaiser' was the first demand in which he joined; make Germany pay reparations the second. Beyond that his programme owed nothing to any party manifesto but was the old familiar blend of socialist measures like nationalisation of the mines and the eight hour day joined to a call for Scotland to be granted Home Rule. He did not respond to anything Sir Harry Hope said of him. The scorn, the wit, the innuendo were reserved for the third candidate in Stirling West, Thomas Johnston of the Independent Labour Party. In 1918, the local paper was the <u>Stirling Observer</u> whose reporters followed him about , recognizing a source of good copy when they saw one. At this distance in time his conduct appears bizarre, not simply in the act of standing against Johnston but in the manner of so doing. His campaign descended to a level his younger self never would have contemplated. There was hardly any debate about issues - how could there be since both were virtually in agreement as to policy. Instead Graham poured scorn on the younger man for his role as a conscientious objector during the war, promising 'conchies' like him silk stockings, suspenders and 'a petticoat at the national expense'. This kind of sneering would have been more understandable if directed at Robert's pet abominations; businessmen and sweaters. That it was aimed at a colleague who held the same broad socialist views as he did; who, for instance, had joined him in supporting James Larkin in 1913, and who had campaigned on his behalf the following year when he stood (unsuccessfully) as Rector of Glasgow University, was baffling. The conclusion his biographers, Cedric Watts and Laurence Davies advanced was that Graham's behaviour was an aberration arising from an aging man's desire to regain his former prestige by whatever means.

There is, however, another possible explanation that the passage of time has all but obscured: it lies in the immediate past of Thomas Johnston. Because of this his appearance on the hustings at Stirling West must have been regarded as a personal challenge by the man whose place of origin this was. Johnston's connections with the constituency were not as close as that but they were not far off. He was born into a family of prosperous grocers at Kirkintilloch, went to Glasgow University where he acquired left wing opinions and friends, afterwards becoming a local councillor. In 1906 he inherited a printing works at which point, rather as the young Graham did, he discovered an unsuspected flair for journalism. He founded a weekly paper, <u>Forward</u> which became the mouthpiece of the ILP in Glasgow. Under Johnston's effective editorship it soon wielded more influence on its home ground than did Keir Hardie's <u>Labour Leader.</u> By 1909 it had a circulation of 10,000. Among its contributors was the group of ILP councillors, trades unionists, and other labour activists whose regular meetings were held in Kate Cranston's celebrated tea rooms newly decorated by a rising young architect, Charles Rennie Mackintosh. After 1914 when workers in Glasgow, including those in the crucial munitions and shipbuilding industries began to demonstrate their lack of enthusiasm for the prosecution of the war, this group became their leaders and as such the objects of acute class hatred in the rest of Britain. By 1915 Johnston himself, Emmanuel Shinwell, William Gallagher, David Kirkwood, John Maclean and James Maxton, among others, stood accused of conduct bordering on treason for organising strikes for better pay and conditions in the Clydeside factories and against the high rents prevailing in the Glasgow slums.

At the beginning of the war those who had no idea of the desperate conditions prevailing on the Clyde blamed Marxist propaganda for the workers' disaffection; in 1917 the October revolution in Russia gave them a new word 'Bolshevism'. That the Clydesiders had been seduced by this dangerous belief into sabotaging the war effort became an article of faith in the rest of the country, and one shared by Cunninghame Graham. Asked if he would be prepared to recognise the new regime in Russia his reply came smartly - he would be delighted to recognise Lenin and Trotsky 'at the end of a long piece of hard rope'. Here was another apparent inconsistency: for the last forty years Robert had maintained close contacts with activists in Russia opposed to the Tsarist regime, contacts that benefited from the knowledge he acquired from his editor, the Russophile, Edward Garnett. Like many others who had befriended Russians exiled to Britain in the 1880s, he welcomed the first upheaval in March 1917 that brought Alexander Kerensky to power. But the revolution that took place the following October was a different matter: a disaster, not only for the

Russian people, but one that seriously threatened to undermine the Allied cause at a most difficult moment in the war with Germany. Once more his reaction was extreme: he turned upon the people in whose interest he had campaigned so vigorously twenty five years before. 'This was not a war of capitalism', he told his audiences in 1918, 'it was the working men of Germany who sang the hymn of hate'. Harsh words from one hailed by Friedrich Engels as a fellow Marxian who, a frequent visitor in the 1880s, had drunk a Maibowl at 100 Regents Park Road with Engels and his guests, Auguste Bebel and Wilhelm Liebknecht, leaders of those same workers.(43)

To vent his displeasure, hastily and without considering the consequences had got him into trouble all his life - this was Don Roberto, lance in hand, galloping full tilt at his adversary – a performance endearing to some, John Galsworthy for instance who praised what he called Graham's knight errant philosophy. Others were repelled by his failure to take into account circumstances different from his own which were so privileged, a fault line in the approach of an aristocrat to the modern world. Whether this influenced the result in Stirling West cannot now be determined but when the electorate delivered its verdict on 11 December the official coalition candidate, Sir Harry Hope was found to have won with 6,893 votes, Thomas Johnston was second with 3,809, Cunninghame Graham last with 2,582. Five weeks later the Red Clydesiders called out 80,000 Glasgow workers in support of a shorter working week; the city was in turmoil; rumours abounded that a Bolshevik uprising was about to happen; on 31 January 1919, demonstrators in George Square were scattered by a police baton charge; the new government sent in tanks and soldiers armed with machine guns. Though the eight hour day had been central to Robert's political philosophy, some he preached frequently on Glasgow Green, this time he was nowhere to be seen. A letter exists, written later in the year in which he sets down the reasons for his disaffection. To an old friend, one of his fencing companions, the actor manager, Henry Arthur Jones, he wrote; 'I had hoped in Socialism to find a gradual demise of selfishness and the gradual establishment of a better feeling between man and man. You may remember that then (28 years or more ago) the sweater was excessively aggressive, hours were long, and there was a brutal spirit of materialism about...You will admit, I think, that my ambition was not a low ambition. That I was deceived and that all the golden dreams of Morris have vanished in the nine bestial and inarticulate years of the reign of King Edward, the war and now in the increasing inartisticness (sic)of everything, the prostitution of the stage and literature, and now in the ever increasing selfishness and lack of patriotism of the working classes [has] not been my fault' (44)

It was not his fault but his misfortune to have failed to bring about the fundamental improvement in social circumstances he had so earnestly desired. Now that he had grown old he was confronted with the disagreeable necessity of standing by while ideals he had held dear were translated into the kind of reality he could not approve, by people he disliked and whose motives he distrusted.

Notes to Chapter 15

1. NLS. Acc.11335/78, Rothenstein to RBCG, - Sept. 1906.
2. National Library of Scotland; Acc 11335/70 , Maya de Frias to RBCG, 27 Mar. 1908.
3. Watts/Davies, op.cit.; RBCG to Morel, 10 Dec. 1906
4. Benn, Caroline, 'Keir Hardie', Hutchinson, 1992, p. 251
5. Blunt, W.S., 'My Diaries', Martin Secker, 1919. p 611
6. BL, Add 46310, Burns Papers; RBCG to Burns, 26 May 1890.
7. The Times, various dates in July, and esp. 16 Aug. 1911.
8. Ensor, R.C.K. 'England 1870-1914' OUP 1964, pp 472-3
9. NLS,Acc.11335/71, n.d.
10. Brotherton Library, Leeds, Gosse Papers, RBCG to Gosse, 1 July 1918.
11. The Times, 12 Jan. 1906
12. ibid., 3 Aug. 1914.
13. The Veterinary Services with the Uruguay Remount Commission. HMSO 1925.
14. NLS Acc 11335/35, RBCG to Charles CG., - Feb. 1915.
15. Quoted in Thompson, L., 'The Enthusiasts', Gollancz, 1971, p 209.
16. NLS, Acc. 11335/35, RBCG to Charles CG, 24 May 1915.
17. NLS Acc 11335/ 35 RBCG to AEB, 26 Mar 1915
18. Cunninghame Graham, R.B., Bopicua in 'Brought Forward', Duckworth, 1916 pp 185-205
19. NLS, Acc. 11335/35, RBCG to AEB, 26 Mar 1915.
20. Uruguay Remount Commission, op.cit.
21. NLS, Acc. 11335/35, RBCG to Blunt,16 May 1915.
22. Cunninghame Graham, R.B., 'The Horses of the Conquest', Duckworth, 1930, Dedication.
23. Blunt, W., 'The Land War in Ireland' Stephen Swift,1912. p.
24. Wilson, J., 'Lawrence of Arabia' Mandarin Press, 1990, pp 165-6.
25. ibid.
26. Daily News 1 Mar 1915.
27. NLS Acc 11335/77,Lawrence to RBCG, 6 June 1921.
28. Rauner Special Collections Library, Dartmouth College; West papers, Series I, Box II, Folder 3, RBCG to Lawrence, 7 June 1921. And see, NLS Acc 11335/35, RBCG to AEB, 18 Mar. 1915 for the Labour Party reaction to his letter.
29. Cunninghame Graham, R.B., With the North West Wind in 'The Ipane', op.cit.
30. Cunninghame Graham, R.B., With the North East Wind in 'Brought Forward', op.cit.
31. NLS, Acc. 11335/56, [Handwritten].
32. Cunninghame Graham, R.B., 'Cartagena and the Banks of the Sinú', Heinemann, 1920.
33. NLS Acc 11335/ 108, Grey to RBCG .,18 Feb. 1916.
34. Cunninghame Graham, R.B., 'Cartagena' op.cit.
35. Harry Ransom Humanities Research Center, University of Texas at Austin, RBCG to Garnett, 21 Aug. 1927.
36. NLS, Acc. 11335/25, AEB to RBCG, 19 Sept. 1917.

37. ibid., Acc. 11335/137, GCG to AEB, various dates 1900 - 3.
38. ibid. Acc.11335/55, various dates, 1890- 5, GCG to RBCG
39. SRO, GD22/4/36, Cunninghame Graham, Angus; 'Notes on Ardoch and Associated Families'.
40. NLS,Acc.11335/ 48, AEB to RBCG , 27 Sept. 1911.
41. Tschiffely A.F., 'Bohemia Junction',Hodder & Stoughton, 1950.
42. <u>Stirling Observer</u> ,various dates in Nov. Dec. 1914
43. Johnston, T., 'Memories', London, 1952.
44. Jones, D., ed., 'The Life and Letters of Henry Arthur Jones' Gollancz, 1930, pp 303-5.

Chapter Sixteen

Nationalism

As one who claimed descent from the Kings of Scotland, the idea that circumstances could arise in which the country's independence might be restored was always present in Robert's mind; part of his dream of chivalry that led him to believe he, personally, was called upon to play a part in such an enterprise. With Keir Hardie he had been the principal begetter of the Scottish Home Rule Association in 1886. While the kind of nationalism they envisaged was meant to be a unifying force within Scotland it hardly threatened English institutions. Several attempt to pass legislation giving effect to Scots ambitions having come to nothing in the early years of the 20th century, the most promising to come before Parliament had to be postponed due to the outbreak of the war. After 1915 when it was understood that the leaders on the Clyde were intent on bringing social reform to Scotland on their own terms, the new structure these terms would bring about was perceived by the country at large as owing far too much to their socialist colleagues in other countries, not least those shortly to come to power in Russia. So it was in Ireland too, where the kind of picturesque nationalism Robert had derided in 1913 vanished after the outbreak of the war to be replaced by the deadly commitment of, among others, Roger Casement and James Connolly, Commander of the Citizen's Army; with both of whom Robert was well acquainted. After the collapse of the Easter Rising in 1916 Connolly's terrible death by execution for treason [helpless from a wound he had sustained during the fighting in the GPO he was taken before the firing squad in a wheelchair], was partly the reason for Robert's denouncing nationalism as conceived by the new generation of Irish leaders. In his eyes their beliefs were just as extreme as those sustaining the brutal civil which he had witnessed as a young man in the Argentine and Uruguay. When after the war the time came to try to establish a framework of government in Ireland capable of restoring peace in a country devastated by a culture of revenge and acts of savage reprisal on both sides, like many politically aware persons on this side of the water, including Winston Churchill, he was deeply suspicious of the Irish leaders' intentions. If the likes of Eamonn de Valera had their way the new state would be well on the way to Bolshevism.

In the winter of 1920-21 the running battle between the IRA and British auxiliary forces, including the Black and Tans and undercover intelligence officers reached new depths of brutality. In the early morning of Sunday 21 November, as an act of revenge for the shooting by the British of several of its leading volunteers, the IRA forced entry into eight houses in Dublin where members of the British Secret Service were reported to be living. Nineteen young men were roused from sleep and shot, some in the presence of their wives. Afterwards it transpired not all were agents. Inevitably the day on which the murders took place became known as 'Bloody Sunday'. Two days later, Robert Cunninghame Graham wrote a furious letter to Roland Muirhead,

Secretary of the Scottish Home Rule Association, resigning as its President. He was reacting to a meeting held by the Association at which the recourse to reprisals by both sides was condemned, a point he ignored. The letter is valuable for the declaration it contains regarding his attitude to nationalism. 'I do not think for a moment that the [British] government is encouraging reprisals in Ireland' it began, and in a phrase that recalls his forbearance towards the Metropolitan Police in 1887 on the first Bloody Sunday, when in spite of their rough treatment of himself and John Burns, he excused them as they were acting under orders; 'Policemen and soldiers are only human, and it is (though not admirable) still not unnatural when they see their comrades and officers basely assassinated from behind hedges...they occasionally hit back. The last horrible and cold blooded murder of 19 young men, unarmed, in bed, and some instances under the eyes of their wives, is enough to fill any decent man with horror and indignation'.

'I have been, and shall continue, I hope, undisturbed by the violence of these criminals, a convinced Home Ruler. I have no objection to Dominion Home Rule so long as the British Empire is master in its own house and controls the ports and armed services of the Crown. As a Scotchman I detest assassination and despise those who resort to it, and I believe no nation was ever freed by recourse to such dastardly methods.

'Such were not the ways employed by Wallace [at whose memorial near Glasgow he had given the annual speech] and by Bruce'

'I much fear I must ask you to remove my name from the Scottish Home Rule Association'.

Thus far, although there was no mistaking the depth of his feeling, his tone was measured. But there came a moment in the same letter when anger and contempt overcame him. Of course he had no idea of imputing complicity in murder to the Jews as a race, he remarked, but he believed; 'these murders are instigated chiefly and certainly paid for by the band of international Jews grouped round their fellow Jew, Mr 'De' Valera in New York'. At once he knew he had gone too far and added a PS;' I have no thought of impuning Jews as a race only those who 'run' 'de' Valera in New York'(1). This was not enough; the first allusion to Jews in the body of the letter had a most unfortunate impact on his reputation - while the postscript was ignored. Once again, as many times previously in the course of his career, he failed to gauge the reaction to such strong words in the mouth of a public figure of his standing. The wisest course would have been to rewrite the entire letter and then refrain from posting it. What was seen as an impulsive and ill judged attack by those who knew him, shocked the public at large ; in retrospect it gives an even worse impression - fixing upon him the label of anti-semitism that, in the context in which it was delivered ,seems to reveal his political philosophy in these later years as tainted with fascism. There is no truth in this. The charge of anti-semitism falls in contemplating his friendship with many prominent English Jews, one of the closest to him being William Rothenstein; it stands revealed as preposterous in the MP who damaged his standing in the Commons by his solitary fight to preserve Israel Lipski from the gallows. That, however, was an episode already grown dim in most people's minds and entirely forgotten in the present day, while his reckless language about the Jews is taken as a kind of shorthand indicating a subscriber to the views of people like Oswald Mosley: the comparison still surfacing from time to time is inaccurate and unfair.

As with other fits of political bad temper Robert's estrangement from the SHRA did not last and he continued to speak and write on its behalf . But during the decade of the 1920s his commitment was not especially enthusiastic. The violence of the workers' demonstrations in Glasgow in 1919, the return to Parliament in 1922 of members of the Red Clydesiders, among whom were William Gallagher, Emmanuel Shinwell and other leaders of the wartime disturbances caused the kind of nationalism they endorsed to be seen by many Scots as lacking in that necessary virtue - respectability. At the same time, watching the horrors of the struggle for independence in Ireland from an uncomfortably close vantage point, many were profoundly thankful for their separate status and less turbulent past .

When the Anglo-Irish Truce was declared in July 1921 Robert chanced to find himself with a privileged inside view of the next stage. Negotiations between the British and Irish had to take place to establish the terms of a Treaty. The problem was to find a venue. Members of the delegation chosen by the Dail were former guerilla leaders who were persona non grata in London. It was at this point that Lavery, the painter, offered his house in Cromwell Place as 'neutral ground where both sides might meet.' It was an inspired gesture; both Lavery and his wife, Hazel, were of Irish origin; he from Belfast, she from a County Galway family. In the ensuing months her talents as a brilliant hostess contributed a very great deal to easing the tension between the two sides. Lloyd George, Winston Churchill, Lord Birkenhead for the British; De Valera, Arthur Griffiths, Erskine Childers and Michael Collins for the Irish, thrashed out their differences in the opulent privacy of her drawing room, one of the places where, as it happened, Robert had, for many years, felt completely at home.

Lavery remained one of Robert's closest friends though gone were the days when the young MP had coaxed his better known colleagues, including Parnell, to sit to the young and struggling portrait painter. He had prospered mightily over the years, acquiring a knighthood and the entrée to most of the great houses in London, especially 10 Downing Street when Asquith was Prime Minister. His acquaintance with Robert had begun in Morocco in 1894 when he was one of a party, including Walter Harris, who rode together via Arzila and Bibi Carleton's stronghold, Alcazar el Kebir, to Fez, a journey Lavery described in detail in his memoirs and which inspired him with such a liking for the country and its brilliant light he bought a house outside Tangier where Robert was a frequent visitor. They supported each other; when the struggle to hold on to Gartmore was at its height it was to John Lavery that Robert confided his impulse to escape by committing suicide. In 1909 when Lavery married the beautiful - and much younger - Hazel Trudeau Robert was one of the very few people at their wedding at the Brompton Oratory. With his special knowledge of recent Irish history he was allowed a close view of the crucial negotiations under way in the familiar surroundings of 5 Cromwell Place which lasted through the summer and autumn of 1921. When, as a consequence of the signing of the Treaty - which de Valera rejected thus making civil war inevitable -

one of its principal advocates, Michael Collins, was shot, and when four years later, Kevin O'Higgins, another of Ireland's new leaders who might have done great things, and whom Robert came to know well , was also murdered, he was reinforced in his determination, in so far as it would be in his power, to help to preserve Scotland from a similar disaster.(2)

To that end he held to the position he laid down in his letter to Muirhead. That, while Scotland should be granted Home Rule in the form of her own Parliament, defence and foreign affairs should continue to be conducted from Westminster. Sadly for his posthumous reputation his moderation was obscured, partly by the violent language in which the reference to de Valera was couched, largely because of the company he kept. During the latter part of the 1920s after the Labour Party virtually lost interest in the subject, the two principal organisations involved were the Scottish Home Rule Association and the Scottish National League. Members of these two held widely differing views of nationalism - what it was and how it was to be achieved. In 1928 they merged - uncomfortably - to form the National Party of Scotland. At the age of 76 Robert accepted an invitation to become President. In the general noise and confusion generated by the new situation some were better at making themselves heard than others: those who shouted loudest were perceived by the public to typify the organisation. Prominent on the fundamentalist wing of the National Party of Scotland was Christopher Grieve, better known today as the poet, Hugh McDiarmid. So far as his political beliefs were concerned Grieve's behaviour was that of a particularly well lubricated weather cock. During the time Robert presided over the Party his beak was firmly in the right wing quarter. According to the historian, Richard Finlay, 'Grieve expressed strongly anti-democratic and intolerant ideas which resembled some of the more inane early writings of the Scots National League'. He called for a small elite to direct activities in a 'powerfully, spiritually dynamic way...aristocratic standards must be re-erected. We in Scotland have for too long been grotesquely over-democratized. What is wanted now is a species of Scottish Fascism'. Quotes like these, together with Grieve's open admiration for 'big men' like Mussolini and his announcement in 1930 of the founding of Clann Albann, a paramilitary nationalist organisation that would undertake unorthodox special duties - a concept dangerously close to Mosley's Blackshirts - eventually caused Grieve to be expelled from the Party. But before that happened, as President, Robert Cunninghame Graham had become associated with these views. (3) The impression was reinforced by the fact that, from 1928 to about 1933 he was often in the company of another young fundamentalist member of the Party's Council, the writer, Compton Mackenzie.

He makes several appearances in Mackenzie's best selling memoirs; in Robert's ancient motor the two of them bring up the rear in nationalist processions, they spend evenings in chilly hotel dining rooms waiting for election results while Don Roberto, as Mackenzie always referred to him, relives occasions in these same rooms with John Burns, Charles Stuart Parnell and Keir Hardie. Not everything takes place in the distant past however. In 1928 Mackenzie sits with him in the Caledonian Hotel in Edinburgh waiting for the result of the Glasgow Rectorial Election. When the telegram comes Robert opens it to discover a sensation: he has come second, only 66 votes behind the Prime Minister, soundly beating the Liberal, Sir Herbert Samuel, and the Labour candidate, Rosslyn Mitchell . 'Cunninghame Graham had a majority of 211 among the men; the women supported Baldwin', Mackenzie tells his daughter(4) 'The ladies voted against me' Robert explained to Edward Garnett, 'because Mr Baldwin had just given them the franchise'. As in the case of his efforts on behalf of Israel Lipski his longstanding support of votes for women had long since vanished from the public memory. When the National Party of Scotland decided to run 5 candidates in the 1931 general election the President took an active part in the campaign (though he drew the line at riding a white horse at the head of a procession to Stirling Castle). He thoroughly enjoyed himself. 'Quite your Party leader. Back to the soap box again. It is amusing' he told Garnett in October 1931. Ten days of strenuous electioneering left him under no illusion as to the result. 'I fear we shall be snowed under as were the Moseleyites'. He was right; while three of the National Party saved their deposit, the other two polled only 10 % of the vote.(5) Undaunted he continued to lend his romantic presence to the Party gatherings; thin, upright, and amazingly spry for his age he was equally at home with a microphone in front of crowds picnicking beside their cars, as he had once been 'roaring' on Glasgow Green. But as Nazism took hold of Germany the mention of race in the context of politics - as in the Celtic Scots versus the Teutonic English - which had been well enough received in the early days of the movement, became increasingly unpopular to the point where, on the outbreak of the Second World War the Party's Chairman, Roland Muirhead (who had succeeded to the position on the amalgamation of the SHRA with the Scottish National League in 1928) narrowly escaped internment. And probably this was the reason why when Aimée Tschiffely's biography was published in 1937, shortly after Robert's death, though practically all the newspapers and journals in the country reviewed it at great length, there was hardly any mention of his Nationalist activities. (6)

Robert was fortunate in that 'politicking' was something he could enjoy well into old age so long as he was capable of memorizing the speeches he, as President, was called upon to make. That was essential after the age of 60, he told Compton Mackenzie; 'the voice goes'. One of the most enjoyable aspects of the various gatherings was the number of young people who turned up. In sharp contrast to these sociable occasions the time he devoted to his other career - of writer - had to be spent alone, either at Ardoch, or at the house he inherited on the Isle of Bute. Judging by most of the work he produced in the post war years the effort was considerable; the ideas no longer jostled for attention; the words came far less readily. Although many of his prefaces insist that he writes for pleasure only, the impression is that pride in his established reputation, the determination not to surrender to advancing years were equally important. The regular publication of collected sketches ceased with 'Brought Forward' in 1916 which Frank Harris, for one, thought not among his best work. More than ten years were to elapse before Heinemann brought out 'Redeemed and Other Sketches 'in 1927.

'Redeemed' which was dedicated to Elizabeth Dummett, reveals significant changes in Robert's life. Morocco is not the background here, the scene has changed to Spain. In the 1920s he spent weeks each year at the isolated farmhouse, El Dehison del Encinar, in the shadow of the Sierra de Guadarrama. Reached by fording a stream, surrounded by miles of uninhabited countryside where foxes and wolves roamed, it was almost all that remained to his spendthrift friend, Dino, Duque de Frias, the place where he took refuge after his return from Mozambique in 1909 and where he died of pneumonia. Afterwards Robert who remained a close friend of his widow, Maya de Frias, made regular visits to a place that helped to assuage his nostalgia for the wilderness. (7) Walter Harris is remembered in this volume by a detailed description of Dar el Jinoun, the house on the beach near Tangier that, more than anything he wrote , was the truest expression of his personality. (8) This was something Robert did not succeed so well in doing with either Wilfrid Blunt or Joseph Conrad, whose deaths are recorded here. Both the straightforward obituary of Blunt and the account of Conrad's funeral seem forced, with an uncharacteristic hint of sentimentality. 'Inveni Portum' is a return to the style he used first in 'With the North West Wind' but, though he recounts the progress of Conrad's funeral cortège through Canterbury to the Cathedral in similar detail, the sense of greatness passing so brilliantly conveyed with regard to William Morris, is lacking here to the extent that Conrad's memory loses by it. 'Redeemed' is also the volume in which <u>A Hundred in the Shade</u>, the account of the New Orleans courtesan with its scattered clues - appears, a deliberate attempt to lead the few who knew his true history to identify in her a portrait of his wife.

In 1929 Edward Garnett, then working for Duckworth, Robert's former publisher, persuaded them to republish thirty tales and sketches of his choosing(9). The only other similar work its author lived to see was 'Mirages' published by Heinemann in 1936, the year he died. South America, Morocco, Spain and Scotland form the background to these pieces, as if in farewell. His friends welcomed it if only because it contained a reprint of his portrait of Bibi Carleton that, when it appeared shortly after the subject's death in 1929, was snapped up almost as a collector's item. (10) The sketches in 'Mirages' were the last to meet the principle that guided him when speaking of his own work - that it was autobiographical. Yet in the same years between the ending of the War and his death no less than nine other volumes appeared under his name, witness to his desire not to abandon the occupation that, in his late forties had so suddenly appropriated his spare time and brought him to the attention of the literary world. These were not products of his imagination but the result of foresight: they were cleverly contrived from the privileged information he had made a point of acquiring from the very beginning of his adventures in parts of the world little known to his countrymen but in whose history and landscape they found much to interest them. South America was the background to all but one of these nine, two of which appeared in 1920, each one very different from the other. 'Cartagena and the Banks of the Sinú' was a straightforward, not to say rather dull account of his mission to Colombia in 1916. As such it was admirably well supplied with facts but hardly beguiled the reader into visiting. The other, 'A Brazilian Mystic' turned out to be one of the most curious and absorbing of all his many works. (11)

Antonio Maciel, later to be known as El Consulheiro, the Councillor, was born about 1842 in the small town of Quixerabomin in the Sertão, the high and wild plateau in the backlying country of Brazil, separated from the coast 200 miles away by densely forested mountains. Though his family owned land they made a poor living from raising cattle in contrast to their neighbours, the Araujos, who prospered from the same occupation. Accusations of cattle stealing over the years nurtured a culture of revenge which claimed the lives of members of both families. Antonio, however, resisted the example of his older relatives. Well educated and exceptionally devout, he worked as manager of his father's store in Quixerabomin. Nothing up to the year 1858 gave any sign that the careful storekeeper would be called upon to play the part fate had destined for him, Robert wrote. 'No doubt the blood of his wild family but slumbered and though it never manifested itself in the same fashion as it did with his uncles and grandfather, the taint was certain to appear' (12) - an assessment in which hindsight played a part. Nevertheless Antonio's marriage in 1858 did change everything. His wife is described as of violent temper and loose morals; one in particular of her love affairs drove Antonio to behave like a true Maciel by assaulting the man he believed was the author of his misfortune. It was not his wife's lover but a relative unfortunate enough to come in his way. He was sent to prison but escaped and, for the next ten years, his whereabouts were unknown.

In about 1868 he reappeared, scarcely recognisable. 'Sunburned and worn with fasting, his eyes wide open, fixed and staring, his sunken face and his thin limbs worn with privation gave him the look of a monk...His dress was a long shirt of coarse bluelinen and he leaned upon the classic pilgrim's staff'. As such men do when they wander about among people struggling to make a living in remote and poor areas, he began to attract followers who delighted in telling stories about his power of healing and holiness. Where the parish priests made no objection he began to preach but when he set his followers to rebuilding churches in the small settlements of the Sertão its government decided it was time to curb him. In 1876 he was arrested on the charge of murdering his mother and tried at Bahia. Able to prove she was still living he had to be released. He returned to the Sertão, a martyr, more famous than before.

So far his life resembled that of most religious fanatics, especially those of the East. Robert, who had observed many such in Morocco, described him as fulfilling a self imposed mission; he judged him not mad but not entirely sane; 'probably just on that borderland where dwell saints and visionaries'.(13) In 1889 the abdication of the Brazilian Emperor, Dom Pedro, brought about a remarkable situation in which power over the scattered population of the Sertão devolved upon Antonio Consulheiro to the great alarm of the central government. Dom Pedro's departure into exile in Lisbon (where Robert saw him shortly after his return) occurred in consequence of a military revolt said to have been arranged by people with republican sympathies. The Sertajanos were deeply conservative and monarchist; rumours penetrating from the outside world that a Republic of Brazil would soon be declared lit a bonfire of opposition fuelled not simply by political argument but that most inflammatory element - superstition. In the late 1870s the English explorer, Richard Burton, had come across traces of Sebastianism in remote parts of the country among Portuguese settlers. Its adherents maintained that the young King Sebastian who ruled Portugal from 1554 to 1578, when he fell in battle against the Moors, was not dead but would reappear at the moment he was most needed. This belief in the 'hidden king' now took hold of Antonio Consulheiro In 1893 he withdrew to a ruined farm called Canudos, in a valley guarded by encircling mountains where he set his ever increasing band of followers to build a mighty Church, the place in which their King would reappear. It was surrounded by a fortified settlement all of whose inhabitants carried arms. In the next three years the government sent no less than three expeditions to reduce Canudos. All were defeated with great loss of life. In 1896 an overwhelming force accompanied by field guns slowly forced a way through difficult terrain to the valley where the Church came under bombardment. Soldiers fought their way in to the narrow lanes between the shanties, killing every inhabitant. Antonio Consulheiro's body was found in a shallow grave. 'Dressed in his long blue tunic...his hands crossed...clasping a crucifix against his breast he lay', Robert wrote, 'waiting the coming of the King, that Dom Sebastian who he believed should come to rule the world in glory, blot out injustice, cast down the mighty, and exalt the poor in spirit...His body lay upon a ragged piece of matting and both his eyes were full of sand' (14).

Terrible tragedy though it was, the narrative which is by far the clearest and most vigorous of all his post war work reinforces the impression that Robert was thoroughly at home with the subject. The facts were readily to hand and born out by his own experience. Though so far as we know he had not been into the Sertão, his journey as far as Cruz Alta in the south of Brazil had shown him how the settlers in the back country lived. His knowledge of Portuguese gave him access to everything written about the affair; he was in Lisbon in 1889 when the capital was preoccupied with the plight of the former Emperor, Dom Pedro. During the years he and Gabrielle spent at Vigo they often crossed the border into Portugal where he met people who believed in the return of the 'hidden king' - his sketch, A Sebastianist describes an old man who dreams of the final battle against the Moors. This took place in Morocco at Alcazar el Kebir - Bibi Carleton's town - a place Robert knew almost as well as Tangier, and where he probably first encountered the belief, about which he writes with much sympathy. (15) This being known to some of his friends and acquaintances, they urged him not to neglect the subject. One was Theodore Roosevelt who, when he was President of the United States, having read some of Robert's tales about the gauchos, remarked upon the absence of similar books about the frontiersmen in Brazil. 'Why dont you do it' Robert quoted him as saying in the Preface to 'A Brazilian Mystic' 'you have been there, know them, and speak their lingo. The field is open to you' Roosevelt, whom Robert often encountered as a fellow guest at the Hotel Beau Site in Rome, a favourite of both of them, died in 1909 and his suggestion was forgotten. But, the Preface goes on to explain, in 1915, on his way to buy horses in Uruguay, Robert's ship touched at Bahia in Brazil where a fellow passenger told him the story of Antonio Consulheiro. 'I listened...and when we landed at the capital [Rio de Janeiro] bought books about it, bought more in Santos and as I read and mused upon the tale the letter from the President came back into my mind'. Among the books he bought was one that made the task immeasurably easier. This was' Os Sertões' by Euclides da Cunha. First published in 1902 it was a mighty epic, covering every aspect of Brazil and going into the smallest detail of the tragedy at Canudos. 'Os Sertões' did not find an English translator until 1944 so as one of the few people fluent in Portuguese Robert had the book very much to himself (16). That is not to say he lifted facts without acknowledgment; he was scrupulous in referring to da Cunha as the origin of what he relates. Comparing the two 'A Brazilian Mystic' benefits from the pace and precision of Robert's narrative. Euclides da Cunha, by contrast, pauses by the way to consider the significance of all kinds of secondary facts; flora, fauna, history, religion, while at the same time voicing his outrage at the violence perpetrated by both sides in what was, effectively, an episode of civil war. Robert briskly rejects morality and religion both. When faith, works, philosophy, logic and the rest of the panaceas preached during the last two thousand years fail, he remarks 'all that is left to reasonable men is to pay the bootmakers' and tailors' bills with regularity, give alms to the deserving and to the undeserving poor, and then live humbly under the sun, taking example by the other animals'. (17)

Two histories followed both of Spanish Conquests; the first of New Granada in 1922 the second of the River Plate in 1924 (18). The next which appeared in 1925 was a new departure, a biography of his 18th century ancestor, the first Robert Cunninghame Graham. It cannot have been nearly as enjoyable to write as 'A Brazilian Mystic'. Although he did his best with the papers he had inherited they are hardly substantial documents and have to be augmented with padding that, paradoxically, is interesting since it takes the form of those descriptions of Gartmore and its surroundings quoted at the beginning of this biography. There is no mistaking the affection he continued to feel for the place and regret at having had to sell it. Every detail of the house, its contents, its surroundings and its history is present in his mind twenty five years after he ceased to be its master. In fact the house and the estate are the real subjects of the book rather than the laird whom he somewhat awkwardly calls Doughty Deeds, after the poem his namesake and predecessor wrote which found its way into the anthologies. One suspects this was a publisher's device, something to inspire curiosity about an otherwise obscure and sometimes tedious figure.

The year after 'Doughty Deeds' was published yet another history of the Conquest appeared and this time its author found himself well and truly in the dock. D.H. Lawrence's review of 'Pedro de Valdivia' condemned the book for its construction which he said was shoddy [it is certainly rather muddled] and criticized his translation. But, unusually in a reviewer, he turned the full force of his own personality against the author in a scathing attack upon Graham's character and motives as revealed by what he chose to write about the conqueror of Chile. 'Mr Graham has shown us, not Valdivia, but himself. He lifts a swashbuckling fountain pen, and off he goes. The result is a shoddy, scrappy, and not very sincere piece of work. The Conquistadores were dammed by their insensitiveness to life, which we call lack of imagination. And they let a new damnation into the America they conquered. Yet at least they never felt themselves <u>too good</u> for their job, as some of the inky conquerors did even then, and do still'. Graham - an old Don in a caracoling armchair - had shown himself trivial and complacent in relating the cruel treatment of the Indians by Valdivia and his men and not condemning it, but that was the sort of thing to be expected of men of action who, Lawrence declared were usually deadly failures in the long run. 'Their precious energy makes them uproot the tree of life, and leave it to wither and their stupidity makes them proud of it', Their precious energy - when he wrote that Lawrence was 41, consumed by TB, with only three more years to live. (21)

1933 was the year Nazism came of age in Germany, when Hitler took over as Chancellor. It was also the year that Robert's last book , 'Portrait of a Dictator Francisco Solano López' was published. It is a damming indictment of the misuse of power by an individual in sole control of a country's resources. Part of the reason why he wrote it was to warn his contemporaries of the risk of being seduced by pomp and a show of nationalistic fervour into allowing a cruel, barbaric regime to take over. According to 'Portrait of a Dictator', as time went on in Paraguay, López as leader steadily gained in respectability so that when Robert came to write the book 60 years after the events it described, the Marshal/President was revered as a national hero. It was his purpose to set the record straight. How well he succeeded must be a matter of some dispute. Owing to his ability to speak Spanish and Guarani his observations proceed from a more secure foundation than those of most foreigners. But he did not enter the country until 18 months after the war was over, and his major sources are for the most part in English, memoirs of expatriates who were trapped in Asunción at the outbreak of the war and became victims of López' brutality. As in the case of 'A Brazilian Mystic' the book gains in dramatic tension from its focus on individuals - López and the intriguing figure of his mistress, Madame Lynch. The penultimate scene is at Cerro Corda where the remnants of the Paraguayan army were ambushed by Brazilian forces. López, mortally wounded, dies in the arms of Eliza Lynch. (22)

The historians stop there; at a scene well known all over South America; that people celebrate as a symbol of plucky small nations pitted against the large. But Robert continued his narrative, emphasizing his status as one of the very few people left alive who knew what befell those who survived the celebrated battle of Cerro Corda. Madame Lynch appears to have lived prosperously, if not happily, ever after. She bought a fine house in the Rue de Rivoli in Paris. 'I saw her several times in London in 1873 or1874, 'Robert wrote, 'getting into her carriage. She was then apparently about forty years of age. Of middle height, well made, beginning to put on a little flesh, with her abundant hair just flecked with grey. In her well made Parisian clothes she looked more French than English and had no touch of that untidiness that so often marks the Irishwoman'.[there spoke the husband of Gabrielle] Still handsome and distinguished looking she did not appear like someone who had looked death in the face, lived for so long in circumstances so strange and terrifying and buried her lover and her son with her own hands.(23)

'Portrait of a Dictator' was Robert's 27th book. Together with prefaces to other people's books, articles in newspapers and journals this was a considerable body of work that made him a figure to be reckoned with on the English literary scene. One of those who recognized his potential in advance of the majority was an ambitious young American student of literature. When Herbert Faulkner West came to England in 1929 he was looking for what the young Robert called 'an oppening' to make his mark in his chosen profession. (24) Certain contemporary English writers had already caught his eye as promising. Henry Williamson was the first he approached. Cunninghame Graham was next. Kind and helpful as he always was to those who asked him for an interview or advice, especially the young - Robert invited West to lunch at Martinez' Spanish restaurant just off Regent Street. The two got on famously together; Robert liked talking to the young man who regarded him with awe. Upright and alert with a thin aquiline face and wavy white hair 'he was like an eagle'. Mutual respect turned to liking. In due course Don Heriberto was invited to stay at Ardoch where following long conversations the idea was proposed and, though cautiously received, not instantly rejected, that West should write the first biography(25)

In September West returned to the Ivy League establishment that was to be his place of work and home for the rest of his life. Dartmouth College at Hanover, New Hampshire was the epitome of East Coast privilege with a library on which no expense was spared over the years to put together books and a significant collection of manuscripts. From here West sent questions to his subject who sent his answers back after carefully considering them. It had dawned on Robert that this was the way to ensure posterity would remember him as he wanted, and only as he wanted. For instance, at the point where West proposed to say his father, William Bontine, had been injured in 1880, a date Robert obviously regretted giving him, he had recourse to that old, much loved device which appears so often in his own reminiscences. No, he told West, the injury was much earlier. 'You might say during his service with the Scots Greys in Galway his horse fell on ,stepped on his head. Or something of the kind' (26) West was not in a position to challenge him. And so, as well as its silence on the subject of William Bontine's mental derangement and his long incarceration, his book is the first source of the impression that Robert was brought up by his Spanish grandmother, spending much of his time with her side of the family in Spain. It has the first account of the [fictional] meeting with his future wife in Paris, and of the winter after the marriage being spent at Gartmore. These details are proved wrong by the papers deposited years later by the Graham family in the National Library of Scotland and even more importantly by the official records of the Court of Session at HM Register House in Edinburgh.(27) But West's own correspondence which on his death was deposited in the Baker Library (now the Rauner Special Collections Library) at Dartmouth College also call certain assertions in his biography into question. For instance, Robert's closest relation, his nephew, Angus Cunninghame Graham, found it hard to swallow West's description of Robert lisping Spanish at Catalina's knee, or that he stayed in her family house in Spain. Where did he get the information that Robert was brought up by her? Angus, by then an Admiral of the Fleet, somewhat peremptorily asked West. So far as he knew Catalina spent the years in question with her second husband, Admiral Katon, on the Isle of Wight. She died there and was buried in the Anglican churchyard in Ryde. Robert and Charles [his father] were brought up, first at Finlaystone, then Gartmore, with visits to London in between. He knew this from countless stories of their doings. Nor, so far as Angus knew, were there visits to Catalina's family in Spain: she had very few relations in that country. Aunt Jimenez was the only one, he, Angus, ever knew. (28)

When West's biography appeared in 1932, even Robert found it dull, while the younger generation was dismissive of both book and subject (29). Writing to the publisher, C.J. Greenwood in October 1932 T.E. Lawrence told him; 'The Cunninghame Graham duly arrived. It is a disappointing book. Anything about the old Don should have been written with a swagger. He is an artist thereat as you see if only he takes off his hat to a lady in the street. His pen swaggers too; and he cannot therefore sustain a book; though he writes the best five or six pages imaginable...A wonderful old man...Not much brain you know, but a great heart and hat and what a head of hair!' That this condescending missive earned a place in the Selected Letters was probably due more to the dislike the Editor, David Garnett, felt for Graham, his father, Edward's, close friend, than to any contribution it might make to an understanding of that complex character, Lawrence of Arabia (30).

Perhaps a man of action could write more interestingly than a professor about a man whose life had been almost all action? When they met in about 1934 Aimée Tschiffely was already famous for an adventure he had conceived and singly handedly carried out seven years before when, with two horses, Mancha and Gato, he had ridden the 15,000 miles from Buenos Aires to New York. Newspaper accounts of this exploit had so impressed Robert at the time that, without having met the Swiss, he wrote an account 'Tschiffely's ride'. (31) Again the two became friends. One of the younger man's great attractions was he had spent years in the Argentine roaming the pampa, working with gauchos. Once more a biography was mooted and as West had, Tschiffely found himself being fed with reminiscences. His remit was wider than West's, more detailed, delivered with a heightened sense of drama that was instinctive in him. When it appeared in 1936 shortly after Robert's death, but with a preface by him, it received long and enthusiastic reviews in countless journals and newspapers across the English speaking world - 'the adventure of being Cunninghame Graham' as G.K. Chesterton put it, providing a thoroughly good read.(32) One or two reviewers aired their suspicion that there was a great more to be told. And indeed there was for Tschiffely did not probe further than Robert wanted him to go; he reproduced the accepted version of the meeting with Gabrielle; he asked no question of those who might have provided a different viewpoint of Robert's activities - as a MP for example. Most significantly he omitted all mention of business enterprises like those in Southern Morocco as was Robert's clear intention since it, and others like it, were out of keeping with the image of Don Roberto, that cherished creation on which so much effort had been lavished. As with Herbert Faulkner West subject and biographer became close friends; 'hardly a day passed without our meeting, telephoning , or corresponding with each other' Tschiffely wrote later. 'Once when I asked him why he wasted his time on me, he told me that, since his friend, W.H. Hudson had died, until he met me, there had been no one with whom he could talk about gauchos and the pampa which were [his]spiritual home'. On one visit to Tschiffely who had lodgings in a dilapidated part of Notting Hill, Robert dispensed with his chauffeur and the two of them walked to a house nearby, No 40 St Luke's Road, where Hudson had lived until his death in 1922, and where Robert had visited him, braving the desert of macadam, mud and fog which was how Hudson described the neighbourhood. 'For some time Cunninghame Graham and I stood in St Luke's Road, talking about Hudson, Tschiffely wrote, 'and before seating ourselves in the car my companion tiptoed up the steps leading to the entrance to No 40 and, having gently touched the doorknob, rejoined me'. (32)

The gesture was a mark of esteem for a departed friend, similar to the brand he drew beside the signatures of others or the letters R.I.P. Hudson who was born and lived the first twenty five years of his life in Argentina , came to England in 1874 where for many years he lived in penury while composing the works that made him famous; novels like 'The Purple Land' and 'Green Mansions', and books about birds. His dedication to and knowledge of natural history was unusual at the time, this, together with his reclusive, rather mysterious personality - partly the result of precarious health due to a bad heart- and his extreme poverty made him a cult figure in London's artistic and literary world. William Rothenstein who painted him in 1906 was hard put to describe the effect he had. 'His peculiar mysterious charm was indescribable. Something about him tore at one's heart so lovable he was. Yet he never invited affection. He was a lonely man with something of the animal about him, walking away and returning with the nonchalance of an animal, and then disappearing again'. (33). The same quality of naturalness was remarked by Joseph Conrad who said his writing was like 'the grass that the good God made to grow and when it was there you could not tell how it came.' (34). Robert, who began to correspond with Hudson in 1890, did his utmost to promote him as a writer by means of reviews, by introducing him to friends like Conrad and Violet Hunt, and in the prefaces he wrote for his later works. In return Hudson dedicated one of his strangest and cruellest stories, 'El Ombú' to him, perhaps because he recognized the latter's own capacity for brutal realism. 'To my friend, R.B. Cunninghame Graham' the dedication read, 'Singularismo escritor ingles' , words that Robert cherished. Frequently repeated they have contributed a great deal to enhancing his own standing as a writer.

As the second most enthusiastic 'Hudsonian' - the writer, Morley Roberts was generally acknowledged to be the first - as well as a noted connoisseur of contemporary art, and a public figure , Robert was the natural choice as Chairman of the Hudson Memorial Committee. A protégé of his, the American born sculptor, Jacob Epstein, was commissioned to produce a piece of sculpture for the bird sanctuary in Hyde Park. What could be more appropriate? But Epstein's concept of Rima, the spirit of nature celebrated by Hudson in 'Green Mansions' as a bare breasted female attended by four birds, provoked such a storm when it was unveiled by the Prime Minister, Stanley Baldwin, every ounce of Don Roberto's famous insouciance was needed to withstand it. This was forthcoming; not only was he a dedicated admirer of Epstein's style - 'stark, massive, Assyrian-Modernist' but one of the staunchest of the few supporters at the time of Cézanne, Matisse and other Post-Impressionists whose object in painting was in sympathy with Epstein's approach to sculpture. According to the latter, no stranger to controversy, the uproar that greeted the unveiling was 'unequalled in venom and spite' (35). The main complaint concerned the figure's ample proportions. As Violet Hunt pointed out Hudson had stressed Rima's buxomness, her 'aptness for motherhood', and Epstein with something like second sight, according to Hunt, had represented this so faithfully that when Baldwin, having pulled the cord, turned to contemplate the relief, he was observed to flinch(36). The press had a field day 'TAKE THIS HORROR OUT OF THE PARK' was a typical headline. Even some of Hudson's closest friends and supporters (who were also Robert's friends) the Ranee of Sarawak, Hilaire Belloc, Arthur Conan Doyle, declared the only thing to do with such a repellent object was to remove it. This demand provoked the architect, Muirhead Bone, to organize a counter petition to preserve it. This appeared in The Times whose art critic was in no doubt it was one of the most beautiful memorials in the country. As well as Robert Cunninghame Graham those who signed were Bernard Shaw, Edward Garnett, Augustus John, Ramsay Macdonald, John Lavery, Sybil Thorndike and Ben Tillett (37).

That was not the end of the connection; his friendship with W.H. Hudson was to have a significant effect upon the manner of Robert's own death eleven years later. In November 1934 he told Edward Garnett that a Dr Pozzo, 'a young enthusiastic Argentinian Hudsonian' had written to tell him he had located the house where Hudson had been born. Pozzo was very keen that, as Chairman of the Memorial Committee, Robert should make a ceremonial visit to it when there would be an opportunity for him to help with the Spanish translation of Hudson's work. At the same time his own would be honoured: it was precious to those who cared for the history of the pampa in the 1870s before the flood of emigrants from Europe overwhelmed its unique way of life. Such a visit began to be seriously talked about. Though Robert had turned 82 in May 1934 he was still remarkably fit - Tschiffely described how he took the three flights of stairs to his house in Notting Hill without visible distress. But the following year marked the onset of symptoms of decline. His hands were colder than ever after a walk in the Park, he complained to Garnett in October 1935, and again 'It is so cold I can hardly write and the Judaeo-Gothic script [his handwriting] is worse than ever (38) Perhaps high summer in the Argentine would provide the warmth he so obviously needed. Accompanied by Mrs Dummett and her sister, Louisa Miéville, he left Liverpool in January 1936. At the Spanish port of La Coruña where the ship touched before crossing the Atlantic he found Gabrielle's old friend, Emilia Pardo Bazán presiding in the form of a statue. Rio de Janeiro amazed him so greatly had it changed as did Buenos Aires, now ,like Rio, a thriving modern city. As soon as Dr Pozzo met them at the steamer he had hardly a moment to himself' everyone wants to be my friend.' The constant social whirl had undesirable consequences; 'At present I am in bed with a slight touch of bronchitis' he confessed on 6 February in his first letter to Edward Garnett since reaching South America. Before succumbing he had been out to see Hudson's house at Quilmes, some ten miles from the city. 'Although the plain is cut with fences [which nowhere existed the last time he had been there] 'the effect is very fine'. He sat down at a small table on the brick floor and wrote a letter to Hudson's old friend, Morley Roberts. Although the letter to Garnett, the last in a correspondence that had continued for forty years, was dictated, he added a postscript in his own hand. 'We sail for home on the 26th [March] in the Almeda Star.. (due April 15)'. His first letter to West was not written until three weeks later, on 1 March, when he made a point of repeating the dates he had given Garnett - 'I sail for home on the 26th in the Almeda Star'. He told 'mi querido Heriberto' his visit to Hudson's birthplace had been extraordinarily interesting. 'It is a small rancho near a wood and the great plain surrounds it like a sea. Some day I hope to send you my account of it'. Why the delay? Why not one of those brief but vivid pictures of the kind he used to send his mother? The answer lay in the letter. 'We are going through a heat wave that is rather trying' he told West, 'and the sun has inflamed my eyes which makes my writing worse than ever. However it is nothing much and is passing off' (40)

It did not pass off. Pneumonia set in from which he died on 20 March. His body lay in state at the Casa del Teatro; crowds filled the street outside and the President of the Argentine Republic paid his respects. A procession followed the coffin on the way to the docks ; at its head walked Mancha and Gato. The Almeda Star sailed according to her schedule on 26 March. In late April the coffin arrived at Port of Menteith . After a service held in the church pipers accompanied it to the jetty where it was put on board a small boat and rowed over the lake to Inchmahome. There in the chancel of the ruined Priory Robert was buried beside Gabrielle.

It was a private occasion yet whose significance in terms of his ancestral descent, could not have escaped those who attended. As such one may venture to suppose, it would have pleased the dead man whose instinct at his first visit to the island as a boy had been to claim it as a sanctuary.

Barely a year later the publication of Tschiffely's' Don Roberto' had every book reviewer in the country clamouring for extra space. The majority were undiscriminating in their acceptance of the story Tschiffely had to tell and gave him rather more credit than he deserved for producing the kind of rattling good yarn that, all too seldom, came their way. Robert dead became instantly more famous than in life. His striking appearance, his dash, his versatility, his knowledge and skill with horses, his literary ability, his social conscience - these combined made his life story irresistible. 'The kind of man every boy wants to be', 'Don Roberto, the human dynamo', 'Man of Swagger' were some of the headlines and, of course, there were countless variations on the theme of Don Quixote. Only his adversaries - the Noncomformists, for example, were less than enthusiastic; 'A noticeable man' was as far as the Methodist Recorder, for example, was prepared to go. The Times also had reservations "The biography is in essence an autobiography', the newspaper warned its readers, Tschiffely was merely acting as editor of the material Cunninghame Graham had given him. The 37 year old V.S. Pritchett was more specific in his doubt. 'They were, those who knew him, inclined to soft pedal the Spanish grandmother; at the gaucho they raised their eyebrows a little', he revealed. But, if any of these people noticed more serious errors or omissions in the book either they remained silent, or their comments have since been lost. One of the most striking discrepancies between the life as lived, and as recounted is that of Robert's marriage when Tschiffely accepted without question his fictitious account of the meeting with Gabrielle de la Balmondière in Paris. Even though husband and wife were both dead by 1937. so far as is known, no one, not even a member of the Horsfall family sought to correct the record. Even so, in spite of their discretion or, it may have been, their ignorance of the true history of the doctor's daughter from Masham, over time an impression emerged that Robert Cunninghame Graham's taste for adventure joined to his flamboyant personality, sometimes betrayed him into exaggeration and, occasionally, into fantasy.

That Robert foresaw this effect is evident in the Preface to 'Writ in Sand', which came out in 1932, the same year as West's biography. In it he expressed his distaste for the public's avid desire for details of a writer's life, a public he dismissed as 'thinking perhaps, but absolutely falsely, that [the details] assist it to understand the man, or perhaps out of lewd curiosity - the curse of common minds' Close friends though they both became in the process of writing about him, neither West nor Tschiffely were allowed the slightest insight into the illness of William Bontine. Robert's desire to erase this long drawn out and devastating experience from his own memory as well as to spare his mother the condescending pity visited on the relatives of those afflicted by a fearful disease, gave rise to awkward moments in later life when he had to make shift to conceal his movements at certain times or risk exposure. Having put up with this necessity for many years he went on the attack in 'Writ in Sand'. 'It is a natural instinct in the majority of men to keep a secret garden in their souls, a something they do not care to talk about, still less to set down for the other members of the herd to trample on', he declared; it was an instinct most manifest in those who wrote their own biographies, memoirs, or confessions.

Such a challenge must be answered by those who disagree with the strictures in the Preface. This writer believes the details of William Bontine's illness are crucial to an understanding of his eldest son's character, and of the course of subsequent events. The fact that it was monitored in documents drawn up by officials of the Court of Session provides an invaluable point of reference for the other sources. Avid a biographer may be, and curious, but with a view to describing circumstances that could have halted the boy's development at a crucial moment and damaged his health and well being beyond repair. That it did not is a tribute to the steadfastness of Robert's character, a quality doubtless inherited from his mother - and something his Great Uncle Mount would have rejoiced to see. Even as a boy he had a well developed sense of responsibility towards his family from which sprang his passionate desire to repair the damage his spendthrift forbears had wreaked upon its fortunes. Yet almost everything he did was of his own choosing. Thus, in 1870 he went to South America in the teeth of strenuous opposition by his elders, not least his mother. Afterwards he resisted whatever course of action they proposed whether service in a 'good' regiment in India, tea planting in Ceylon, whatever helpful suggestions his mother's legal adviser, Mr Wright, was minded to advance, and anything at all the Curator favoured, to the point where Jamieson was given little idea of where he was or what he was doing. Letters written at the time of Robert's first adventures reveal a young man who is brave, resourceful, inquisitive and tough, capable of enduring harsh and intimidating conditions - long hours in the saddle, little food, the very real threat of attack by hostile forces; a young man who - reprehensibly - ignores the constant frights he gives his mother with tales of the perils he has narrowly escaped.

But that picture is too simple; the evidence thus made available incomplete, a fact that in itself points to something undeclared, it may well be, hidden. There were times when Robert went to ground, when whatever he was engaged in doing came to a sudden halt and, even - as we know from the Court of Session records, - had to be abandoned. More than once the Court cites an unspecified illness as the reason. Robert, who in writing letters to his family, often had recourse to a personal kind of code, almost always described the times he was obliged to lie up as resulting from a horse related mishap - either it fell on him, or he fell off it. The possible true cause of these occasions when he disappeared from view surfaces only once in the Court of Session records. In 1881 something about Robert on his return from Texas prompted Jamieson to send him to a doctor whose verdict was that it would be some time before he was able to lead a normal life. Joined to the evidence of his low state of mind in the letters he wrote from Texas after Gabrielle left him, this seems to point to an episode of severe depression. At other times his famous volatility was manifest in sudden outbursts against his political and parliamentary colleagues when he stormed out of meetings like the one in Dundee in 1888. These add weight to the supposition that his was a manic-depressive personality. both aspects can be traced in the comments of those who knew him well. In his memoirs the painter, John Lavery, recalls the time when Robert ,struggling with the Gartmore debts, was under so much pressure he threatened to commit suicide. The manic aspect emerges from the many accounts of his furious energy and from his mother's surrender to his desire to go to South America due to her apprehension of the effect her continued refusal would have upon him. Like so many people who fall into this category, when he was in spirits Robert displayed an abundance of gifts - wit, expertise in several different directions, artistic flair, compelling charm that won him many admirers, but when his mood turned down his instinct, like an animal's was to lick his wounds in solitude.

While the habit of pleasing himself, of speaking exactly what was in his mind secured him a place while he was still young among the rising generation of political activists, causing him to be regarded as a coming leader of the newly enfranchised working class, this same aspect of his temperament ensured his moment would be brief. It was not long before what they regarded as his unreliable behaviour and injudicious remarks became more than his colleagues were prepared to tolerate. He became a liability just at the moment when electoral gains seemed to promise the realization of their ambitions. So, at the same time as his erstwhile protégés, Keir Hardie and John Burns, achieved positions of real power, Cunninghame Graham was quietly left to his own devices. His political career begun so early and with such passionate effect upon the hearts and minds of the industrial workers of the West of Scotland, ended at the summer outings of the National Party of Scotland where, a painfully thin but still upright and dapper figure, microphone in hand he bid for the attention of the picknickers around him.

The Chancel, Inchmahome Priory, burial place of Robert and Gabrielle Cunninghame Graham. Historic Scotland.

Notes to Chapter Sixteen

1. DC; Series I, Box II, Folder 3 RBCG to Muirhead; 23 Nov. 1920.
2. McCoole, S., 'Hazel: A Life of Lady Lavery 1880-1935', Lilliput Press, 1997, p 72 et seq.
3. Finlay R., 'Scottish Politics and the Origins of the SNP 1918-1945' John Donald,1994, p 87
4.. Mackenzie, C., 'My Life and Times' Octave 6, Chatto & Windus,1967, p 157-8
5. Austin; RBCG to Garnett, 30 Sept. 1929.
6. Tschiffely, A.F., 'Don Roberto', Heinemann, 1937.
7. Cunninghame Graham, R.B., Fin de Race in 'Writ in Sand', op.cit pp 115-152..
8. Cunninghame Graham, R.B., Dar al Jinoun in 'Redeemed and Other Sketches', Heinemann, 1928.
9. ibid.
10. Cunninghame Graham, R.B., 'Thirty Tales & Sketches', Duckworth, 1929
11. Cunninghame Graham, R.B., 'A Brazilian Mystic Being the Life and Miracles of Antonio Consulheiro'., Heinemann, 1920.
12. ibid., pp 62-64.

13. ibid., p. 68.
14. ibid., pp 237-38.
15. Cunninghame Graham, R.B., A Sebastianist in 'Hope', Duckworth, 1910, pp29-39
16. Samuel Putnam,tr. ' Rebellion in the Backlands' [Os Sertãos} Chicago Press, 1944.
17. Cunninghame Graham, RB., 'The Conquest of New Granada Being the Life of Gonzalo Jimenez de Quesada' Heinemann, 1922. 'The Conquest of the River Plate', Heinemann, 1924.
19. Cunninghame Graham, R.B., 'Doughty Deeds An Account of the Life of Robert Graham of Gartmore', Heinemann, 1925 p.164
20. Curle.R.,ed., 'W.H. Hudson's letters to R.B. Cunninghame Graham,' Golden Cockerel Press, 1941.Hudson to RBCG, 2 Dec. 1900.
21. Lawrence, D.H., The Calendar 3, January 1927,pp 322-6.
22. Cunninghame Graham, R.B., 'Portrait of a Dictator Francisco Solano López Paraguay 1865 - 1870' Heinemann, 1933.
23. ibid., p 242.
24. NLS, Acc11335/20, RBCG to AEB,20 April 1873.
25. DC; Series I, Box 2, Folder
26. ibid., 8. April.31
27. West, H.,F., 'A Modern Conquistador Robert Cunninghame Graham His Life and Times', Cranley and Day, 1932.
28. Scottish Record Office; GD22; Court of Session 94 and 96. National Library of Scotland, Acc. 11335, 1-205
29. DC; Series I, Box II Folder 2, Angus Cunninghame Graham to West, 8 Jan. 1964.
30. Garnett, D., ed., 'Selected Letters of T.E. Lawrence , The Reprint Society, 1941, p.341. And see ,DC Series I, Box II, Folder 3, 23 Feb 1933 'The book, our book is a great disappointment'.
31. Chesterton, G.K., 'Autobiography' Hutchinson, 1936, p 271.
32. Tschiffely, A.F., 'Bohemia Junction', op.cit., pp 246-7.
33. Tomalin, Ruth, ' W.H. Hudson A Biography' OUP 1984 p 211.
34. Ford, F.M., 'Joseph Conrad A Personal Reminiscence' Duckworth, 1924, p 197.
35. Tomalin, op.cit., p 24.
36. Hunt, Violet, 'The Flurried Years', Hurst and Blackett nd p. 271.
37. Tomalin, op.cit., p.24
38. Harry Ransom Humanities Research Center, University of Texas at Austin; Graham/Garnett correspondence; RBCG to Garnett, 5 Oct. 1935.
39. ibid.,the same to the same, 6 Feb. 1936.
40. DC, Series I Box II, Folder 3. RBCG to West 1 March 1936 . Note West had 40 copies made of a 'last letter' to him from RBCG containing many details of Hudson's house at Quilmes. This does not accord with the 1 March letter in which Robert appears too sick to write at any length.

Select Bibliography

Principal unpublished sources

Edinburgh.
National Library of Scotland; Cunninghame Graham Papers; Acc. 11335/1-203
Scottish Record Office; Cunninghame Graham Muniments; GD22.
Court of Session Papers; CS 46 and CS96

London.
Public Record Office; Home Office; 144/204 (Bloody Sunday)
Foreign Office; 84/1500 (North West Africa Company)
Foreign Office; 99/298, 310 (Morocco).

British Library; Add. 46284, 46288, 46310 (papers of John Burns).

In private hands; Horsfall Family Papers.

United States.

Rauner Special Collections Library, Dartmouth College, Hanover, New Hampshire.
Herbert Faulkner West Papers.

Harry Ransom Humanities Research Center, University of Texas at Austin; Gabrielle Cunninghame Graham to Mary Evans; Robert Cunninghame Graham to Evans, Smith.
Robert Cunninghame Graham, Anne Elizabeth Bontine to Edward Garnett.

Published Works.
Note. For a chronological bibliography of works about RB Cunninghame Graham see Professor John Walker in The Bibliothek, Vol 4, No 5, (1965).

Benn, Caroline, 'Keir Hardie',(Hutchinson, 1992).
Blunt, W.S., 'The Land War in Ireland', (Stephen Swift, 1912).
ì ì 'My Diaries', (Martin Secker, 1919).
Bottigelli, E., ed., 'Friedrich Engels, Paul and Laura Lafargue: Correspondance' (Editions socials, 1956-57).

Broadhurst, H., 'From a stonemason's bench to a Cabinet bench', (Hutchinson, 1901).
Buchan, John, 'Greenmantle', (Hodder & Stoughton, 1939, first published 1916).

Campbell, A.B., 'The Lanarkshire Miners. A Social History of their Trades Unions, 1775-1874 (J. Donald, 1979).
Claraz, Georges, 'Ensayos de un concociemento geognostico-fisico de la Provincia de Buenos Aires' (1863).
Colebrook, T.E., 'Life of the Hon. Mounstuart Elphinstone' (John Murray, 1884).
Collier, E.F., 'A Victorian Diarist' (John Murray, 1944)
Conrad, Joseph, 'Nostromo', (Penguin, 1963).
Chesterton, G.K., 'Autobiography', (Hutchinson, 1936).
Critchley, T.A., 'The Conquest of Violence', (Constable, 1970).
Crowley, W., 'The Crofters' Party 1885-1892' in Scottish Historical Review Vol 35.
Curle, Richard, ed., 'W.H. Hudson's letters to R.B. Cunninghame Graham (Golden Cockerel Press, 1941).

Davies K. and L., eds., 'The Collected Letters of Joseph Conrad', Cambridge University Press, 1983).
Drummond P., and Smith, J., 'Coatbridge Three Centuries of Change' (Monklands Library Services Department, 1983).

Emily, Shereefa of Wazzan, 'My Life Story' (1911).
Ensor, R.C.K., 'England 1870-1914' (Oxford University Press, 1964).
Erskine, Mrs Stuart, ed., 'Memoirs of Sir David Erskine of Cardross' (Fisher Unwin, 1926).

Finger, Charles, 'Seven Horizons', (Doubleday Doran, 1930).
Finlay,Richard, 'Scottish Politics and the Origins of the SNP 1918 –1945).
Flint, J.E., 'Sir George Goldie and the Making of Nigeria' (Oxford University Press, 1960).
Ford Madox Ford, 'Joseph Conrad A Personal Reminiscence', (Duckworth, 1924).
Friedland, M., 'The Trials of Israel Lipski' (Macmillan, 1984).

Garnett, David, ed., 'Selected Letters of T.E. Lawrence' (Jonathan Cape, 1938).
Glasier, J. Bruce, 'J. Keir Hardie A Memorial' (Independent Labour Party, 1919).
Glen, R.C., ed., 'Reports of Cases in Criminal Law 1886-1890' Vol XVI (H. Cox, 1890).

Harris, Frank, 'Contemporary Portraits' Third Series, (Published by the author, New York, 1920).
Harris, Walter, 'Morocco That Was'. (Blackwood, 1921).
Hemingway, M., 'Emilia Pardo Bazán The Making of a Novelist', Cambridge University Press, 1983).

Holroyd, Michael, 'Augustus John A Biography' (Penguin, 1976).
Hunt, Violet, 'The Flurried Years' (Hurst and Blackett, n.d.).
Hyndman, Henry, 'Further Reminiscences' (Macmillan, 1912).

Jacomb-Hood, G., 'With Brush and Pencil' (John Murray, 1925).
Jefferson, G., 'Edward Garnett A Life in Literature' (Jonathan Cape, 1982).

Kapp, Y., 'Eleanor Marx' Vol 1. (Virago, 1979).
Kellas, J.G., 'The Mid Lanark By Election and the Scottish Labour Party' in Parliamentary Affairs, 18, 1964-65.
Kelly, E.R., 'Post Office Directory of the North and East Ridings, 1872'
Kelvin, J.,ed., Collected Letters of William Morris' (Princeton University Press, 1987).
Kolinski, D.J. 'Independence or Death The Story of the Paraguayan War' (University of Florida Press, 1905).

Laurence Dan H., ed., 'Bernard Shaw Collected Letters 1874-1897 (Max Reinhardt, 1965).
Lavery John, 'The Life of a Painter' (Cassell, 1940).
Lindsay, J., 'William Morris' (Constable, 1975).
Loch, G., 'The Family of Loch' (Edinburgh,1934).
McCarthy, Fiona, 'William Morris A Life for Our Times' (Faber, 1994).
MacDiarmid, Hugh, (Christopher Grieve) 'Cunninghame Graham A Centenary Study' (Caledonian Press, 1952).
Mackenzie, Compton, 'My Life and Times Octave 6', (Chatto and Windus, 1967)
Mackenzie, Donald, 'The Khalifate of the West', (Simpkin Marshall, 1911).
Maitland, Alexander, 'Robert and Gabriela Cunninghame Graham' (Blackwood, 1984).
Masterman, G.F. 'Seven Eventful Years in Paraguay' (Sampson Low Son and Marston, 1869).
McCoole, S., 'Hazel A Life of Lady Lavery 1880-1935', (Lilliput Press, 1997).

Newall, C., 'The Grosvenor Gallery Exhibitions' (Cambridge University Press, 1955).

Parliamentary Papers; 1884, Vols XXXII-XXXVI, 'Report by the Commissioners of Enquiry into the condition of the Crofters and Cottars in the Highlands and Islands of Scotland' (Napier Report).
Parsons, F., 'The Origins of the Morocco Question 1880-1900' (Duckworth, 1976).
Parsons, F.W., 'The North West Africa Company' in Historical Journal, 1958.
Pearson, H., 'Bernard Shaw His Life and Personality', (Reprint Society, 1948)
Pelling, H., 'Henry Champion' in Cambridge Journal VI, 1953.
Putnam Samuel, trans., 'Rebellion in the Backlands' (Os Sertãos) (Chicago University Press, 1944).

Rothenstein, William, 'Men and Memories Recollections of William Rothenstein 1872- 1900' (Faber and Faber,1931).

Rostov, W.W. 'British Economy of the 19th century' (Clarendon Press, 1948).

Smillie, R., 'My Life for Labour' (Mills and Boon, 1924).
Sommer, D., 'Haldane of Cloan His Life and Times 1856-1928 (Edinburgh, n.d.).
Stevenson, George, 'Benjy' (John Lane/The Bodley Head, 1917).
Strang, William, 'Etchings' (George Newnes, 1907).

Thompson, E.P., 'William Morris Romantic to Revolutionary', (Pantheon Books, 1976).
Thompson, George, 'The War in Paraguay', (Longmans Green, 1869).
Tomalin, Ruth, 'W.H. Hudson A Biography' (Oxford University Press, 1984).
Torr, Dona, 'Tom Mann and his Times', (Laurence & Wishart, 1956).
Tschiffely, A. F. 'Don Roberto', (Heinemann, 1937).
   'Bohemia Junction' (Hodder & Stoughton,1950).
Tsuzuki, C., 'Tom Mann' (Clarendon Press, 1991).

Walker, John, ed., 'The South American Sketches of R.B. Cunninghame Graham' (University of Oklahoma Press, 1986).
Walker, John, ed., 'The North American Sketches of R.B. Cunninghame Graham (Scottish Academic Press, 1986).
Watts, Cedric, ed., 'Joseph Conrad's letters to R.B. Cunninghame Graham', (Cambridge University Press, 1969).
Watts, Cedric and Davies, Laurence, 'Robert Cunninghame Graham, A Critical Biography', (Cambridge University Press, 1979).
West, Herbert Faulkner, 'A Modern Conquistador Robert Bontine Cunninghame Graham His Life and Works' (Cranley and Day, 1932).
Williams, W.W., 'The Life of Sir Charles Warren' (Blackwell, 1941).

Newspapers and Journals
The Airdrie Advertiser
Contemporary Review
The Commonweal
Daily Graphic
Glasgow Observer
Justice
Labour Elector
The Queen
Saturday Review
Stirling Advertiser
Stirling Observer
The Times.

Works by R.B. Cunninghame Graham

Notes on the District of Menteith, (A & C Black, 1895).
Father Archangel of Scotland – with Gabrielle (A & C Black, 1896).

Mogreb-el-Acksa (Heinemann, 1898).
The Ipané, (Fisher Unwin, 1899).
Thirteen Stories (Heinemann, 1900).
A Vanished Arcadia (Heinemann, 1901).
Success (Duckworth,1902).
Hernando de Soto (Heinemann, 1903)
Progress (Duckworth, 1905).
His People (Duckworth, 1906).
Faith (Duckworth, 1909).
Hope (Duckworth, 1910).
Charity (Duckworth, 1912).
A Hatchment (Duckworth,1913).
Scottish Stories (Duckworth,1914).
Bernal Diaz de Castillo (Eveleigh Nash, 1915).
Brought Forward (Duckworth,1916).
A Brazilian Mystic (Heinemann, 1920).
 Cartagena and the Banks of the Sinú (Heinemann, 1922).
The Conquest of New Granada, (Heinemann, 1922).
The Conquest of the River Plate (Heinemann, 1924).
Doughty Deeds (Heinemann, 1925).
Pedro de Valdivia (Heinemann, 1926).
Redeemed (Heinemann, 1927).
José Antonio Paez (Heinemann, 1929).
Thirty Tales and Sketches – selected by Edward Garnett (Heinemann, 1929).
The Horses of the Conquest (Heinemann, 1930).
Writ in Sand (Heinemann, 1932).
Portrait of a Dictator, (Heinemann, 1933)
Mirages (Heinemann, 1936).

Works by Gabrielle (Gabriela) Cunninghame Graham

Spain A Lecture (Modern Press, 1890).
The Science of Tomorrow and Medieval Mysticism (J. Miles, n.d.)
Santa Teresa: Being some Account of her Life and Times (A & C Black, 1896).
Father Archangel of Scotland – with R.B. Cunninghame Graham (A & C Black, 1896)
The Christ of Toro (Eveleigh Nash, 1908).
Rhymes from a World Unknown (privately printed, 1908)
The Dark Night of the Soul, (Watkins, 1908).
Genera (in MS, now lost?).

The People's Laird:

Index

A
Aberdeen, Marquis of, 143
Abdul Kerim Bey,(Captain Geyling), 265-6, 282
Abraham, William, M.P. (Mabon), 157, 158
Adam W,P., 118, 138
Adrar, 261, 281, 287
    Concession, 284
    1904 collapse 288
Airlie, Countess of, 32
Airdrie Advertiser, 24(n), 126, 127, 139, 140, 144, 156
Alcorta & Co., 49, 58, 59
Allman, James, 171
Alps S.S., 48
Alvaredo, Pedro de, 47
Angelo's (fencing club), 103, 279
Annual Register, 134
Arbuthnot, Sandy, 259
Ardoch, 11, 18, 48, 112, 113
    Sale, 134, 229
    repurchased, 289, 308-9
Argyll, Duke of, 122
Asquith, Herbert, M.P., 181, 183, 184, 216, 319
Auracania, 251,266
Aveling, Edward, 167, 211, 214, 221, 222
Avila, St Teresa of, 217, 236, 237-8
    GCG's biography of, 238-9, 241-3, 295

B
Bagot, Barbara, see Cunninghame Graham, Barbara
Banda Oriental (Uruguay), 74
Bashir el Bairuk, Sheik, 261, 262, 264, 272
    Concession, 281, 282, 284
Baird, Alexander, 123, 124
Baird, William &Co., 124-5
Baird, John M.P., 125, 126, 127
    1885 election 128, 129
    1886 election 139, 140
Balfour, Arthur M.P., 162, 163
Balmondière, Francis de la, 85,86,87
Balmondière, Gabrielle de la, (1858-1906), RBCG's wife; 85-93, 111, 116, 129, 141, 232
    Marriage, 91
    Mexican journey 95-99
    As writer, 96, 187-8
    In New Orleans, 100
    RBCG,s description, 102
    And religion, 102
    Clothes, 103, 326
    As Chid, 105, 242, 295
    And mother in law, 112, 182, 231, 233
    And servants, 113,
    Health, 142, 182, 206, 209
    And politics, 209, 214, 223
    Biography of St Teresa, 217, 229, 236-8, 241-3, 295
    And Gartmore , 233, 285, 286

  And 'Nostromo', 8, 279-8
  Last illness, 288-9
  ' Don Juan Tenorio' 288
  as speculator, 308
Barham, H,.M.S., 15 ,30, 31
Barnard, T.J., 245
Barry, Maltman, 199, 200, 202, 211, 216
Bateman, J La Trobe, 230
Bax, Ernest Belfort, 136, 162
Benn, C.W., 296
Besant, Annie, 153, 154, 166, 167, 172, 173, 176, 186, 187, 188, 191, 203, 209
Bickmore, Dr., 20, 307
'Bitter Cry of Outcast London', 173
Black, Adam & Charles, 235, 236, 242-2
Blackie, John Stuart, 122
Blanqui, Louis, 211
Blunt, Wilfrid Scawen, 163,267,296,302-3,322
Bontine, Hon Mrs Anne Elizabeth, (1828-1925) RBCG's mother, 13-17, 31, 40, 43, 47, 51, 67, 84, 107, 129, 178, 189, 243, 259, 277, 286, 308, 332
  And in-laws, 22
  Continental journey, 23-4
  Stillborn child, 27
  Jointure, 28, 29, 111, 134, 229
  And RBCG's marriage, 86, 92, 101, 104
  And Malise'death, 133
  And Gartmore, 231, 232, 285
  And 'Pygmalion', 287
  And Ardoch, 309
  Death, 309
Bontine, William, (1825-1883)' The Strix', RBCG's father; 12-13, 16-17, 75, 85, 230, 327, 332
  Illness, 19-21, 22
  Continental journey, 23-4
  'Reminiscences', 24(n),
  at Dumfries, 27, 67
  Death, 106,
  Will, 111
Bradlaugh, Charles, M.P., 127, 142, 154, 158, 176, 181, 182, 193, 195
Bradly, Mr, 27, 29
'Brazilian Mystic A', 322 et seq.
Broadhurst, Henry, M.P., 157, 158, 213-4
Bryant & May, 202-3
Buchan, John, 259, 303
Buenos Aires, 71-73, 100, 330-31
Burgess, Joseph, 135, 137, 153, 177, 212
Burne Jones, Edward, 105, 153
Burns, John, M.P., 134, 136, 137, 177, 189, 220, 101, 211, 212, 220, 296, 298, 305, 318, 320, 333
  Trial, 181, 183, 184
In Pentonville, 188, 191, 194, 200, 201, 211, 212
  And Dundee, 214-15
  And Battersea, 215, 296
Burns, Mrs Pattie, 185, 188
Burt, Thomas, M.P., 157, 166 , 213
Burton, Sir Richard, 47, 49, 267, 323
Butler, Dr., 23

C

Campbell, Arthur, W.S., 12, 20, 112
Campbell, George, W.S., 231, 232
Camlachie, 118,123,124

1892 election, 222-3, 224
Cape Juby (Tarfaya), 70, 261-2, 262-3, 264, 306
Carleton, Edward, 'Bibi', 253, 256, 257, 259, 262, 267, 284, 309
    'Bibi', 322,324
'Cartagena and the Banks of the Sinu', 322
Casement, Roger, 317
Cave, Mr Justice, 137
Cayzer, Sir Charles, 285, 286, 288
Chamberlain, Joseph, M.P., 138, 281
Champion, Henry, 134,144, 173, 191, 199-200, 202, 211, 212, 213, 223, 305
    Family/career, 136-7
Charles, Mr. Justice, 183
Chicago Seven, 153, 175, 205, 209
Chideock, Dorset, 105
Childers, Erskine, 319
Churchill, Winston, 317, 319
Clann Albann, 320
Claraz, Georges, 72
Clark, Gavin, M.P., 121, 141, 200,202
Clerici, Enrico, 61,78,279
Coal Mines Regulation Bill, 157-8, 159, 103, 166
Coatbridge, 123-4, 129
Cody, Col. (Buffalo Bill) 100, 156, 179
Collazo, Peregrina, 104, 113, 209, 217, 239-40, 259
Collins, Michael, 319, 320
Colombia, 305-7
Commonweal, The, 126, 151, 152, 173, 184
Connolly, James, 298, 317
Conrad, Joseph, 8, 21, 61, 267, 277, 281, 283, 284, 329
    RBCG and 'Nostromo', 8, 279-280
    RBCG obit., 322
Contemporary Review, 198
Consulheiro, Antonio, 323, 324
Conybeare, Charles, M.P., 171, 199, 200, 201, 206
Córdoba, 43
Corpus Christi, 94
Court of Session, 28, 29, 32, 43, 80, 85, 97, 103, 327, 332, 333
Cowen, Joseph, 213
Crane, Walter, 179, 300
Cradley Heath, 203, 205-6, 209
Crawford, Donald, M.P., 142, 157, 158
Crawfurd, Oswald, 106, 243
Crawhall, Joseph, 250
Crofters' Party, the, 121-2, 124, 125, 146, 200
Cunninghame Graham, Anne, 24(n), 229
Cunninghame Graham, Admiral Sir Angus, 285, 307, 327
Cunninghame Graham, Barbara, 178, 182, 189, 230, 231, 307, 308
Cunninghame Graham, Charlotte, 111, 229
Cunninghame Graham, Charles, (1854-1916) RBCG's brother, 17, 22, 23, 27, 29, 48, 67, 84, 103, 116, 129, 182, 189
    In Texas 1881, 101
    Marriage 107
    Inheritance,107(n), 111,116
    sale of Gartmore, 285
    death, 307,
    character, 307-8
Cunninghame Graham, Gabrielle, RBCG's wife, see Balmondière de la
Cunninghame Graham, Laura, (RBCG's grandmother) 22, 28, 31
Cunninghame Graham, Olave, 230, 231, 307

Cunninghame Graham, Malise, RBCG's younger brother, 20-21, 29, 101, 104, 105, 111, 116,
    Death, 129, 133, 134
Cunninghame Graham, Robert , 6th laird ,'Doughty Deeds', 10, 11, 24(n), 116, 117, 308
Cunninghame Graham, Robert Cunninghame, 'Uncle Bobby', 19, 22, 28, 32, 43, 47, 48, 63, 75, 80, 107, 235
  Majorca Land Scheme, 230
Cunninghame Graham, Robert, 8th laird, RBCG's grandfather, 12, 13, 16, 20, 111
Cunninghame Graham, William, 7th laird 'The Swindler', 11, 12, 21, 111, 124
Cunninghame Graham, Robert Bontine, (1852-1936)
    Ancestry, 21, 317
    Appearance, 7
    And religion, 139, 234, 235, 264
    And socialism, 7, 67, 124, 126, 135 et seq., 152, 193
    And Ireland, 7, 13, 138, 219
    And Parnell, 8, 217, 218-221
    Character, 28, 28, 332-3
    In the Argentine, 32-43
    In Paraguay, 49 et seq.
    Iceland, 67, 68,
    West Africa, 69-70
    Buenos Aires, 1875, 71-73; 1881,100; 1936, 330-31
    In Brazil, 76-77
    As writer, 77, 192, 234, 251, 277 et seq.,
    Allowance, 80, 83, 93, 103
    Marriage, 85-93, 217
    Texas, 93-101
    Exiled to Spain, 101
    Describes his wife, 102
    Inheritance,107,111
    Political programme, 123, 126-7
    Candidate for NW Lanarkshire, 124
    On war, 127, 299
    And animal rights, 144, 158
    And alcohol, 141
    Maiden speech, 144
    And clothes, 152
    And 8 hour day, 157-8
    Lipski case, 159-162
    Bloody Sunday, 171-180
    Imprisoned, 185-6
    And Mid-Lanark, 200-1
    Scottish Labour Party, 201-2
    And Labour Elector, 203, 209
    And Great Dock Strike, 213-4
    Finances, 1893, 229-30
    Health, 230
    Travels in Morocco, 255, 259, 268 et seq.
    As Don Roberto, 278-9, 313, 320, 328
    And Shaw, 286, 287
    And GCG's last illness, 288
    and her death, 295
    in Uruguay, 1914-15, 300-02
    And Middle East, 304
    And Colombia, 305-6
    And 1918 general election, 311
    Glasgow Rectorial election, 321
    Death, 331
Currie, Sir Donald, M.P., 117
Cruz Alta, 76-7, 324

D

Dajory (de l'argent), 83, 93
Daily News, 304
Davidson, Thomas, 136
Davies, Laurence, 312
Davitt,Michael, 122, 144, 146, 163, 188, 191, 195, 196, 197, 220, 223, 299
De Mendoza, Pedro, 39, 71
De Ojeda,Emilio, 284, 285
De Rosas, Juan Manuel, 35
De Urquiza, Justo Jose, 35, 39, 54
De Valera, Eamonn, 317, 318, 319
Devonshire Club, 83-4, 85, 103, 134, 135
Dilke, Sir Charles, 216-7, 219, 260, 263
Dillon, John, M.P., 163
'Don Juan Tenorio', 288
'Doughty Deeds', 325
Drummond Hay, Sir John, 251, 252, 255
Dummett, Mrs Elizabeth,'Toppy', 310, 321, 330

E

Edward, Hay, 73
Eight Hour Day, 158, 159, 193, 211, 217, 222-3, 296, 313
Elphinstone, Hon. Mountstuart, 13-14, 15, 16, 17, 19, 25(n), 31, 111, 332
Elphinstone, 11th Lord, 15
    14th Lord, 29
Engels, Friedrich, 87, 210-11, 212, 222, 225
Ensor, R.K., 298
Entre Ríos, Province, 34, 36, 40, 73, 127, 185
Erskine, Hay, 44(n)
Erskine, Helen, 47
Erskine, Admiral Sir John, 106, 116
Erskine, Keith, 47
Epstein, Jacob, 7, 24(n), 329-30
Euan-Smith, Sir Charles, 257-8, 262
Evans, Bernard, 105
Evans, Mary, 105, 111, 113, 133, 141, 206

F

Fabian Society, 137, 187, 200, 299
Fair Traders, 134-5, 182
Faisal, Emir, 303-4
Fane, Blanche, 101, 308
Federation of Celtic Societies, 121
Fellowship of the New Life, 136-7
Fenwick, Charles, M.P., 157, 158, 166, 213
Ferguson, John, 128, 180, 196, 197, 202, 305
Feus, 116, 133, 230, 232, 233, 239, 285, 291, 309
Finger, Charles, 153, 154, 177
Finlaystone, 17, 30, 48, 308
Fitzmaurice, Lord Edmond, 121, 128, 263
Flahaut, Comte de, 14, 24
Flahaut, Mme de, 14, 15, 17, 31, 121
Fleeming, Doña Catalina, see Katon
Fleeming, Admiral the Hon. Charles Elphinstone, RBCG's grandfather, 15, 16, 27, 30, 31, 129, 133, 247
Fraser-Mackintosh, Charles, M.P., 120, 121
Ford Madox Ford, 279

Ford, Richard, 104
Fortnightly Review, 67, 240
Francia, Dr., 53
Frias, Duque de, (Dino) 250, 251, 282, 322
Frias, Duquesa de, 282, 295, 322
Friedland, Professor Martin, 160, 161, 162

G

Gallagher, William, 312, 319
Galsworthy, John, 277, 313
Garibaldi, Giuseppe, 36, 61
Garnett, David, 328
Garnett, Edward, 24(n), 272, 275, 277, 279, 280, 283, 284, 285, 289, 295, 312, 322, 330
Gartmore; House, 8, 113, 244, 325
    Estate; 10, 12, 20, 93
    Curator's administration, 28,31,32,41,43, 106,111
    Burial ground, 111
    Farms, 114
    Village; 114, 235
    Agricultural depression, 229 et seq.
    Sale 230-32, 285-6
'Genara', 295
George. Henry, 122, 136
Gladstone, W.E., 117, 118, 193,
    And Irish Home rule, 137
    1886 election, 139
    and Bloody Sunday, 171, 172, 179
    and Parnell, 218-19, 221
    and eight hours day
Glasgow Green, 117, 146, 197, 299, 321
Glasgow Daily Mail, 216
Glasgow Herald, 139, 223, 299
Glasier, John Bruce, 147, 152, 156, 287, 296, 301
Globe Venture Syndicate, 266, 268, 269, 271, 284
Goldie, Sir George, 136, 281
Gosse, Edmund, 299
Gould, Mr., 57
Graham, Nicol, 10, 115
Grey, Sir Edward, 303, 306
Grosvenor Gallery, 86, 105-6, 249, 250
Grove, Emily, 47, 86
Grove, Capt. Ross, 47, 58, 63, 86, 281
Gualeguaychú, 36, 37, 41, 43, 45(n), 71, 99, 301
Gulliver, Mr., 22, 307

H

Haldane, R.B., 179, 195, 220
Hallé, Charles, 105
Hardie, James Keir, 142, 146, 158, 165, 166, 202, 211, 213, 214, 217, 220, 320, 333, 300, 317
    Mid-Lanark by-election, 196,197,198,199,201,
    West Ham, 225
    As labour leader, 296, 297
    RBCG's obit., 305
Harkness, Margaret, (John Law), 200, 211
Harris, Frank, 7, 24(n), 234, 321
Harris, Walter, 255, 257, 260, 267, 284, 319
    RBCG on, 322
Harte, Bret, 77, 94

Highland League, 121
Headlam, Stuart, 153, 173
Henderson, Sir Edmund, 173, 174
Holland,Jacques, 47, 49, 59, 61, 62, 63, 86, 281-2, 306
Homer, Fraulein, 29, 103, 134
Hope, Col. William,V.C.,19, 22, 28, 32, 47, 58, 111, 112, 178, 230
Hope, Margaret, 111
Horsfall, Caroline Stansfield, see Balmondière, Gabrielle de la
Horsfall, Grace ,Gabrielle's sister, 88
    And 'Benjy',90-93,102
    Marriage to George Stevenson,91
Horsfall, Dr. Henry, Gabrielle's father, 87, 88, 91
Horsfall, Mary Stansfield, Gabrielle's mother, 88, 89, 90, 91, 92
Horsfall, Mary, Gabrielle's eldest sister, 91, 289, 290, 291
Horsfall William,Gabrielle's brother, 289, 290, 291
Hudson, W.H., 277, 279, 329
    Memorial Committee, 329, 330, 331
Hume, Major Martin Sharpe, 239, 283-4
Hussein, Sherif of Mecca, 303, 304
Hunt, Violet, 105,
Hyndman, Henry, 134, 135, 172, 175, 200, 211, 300

I

Inchmahome, island of, 21, 67, 114
    GCG burial, 290, 295
    RBCG burial, 331
Independent Labour Party, 223, 224, 311, 312
International Socialist Labour Congress 1889, 211
International Workers' Congress 1889, 211-2
Ireland forgeries, 11, 24(n)
Irish National League, 163, 175, 180, 187, 198, 223
Irish Republican Brotherhood, 197
Irving, Henry, 86, 91, 104

J

Jack (fox terrier), 94, 100, 133, 233, 286
Jacomb-Hood, George, 85, 209
Jamieson, George Auldjo, <u>Curator Bonis</u>, 28, 31, 32, 41, 43, 47, 48, 64, 67, 69, 75, 80, 84, 85, 97, 101, 103, 107, 113, 116
333 Evidence to Napier Commission, 119-20
    And Malise Cunninghame Graham, 129
    Career, 231-2
Jenkins, Revd Mr., 29
Jesus, Society of, 51, 61-2
    <u>Reducciones</u>, 52, 77, 78, 79, 121, 236
Johnston, Thomas, 311, 312, 313
Jones, Henry Arthur, 313
Jordán, Lopez, 35
<u>Justice</u>, 126, 137, 188, 235

K

Kaiser Wilhelm II, 302, 303
Katon, Doña Catalina, RBCG's grandmother, 14, 16, 23, 25(n), 27, 102, 133, 259, 277, 327
    Death, 100
Katon, Admiral James, 14, 16, 29
    At Ryde, 29-30, 31, 77, 327
Kelmscott House, 209, 215
Kintafi, Caid of, 269-70

Kitchener, Lord, 303, 304
Kirkwood, David, 312
Kisbany, Najim, 264, 265, 282, 284, 285
Knoydart, 124, 125,1 28
Knox, John, 17, 139, 235

L

Labalmondière, Col. Douglas, 86, 87, 173
Labalmondière, Joseph, 87
Labalmondière, Margaret, 86
<u>Labour Elector,</u> 202, 203, 211-2, 215, 217, 219, 238
Langdale, Lady, 31, 33
Landsdowne, Marquis of, 84, 121
Larkin, James, 298-9, 312
Law &Liberty League, 187-8, 191
Lavery, Hazel, 319
Lavery, John, 7, 106, 251, 253, 300, 319-20, 333
Lawrence, D.H., 277, 325
Lawrence, T.E., 303, 304, 328
Lee, Henry, M.P., 261
Lee Sir Joseph, 261
Lina, 86
Lindsay, Jamieson, & Haldane, 113, 133, 229, 231
Lipski, Israel, 159-162, 163, 167, 184, 318
Loch, Henry, 18-19, 23, 27, 28, 111, 112
Loch, James, 122
López, Francisco Solano, 54, 56, 57-8, 62,79, 326
Lowe, David, 214, 215
Lushington, Godfrey, M.P., 160, 172, 180
Lutaif, 269, 271
Lynch, Eliza, 54, 55, 56, 57, 58, 326

M

Macdonell, H.G., 33, 34, 41, 42,
Mackenzie, Compton, 320, 321
Mackenzie, Donald, 261, 263, 264, 281
Mahkzen, The (Moroccan govt.) 253, 254, 255, 260, 268, 299
Mahon, John, L., 204
Mann, Tom, 199, 212, 213, 215, 297, 305
Mansel, George, 69, 70, 71, 76, 80, 83, 99, 102, 105, 266, 285
Majoribanks, Edward, 215, 217, 223-4
Marx, Eleanor, 136, 167, 211, 214
Marx, Karl, 211
Masham, Yorks., 89 et seq., 238
Mason, Stephen, M.P., 142, 152, 196, 198
Masterman, George, 54, 55, 56
Matthews, Henry, M.P., 154, 156, 157
    And Lipski, 160-161
    And Trafalgar Square 167, 169, 192, 193
    And Bloody Sunday, 171-186
McDiarmid, Hugh (C. Grieve), 320
McGhee, Richard, 196
McOnie, William, 116
Maxwell, Shaw, 121, 202
Mid Lanark, 196-98, 201, 210
Meakin, Budgett, 267-08
Menken, Ada Isaacs, 102
Menpes, Mortimer, 106, 250

Metropolitan Radical Federation, 167, 171
Mexico, 1879, 92-93
Miéville, Louisa, 309, 330
'Mogreb el Acksa', 266, 267-8, 270 et seq.
Morocco City, 258, 260, 269
Morocco, Sultans of, 254
    Moulay Hassan 256, 262, 265
    Abdul Aziz, 257, 264, 265, 266
Morris, William, 62-68, 126, 136, 151, 152, 153, 158, 162, 172, 176, 178, 179, 182, 184, 188, 191, 195, 287, 313
    Funeral, 276, 305, 322
Muirhead, Roland, 317-8, 320, 321
Murdoch, John, 120, 121-2

N

Napier Commission, 119-121, 122, 125, 128,
National Secular Society, 153, 175
National Party of Scotland, 321
New Orleans, 93, 100
Nicolson, Sir Arthur, 266, 269, 270, 271, 272
North West Africa Co., 261, 262
    At Tarfaya, 263-4, 265
North West Lanarkshire,
    1885 election, 124
    1886, election 138-9, 140
    1892 election, 225
'Nostromo', 8, 279-80, 283
'Notes upon the District..', 234

O

O'Brien, William, M.P., 163, 165, 167, 175, 179, 191
Ogilvy, Edward, 32, 37, 40, 41, 42
Ogilvy, James, 32, 36, 37, 40, 41, 42
O'Shea, Capt., 218, 220
Overseas Library, The, 275

P

Pall Mall Gazette 160, 162, 184, 186
Pampa, 133, 233, 234, 254, 286, 302
Pardo Bazán, Emilia, 240, 241, 243
Parnell, Charles Stuart, 118, 121, 122, 128, 139, 141, 142, 143, 161, 197, 217, 223, 299, 319, 320
    And Mid Lanark, 198
    O'Shea divorce, 218-220
    Death, 222, 260
Pedro II, 58, 217, 218, 323, 324
Pelling, Dr. Henry, 136
Pentonville Gaol, 184, 185
Philips, John, 197, 201
Peregrina, see Collazo
Pickles, Fred, 151
Plan of Campaign, 155, 162, 163
'Portrait of a Dictator', 54, 326
Pozzo, Dr., 330
Pritchett, V.S., 331
'Pygmalion', 287, 291

R

Ratto, Pepe, 266, 269, 271
Reed, Sir Edward, M.P., 176, 177, 180, 181
'Remarks on the River Plate Countries', 34-5, 44(n)
Rio de Oro, 265, 281 et seq.
Robertson, Chisholm, 166, 196, 223
Robinson and Fleming, 28, 63
Roca, Gen., 73
Roosevelt, Theodore, 324
Rosebery, Earl of, ' the people's peer', 138, 141, 256
Rothenstein, William, 7, 253, 254-6, 279, 295, 300, 318, 329
Royal Niger Co., 261, 281, 282

S

Salisbury, Marquis of, 118, 128, 139, 141, 161, 174, 192, 252, 262, 270, 284
<u>Saturday Review</u>, 67, 234, 235, 242, 243, 275, 276
Sauce Grande, 72-74, 123
Schnadhorst, Francis, 197
Scott, Walter, 10
Scottish Home Rule Assoc., 317, 319, 320
Scottish Labour Party, 166, 201-2, 217, 220, 221, 225
Scottish Land Restoration League, 121
Scottish Nationalism, 140, 146, 165, 317 et seq.
Sesame Club, 237
Small, William, 146, 147, 166, 305
Spiridon, 264-5
<u>Star,</u> The, 183, 212
Stevenson, George/Grace, see Horsfall, Grace
Stevenson, Martha, 91-2
Shaw, G.B., 8, 105, 135, 137, 166, 173, 176, 186, 209, 234, 237, 280
    RBCG his model, 279, 287
Shinwell, E., 312, 319
Sidi bu Bekhr, 260, 271
Simancas, 84, 97, 240
Sioux, 236
Smillie, Robert, 196, 197, 201
Social Democratic Federation, 126, 135, 136, 137, 153, 154, 155, 167, 175, 187, 188, 199-200, 211
Socialist League, 136, 146, 147, 153, 171, 175, 187, 200, 204
Spilsbury, Major, 266, 267, 269, 270, 272, 282
Stead, W.T., 160, 179, 186, 187, 195, 219, 240
    Character/appearance, 186, 187
Stewart, Andrew, 126
Stewart, George, 58, 63-4
Stewart. Dr William, 58
Sharpe, Dr., 67, 111
<u>Stirling Advertiser,</u> 116, 291
<u>Stirling Observer,</u> 311
Sus, 260, 262, 269, 270, 282
Stephen, Mr Justice, 160, 162

T

Talla, 13, 141, 233, 286
Tamasluougt, Sheikh of, 260, 264, 271
Tangier, 218
Teleki, Countess, 31, 33, 41
Theosophy, 237
Thompson, E.P., 67, 68, 204
Thompson, Lieut Col. 58

Thornton, Sir Edward, 270, 271
Tillett, Ben, 213, 297, 300
Times, The, 12, 63, 180, 218, 220, 255
    Letter on Germany, 300
    On ' Don Roberto' 331
Timms, James, 171, 193
Tiris, 261
Tschiffely, A. F., 32, 74, 80, 87,
    'Don Roberto', 85, 92, 93, 97, 100, 321, 328, 329, 331
Trafalgar Square, 171-187, 191, 193, 195
Triana, Perez, 279, 306

U

Urquhart, David, 136, 202
Uruguay Remount Commission, 300-02

V

'Vanished Arcadia, A', 277, 284
Victoria, Queen, 118, 138, 141, 156
Vigilance Assoc., 166, 167
Vigo, 104, 139, 263, 324
Vanity Fair, 144
Viola, Georgio, 61, 279
Villiers, Francis, 23, 256

W

Walker, Supt., 135, 172, 174
Ward, Miss, 286, 295
Warren, Sir Charles, 135, 156, 162, 166-7
    And Bloody Sunday, 171-3, 183, 184
    Career, 173-4
Watts, Dr Cedric, 288, 312
Wazzan, Shereef of, 256
Wazzan, Emily, Shereefa, 256
Webb, Beatrice, 200, 202, 214
Wells, H.G., 234
West, Herbert Faulkner, 85, 87,
    Biography of RBCG, 327, 328, 329
    RBCG's last letter, 331-2
Wilde, Oscar, 179
Williams, John, 134, 136
Workman's Times, 135
Wright, Robert, 13, 93, 95, 100, 101, 107, 184, 231, 332
Yeats, W.B., 87, 337